Disability Drama in Television and Film

Disability Drama
in Television and Film

by
Lauri E. Klobas

McFarland & Company, Inc., Publishers
Jefferson, North Carolina, and London

Library of Congress Cataloguing-in-Publication Data

Klobas, Lauri E., 1954–
 Disability drama in television and film / by Lauri E. Klobas.
   p.   cm.
 Includes index.
 ISBN 0-89950-309-8 (lib. bdg.)
  1. Handicapped in television. 2. Handicapped in motion pictures.
 3. Handicapped—Public opinion. 4. Stereotype (Psychology)
 I. Title.
 PN1992.8.H36K56 1988
 791.4′0880816—dc19   88-13296
                                                                  CIP

© 1988 Lauri E. Klobas. All rights reserved.

Printed in the United States of America (50# acid-free natural paper)

McFarland & Company, Inc., Publishers
 Box 611, Jefferson, North Carolina 28640

To the small "army" who helped along the way—
Suzy; Michael and Buzzie and their phone bills;
Marit; Melissa; Wayne; Nancie; Laurie; and *The Disability Rag*.
With love to Mom and Dad who worried but let me go my own way.

Contents

Acknowledgments ix

Introduction xi

Disability Dramas
    1. Blindness 1
    2. Wheelchair-Users 114
    3. Deafness 195
    4. Amputation 272
    5. Developmental Disability 313
    6. Small-Stature 341
    7. Other Disabilities 369
    8. Multiple Disabled Characters 413

Endnote 437

Appendix: Additional Disability-Related Productions 439

References 459

Index 461

Acknowledgments

A special thanks is owed to some people for their help in providing information, insight and proofreading:

Gayle Rubenstein, M.A.
Sheila Killian
Troy Hammond
Thomas Compton, M.A., A.B.D., M.S.
Jonathan Levy, M.A.
Harry O'Wanty
Dr. Michael Bryan Kelly, M.A., PhD
Nancie Attwood
Laurie Luedtke

Introduction

The dramatic use of characters who have a physical disability is a theatrical tradition rooted in antiquity. It has been carried on through past centuries in plays and continues to our own era via moving pictures and television. The theme of disability is a popular and recurring film and TV staple. "Affliction dramas" or "three-hankie dramas," as critics often call disability pieces, are not uncommon.

Television and film perceptions of people with disabilities are narrow and, in some cases, damaging to the lives of actual citizens with limitations. Their celluloid personas are more familiar to society than their real-life counterparts by warrant of screen repetition.

The influences of film and television are seen in fashion, attitude, and popular vernacular. Madison Avenue and Hollywood have generated a spillover that has been absorbed in every corner of the country where there is a film projector or an antenna sucking in a signal. This spillover, as measured in consumer dollars, is immense. But while the film and television media applaud themselves for the dollars and audience they are capable of generating, they similarly recoil when outside sources suggest that the overflow extends to attitudes and influences that negatively affect society.

Unrelenting static images and situations have created a compound picture of a disabled person in the minds of the audience. "People ask me if I want to feel their face," complained a college student who is blind, referring to the plethora of blind screen characters who touch faces to "see" them. "They've gotten mad when I tell them I don't do that."

The inclusion of characters depicted as disabled on screens large and small is welcome since they represent a portion of society. But the stereotypical traits and personalities of these characters and ways they deal with repetitive situations deserve investigation and criticism.

An immense chasm exists between disabled people and their screen counterparts. People with physical limitations are fighting for civil rights in a "disability rights" movement. They strive to effect change in political definitions and legislation. They attempt to draw the camera lenses away from a voyeuristic study of their physicality to such realities as their denied physical access to public buildings, public transit, and other facilities supported by their taxes. They often face discrimination in education and the workplace. Censorship has recently become an issue after a politician complained that *Playboy* was available in Braille. The magazine is no longer available to those who don't read print. Until recently, disabled patrons of one particular Canadian airline were not permitted to travel without a companion. While these battles rage, the screen's reflection of people with disabilities is often a rerun of stories seen in previous years. Contemporary roles, abilities, issues, and problems confronting people with disabilities are ignored. They work to carve a niche in a society that prefers to dwell on emotions and physicality while neglecting real-life issues.

Situations of an obvious nature are illustrated onscreen. Life-changing accidents are difficult to accept. Loss of a physical capacity long taken for granted is painful. The natural and righteous anger that accompanies traumatic change is easy for a writer to synthesize and depict. A non-disabled writer imagines how he or she would feel and writes about it. The miracle of a cure is a boon to a creator who imagines being able to see after a period of blindness or being able to run after a time of using a wheelchair. This non-disabled point of view is the main problem with disability drama. Explorations of real problems are sidestepped while soaring "miracles" or stories of courage prevail.

Another difficulty is conflict. The difficulties of facing a new disability are many and provide much "conflict"—a dramatic necessity in any production. Again, that is the obvious. The point of view from *inside* disability, with more reality-based conflicts, is sadly lacking. Without this perspective, dramas with or about people with disabilities are doomed to wallow in "inspirational" tears.

The "cultural" chasm between real-life and screen disability can be graphically defined by looking at disability not as a physical/personal problem, but as one of human rights. A simplistic parallel argument would be to state that the reason black Americans did not vote in previous decades, could not use all public bathrooms, and had to sit at the back of the bus was because they had not "accepted" the reality they were black. Their anger resulted from not "overcoming" their race. Obviously, this was never the case and it sounds ludicrous to state the same. However, it is happening to the nation's disabled citizens. Their social problems and individual idiosyncrasies are ignored, while easy emotional stories of "bitterness," "overcoming," and "courage" abound. Contemporary pieces more resemble previous productions than the reality in society.

Biograph released *The Light That Came,* in 1909. In it, a young woman with a "scarred" face falls in love with a blind musician. She wants to finance an operation to restore his vision—but fears if he has sight, he will shun her like all the rest. The man has the operation and regains his sight. He assures the woman he loves her despite her appearance.

The modern world is far different from the one in which *The Light That Came* was released. For people with disabilities, great progress in medicine, rehabilitation, and legislation has been made. Attempts continue to eliminate physical and attitudinal barriers—often more handicapping than the limitations themselves—to permit people with disabilities true equality in society. However, in 1985, the TV series *Highway to Heaven* featured "The Monster." In it, a young man with a large port wine stain birthmark covering half his face falls in love with a blind girl. He is concerned when she tells him an operation could restore her sight. He fears she will not love him anymore. When she sees him after successful surgery, she assures him she loves him.

Introduction

Seventy-six years separate *The Light That Came* and "The Monster." A story made about women in 1909 would require reshaping to appeal to a contemporary audience. A piece made in 1909 about black people would require a massive overhaul to be palatable for today's viewers. Although the rights of the disabled have undergone as many changes as the women's movement and the civil rights movement, television and film have, for the most part, remained ignorant of this progress. The media have fallen back on the tried-and-true imagery with which they are familiar and comfortable.

Television and film's disabled characters have benefitted only marginally from recent social changes. Stories are bound to a confining formula treatment where disability is a personal problem one must overcome. Viewers seldom see disabled characters as multifaceted human beings for whom physical limitations are a fact of nature. Disability is not depicted as being integrated into a busy and full life. For every piece which shifts the focus to the realities and social issues that disabled people face, there are ten fictional TV stories which convey that the *real* problem is emotional. The character has not accepted his/her disability and must overcome the difficulty.

One significant desultory effect of this screen imagery surfaces in articles about people with disabilities in TV news reports or newspapers. Disability is forever relegated to "human interest" status. News stories are about "overcoming" and "triumph" and the one-in-a-million person who is "cured" of disability. Despite the content—from civil disobedience to civic-minded action—the people involved are described as "courageous" in "poignant" stories that skirt the issues at hand; just as the fictional stories do. Mary Johnson, editor of *The Disability Rag* magazine, states these pieces serve to "comfort society—reminding the not-yet-disabled that, if they are injured, or fall prey to disease, they, too, may be able to return to normal ... the repeated telling of these stories, using a formula so exact as to be almost ritualistic, also serves to protect non-disabled society. Telling them serves as a charm to ward off the awful reality—that everyone is just a slip away from disability." The simultaneous bombardment from fictional television and nonfiction TV/newspaper/magazines ensures continued repetition—because it sells. Above all, it is "safe." But entertainment writers do not seem to understand what it is they are perpetuating. In an informal survey, only 2 percent of the adult students in a screenwriting workshop expressed they had contact with disabled people. The rest gleaned their information from movies and television.

A perusal of film and television productions featuring disabilities is not only historically revealing but relevant. The magic of reruns has allowed many older television and film pictures to be seen repeatedly. With the explosion of cable TV, stations are crying out for more product to fill their schedules. Programs in syndication can be viewed by an audience as "new" in that they have not been seen by the watcher.

Between syndicated reruns of films/TV shows and network first-run offerings, an average of three disability-oriented pieces are aired every week. First-run programming on the three major networks usually delivers one "affliction drama" a week. Disability is prominently portrayed in one or two feature film releases every year. Given this visibility, audience size, and the mostly stereotypical nature of these characterizations, the ramifications of erroneous messages are enormous — and frightening.

Watching a large number of pieces that deal with disability reveals an astonishing degree of repetition. Speeches and scenes resemble others a great deal. Pieces are often so similar that the outcome can be predicted within the first ten minutes.

Any critic worth her/his salt will argue that for the most part, film and television stories *are* repetitive regardless of subject matter. That may be true, but those pieces play to an audience that can evaluate what is being seen from personal experience. On the other hand, the general audience is uninformed about persons with disabilities and has little cautionary discretion for guidance.

People with disabilities are broadly defined onscreen as falling within one of two character types: They are defeated, angry people who require help, or they are "never-say-die" types who accept disability as a "physical challenge" and go out to conquer the world. The former types resist aid out of angry pigheadedness; the latter reject it with strength of character. With such heavy screen focus on two ends of a spectrum, there is little room for shading. The nuances of character taken for granted in non-disabled roles are missing. Any character with a disability is perceived to be less than or better than average. The pitfall is that the audience finds these stereotypes unapproachable. They cannot always identify with constant depression and misery; nor do they relate to shining stars who always triumph.

Certain elements show up consistently in screen disability stories. A characteristic overused in disability portrayals is one termed as "devaluation." People with disabilities are illustrated as hating themselves and their limitations. They use poor language to further hammer home the point that they are, in their own eyes, less than human. "Freak" is a word of popular usage among screen characters. "Look at me!" is another term they employ, suggesting their appearance is inherently disgusting. It also serves the unspoken purpose of frightening a non-disabled audience as they see a nervous non-disabled character fighting back tears or painful outcries as they view the sight. This cancels out the possibility that disabled people assimilate their own physicality and actually like themselves without the aid of an omniscient non-disabled person who helps them acquire understanding.

Devaluation also indicates mental instability on the part of disabled characters. They require help and aid to regain full personhood status. They are subordinated to characters without disabilities who help turn their lives around. This amazing capacity of heart and understanding to effect change is referred, in this work, as the non-disabled catalyst syndrome. A non-disabled person often assumes the responsibility of helping a devaluing and depressed disabled character to change attitudes about self and the world in general. Miraculously, self-respect is restored (this role is infrequently assumed by another character who is disabled).

The aspect of a catalyst too easily assumes that problems relating to disability are exclusively ones of personal adjustment. This neatly sidesteps such pertinent social issues as physical access and attitudinal barriers. It also

Introduction

helps pigeonhole a portrait of disability. If the character is angry, he/she must be angry because of a personal limitation—or so this attitude assumes. (If the black character is angry, it must be because he/she is black, and not because of the prejudices and lack of choices foisted upon him/her by the community.) A writer's own naivete prevents the audience from learning that anger may be resultant from things other than the limitation itself.

This writers' block seems to be never-ending. A non-disabled writer's imagination takes over by visualizing life with a sudden sensory or physical limitation. Thus, characters who within the story have had limitations since birth or for many years, wish for sight, for the ability to dance, or to just once hear the sound of music. This myopic approach renders the perceptions from a point of view *within* disability as impotent, unimportant, and invalid.

The easy way out of this dilemma for many writers is a cure. Miraculous operations abound. But when they don't, an exceptionally strong will to "overcome" substitutes—indicating disability, anger, and even societal attitudes resulted from not trying hard enough to return to "normal." The "quick fix" syndrome has its roots here. If an ice skater who loses her vision is able to skate again *(Ice Castles)*, she will be fine. If a major leaguer can pitch a pro game after losing a leg *(The Stratton Story)*, he will be able to go on with life. Again, this invalidates perceptions and experiences from within the disability.

This results in a "them" and "us" situation. "They" are the people with disabilities who are bitter and full of rage at what life has dealt them. The audience is "us," the non-disabled majority who see film and TV reiterate that "they" require help, be it a TV telethon asking for money or a character on a sitcom who needs the kindly star to change his/her life. The "SuperCrip" stories of overcoming also set "them" apart from "us." "They" are disabled and have somehow garnered exceptional wisdom and courage, which elevate them far and beyond the realm of "us" mortals. They do everything "we" do and even more, even though "they" are disabled. Such common devices divorce a well-meaning audience from "them." "They" need help or encouragement; "they" inspire us with incredible courage. "They" are rarely depicted as average citizens in an ordinary everyday way. The audience is not permitted the luxury of understanding them on a personal level. "They" are not wild and crazy people with senses of humor, nor are "they" impetuous geniuses or even strait-laced salt-of-the-earth types. "They" are disabled characters, living examples of pain, tragedy, and courage. Any personality traits they may possess are secondary.

Trauma is drama, the meat and potatoes of film and television. Often depicted are scenes of characters experiencing life-changing accidents and fighting their way up the comeback trail. Many such pieces are "based on a true story" but have more in common with other disability pieces than the actual person or his/her life.

Every attitude or situation depicted onscreen has its root in reality. The solutions committed to film have happened to someone, somewhere. Someone once reacted in a similar way. But, as the analyses of separate depictions will illustrate, they are done to the point of running a dead horse into the ground. "Ritualistic" scenes are constantly redone. One formula device is curiously voyeuristic. Disabled characters often describe to complete strangers how they became disabled. This seems to illustrate that such persons are completely absorbed in their own physicality. In the course of a relationship, a description might come up. But on film and television, characters often offer detailed explanations for no reason. The story is not moved along by such an admission; it exists to satisfy curiosity. This is more of the "us" and "them" syndrome. In the TV film *First Steps,* a researcher working on a computer device to stimulate muscles in persons with spinal cord injuries speaks to potential candidates for testing. A number of nonessential characters describe in great detail what has happened to them. Afterward, the researcher painfully marvels in wonder to a colleague at what they'd been through. The scene was screen voyeurism of the worst kind. When such an "explanation" scene occurs, the text will note that the "cause of disability is discussed."

Another prevalent characteristic of film and TV pieces is the use of offensive, erroneous, and often outdated terminology regarding disability. Characters have been described as "stone blind" *(The Waltons,* "The Job"), "stone deaf" *(Hart to Hart,* title unknown), and worse. This poor language is often accompanied by erroneous ideas. "'I'm only twenty-one and I'm a helpless cripple'" and "'How can I sentence her to pushing a wheelchair...'" *(Leave Yesterday Behind)* are prime examples of the same. This is only excused when a character is used as a mouthpiece for prejudice toward a person with a disability. It is also a gauge denoting that the writer is not familiar with the appropriate terminology preferred by actual people with disabilities. Poor choice of vocabulary will be especially noted in the drama reviews that follow.

Many pieces illustrate special aids available that allow people with disabilities access to various activities of daily or recreational living. Such items of "special equipment" that are used in the course of a film or TV program are described in the individual annotated reviews. Despite this welcome attempt from creative personnel to update imagery, it is disheartening to note how often the same is misused within the course of the story. The most common offenders are mobility canes used by persons with low vision. They are often waved like rapiers, stabbed, beaten, and poked at the ground, posing a threat to oncoming pedestrians. This "misuse" of a device negates the usefulness of the tool to a non-disabled audience. Details of equipment misuse will be noted in pieces which illustrate the same.

A more positive trend that has taken hold in Hollywood is the use of performers with disabilities to play the same. Not only does this add a sheen of authenticity to a production but the inclusion of these performers sometimes permits them to make small improvements for the better in the script or staged action. Pieces utilizing this portion of available talent will be noted. Another welcome step forward has been the use of characters with disabilities in "incidental" roles, that is, small parts that are not designated as disabled roles. In *Cagney and Lacey's* "Hot Line" episode, a man the female cops approached for information just happened to use a wheelchair. (Incidental role will be noted in the "review" section of the book only if they are speaking roles. Characters with disabilities who appear as atmospheric background are appreciated but

Introduction xvii

not mentioned in this work.) The progressive equal access in hiring of performers with limitations in major character roles is refreshing, although their presence does not necessarily insure a piece will avoid the pitfalls of diability drama.

The Reviews

This work does not purport to be an analysis of *every* piece about disability, nor does it stake a claim at having researched all the "important" pieces. It is a collection of films and programs that came to my attention in one way or another over an eleven-year period.

Pieces are noted by title of the film (feature or made-for-TV) or the name of the television series and the specific episode title. They are arranged chronologically to better suggest what may have been seen in the past which could have influenced the writer. When a precise airdate is not available, pieces appear alphabetically after productions of the same release year.

The sections are titled by the disabilities displayed, in order of visibility: Blindness, Wheelchair-Users, Deafness, Amputation, Developmental Disability, Small-Stature. "Other Disabilities" comprise the last category. Productions featuring more than one major disabled character appear in the "Multiple Disabled Characters" category.

An introduction leads off each disability section, noting special characteristics and stereotypes peculiar to portrayals of that particular limitation.

Credits for Executive Producer, Producer, Director, and Writer have been included whenever possible. Some are missing since a few pieces from television were caught during random channel switching. Also, during the early years of this collection, the writer alone was noted. The pieces could not be tracked down again to fill in the holes.

A plot briefly describes the story when applicable. The character is noted by sex, race, and disability for those drawing statistics of any of the above.

The description of the stories and of the role played by the disabled character is based on my observations of the productions and may not be the intent the original creative personnel hoped to impart. Any misspelling of character names is my responsibility with apologies to the writers. Quotes made by characters to express a point are *not* from a script but from careful notes taken while watching the piece. Obviously, the story and quotes are attributed to the writer/s of the stories; the related description of action and impressions are my own. The segment that appears after a three-starred (***) break is a review of the offering as it relates to disability. It is *not* meant to be taken as a criticism on the quality of the direction, acting, writing, or overall product.

Any personnel names that are mistakenly spelled, noted in the wrong technical position, or omitted are my own mistake due to faulty notes in the pre–VCR days!

Additional television episodes, feature films, and made-for-TV movies revolving around disability (or which briefly feature a character with a disability) that do not appear in the main text are listed in the Appendix. This list is to aid any researchers interested in locating/identifying other pieces for their own projects.

And now, a look at how disability has been portrayed on screens large and small.

Blindness

Helen Keller is probably the most familiar person associated with blindness. Nearly everyone has heard of the woman who lost her vision and hearing at the age of nineteen months and went on to become a learned and traveled person.

Helen's education began at the age of seven when Anne Sullivan, a partially sighted teacher from Boston, broke through to a young mind without language. Helen Keller became a celebrity in the days of pre-electronic media. I have formulated a theory that her visibility may be the single most contributing factor to particular characteristics of blind characters seen onscreen.

Three weeks after Anne Sullivan's arrival at the Keller home in Tuscumbia, Alabama, in early 1887, Helen understood the shapes fingerspelled in her hand to be words. The exceptionally bright child gathered a vocabulary at a rapid rate. One month after the breakthrough, Helen became "known" when a newspaper in Boston printed a story about her.

Letters written by Helen were published in magazines. People bent over backwards to give her opportunities. At a circus, Helen was allowed to touch all the tame animals to gain firsthand knowledge about them. At a world's fair, a letter from the president of the function permitted her access beyond ropes to touch any and everything. At an art museum, a ladder was set up so she could climb and touch a bas relief work that was a part of a wall. And wherever Keller went, reporters followed.

She was the correspondent of such famous literary persons as Mark Twain and John Greenleaf Whittier. She met them and spoke to them by using her voice. She followed their replies by placing her hand on the lips of the speaker to tactually follow lip movements and vocal vibrations. The method was difficult and often imprecise, but it added to the mystical aura that surrounded Keller. Many photos were taken of her with one hand gently resting on the lips of the person with whom she was posing.

Keller was also a prolific writer. Her early pieces were flowery as was the style of the period. Perhaps to conform to the stylistic trends of the time, perhaps "sweetened" by others around her, she discussed her disabilities, referring to her world of "darkness" and the "dungeon" of her silence. All of this helped to make Helen the living prototype of popular novels of the late Victorian era—isolated, intelligent, brave, and tragic.

Perhaps it is coincidence or perhaps it is directly related to the amount of visibility Keller had during her youth and adulthood that blindness emerged as a "popular disability." Blindness is the most frequently seen physical limitation onscreen. It is characterized as a condition of total darkness, when, in reality, a clinical definition of blindness encompasses varying degrees of vision. Statistics collected by Dr. Samuel Genensky at the Center for the Partially-Sighted in Santa Monica, California, indicate less than 6 percent of the nation's visually impaired population is "functionally blind," a category which includes "total" blindness. On TV and in film, less than 6 percent of visually impaired characters have a degree of usable vision. This 180-degree swing from reality suggests writers are not aware of the range of blindness and have never explored it for their projects. A second possibility is that limited vision—as opposed to the romantic notion of total blindness—is thought to be unsalable. Keller's world of "perpetual night," as she once called it, may be easier for nondisabled writers to imagine than a life with partial sight.

Another popular characteristic that could possibly relate to Keller is a habit blind characters have of "face-feeling." Characters onscreen will touch the face of a person with whom they are speaking. This is not done as a caressing exploration between lovers. It is seen as a prerequisite for establishing a relationship. "You have me at a disadvantage," says Faye Conners in *Harry-O's* "Second Sight." "I don't know what you look like." In *Highway to Heaven's* "The Monster," Rachel asks Julian, "Could I touch your face? ... it makes it easier to talk to someone if you know what they're like." A person who is blind might caress the face of a lover much like any other person in a relationship, but they do not, as a rule, feel faces. Yet, this shows up frequently in portrayals of blind characters. It is possible that photos of Keller with her hands touching the lips of companions and her own personal penchant for touching faces contributed to this erroneous notion.

Now established, the trait of face-feeling has gained a life of its own. Actors playing a blind character who are required to touch a face recall the films where they have seen the same and copy the technique. The "mannerism" is similar from piece to piece, all completing the stage direction in virtually the same way! Thumbs trace the brow bones then slide down the nose while the fingers rest on the cheeks. Yet, three professionals with a cumulative twenty-six years of working with people who are blind revealed they had never had their face touched in this manner.

Visually impaired characters are often depicted as having compensatory sensory abilities to make up for their lack of sight. Their alleged acuteness of hearing enables them to identify criminals by the sound of shoe heels *(T.J. Hooker,* "Blind Justice"); their sense of smell permits them to identify a car's exhaust fumes *(Simon and Simon,* "I Heard It Was Murder"). This attribute also applies to the blind character who has an abundance of special talents which seemingly make up for a lack of sight. These figures then transcend to a "special" realm, separate from the viewers.

In *Wait Until Dark,* a 1967 feature film release, a blind woman is stalked in her apartment by criminals. She breaks all the lights in the dwelling in order to "handicap" her assailants. A number of blindness programs feature a rendition of this famous scene and are noted as such. This action precludes the notion that blind persons have degrees of vision and require light. *Wait Until*

Dark was not the first piece to use this scene (an early *Rawhide* featured a version of it), but in my opinion, it is the most famous.

Blind characters often affect what is termed in this work as a "wooden stare." They hold their head in a fixed and rigid position while their eyes stare unflinchingly ahead. Many characters who lose their vision in stories adopt this odd habit just moments after becoming blind. They do not turn their heads toward aural stimuli nor do their eyes move.

Characters who are blind utilize various items termed as special equipment:

Mobility Cane — A long and slender lightweight hollow "sensor" which is gently swung in front of a pedestrian who is blind. The cane permits detection of physical obstacles, curbs, trees and so on. It is white to permit visibility by drivers. It is commonly misused onscreen in a variety of ways. Also, pieces of recent vintage which illustrate a standard orthopedic cane (wooden with a curved top on which to lean) painted white constitute misuse of special equipment since the short length negates the cane's function and usefulness (such canes are used by elderly blind persons who require support; onscreen, they have been seen used by those not requiring an orthopedic aid). Some persons with visual limitations prefer the term "white cane" to "mobility cane." However, the term "mobility cane" is used since it describes the function of the tool and not its appearance. Many characters refer to a "white cane" as a badge of inferiority and not a handy aid.

Sighted Guide — A mobility technique by which a blind person takes the elbow of a sighted person and remains a step behind the guide. In this manner, he/she is able to easily detect a step up or down or a change of terrain. In a narrow area, the guide moves his/her arm farther back so that the two continue in single file. This technique is often misused and misunderstood. Blind screen characters often taken an arm as a woman might take an escort's arm. Or, a sighted person takes the arm of the blind. This negates the usefulness and function of the technique.

Dog Guide — A specially trained canine companion that uses its own vision and intelligence to discern obstacles and visual dangers and to guide the blind user around them. (NOTE: The terms "Guide Dog" and "Seeing Eye Dog" are, essentially, "brand names" for two different training centers.)

Braille — An embossed system of dots which persons without usable vision learn to read by touch. Playing cards and an endless variety of parlor games with Braille markings permit players who are sighted and nonsighted to compete with each other. A Braille watch is a timepiece whose crystal pops open to let a blind user read the time by touch, feeling the watch's hands and an orientating dot on the watch face that delineates the hour. A Braille slate and stylus is a portable method to write Braille; a Braillewriter is a manually operated machine to permit rapid mechanical creation of the same.

Talking Book — Books-read-on-record/tape that are used by blind readers.

Talking Clock — A high-tech piece of equipment which relays the time via a synthesized voice.

Handwriting/Signature Guide — A lightweight solid square with cutout areas so that a blind user can set a pen or pencil on paper and write evenly or sign documents and checks.

In addition to the programs listed in this section, other blind characters can be found in: *Amy; Beg, Borrow . . . Or Steal; Code Red* "Dark Fire"; *Little House: A New Beginning* "Marvin's Garden"; *Mask;* and *Highway to Heaven* "The Monster."

City Lights / 1931 / United Artists

Director: Charles Chaplin
Writer: Charles Chaplin
Category: Feature Film — Comedy-Drama

* Blindness
* Single White Female
* Cure

Plot: A Tramp falls in love with a lovely blind flower girl.

The Little Tramp meets a pretty young flower vendor, selling buds from a basket. He discovers she is blind. He impresses her with money and a car provided by a drunken millionaire. When the millionaire is sober, he takes back the car and leaves for Europe.

The Tramp acts as the non-disabled catalyst by getting a job to support the blind girl, who is recovering from a fever. He reads to her about a doctor who can restore sight with an operation. He also discovers a letter the girl's grandmother had hidden, threatening eviction if the rent is not paid. The Tramp promises to take care of it.

The Tramp loses his job and fails in his attempt to win money by boxing. A chance meeting with the drunken millionaire leads him to confide about the blind girl. The millionaire gives him a thousand dollars, which, when sober, he accuses the Tramp of stealing. The Tramp snatches the money and runs. He gives it to the girl to pay the rent and to have an operation. He is jailed for theft.

Months later, he is released. His ragged appearance brings laughs from the owner of a new flower shop who is the girl, now sighted. She gives the sorry apparition a rose and a quarter. Hypersensitive perception is seen when she recognizes him by the touch of his hand.

* * *

City Lights was a silent film. The blind character appeared to be a happy and energetic young woman, raising flowers and taking care of them to sell. She was employed, although streetcorner selling can also be perceived as a stereotype—but not inappropriate for the time period.

The Tramp was attracted to the girl, but his affection was motivated by pity. He did not see her as an average woman and did not relate to her in a natural male/female relationship.

It was also interesting to note that as a blind flower seller, the girl worked on a street corner; as a sighted person, she owned an entire shop and made elaborate floral arrangements. It was assumed some of the money The Tramp snatched from the millionaire helped establish this enterprise, but the rise in status implied a visually-impaired person could not have carried out such a feat without the benefit of sight.

City Lights was a sweet and funny film and gave a rather fair although melodramatic portrayal of a blind person.

The Light That Failed / 1939 / Paramount Pictures

Producer: William A. Wellman
Director: William A. Wellman
Screenplay: Robert Carson
Based on Book by: Rudyard Kipling
Category: Feature Film—Drama

* Blindness
* Single White Male
* Equipment: Sighted guide
* New Disability

Plot: An artist loses his sight after painting his masterpiece.

Fighting a war in the Sudan, Dickie Heldar is struck in the head. Pressure on his optic nerve will lead to "complete degeneration" and blindness. Dickie becomes an artist but never achieves perfection until he uses Bessie, a Cockney street girl, as his model for a work he calls "Melancholia." He belittles and angers his model. He finishes his painting and goes to bed. Bessie sneaks back in and destroys "Melancholia" by smearing turpentine across her own painted face.

Dickie wakes up to find his vision gone. A new disability is incurred.

> DICKIE: It's black, quite black.... I'm blind and the darkness won't go away!

Heightened sensory perception helps him recognize a female visitor at his door simply by touching her face with his hand.

DICKIE: Maizie!

Negative connotations and poor language are in evidence.

DICKIE: [You came to] join me in my prison? ... I won't sentence you, Maizie, you're pardoned.

He is eager to show Maizie his masterpiece. Maizie gasps when she sees the ruin. She lies and says "Melancholia" is magnificent.
Dickie indicates there is no existence left for him.

DICKIE: I have a lot of life to forget.

Bessie comes by and admits she spoiled the painting. Dickie is quietly dismayed to realize everyone has deceived him. He leaves for Africa where a war is in progress. He asks to be able to mount up with a cavalry unit. He dies in the battle.

* * *

The Light That Failed had some interesting independent images of blindness, particularly when considering its vintage and the number of "helpless" melodramas that later followed it on film and television. Dickie was quite mobile after losing his vision. Although he seemed to remain in his flat a great deal of the time, he continued to entertain and exhibited curiosity about friends and events. He was independent enough to travel alone from England to Africa.

The cruel deception of lying about the picture was interesting. It seemed to indicate that all those involved with him believed him too fragile to hear the truth. They were silently cutting him off from the real world by their "kindness," indicating he was no longer in the mainstream.

Special equipment was misused. Beaton, Dickie's butler/aide, took Dickie's arm in an inappropriate sighted-guide technique.

It was disappointing that death was the only way out for a youthful and healthy man who still enjoyed his friends and travel despite his visual lack. It indicated there was nothing left in life for this man—and he would be better off dead. *The Light That Failed* portrayed blindness as a stop-off just prior to the end of life.

Pride of the Marines / 1944 / Warner Bros.-First Nat'l Pictures

Producer: Jerry Wald
Director: Delmar Daves
Screenplay: Albert Maltz
From a Book by: Roger Butterfield
Adaptation: Marvin Borowsky
Category: Feature film—Drama

* Blindness
* Single White Male
* New Disability
* Based on a True Story

Pride of the Marines

Plot: A Marine heroically staves off the enemy on Guadalcanal and loses his sight when a grenade is lobbed in his face.

Philadelphian Al Schmid leaves home and girlfriend Ruth Hartley to fight the war. On Guadalcanal, frontal defenses are gone. Schmid battles back a line of the enemy. A grenade explodes in Al's face. A new disability is incurred.

> AL: My face! I can't see! My hands—I can't see.

Al is transferred to the Naval hospital in San Diego. A doctor snips his bandages off. Al opens his eyes.

> AL: No! Not a darn thing! ... No! I can't be blind! Not my whole life!

The doctor promptly gives Schmid a card with Braille on it. The veteran rejects it.

> AL: This is for blind people! I don't want any of this stuff. I want to stand on my own!

The doctor tells Schmid about a friend of his, a psychiatrist who is blind, married, *and* a father.

> DOCTOR: A blind man isn't helpless. He just has to do some things differently from the rest of us.

Al writes Ruth, telling her he is not coming back to Philadelphia. He uses devaluation when he confides to a Red Cross worker:

> AL: [Give Ruth time] to decide what? How to ruin her life.... I won't have her being a seeing eye dog for me.

Al is being awarded a medal for his heroics. To his distress, he finds he must return to Philadelphia to receive it. He vows not to call Ruth.

> AL: As long as I can't see, I don't want to marry anyone.

On the train trip east, pal Lee Diamond mentions Al might have problems finding a job he's qualified for because he's blind—just as Lee himself might be denied because he is Jewish. Ruth meets Al's train. He believes she is a driver taking him to the Naval Hospital. He is angry when he discovers the deception. He has it out with Ruth, again devaluing himself.

> AL: You think I want to live out my life knowing every day of the year that you married me out of pity? I got too much pride for that. I'd rather live alone.

Ruth gets angry at him, becoming the non-disabled catalyst.

> RUTH: ...You WANT to feel sorry for yourself.

Angry, Al stalks off for the phone, intending to call a cab to take him to the hospital. He knocks down a fully trimmed Christmas tree. He admits to Ruth that he *does* love her.

* * *

Pride of the Marines was a typical "overcoming" story. The newly disabled person exhibited every angry emotion in the book, only to be assured by the loved one that "it doesn't matter."

Al did not undergo any rehabilitation after being blinded, but he evidenced some training by using special techniques to light a cigarette or check the level of liquid in a glass just poured. There was no evidence he was heading for rehab, either—this, despite comprehensive retraining available for war-blinded veterans (see *Bright Victory*).

Most annoying about the portrayal was the actor's wooden stare and unmoving head. Two minutes after having the grenade tossed in his face, he stopped moving his head in the direction of sounds.

Al was illustrated as having a degree of light perception which improved a bit during the film. The "eye trouble," as he called his limitation to minimize it to others, would still be with him though.

Pride of the Marines was more of a wartime morale picture built upon a real-life hero than an honest depiction of a man facing a life with a visual limitation. (See *Ordinary Heroes* for another version of this story.)

Night Song / 1947 / RKO Radio Pictures

Executive Producer: Jack J. Gross
Producer: Harriet Parsons
Director: John Cromwell
Story: Dick Irving Hyland
Screenplay: Frank Fenton and Dick Irving Hyland
Adaptation: DeWitt Bodeen
Category: Feature Film—Drama

* Blindness
* Single White Male
* Face-feeling
* Cure

Plot: A rich society girl falls for a blind pianist who doesn't want anything to do with her so she secretly sponsors him to rebuild his confidence.

A gang of socialite friends stops at a cheap dive to enjoy a band. Cathy Mallory is taken by the music played by pianist Dan Evans during an intermission. She goes to talk to him and realizes he is blind. She stands in awkward silence. Evans devalues himself.

EVANS: I'm Exhibit A around here. I'm the blind piano player. She wants to know how I can find the keys with only my fingers ... it's a Braille piano.

At home, Cathy tells her aunt about the blind musician.

After talking to bandleader Chick Morgan about Evans, Cathy formulates an idea. She meets Chick and Evans as they stroll on the beach. She tells Evans that her name is "Mary" and that she is blind. She invites the two to the "clean but crummy" apartment she has rented for the masquerade.

The cause of Evans' disability is described as a hit-and-run accident. Since Evans would never accept money for an operation that could restore his sight, Cathy creates the "Mallory Prize," a $5,000 sum to be awarded in a contest searching for a composer. "Mary" urges him to enter. Evans wins the prize and plans to finance an operation to restore "Mary's" sight. She tells him to use it for himself. Surgery is successful. Evans is reluctant to contact "Mary." He "meets" Cathy Mallory and falls in love but confides that he also loves a blind girl. He is delighted to find "Mary" and Cathy are one and the same.

* * *

Night Song packed nearly every cliche about blindness into one film. Evans was self-pitying, rude, surly and angry. He had lost his will to compose since losing his vision. Cathy/Mary was the non-disabled catalyst, getting him interested in music again, then motivating him to try for the "Mallory Prize." Both Chick and Cathy's aunt supported the deception played on Evans—presumably, as in *The Light That Failed* and *Pride of the Marines,* that *not* knowing the truth was for his own good.

As a blind man, Evans was sour and angry. After regaining his sight, he was a charming and delightful man.

Night Song was a dull soaper and a poor portrayal of a person who is blind.

Union Station / 1950 / Paramount Pictures

Director: Rudolf Mate
Story: Thomas Walsh
Writer: Sidney Boehm
Category: Feature Film—Crime Drama

* Blindness
* Single White Female

Plot: Police search for the thugs who are holding a young blind woman for ransom.

Wealthy Henry Murchison's blind daughter Lorna is kidnapped. Her overnight bag and clothes are found in a locker at Union Station, a large train terminal. An army of plainclothes cops, led by Lieutenant Calhoun, are planted in the station and on trains to try and catch the kidnappers with the help of Joyce Willicombe, who can identify the criminals.

Calhoun wants to see pictures of Lorna to distribute to his men.

MURCHISON: There aren't any. Not since she lost her sight.

Murchison eventually comes through with home movies of a younger, sighted Lorna. She is shown as an active, cheerful person. Murchison grieves as he watches the old images.

Lorna is being held in an apartment. She feels her way across the room, and falls over a chair. Kidnapper Joe Beacom's girl comes into the room.

WOMAN: Now I gotta tie you up again . . . you got a chance to live because you're blind, don't you understand that?

She ties Lorna up again. To stop Lorna's sobbing, Beacom knocks her out.

Murchison drops the ransom at the station as directed. Beacom takes Lorna to a deserted municipal tunnel that runs under the city. Lorna is in a baggage wagon. Beacom thwarts her from escaping, telling her she is close to: "...a flock of high tension wires.... You'll fry so fast it'll curl your hair." Beacom picks up the money in the station. Lieutenant Calhoun follows him in the tunnel.

Lorna climbs out of the baggage wagon. She screams and cries as shots are fired. Calhoun tells her to run. She does and trips over a rail. Beacom is killed. Lorna is reunited with her father.

* * *

Union Station presented a blind character as a helpless victim. Lorna's only personal solution to the terrible situation was to scream and cry, which she did whenever she wasn't gagged. Her complete lack of control established her as nothing but a helpless pawn in a game between the police and the kidnapper. The lasting impression was that a sightless person was as good as dead in such a situation. Whenever Lorna tried to move independently, she would fall—and cry. Her only hope was to be saved.

The story indicated that when Lorna was sighted, her father had taken movies of her many activities. As a blind woman, there were no pictures and no mention of any activities that could have given Lorna even a minuscule edge during the kidnapping. Her life had all but ended with the loss of her sight, or so Murchison seemed to think. (In fairness, Lorna's role was a small one. The story did not permit discussion of her life. She was missing and time was of the essence.) *Union Station* was a typical blind-woman-as-victim story.

Bright Victory / 1951 / Universal-International

Producer: Robert Buckner * Blindness
Director: Mark Robson * Single White Male

Screenplay: Robert Buckner
Based Upon the Novel: *Lights Out* by Baynard Kendrick
Category: Feature Film — Drama

* New Disability
* Equipment: Mobility cane; Talking Book; Handwriting guide; Low vision techniques; Sighted guide; Braille watch

Plot: A newly blinded war veteran learns to live without vision.

* * *

Bright Victory was an interesting and detailed study of a World War II veteran after he was blinded by an enemy sniper. The film managed to avoid cliches about blindness. Veteran Larry Nevins was distraught at his situation and even tried to slit his wrists in a fit of passion. However, he bypassed the natural and obvious type of depression his limitation caused and moved on.

Nevins was a patient at Valley Forge General Hospital in a ward full of blinded men. These peripheral characters were active, busy men, discussing their lives and offering support to one another. An amusing segment occurred when one hot make-out artist lusciously detailed his date with a woman, only to be thwarted when she turned out the lights. He didn't know he had a luminous watch dial and the lady noted it was time for his bus!

Nevins was given mobility training and learned the route about the base. He had difficulty admitting over the phone to his parents that he could no longer see—but was forced to do so by a blind officer.

A sharp and poignant lesson about prejudice was inserted in this story of rehabilitation and shaping a new life. Nevins struck up a friendship with another vet, enjoying swimming and bowling with him. He was shocked to discover Joe was black. The revelation tore the friends apart. Nevins later reunited with Joe, having learned his prejudice was based on his upbringing and beliefs, not Joe's value as a person.

Nevins also discovered love in the person of Judy Greene. He cared for Judy but had a girlfriend waiting at home. He was disappointed to discover his old girl couldn't deal with his limitation. Her industrialist father didn't like the idea of his daughter marrying a blind man. The crumbling relationship was interesting. Instead of cliche scenes of "love conquers all," the two tried to hang onto what they had once had and could not. Nevins was offered a "charity" job in the father's factory for which, the older man told him, he should be grateful.

Nevins made the difficult decision to go into law practice and marry Judy in a world where he could make or break it on his own.

Bright Victory utilized research and a reality base in its story. Where the emotional thrust of *Pride of the Marines* sought audience sympathy by illustrating Al Schmid as a defeated man who couldn't even feed himself, *Bright Victory* looked for respect. Nevins was making the best out of a bad situation and finding it wasn't the worst. He was learning to regain control over his life.

Also nicely done was Nevins' first meeting with his parents. His mother tried to ignore the differences and chattered on incessantly. His father rescued his son from her clutches and the two went to a bar. The older Mr. Nevins listened to his son's complaints and honestly told him that neither he nor his wife wanted to see him, fearful of the changes. Mr. Nevins reminded him that all of them had been affected by the war and its aftermath.

Bright Victory wisely found its conflict outside of the obvious. Nevins was going to survive the trauma and live a good life. But he had many beasts to fight back — ones he never imagined or would have met before losing his vision. *Bright Victory* was an honest portrayal of a newly blinded veteran. Nothing was pat or blatantly obvious. Nevins was a realistic person who was unable to see, not a "blind" character created by cliche. Unfortunately, the quality of the message seemed to have been ignored in many other pieces produced after it.

The Blue Gardenia / 1953 / Warner Bros.

Producer: Alex Gottlieb
Director: Fritz Lang
Story: Vern Caspary
Screenplay: Charles Hoffman
Category: Feature Film — Drama

* Blindness
* White Female

Plot: An interested newspaper reporter helps out a woman who is accused of murdering a ladies' man.

A womanizer takes a woman out to eat at the Blue Gardenia Restaurant. They purchase a signature blue gardenia from a roving flower vendor, a woman who is blind. After the playboy is found murdered, a reporter begins helping out the woman accused of the crime. He goes to the Blue Gardenia in search of clues. He speaks with the flower vendor, handing her a bloom.

> VENDOR: A blue gardenia. Just like the one I sold to Mr. Preble last night.

Hypersensitive sensory perception is assumed by the newspaper man.

> REPORTER: And the girl with him. Can't you remember anything about her? Her ... perfume maybe?

> VENDOR: No, and that's usually the first thing I ... oh, yes, her dress — taffeta. Taffeta has a voice of its own. It rustles, like no other material.... And I remember her voice, too. It was a friendly voice.

* * *

The Blue Gardenia used a blind woman in two scenes. The flower vendor was an ethereal character who spoke slowly with an accent and in a manner that indicated her spare time might have been spent on Jupiter. Her "ear" for details was dangerously close to the almost-extrasensory perception blind characters often possess. Her employ was rather stereotypical, especially for the post–World War II period of opening opportunities for disabled veterans. *The Blue Gardenia* used a blind character as part of the population of a busy nightspot — albeit a somewhat wispy and detached one.

Superman / "Around the World with Superman" / 1953 / Syndicated

Producer: Whitney Ellsworth
Director: Thomas Carr
Writer: Jackson Gillis
Category: Series Television; Adventure

* Blindness
* White Female Child
* Face-feeling
* Cure

Plot: A young blind girl wins a contest to go "around the world with Superman."

Anne Carson is a blind girl who wins the *Daily Planet*'s contest to go around the world in a brief jaunt with Superman. Anne doesn't care for the prize herself — it's for her mother.

> ANNE: I don't wanna go around the world. I'm blind.

The cause of Anne's disability is described as an auto accident.
When Anne finally meets Superman, she does not believe he has superpowers.

> ANNE: The only ones who believe in you are the ones that can see you.

Anne also seems to possess some hypersensitive perceptions.

> ANNE: Mommy's coming! I can tell by her footsteps!

Anne's plight has touched the hearts of readers. An operation is performed on her. Glass lodged in her optic nerve is removed and she can see. Now, she travels around the world with the Man of Steel.

* * *

"Around the World with Superman" painted a portrait of a blind child as one who is forever tragic. Anne pitied herself, as did her mother. Mrs. Carson described her as "poor little Anne."

When Superman first came to see Anne, she was alone. He did not remove the clothing and glasses that identified him as Clark Kent—thus promoting the idea that all blindness is total and Anne would be unable to see shape or color that would reveal he was not in his super-garb.

Lois Lane had difficulty facing the child and expressed heartache when she did. This turned a blind child into an object and subordinated her personality to a disability. Of course, the character was quite pitiable due to the non-disabled writer's point of view.

Anne's intelligence and interests were also unimportant in the face of her blindness. Perry White of the *Daily Planet* worried that Anne had won the contest and wouldn't even be able to see anything along the way. This invalidated a blind child's perceptions and needs, again on the basis of sight, which was quite unrealistic.

"Around the World with Superman" presented an uninformed point of view about blindness. A sad image of a child without vision emerged. The little girl's life was forfeit without sight.

Magnificent Obsession / 1954 / Universal-International

Producer: Ross Hunter
Director: Douglas Sirk
Screenplay: Robert Blees
Based on the Screenplay by: Sarah Y. Mason, Victor Heerman
From the Novel by: Lloyd Douglas
Category: Feature Film—Drama

* Blindness
* Widowed White Female
* New Disability
* Cure

Plot: Indirectly responsible for the death of a young woman's husband, a playboy tries to make it up to her. After she is blinded in an accident, he dedicates himself to her—and medicine—without revealing his identity.

When reckless playboy Bob Merrick is injured in a boating accident, needed medical equipment is not available for pillar-of-the-community Mr. Phillips. The entire town mourns his death. Merrick tries to atone to the young, widowed Helen Phillips. While avoiding the conscience-stricken playboy, Helen is injured when an oncoming auto strikes her car door. A new disability is illustrated. Helen is blind.

Merrick decides to return to medical school. He develops a friendship with Helen and deceives her, introducing himself as "Robby." Helen goes to Switzerland for an operation to restore her sight. It fails. Blindness as a lightless condition is reinforced.

> HELEN: I know when I wake up in the morning, there won't be any dawn.

"Robby," remains with Helen and proposes marriage. She devalues both him and herself.

HELEN: I couldn't have you pitied because of me.

Although Helen is tempted to accept the marriage proposal, she can't. She leaves, writing Bob a letter, saying he has his "study and work now and I could only be a burden." She flees. Bob can find no trace of her. He buries himself in his work until, years later, he is contacted to come to Helen. She is deathly ill. His medical skills save her life and restore her sight.

* * *

Magnificent Obsession depicted a blind woman as one who was intelligent and ready to try new things, yet who constantly searched for a cure and felt she was only a burden.

Bob's ("Robby's") devotion under an assumed name made the viewer wonder if he really loved Helen — or did indeed pity her and hate himself for being responsible for much agony in her life. A deception was again played on an unsuspecting blind character, supposedly for her own good.

Magnificent Obsession was soapy, making a blind character out as one who was forever tragic and destined for misery unless sight was restored.

Bonanza / "Gabrielle" / 1963 / NBC-TV

Producer: David Dortort
Director: Thomas Carr
Writer: Anthony Lawrence
Category: Series Television — Western

* Blindness
* White Female Child

Plot: Hoss and Little Joe Cartwright discover the wreckage of a small caravan, along with a sole survivor, a young blind girl.

Hoss and Joe Cartwright discover a blind girl has survived a wagon train accident which killed her family. Gabrielle Wickham is taken to the Ponderosa by the Cartwrights, who learn her family was trying to locate the girl's grandfather, a hermit.

The all-male Cartwright clan is at a loss to know how to handle a girl — let alone a blind one. However, assertive Gabrielle lets them know how best to help her, as Hoss indicates:

HOSS: Joe, she don't need no help . . . just walk along in front of her. She don't like to hang on.

Grandfather Wickham breaks Gabrielle's heart when he says he doesn't want her. Ben Cartwright must then find a home for the child. He approaches the Pasters family, who agrees to take her in. Gabrielle is shy around her new family but opens up to her "brother," Jeremy. Lack of educational opportunity for blind children in another era is quietly expressed when Jeremy finds out Gabrielle has never been to school. The girl is also realistic about herself.

> JEREMY: Have you been blind long?
>
> GABRIELLE: All my life. But I don't mind. You don't miss something you've never had.

Gabrielle is protective of her own independence and mentions attitudinal barriers.

> GABRIELLE: Everybody treats me like a baby, just because I can't see. That's why I want to go live with my grandfather.

Her energetic independence asserts itself when she goads Jeremy into taking her up to the mountain in a bid to convince Grandfather Wickham he needs her. She is left alone when the old man frightens Jeremy off. Gabrielle goes into Wickham's cabin while he is gone and begins to clean house and mend his shirt. The old man refuses her help, but later has a change of heart and takes her in.

* * *

"Gabrielle" presented a refreshing and nontragic portrait of a girl who simply wanted something. Her obstacle was not her disability, but the grown-ups around her who wished to protect her from more pain. The excess baggage of teary, melodramatic scenes was absent. Gabrielle's visual limitation was almost purely incidental.

"Gabrielle" positively illustrated a blind child as one with a strong will and self-direction. She was not particularly different from any other youngster.

Bonanza / "Bullet for a Bride" / 1964 / NBC-TV

Producer: David Dortort
Director: Tay Garnett
Writer: Tom Seller
Category: Series Television — Western

* Blindness
* Single White Female
* Temporary Disability

Plot: Little Joe blames himself for a woman's blindness.

Little Joe shoots at a mountain lion as it is about to spring on a passing wagon. The bullet ricochets and a young woman clutches her face. A new disability is incurred.

> TESSA: Papa, my eyes! I can't see! Papa, I can't see anything!

Marcus Caldwell and his adult children, Lon and Tessa, are brought to the Ponderosa. Little Joe suffers terrible guilt.

> JOE: I'm to blame. It was my bullet that blinded her.

The wealthy Cartwrights are Marcus Caldwell's chance for the ever-elusive rainbow. He lies, telling them Tessa's mishap has caused him to lose a job and Tessa to lose a fiancé. Little Joe feels worse. He takes solicitous care of Tessa. He says that he loves her. Devaluation is indicated in Tessa's reply.

> TESSA: [A man] might mistake love for pity.... I just don't think that would be a very sound basis for a marriage ... a woman wants a man to love her for herself alone—not because he feels sorry for her.

> JOE: You talk as though you don't believe a man could love you just for yourself alone.

Joe feels Tessa needs a husband to take care of her and proposes. She puts him off, wanting to think about it.

Tessa traverses the stairs and falls. Her vision is restored.

> TESSA: Papa, this changes everything ... I'm whole again. I'm the way [Little Joe'd] want me to be.... He won't feel guilty anymore.

Papa convinces Tessa to play "blind" until after the marriage.

> CALDWELL: It's our last chance to get anything!

Tessa goes along with the ruse and accepts Joe's proposal. As they stand at the altar, she bolts. She blurts out her father's lies to him. Joe is relieved, admitting he really didn't want to get married.

* * *

"Bullet for a Bride" presented a woman who was blind as one who needed to be handled gingerly and taken care of. After becoming blind, Tessa adopted the typical stiff neck and wooden stare associated with screen blindness. After regaining her vision and playing blind, she still retained these characteristics but relaxed since she was "peeking."

Joe's exceptional guilt for a freak accident was understandable. His youthful desire to make everything the way it had been motivated his marriage proposal. His desire to help Tessa by "being your eyes" was certainly a poor rationale for getting married—and one that no one attempted to dissuade him from, with the exception of Tessa herself.

As a blind person, Tessa was carefully handled by all. They held her hands as they guided her to chairs, etc. Joe cut her meat for her at the table. The only independence she demonstrated was the ability to walk up and down the staircase alone. She was able to maintain a seat on a horse but was knocked off by a low-hanging tree branch. Everyone took Tessa's arm to lead her.

"Bullet for a Bride" supported the erroneous notion that the only option available for a blind woman was finding a love who would sacrifice himself for her.

A Patch of Blue / 1965 / MGM

Producer: Pandro S. Berman
Director: Guy Green
Adapted for Screen by: Guy Green
Based on the Novel: *Be Ready with Bells and Drums* by Elizabeth Kata
Category: Feature Film—Drama

* Blindness
* Single White Female
* Face-feeling

Plot: An abused, undereducated blind girl meets a man unlike any she's ever known in a park.

Selina D'Arcy, who is blind, sits doing her bead-stringing work. Whorish mother RoseAnn harps at her for having the place dark. Blindness as a lightless condition is suggested.

> SELINA: Dark's nothin' to me! I'm always in the dark.

Selina goads her grandfather, Ol' Pa, to take her to the park. She works on her beads, sitting under a tree. A friendly black man passing by rescues her from a caterpillar that has fallen down her back. He is Gordon Rau. He is intrigued by the uneducated young woman.

The cause of disability is discussed. RoseAnn tossed acid in Selina's face when she was five—acid meant for her own two-timing husband.

Daily, Gordon looks for Selina in the park and helps her with the beads. He initiates the knowledge-hungry girl into a different world. He is amazed to learn she's never been to school. Selina has a reason for that:

> SELINA: Well, bein' blind and all....

Selina's days in the park become wonderful adventures. After reading a book on blindness, Gordon teaches her how to find her own way about and how to cross streets. He takes her to the market. He introduces her to new foods and ideas. She thrives under his attention. Gordon wants to find a school for Selina. His brother vetoes the idea.

> MARK: You plannin' on educating a white girl? Man, that's not your job. Let Whitey educate his own women. They've never given us anything but a hard time.

GORDON: ...this is a personal matter.

When RoseAnn and her friend Sadie plan to get a place of their own and set themselves up as prostitutes, Selina escapes the apartment and meets Gordon in the park. He takes her home and arranges for a school to take Selina, despite her age. She wants to remain with Gordon, saying she's in love. She feels his face.

SELINA: I know you're good and kind, I know you're colored and I think you're beautiful.

GORDON: Beautiful? Most people would say the opposite.

SELINA: That's because they don't know you.

Selina leaves for the school—and hopefully, a chance at life.

* * *

A Patch of Blue indicated that the things handicapping a young blind woman were her family and their ignorance—not her disability. Selina was a curious and bright person who knew only what RoseAnn had let her know. She was a capable household worker; she was virtually RoseAnn's slave, doing the ironing, cleaning, and cooking. The only bright spots were Selina's days in the park—which became brighter when she met Gordon. She was eager to learn everything he could teach her. He was, she said, the first friend she'd had since she was nine.

Gordon was clearly the non-disabled catalyst in Selina's life—but that was the point of the movie. The gentle black man was better for her than her white family—and more concerned.

A Patch of Blue was a unique look at societal handicaps—ignorance and prejudice—more than a study of disability.

Wait Until Dark / 1967 / Warner Bros.

Producer: Mel Ferrer
Director: Terence Young
Screenplay: Robert & Jane-Howard Carrington
Based on the Play by: Frederick Knott
Category: Feature Film—Thriller

* Blindness
* Married White Female
* Equipment—Mobility cane; Braille slate and stylus

Plot: A blind woman is terrorized by three men who are looking for a doll they insist is in her apartment.

20   Blindness

Susy Hendrix, a young blind housewife, plans to meet her husband, Sam, a photographer. She calls him on the phone and tells him about her day:

> SUSY: I was the best in blind school today.... Can I tap my way over to your studio?

Sam agrees to meet her in a coffee shop.

> SUSY: Won't be hard to find me. I'll be the one reading *Peter Rabbit* in Braille.

Unbeknownst to Susy, three men are in her apartment looking for a doll stuffed with heroin, which an unsuspecting Sam brought home from the airport. A strange woman gave him the toy, a woman whose body is now in the Hendrixes' closet.

When Sam is called out of town, Susy becomes the focal point of a bizarre and complex ploy woven by three creative criminals to locate the doll. Mike Talman gains her trust by pretending to be a friend of Sam's who protects her from Harry Rote, Jr. Rote claims Sam is having an affair with his wife. "Sgt." Carlino is a "cop" investigating a break-in at the apartment.

Susy discerns the plot and tells Talman the doll is at Sam's studio. He leaves with Rote to find the doll. Susy takes control of the situation and dispatches teenaged neighbor Gloria to the bus station to meet Sam. Her phone is dead; she prepares her apartment for the inevitable return of the men. She pours a bottle of Sam's photo chemicals into a large vase. When she accidentally breaks a lamp, she is seized with an idea. She rapidly destroys every light in the apartment and in the outside hall.

Carlino is out; Talman has been killed. It's Susy versus Rote. Susy gains control and has Rote at bay in the dark—until he opens the refrigerator for a source of light. He is stabbed by Susy but is still able to pursue her. She pulls the plug on the refrigerator and survives a nightmare when the killer dies of his wounds.

* * *

Wait Until Dark featured a recently-blinded woman who was intelligent, independent, in love and showed no remorse at her loss. The cause of her disability was described as a fire following a car accident a little over a year before. She was going to school to learn to live with her situation. She functioned comfortably in her home.

Susy figured out that Mike Talman was NOT an old Marine buddy of Sam's; that Carlino was NOT a cop; and that the blustering Harry Rote, Sr. and humble Harry Rote, Jr. were one and the same (in typical fashion, one of Rote's shoes squeaked). Despite her fear and recognizance of danger, Susy maintained a fair semblance of calm.

Although the story could be looked at as a blind-woman-as-victim story, it was quite different—mainly in that Susy was someone the criminals had to contend with. She fought back. Blindness worked in this piece as the heavies were playing on the fact that they believed she could be easily deceived. Susy didn't seem too limited by her disability. She was completely aware of the strange things going on: the men "fooling with" the venetian blinds which they were using as a signal and "Sgt." Carlino's "dusting" her apartment when he was wiping away his fingerprints.

Susy survived because of her own quick thinking and resources. She was not saved in the nick of time by husband or police. They arrived when the danger had passed.

Wait Until Dark used a blind character who was cunning and quick. Susy began as a pawn and out of self-defense became a predator.

Night Gallery / "A Portrait" / Nov. 8, 1969 / NBC-TV

Producer: William Sackheim
Director: Steven Spielberg
Writer: Rod Serling
Category: Made-for-TV Movie—
    Occult

* Blindness
* Single White Female

Plot: A blind woman bribes a doctor to do an unethical transplant to allow her a few hours of sight.

Claudia Menlo is "a blind queen who reigns in a carpeted penthouse on Fifth Avenue [and] who will soon find a darkness blacker than blindness." Blind-since-birth Claudia built an apartment building on Fifth Avenue in New York and installed herself as the sole tenant. She wants a doctor to do an experimental operation to graft donor optic nerves onto her own for eleven or twelve hours of sight. She blackmails the reluctant doctor to perform the operation.

    CLAUDIA: I want to SEE something—trees, concrete buildings, grass, airplanes, COLOR!

Sidney Resnik is the hood who needs money and will sacrifice his eyes. He shrugs off the idea of blindness with stereotypical images.

    SIDNEY: White cane, tin cup, pencils?

The surgery is performed. Claudia has paintings and statues all lined up, things she wants to see. Alone in the apartment at night, she removes the bandages at the designated hour and ecstatically sees artificial room light. Suddenly, the room and city are plunged in darkness.

Ironically, New York has suffered a power blackout. Claudia is awakened by the sunlight on her face. She experiences a few moments of golden yellow vision before the eleven hours of sight fades away into blindness.

"A Portrait" was a moral story with a macabre twist. As a blind person, Claudia Menlo was a rich and aloof woman. She wanted no one near her. She treasured her privacy so much that her entire apartment building was empty. She also had no reservations about someone else sacrificing his sight forever simply so she could experience vision for a brief time. She was ruthless and unsympathetic, thinking only of herself. The piece suggested Claudia Menlo had nothing in her life to sustain her except a dream of being able to see.

This episode was a nice piece, but presented a blind person as a selfish one out of touch with emotions, reality or life.

Hawaii Five-O / "Blind Tiger" / 1969 / CBS-TV

Executive Producer: Leonard Freeman
Producer: Leonard Katzman
Supervising Producer: Frank Barton
Story: Jerome Coopersmith & Robert Yates
Teleplay: Jerome Coopersmith
Category: Series Television—Police Drama

* Blindness
* Single White Male
* Temporary Disability
* Equipment: Sighted guide; Handwriting guide

Plot: Detective Steve McGarrett is blinded by a would-be assassin's bomb.

An enemy plants a bomb in Steve McGarrett's car. It explodes when the detective is close to the vehicle. He is attended to by comrade Lt. Dan Williams. A new disability is incurred.

> McGARRETT: Danno, I can't see. I can't see.

At the hospital, it is discerned that Steve may regain his vision or remain visually-impaired. McGarrett also knows he is still a target for the man who tried to kill him. He uses stereotypical imagery.

> McGARRETT: I don't intend to sit here waiting for him with a tin cup and dark glasses.

McGarrett wants to leave the hospital—the day after the bombing—and get back to work. A non-disabled catalyst appears in the person of hard-boiled Nurse Levello. She makes McGarrett go to the closet for his clothes and use the telephone; she stops his police guards from doing for him. He claims he is perfectly capable. McGarrett begins to walk down the hospital corridor. He knocks down any obstacles encountered. He falls over a table and chairs and gives up.

McGARRETT: Take me back to my room.

LEVELLO: Get on your feet.

McGarrett tells the governor he can run Five-O's investigation from the hospital. After a big speech about his capabilities, he demonstrates helplessness when he replaces the telephone on a table and sends a large vase crashing to the floor. McGarrett reluctantly turns to Levello for assistance.

McGARRETT: I understand there are things to learn, ways of getting on in this condition.

Levello begins walking him through the hospital. She dispels a misconception about blindness.

LEVELLO: Don't expect a sixth sense, Mr. McGarrett. Don't expect your other senses to automatically compensate. Those things don't happen. They're myths. But you can improve your perceptions by concentration and hard work.

They go on, McGarrett's "improved concentration" resembling heightened sensory perception as he identifies a food tray with Portuguese sausage on it. He walks into a lounge and Levello asks him what kind of visitors are present. McGarrett sniffs the air.

McGARRETT: I smell perfume. Obviously a woman. I smell something else, sweet like sugar but not exactly.

McGarrett sniffs again. The sound of a pop helps him identify the smell as bubblegum.

McGarrett and Nurse Levello are cornered by the man trying to kill Steve in the therapy room. In a *Wait Until Dark*-type sequence, Levello cuts the lights. In the darkness, McGarrett gets his man. McGarrett's vision returns. He passes Levello in the corridor, never knowing who she is.

* * *

"Blind Tiger" had McGarrett retaining his heroic status despite the difficulties he was encountering. An interesting TV concept of a new disability appeared in "Blind Tiger" where a friend or a nurse takes over the rehabilitation process. There was no evidence of psychological counseling or specialty guidance. As it was, McGarrett had a crusty floor nurse who just happened to have the stomach and know-how to get him on the comeback trail.

McGarrett retained his sharpness and businesslike demeanor during his brief disability. However, within the compressed time frame of the story, McGarrett became competent with his disability days after incurring it. It was hard to buy.

"Blind Tiger" was routine, an inspiring attempt by the star to overcome any and all obstacles thrown at him.

Here Come the Brides / "Two Worlds" / 1969 / ABC-TV

Executive Producer: Bob Claver
Producers: Paul Junger Witt and Stan Schwimmer
Director: Lou Antonio
Writers: Jack Miller and Shelley Mitchell
Category: Series Television — Romantic Period Drama

* Blindness
* Single White Female
* Cure

Plot: Joshua Bolt arranges for blind Callie Marsh to have an operation that may restore her sight.

Mountain man Jacob Marsh and his blind daughter, Callie, go to 1870's Seattle on business. Joshua Bolt talks to Callie. He's gotten an answer to a letter sent to an eye doctor in San Francisco. Joshua Bolt speaks to Jacob.

JOSHUA: [The doctor]'ll see Callie.

JACOB: No, he won't.

Jacob fears if Callie can see, she will be disappointed in him. He wants to keep her, the only thing he has in the world. Joshua tries to convince Callie she needs this operation. There are so many beautiful things she could see. Callie gives evidence of the disabled person's viewpoint.

CALLIE: Maybe [I can't see] your kind of beauty.... I can see in my own way.

Joshua describes color to her. He tells Jacob that Callie has the right to see. Callie decides she wants the operation. Joshua takes her to San Francisco. The big city is a revelation to Callie.

CALLIE: It's like nothin' I've ever heard before.

Callie has the operation and experiences a cure. Blindness as a lightless condition is reinforced as the bandages come off.

CALLIE: It's gettin' lighter! It's gettin' lighter!

With glasses, Callie now possesses useable vision. Joshua takes her to see everything.

Back home, Callie has a rude awakening. Her home, the "castle" she imagined, is a cramped and dingy place.

>CALLIE: I didn't think it would look like this.

Callie pulls off her glasses, not wanting to see.
Joshua is again the non-disabled catalyst. He forces Callie to face the fact that this is life. And, as far as Callie loving him as she claims:

>JOSHUA: I'm the first man that you've seen [so you can't really love me].

Callie learns to accept life as it is — and not as she wants it to be.

* * *

"Two Worlds" had some different elements in it. Notable was Callie's cure. It was not a "complete" cure. Callie still had impaired vision.

As a blind young woman, Callie possessed poise and a sense of self. However, within the story line and in the eyes of non-disabled catalyst Joshua, her ability to see in her own way was discounted. When her vision was restored, Callie suffered severe emotional problems in learning to deal with sight — an occurrence seen by psychologists working with persons who have sight restored.

Callie's difficulties in assimilating what she had imagined with real life were too easy. A person born without vision would not have preconceived parameters of visual beauty or sighted concepts. Establishment of visual standards would take time.

As a "cure" story, the piece was different, although it was still played for the heart-tug. Joshua's indication that since his was the first face she had seen, she didn't really love him, was a little hard to swallow. After all, their friendship had been established prior to her regaining her sight. This suggested that his friendship itself was motivated by pity. In this way, a blind person was not valued for herself, only for the benefit of helping another character do good deeds.

"Two Worlds" used a different psychological approach to a fairly routine story.

How Awful About Allan / Sept. 22, 1970 / ABC-TV

Executive Producer: Aaron Spelling
Producer: George Edwards
Director: Curtis Harrington
Teleplay: Henry Farrell
Based on the Novel: *How Awful About Allan* by Henry Farrell

* Blindness; Partial
* Single White Male
* Hysterical Disability

Category: Made-for-TV Movie — Drama

Plot: After months in a mental institution, a blind man returns home to live.

Allan Cauley is released from the mental institution where he's been for eight months. A bad fire has left him with impaired vision. He has blamed himself for leaving paint cans near a heater which exploded. His father died in the fire.

Allan is uneasy about returning home. He is upset to find his sister Kathryn has been renting a room to students. In fact, a new boarder is moving in. Allan is paranoid about how the student roomer will look at or think of him. When he hears something or someone calling his name, he believes the roomer is trying to bedevil him.

Allan's paranoia severely affects him. While sitting in girlfriend Olive's car, he hears the voice calling his name. He starts the car up and drives recklessly to escape until he hits a lamppost. He wonders about the roomer and devalues himself.

> ALLAN: Doesn't he mind living in the same house as a crazy blind man?

A black shadowy figure has begun to appear and is physically touching Allan, trying to pull him down the stairs. He grapples with the figure, and suddenly his vision is restored. The culprit is Kathryn. She wanted retribution because of their father's death.

Months later, Kathryn writes that she will soon be released from the mental hospital and will come home. Allan's vision then blurs back into blindness.

* * *

How Awful About Allan illustrated blindness as a condition with light and color, but distorted so much that vision was unusable. In a typical fashion, the blind victim was harassed in a way that would never occur if sight was present.

Allan was an intelligent character who functioned well with his limited vision. He seemed more preoccupied with his mounting paranoia than his vision problems. His sight presented difficulties, such as when he tried to escape the voice one stormy night and fell over bushes in the yard before being knocked out by a falling tree limb. Such staging was created to put Allan at a disadvantage; any other time, he would have stayed on the walkway and not headed across a potentially hazardous area.

How Awful About Allan was interesting in that partial blindness was illustrated. Allan discussed his mental status more than his visual (which he knew to be a result of the same). Other than that, it was a beleaguered blind victim at someone's mercy with little hope of recourse—until sight was restored.

See No Evil (a.k.a. Blind Terror) / 1971 / Columbia

Producers: Martin Ransohoff and Leslie Linder
Director: Richard Fleischer
Writer: Brian Clemens
Category: British Feature Film—Drama

* Blindness
* Single White Female
* Equipment: Braille watch

Plot: A blind woman finds her family has been murdered—and she is next on the list.

Sarah returns to her uncle's country estate in England a year after being blinded by a fall from a horse. Young cousin Sandy has a question for Sarah.

SANDY: Sarah, what's it like?

SARAH: It's bloody awful.

Sarah has a date with Steve, a young man she was seriously dating before her accident. They go horseback riding. Steve wants to pick up their relationship where they left off. Sarah devalues herself.

SARAH: It's not just today. It's something you'd be burdened with forever.

STEVE: Don't go, Sarah.

Sarah returns home where she discovers, one by one, that all the family members have been murdered in her absence. She retrieves a broken ID bracelet the dying gardener tells her belonged to the killer. Sarah takes her horse and attempts to ride to Steve's. She is imprisoned in an abandoned shack by a sleazy "gypsy" who thinks his brother was the murderer. Her horse returns to Steve's; he manages to find her in the countryside after she has broken out of the abandoned shack. The killer tries to do her in, but Steve saves her in the nick of time.

* * *

See No Evil portrayed a blind woman who was making the best out of a difficult situation. Sarah was not happy about being blind—however, she was re-entering life. She insisted to the family that she could manage herself. She navigated well in the large, two-story house. She poured herself a glass of wine from George's bar, got herself a cup of coffee, and was at ease in familiar surroundings. She was game to try riding again although she admitted she was nervous. Once she found she could keep her seat, she became confident in the saddle.

Sarah was realistic, looking ahead to how she would support herself. She had more trepidation about remaining with Steve than going off to the big city for training in a new profession.

Despite the horrible situation Sarah found at the house, she kept her head. When the killer returned for his broken ID bracelet, she got out of the house and concealed herself in the stable. He did not see her. She got away and would have made it to Steve's—the horse's home—but, in typical manner, was brushed off the horse by a tree branch. She wandered barefoot in the countryside. After being locked in the abandoned shed, she broke out. She found wreckage of a car and banged on it, a noise that alerted Steve, who was searching for her.

See No Evil presented a fair portrait of a blind woman coping with a new disability and hideous circumstance—in the tiresome blind-woman-as-victim mode.

Butterflies Are Free / 1972 / Columbia Pictures

Producer: M.J. Frankovich
Director: Milton Katselas
Screenplay: Leonard Gershe
Based on the Play: *Butterflies Are Free* by Leonard Gershe
Category: Feature Film—Comedy

* Blindness
* Single White Male
* Face-feeling
* Equipment: Mobility cane; Sighted guide; Braille watch

Plot: A young blind man finds his fight for independence fueled when he falls in love.

Don Baker, living in a funky San Francisco apartment, meets Jill Benson Tanner, a hippie-dippy actress who has just moved in next door. He is utterly enchanted by the free spirit who waltzes into his life; she is embarrassed when, after having been with him for fifteen minutes, she suddenly discovers he is blind. Don assures her it's no big thing and they move on to other more interesting subjects—including a picnic on the floor which leads to romance.

Face-feeling is illustrated.

JILL: Am I not the image of Elizabeth Taylor?

DON: I dunno. I've never felt Elizabeth Taylor.

The tender exploration gets scary for Don as Jill's false "fall" becomes unloosed from her hair and a false eyelash comes off in Don's fingers. Jill then places his hand on her breast, assuring him it's real. Don immediately backs off and devalues himself.

> DON: What is it? "Be Kind to the Handicapped Week" or something? You've been feeling sorry for me ever since you came in here this morning. Take the poor guy out shopping, show him a good time, get him into the sack and that'll take care of my social work for the next six months. Well, thanks a lot but don't patronize me! And don't feel sorry for me!

Jill assures him of her sincerity and they make love. Their idyllic encounter is interrupted when Florence Baker, Don's overprotective mother, barges in the next morning after promising she would stay away for another month. Mrs. Baker is not amused by Don's bohemian surroundings or Jill.

Jill misses her dinner date with Don, showing up very late with the director of her new play, with whom she plans to move in. Defeated, Don asks his mother to take him home. Mrs. Baker convinces both herself and her son that he needs to learn from this. She leaves him alone. Jill, at the last moment, changes her mind and returns to Don.

* * *

Butterflies Are Free was an upbeat look at the life of a young blind man. Unfortunately, it never completely escaped formula. Don was an attractive and intelligent young man who was eager to try striking out on his own, far away from the wealthy and protected neighborhood in which he had grown up. Much like any other fellow his age, he was full of dreams and hopes, both real and grandiose. The fly in the ointment was his mother.

Don functioned very well in his apartment—so well that Jill, dizzily outlining her own life, had no idea he was blind. After she realized he could not see, the movie took a light-hearted turn to prove Don was capable. It became belabored and overdone, particularly when he "proved" he knew his way around the apartment by giving a guided tour—all the way down to the bottles in the kitchen.

Face-feeling was seen although certainly one of the less offensive versions of this tedious scene, where Jill's various beauty aids came off one by one. Don insisted to Jill that he was just like any other guy. His sudden devaluation did not belong in the piece. After all the tedious making of the point that blindness was Don's natural state in which he was comfortable, it was jarring to see him jerk back and launch into the "Be Kind to the Handicapped" spiel. It was a concession to traditional "blind" formula.

Butterflies Are Free seemed to be an ice-breaker for sighted audiences, giving them the freedom to laugh WITH a blind character. But it never truly permitted them the luxury of letting go of his disability.

Barnaby Jones / "See Some Evil ... Do Some Evil" / 1973

Executive Producer: Quinn Martin
Producer: Gene Levitt
Supervising Producer: Adrian Samish
Director: Lawrence Dobkin
Writer: George F. Slavin
Category: Series Television—Crime Drama

* Blindness
* Single White Male
* Fake Disability
* Equipment: Mobility cane

Plot: Detective Barnaby Jones suspects a blind musician of masterminding a murder.

Mr. Stan Lambert is a blind pianist who entertains at a nightclub. When detective Jones comes to the club looking for clues to a murder, Lambert illustrates an ultrasensitive sense of smell. He speaks to Jones and then to singer Jenny Lynn.

> LAMBERT: That aftershave lotion you're wearing—that's pine, isn't it?... That crazy perfume—I'd know it in a crowd.

Jenny had been having an affair with Henry, the murdered man. No one knew who he was; the man gave Stan a lift home one night but he introduced himself to the blind man with another name "so Stan couldn't possibly know who Henry was."
The detective doubts the deception could have fooled Lambert.

> JONES: Blind men pick up awful fast. Now Stan, he got me on shaving lotion and footsteps.

Henry Warren had correctly suspected Stan Lambert wasn't blind; Stan was blackmailing him and had to kill Henry. Jones goes to the club. Lambert identifies him by his aftershave—which is different from before.
Jones goes to visit Lambert. At the sound of the doorbell, Stan shuts the baseball game off from the TV and turns on the radio. He replaces his dark glasses. Jones feels the heat from television set. As the clues mount up, Jones pulls a gun on Lambert. When the man reacts, Jones knows for sure that Stan is sighted.
Erroneous myths are reinforced when Jones explains what tipped him off.

> JONES: ...you recognized me with a different aftershave, the TV set was warm ... a blind man doesn't normally look at television.

Stan was once blind but had his vision restored, a move he termed the "biggest mistake I ever made."

STAN: When you've been a blind musician all your life, well, you're something special. An oddity. A commodity. You can always get work, someone always wants to book an attraction like that.... With my sight, I'd just be another club date musician, standing in line, scratching for work....

* * *

"See Some Evil ... Do Some Evil" depended wholly on public mythology in order to work. Since the super sense of smell which blind persons are believed to possess onscreen was off, Jones immediately suspected Lambert wasn't blind. And particularly since the man's television had been on, Jones' suspicions were founded. Such story lines indicate the prevailing "baseline" knowledge afloat in public about persons with visual limitations.

Misuse of special equipment was seen. Jones was never tipped off by the too-short white cane Lambert used or the awkward way he poked it in front of himself — clues much more revealing than a warm television set!

"See Some Evil ... Do Some Evil" never took into account the possibility that blind people do not sniff out everyone they meet; nor the fact that those with limitations watch television with the rest of the populace. Regardless if Lambert was truly blind or not, the piece was a poor image of blindness and laughable.

The Eyes Have It / 1974

Executive Producer: Cecil Clarke
Producer: John Sichel
Director: Shaun O'Riordan
Story: Brian Clemens
Writer: Terence Feely
Category: British Made-for-Television Movie — Drama

* Blindness
* Group Portrayal; White adults

Plot: Terrorists take over a school for the blind in England to assassinate a leader slated to pass by the building in a parade procession.

The Clinical Training Centre for the Blind is virtually deserted as all staff members have gone off to see the motorcade procession due in town. Instructor George Mullard remains in the anatomy lab. He is murdered by a strange man, Andersen. Andersen replaces the anatomical dummy on the lab table with Mullard's corpse.

Sally, a blind woman, enters the lab. Andersen introduces himself as a visiting friend of Mullard who is "upstairs." He admits two accomplices into the building who carry large boxes. Sally is told they are plumbers. Upstairs, the terrorists target the parade route with rocket launchers.

In the lounge, the students discuss the parade, listening to radio coverage. Sally tells the others she doesn't really believe the visitors are plumbers.

SALLY: Come to think of it, they didn't smell right.

Although some distance from the men, Sally noted they didn't smell of sweat or a "work-y" smell. She has, though, detected the smell of gun oil. She tells the others something is wrong.

The students think Sally is overreacting—until she discovers Mullard's dead body. The villains imprison the students in the day room. Iron gratings cover the windows. Poor imagery is used:

FRANK: If we could just get a GLIMPSE of the world—some gray through the darkness—we might just as well be helpless babies.

They discern why the men have come and are desperate to escape. When Andersen returns to the locked room, he is jumped by the students. Sally locates his gun.

SALLY: What good is a gun to us?

FRANK: Well, you never know.

Sally and Frank creep upstairs. They open the door and shoot a villain. His rocket screams off harmlessly as the motorcade passes by.

* * *

The Eyes Have It presented a group of blinded adults as easy pawns. They were victims of sighted perpetrators.

Contradictions appeared within this story. Sally's hypersensitive perception kicked in when she noted the supposed plumbers—some distance away—did not "smell right." However, when standing in a closed room with a dead body on the slab and a live one scrunched against the wall, she noted nothing. Sally's abilities were manipulated to suit the writer's needs.

The blind students saw themselves as impotent in the face of danger. As it was, their feat became "remarkable" rather than an illustration of a group of intelligent, concerned adults doing their civic duty.

Another curious aspect occurred. The Centre was devoid of staff with the exception of Mullard. But it would seem the students did not classify for attendance at the parade. They remained at school and listened to coverage on the radio. This erroneous notion was similar to the concept in *Barnaby Jones'* "See Some Evil ... Do Some Evil": the blind do not own or watch television since they cannot see it. The students were not present at a parade they could not see, precluding they could enjoy a busy, public outing. They appeared to be cut off from daily life.

The sighted writer's viewpoint was illustrated in a tedious scene about color. Blindness was expressed as a lightless condition when "purple" was said to be a dark color. "That's something we do know about—dark," maintained a student.

The Eyes Have It used poor imagery that was based on all the negatives a writer could imagine about blindness.

Good Times / "The Encyclopedia Hustle" / 1974 / CBS-TV

Executive Producer: Norman Lear
Producer: Allan Manings
Director: Herbert Kenwith
Writers: Bob Shayne & Eric Cohen
Category: Series Television—Situation Comedy

* Blindness
* Black Male

Plot: The Evans family has trouble resisting the pitch of a blind encyclopedia salesman.

Unable to pay the bill, the Evanses' phone is disconnected. Money is tight. A salesman selling a set of Black History encyclopedias invites himself into the apartment. He falls over a chair, indicating he cannot see.

> MICHAEL: Mama, he's b-l-i-n-d!

> J.J.: But Michael, he can still h-e-a-r.

Florida suddenly warms to the man. She offers him coffee and a doughnut. Virtually unprompted, the salesman begins talking about his disability. Hypersensitivity of senses is brought into play.

> ANDERSON: I may be unsighted but I still have my other senses to compensate. For instance, I'd say the young man is twelve years old, about five feet and extremely intelligent ... sometimes I can see things sighted people can't ... there's also a young lady in the room.

> THELMA: How'd you know that?

> ANDERSON: By your perfume.

When father James Evans returns, he has no interest in the encyclopedias and goes to throw the salesman out. When Anderson falls over a coffee table, James realizes he is blind and becomes friendly. He decides to sign a contract for the encyclopedias. When Anderson leaves and James reads the contract, he realizes he's been had. He guesses the salesman was actually sighted and plans to prove it.

James orders J.J. to lay on the floor in front of the door. When Anderson comes in to deliver the encyclopedias, he steps over J.J. How did he avoid the teenager? Hypersensitive perception is suggested.

ANDERSON: If you're talking about that person on the floor, I heard him breathing.

Anderson proves he is blind by showing James a photocopy of his Korean war record. With his finger on the switchhook of the disconnected phone, the huckster "calls" his boss to cancel the contract. He tells the Evanses it's too late. Playing Anderson's game, Florida pretends to call the bunko squad. Anderson tears up the contract.

FLORIDA: Mr. Anderson, you may be blind, but . . . you're a liar, a cheat and you steal. You're a disgrace to blind people—in fact, you're a disgrace to ALL people.

ANDERSON: . . . Blind people are just like everybody else. You take the good with the bad.

* * *

"The Encyclopedia Hustle" had one or two good points but the majority were bad. Anderson stated the good points himself: blind people are just like everyone else, including hucksters and con men. The bad points were all the bizarre statements made by Anderson. Even J.J. concluded that Anderson's sensory capabilities had the "Six Million Dollar Man" beat.

Anderson was a good salesman, complimenting and stroking his prospective customers, but he also was allowed to reach that point only after it was discovered he was blind. Had he been sighted, he would have been thrown out by Florida.

Anderson had no cane or dog guide to help him make his unappointed rounds. Perhaps his falling over furniture was a sympathy ploy to snare otherwise uninterested customers like the Evanses. "The Encyclopedia Hustle" was a bizarre image of a person who is blind.

Harry-O / "Eyewitness" / 1974 / ABC-TV

Executive Producer: Jerry Thorpe * Blindness
Producer: Robert E. Thompson * Black Male Teenager
Director: Richard Lang
Writer: Herman Groves
Category: Series Television—Crime Drama

Plot: A blind "witness" to a murder helps Harry Orwell on a case.

Offbeat retired cop Harry Orwell takes the case of James Drew, who has been arrested on suspicion of murder. Harry backtracks to the scene of the crime, a ghetto apartment building. He is looking for witnesses. The only person willing to help is Adams. Harry opens the apartment door. He finds it dark inside.

> HARRY: You want the lights on?

Blindness as a condition without light is reinforced.

> ADAMS: What difference does it make?

Adams makes comments intended to help the audience recognize his potential as a witness.

> ADAMS: You're white, aren't you?
>
> HARRY: How'd you tell?
>
> ADAMS: Your voice.

Adams helps Harry solve the case.

* * *

"Eyewitness" used an astute blind character in the time-honored role as the best witness for the job. Adams' sensory capabilities became hysterically funny when he noted Harry had hurt his back. Adams, of course, could tell by the sound of Harry's footsteps! "Eyewitness" was a stereotype.

Look Back in Darkness (a.k.a. The Next Voice You See) / 1974

Producer: Ian Fodice
Director: Robert Tronson
Original Story: Brian Clemens
Writer: Terence Feely
Category: British Made-for-TV Movie—Thriller

* Blindness
* Widowed White Male
* Equipment: Braille watch; Sighted guide

Plot: Pianist Stan Kay overhears a voice at a party—the voice of the man that killed his wife and blinded him ten years before.

American jazz pianist Stan Kay plays for a party at Sir Peter Hastings' mansion in Britain. Kay stops playing when he hears a voice discussing wine. He recognizes the voice—it is the man who, ten years previous, killed Kay's wife and blinded the pianist. His assistant Julie is reluctant to believe him.
Kay wants to locate the man.

> KAY: Would you steer me around this place so I could listen?

Julie is convinced Kay is on to something when he is beaned on the head by the villain and pushed down the steps. Julie patronizingly seats Kay.

> JULIE: Now stay here—out of trouble.

Sir Peter takes Kay down to the cellar to try his wines. When Sir Peter is called upstairs, the killer strikes but is battled off by Kay's well-brandished bottle of wine.

> KAY: Ten years of hatred. Ten years I wanted to kill him. Now I'm glad I didn't.

* * *

Look Back in Darkness was a long and not very thrilling thriller. Kay's blindness was an obstacle to a quick and easy identification of the man who had killed his wife. In that sense, his disability worked as it created the tension in the piece.

Special equipment was misused. Both Julie and Sir Peter took Kay's arm and led him about. They both handled him as if he were a fragile and breakable object. Oddly enough, when Kay was led by Julie, he maneuvered the stairs quite well. Yet, when on his own with his hand on the rail, he could barely manage them.

Look Back in Darkness presented a strange image of a blind man as one who was dependent on others.

The Waltons / "The Job" / 1974 / CBS-TV

Category: Series Television—
Family Period Drama

* Blindness
* Single White Female

Plot: John-Boy Walton gets a job as a reader for an embittered young blind woman.

John-Boy answers a newspaper ad to become a reader for Ruth, a young blind woman. Ruth explains the nature of the job. She is rude to the young man and walks out. Her mother begs for John-Boy's understanding. He is reluctant to accept the position. Teenager Mary Ellen can't understand why her brother is reluctant about accepting the job.

> MARY ELLEN: ...blind like her, I don't see what you have to think about ... she must need help.

Mary Ellen is intrigued by Ruth and blindfolds herself. She attempts to carry a pie and drops it.

MARY ELLEN: It's terrible! It must be terrible to be blind!

Ruth's mother discusses the cause of Ruth's disability with John-Boy — a "severe case" of scarlet fever four years before. John-Boy suggests outdoor activities to Ruth.

JOHN-BOY: We could go for walks.

RUTH: I prefer not calling attention to myself tapping along the sidewalk.

The Walton family discusses the girl and recalls someone they used to know who had lost his sight.

JOHN: ...became a mean, bitter person.

Mary Ellen finds a lovely smooth stone in a brook. Intrigued by the shape and texture, she gives it to Ruth, wanting to be friends. Poor terminology is used.

RUTH: A perfect gift. How appropriate — a stone for someone who is stone blind ... something to remind me I'm blind.... I want my life back!

Ruth stays with the Waltons. While on a bridge with Elizabeth, she doesn't realize the child has climbed on the railing. Elizabeth falls in the stream. Ruth tries to help, crying for John-Boy to help. She tumbles over the rail. The two are saved; John-Boy acts as the non-disabled catalyst to tell her life is worth living, whether she can see it or not.

* * *

"The Job" depicted a blind person as a self-pitying, angry whiner without interest in life. Ruth was incapable of doing or saying anything constructive, it seemed. Her angry lashing out at young Mary Ellen about the pretty stone indicated that blindness had affected her mental stability. Her mother had described her prior to her illness as "outgoing, energetic" to John-Boy. Clearly, blindness had hastened the sad decline. Presumably, the only good thing to happen to her in four years was the advent of John-Boy Walton.
"The Job" was a poor image of blindness, using traditional helplessness, bitter anger, and self-devaluation in an attempt to construct a plot.

Harry O / "Second Sight" / June 5, 1975 (rerun) / ABC-TV

Writers: Gene Thomsen; Barry Trivers

* Blindness
* Married White Female

Category: Series Television—Crime Drama

* Face-feeling
* Equipment: Braille book; Mobility cane; Sighted guide

Plot: The plots of a blind authoress are suddenly coming true.

Authoress Faye Conners is concerned about an odd coincidence: her stories are coming true. She calls upon Harry Orwell to find out who is going to such pains to scare her.

Harry is surprised to drop in and find that Faye is out for a walk.

HARRY: By herself?

HELPER: Yes, she's quite capable.

Faye is quite mobile in her own surroundings. The familiarity she illustrates in her own dwelling leads a doctor to theorize she may have vision.

HARRY: Are you telling me that Faye Conners isn't blind?

The doctor notes that Faye never "runs into furniture" and theorizes her blindness is selective and hysterical.

Face-feeling is seen when Faye tells Harry:

FAYE: You have me at a disadvantage. I don't know what you look like.

Faye is cleared from all accusations that she is setting herself up.

* * *

"Second Sight" was rather laughable due to the unlikely premise that maybe Faye was hiding something—her sight. A statement such as the one made by the doctor completely precluded the possibility that a blind person may have a degree of usable vision. And not running into furniture? Most persons familiar with their homes, regardless of visual ability, do not run into furniture! Such a statement indicates inability of blind persons to function independently.

Special equipment was misused as Harry took Faye's arm.

"Second Sight" would probably have been a better mystery had the writers not concerned themselves with a situation they appeared to not be familiar with and concentrated on the story.

Medical Story / "Million Dollar Baby" / Oct. 23, 1975 / NBC-TV

Writer: E. Arthur Keane
Category: Series Television—Medical Drama

* Blindness
* Single White Female

Medical Story

Plot: A woman whose blindness was caused shortly after birth, sues the hospital as an adult.

Alma Geary was premature at birth and placed in an incubator. Prolonged exposure to a high concentration of pure oxygen from the incubator caused her blindness. She is suing for malpractice as an adult.

Alma is bitter and manipulative when she discusses her reasons for filing suit.

> ALMA: Only thing I got going for me is that I'm blind.... [This lawsuit is a] way for me to get ahead.

Alma indicates she had to go through extraordinary measures.

> ALMA: I learned Braille and all....

A lawyer is concerned about pre-publicity and a sympathy vote reaction in a case like this.

> LAWYER: [They] see the picture of a blinded girl in the newspaper and you've lost [the case].

* * *

"Million Dollar Baby" gets a ten-cent nod for exploring a hot issue that was in the news at the time. Malpractice suits against doctors and hospitals were all over the papers — filed by everyone including "RLF babies" (retrolental fibroplasia, caused by prolonged exposure to pure oxygen). Alma could be considered political in asserting her right to damages; however, her indication that winning a large cash award was a "way to get ahead" shifted her to the greedy category. She did not express that the medically induced blindness may have put her in contact with societal barriers that had prevented a healthy young woman from getting ahead.

Alma's having to "learn Braille and all" was odd. For a child who had been functionally blind all of her life, Braille would have been as natural to her as reading print is to a sighted child. Therefore, by context, it was assumed that Braille was a hardship for Alma Geary. It registered as a negative aspect in this story.

The legal people involved in the case were all quite concerned about the possibility of a jury automatically awarding a settlement to a person with a disability on warrant of sympathy. This silently expressed that a blind person was socially impotent, with no importance or value, who required special care. A more realistic approach would have been to base the case on the fact that medical error had denied Alma many civil rights simply because she was blind. But since lawyers don't do that in real life, there was no reason to expect their TV counterparts to be any different.

"Million Dollar Baby" presented blindness as unfortunate and extremely pathetic.

Petrocelli / "To See No Evil" / Oct. 29, 1975 / NBC-TV

Category: Series Television—Legal Drama
* Blindness
* Single White Female
* Face-feeling

Plot: A blind woman is accused of murder when a man is found dead in her room with a bullet through his heart.

Julie Carter is awakened by the sound of an intruder in her dark apartment. She pulls a gun from the nightstand drawer and fires. A man is found dead, shot through the heart. Tony Petrocelli takes the Carter case. He admits to the jailed woman that he has a problem understanding how she could have put a bullet through a man's heart in a dark room. Blindness as a visionless and lightless condition is reiterated.

> JULIE: All rooms are black to me.

Tony realizes Julie is, indeed, blind.
Face-feeling is illustrated:

> JULIE: Would you mind if I touched your face? ... you have a nice face, Tony, strong and gentle.

Julie is employed as a teacher at the school for the blind. She walks across the campus with one of Tony's assistants and sniffs. Hypersensitive sensory perception is suggested.

> JULIE: Don't you love the smell of children?

The case against Julie is dropped when it is discovered the man she "shot" was already killed by someone else and planted in her room.

* * *

"To See No Evil" used welcome new additions to traditional imagery by illustrating a blind woman as vivacious, busy, and self-assured. She was employed and got along fine on her own. Still, the old stand-bys had to be inserted—the "all rooms are black to me," the face-feeling, and the odd lines suggesting a sixth sense. "I feel like I can see the [jail] bars around me ... don't you love the smell of children," etc.

Julie was seen doing routine household chores, such as going shopping with the aid of a delivery boy to select the appropriate items desired. This episode's tentative steps toward modern imagery perked up this story.

Medical Center / "A Touch of Sight" / Feb. 16, 1976 / CBS-TV

Writer: Howard Dimsdale
Category: Series Television — Medical Drama

* Blindness
* Married White Male
* Equipment: Mobility cane
* New Disability

Plot: A doctor is blinded.

Doctor Nick Battero is blinded when attacked by a criminal. Helplessness is illustrated and blindness is described as a lightless condition.

NICK: I can't DO this . . . and it's dark in here!

Nick goes back to the hospital and makes patient rounds with Doctor Joe Gannon. He makes a correct diagnosis while listening to chest/heart sounds through a stethoscope. Nick Battero's employment is resumed.

GANNON: As of tomorrow morning, you're back on my service.

Nick's fear permits him to speculate negatively on the life condition he now experiences.

NICK: It's bad enough that I'm blind, but to live scared — I'm not gonna hang around and be a bad [doctor] because people pity me.

Nick's confidence is shattered when he misdiagnoses a patient. He devalues himself and refers to pejorative, stereotypical imagery.

NICK: If I had eyes, if I could see, it never would have happened. . . . Do they have a book on how to rattle a tin cup and sell pencils? . . . When you're blind, your options are limited.

* * *

"A Touch of Sight" placed the powerful voice of the media into a character ill-equipped to deal with his situation. No evidence of counseling or rehabilitation appeared in this piece. Nick was blinded; suddenly, he was awarded with a mobility cane.
Nick said if he had eyes, he wouldn't have misdiagnosed a patient. One must wonder whose brilliant idea it was to place a traumatized individual in such an important and stressful position. He was in no condition to deal with it. (It is interesting to note that while Nick and other TV/film counterparts have had their jobs restored after incurring disabilities, real-life people seem to LOSE jobs after becoming disabled.)
"A Touch of Sight" was depressing and written from the sighted person's standpoint. It wrongly assumed that a "quick fix" — a resumation of employ — would ease Nick's difficulties.

ABC Afterschool Special / "Blind Sunday" / Apr. 21, 1976 / ABC-TV

Producer: Daniel Wilson
Director: Larry Elikann
Story: Bob Kennedy
Writers: A. Barron and Lawrence Pressburger
Category: Made-for-TV movie — Children's Programming

* Blindness
* White Female Teenager
* Equipment: Mobility cane; Braillewriter

Plot: A high school boy spends a day blindfolded to try and better understand the world of a blind friend.

Jeff meets an attractive teenaged girl at the swimming pool. He is surprised to discover that she is blind. Jeff likes her, but is a little uneasy. He later sees Lee walking and impulsively invites her out for a hamburger. They go to a snack shop. Attitudinal barriers are indicated.

> WAITER: What is she gonna have?
>
> LEE: SHE will have a cheeseburger, vanilla shake and French fries.

Jeff is quite attracted to Lee. He is thinking of asking her out on a date. His own attitudes are explored.

> JEFF: But Dad, I'd feel funny about asking a blind girl for a date. Everybody would be staring at us. They'd think I was desperate for a date.
>
> FATHER: You care more about what they think than what you think.

At the pool, Jeff sneaks up on Lee and tosses her in the water; he is surprised when she becomes hysterical. Lee's resource teacher, Miss Hayes, advises Jeff to shut his eyes. Jeff accepts the challenge of being sightless. He bandages his eyes and manages to travel to Lee's via taxi, a cane, and a long period of groping.

> LEE: Why didn't you ring the doorbell?
>
> JEFF: I couldn't find it ... I'm blind.

Lee takes him out. He is completely disoriented.
Lee explains the difference between being born blind and becoming blind. She herself can't ever recall seeing.

LEE: It's harder for people who lose their sight.

While Lee is in a phone booth, Jeff thinks he hears a "vicious dog," a pooch who turns out to have the fearsome name of "Fluff."
Face-feeling is illustrated as Lee touches Jeff's face.

LEE: All in all, it's a nice face.

Discrimination is illustrated when a concessionaire won't let the two ride on the merry-go-round at the park.

MAN: ...you gotta get off.... It ain't allowed. I can't have blind people on the horses.... I don't have insurance for your kind.

At a busy street corner, Jeff is afraid to cross. He endangers them both by holding Lee back.
Lee introduces him to flowers. She asks him to uncover his eyes to identify them for her. Everything he sees is beautiful. Jeff invites Lee to be his date for the dance.

* * *

"Blind Sunday" was an adventurous one-hour movie. Lee was a bright teen, integrated in public school and worried about boys. She discussed difficulties about the same, such as boys "don't ask me out." She was capable and independent.
Two messages could have been perceived by Jeff's experiment. One was "isn't this terrible?" being pursued by imaginary attack dogs, afraid to cross a street, etc. Jeff was very frightened and had to cling to Lee for guidance and support. All he gained was an appreciation for his own sight.
Another message might have been an understanding of the different perceptions Lee had as opposed to Jeff's when blindfolded. She was not terrified or disoriented. It would seem that the former message might register more deeply with young viewers than the latter.
This piece was valuable, however, in that it did illustrate these perceptive differences. Jeff could not hope to gain an understanding of life without usable vision by spending a day being blindfolded. However, Lee was able to guide him and take care of him during the odyssey simply because she was navigating in the world in which she was completely familiar.
"Blind Sunday" was different and interesting. A blind teen was seen at ease in the world although she had to put up with the limiting perceptions and expectations of those around her.

Little House on the Prairie / "The Hunters" / Dec. 20, 1976 / NBC-TV

Executive Producer: Michael Landon

* Blindness
* Widowed White Male

Blindness

Producer: John Hawkins * **Equipment:** Walking staff
Director: Michael Landon
Writer: Harold Swanton
Category: Series Television —
Period Drama

Plot: When Pa Ingalls is injured in an accident, daughter Laura must depend on an old blind man to help her find aid.

Laura begs to go hunting with Pa. On their trek, they say hello to trapper Ben and his old blind father, Mr. Shelby. When Pa is accidentally shot, Laura goes back to Shelby's cabin, only to find Ben has gone trapping. Shelby doesn't think he can help. Helplessness is indicated as well as blindness as a lightless condition.

> SHELBY: I don't know what I can do for you. I know my way around the cabin here but that's as far as I can go ... I can't go out there. I can't see a lick ... I haven't been a hundred feet from this cabin in five years ... I can't walk in the dark.

Laura goads him. Shelby gets his staff and the two reach Pa. Shelby devalues himself.

> SHELBY: I ain't got much to offer but I'm all there is.

The two get Pa to the cabin. Laura then depends on Shelby's old recollection of mountain paths to try and find help for her rapidly declining Pa. Laura and Shelby get lost.

> SHELBY: I'm afeerd, child.
>
> LAURA: Then we'll be afraid together.

The two are found by Shelby's son. Pa will survive.
Shelby indicates to son Ben that perhaps it is time he went trapping with him again.

* * *

"The Hunters" presented a blind character as one unable to cope with a serious situation. Laura acted as the non-disabled catalyst as she told Shelby he *had* to help. The strong-willed child was in control. Her fear for her father's life drove her.

Shelby demonstrated extremely poor judgment when he took on the chore of attempting to find the way out of the mountains since he admitted he hadn't been far from the cabin in years. The action of going out seemingly restored some long-gone confidence as Shelby later indicated he wished to join Ben trapping.

"The Hunters" subordinated a blind adult to a child. Shelby's helplessness was self-inflicted due to an inability to accept his limitation. A mountain man who had to live by his wits was devoid of judgment without the benefit of sight—or so this piece suggested.

Barney Miller / "Community Relations" / 1977

Producer: Danny Arnold
Director: Noam Pitlik
Teleplay: Tony Sheehan
Category: Series Television—Situation Comedy

* Blindness
* White Male
* Equipment: Mobility cane

Plot: A blind shoplifter is arrested.

The cops at the 12th Precinct have arrested a blind shoplifter.

> BARNEY: Considering your handicap, how did you think you could get away with it?
>
> MR. ROTH: ...I was counting on the element of surprise.
>
> YEMANA: I was surprised.

A play on hypersensitive perception appears when Roth explains why he went ahead with the crime.

> MR. ROTH: I didn't smell anyone around.

Mr. Roth has been continuously ripped off. A revenge motive surfaces as he indicates it's his turn to steal. More heightened sensory perception is illustrated as Mr. Roth zeroes in on Harris and the Asian Yemana.

> MR. ROTH: You're over six feet tall and you're a chain smoker.... You're cool and collected ... intelligent ... either that or you're Japanese.

Mr. Roth illustrates he is somewhat independent yet needs help.

> MR. ROTH: Someone's got to get me down on the street. Once I'm on First Street, I'm okay ... I'm usually very independent.

Mr. Luger, a displaced veteran, has been arrested. Since Mr. Luger has no place to live and Mr. Roth indicates living alone makes him a target, the two agree to move in together.

* * *

"Community Relations" was a funny story which characterized a blind man as a wisecracking—yet sharp—citizen. Despite the sensory capabilities Mr. Roth possessed, they can be halfway dismissed due to the exaggeration present in such sitcoms; however, use of the same in comedy must be noted. A sharp-tongued petty criminal who was blind—despite the stereotypes in the program—was a welcome change.

M*A*S*H / "Out of Sight, Out of Mind" / 1977 / CBS-TV

Executive Producer: Gene Reynolds
Producer: Burt Metcalfe
Director: Gene Reynolds
Writers: Ken Levine and David Isaacs
Category: Series Television—Situation Comedy/Drama

* Blindness
* Single White Male; Series lead
* Temporary Disability

Plot: Surgeon Hawkeye Pierce discovers a new world after he is blinded in an explosion.

Hawkeye goes to fix a stove for freezing nurses battling the Korean winter. The contraption blows up in his face and he is blinded. Bandaged, he worries that the condition might be permanent.

Hawkeye discovers the young man in the next bed in post-op is Tom Straw, also blind. Straw is depressed about his upcoming release from the hospital.

>TOM: I'm looking forward to getting back and NOT seeing the Golden Gate.

Despite fear and anxiety that his surgical career may be at an end, Hawkeye has made some discoveries.

>HAWKEYE: Something fascinating's been happening to me. One part of the world closes but another opens up.... [I] listened to that rainstorm ... [and] was a *part* of it—you wouldn't believe how funny it is to hear someone slip and fall in the mud.... I've never spent a more conscious day in my life.... You ought to sit back and listen to the war.

Hawkeye's eyes are unbandaged and he finds that he has his vision.

>HAWKEYE: I was lucky twice. First I got the chance to see without my eyes. Then I got 'em back.

* * *

"Out of Sight, Out of Mind" was a completely different type of leading-character-becomes-disabled-for-a-day story. The formula of a principal character suffering a brief disability was offset by the unique humor of Hawkeye. The surgeon was afraid, yet too much of the rebel to let it get him down.

Hawkeye's discoveries excited him in the midst of his depression. He was realizing that there was an existence after disability. Fortunately for him, his vision was retained — but he had truly acquired some valuable perceptions from the difficulty.

Hawkeye referred to stereotypes of blindness, such as mentioning he visualized himself "sitting on a corner with a tin cup selling thermometers" but quickly negated such an image by indicating how aware he was becoming of everything around him.

A performer with a disability was cast in the role of Tom Straw.

"Out of Sight, Out of Mind" dealt with a temporary disability quite fairly and with both poignancy and humor.

The Love Boat / "Eyes of Love" / Jan. 21, 1978 / ABC-TV

Executive Producers: Aaron Spelling; Douglas Cramer
Producers: Gordon and Lynne Farr and Henry Colman
Director: Allen Baron
Writer: Tony Webster
Category: Series Television — Romantic Comedy

* Blindness
* Single White Female
* Equipment: Mobility cane; Braille book; Braille cards; Sighted guide

Plot: A young blind woman re-meets her high school love on the cruise ship.

Jenny Lang is surprised to meet old boyfriend Steve on the *Pacific Princess*. She explains the relationship to ship's employees Gopher and Julie.

JENNY: Steve and I went to the same school for the blind.

Gopher and Julie exchange looks because Steve can see. Jenny exits, planning to meet Steve later for a drink. Steve explains to Gopher and Julie that an operation restored his vision.

Steve tells Jenny that he has his sight. Their mutual attraction grows during the cruise. Jenny devalues herself when Steve does not pick up on her advances.

JENNY: You have your sight now. Why should you be saddled with a blind girl?

48 Blindness

Steve admits he is engaged.

Jenny has said goodbye to Steve at Puerto Vallarta, where he will meet his fiancée. She is reading in her cabin when he comes in. He has broken his engagement because he loves Jenny. She again devalues herself.

> JENNY: You're crazy! You could have a normal, happy marriage with that girl!

> STEVE: What makes you think that marrying a girl who can see guarantees a happy marriage?

Jenny is well-liked by all the crew members. Her personality is subordinated when Doc Bricker notes:

> BRICKER: She's quite a girl—it's a shame she's blind.

Jenny overhears the empty, materialistic talk of a rich couple on board and reports the conversation to Steve. The couple listens in and realizes they've lost sight of love. The large diamond the wife has will be donated to "charity."

> HUBBY: I understand there's a school for the blind that does wonderful work.

Jenny proposes to Steve and they will be married.

* * *

"Eyes of Love" presented a young woman who was blind as independent, capable and possessed of a personality. She had taken the cruise alone; she indicated to Gopher if he took her around the ocean liner once, she wouldn't require his aid again. She navigated independently about the ship.

Special equipment was misused. Jenny inappropriately used a cane which was also too short for her.

Jenny was handled very carefully by everyone as if she might break. Even Steve, a person who had been sightless himself, handled Jenny as if she were fragile. Jenny sometimes moved in a tentative way which added to this overprotectiveness. (It seemed the sighted actress was working with her eyes closed in some scenes to perhaps better "feel" her character.)

The action of the fellow passenger who stated he was donating to "charity," then mentioning a school for the blind, erroneously indicated education for the visually impaired is strictly a segregated institution supported exclusively through fund-raising and not public monies. It is a small point but one worth noting. "Eyes of Love" presented a blind young woman as independent and emotional yet who required special handling and attention because of her disability.

Family / "See Saw" / Jan. 28, 1978 / ABC-TV

Executive Producers: Aaron Spelling; Leonard Goldberg
Producer: Nigel McKeand
Director: Philip Leacock
Story: Len Jenkin
Teleplay: Barbara Elaine Smith
Category: Series Television — Drama

* Blindness
* Single White Male
* Equipment: Mobility cane

Plot: Kate begins to mother a blind young man who wants to be helpless.

Kate Lawrence reads at a center for blind persons on Fridays. Director John Krieger approaches her for help on a special project.

> JOHN: I need someone to work with a young man in our rehabilitation program.... A year and a half ago ... he was involved in a ... tragic accident and it left him blind permanently.... Now he's ... ready to start back [to college].

John and Kate enter the day lounge, a room full of people in dark glasses. Sensory capabilities are solicited when John says:

> JOHN: You're all wondering who just came in with me.

Alex, an older blind man rises.

> ALEX: It's a woman!

John tells Kate she will be working with Robert Pearson, the young man playing the piano. Bitterness is evident in his introductory speech.

> ROBERT: She's seen me and admired me from near, but I, of course, have seen nothing of her devotion.

John leaves Kate in the lounge. Robert and Alex engage in a battle of exceptional sensory perceptions.

> ROBERT: Don't move, Katherine Lawrence. I'll find you. Your perfume is lilac.

> ALEX: Lilac, my foot. It's carnation. What's the matter with your nose?

Robert casts negative shadows over the life of a person who is blind when he tells Kate:

> ROBERT: You don't know what it's like always having to be at it, always trying to overcome something, trying to make sense of pages full of bumps and dots, always having to listen for every sound and squeak ... you don't know how much pressure has been put on me.... I feel very safe with you.

Robert becomes dependent on Kate and manipulates her to do things *his* way, such as deferring a mobility trip to the college campus where he is to register on Monday. When, at last, they go, Robert fails miserably. After bumping into both a wall and a girl, and scaring a child, he sits on the ground, defeated.

> KATE: You don't have to do anything you don't want to.

Kate takes him back to the center. Robert is seen as willingly dependent and helpless as Kate gets his food in the cafeteria and feeds him.

Kate goes to the center after discovering she has let herself become Robert's patsy. She refuses to listen to Robert's promise to register "next semester" and assumes the role of the non-disabled catalyst. She uses pejorative notions in her speech.

> KATE: You'll find someone else as foolish as I am. You'll stay right where you are in a darkness, darker than your sight.

> ROBERT: There's nothing darker than that.

> KATE: Don't feel so sorry for yourself. Your mind isn't dark, your imagination isn't dark, but they will be unless you struggle to free them. Give them light to be educated. If you avoid that struggle, where will the light come from to you? You're blessed, having the capabilities to get to a university. How dare you not take advantage of them?

Kate goes to her car. As she starts her engine, Robert appears, ready to leave and register for college.

* * *

"See Saw" was an exceptionally poor depiction of life with a visual impairment. The new limitation was frightening for Robert, but instead of exploring his fears and offering solutions, the story focused on all the negatives he was facing.

Special equipment was misused. Both Robert and Alex used their mobility canes inappropriately. Also, the use of an untrained professional like Kate for mobility training at a college campus was also misuse of special equipment.

"See Saw" presented no factual information in its pitiful portrayal of blindness.

Little House on the Prairie / "I'll Be Waving As You Drive Away" / Mar. 13, 1978 / NBC-TV

Producer: William E. Claxton
Writers: Carole & Michael Paschella
Category: Series Television — Period Drama

* Blindness
* Single White Female; Regular character
* New Disability
* Face-feeling
* Equipment: Braille

Plot: Mary Ingalls goes blind.

Young Mary Ingalls loses her sight — and her hopes of becoming a schoolteacher. The cause of disability is described as the strain of a long-ago bout with scarlet fever.

Mary isn't keen on going away to a school for the blind. Devaluation, negative aspects, and an indication of blindness as lightlessness show up in an outburst.

> MA: ...you can't spend the rest of your life sitting in that chair.
>
> MARY: Why not? Why can't I just sit here? There's nothing for me to see. It's dark. No matter where I go, darkness.

At the school for the blind, Mary meets instructor Adam Kendall. She prefers to dine alone but Adam squelches that thought.

> ADAM: Just because you're blind doesn't mean you have to eat like an animal ... all you can think about is being blind ... blind people are just as good or bad as anybody else ... you're not special.

Face-feeling is seen as Mary and Adam get to be friends. Mary worries that she does not know what Adam looks like. She touches his face and has him describe himself. Mary discovers Adam is blind when he asks her to describe herself.

Mary will become a teacher for blind children in the new school Adam will set up.

* * *

"I'll Be Waving As You Drive Away" was unique in that it featured a regular character in a series incurring a disability — one who did not get cured. For the remainder of the run of *Little House,* Mary Ingalls remained blind. She married Adam, had a child and was a teacher. Adam's sight was restored but Mary remained blind.

Most refreshing in this piece was the role of Adam. He appeared quite relaxed and natural; in contrast, Mary and the children at the school all stared straight ahead in a wooden manner.

Special equipment such as Braille was seen as well as different methods a person with low vision might use for various chores. (Although Braille materials seen in the production were historically inaccurate, it is much more important that the message get across to viewers that blind children could read.)

"I'll Be Waving As You Drive Away" had its share of melodrama as well as good information.

Little House on the Prairie / "Blind Journey" / Nov. 26, 1978 / NBC-TV

Executive Producer: Michael Landon
Producer: William F. Claxton
Story: John T. Dugan
Writers: Michael and Carole Paschella, John T. Dugan
Category: Series Television — Period Drama

* Blindness
* Group portrayal; Black and white children

Plot: Winoka Academy for the Blind and its children find a new home in Walnut Grove.

When the Winoka Academy for the Blind is sold, blind headmaster Adam Kendall accepts the invitation of Walnut Grove to adopt the school. Adam goes to buy a couple of horses for the trip. His father-in-law, Charles Ingalls, looks over the sorry nags purchased.

> CHARLES: There're two things the blind should stay away from — buzz saws and buyin' horses.
>
> ADAM: Are you trying to tell me only a blind man would buy those horses?

The children travel holding onto a long rope tied to a wagon.

The school joins up with Hester Sue Terhune, a woman with a school of her own for blind black children. Hester Sue is black, much to the chagrin of prejudiced Mrs. Oleson, who thought she was going to be assisting a society woman, not an ex-slave.

The children cross over river and dale and arrive safely in their new home.

* * *

"Blind Journey" illustrated a group of sightless children as quiet, gentle, and ever-obedient kids with wooden stares.

Blindness as a metaphor for lack of prejudice was seen as a small black boy asked why white people didn't like black people—since all people "looked" the same to him.

"Blind Journey" presented blind children as a group apart from their young sighted contemporaries, kids who would never disobey or refuse to do their homework. Their blindness set them far apart from average children. They did not mirror the prejudices of society.

Little House on the Prairie / "The Enchanted Cottage" / 1978 / NBC-TV

Executive Producer: Michael Landon
Producer: William Claxton
Director: William Claxton
Writer: Don Balluck
Category: Series Television—Period Drama

* Blindness
* Married White Female; Series regular

Plot: Mary Ingalls Kendall begins to see light and dreams of getting her vision back.

Mary believes she is regaining her sight. Her blind husband, Adam, is very quiet about the prospects. Mary is ecstatic and tells him she wants:

MARY: To be able to see your face ... really see it.

Adam begins exhibiting clumsy behavior. He knocks over a bowl of fruit.

CAROLINE: Let me give you a hand with this.

ADAM: No, I can manage by myself!

Father Charles Ingalls takes Mary to see an eye specialist. She rhapsodizes about all the things she will see. She wants to see, she insists, for Adam.

MARY: I'm gonna see ... Pa. I *am.*

Mary is tested by a doctor and preliminary results are encouraging. Pa sends a telegram home. Adam seems distressed by the news. Caroline finds him alone in the church, crying.

ADAM: Ever since Mary told me ... I've just been afraid.

CAROLINE: Of what?

Adam devalues himself and the love he and his wife share.

> ADAM: If she could see, she could go anywhere, do anything she wants. I'd just be a burden to her ... I don't know if I want her to see again.

Caroline becomes the non-disabled catalyst.

> CAROLINE: ...Being blind together isn't your strongest bond with Mary.

Mary is devastated when further tests prove that she is only imagining she is seeing light.

> MARY: I can see the light!!! He's wrong!

Mary throws herself spread-eagled against a bright window and sobs despondently.

Back home, Mary goes to the little cottage that Laura was readying for her older sister's sighted homecoming. Mary squelches any possible sentimentality.

> MARY: I'm blind and you better get used to it because that's the way it's going to be.

* * *

After Mary Ingalls lost her sight on *Little House,* there were numerous stories about blindness. Nearly every formula aspect described in this work showed up on the family drama. "The Enchanted Cottage" was one such episode.

Mary was typically hoping for a cure. Adam was typically concerned he would be "a burden" to a sighted wife. Oddly enough, in a future episode when Adam's sight was restored, Mary devalued herself and felt Adam wouldn't love her and that she would be "a burden" to a sighted husband! These types of scenes actively created a mentality that people with a lack of vision exist in their own subculture. "The Enchanted Cottage" was an exercise in emotions and heartstring tugging.

Happy Days / "Fonzie's Blindness" / 1978 / ABC-TV

Executive Producers: Thomas L. Miller; Edward K. Milkis; Garry K. Marshall
Producers: Jerry Paris; Bob Brunner

* Blindness
* Single White Male; Series lead
* Temporary Disability

Director: Jerry Paris
Writers: Ron Leavitt & Richard Rosenstock
Category: Series Television — Situation Comedy

Plot: A bump on the head causes the Fonz to go blind.

At Arnold's Restaurant, Al turns around and bashes Fonzie in the head with a tray. Fonzie is stunned. He claims he's all right — but collapses. Fonzie is wearing dark glasses after seeing the doctor. He claims it's to give his eyes a rest. Richie sticks close. He goes upstairs to the Fonz's apartment the next morning.

>   RICHIE: Well, ready to start off the morning with a good hearty breakfast?

>   FONZIE: No ... Richie, I'm blind.

Ralph explains to the gang what's happened to Fonzie, the knowledge courtesy of his father.

>   RALPH: What Fonzie's got is optic neuritis. And with treatment, he could get his sight back.

Richie primes the gang at Arnold's for Fonzie to come in, to show him everything is the same. He sits Fonz at his booth. Al approaches for a greeting. Fonz reaches up and feels Al's nose. He fondly pats it.

>   FONZIE: How ya doin', Al?

Potsie and Ralph are uneasy around Fonz and stumble over their references to things visual. Fonzie can't take it. He yells at Richie to get him out of there.

At the Cunninghams, Fonzie continually asks for help at the dinner table until Richie stops him.

>   RICHIE: The doctor said Fonzie's got to start doing some things for himself now.

Richie acts as the non-disabled catalyst, telling Fonz he isn't even trying to cope.

>   RICHIE: You're a coward!

Fonzie leaps up in anger. He starts throwing things as he verbally devalues himself.

FONZIE: I'm useless! I'm blind!

Richie dismantles Fonzie's beloved motorcycle and dumps the pieces on the floor of Fonzie's apartment. He goads his friend to put it back together. Fonzie successfully reconstructs his bike and thanks Richie for his help. He knows there are places and things that can help him.

FONZIE: Well, maybe I can get a Seeing Eye Chick — as long as she ain't a dog.

Fonzie's sight begins to come back. He will be completely recovered in a few days.

* * *

"Fonzie's Blindness" was predictable. Fonzie, after losing his sight, became angry, surly, self-pitying, and bitter. It took Richie to break him out of his blue funk. This approach again condenses the disability into a personal problem. Friends with patience and understanding like Richie could help the person through. The "quick fix" of assembling a motorcycle was used to restore Fonzie's self-confidence.

"Fonzie's Blindness" possessed nothing that was new, different, or compelling.

Three's Company / "Jack's Navy Pal" / 1978 / CBS-TV

Director: Bill Hobin
Story: Paul Wayne & George Burditt and Alan J. Levitt
Teleplay: Paul Wayne & George Burditt
Category: Series Television — Situation Comedy

* Blindness
* White Male
* Equipment: Mobility cane

Plot: An old Navy acquaintance of Jack's comes to settle an old score.

The Ropers are going to raise Jack, Janet, and Chrissy's rent $75 a month. To butter up their landlord, the Ropers are invited to dinner.

Jim Walsh, an old nemesis of Jack's, shows up. He is blind. He reaches out to touch Jack's face.

WALSH: Yeah, that's you.

Satisfied, he punches Jack in the jaw and challenges Jack to hit him. He says Jack won't hit a blind man.

The Ropers show up for dinner and wonder why Walsh is there.

WALSH: ...I'm just waiting for Jack to hit me.

The cause of Walsh's disability was an explosion when his still blew up. The doctor thinks it's only temporary.

ROPER: Bet you can't wait to see us all.

WALSH: You lose.

In an attempt to get rid of the unwanted guest, Jack and the girls try to ignore Walsh. It turns out to be very hard to do that — especially when Walsh pours Roper's wine all over Roper; sniffs out Roper's dinner plate and tosses it over his shoulder; takes his cane and misuses it, swinging it to purposely break objects and furniture, trashing the apartment. Fed up, Jack goes to hit Walsh, who blocks him and lands a punch on poor Jack.

WALSH: Serves him right for trying to hit a blind man.

* * *

Not only was "Jack's Navy Pal" a bizarre image of blindness, it was a story that made little sense. Jim Walsh was bent on annoying Jack Tripper whom he hadn't seen in years. Now blind, he showed up at the door and belted Jack, demanding to be hit in return. Jack, the eternal nice guy, refused and was virtually terrorized by Walsh.

Special equipment — in this case, Walsh's outdated standard orthopedic cane painted white — was badly misused, breaking everything in sight. Obviously, Walsh was meant to be a parody, but why? Again, the story was weak and senseless. A bizarre image of blindness emerged. "Jack's Navy Pal" presented a ridiculous image of blindness for unknown and misguided reasons.

Ice Castles / 1979 / Columbia Pictures

Executive Producer: Rosilyn Heller
Producer: John Kemeny
Co-Producer: S. Rodger Olenicoff
Director: Donald Wrye
Story: Gary L. Baim
Screenplay: Donald Wrye and
   Gary L. Baim
Category: Feature Film — Drama

* Blindness; Partial
* Single White Female
* New Disability

Plot: A promising figure skater loses her vision in an accident.

Alexis "Lexie" Winston, an untrained but exceptionally skilled skater, catches the eye of an Olympic coach. The coach wants to train this unlikely young hopeful for the skating nationals and the Olympics. Lexie is groomed by coach Deborah into a skater but needs a recognition factor. Deborah arranges a media blitz.

Lexie is snubbed by her old boyfriend Nick, who can't cope with her sudden leap to stardom. At a special party thrown for her by sponsors, she straps on a pair of skates and goes to a private outdoor rink. She risks a dangerous move. Lexie spins out of control and falls, banging her head against some wrought iron fixtures. A new disability is incurred. The doctors tell Lexie's father her vision is impaired.

Lexie returns home to the quiet house she shares with her father. She shuts herself up in her room, ignoring her appearance. She refuses telephone calls from Deborah.

Beulah, the owner of the local skating rink who had originally taught Lexie, goes to the Winston home upon Marcus Winston's request. She finds Lexie in the attic, cradling old clothes belonging to her dead mother, lost in a regressive, childish haze. Beulah becomes a non-disabled catalyst, forcing Lexie to face herself. Lexie breaks down and begins to look after herself. She leaves her room.

Nick comes to the farm to spy on Lexie where Marcus has gotten his daughter to strap on her skates and move across the frozen pond on their land. Nick takes over and despite the animosity between Lexie and him, he works to teach her to skate again. He works with her on Beulah's rink until she's ready to try skating at the regionals—which she does, successfully, as the crowd roars approval.

The audience tosses flowers on the ice. Unable to see them, Lexie stumbles and skids on the stems. The audience sits in stunned silence as Nick goes to help Lexie to her feet—and they realize what they've just seen.

* * *

"Ice Castles" featured a young blind woman who was angry and frustrated with her life until she regained competence in what she did best—ice skating. Lexie's accident left her with the ability to see light and shadows. Her partial blindness brought up a unique situation rarely touched upon in dramas: her residual vision hindered her in many ways. Although she had light perception, Nick persuaded her to skate with her eyes closed to block out the visual distractions. She concentrated so hard on trying to see, she handicapped her own efforts to skate. She learned to trust Nick's directions, using his help to gauge the skating area available on a rink.

After losing her vision, Lexie went straight home with her father. No evidence of rehabilitation or counseling was seen. Lexie was able to achieve on the skating rink after her accident, but could she manage her own personal mobility? This was ignored in favor of a "quick fix."

The "overcoming" focus of this story limited the audience's perception of disability—Lexie's problem was not being able to skate. Her life was suddenly forfeited. However, Lexie's mental state just prior to her accident indicated she had lost reason and was possibly hoping to hurt herself. Learning to skate again was *not* the solution to an emotional difficulty.

Ice Castles presented a blind character as one who triumphed, but who was ultimately a tragic figure.

Mork and Mindy / "Mork Learns to See" / 1979 / ABC-TV

Executive Producers: Garry K. Marshall, Tony Marshall
Producer: Dale McRaven and Bruce Johnson
Director: Howard Storm
Writers: Ed Scharlach & Tom Tenowich
Category: Series Television — Situation Comedy

* Blindness
* White Male
* Performer with a Disability
* Equipment: Braille; Braille watch; Dog guide

Plot: Mork and Mindy's crusty neighbor avoids his visiting blind son.

Mork and Mindy go to Mr. Bickley's apartment to meet his visiting son. They enter at Tom's invitation and find him sitting in the dark. Blindness as a lightless condition is reinforced.

> MORK: Why are you sitting in the dark?
>
> TOM: I'm sorry. The switch is on the wall by the door.... I was just reading.
>
> MINDY: You shouldn't read in the dark. You'll go—

The light goes on. Mindy sees the Braille book on Tom's lap and the dog at his side.

> MINDY: —bl—bl—bl
>
> TOM (laughing): I've been bl—bl—bl for quite some time now.

Tom is a singer performing at a local club. Mork and Mindy go to see his act. Tom is illustrated as athletic. He says he plays golf, water skis, and likes to jog. He's also gone sky diving.

> MORK: I'll bet the hard part is to keep your dog from screaming on the way down.

Tom admits he has not seen his dad for twelve years.

> TOM: I guess having a son with a handicap is more than he can face.

Bickley feels Tom's been better off without him. Bickley sent Tom away to school, got him the best doctors, sent him a card every Christmas, took a second job to pay for the school. He thought it made his son independent.

> BICKLEY: You don't know what it's like to have a child born blind. What do you do? Keep him inside so he'll be safe? Or freeze every time you hear a car horn? I had to make Tommy fend for himself.

Mork and Mindy go to the club to pick up Tom to take him to the airport. Bickley tags along, but doesn't want Tom to know he's in the room.

Mork and Mindy and Mr. Bickley come into the club. Tom reminisces about his father. Bickley gets misty.

> TOM: That was for you, Dad.

> BICKLEY: How—how did you know I was here?

Hyper-sensitive perception is played upon.

> TOM: You're still wearing that awful-smelling aftershave. I could find you when I was lost at the circus. It doesn't take a lot to find you in an empty room.

* * *

"Mork Learns to See" was a nice story, due to the fact it illustrated a man who was blind as funny, attractive, energetic and who had problems like everyone—in this case, his father. The easy jokes made by Tom set the audience at ease. Those things, combined with Mork's unconventional sense of the silly, made this a very watchable episode.

Mr. Bickley's uncharacteristic vulnerability when it came to his son was nicely done, indicating a different kind of problem. "Mork Learns to See" was different and fun beyond the mild schlock.

The Rockford Files / "Black Mirror" / 1980 / NBC-TV

Executive Producer: Meta Rosenberg
Producer: David Chase
Supervising Producers: Stephen J. Cannell and Charles Floyd Johnson
Director: Harold Laven
Writer: David Chase

* Blindness
* Single White Female
* Equipment: Mobility cane; Braille clock

Category: Series Television — Detective Drama

Plot: Someone is trying to scare a blind psychologist upon whom private investigator Rockford has a major crush.

Jim Rockford is attracted to Megan, a woman he meets on the beach. She later employs him to find who is harassing and scaring her. On a consult to her apartment, Rockford discovers she is blind. He takes the case.

He finds her sexually attractive and begins a personal relationship with her. As he himself states:

> ROCKFORD: ...It's almost like she's not blind—she's free, she's savvy, she's independent.

Megan is a professional psychologist and a perfectionist. She refuses to share any "confidential" information about her patients, any one of whom, surmises Rockford, could be after her.

Attitudinal barriers are evident at a restaurant when a waiter asks Rockford if Megan would like Parmesan cheese on her dish. Megan neatly tips the man off that sight has nothing to do with decision-making.

A little devaluation shows up after Megan realizes she may have badly misdiagnosed a patient. Rockford's evidence points to the man pulling a fake multiple personality act to use later as an alibi for a killing. Megan, angry at herself, drops a bowl and lets off steam, refusing to be comforted by Rockford.

> MEGAN: Look, you wanted me, you got me. This is the reality, knocking over dishes, banging into furniture, victim to just about everything.

Rockford's "diagnosis" is correct. He saves Megan from her patient.

* * *

"Black Mirror" was an utterly refreshing illustration of blindness simply because of its lack of attention upon Megan's visual limitation. She was a bright, vivacious, and humorous woman who was a professional. She had her own private psychological practice and handled herself quite well. Her limitation was almost purely incidental.

The brief devaluation scene was out-of-character for Megan—but as a staunchly independent perfectionist, her misdiagnosis was a severe blow to her ego. Rockford did not act as the non-disabled catalyst to break her out of it; he responded as a partner in a relationship, with anger, sarcasm, and affection.

As a love interest to Jim Rockford, Megan was a decent match. The road they took was by no means easy, due to the personality dynamics of the two.

"Black Mirror" was a neat story, despite the blind-woman-as-victim plot. It was a bit of a thriller with a twist and a satisfying romance to boot.

The Rockford Files / "Love Is the Word" / June 27, 1980 (rerun) / NBC-TV

Executive Producer: Meta Rosenberg
Producer: David Chase
Supervising Producers: Juanita Bartlett; Stephen J. Cannell; Charles Floyd Johnson
Director: John Patterson
Writer: David Chase
Category: Series Television — Detective Drama

* Blindness
* Single White Female
* Equipment: Mobility cane

Plot: Jim Rockford is again called into service by Megan Dougherty, the blind psychologist.

* * *

"Love Is the Word" featured the incidental role of a blind woman. Dialogue indicated Megan and Rockford had not seen each other for some time. The duration was clear to Rockford when he discovered Megan had become engaged since he'd last plopped down on her couch and helped himself to a beer from her fridge.

Megan was a professional psychologist who was very attractive to both Rockford and her new love. She was a person far and beyond her disability. Her blindness, in fact, was only mentioned once in the story when someone asked if she'd seen a blue jacket. She lightly replied she didn't know anything about jackets, "let alone which one's blue!"

"Love Is the Word" positively illustrated a blind woman as one with feelings and emotions she needed to deal with; as one with a challenging career; and one who had fallen in love and wanted to marry.

Barnaby Jones / "A Focus on Fear" / 1980 / CBS-TV

Executive Producer: Philip Saltzman
Producer: Robert Sherman
Director: Kenneth C. Gilbert
Writer: Jack V. Fogarty
Category: Series Television — Crime Drama

* Blindness
* Single White Female
* Equipment: Sighted guide
* Temporary Disability

Plot: A fashion photographer is blinded by a criminal.

While developing photos in her darkroom, fashion photographer Gwen is attacked by a man who throws acid in her face. A new disability is incurred. Gwen returns home with dark glasses; the doctor says the glasses are a precaution against a sudden rush of light should her sight return.

Negative aspects and erroneous connotations are evident when Gwen chides Barnaby's assistant, J.R. Jones.

> GWEN: That's easy for you to say. You're not stumbling around in the dark, twenty-four hours a day.

Gwen's fashion photos shot at an airfield feature a plane in the background that crashed that same day. J.R. uncovers a freight/insurance scam. As he is being attacked by villains, Gwen's vision blurrily returns. She helps battle the bad guys.

* * *

"A Focus on Fear" was one of those tired stories where a frightened and angry newly disabled person was taken under the wing of a protective series star.

J.R. inappropriately took Gwen's arm to guide her in a misuse of the sighted guide position.

No information about disability was seen; no possibility of life within disability was seen. The character with the limitation was helpless and lost. The timely cure saved the day and the career of a photographer.

The Love Boat / "Eye of the Beholder" / Feb. 21, 1981 / ABC-TV

Executive Producers: Aaron Spelling; Douglas Cramer
Producers: Ray Allen and Harvey Bullock and Henry Colman
Director: Harry Mastrogeorge
Writer: Sid Morse
Category: Series Television — Romantic Comedy

* Blindness
* Single Black Female
* Face-feeling
* Equipment: Braille book; Braille watch

Plot: A man falls in love with a bitter blind woman on a cruise to Mexico.

Assistant Purser Gopher Smith meets Callie Reason, a blind woman on the arm of her helper, Dora.

> GOPHER: I have your cabin assignment for you.

Callie exhibits anger and self-pity.

> CALLIE: No point telling it to me, Mr. Smith. I'd bump into too many walls trying to find it. You'd better give it to my seeing eye lady—if she's anywhere around.... I want you all to just leave me alone.

As Callie leaves, Allan Christianson steps up.

> ALLAN: Poor girl's just hitting out at everybody in frustration.

Allan sees Callie in lounge. He asks if he may sit with her.

> CALLIE: I'd rather you didn't ... I'd like to be alone, okay?... I'm just not in the mood for sympathetic conversation ... I just want to be left alone.

Later, Callie is reading from a Braille volume on deck. Allan silently takes the seat next to hers.

> CALLIE: You're staring, Mr. Christianson. Haven't you ever seen someone trying to read Braille before?

> ALLAN: It's Allan. And how did you know it was me?

Sensitivity of another sense is illustrated.

> CALLIE: You wear a very distinctive cologne.

Callie accepts Allan's invitation to join him at dinner. Later, they go out on deck where a dance is in progress. Callie devalues herself.

> CALLIE: Allan, you're making me feel guilty. You should be out there dancing.... You've been very sweet but I don't expect you to babysit me for the rest of the cruise.

Allan convinces her to dance. She panics when they are separated on the dance floor. She retreats to her cabin, refusing to see Allan. He finally goes to talk with her. He begs her to come with him to see Mazatlan, where the ship has docked. Callie exhibits more anger and self-pity.

> CALLIE: Show me Mazatlan. How can I see it?

> ALLAN: I'll see it for you, Callie. I'll be your eyes.

On deck, in the moonlight after a wonderful day in Mazatlan, Callie turns to Allan and reaches up to feel his face. Allan proposes marriage to her. She accepts and they leave the ship together for Allan's ranch and a new life.

* * *

"Eye of the Beholder" was one of the poorest portraits of blindness ever committed to film.

Callie was angry, bitter, self-pitying, and quick to reprimand everyone around her. Allan was the non-disabled catalyst in every way, shape, and form. He alone found something worth salvaging in Callie. It seemed others on board were rooting for the relationship. When Captain Stubing saw the two on the dance floor, he admitted he thought Allan's getting her to dance was "good therapy."

Callie did not learn how to assimilate her limitation. She simply learned to trust another human being — in this case, Allan. Therefore, without Allan, she would again be as miserable as she was prior to meeting him.

Callie was not explored past her dashed future as a high fashion designer and her fear at facing the world with a disability. Allan was simply a kind soul who, for reasons unknown by the viewer, was attracted to the whining woman.

An interesting footnote to this piece was revealed in an examination of the first draft script of this program. In it, Callie was even *more* angry and self-pitying. "Eye of the Beholder" was a poorly conceived, damaging, and short-sighted depiction of a person who was blind.

The Incredible Hulk / title unknown / Apr. 25, 1981 / CBS-TV

Executive Producer: Kenneth Johnson
Supervising Producer: Nicholas Corea

* Blindness
* Single White Female

Plot: David Banner rescues a blind girl in a creek and tries to hide his ability to turn into the Hulk from her.

A girl is floundering in a creek. On-the-run scientist David Banner rescues her and discovers she is blind. Katie Maxwell is her name. The cause of her disability is discussed.

> BANNER: Were you born without sight?
>
> KATIE: No — seven months, three weeks, two days. A drunken driver, damage to the optic nerve. I wake up blinded.
>
> BANNER: You've got quite a memory.
>
> KATIE: I've got no choice.

Katie indicates blindness is a lightless condition when she explains why she moved to this rural area after her accident.

KATIE: I couldn't take the city after the lights went out.

A professional pianist, Katie bitterly describes her future.

KATIE: I'll sit at my piano and play odes to springtime.

Self-devaluation is evident after she runs into her piano. She tells Banner someone will make a Katie Maxwell doll that one can wind up to send crashing into a piano. Banner acts as the non-disabled catalyst, taking Katie outside and teaching her how to locate the sun.

A meteor causes Banner to partially metamorphose into his alter-ego, the Hulk. The army is on his trail. A derivation of face-feeling occurs when Katie touches his face in mid-transformation. The scientist is trapped halfway between his average self and the Hulk. He needs her help.

The army evacuates Katie. She slips away to try and find her way back to assist Banner. Listening to sounds and locating directions by the sun on her face, she finds Banner and saves the day.

* * *

This episode of *The Incredible Hulk* portrayed an angry and bitter blind woman who shut herself away. It took the untrained David Banner to turn Katie around and give her some hokey pointers on mobility in her own surroundings. It would seem that after acquiring her disability, Katie received no counseling or rehabilitation training.

There was no indication from Katie that there was anything worth striving for after losing her sight — not even her music career. This episode of the series presented no information about blindness.

Hart to Hart / "Hart of Darkness" / 1981 / ABC-TV

Executive Producers: Aaron Spelling; Leonard Goldberg
Producer: Matt Crowley
Director: Karen Arthur
Writer: Lawrence Hertzog
Category: Series Television — Crime Drama

* Blindness
* Married White Male; Series lead
* Equipment: Mobility cane
* Temporary Disability

Plot: Jonathan Hart is blinded by a deranged would-be assassin.

Multimillionaire Jonathan Hart is blinded by an assailant who dumps a burning chemical into his swimming pool. In the hospital, the villain goes into Jonathan's room and moves all the furniture around to confuse him.

Jonathan calls Jim Blye, his old professor who is now blind. Jim uses poor language while talking to Jonathan, whose eyes are bandaged.

> JIM: So Jonathan, how does it feel to be groping around in the dark?

Jim acts as a disabled catalyst. He discusses having a visual limitation. He indicates there is life after blindness.

> JIM: The word *handicapped* is a bit overstated. It all depends on how you look at it.

Jennifer reacts.

> JIM: Sorry — how you *perceive* it. I said I don't feel handicapped — there're things I can do now that I never dreamed of when I was sighted.

Jim dispels the notion of blind people having a sixth sense.

> JIM: See, when you're sighted, the other senses can relax. There's a tendency toward laziness.

Jim introduces Jonathan to a mobility cane and takes him to the hospital cafeteria.

> JIM: What do you smell?
>
> JONATHAN: Food. Specifically? I'm not sure.

Jim indicates hypersensitive perception.

> JIM: Fish. Definitely broccoli, salad, Roquefort dressing.

Jonathan returns home with wife, Jennifer. He indicates helplessness.

> JONATHAN: You'll have to take care of me.

The assailant stalks Jonathan as Jennifer is taking a shower. Jonathan kills the lights to have an equal advantage in a *Wait Until Dark* sequence. The would-be killer lights a fire for illumination. Jonathan beats him up and removes his bandages. He can see.

* * *

True to TV tradition, Jonathan Hart received no counseling after losing his sight in "Hart of Darkness." He was left on his own. He called Jim Blye, who helped Hart make a simplistic and too-easy transition to being nonsighted. His experience would have been better suited to verbal counseling than mobility training. His deliverance of a cane to Hart implied that such duties are handled by friends in this type of situation and not trained professionals.

Jonathan retained his personality and self-assurance after losing his vision, as do most series leads when facing a devastating life change. They differ from the average guest star who has serious difficulties in assimilating a disability. "Hart of Darkness" was typical and dull.

VEGA$ / "Out of Sight" / 1981 / ABC-TV

Executive Producers: Aaron Spelling; Douglas Cramer
Producer in Vegas: Jeffrey Hayes
Supervising Producer: E. Duke Vincent
Director: Cliff Bole
Writer: Anne Collins
Category: Series Television—Crime Drama

* Blindness
* Single White Male; Series lead
* Temporary Disability
* Equipment: Mobility cane; Sighted guide

Plot: Dan Tanna is blinded in an attempt on his life.

Private eye Dan Tanna is shot in the desert and left to die. He is rescued by some bikers and awakens in the hospital with a new disability.

TANNA: I can't see—I'm blind and I can't see.

Tanna also cannot recall what happened in the desert. The doctor believes Tanna's visual and recollection problems are the result of emotional stress. Tanna packs to leave the hospital. At home, he tries to track down whoever was responsible for the attack.

Tanna narrows down leads. He is getting too close to the truth and expects a "visit" from criminals that night. With assistant Binzer's help, they set up a plan, à la *Wait Until Dark*. When the would-be assailants come in, Tanna will cut the lights using the fuse box, then blind the attackers with high-powered bursts from a strobe light.

The villains come in and although the plan is foiled, Tanna gets the edge. In fear, he regains his sight.

Las Vegas, with its shows and lights, is food for Tanna's eyes.

TANNA: These lights never looked better to me.

* * *

"Out of Sight" differed from most star-becomes-temporarily-disabled stories. Usually, the series lead maintains his heroic status by coping exceptionally well with the difficulty. Tanna's disability was psychologically caused and he refused to deal with that fact. He told Binzer that being blind was not his "style."

After being blinded, Tanna adopted the typical wooden stare and stiff neck the media blind possess. Tanna grew frustrated and did a typical "helpless" scene—in this scene, dropping a glass and breaking it before swinging his cane in anger.

Special equipment was misused. Tanna utilized a white cane that was much too short for a man of his stature. Binzer took Tanna's arm in a misuse of the sighted guide mobility technique. He also handled Tanna carefully as if the man had become fragile.

"Out of Sight" was more interesting than the basic star-becomes-disabled story, but it still left much to be desired.

WKRP in Cincinnati / title unknown / Aug. 9, 1982 (rerun) / CBS-TV

Executive Producer: Hugh Wilson
Category: Series Television—Situation Comedy

* Blindness
* White Male
* Performer with a Disability

Plot: Herb Tarlek's job may be down the drain when he alienates a big sponsor of the station.

Herb Tarlek's ego gets him in trouble when he insults Mr. Sherman, a big executive, who threatens to pull a large advertising account from the station. Herb begs and pleads for receptionist Jennifer Marlowe to go and visit Mr. Sherman and use her feminine wiles to get him off of Herb's back. Jennifer reluctantly agrees.

Jennifer waltzes into Mr. Sherman's office and discovers her strategy is dead when he turns out to be blind and oblivious to her body language. He finds Jennifer attractive.

> MR. SHERMAN: May I feel your face?
>
> JENNIFER: Is this some kind of sightless come-on?

* * *

This episode of *WKRP* was amusing but sometimes at the expense of Mr. Sherman, such as when Herb returned to apologize and made faces and rude gestures to the blind man. However, he got his when he left the office and Sherman called him back—to thumb his own nose at Herb!

Most amusing was Herb's reaction to the news that the dreaded Mr. Sherman was blind. He became cocky and cheerful, figuring he had the situation in the bag. As usual, he was wrong, for Sherman was an executive of barracuda nature (and he did *not* feel Jennifer's face).

This episode of *WKRP in Cincinnati* illustrated a blind character as a headstrong professional who was not to be dallied with and who had a sense of humor.

T.J. Hooker / "Blind Justice" / Oct. 23, 1982 / ABC-TV

Executive Producers: Aaron Spelling; Leonard Goldberg
Producer: Jeffrey Hayes
Supervising Producer: Rick Husky
Director: Don Chaffey
Story: Joe Viola, Stephen Downing and Walter Dallenback
Teleplay: Joe Viola & Stephen Downing
Category: Series Television—Police Drama

* Blindness
* Single White Female
* Equipment: Mobility cane; Sighted guide

Plot: A blind woman is the only witness to a robbery.

A woman disembarks a city bus outside a theatre where a box office robbery is taking place. The woman cowers near a building and is shot at by criminals. Sergeant Hooker and his sidekick, Vince Romano, responding to a silent alarm, give chase. They lose the perpetrators and return to the theatre. Hooker questions Anne Perry.

ANNE: I didn't see anything, Sergeant. I'm blind.

Vince Romano is distressed as Anne leaves the scene.

ROMANO: Blind! And I was so sure we had a witness.

HOOKER: I'm not so sure we don't.

Hooker does some legwork and discovers Anne works teaching "sensory awareness" to blind children. He interrupts her class on the beach and is impressed when Anne approaches him and calls him by name. Heightened sensory perception is evident.

HOOKER: You recognized me!

ANNE: I remember your cologne from the other day. And you're not alone.

HOOKER: No, I brought my partner with me.

ROMANO: I'm Vince Romano. Pleased to meet you, Miss Perry.

ANNE: Oh, it's Anne. And you're from South Philadelphia, aren't you?

ROMANO: Yeah. Yeah, how could you tell?

ANNE: I went to school outside Philadelphia . . . linguistics was my passion in college.

Anne insists she cannot help Hooker's investigation.

The criminals knock off another box office, this time committing murder in the process. Hooker tries again to enlist Anne's help—as the perpetrators trail him to her home. Anne breaks down and uses amazing sensory perception as she tells Hooker:

ANNE: There were two of them. One black, one white . . . the white one—I'm pretty sure—is from the southwest, probably Oklahoma. And his friend is from the south, maybe Louisiana. . . .

The killers wait for their moment outside of Anne's house. They cut the telephone wire and knock on her door. One identifies himself as "special delivery." Anne recognizes the voice.

The baddies burst in the dark house. In a *Wait Until Dark* sequence, Anne knocks out the lights and switches off the fuse box. The criminals discover her mobility cane and decide she's no threat.

Anne is now ready to help the police. She uses more sensory recall. She remembers the Caucasian's name is "Bobby Joe."

HOOKER: Nothing on the other guy?

ANNE: Except the odor. I recognized the smell from the theatre robbery. It was liniment like athletes use.

HOOKER: Anything else?

ANNE: Boots. The small Caucasian wore high heeled boots, probably Western.

Hooker has enough leads that he is able to track the criminals and stop them after they rob the Amphitheatre's box office where the Beach Boys are playing a sold-out show.

* * *

"Blind Justice" was another of the endless blind-woman-as-victim pieces. Anne's sensory prowess was grossly exaggerated. Her abilities to sniff liniment and geographically place accents of two individuals during a heated moment where she heard only two sentences spoken were laughable. She recognized Hooker's cologne (unannounced; fifteen feet away at the beach) and discerned Romano's accent (believable, since she grew up in the same area). Her notations on bootheels all added to the mysterious sensitivity blind characters on screen possess. Details of this episode evoke roars of laughter from people who are blind.

Anne described the cause of her disability as a bad fire caused by mobsters when she was a child.

Actual visually-impaired children were featured in the background as Anne's class. The hand-holding and singing of "He's Got the Whole World in His Hands" set these youngsters apart from any sighted children their age. The lesson taught by Anne as she passed around a conch shell ("Paco, does this conch feel like your new kitten?" "No, my kitty's soft.") was age inappropriate for a group illustrated as eight, nine, or ten years old.

"Blind Justice" used a modern image of a bright, busy blind woman, but socked her in the old tried-and-true mold with stereotypical traits.

Fame / "Solo Song" / Nov. 11, 1982 / NBC-TV

Executive Producer: William Blinn
Producer: Mel Swope
Supervising Producer: David De Silva
Director: Mel Swope
Writer: Linda Elstad
Category: Series Television—Drama

* Blindness
* Single White Male
* Performer with a Disability

Plot: A blind substitute teacher clashes with dance teacher Lydia.

Jim Landon has been hired as a substitute teacher for a music class at the high-energy School for the Performing Arts. Student Doris is amazed to find Landon is blind and develops a crush on him.

Landon's active choral class is disrupting Lydia Grant's dance session. She fumes to Elizabeth Sherwood about the interruptions. Elizabeth reminds her he's blind.

LYDIA: That doesn't give him any right to disrupt my classroom.

Landon quickly learns to identify Elizabeth, calling her by name in the lunchroom. He plays upon extraordinary sensory perception when asked how he knew it was Elizabeth.

LANDON: It's her breath. It could stop a truck.

He goes on to demonstrate a hypersensitive sense of smell by admitting it was her cologne.

During a fire drill, Landon exhibits professionalism as well as athletic agility. He tactually checks every seat to be sure it is empty, refusing to accept a student's word that the kids are out. Landon becomes hysterical in the face of panic. Lydia silently watches him cry as he realizes it was just a fire drill.

Doris' crush on the teacher grows. Drama teacher Reardon approaches Landon to tell him to nip it in the bud. Landon does not appreciate Reardon's "advice." He indicates an attitudinal barrier.

> LANDON: [If I was sighted, would you think I could handle it myself?] ... your attitude is condescending and parental [and I resent it].

In anger, Landon retreats from Reardon into the restroom—the girls'. He comes out where Reardon is waiting, indicating he knows Reardon saw the gaffe. The two men laugh and reach a new understanding.

Lydia convinces Landon to join her in a project, insisting she can teach a blind person to do a complex dance routine with her. She gets mad at him.

> LYDIA: I wish you could see. Then I wouldn't feel so guilty about wanting to make faces at you!

Landon's performance with Lydia impresses the school board about the school's teaching methods.

* * *

"Solo Song" was a very different and refreshing look at blindness. Landon was a character *first,* and a blind person second. Societal barriers were evident, as the staff wanted to be open-minded about having Landon in their ranks but constantly watched and worried over him. Consequently, Landon was very protective of his own independence, forced to work twice as hard to prove he was capable. His anger was directed toward the reactions of others.

The story charmingly kicked formula around, such as the "her breath could stop a truck" line. Lydia's "I wish you could see...," a staple, was turned around. Sight was desired so she could make faces at him without guilt.

Landon was a flawed human being, displaying his shortcomings as well as his virtues. He moved easily about the school and classroom. Most importantly, he was seen as a professional, a good teacher who had gained the trust of his pupils. The use of an actor without sight was also a plus. The active role served as a reminder that the blind are not quiet, sedentary beings.

"Solo Song" used humor and a story with a reality base. It was skillfully done and worth seeing despite one or two concessions to formula.

Little House: A New Beginning / "Love" / Nov. 29, 1982 / NBC-TV

Executive Producer: Michael Landon
Producer: Kent McCray
Director: Victor Lobl
Writer: Paul W. Cooper
Category: Series Television— Period Drama

* Blindness
* Single White Female
* Face-feeling
* Cure

Plot: Isaiah Edwards falls in love with a blind woman who is twenty years younger than he.

Jane Caulfield travels to Walnut Grove via stagecoach. She asks if the boy traveling in the coach is a big boy.

JANE: I have to ask because I'm blind.

Laura Ingalls Wilder meets Jane at the coach stop. The two young women have a tearful reunion.

JANE: You sound wonderful!

Jane touches Laura's face as well as that of baby Rose.

JANE: Oh, Laura, she's beautiful.

Jane has lined up a job with Hester Sue in Mrs. Oleson's hotel, working on the switchboard. Gruff and grizzly Isaiah Edwards sees Jane at the hotel. At a dance, she brings Isaiah a pie she baked. There is a quick attraction between the two. They spend time together.

JANE: May I look at you?

ISAIAH: I ain't much to look at.

Face-feeling is demonstrated as Jane touches Isiah's face.
Jane gets a letter from a doctor in Chicago who is looking for blind patients to help perfect an operation. Jane has trepidation about surgery.

JANE: I've learned to accept my life the way it is.

But then again, she admits:

JANE: I've had one dream—to see the light of one sun-filled day—

LAURA: Then have the operation.

JANE: I can't. I won't. I'm sorry. I won't be disappointed again.

Isaiah jumps on the bandwagon and urges Jane to have the operation. She makes the decision to go through with it for him.

Jane's vision is restored. When she returns to Walnut Grove, Laura is there to meet her.

JANE: You're so pretty.

LAURA: Well, how about you?

JANE: I'm pretty, too.

When she sees Isaiah for the first time, she must close her eyes and touch his face to assure herself of his identity. He spurns her, telling her she has opportunities now and should not be tied to an older man. Jane leaves Walnut Grove.

* * *

"Love" featured a blind character as one who was independent enough to take a long stagecoach trip alone, get a job and do it well, and was self-assured enough to fall in love. However, these qualities and characteristics were overshadowed by the formula treatment. Jane had to experience a cure.

Special equipment illustrated included a Braille listing of numbers which Jane utilized at the telephone switchboard. She used a walking stick as a mobility aid. Special equipment was misused when Isaiah took her arm to guide her.

Isaiah's feeling that Jane's vision canceled out her feelings of affection was reminiscent to that of Joshua Bolt denying Callie Marsh's love in the "Two Worlds" episode of *Here Come the Brides*. "Love" was a typically superficial and syrupy look at blindness.

Simon and Simon / "I Heard It Was Murder" / Oct. 13, 1983 / CBS-TV

Executive Producer: Philip De Guere
Producer: Richard Chapman
Associate Producer: John G. Stephens
Director: Christian Nyby II
Story: David Douglas Sher
Teleplay: Bill Dial

* Blindness
* Single White Female
* Performer with a Disability
* Equipment: Mobility cane; Sighted guide; Braille
* Face-feeling

Blindness

Category: Series Television — Detective Drama

Plot: A blind woman is the only witness to a murder.

Dr. Rebecca Towne, a blind researcher at the university, is visiting a special sculpture exhibition for the visually impaired. Her tactile perusal of a marble bust is interrupted as two men pass by. Rebecca hears surprised voices, a third man and two shots. Two leave by a side door. Rebecca follows them and hears them get into a vehicle with a loud engine clatter.

Detective brothers Rick and A.J. Simon are assigned to protect the witness, even though the police seriously doubt her ability to help. Rebecca expresses to the two that she is valuable.

> REBECCA: I heard everything. I can identify the killers by the sound of their voices.... I want you to help me convince the police I *can* help.

The three are riding in Rick's pick-up. A noisy truck rattles by. Despite its distinctive sound, Rebecca shows indication of heightened sensory abilities.

> REBECCA: That's it!... The car ... the killers drove. It's making the same kind of noise ... I smell the same exhaust fumes, too!

Rebecca recalls the crime with amazing sensory abilities.

> REBECCA: One was carrying keys and he had a nervous habit of jingling them.... I was the last one there that day. Two men came into the gallery.... One of the men was wearing new shoes. In the gallery, they met a third man. He was carrying some kind of tools, I think. He unzipped his jacket, then there was some sort of scraping sound. I think the old man knew what was about to happen. There were two shots, more like thumps, really.... I heard them get into the truck, the truck with the valve clatter that we found this morning.

Rick is attracted to Rebecca and makes her a romantic dinner. She feels his face to see what he looks like prior to a kiss.

Rebecca is stalked by the criminal and escapes by going down to the laundry room in the garage of her apartment building. In a small scene reminiscent of *Wait Until Dark,* she turns off the lights so she has an advantage when she tosses bleach into the man's face. Rick and A.J. arrive to save her in the nick of time.

* * *

"I Heard It Was Murder" was a blind-woman-as-victim story. The negatives from the portrayal were derived from the staple elements. The truck

Rebecca identified for the private eyes *did* have a distinctive rattle, although Rick himself suggested that a thousand other vehicles in town also needed a valve job. Rebecca was almost childishly adamant, insisting it was *that* truck. And, seated between two men in the close quarters of a pick-up truck's cab, it seems unlikely that she could have smelled "the same exhaust fumes, too!" Her remarkable sensory perception added to the "sixth sense" myth that persons with visual impairments supposedly have. The amount of details Rebecca pulled out about a happened-so-fast moment were too much to be believed.

An extensive color sequence was inserted where Rick, at dinner, described colors to Rebecca. This seemed to express that even highly educated blind persons like Rebecca never learn about color; it also invalidated perceptions she may have had from within her disability.

"I Heard It Was Murder" plugged an intelligent blind woman who was full of life and energy into the routine mold.

Alice / "Alice's Blind Date" / Oct. 23, 1983 / CBS-TV

Executive Producers: Madelyn Davis & Bob Carrol, Jr.
Producers: Mark Egan, Mark Soloman & Jerry Madden
Director: Delores Ferraro
Writer: Bob Stevens
Category: Series Television—Situation Comedy

* Blindness
* Single White Male

Plot: Alice makes a date with an old flame—not knowing he has lost his sight.

Alice, feeling lonely, sees a familiar name in the newspaper. She wonders if it's her old boyfriend. She calls and discovers Rob McGregor *is* her old love. She makes a date to get together with the successful businessman.

Alice is thrilled to see Rob when he comes by Mel's Diner to pick her up.

ALICE: You look great!

ROB: I'm sure you do too ... how does Alice look?

MEL: Whatsa matter? You blind?

ROB: Yes, I am.

Alice is a bit rattled to discover Rob has lost his sight. She leaves with him in his limousine. Rob's blindness is a benefit, decides Mel.

MEL: At least he won't be able to see how old Alice looks.

Rob and Alice have a delightful time at dinner. Rob shows Alice photos in his wallet.

ROB: This is either [my daughter] or my house in Connecticut.

Rob describes the cause of his disability as retinitis pigmentosa. There have been some disadvantages.

ROB: My friends won't play darts with me anymore.

Rob surprises Alice by announcing their waiter is coming. How did he know?

ROB: His shoes. They squeak.

The evening proves to be an eye-opener for Alice. She is so excited by what she has learned, she goes to the diner the next day to lead a sensory awareness lesson. She and the other employees blindfold themselves to test their awareness. And while they are identifying sounds, they hear the cash register open as they are robbed. The thief is caught as he bolts out the door smack into Rob. Rob has a word of advice for the sensory "trainees."

ROB: You should leave being blind to the professionals.

* * *

"Alice's Blind Date" was a pleasant story. Rob was a charming and successful man who had made peace with a difficulty in his life. He was attractive to Alice and the other waitresses in the diner.

The easy identification of the waiter in the restaurant by his squeaky shoes is a staple element in blind stories. One wonders how people with limited vision can get along in this world if others have shoes that do *not* squeak!

The sensory awareness lesson Alice gave her co-workers was rather contrived and silly, although it was well-intentioned. "Alice's Blind Date" presented a fair and interesting picture of a man who was blind.

The Love Boat / title unknown / Mar. 3, 1984 / ABC-TV

Executive Producers: Aaron Spelling; Douglas Cramer
Category: Series Television — Romantic Comedy

* Blindness
* Single Black Male

Plot: Isaac competes with a blind passenger for the affections of an attractive woman.

The Love Boat

Darnell is a blind passenger on the cruise ship. Both he and ship's bartender, Isaac Washington, are interested in cultivating a relationship with Terri, an attractive traveler.

> DARNELL: Since I'm blind and can't see her anyway, I'm gonna take her off your hands.

Isaac reveals to Captain Stubing he feels awkward about this situation.

> ISAAC: I feel kind of strange, competing with a guy who's blind.

> CAPTAIN: Don't think of Darnell as a blind man. Just think of him as a man.

Darnell pretends to be helpless as he helps himself at the breakfast buffet table. Terri rushes in to help.

> TERRI: Let me fill [your plate] for you.

Darnell notes he has good table manners because:

> DARNELL: You'd be surprised how surly people get when I touch their food to see what it is.

Darnell continues to play helpless to garner Terri's sympathy. Isaac watches these developments and sees that Terri gets a perverse satisfaction from helping Darnell. He pulls out of the competition.

> ISAAC: I like Terri but she seems [to be the kind that needs to be needed. She can help you and that will make her happy].

Darnell realizes what he has done is wrong and admits the ruse to Terri.

> DARNELL: It was just to get your sympathy so you'd like me instead of Isaac.

Terri and Darnell leave the ship together.

* * *

This episode of *The Love Boat* was amazing. The mere fact that someone would write such a piece in the 1980s was almost beyond belief. It presented a poor and damaging portrait of a blind person who is manipulative and spoiled. The "helpless" act was particularly offensive. Even the "jokes" were stale, such as Darnell indicating he groped through other people's plates. This episode presented a poor and grossly unfair portrait of blindness. It has to be seen to be believed.

Second Sight: A Love Story / Mar. 13, 1984 / CBS-TV

Executive Producer: Barry Krost;
Doug Chapin
Producer: William Watkins
Director: John Korty
Story: Susan Miller
Teleplay: Dennis Turner
Suggested by the Book: *Emma and I* by Sheila Hocken
Category: Made-for-TV Movie — Drama

* Blindness
* Single White Female
* Face-feeling
* Cure
* Equipment: Mobility cane; Braille clock, cards, and watch; Sighted guide; Dog guide; low vision techniques

Plot: A blind woman finds love.

Alexandra McCabe is a tersely independent blind woman. She lives a quiet, single life in her own apartment. She is employed as an information clerk at the art museum. Her special hobby is teaching blind children about sculpture to "make it more comprehensible" to them. She catches the eye of Richard Chapman, a successful art dealer. He asks her out. Alex devalues herself.

ALEX: Why don't you give it some very careful thought for a couple of days — and if you still want to have lunch . . . I'll be waiting for you here. . . .

The date ends in disaster when Alex storms off, angry to have been asked about her blindness by Richard, which he acknowledges as "a part of you."
Alex goes to stay with her brother Mitchell and his family after an intruder breaks into her apartment. Mitchell again tries to persuade her to go for an operation that might restore her sight. Alex, like her father, is blind from congenital cataracts. She notes her father was always chasing a rainbow to find a cure that did not exist.

MITCHELL: He was a fighter!

Alex, feeling vulnerable after the break-in at her apartment, applies and is accepted at a school to obtain a dog guide. Richard comes to see her and asks her out. Alex again devalues herself, introducing her dog to Richard.

ALEX: Emma, say hello to a weirdo. If he likes blind ladies, he must be crazy about guide dogs.

Face-feeling is seen after a successful date with Richard.
Alex and Richard enter into an intimate relationship, until he leaves for a business trip he didn't tell her about. Alex refuses to see him when he returns. She comes to her senses and apologizes to him. She also goes to the doctor Mitchell has discovered. She is a good candidate for surgery. Richard admits

life with her would be "more fun, more convenient" if she could see—but if the operation does not succeed, so be it. Alex again devalues herself.

>   ALEX: You're not signing up for forty years of martyrdom, are you?

Surgery is successful and Alex can see for the first time since she was sixteen. She makes the sad decision to return Emma to the school so that the dog can help another.

* * *

Second Sight: A Love Story illustrated a blind woman who was comfortable and at ease in her existence, so much so that she had virtually shut out any intrusions. The introduction of a dog guide in her life was to let down a large barrier. From that angle, the story succeeded. Alex was not willing to bend for anyone or anything until Emma softened her up. Had the piece stayed with that approach—and slowly allowed the man into her life—it would have been a story about a person who was blind and who worked out personal problems like the rest of the world. Instead, formula crept in. Mitchell constantly harped on Alex to go in for surgery. His indication that his father was "a fighter" indicated that Alex was immature for giving up hope. Alex actually seemed more realistic, recognizing her father had wasted years in search of a fruitless dream.

Her cure was melodramatic, where she spent long minutes peering at her loved ones and commenting on appearances of things around her. Quite uncalled for was Richard's associating Alex's own inaccessibility with the special little techniques she used to achieve her independence, such as knowing the number of steps from one place to another. It seemed to suggest that the—as he called them—"compartments" in her life made her unspontaneous and inflexible.

Actual blind children were used in a small scene; blind persons appeared as background atmosphere in the guide dog training center setting.

Second Sight: A Love Story portrayed a blind woman as capable, emotional, and able to make mistakes. It also assumed that life was not complete without the removal of disability.

Matt Houston / "The Outsider" / May 18, 1984 / ABC-TV

Executive Producers: Aaron Spelling; Douglas Cramer; Lawrence Gordon
Producer: Calvin Clements, Jr.
Executive Supervising Producer: E. Duke Vincent
Supervising Producer: Michael Fisher

* Blindness
* Single White Male
* Fake Disability
* Equipment: Mobility cane; Sighted guide

Blindness

Writer: Calvin Clements, Jr.
Category: Series Television — Detective Drama

Plot: Detective Matt Houston is intrigued with a blind psychic who locates missing persons.

Detective Matt Houston is stymied on a kidnapping case. A call to the police switchboard from a psychic draws attention. Blind nightclub psychic Adrian Harcum claims the kidnapped girl is at an auto wrecking yard. Harcum, hidden behind large dark glasses, leads police about the wreckage-strewn lot. He locates the girl.

Houston wonders if Harcum is truly blind. He suspects the psychic of masterminding the kidnapping.

COP: Harcum a kidnapper? The man's BLIND.

At a press conference where Harcum is being courted by the press, Houston jams a hand in front of Adrian's face, expecting to see him flinch, indicating blindness can only be a condition of complete sightlessness. To prove he *is* blind, Harcum whips off his dark glasses to reveal white, irisless eyes. He also indicates another child has been snatched.

Harcum's disability is revealed as fake when he pops out opaque contact lenses. He is the brains behind the kidnapping. His flunky pulls off the legwork. Harcum kidnaps the children of wealthy families and accepts monetary rewards of thanks when he "finds" their loved ones. He "locates" the missing boy. Houston cleverly frames Harcum and the killer/kidnapper is arrested.

* * *

Despite the fact that "The Outsider" faked a disability, it must be noted as part of the genre of physical disability in show business. The difference was meant to remove suspicion from the perpetrator, an indication of screen schizophrenia. In this case, disability indicated innocence; in others, it denotes malevolence.

Harcum misused a too-short mobility cane badly; a sharp detective like Matt Houston should have noted that a person who was blind would never have awkwardly poked a cane thusly. It was not a point of debate in the story.

Great offense and negativity were present in the scene where Houston jammed his hand in front of Harcum's face to see if the man would draw back. The music peaked and the director used a close-up of Harcum's irisless eyes to shock and draw a gasp from the audience. It was poorly conceived and an affront to persons whose eyes may not be average.

"The Outsider" used a bad depiction of blindness to further a story line.

Finder of Lost Loves / Sept. 1984 (debut episode) / ABC-TV

Executive Producers: Aaron Spelling; Douglas Cramer
Producers: Ben Joelson & Art Baer
Category: Series Television — Romantic Drama

* Blindness
* Married White Male

Plot: James Osborne engages the services of Maxwell Ltd. to locate Kathryn, an old flame.

Private investigator Cary Maxwell locates the woman James Osborne never got over. Kathryn is married to Galen, a man who is blind. The cause of Galen's disability is described as an auto accident.

> KATHRYN: [The accident] happened — long after James disappeared....

James re-meets Kathryn. He wonders if she really loves Galen.

> JAMES: Are you saying you married him out of guilt?

Kathryn assures him that she loves Galen deeply and has no wish to resume a relationship with James.

* * *

The debut of *Finder of Lost Loves* used a blind character at the tail end of the story as a vehicle to prove that Kathryn really loved her husband. The writer of this episode wisely utilized a blind character as an average citizen and husband with little regard to his visual capacity. James was the person with the problem. Galen was an appropriate husband for Kathryn.

The Love Boat / "The Light of Another Day" / Oct. 13, 1984 / ABC-TV

Executive Producers: Aaron Spelling; Douglas Cramer
Producers: Ben Joelson, Art Baer and Dennis Hammer
Director: Don Weis
Writer: Lan O'Kun
Category: Series Television — Romantic Comedy

* Blindness
* Single White Female
* Face-feeling
* Equipment: Mobility cane; Braille book; Sighted guide

Plot: A blind woman relives an old college crush while on the cruise ship.

Blindness

A blind woman stands at the rail waiting for Doc Bricker. A man smoking a pipe stands upwind. Millie Constant reacts.

> MILLIE: Is there a Mr. Washburn here somewhere?
>
> WASHBURN: I'm a Washburn.
>
> MILLIE: I would have recognized that tobacco anywhere.
>
> WASHBURN: This is my own blend.
>
> MILLIE: I know. And I haven't smelled it in eighteen years.

Millie was a sighted and shy admirer of Sam Washburn in college. She always knew he was in the vicinity by his tobacco. Millie expresses she's been blind for ten years, the result of a gradual deterioration of vision.

> MILLIE: I remember college, though. The campus, my friends — and Sam Washburn — who I never had the nerve to talk to ... I used to fantasize about you, dream about you — I've never forgotten over all of these years.

They begin to spend time together. Face-feeling is illustrated.

> MILLIE: Would you mind if I touched your face? ... You're not wearing your glasses.

After a brief courtship, Millie discerns the man is not Sam Washburn. She will not let him explain. He later apologizes. Millie asks if he will join her fantasy and be Sam Washburn for the remainder of the trip. Washburn agrees, although the deception gets harder and harder for him.

> WASHBURN: I'm not happy this way, as Sam. I'm in love with you.

Millie responds with devaluation.

> MILLIE: ...I don't want pity disguised as love.
>
> WASHBURN: I'm not that sort. I'm telling you the truth.

Millie refuses to listen. Washburn corners her and tells her Sam is dead. He is Sam's brother, George. And he loves Millie.

They leave the ship together. George has changed his special blend of tobacco to something new.

* * *

"Light of Another Day" was a bizarre story about blindness. Although Millie had been without sight for years, she still spoke extensively about it during her first real conversation with Washburn. Although she was attractive, well-dressed, and assumed to be successful in order to afford a cruise, she never mentioned being employed (in fairness, neither did Washburn).

Her identification of the special blend of tobacco used by Sam and his brother was not considered an illustration of a hypersensitive sense of smell since she indicated she was able to discern the tobacco back in college. And, since the sense of smell has a wonderful "memory" and often evokes entire screenplays of past events in one's mind, Millie's quick identification of the smoker's tobacco was plausible.

Millie, like many blind characters, was carefully handled by Doc Bricker and Washburn. She appeared fragile. She also misused special equipment. Her too-short white cane was jabbed tentatively in front of herself.

"Light of Another Day" presented a somewhat flaky portrait of an attractive blind woman whose disability permitted her the leisure of carrying out a fantasy past its prime. She seemed to be living in the past, a time, she said, when "everything was bright and full of colors."

Aurora / Oct. 22, 1984 / NBC-TV

Executive Producer: Roger Gimble, Tony Converse
Producer: Alex Ponti
Supervising Producer: Alessandro Van Normann
Director: Maurizio Ponzi
Teleplay by: John McGreevey
Written by: Ferrini, Menom, Maurizio Ponzi
Category: Made-for-TV Movie — Drama

* Blindness
* White Male Child
* Cure
* Face-feeling
* Equipment: Braille watch and book

Plot: An Italian woman searches for her ex-lovers to tell each about "his" blind son in order to tap into their guilt to finance an operation to restore the boy's sight.

Aurora talks to her eleven-year-old blind son, Ciro, telling him they will try to locate his father — in order to help him see.

AURORA: Isn't it what we both want more than anything?

Ciro rises when his prospective "papa" comes into the room. At a cue from his mother, he heads for a hug and trips over a strategically placed ash tray to express to the shocked "papa" that he is, indeed, blind. The ruse is played again on Andre, another old lover. Ciro trips.

AURORA: Our son is blind.

Andre passes a cigarette lighter in front of Ciro's eyes. Aurora implies having a child with a disability is a burden.

AURORA: I spared you. I suffered alone.

From Andre, Aurora gets ten million lire and a painting.
The cause of Ciro's disability is described as a fall from a third floor balcony at age two. He is able to discern light and shadow.
Face-feeling is illustrated when Ciro feels another prospective papa's face. Ciro also touches the face of his mother.

CIRO: Don't worry. You're very beautiful.

Ackermann, an American pilot, is next on Aurora's list. Ackermann takes Ciro up in his helicopter. He is moved by "his" son.

ACKERMANN: I want to satisfy his craving for color, all at once.

Aurora admits to Ackermann that she really doesn't know who Ciro's father is. The rekindled love interest flickers out.
Ackermann has helped Aurora reach her goal. She checks Ciro into a hospital and goes to have her hair done. A nurse nods.

NURSE: Ciro will see you looking your very best.

Ciro awakens after surgery and pulls off his bandages. He can see. He walks down the hall, his hand resting on the wall. Down in the waiting room, he sees a woman asleep, leaning against the wall, and recognizes her as his mother.
They return to Italy. Now, as a sighted child, Ciro leaves their trailer at night — something he never did before. He locates the constellations to study the stars he's always dreamed about.

CIRO: You just have to see them to know how perfect they are.

* * *

Aurora was an amusing movie despite the basic "cure" formula. As a taxicab driver, Aurora had little money to seek medical treatment for her son. She used her wits to obtain financial assistance. The ploy with the ashtray was funny and immediately hooked Aurora's prospective prey.
Ciro was an intelligent and curious boy. He had a great interest in everything around him. He even indicated he had no desire to see; it was Aurora's fantasy. He seemed every bit the average red-blooded boy. He had his own perceptions, such as telling Ackermann "it's beautiful up here" when flying in the helicopter.

The ending was syrupy as a boy without visual perceptions for nine years walked down the hall and recognized his mother. It was played for the heart-tug.

Aurora deserves credit for allowing a young boy who was blind to be a boy—and to whom this larcenous search was adventure. However, it lost credibility when it relied on staple formula.

T.J. Hooker / "Target: Hooker" / Nov. 17, 1984 / ABC-TV

Producers: Stephen Downing & Chuck Bowman
Co-Producer: Kenneth Koch
Supervising Producer: Rick Husky
Director: Vincent McEveety
Writer: Simon Muntner
Category: Series Television—Police Drama

* Blindness
* Single White Male; Series lead
* Temporary Disability

Plot: Police Sergeant Hooker's partner, Vince Romano, is blinded by a bomb.

Criminals toss a bomb in Hooker and Romano's squad car. Romano is hurt by the blast.

ROMANO: I can't see—Hooker, I can't see!

Romano is hospitalized with bandaged eyes. His prognosis is up in the air. Meanwhile, Hooker hunts down the perpetrators.

A disabled catalyst is seen in the person of Lieutenant O'Brien, a cigar-chomping, hard-bitten cop who uses a wheelchair. O'Brien cautions Romano to watch his terminology. Romano is not, says the lieutenant, handicapped.

O'BRIEN: Challenged—never handicapped.

Romano asks if it was different for O'Brien when he sustained an injury.

O'BRIEN: Of course there were times. That was the challenge....

Negative aspects are suggested as Romano remembers being with his girlfriend. He recalls physical things, running and playing, erroneously feeling these things are not possible without usable vision. In frustrated anger, he shoves a pitcher and water glass off the bed tray to crash on the floor.

Romano's bandages are removed. His vision is intact.

* * *

"Target: Hooker" used a staple theme of the star experiencing a brief disability. This episode differed little from others of the genre with the notable and welcome exception of Lieutenant O'Brien as a disabled catalyst to help Romano along (the role was played by an actor with a disability). However, it would be hoped that a person familiar with different aspects of disability would not use a pejorative line about the benefits of working rather than holding "a tin cup on some corner," as did O'Brien. Other than the use of a disabled catalyst, "Target: Hooker" was quite predictable.

Places in the Heart / 1984 / Tri-Star Pictures

Executive Producer: Michael Hausman
Producer: Arlene Donovan
Director: Robert Benton
Writer: Robert Benton
Category: Feature Film — Drama

* Blindness
* Single White Male
* Equipment: Sighted guide; Talking Book records

Plot: The young widow Missus Spaulding attempts to make ends meet during the Depression.

Desperate to make money after the accidental death of her husband, Missus Spaulding takes in a boarder. Mr. Denby arrives at the farmhouse with a man on his arm, Will. Missus Spaulding is ill at ease when she sees Will is blind, but she needs the money. She agrees to take him in. The cause of Will's disability is discussed.

DENBY: Will lost his sight in the Big War ... he was a real war hero.

He also is self-employed, although in typical "blind" fashion.

DENBY: Will makes a fine living caning chairs and making brooms.

Despite being bushwhacked to move into the farmhouse and Missus Spaulding's reluctance at taking in the boarder, all goes well—until Frank and Possum Spaulding sneak into Will's room and put his Talking Book library records on the phonograph and scratch one. Will discovers the crime and bursts into the kitchen to confront Missus Spaulding, not realizing she is soaking nude in the tub. She attempts to remain still so as not to slosh water. Devaluation and pejorative language appear in his outburst.

WILL: I am not some kind of freak that is here on display for the amusement of those hooligans you call children!

He is embarrassed when he discovers Missus Spaulding is in her bath and sheepishly bows out of the room.

Will is able to pull Possum from the wreckage of the attic when a twister hits the house. He becomes a full-fledged and useful member of the household. Will takes over some cooking chores when Missus Spaulding and Moses, the black hired hand, begin to pull in the harvest of cotton. He remains when local prejudice forces Moses to leave town.

* * *

Places in the Heart used a blind character as a man who was able to hold his own in a difficult time. Will, despite his intelligence and hunger for knowledge, was more limited by society than his visual handicap. Will's means of employment was traditional but not unsuited for the time depicted in the film. He was shown as capable in his employment, able to take initiative in the face of a natural disaster and, due to the desperate financial condition of the Missus Spaulding, allowed to assert himself in matters of the house.

Whenever Will took another character's arm in the sighted guide position, they continuously told him to "step up," "step down" to the point of being tiresome. After Will had rescued Possum from the wreck of the attic after the tornado struck, he was suddenly subordinated as the little girl led him down the stairs calling, "step down, step down."

A variation on a face-feeling scene occurred where Will approached a dead-tired Missus Spaulding in the kitchen, asking her what she looked like. She complied with a verbal description. The scene was out of place and probably used as a tool to inform the audience what the plain-Jane woman discovering her resources thought of herself.

Places in the Heart positively illustrated a blind character as one to be trusted and one who had a great deal of worth.

Hello / 1984 / Motown Productions

Category: Music Video

* Blindness
* Single Black Female
* Face-feeling
* Equipment: Mobility cane; Braille book

Plot: A teacher at a school for the arts has a secret crush on a talented blind student.

Mr. Reynolds has his eye out for a lovely young blind woman. She plays the flute, dances and is a sculptor. She and another student work on reading a dramatic passage. Reynolds finally breaks down and calls her to say "Hello—is it me you're looking for?"

Reynolds is interrupted by another student who calls him in to the sculpture studio for something he should see. He walks in and sees the young woman, working on a clay bust—of him.

GIRL: Tell me what you think.

MR. REYNOLDS: It's wonderful!

GIRL: This is how I see you.

Face-feeling is illustrated as she reaches out to touch his face.

*   *   *

"Hello" introduced a whole new realm of disability drama: the use of disabled characters in music videos so popular with teenagers. The character in "Hello" was a bright and talented young woman, illustrating ability in a variety of artistic endeavors—art, dance, music and drama. It was no wonder Reynolds was struck by her.

Despite the woman's overall capabilities, it brought to mind the "overcompensation" myth—that loss of one sense heightens all others. The exceptional talents of the woman could be considered compensatory for the loss of her sight. "Hello" positively used a blind woman as one worth admiration and attention.

Love Leads the Way / 1984

Executive Producer: David Permut
Producer: Jimmy Hawkins
Director: Delbert Mann
Story by: Jimmy Hawkins and Henry Denker
Teleplay: Henry Denker
Based on the Book: *First Lady of the Seeing Eye,* by Morris Frank and Blake Clark
Category: Made-for-Cable Movie—Drama

* Blindness
* Single White Male
* New Disability
* Based on a True Story
* Equipment: Mobility cane; Braille slate and stylus; Braillewriter; Dog guide

Plot: A newly-blinded young man finds an adequate substitute for his eyes with a dog guide.

In Nashville, 1927, Morris Frank jogs to the gym and goes for a practice boxing round in the ring. Tommy knocks Morrie out. A new disability is incurred. The doctors say he is blind.

Girlfriend Beth comes to visit. Morrie displays hypersensitive perception and devalues himself with poor language.

BETH: How did you know it was me?

MORRIE: Your perfume.... I don't want your pity.... Why do you want to be burdened by a cripple all your life? Out of loyalty? Afraid people will say you deserted me?

Beth leaves at Morrie's insistence.

Morrie, outfitted with white cane and dark glasses, goes to the Institute for the Blind, where he is told he must accept and adjust to his blindness. Erroneous notions are stated when the man tells Morrie that although he can learn Braille, he must reconcile himself to a sedentary life.

Morrie hires a teenaged kid to be his guiding eyes to resume his door-to-door insurance sales career. Societal discrimination is nicely illustrated when people look through the window and see a blind man on their doorstep and refuse to open the door.

MORRIE: They just didn't want to face a blind man, did they? *Did they?*

Morrie turns down a date with Beth and she yells at him for being "bitter and sarcastic." Morrie expresses his feelings to his mother. He devalues himself.

MORRIE: I don't wanna waste Beth's time.

Morrie learns about a woman in Switzerland who is advocating using trained dogs to lead the blind. He is so enthused, he writes to Dorothy Eustis. Morrie goes to Switzerland and trains with Buddy, his dog guide. It takes a while for him to learn to trust the animal. Returning home, discrimination is illustrated when Morrie must ride in the baggage car of the train. The rule of "no dogs allowed" will not be bent. He is also refused a ride in a taxicab for the same reason.

Morrie cannot convince the Institute for the Blind to help. He begins to work for The Seeing Eye and meets a girl, Lois, to whom he is attracted. On their second meeting, he touches her face.

MORRIE: You ARE beautiful.

After much work, Morrie and Buddy finally get an appointment with the state legislature to demonstrate Buddy's capabilities. After years of fighting, legislation is passed to enable blind persons to have full societal access with their dogs at their side.

* * *

Love Leads the Way began as a typical melodrama but evolved into something else. After all the staple scenes of devaluation and anger came some very pointed ones about discrimination. The film illustrated that it required such fighters as Morris Frank to change a perception of society to allow blind persons access to public places with their dogs.

Special equipment was misused. Morrie exaggeratedly swung his white cane.

A small-statured man was seen briefly as a news vendor whom Morrie crashed into. The man safely saw him home.

Love Leads the Way would have done better to concentrate more on politics and less on emotional scenes already seen too many times in other dramas. However, it deserves a large nod for seriously addressing some political issues after the tears stopped flowing.

A-Team / "Waste 'Em!" / Mar. 4, 1985 / NBC-TV

Executive Producer: Stephen J. Cannell
Producer: John Ashley
Supervising Producer: Jo Swerling, Jr.
Director: Sidney Hayers
Writer: Stephen Katz & Marc Jones
Category: Series Television—Adventure

* Blindness
* Single White Female
* Face-feeling

Plot: The A-Team helps a young businessman and his blind sister.

A.J. Perry and his blind sister, Lisa, own and run the Speedy Delivery service. For reasons unknown to them, Ike Hagen is trying to run them out of business. A.J. calls upon the A-Team to help them out of this jam after two trucks nearly kill him and Lisa. The team meets the Perrys. Face holds out his hand to Lisa in greeting. A.J. steps in when Lisa does not respond.

> A.J.: My sister is sightless.

> LISA: You had your hand out, didn't you? I'm sorry, sometimes I don't notice.

The A-Team challenges Hagen. They wait for leader Hannibal to be picked up by Hagen's henchmen. In the back, Face watches Lisa. She asks him why he's staring. How did she know?

> LISA: When you've been blind most of your life, you develop perceptions other people don't have. Like, you know when someone is standing behind you. You know when someone is looking at you.

> FACE: Can you tell when they're smiling?

> LISA: Most of the time.

Face-feeling is illustrated as Lisa touches his face.

> LISA: You're very handsome.
>
> FACE: And you — are very beautiful.
>
> LISA: I guess I'll just have to take your word for it, huh?

Face wants to kiss Lisa but pulls back. She notices and gently remonstrates:

> LISA: You know, blind people kiss just like everyone else.

They kiss.

The A-Team discovers Hagen's rubbish disposal company is dumping toxic waste for a chemical company. The dumping is done in an abandoned sewer line that runs underneath the Speedy Delivery company. When A.J.'s loan goes through for the building of an underground garage, they will discover the sewer.

The Perrys are kidnapped by Hagen and his men. They are rescued by the A-Team's ecletic assortment of flamethrower, bazookas, firearms, and physical combat. The Perrys are safe and the hoods will be prosecuted. Lisa thanks the vigilantes with a curious statement.

> LISA: You know, when you're sightless, you tend to associate people with feelings instead of physical things — I don't know what any of you look like but you all feel wonderful to me.

*   *   *

"Waste 'Em!" presented a blind character in an almost incidental way. Lisa's blindness really had nothing to do with the story. She was simply A.J.'s sister and she was unable to see. Lisa indicated she had worked and supported herself as a dispatcher for the delivery service before A.J. had bought the company. She and her brother worked as a team.

The casual representation of a blind character was proof that progress in disability depictions can occur, even in curious places. It also reinforced that some scenes — such as the face-feeling and the odd "you all feel wonderful to me" — are understood as part of the blind experience, at least, in the minds of writers. Lisa also stared woodenly ahead and rarely moved her face toward the direction of whoever was speaking. Despite this and the other concessions to formula, the overall impression was that Lisa was a self-assured, independent young woman whose disability did not hinder her.

"Waste 'Em!" illustrated a blind person as an interesting part of the community whom the A-Team had to support by their amazing firepower.

Divorce Court / 1985 (Syndicated)

Executive Producers: Peter Locke; Donald Kushner
Producer: Sue Perry
Supervising Producer: Barry Cahn
Director: Randy Cohen
Story adaption and teleplay: Lisa Stewart
Category: Series Television—Drama

* Blindness
* Married Black Male

Plot: A blind man sues his wife for divorce claiming mental cruelty after she has regained her sight.

Judge William Keene presides over the case of *Dixon vs. Dixon*. Stephen Dixon wants to divorce Jill and get custody of their ten-year-old son, Bobby.

> MR. BRYANT: Your Honor, Mr. and Mrs. Dixon were both blind until Mrs. Dixon miraculously regained her sight. She then proceeded to exclude and neglect her husband and her son, treating them as if they were burdens to her. She often humiliated her husband in front of her new sighted friends. My client seeks a divorce on the grounds of mental cruelty and abandonment.

Judge Keene grants the divorce in Jill's favor, but Stephen regains custody of their son.

* * *

Their installment of *Divorce Court* would have been hysterically funny—except it was meant to be a drama. The "based on fact" divorce case was fraught with misconceptions about blindness.

After being cured, Jill Dixon was too busy for her husband. She cultivated a new circle of sighted friends and excluded her husband. She now went to foreign films since she could read the subtitles! She moved furniture around and disturbed the order of Stephen's clothes. Jill claimed Stephen was "bitter" and "jealous" of her good fortune. He became so angry that he was helpless. To top off that, he tried to kill himself.

The cause of Stephen's blindness was described as an Air Force accident when a test battery blew up in his face.

The writer had some odd notions about the lives of people who are blind. For example, it was noted that their son, Bobby, was proud of having taught his mother how to play checkers—after the miraculous operation. This completely negated the popular existence of parlor games used by the visually-impaired that permit them full participation with players both sighted and blind. Bobby also combed and parted his mother's hair for her. Many more completely ridiculous ideas about blindness appeared—too many to be repeated here.

Divorce Court indicated that the life of a blind couple was less than average. It also suggested that a blind man was helpless. He was angry and bitter that "good fortune" had not befallen him. The relentless negative and erroneous imagery sank this one to the depths as one of the worst pieces ever produced on blindness.

All of Me / 1985 / Universal Films

Producer: Stephen Friedman
Director: Carl Reiner
Screenplay: Phil Alden Robinson
Adaptation: Henry Olek
Based on the Novel: *Me Two* by Ed Davis
Category: Feature Film—Comedy

* Blindness
* Black Male
* Face-feeling
* Equipment: Mobility cane; Dog guide

Plot: An attorney finds he is sharing his body with the spirit of a dead woman while she seeks the appropriate reincarnation vessel into which to move.

Attorney/musician Roger Cobb's musical buddy is Tyrone, a saxophone player who is blind. He and Roger play in the same band. Tyrone is a member of the musician's union although he still plays on the street for money.

Roger's life is a shambles. Face feeling is illustratred as Tyrone touches Roger's cheeks.

TYRONE: Hey, look at this face! ... this is an unhappy face.

ROGER: ...don't pick my nose.

Life gets even worse as filthy rich Edwina Cutwater's life entity is accidentally transferred into Roger's body. When Edwina's life energy is zapped out of Roger into a pail of water, Roger pours the water into a pitcher and asks Tyrone to take care of it. Tyrone drinks some water and Edwina finds herself inside yet another body. Blindness as a lightless condition is implied.

EDWINA: It's dark in here!

The appropriate body is procured and Edwina is safely transferred into a young healthy person, ready to start again.

* * *

All of Me illustrated a blind man as one who was wary and savvy. His blindness was a part of him.

The myth of heightened sensory perception was played upon near the climax when Tyrone, an observer of the young woman refusing to accept Edwina's life entity, gave his perceptions of what was going on. "Furniture's falling," he reported, and so on.

Although Tyrone's employment was along rather traditional lines for blind characters, and although he fulfilled a stereotypical role as a streetcorner artist, the character was portrayed with a great sense of humor and as a full-fledged member of the human race.

Crazy Like a Fox / "Hearing Is Believing" / Jan. 15, 1986 / CBS-TV

Executive Producers: Frank Cardea & George Schenck, John Baskin & Roger Shulman
Director: Paul Krasny
Writer: Julie Friedgen
Category: Series Television—Crime Comedy/Drama

* Blindness
* Single White Female
* Equipment: Mobility cane

Plot: Harry and Harrison set out to help a blind writer who overhears a murder plot in a busy restaurant.

Authoress Joanna Blake and her mother, Neva, are dining at an expensive San Francisco restaurant. Neva leaves to go to the ladies' room. To amuse herself, Joanna, who is blind, eavesdrops on other diners. She freezes when she hears a murder being planned. Her shock precludes her from hearing the details. Joanna goes home and immediately types a word-for-word transcript, which she shows to her lawyer, Harrison Fox. Harrison's exuberant, never-say-die father, Harry, who is a private detective, wants to help.

Harry wants to check out the restaurant's guest book for the night before. Joanna compliments him on his appearance. Harry is perplexed. A derivation of the sensory capabilities trait appears.

> JOANNA: It's your cologne. It's imported, right? Well, you wouldn't waste that on anything but your best suit, right?

In an attempt to locate the guilty parties, Harry has Joanna on the extension phone as he calls people from the register swiped from the restaurant. Joanna fails to recognize the voices. After another lead pans out, Joanna tells Harry not to get discouraged. Another derivation on the sensory awareness capacity surfaces.

> HARRY: How did you know I was discouraged?

> JOANNA: Your walk. It's much heavier than when we got here.

A man speaking in an elevator is identified by Joanna as one of the men at the restaurant. A man named Carnie is killed, just like Joanna had predicted. Harrison and Harry are convinced they have nailed the killer.

> HARRISON: She may not be able to see, but her hearing is so accurate, there isn't a court in the world that wouldn't be convinced by it!

Joanna's innocent request for information about who was sitting at the other table leads Patrick, the guilty maitre d', to go after her before she can finger him. Arriving home from the restaurant, Joanna goes to her bedroom. Patrick slides through the door and steps inside her room. She detects movement.

> PATRICK: Your hearing is truly remarkable.

Joanna tries to blind him by shining a bright light in his face. She immediately breaks her lamps in a rendition of the famed *Wait Until Dark* scene. Patrick lights a box of long matches as a torch to see by.
Harry and Harrison arrive at the house as Patrick finds Joanna. Off guard when Harry and Harrison break in, Joanna is able to bean Patrick. She is safe.

* * *

"Hearing Is Believing" was a twist on the blind-witness-to-a-murder theme in that Joanna heard the plans to kill an individual before it occurred. Joanna Blake was depicted as a bright, well-to-do writer who lived in a lavish home, dressed well and ate at the finest restaurants. She was poised and cultured. Her hearing was, as Patrick noted, "truly remarkable." Her memory was just as good, able to type out a word-for-word transcript of the conversation she heard. This seemed related to heightened sensory awareness.
Joanna misused special equipment by using a standard orthopedic cane painted white as a mobility tool. She waved it in front of herself like a sword.
As for Joanna detecting Harry's footsteps as "discouraged," it would have made more sense for her to note the heavy sigh as he released, rather than his gait.
"Hearing Is Believing" featured a blind-woman-as-victim in a piece that was neither creative nor different.

The Twilight Zone / "To See the Invisible Man" / Jan. 31, 1986 / CBS-TV

Executive Producer: Philip de Guere

* Blindness
* White Male

Blindness

Producer: Harvey Frand
Supervising Producer: James Crocker
Director: Noel Black
Teleplay: Steven Barnes
Based on the Short Story by: Robert Silverberg
Category: Series Television — Occult

* **Equipment:** Mobility cane

Plot: A man is sentenced to one year of invisibility for his "coldness" to other human beings.

In some parallel world, Mitchell Chapman is marked with "invisibility" by an applied lesion on his forehead for his "lack of caring and concern" to others. His sentence is to spend one year as a "non-person." No one is permitted to speak to an "invisible" person, nor may they react. Chapman finds himself alone in a crowded world of people.

Day 106 — Chapman goes to a cafeteria to eat. He sits at a table and is surprised to hear a man asking if he may sit with him. Chapman sees the white cane in the old man's hand and realizes the man is unable to see the lesion. Chapman is dizzy with excitement to have someone acknowledge him. He invites the man to join him.

The blind man sniffs as he sits. Heightened sensory perception might be assumed when he says:

> BLIND MAN: Oh, yes, you're having that ham and bean soup, aren't you?

Seeing the man's meager plate, Chapman offers to share his soup with the older man, who is profoundly grateful.

A nearby waitress realizes the blind man is unwittingly being involved in a social crime. She whispers to him.

> WAITRESS: Invisible!

The blind man freezes.

> BLIND MAN: Damn you!

He angrily rises and leaves.

* * *

"To See the Invisible Man" used a blind character in a different way. In this piece, blindness was not a metaphor to illustrate lack of prejudice (see *Little House on the Prairie,* "Blind Journey"; *Mask* for examples of the opposite). Instead, it was used to hammer home the fact that prejudice is caused by social convention, whether differences can be seen or not. The scene was dramatically powerful and fit well into the story.

Special equipment was misused when the man angrily rose from the table. He swung his white cane in a dangerous fashion as he rushed away.

This episode's use of a blind character added an extra facet to the story and provided some juicy food for thought.

The Cosby Show / "A Touch of Wonder" / Feb. 20, 1986 / NBC-TV

Executive Producers: Tom Werner & Marcia Carsey
Co-Executive Producer: John Markus
Producer: Carmen Finestra
Director: Jay Sandrich
Writer: Matt Williams
Category: Series Television—Situation Comedy

* Blindness
* Black Male
* Performer with a Disability

Plot: Teenagers Denise and Theo are in a minor car accident when they are hit by singer Steve Wonder's limo.

* * *

"A Touch of Wonder" presented a blind man as a "happens-to-be" person in this family comedy. Performer Stevie Wonder played himself in a cute story. The Huxtable teenagers were excited to no end to have met the star. They were equally as thrilled to be invited to a recording session where Wonder programmed their voices into a synclavier against a rhythm. He was a gracious host, rising when meeting their mother, Claire Huxtable, accepting a paper giraffe from little Rudi, etc.

"A Touch of Wonder" presented a blind person as one with special talents and interests without regard to disability.

Mr. Belvedere / "Heather's Tutor" / Feb. 21, 1986 / ABC-TV

Executive Producers: Frank Duncan, Jeff Stein, Tony Sheehan
Producer: Patricia Rickey
Director: Noam Pitlik
Writer: Lissa Levin

* Blindness
* White Male Teenager
* Equipment: Mobility cane
* Face-feeling

Plot: Teenaged Heather is amazed to discover her new peer instructor is blind.

Heather Owens is not looking forward to having a French tutor come by the house, until she imagines that maybe he is a good-looking sophomore with a car. To her amazement, Kyle shows up at the Owenses door with a white cane in hand.

Hyper-sensitive perception could be implied by Kyle's joking reaction:

> KYLE: Oh, I can tell by your breathing that nobody told you I was blind.

Heather leaves the room for a few minutes. Her bratty brother, Wesley, pops in and inquires to the identity of the boy at the table.

> KYLE: I'm Heather's tutor.
>
> WESLEY: Oh, I feel sorry for you.
>
> KYLE: Because I'm blind?
>
> WESLEY: No, because you're stuck with my sister.

The first tutoring session is such a success that Kyle asks Heather out on a date. Heather accepts.

> KYLE: Can I ask you a sort of personal question?
>
> HEATHER: Sure.
>
> KYLE: What do you look like?... Do you mind if I feel your face?

Kyle feels Heather's face then kisses her. Heather pulls away. She tells her friend Angela that she likes Kyle but he is coming on too strong.

With housekeeper Mr. Belvedere's help, Heather manages to let Kyle know she likes him, but doesn't want to go too far.

* * *

"Heather's Tutor" was a cute story. It dealt with an attractive and intelligent boy who was blind. And like others his age, he was very interested in girls. He pushed Heather; she was afraid if she repulsed his unwelcome advances, he would think she didn't like him because he was blind. She had to learn to find a delicate balance to let him know she *did* like him — but that she wasn't crazy about his actions. The two managed to strike a harmonious balance.

"Heather's Tutor" used a person who was blind as a character. His limitation was of little consequence.

Mr. Sunshine / pilot / Mar. 28, 1986 / ABC-TV

Executive Producers: John Rich; Henry Winkler
Director: John Rich
Writer: David Lloyd
Category: Series Television — Situation Comedy

* Blindness
* Single White Male; Series lead
* Equipment: Mobility cane; Braille; Braille watch

Plot: A divorced college professor who is blind moves into a new apartment.

Professor Paul Stark moves into an apartment in Mrs. Swinford's house near the university. Mrs. Swinford is shocked to find her new tenant is blind. Mrs. Swinford isn't sure about keeping this new tenant. She talks to Paul's typist, Grace D'Angelo:

> MRS. SWINFORD: Blind wasn't what I had in mind.
>
> GRACE: Wasn't what he had in mind, either.

Grace has finished a project for Paul.

> GRACE: I finished your article. You want to proof-feel it?

Grace is encouraging Paul to start dating again. She goads him to go to a singles club. He meets Janice.

> JANICE: Are you really blind?
>
> PAUL: Bats use me as a role model.

Paul discusses his divorce.

> JANICE: What kept you [and your wife] together?
>
> PAUL: Pity, apparently. I went blind and she felt she couldn't desert me.

Paul embarrasses himself by accidentally dancing with a man and tripping when he insists on getting drinks. He wants to leave. Janice becomes the non-disabled catalyst.

> JANICE: You know what your problem is, Paul? You're so afraid of pity that you can't accept caring.

* * *

Preliminary blurbs about *Mr. Sunshine* indicated that the program would be about a newly-blinded bitter college professor who was coping with the single life and a teenaged son. This formula was deemed so touchy that Lewis Erlicht, then-president of ABC Entertainment, was quoted in the April 20–26, 1985, issue of *TV Guide* as saying "we have to make sure" that viewers "are not uncomfortable." Erlicht was described as "wary of the concept." It seemed the show would either be a disaster or a strikingly different image of blindness.

Mr. Sunshine possessed some different qualities. Paul Stark was independent, a parent (at least in the debut episode; his son seemed to vanish from subsequent stories) and a white-collar professional. The sighted actor portraying him made promotional appearances on radio and TV programs, expressing how he had spent a great deal of time at an organization for people with visual limitations to learn about the disability he would be portraying. Hence, it was disappointing to find him badly misusing a white cane. He poked it in front of himself.

His blindness was the butt of many of the jokes. Examples were when an angry Paul tried to march out of the room and went into a closet. Or, when he appeared in hopelessly outdated and inappropriate clothes.

Some of the heavy-handed humor was found to be tedious by those familiar with the disability Paul had. Lines such as Grace's "Do you want to proof-feel it?" or the "bats use me as a role model" had the effect of breaking the ice with the audience—and annoying persons who were, themselves, visually impaired.

Paul had a searing sense of humor that was fueled on by drippy Mrs. Swinford and the acid-tongued Grace. The situations illustrated on *Mr. Sunshine*'s eleven episodes were the typical sitcom variety. They usually had little to do with Paul's disability although this was not a rule.

Mr. Sunshine presented a different image of blindness. It also fell far, far short of its potential by not permitting the audience to forget Paul had a limitation.

New Love American Style / "Love & Reading Music" / 1986 / ABC-TV

Executive Producer: Gordon Farr
Producer: David Yarnell; Linda Morris; Vic Rauseo
Supervising Producer: Arnold Kane
Coordinating Producer: Tom John
Director: Lee Bernhardi
Writer: Gregory Van Boom
Category: Series Television — Romantic Comedy

* Blindness
* Single White Male
* Equipment: Sighted guide
* Face-feeling

Plot: A blind concert pianist falls in love with a tough deli delivery girl.

Concert pianist Chester Burrows accepts a deli delivery from crusty Alice Clipton. He hunts through his pockets for money. Alice waves the bag in his face.

ALICE: What are you, blind?

CHESTER: Yes.

Alice bows out quickly but returns with Chet's newspaper. She hands it to the musician.

ALICE: Why do you get a newspaper?

CHESTER: My secretary reads it to me.

Chester wants Alice to read him the review of his previous night's concert. Alice fudges then relates a brief and immature review. When his agent calls, Chet learns what the critic actually said. Chet is angry at Alice and asks about her "reading." Devaluation surfaces.

CHESTER: Is it "Make Fun of the Blind Guy" week?

ALICE: No. That's not why I did it ... I can't read.

Alice is a drop-out who claims she is "too old" to go back to school.
Chet tags along with her to a country and western barn. They are getting along famously. Chet steps up to the piano during the band break and begins to play honky tonk. The band returns and accompanies him. He is cheered by the response of the crowd and turns to Alice.

CHESTER: I don't know what you look like.

Face-feeling is seen as Chet rises and touches Alice's cheeks. He feels her face.

CHESTER: Just as I thought. You're beautiful.

Chet purchases the bar but needs a partner to help run it while he's on the road. Alice is interested — *if* he gives her time off to go back to night school to get her diploma.

* * *

"Love & Reading Music" was a brief vignette which illustrated a blind person who was intelligent, talented and possessed of a range of emotions. The welcome new awareness was lost in a story full of formula "tactics."
The successful man was illustrated as being fixated on himself — Alice's

gaffe could only mean she was mocking him and his limitation. Such staging suggests that a disability never becomes second nature.

It was jarring when, after a cheerful little impromptu gig at the country bar, Chet suddenly—and out of context—told Alice he didn't know what she looked like. Thus, the curious and potentially intriguing relationship of the cultured pianist and the street-wise gum-snapper was lost as the prevailing romantic image of blindness popped up. Chet was no longer a man, he was a blind man.

"Love & Reading Music" used some positive aspects within a tired image of blindness.

The Wizard / "Seeing Is Believing" / Sept. 30, 1986 / CBS-TV

Executive Producers: Douglas Schwartz & Michael Berk
Producer: Peter H. Hunt
Co-Producer: Rick Mittleman
Supervising Producer: Paul B. Radin
Director: Peter H. Hunt
Writers: Dale Kern & Douglas Barr
Category: Series Television—Fantasy Adventure

* Blindness
* Single White Female
* Equipment: Mobility cane; Braille book; Dog guide

Plot: The robotic dog guide developed by genius Simon McKay is wanted by villains.

Genius inventor Simon McKay has created a robotic canine, a dog that will never die.

SIMON: He's going to be a perfect Seeing Eye dog.

The dog is desired by Dyer, an arms dealer who wants to reprogram it as the ultimate attack machine.

Jennifer Dunn, a young blind woman, has agreed to test the dog. She is surprised at Aegis' performance—but doesn't trust him. Jen uses a bracelet to activate and deactivate Aegis. She can send him a homing signal should they be separated.

At home, Jen plugs Aegis in to recharge him. She hears Dyer's hoods breaking in. She escapes from her room and goes to the kitchen. In a scene reminiscent of *Wait Until Dark,* she kills all the fuses. The villains snatch her and Aegis.

She refuses to cooperate with Dyer. He threatens her with a knife.

DYER: Imagine what it would be like to be deaf—as well as blind.

Jen uses her bracelet to later activate Aegis. She orders him to return to Simon. The dog takes off and gets Simon. The inventor locates Jen. Now she trusts Aegis.

* * *

"Seeing Is Believing" used a blind character in a natural way, although the tried-and-true blind-woman-as-victim element was used again. Jennifer Dunn was an attractive, modest young woman who lived alone and was completely at ease with herself. She was leery of Simon's robotic dog but was willing to give it a try. She indicated she had been "sightless" since she was five.

Although she was frightened at being taken hostage by the villains, she remained clear-headed and able to think throughout the dilemma, a distinct difference from such earlier blind victims as "Lorna Murchison" in *Union Station*.

Actual blind persons were seen in the background of this piece. "Seeing Is Believing" used a blind character well. Jen was a perfect and appropriate test case for Simon's experimental dog.

Can You Feel Me Dancing? / Oct. 13, 1986 / NBC-TV

Executive Producers: Robert Greenwald; Jonathan Bernstein
Co-Producers: Diane Walsh; Cleve Landsberg
Supervising Producers: Philip K. Kleinbart; Kent Bateman
Director: Michael Miller
Writers: J. Miyoko Hensley & Steven Hensley
Category: Made-for-TV Movie — Drama

* Blindness
* Single White Female
* Equipment: Mobility cane; Braille

Plot: A young blind woman discovers who she is.

Karen Nichols, a young woman who has been blind since birth, anticipates support from her family for her college plans. They've always encouraged her to try her own wings, getting her involved in water skiing, hang gliding, etc.

Karen's mother is concerned about Richie, a young man who wants to date Karen. Joan indicates to him that a date with Karen is less-than-average.

> JOAN: Have you ever dated a blind girl before? Did she mention she's never been out with a sighted boy before?

A wonderful reversal on face-feeling occurs.

RICHIE: Karen, do you want to feel my face so you know what I look like?

Karen bursts out laughing.

KAREN: No, I don't! It's not necessary.

Karen's mother devalues her daughter.

JOAN: I think it's possible he gets some ego satisfaction out of helping you and then what happens if the novelty wears off?... I just think you have to realize it's not as easy for a sighted boy to understand what you go through and he may not want the responsibility in the long run.

Karen is accepted to the college of her choice in New York; however, her parents refuse to foot the bill unless she goes to a local school. She is determined to win a scholarship, as determined as she is to learn to dance from Richie. She learns a dance routine and moves in with Richie.

A rehabilitation counselor deems Karen ineligible for a scholarship. Although she can hang-glide and water ski, she has never taken a bus by herself. She does not know the basics of independent living skills.

Karen sets her own destiny, learning how to manage daily skills. She wins the scholarship to go and build her own future.

* * *

Can You Feel Me Dancing? was a refreshingly different portrait of blindness. Karen was groomed by her parents to be a model blind person, the kind profiled in "inspiring" dramas. She was afraid of nothing, but they had protected her from daily life which handicapped her more than her disability.

Karen's father wouldn't permit her to work in the family printing firm — even after a crisis where the employees had to be laid off. Mel told her he could do things "faster" if Karen stayed out of the way. He would take her mobility cane away, telling her, "You don't need that here," until she finally rebelled.

Her love affair with Richie was as much an act of rebellion as one of love. She cared for Richie; he let her do things although in his own way, he was as overprotective as her family.

Karen was a resourceful and intelligent young woman. When her parents wouldn't foot the bill for her to go to school, she looked for a scholarship. When she wasn't eligible, she made herself acceptable. When she was mugged, she took self-defense. Despite her successes, she was not an overachieving character. She took her knocks and learned the hard way.

A nice scene was one when she and Richie went to a nightclub and won a dance contest. In the flush of victory, Richie proudly announced to the crowd that Karen was blind. The pronouncement made Karen decide to leave him. It was the same thing she had suffered with her family—being a model showpiece.

Actual people with visual impairments were seen in the background of the film; the roles of the rehabilitation counselor and a teacher at the center for the visually impaired were played by actresses with limitations.

Can You Feel Me Dancing? benefitted strongly by technical advice from persons who were blind. The story dealt with issues of independence. A nice picture of growing up as experienced by a blind young woman was illustrated—not simply the disability itself.

The Equalizer / "Nocturne" / Oct. 15, 1986 / CBS-TV

Executive Producer: James McAdams
Producer: Alan Barnette
Co-Producers: Coleman Luck and Scott Shepherd
Co-Producers in New York: Daniel Lieberstein; Peter A. Runfolo
Supervising Producer: Ed Waters
Director: Richard Compton
Writer: Carlton Eastlake
Category: Series Television—Crime Drama

* Blindness
* Single White Female
* Equipment: Braille watch; Braille slate and stylus; Braille labels; Writing guide; Mobility cane

Plot: A blind woman hears the voice of the man who blinded her eight years before.

Sightless music critic Kate Parnell takes a call from a would-be admirer. She turns down his request for a date with devaluation.

> KATE: I think you might be getting into something here that you're not gonna want to cope with.

Kate gets on a jammed elevator. She hears a voice and panics.

> KATE: Let me through! Please let me through—that's him! ... the man who did this to me! Don't let him get away!

Kate reveals the man was responsible for blinding her eight years previous.

The police can't help her. At home, she finds items on her desks are out of place and she hears a door close. She knows the man on the elevator is tormenting her. A friend of hers calls Robert McCall, The Equalizer. McCall convinces his disillusioned friend Logan to help watch Kate and offer protection.

Kate explains to Logan that the cause of her disability was a severe beating from the man who attacked her. She recognized his voice because he had taunted her for hours before raping and beating her.

    LOGAN: You haven't—dated anybody since—?

    KATE: That's right. No, I guess I haven't been in the mood.

McCall assumes the man must have a high public profile where there is a possibility his voice could be heard. Using a high tech voice synthesizer, Kate helps a technician to duplicate the voice she heard. The police send out copies of the synthesized voice, although

    ISADORE: That tape isn't really evidence.

The would-be murderer is trapped by matching voice patterns from telephone lines coming into the building with the synth voice. In a showdown at Kate's apartment, McCall shoots out lights to give Kate a better advantage in the laundry room. Between Kate, Logan, and McCall, the man is felled.

* * *

"Nocturne" presented a fair image of a blind woman in a rather far-fetched blind-woman-as-victim story. Kate was perceived to be completely independent, holding down a prestigious job at a magazine as a critic. She navigated easily and well at work and within her apartment. She was at ease with herself. She appropriately used such aids as a Braille slate and stylus while making notes on the concert she was attending, wielded her cane correctly, and used handwriting guides to enable her to write in script.

While her rebuff of a date with an admirer can be noted as devaluation, it was later explained that Kate had a great fear of men after her rape and beating. However, at the outset of the program without such knowledge, it could only be defined as devaluation. The inclusion of yet another version of the *Wait Until Dark* scene makes one wonder if "Turn Out the Lights When in Danger" is assumed to be part of the basic education for people with severe visual impairments!

"Nocturne" presented a blind woman as one who was capable and relaxed with herself (see "Look Back in Darkness" for a similar story line).

Ordinary Heroes / Oct. 19, 1986 / ABC-TV

Producer: Ira R. Barmak
Director: Peter H. Cooper
Screenplay: Ira R. Barmak
Category: Feature Film (not released to theatres; aired on television instead)—Drama

* Blindness
* Single White Male
* New Disability

Plot: A Vietnam vet blinded in the war returns home.

Just four days before his draft enlistment is up in 1973, Tony Kaiser saves the life of a drunken friend in Vietnam and is blinded in the process. At home, girlfriend Maria Pezzo is worried because she hasn't heard anything.

After surgery in California, Tony's sight has not been restored. Depressed, he has no desire to return home. To his chagrin, he is sent home at Christmastime by the Army to receive the Silver Star.

At home, the driver of the "official car" taking him to the hospital turns out to be Maria. She has deceived him. He is forced to dine with friends and tells Maria he doesn't love her anymore. He gets up to go to the phone in order to call a cab and exhibits extreme helplessness when he knocks down the Christmas tree. He admits to Maria he loves her.

* * *

Ordinary Heroes appeared to be a remake of 1944's *Pride of the Marines*. After Tony was blinded, some scenes played identically to the original—right down to knocking down a Christmas tree. The updating of the story took it from World War II to Vietnam. Tony and Maria were live-in lovers. In the war, Tony was not quite the hero Al Schmid was, but he did save his best friend, Ken ("Lee" in *Pride of the Marines)*.

For some reason after losing his sight, Tony had also lost the ability to locate his mouth. An orderly fed him and Tony made a culinary mess all over his pajamas. In a major departure from the original, Maria flew to California where the doctor let her see Tony without revealing her presence. She saw him after a creative food session, unshaven and with his dinner all over him. She fled quickly and admitted she thought of him as an anchor to strip her of her independence. Other than that, the two stories were identical.

After forty-two years of social change, technological advances, and opportunities for people with visual limitations, the same story was made; within the realm of media's version of disability, it still played. Such easy duplicity is a clear indication of how little the film industry understands (or cares to understand) about disability in some circumstances. Could certain ethnic roles of the forties still be valid in contemporary cinema with only a change of name?

People with disabilities were seen in the background of hospital segments.

While *Pride of the Marines* in 1944 did not take advantage of then-current rehabilitation technologies in dealing with the war-blinded, neither did *Ordinary Heroes*. Not only did the movie ignore World War II rehab techniques, it also ignored the twenty-five years of progress separating the time frames of the two pictures! *Ordinary Heroes* was a tired and ludicrous stereotype that was played for all the tears it was worth.

ALF / "For Your Eyes Only" / Nov. 3, 1986 / NBC-TV

Executive Producer: Tom Patchett and Bernie Brillstein

* Blindness
* Single White Female

Blindness

Producer: Paul Fusco
Co-Producer: Laurie Gelman
Supervising Producer: Thad Mumford
Director: Peter Bonerz
Writers: Mitzi McAll and Adrienne Armstrong
Category: Series Television — Situation Comedy

Plot: ALF, the alien being from the planet Melmac, befriends a blind woman.

ALF is left alone when the family with whom he is living goes out for various activities. He turns on the radio for companionship and hears a lonely woman named Jody talking to psychologist Dr. Schrock. Jody says she is overwhelmed by Los Angeles.

> JODY: Moving here was like moving to a different planet.
>
> ALF: I can relate.
>
> JODY: I'm just so afraid of rejection. People react funny when they find out I'm not like them.
>
> ALF: I can relate to that, too.

ALF calls up the radio station and leaves his number. He wants Jody to call him. The two strike up a phone friendship.

ALF's host family is concerned when ALF makes a date with Jody. After all, no one but the family knows about ALF and his alien origins. No sweat, informs ALF.

> ALF: That's where I lucked out. Jody's blind.

ALF goes to see Jody. When she answers the door, she notes the voice from the diminutive alien is near the floor.

> JODY: Please you don't have to bow.

Jody enjoys her evening with the unconventional ALF, never suspecting he is less than human until he goes to leave and shakes her hand. She is left wondering about the small, fuzzy paw.

* * *

"For Your Eyes Only" was a curious story. Jody was intelligent, alert, independent and needed a friend. She wasn't much different from anyone else.

Jody noted the low physical placement of ALF's voice when he entered; she never made any mention of it as the evening wore on. She didn't think it odd when he literally swallowed a whole tray of hors d'oeuvres in one bite. Nor did his distinct musical favorites seem out of the ordinary—ALF wanted to hear The Chipmunks.

In one sense, Jody could have just been appreciating ALF's unique humor and outlook. Perhaps she thought he was small-statured. But she never questioned him. Her ignorance of his difference was a new rendition of the old deception game—where it was "safe" to not let blind persons know the truth for their own good.

Despite an amusing story and a blasé, humorous depiction of a woman who was blind, the piece fared badly in its assumption that a person without vision could be so easily gulled.

"For Your Eyes Only" was created from a sighted writer's viewpoint. Laughs were not at the expense of the blind character in this strange story.

The Equalizer / "Counterfire" / Nov. 19, 1986 / CBS-TV

Executive Producer: James McAdams
Producer: Alan Barnette
Co-Producers: Coleman Luck and Scott Shepherd
Co-Producers in New York: Daniel Lieberstein; Peter A. Runfolo
Supervising Producer: Ed Waters
Director: Alan Metzger
Writers: Scott Shepherd & Coleman Luck
Category: Series Television—Crime Drama

* Blindness
* White Male
* Equipment: Mobility cane

Plot: Robert McCall is framed with the help of a blind man.

Stopping to go investigate an address in an harassment case, McCall is deterred by a blind man who runs his hands over McCall's car and identifies it as a Jaguar. After an unsuccessful visit with a possible suspect, McCall gets in his car and leaves. The blind man suddenly jumps in front of McCall's car and is slightly injured. A crowd gathers. To a policeman, McCall claims the man leapt in front of his car. Furthermore, he doubts the man is blind. He rips off Clark's dark glasses. Seeing Clark's eyes are not average in appearance, McCall realizes he was mistaken.

He rides an elevator in a building. At one floor, he is shocked to see Clark stumble in, bleeding from the stomach with a gun in hand. The blind man slumps to the floor and dies as McCall takes the gun. The door opens up and policemen see McCall with a gun in hand, a dead man at his feet. The frame-up has been locked tight.

* * *

"Counterfire" used a blind man as a confederate in a con. When a sighted confederate gave the word, Clark would jump in front of a car.

It never occurred to either McCall or the policeman that it was odd for a blind man to step off a curb in the middle of a block—a perilous location. A corner crossing would permit him to aurally monitor the movement of traffic to cross safely. Since he was not out for a stroll but involved in a crime, he walked into traffic. No one ever suspected something was amiss—a silent assumption that blind persons are so easily disoriented that they may wander out into traffic.

The segment where McCall ripped off Clark's dark glasses was offensive and an insult to persons with less-than-average-appearing eyes. It also discredited the possibility that Clark could be blind and have average-looking eyes or have any usable vision. Clark's walk into traffic was more of a clue than his eyes. Public mythology on the part of the characters' beliefs and the audiences' was necessary for this piece to work.

"Counterfire" was a neatly crafted story of a frame which used an outdated and stereotypical image of a blind person to propel the plot.

Taxi / "Louie and the Blind Girl" / date unknown / ABC-TV

Executive Producer: Stan Daniels
Producer: Simon Aediken
Director: Noam Pitlik
Writer: Ken Estin
Category: Series Television—Situation Comedy

* Blindness
* Single White Female
* Cure

Plot: Louie's blind girlfriend goes for an operation to get her sight back.

Caustic Sunshine Taxicab Company dispatcher Louie De Palma has a blind girlfriend to whom he is thinking of popping the question. Judy is independent, living alone in an apartment. She is cooking dinner for Louie. She tells him she has a surprise for him.

> JUDY: I may be able to see again . . . the doctor . . . wants to operate again . . . with any luck at all, in twenty-four hours, I'll be able to see your sweet, beautiful face.

Louie is depressed as he tells resident philosopher/driver Alex about the operation. He thinks Judy will be disappointed by his appearance.

> LOUIE: I'm gonna get that [rejection] look from somebody I already love.

Louie and Alex go to the hospital where Judy's bandages are coming off.

JUDY: I want your face to be the first thing I see.... Louie, what if I still can't see?

LOUIE: You'll still have me ... Judy, I'm not the best-looking guy in the world.

Judy's surgery is a success. She is cured.

JUDY: I can see—it's blurry—but I can see! Oh, Louie, you're beautiful.

LOUIE: It's still blurry.

Now that Judy can see, the tightwad makes a disappointed realization.

LOUIE: I'll have to buy her a real diamond.

* * *

"Louie and the Blind Girl" was a typical feel-good story that felt oddly out-of-place within this acclaimed comedy. Louie De Palma, the man everyone loved to hate, showing he had a heart and cared for an attractive blind woman? Well, maybe it was character development—or it would have been if Judy had not regained her sight. As it was, it was a ho-hummer and a rendition of the 1909 Biograph feature *The Light That Came*.

Wheelchair-Users

The bulky term "Wheelchair-Users" is a catch-all phrase used in this resource for characters utilizing chairs. Most characters illustrated in this section are those experiencing paraplegia, a paralysis involving the lower extremities. Others experience quadriplegia, or paralysis involving four limbs. Unless particularly noted as the same by the story's writer, no designation will be made as to the existence of paraplegia or quadriplegia since this information is generally lacking within the stories themselves. Any other reason a character may be using a chair, such as having two sprained ankles, will be specifically expressed.

Characters are described in the appropriate terminology of the disabled community as *using* wheelchairs. "Confined to a wheelchair" or "wheelchair-bound" are terms classed in this work as offensive language as an individual is not forcefully bound to a wheelchair with ropes or leather thongs! The chair is a tool which restores mobility and independent movement to those who, for any reason, do not walk.

The most prevailing aspect seen in dramas with wheelchair-using characters is a sin of omission. Physical access to buildings and public transportation continues to be a heated issue for which disability advocates fight. The removal of physical barriers and the addition of ramps, lowered drinking fountain facilities, public telephones, or the inclusion of outfitted "wheelchair stalls" in public restrooms reduce the obstacles a person in a chair encounters and permits him/her to function more easily in society.

Access is rarely discussed in dramas. Also never seen are the sometimes agonizing circuitous "access routes" to public buildings or restaurants—through freight elevators, past garbage bins, or via back alleyways—to which many disabled persons have become forcefully accustomed. A wealth of conflict and story ideas exists in this area alone, which a writer would be wise to learn about.

Wheelchairs are not specifically described as Special Equipment in this section due to the overall classification of "Wheelchair-Users." They will, however, be described in some examples as being misused. The most common "misuse" is the type of chair illustrated. A "hospital chair" is a standard-sized chair with straight arms. Many studios have such chairs in their prop department and sock actors into them without regard to their individual stature. These huge chairs often hinder and further limit a character. Different chairs of different weights, back support and size are the ones seen in the real community. Their selection is determined by several factors, such as appropriate size, what the user's general level of daily activity is, and more commonly these days, aesthetic concerns. Studio prop chairs, besides being inappropriate for the characters seen using them, are extensions of the "hospital" and "patient" designations of people with limitations. (A larger variety of chairs are currently seen on television since more actors with disabilities are playing themselves and bring along the chair that best suits them and enhances their mobility.)

A sometimes seen "trait" in wheelchair-using characters is one described as lack of sexual capacity. A few stories indicate that persons with bodily paralysis have no sexual capabilities. This trait is cited here with criticism since the pieces act as a perpetuation of public mythology. The stories do not indicate this is one person's situation, thus failing to consider the general sexual dynamics of the population under scrutiny. Sexual ability varies due to many factors, a point rarely made in dramas. In "Thou Shalt Not Commit Adultery," the entire story illustrated characters who matter-of-factly "knew" that a man with a spinal cord injury was incapable of enjoying sexual relations. Such a message is damaging to the entire population.

Characters who are Wheelchair-Users utilize various items termed as special equipment:

> **Hydraulic Lift Van** refers to an automotive van fitted with a motorized lift to easily allow a chair-using character inside.
>
> **Car Hand Controls** — Instruments that permit a person who does not use his or her legs to work the accelerator and brake pedals in a motor vehicle. Other instruments may be used to permit people with limited hand movements to easily insert a key in the ignition or manipulate the smaller controls. Other devices permit those with difficulty gripping to grasp the steering wheel and pilot the vehicle.
>
> **Adaptive Feeding/Writing Cuff** — A small tool used by those with limited hand grip to grasp small objects such as pens or silverware by means of a cuff that fits over the palm and snugly holds such slender items as a pen, toothbrush, or fork. The user can then write, brush, or eat using the larger motions of the arm. (The catalog of assistive devices would do Sears and Roebuck proud; this is the most basic and generic description of such a tool.)
>
> **Personal Care Attendant** — A hired aide who assists a person with a disability with routine chores of dressing, grooming, transfer to the chair, etc.

In addition to the programs in this section, other wheelchair-using characters can be found in *Tell Me That You Love Me, Junie Moon; Medical Center* "Albatross"; *Beg, Borrow . . . Or Steal; Code Red* "Dark Fire"; *The A-Team* "Water, Water Everywhere"; *Highway to Heaven* "One Fresh Batch of Lemonade"; *The Twilight Zone* "Healer"; *Highway to Heaven* "The Monster"; and *Highway to Heaven* "A Special Love."

Hands Across the Table / 1935 / Paramount Pictures

Producer: E. Lloyd Sheldon
Director: Mitchell Leisen
Screenplay: Norman Krasna, Vincent Lawrence and Herbert Fields
From a Story by: Viña Delmar
Category: Feature Film—Romantic Comedy

* Wheelchair-User
* Single White Male

Plot: A golddigging manicurist must choose between an impoverished playboy or a wealthy man with a disability.

Miss Reggie Allen is a manicurist at the swank Savoy-Carleton Hotel. Her one dream is to meet a rich man and live a comfortable life. She is summoned to dispense a manicure to Mr. Allen Macklyn up in Room 1502, "where the rich live." Reggie is admitted by Peter, a valet. She is introduced to Allen Macklyn and hesitates momentarily when she sees he uses a wheelchair. She begins to do his nails. Macklyn has carefully kept hands, she notes.

> MACKLYN: Some people play golf to pass the time, some go in for tap dancing, some destroy clay pigeons—I have manicures.

He indicates his life is rather empty.

> MACKLYN: A manicure takes forty minutes. That leaves the day only twenty three hours, twenty minutes long.

Reggie asks if the picture of the handsome aviator she sees is Macklyn's brother. He admits the picture is of himself, taken four years before. He alludes to the cause of his disability.

> MACKLYN: Aeroplanes weren't as safe then as they are now.

Macklyn admits a little discomfort.

> MACKLYN: I'm still rather embarrassed about meeting people.

> REGGIE: Why?

> MACKLYN: Well, frankly, I'm always afraid they'll feel sorry for me.

Reggie looks amazedly about the penthouse terrace.

> REGGIE: What? When you have all this?... I don't feel sorry for you, mister.

Macklyn is smitten and orders his valet to buy him some new dressing gowns more suitable for entertaining.

Reggie thinks she has a chance at her dream when she meets outrageous Theodore Drew the Third. The young man sweeps her off her feet. She is brought back to earth when she discovers he is engaged to be married. She is piqued to discover he has no money and is marrying a rich heiress for her fortune. They discover a camaraderie in their tandem larcenous motives. They also discover each other.

Macklyn plans to ask Reggie to marry him, knowing he can give her everything and then some. She decides to go with the impetuous Drew. Macklyn quietly supports her decision.

* * *

Hands Across the Table was a delightful and unassuming little comedy. Allen Macklyn lived a quiet and lonely life, secluded in his suite. He was attired in dressing gowns, his legs covered by a blanket. His companions were his valet and Reggie, the manicurist. He hadn't been out on his boat for years. He considered his dressing gown wardrobe too shabby to entertain, indicating he never left the suite. He spent time on the terrace. He easily fell for Reggie who was pretty and did not indicate any remorse at his disability.

Macklyn's presence in the film seemed to be a character measure. Reggie wasn't quite the golddigger she imagined herself to be. When she had the choice between a rich man and a poor man, she chose the poor man, who had captured her heart with his outrageous personality.

Macklyn seemed to be on the outside looking in. Reggie responded to him like a brother, confiding in him about her new friend, Drew. And when she announced to Macklyn that she loved Drew, he gamely smiled and hid the engagement ring with which he had planned to surprise her. Macklyn did not imagine himself to be an opponent of Drew's for Reggie's affections. In quiet devaluation, he backed off and wished the couple well.

Special equipment was misused. A lavish art-deco wheelchair was designed to mesh with the set. The result was a huge monstrosity of a chair that further disabled Macklyn.

Hands Across the Table illustrated a man with a disability as one who would quietly acquiesce forever, knowing he was not "normal."

The Men / 1950 / United Artists

Producer: Stanley Kramer
Director: Fred Zinnemann
Story: Carl Foreman
Screenplay: Carl Foreman
Category: Feature Film — Drama

* Wheelchair-User
* Single White Male
* Equipment: Car hand controls
* New Disability

Plot: A paraplegic war veteran is reluctant to continue his life in a chair.

Wheelchair-Users

A year after Ken "Bud" Wilchek has been paralyzed in the war, his girlfriend Ellie attends a seminar at the veterans' hospital. Dr. Brock lays the cards on the table for mothers, wives, and girlfriends of paraplegic veterans. Appropriate clinical vocabulary is used as the doctor discusses physical difficulties the men face as well as possibilities for marriage and fatherhood.

Ellie approaches the doctor about Bud, who has repeatedly refused to see her. She asks for help. Bud is transferred into the ward. Ellie comes to see him. He states erroneous notions and devalues himself.

> BUD: I said look at me. Now, get a good look, Ellie. Does it make you feel healthy? Is that what you want? Okay, you can go home now ... you don't know pity from love ... what do you want to do, wait on me hand and foot all your life? I'm like a baby.

Convinced of Ellie's love, Bud actively works to improve.

Norm Butler, another vet, discusses women. He devalues the population of men with injuries.

> NORM: It's not the nature of a normal woman to be in love with one of us.... Normal is normal and crippled is crippled and never the twain shall meet.

Bud and Ellie plan to marry. Ellie's father erroneously warns her that she will be Bud's nurse for the rest of her life.

> FATHER: He ought to let you go. If he loved you as much as you love him, he'd let you go.

Bud works on parallel bars with braces as he wants to be married standing up. He learns to drive a car with hand controls. He goes bowling and plays wheelchair basketball.

After the wedding, Bud and Ellie retire to their new home. Both are uneasy. Bud badgers Ellie into saying she's sorry she married him. He leaves and goes on a glorious rampage, resulting in a citation for drunk driving after he is in a car accident. Members of the Paralyzed Veterans Association note he is doing them damage and vote to discharge him from the hospital.

Bud realizes he is in charge of his destiny. He approaches Ellie and suggests they talk.

* * *

For all of its devaluation scenes, *The Men* was a different type of disability movie. It covered many, many bases. Before Bud was introduced, the audience had learned about the disability through Dr. Brock's seminar. Brock was no Pollyanna, just simple and straight to the point. After his talk, he was seen doing rounds — and meeting many different men with disabilities — from the cigarchewer Leo, who used his government benefits to play the horses, to the serious Angel, a young Hispanic man who wanted to get a loan to buy a house. Norm Butler was a philosophical member of the Paralyzed Veterans board. The men were illustrated as having diverse personalities and approaches to their disability. Some were irresponsible in their personal care, some were very responsible. Consequently, Bud's anger when introduced was *his* problem and not one of his disability.

Bud and Ellie's situation was one of misunderstanding. She tried to ignore Bud's differences rather than deal with them. However, she was constantly reminded of them, such as when his leg began to shake from muscle spasms or his wheelchair would squeak. Neither was ready for marriage; they learned about their own short-sightedness and resolved to correct it.

Most welcome in this picture was the use of people with disabilities as the catalysts. They were all neighbors in the ward; they depended on each other in a variety of ways. Actual men with disabilities were seen throughout the hospital segments.

The Men was an interesting and absorbing character study that honestly approached questions about disability.

Whatever Happened to Baby Jane? / 1962 / Seven Arts Productions

Executive Producer: Kenneth Hyman
Producer: Robert Aldrich
Director: Robert Aldrich
Screenplay: Lukas Heller
From the Novel by: Henry Farrell
Category: Feature Film — Drama

* Wheelchair-User
* Single White Female

Plot: Ex-child star Baby Jane Hudson has a cruel relationship with her disabled sister.

Mrs. Bates, a new resident in the neighborhood, is continually asking next-door neighbor Jane Hudson about her sister, one-time star Blanche.

> JANE: Mrs. Bates, my sister doesn't ever go out. She's not fit to receive visitors.

Blanche Hudson uses a wheelchair. She is Jane's virtual prisoner in an upstairs bedroom. Hollywood scandal has it that Jane's jealousy caused her to run down Blanche in a car, injuring her.

Jane runs every aspect of Blanche's life. When mad at Blanche for making a telephone call, Jane yanks the phone out of the wall. For spite, she serves her sister lunch — Blanche's little canary, now on a plate. The demented Jane terrorizes the trapped Blanche by putting a dead rat on her dinner plate. When annoyed by the call button Blanche uses to summon Jane, she rips the device out. Jane murders a maid who discovers Blanche has been tied up and gagged and locked in her room.

The cause of Blanche's disability is discussed as a car accident — where *she* attempted to run down Jane.

      BLANCHE: ...snapped my spine.

Jane drags Blanche out of the house and to the beach where, as police approach her, she deludes herself into thinking admirers are surrounding her and starts to perform.

* * *

Whatever Happened to Baby Jane? was a frightening portrait of disability. Blanche Hudson was a prisoner of her insane, sadistic sister. Blanche's life was severely curtailed, one would assume from the film, because of the disability she had incurred. Her world was her room, the view from her window and the hall leading to the staircase. Jane, still jealous of the film stardom Blanche had achieved after little Baby Jane's star had descended, permitted no autonomy from Blanche. She constantly thwarted Blanche's decisions by flawlessly mimicking her sister's voice over the telephone. Thus, Blanche was completely at Jane's mercy.

The only person permitted to see Blanche was Elvira, a maid. When she discovered Jane had bound and gagged Blanche, she tried to help — and got a hammer in the skull for her trouble.

Had Blanche not been totally helpless and dependent upon her sister, there would have been no movie. The story pivoted on Blanche's disability and created a terrible image. A woman like Blanche, still youthful, intelligent and poised, was destined to a restricted half-life in a bedroom, dependent upon a sister who'd lost many bricks from her full load over the years.

As a film, *Whatever Happened to Baby Jane?* was compelling to watch. However, it was an exceptionally poor and erroneous presentation of disability, in the disabled-woman-as-victim mold.

Bonanza / "The Horse Breaker" / 1963 / NBC-TV

Producer: David Dortort
Director: Don McDougall
Writer: Frank Chase
Category: Series Television — Western

* Wheelchair-User
* Single White Male
* Temporary Disability

Plot: One of the Cartwrights' wranglers is injured in a fall from a horse.

Johnny Lightly falls off a horse while riding a bucking bronc and can't move his legs. Indicating that recovery is a matter of will, Doctor Kay says with exercise and hope, maybe Johnny will walk again. In the meantime, Johnny will use a wheelchair.

Since Johnny is alone in the world, the Cartwrights accept responsibility for the injured man. Doctor Kay's assistant is Ann Davis. She stays at the Ponderosa to help get Johnny going again. She is a tough young woman with a blazing streak of independence who takes no guff.

Accessibility is briefly mentioned as Johnny moves into the ranch house on the Ponderosa.

> JOHNNY: Your bedrooms are upstairs.

No problem; Ben makes up a bed for Johnny right in his office. He also creates a paper-pushing job for Johnny so the young man can earn a living. Ann teaches the Cartwrights exercises to help Johnny.

Johnny is attracted to Ann. He discovers she was the girl of Jody Clay, a fellow who was killed robbing a bank. Old Nathan Clay blames Ben Cartwright for his loss of farmland after Jody's death and vows retribution.

Johnny is harassed by Mr. Clay's hired bozos and depends on Hoss to fight them off. He tries to stand late one night and crashes to the floor. Ben puts him back to bed.

> JOHNNY: I can't cut it, Mr. Cartwright. I wasn't made to live this way.

Ben acts as the non-disabled catalyst and tells Johnny he needs to believe in himself.

Johnny gets a revolver from Ben's desk drawer. Ann confronts him. Johnny devalues himself.

> JOHNNY: I do this and I'm not a burden to them anymore.

Ann dares him to kill himself. Johnny puts the gun away.

Ben, Ann, and Johnny are cornered alone in the ranch house one night by Mr. Clay and his hooligans. Johnny knows he is the only hope for the three of them to survive. Suddenly, he begins to move. He gets on his feet. His return of function has saved them all from a terrible end. Johnny and Ann plan to marry.

* * *

"The Horse Breaker" was a routine story. The addition of what could be called a rehabilitation professional offering therapy was the only difference included in this drama. Other than that, it was predictable.

Bonanza / "The Return" / 1965 / NBC-TV

Producer: David Dortort
Director: Virgil W. Vogel

* Wheelchair-User
* Married White Male

Story: Frank Chase and Ken Pettus
Teleplay: Ken Pettus
Category: Series Television — Western

Plot: After ten years in prison, Trace Cordell returns to Virginia City, much to the chagrin of a man in a wheelchair.

Influential banker Paul Dorn is a staunch opponent to the return of Trace Cordell, out of prison after a ten-year sentence. Ben Cartwright is troubled by Dorn's anger. Dorn, a man using a wheelchair, devalues himself.

> BEN: You're not fighting like the man that you used to be.

> DORN: I'm *not* the man I used to be. Look at me! Cordell got ten years — but I got *life*. Cordell is free, but I'm still paying....

In a vengeful move, Dorn puts pressure on local merchants to "freeze" Cordell out of town.
Ben talks to his sons about Dorn's motive:

> BEN: I can understand Paul's bitterness — being confined to that wheelchair, and all — but I sure hoped he'd be a bigger man than that.

Clara Dorn, Cordell's old sweetheart, tells Trace why she married Paul.

> CLARA: I ... thought I could help, because of what happened to him.... Trace, I didn't love him. I still don't love him. I love you.

Trace and Clara plan to run away but Paul finds out. He corners Trace at the hay barn and inadvertently starts a fire. He is trapped. Cordell saves his life. Clara declares her love for her husband.
Ben approaches Dorn to tell him Clara doesn't love Cordell. Dorn refuses to believe it. Ben acts as the non-disabled catalyst.

> BEN: Paul, what's the matter with you? Has your hate so completely blinded you that you can't see what's in front of your face?

* * *

"The Return" was standard disability formula, featuring the angry, embittered person with a disability who refused to believe he was loveable or had any worth beyond what he'd lost. Dorn's anger was directed at Cordell. His fury was not defined — whether it was at Clara for once having loved Cordell, Cordell for having caused Dorn's disability (the syndicated version of this story never expressed the cause of the limitation but all clues indicated Cordell was at fault), or Dorn's self-hatred for being disabled. No matter. "The Return" was a stereotypical depiction of disability.

Long Ago Tomorrow (a.k.a. "The Raging Moon") / 1971 / EMI Film Productions Limited

Producer: Brice Cohn Curtis
Director: Bryan Forbes
Screenplay: Bryan Forbes
Based on the Novel: *The Raging Moon* by Peter Marshall
Category: British Feature Film — Drama

* Wheelchair-Users
* Single White Couple
* New Disability (male)
* Equipment: Hydraulic lift van; Handled ping-pong ball retriever

Plot: A newly-disabled man and a disabled woman fall in love and try to beat the system.

Bruce Pritchard, a brash and sharp-tongued athlete, loses the use of his legs from a disease. He decides to move into a specialized home after hospitalization. His brother is aghast and uses poor language.

HAROLD: But — this is a place for cripples!

BRUCE: A home for the disabled.

Upon arrival at the home, Bruce is angry and sullen. He is surly about the assortment of curious people who wish to play bridge and make handicrafts. All that interests him is Jill Mathews, a pretty woman in a chair who is engaged. But she leaves the home to try again to live with her family. She has no illusions about her future and pragmatically tells her father:

JILL: I'm a thirty-one year old crippled woman with a fiancé who's looking for an out ... he's ... trapped by pity.

Jill breaks her engagement and returns to the home.
Bruce begins to assimilate into the home: first by trying ping pong and then playing chess. He writes poetry and sells some. Bruce is more and more interested in Jill. He indicates a lack of sexual capacity.

BRUCE: The engine's all right but the wheels won't go 'round.

The two get engaged. The home's administrators tell them they are unrealistic. Undaunted, the two begin planning for a future outside the home.
Just as the world is opening up, Jill dies of an infection. Bruce finds he must go on — alone.

* * *

Long Ago Tomorrow had some marvelous undertones. After becoming disabled, Bruce did not receive any type of rehabilitation. His family was at a loss with the whole situation. Bruce did not wish to return to such a strained atmosphere. His only solution was a home for "the welfare of the handicapped." The athletic scrapper was introduced to a world of quiet chess players and empty souls who had no lives of their own.

The film pointedly discussed the dehumanization that occurred in such an institution. Without locks on the doors, residents had no privacy. Bruce and Jill had to meet secretly to spend time exploring one another.

Bruce indicated he was unable to enjoy sex; both he and Jill lamented the fact they would not be able to have children. However, this statement seemed to be a lack of knowledge. On his own, Bruce began researching in medical books and was coming to the realization that sexual options were open. Both he and Jill were victims of polite misinformation, he seemed to believe.

A scene at a church bazaar lashed out pointedly at the charity image constantly linked to disability. Philanthropic patrons smiled nicely at the residents of the home but paid little real attention to them. Bruce and Jill went on an outrageously funny rampage, discussing how all those people had legs—and some were *so* clever, they even learned to manage to dance with them! This explosion of repression was *not* appreciated by those who ran the home!

Jill's death was disappointing. She was on the threshold of real happiness. Bruce was ready to shove the whole institutional system where it belonged; then Jill died. The conclusion of the movie suggested Bruce would go on, but it was not clear what effect her death would ultimately have on him.

Long Ago Tomorrow illustrated the lack of expectations afforded those with disabilities in a society where they had no options. Dehumanizing institutionalization was, at best, a welcome escape from smothering families. Bruce and Jill were not out to climb mountains—they just wanted a life of their own.

The Next Victim / 1975

Producer: Ian Fodice
Director: James Omerod
Writer: Brian Clemens
Category: British Made-for-TV Movie—Thriller

* Wheelchair-User
* White Married Female

Plot: A woman in a wheelchair is trapped and tracked by an unseen tormentor.

Businessman Derek and his American wife, Sandy, live in a nice flat in an apartment building. Sandy uses a wheelchair. Derek talks about money and the things it can do.

SANDY: Can you buy me out of this chair?

Left alone in the apartment, Sandy meets Tom Bartlett. He is a strange young man who does the building maintenance. He notes Sandy's wheelchair.

TOM: My mother spent ten years of her life in a chair—the last years.

Sandy indicates there is a good chance she will recover and not have to spend much more time on wheels.

TOM: I hope it's not a life sentence.

Strange things begin to happen. Sandy finds herself at the mercy of someone who has cut off her means of escape. There is no one else on the apartment floor.

Bartlett turns out to be the culprit. He wants to put Sandy out of her misery so she won't suffer as his poor old mother did.

* * *

The Next Victim was another disabled-woman-as-victim story. Sandy was illustrated as a helpless pawn.

Special equipment was misused. In this case, the actress was socked into a standard hospital chair that was much too large for her frame and hindered her mobility tremendously. The chair did not even have desk arms to permit her to slide under table tops.

The Next Victim was a poor image of a person with a disability.

The Other Side of the Mountain / 1975 / Universal

Producer: Edward Feldman
Director: Larry Peerce
Screenplay: David Seltzer
Based on the Book: *A Long Way Up* by E.G. Valens
Category: Feature Film—Drama

* Wheelchair-User
* Single White Female
* Based on a True Story
* New Disability
* Equipment: Adaptive writing/feeding cuff

Plot: A world-class skier becomes a quadriplegic after an accident on the slopes.

While in competition for a berth on the 1955 Olympic ski team, Jill Kinmont crashes and breaks her neck. A new disability is incurred. Jill is told she will be a quadriplegic, able to use her shoulders and arms but not her hands.

Her best friend, Audra Jo, visits her in the hospital. Audra Jo is a paraplegic who uses braces and crutches/chair after a bout with polio. She acts as a disabled catalyst and uses bad language when Jill worries about her future.

> AJ: Stop playing the heroine ... you gotta see what you are and say what you are ... there's only one thing that kills cripples and that's taking themselves too seriously.

Jill's unofficial fiancé, Buddy Werner, never sees her again when he realizes she will not be walking. But crazy hot-dog skier Dick Buek breezes in and smuggles Jill and her wheelchair out of the hospital. They tear down the street. He sets Jill in the middle of an intersection and begins a serious conversation as cars whiz back and forth.

> DICK: I don't care if you can't ski. I don't care if you can't walk.

Back home in Bishop, California, Dick is her contant companion. He tells her how he's going to build her a ramped house with appliances low to the ground—after they're married. Jill says she can't have kids and is concerned about making love.

> DICK: It's not all it's cracked up to be.

Jill discovers a new direction in life when she realizes the children on the nearby Indian reservation have difficulties finding a teacher for the community.

Jill goes to a rehabilitation center. Jill tells Lee, a fellow student, that all she's known is skiing. He acts as a disabled catalyst, telling her she's got to try for a new future. With his goading, she starts school at UCLA.

Jill finds herself attracted to the children at the rehabilitation center. She works with them and entertains the idea of becoming a teacher. She talks to a school counselor to find out about getting a teaching certificate.

> COUNSELOR: You people are an inspiration to me, an absolute inspiration. The way you carry on in the face of this handicap makes me feel very small indeed.

Yet, despite his admiration, the counselor dissuades her from teaching. Attitudinal and societal barriers surface.

> COUNSELOR: No school will take you ... let's be realistic. It's your handicap.

> JILL: ...my only handicap is you!

Until Jill finds a school that will hire her, he says, she will not be able to get a teaching certificate. Jill finds the reservation school in Bishop will accept her. She decides to marry Dick. He is killed in a plane crash before he sees Jill.

* * *

The Other Side of the Mountain was a melodrama benefitting the tissue industry. The movie so clearly sought the heart-tug, it was difficult to take seriously. After Jill's injury, instead of dealing with the aftermath by hearing from the character or others around her, the audience was treated to unexplained medical recovery procedures which made it seem Jill had been plunged into a mad scientist's workshop rather than a medical facility. Close shots of Jill being rotated in a frame while her arms dangled helplessly clearly illustrated the frightening aspects experienced by a newly-disabled person — and indicated she was no longer a world class skier. The haunting images were fearful and not countered by any explanation of the procedures. The character never voiced worries or concerns.

Jill was seen in physical therapy and learning to use special devices to enable her to write or feed herself. But she never talked about her feelings. She was a very pretty doll. She was ravishing and fun-loving when Dick parked her chair in the middle of a busy intersection. She was cheerful and pretty when she slipped out of her chair onto the ground her first day at college while other students gawked.

Surprisingly, this soaper touched on a matter pertaining to Jill's civil rights — when she was informed no school in the country would hire a teacher in a wheelchair. The guidance counselor's "inspiration" speech countered with his refusal to let her try for a teaching certificate was wonderful irony. But when he spoke of challenges, formula took over. Jill told him he didn't know what a challenge was. It meant, she told him, struggling to pick up a chunk of Jell-O, or being unable to scratch one's own nose or feel a toilet seat under oneself. Particularly since she was trying to convince him she was *capable,* it appeared the counselor gained more fuel for his own fire by Jill's outburst. It also squeezed a few more drops from the audience's eyes.

The peripheral character of Audra Joe misused special equipment by using a wheelchair much too large for her frame.

The Other Side of the Mountain insisted that love existed even for those like Jill. It stated little about life in general for people who are quadriplegics. Jill was doted over by Dick and swung into his arms, silently stating true love conquers all. Jill sat, looked pretty, and life went on.

Eleanor and Franklin / 1976 / ABC-TV

Executive Producer: David Susskind
Producer: Harry R. Sherman & Audrey Maas
Director: Daniel Petrie

* Wheelchair-user
* Married White Male
* Based on a True Story
* Equipment: Braces and crutches

Writer: James Costigan
Based Upon the Book: *Eleanor and Franklin* by Joseph P. Lash
Category: Made-for-TV Movie — Period Drama

Plot: Franklin Roosevelt contracts polio and goes on to become President.

After a busy day out on the boat with the children, Franklin feels weak and tired. He can't move his legs.

> FRANKLIN: I can't seem to move ... at all, now.

Franklin learns he has polio. Devaluation occurs and poor language is used.

> FRANKLIN: I'm a cripple ... there's a good chance I'll be a cripple for the rest of my life ... people don't want cripples in public office. It makes them uneasy, embarrasses them.

Eleanor talks to Dr. Lovett about Franklin's prognosis.

> ELEANOR: Will he ever get better, Dr. Lovett? Will he ever be able to walk or just stand or even sit up by himself?

> LOVETT: I hope so ... if his will is strong enough—if he wants it, wants an active life again, then of course, there's a chance.

Franklin learns to get around using a wheelchair; learns to stand and walk with braces and crutches. He restarts his political career by nominating Al Smith for President. After that, there is no stopping Franklin.

* * *

Eleanor and Franklin was an absorbing story told in flashback, beginning after FDR's death. As usual, Roosevelt went through devaluation and passed through it. The suggestion made by Dr. Lovett, indicating that Roosevelt's recovery would be resultant from his strong will, fit into the FDR legend. According to the drama, recovery had nothing to do with residual muscular function—just the will that would vault him to the presidency.
Roosevelt was shown getting around ably in his wheelchair; his for-the-public bouts with braces and crutches appeared to be difficult.
Eleanor and Franklin had its share of typical language. It was also followed up in 1977 by *Eleanor and Franklin—The White House Years.*

The Love Boat / "Message for Maureen" / Oct. 15, 1977 / ABC-TV

Category: Series Television—
Romantic Comedy

* Wheelchair-User
* Single White Female
* Temporary Disability

Plot: A tennis star is sidelined in a wheelchair, with an injury that may be permanent.

Famous tennis pro Maureen Mitchell is facing risky surgery after an injury. She hopes to be able to walk and play again. For the time being, she must use a wheelchair. While on board the *Pacific Princess,* she runs into antagonistic columnist and ex-boyfriend John Ballard.

Ship's doctor Adam Bricker keeps a close eye on Maureen. He talks to her land-based surgeon and receives bad news. The operation is off and Maureen will never walk again. Ballard overhears the conversation and asks to tell Maureen. He approaches Maureen in her cabin.

> JOHN: There's something you have to know.
>
> MAUREEN: What?

John can't tell her the news. He ad-libs on the spot.

> JOHN: I'd go anywhere in the whole wide world with you anytime. But only as man and wife.

Maureen accepts his proposal. When she learns from Doc that John was told she would never walk again, she suspects pity was the motive behind his marriage proposal.

Maureen's land-based specialist made a mistake. Bricker tells her the surgery is back on. John still wants her.

* * *

"Message for Maureen" was rather benign. Maureen handled her disability well, growing weary of people pussy-footing around her. John's sudden desire for marriage after he discovered the woman might never walk and lose her career was an uninspired story concept, to say the least.

Baretta / "All That Shatters" / Oct. 19, 1977 / ABC-TV

Executive Producer: Bernard L.
Kowalski

* Wheelchair-User
* Single White Male

Producer: Charles E. Dismukes and Alan Godfrey
Supervising Producer: Ed Waters
Director: Don Medford
Writer: Rift Fournier
Category: Series Television — Police Drama

* **Equipment:** Braces and crutches

Plot: Undercover cop Tony Baretta investigates a group of protesting Vietnam veterans who are suspected of planting terrorist bombs at "access barriers."

A protest is going on at City Hall. Judd Parker, a man in a wheelchair, addresses a large group of disabled supporters and news media. Access is discussed.

> PARKER: If you were in a wheelchair or used crutches ... you would either find it impossible to get in this building or you would have to get help. Yet, there is a special elevator in the back — for garbage. We want equal but separate access with the garbage. We want easy access to the libraries, to our schools, to our municipal facilities.

Cop Tony Baretta is at the rally, wanting to break it up. A wealthy philanthropist, Mrs. Carr, approaches him.

> MRS. CARR: ...Yet, these poor people, many of them hardworking taxpayers, only want access to their buildings and public facilities.

Tony has no interest in Mrs. Carr's statement. Suddenly, when the woman's lovely daughter appears and appeals to Tony to let the protestors remain, he agrees to help.

TJ, a man in a chair who also stands with braces, is a busy energetic sort who is single-handedly planting bombs at "access barriers." He figures responsibility will be pinned on the coalition at City Hall. He plans to take a bank and get out of town. Bitterness and a vengeful nature appear in his statement to his supportive, non-disabled girlfriend:

> TJ: I deserve better. And I'm gonna get what I deserve.

More bombs go off. Baretta suspects the coalition as the guilty party.

In an attempt to crack the case, Baretta goes undercover in a chair and lies to a group of vets about a war career in Vietnam. The men with disabilities see through his ruse. He admits he is "the heat" and is looking for the man planting bombs. His terminology is quite interesting, describing the culprit as one who "ain't sittin' around on his stumps." Tony uses more pejorative language when he describes an innocent man injured in one of the bomb attacks.

BARETTA: Now he's a cripple in a wheelchair. He didn't do nothin'.

The vets finger TJ as the culprit.

VET: He don't wanna face up to what he is.

With the help of TJ's girlfriend, Baretta fingers the young man at the bank while an executive is getting the $100,000 demanded. The cop quietly talks TJ down. He acts as the non-disabled catalyst, using offensive and pejorative language.

BARETTA: ...[There] must be something you dig about this world ... [your girlfriend] don't know nothing about cripples. She just loves you. But you got to face it sooner or later.... I talked to people and you got to face it. You're a crip, you're not whole. I got my legs but you got a woman who loves you.

TJ realizes it's all over.

* * *

"All That Shatters" aired five months after a month-long sit-in by disabled persons in San Francisco that pressed the federal government to sign Section 504, a piece of legislation that had been kicked around without enforcement since its inception in 1973. The actions of the protesters resulted in the enactment of 504, which outlined the civil rights of those with limitations. "All That Shatters" drew heavily from that incident, evident by the language used by the protesters onscreen and the very act of illustrating them as political activists demanding their rights. However, the basic story line was rather stereotypical. TJ's problem was one of not being able to accept himself. He was taking on the world with bombs.

Another weakness occurred at the beginning of the production. When Baretta was getting ready to call the chief for help in clearing out the protestors, it was a wealthy matron who spoke to him of access. While support from the non-disabled public is necessary in such social debate, Mrs. Carr's involvement could have been misinterpreted as a rich lady's alternative to Thursday bridge games. Baretta only agreed to help the protest continue after he met Mrs. Carr's daughter whom he couldn't resist.

Offensive and pejorative language was prevalent throughout the episode; however, it must be noted that Tony Baretta was more street-smart than linguistically oriented. Better terminology would have helped this story, but the blunt Baretta was never known for flowery subtlety.

The most interesting aspect of "All That Shatters" was the utilization of a social issue in the lives of people with disabilities within a static bitter-disablee story. This injection of reality gave a different tone to "All That Shatters" and illustrated that TJ's anti-social behavior was the skewed action of *one* misguided individual—and not meant to cast dispersions on the mentality of the disabled community as a whole.

Actual disabled performers appeared in the background of the production.

"All That Shatters" was a fairly routine disability drama. However, the use of important contemporary issues (which, unfortunately, were not resolved or even discussed after TJ was stopped) made it something different. It was also possibly the only production to ever mirror one of the most important chapters in the disability rights movement.

Exo-Man / 1977 / NBC-TV

Executive Producer: Richard Irving
Producer: Lionel Siegel
Director: Richard Irving
Writers: Henry Simoun; Lionel Siegel
Category: Made-for-TV Movie — Science Fiction

* Wheelchair-User
* Single White Male
* Equipment: Hydraulic lift van
* New Disability

Plot: A newly-disabled scientist devises a way to walk so that he may find the villains who disabled him.

Physics professor Nick Conrad is experimenting with a way to power cells to move solid matter. He fails.

While at the bank, Nick sees a robbery. He takes off after the robber and catches him. The Syndicate puts a contract out on Nick's life.

Another test at the lab with Nick's "exo" system fails. A student borrows Nick's car to go and get a pizza to sustain the late-night workers. The car blows up. Nick is placed under police protection. A villain beats and severely injures him. A new disability is incurred.

> DOCTOR: There was very little we could do ... severed nerves in your spine ... resulted in paralysis from the waist down — I'm afraid, for the rest of your life.

Nick is persuaded to testify at the trial of the man he helped capture at the bank robbery.

An ancient suit of armor at a museum inspires Nick. Using the concept of chain-type mail, he attaches his "exos" to a similar garment and finds the suit gives him walking mobility for short periods of time.

His ingenuity helps him to capture those responsible for his injury.

* * *

Exo-Man was a pedestrian science fiction piece. Nick was angry and sullen after incurring his injury. As usual for television, he received no rehabilitation after his injury.

Nick's consuming rage at his physical situation and the criminals responsible directed all of his concentration to finish developing his exo-system to give him the mobility to do in his attackers. This implied Nick could only trail his enemies and be a threat to them as a walking individual.

Nick was seen driving a car independently although a camera angle never revealed how he was able to complete this task. He drove with both hands on the wheel. He was also seen with a hydraulic lift van.

Exo-Man was a new twist on the formulaic revenge-type of story — science gave a person with a disability an edge over his would-be attackers.

Stunts (a.k.a. "Who Is Killing the Stuntmen?") / 1977 / A Robert Shaye and Peter S. Davis Production

Executive Producers: Peter S. Davis and Robert Shaye
Producers: Raymond Lofaro and William N. Panzer
Director: Mark L. Lester
Original Scenario: Robert Shaye; Michael Harpster
Story: Raymond Lofaro
Screenplay: Dennis Johnson and Barney Cohen
Category: Feature Film — Action Adventure

* [Quadriplegic]
* Married White Male
* New Disability

Plot: Someone is trying to kill off stuntmen working on a movie set.

Tampered-with apparatus causes Chuck, a stuntman, to fall from a building during a shoot. He hits the ground. A new disability is incurred. At the hospital, a doctor talks to Chuck's wife, Judy. A couple of stuntmen from the picture stand by.

> DOCTOR: He has a complete fracture of the cervical spine.... His diaphragm is paralyzed. I'm afraid he will always be on the respirator.

Judy leaves in tears. Pal Greg enters Chuck's room where the former stuntman is in bed, hooked up to a respirator. Chuck's eyes are open.

> GREG: Doc says you're alive. That ain't much, Chuck.... The doc says if you wake up, you ain't never gonna move. That's why I'm here, Chuck. A deal's a deal. If it was me, I'd expect you to do the same thing. There ain't nothin' in my life I've been afraid of except bein' where you are right now.... Sweet luck, baby. Sweet luck.

Greg shuts off respirator. Chuck succumbs.

* * *

Stunts utilized a character who became quadriplegic in one scene of this action-adventure film. Without benefit of counseling, factual information, or even permission from Chuck's spouse, Greg evoked some old deal and pulled the plug on Chuck once it was known the severely disabling injury was permanent. Thus, Chuck's value as a person was subordinated. A personal decision made by his uninformed self prior to injury was the determining factor.

Although not important to the story, medical equipment used on Chuck was completely wrong for the type of injury sustained.

Stunts' brief depiction of a man with quadriplegia indicated life with a disability was not worth investigating, let alone living.

America 2-Nite / Apr. 27, 1978 / Syndicated

Category: Series Teleivision —   * Re: Wheelchair-Users
   Satire

Host Barth Gimble discusses his pet peeves on his talk and variety show with moronic co-host Jerry Hubbard.

> BARTH: Do you have any things that bother you?
>
> JERRY: Yes I do. You know something that annoys me are these special skateboard ramps they're putting in on every street corner now. You know, it's dangerous enough walking down a street, a sidewalk today without some kid whizzing by, and knocking you down, maybe putting out an eye or something and without encouraging them by putting in these special skateboard ramps. And what annoys me, they never asked us, the taxpayers, whether they wanted their hard-earned money to be spent on some crazy kids.... I know they didn't ask me and I'm kind of annoyed about it!
>
> BARTH: Well, I think it's well-put, Jerry, and ... I certainly admire your guts for speaking out that way. *However,* I think the ramps you're talking about are put on the sidewalks for our *handicapped* people.
>
> JERRY: That makes even *less* sense! I mean, they're the last people we should be encouraging to use skateboards!

* * *

This wonderfully insane parody of talk and variety shows, *America 2-Nite,* delighted in poking fun at every and anything via savvy host Barth (who, with the help of a battery of lawyers, had escaped some sticky business in Florida) and his moronic sidekick Jerry (who got the job only because his brother-in-law owned the station). Jerry, who in Barth's words, had played "Varsity ball without a helmet," constantly misunderstood and grew indignant over things he thought he knew about. Curb cuts, placed at corners for wheelchair access, were simply another staple of American life for the show to poke fun at in its inimitable way.

Coming Home / May 1978 / United Artists

Producer: Jerome Hellman
Director: Hal Ashby
Story: Nancy Dowd
Writer: Waldo Salt and Robert C. Jones
Category: Feature Film—Drama

* Wheelchair-User
* Single White Male
* Equipment: Hydraulic lift van; Car hand controls

Plot: An innocent military wife grows and changes when her husband goes to Vietnam and she encounters an old schoolmate who has become paraplegic as a result of the war.

* * *

Coming Home was released the first week of May in 1978. Within the parameters of this resource, it is the *best* piece produced about disability. The basic story was simple. A young wife whose husband went to Vietnam became involved with hospitalized veterans. She met Luke Martin, an old schoolmate who had become paraplegic in the war. Sally began to mature emotionally. She and Luke fell in love and began a relationship that satisfied her in a way her marriage did not. When husband Bob returned, she was not the same woman—nor was he the same man. The war had directly and indirectly altered many lives.

Luke was not happy about his situation, but he was moving ahead with his life. He exhibited emotion, passion, humor, and pain—the elements that make up all humans except, it would seem, the cast of disabled characters in numerous dramas. Luke was a very real person.

A marvelous scene occurred when, after time spent on a gurney to permit healing from surgery on the injured spine, Luke graduated to a wheelchair. Instead of the usual sadness associated with chair acquisition, Luke was seen gleefully free, zipping up and down hospital ramps. He had regained mobility and was greatly relieved. Thus, the audience was able to see the wheelchair was not a "prison" or an object of horror. It was a tool that permitted an active young man like Luke to regain control of his life.

Accessibility was discussed in a scene at the supermarket where Luke had to go around the check-out counter to bypass the too-narrow-for-chairs entrance by the cash register. When he visited Sally's little beach house the first time, he had to hitch himself up a few stairs on his hands. When he moved in, the first order of business was the construction of a ramp.

Luke and Sally consummated their interest in each other in a beautiful and honest love scene. It illustrated that perhaps making love with a man like Luke might require a modified technique—but Sally was satisfied by him in a way never accomplished by her brusque husband. The most distressing part of this talked-about scene was the version aired on television long after the theatrical run. A different version had been shot and edited for the network audiences. An anguished cry from Sally when first looking at Luke's nude form could have been easily misunderstood by an uninitiated audience.

With all the honest information quietly doled out about disability was a deep and thought-provoking story about war and its effects on the humans involved. Luke's fellow vets at the hospital discussed the war and the subsequent difficulties in many ways—with open discussion to ribald humor and even the mental implosion experienced by one suicidal vet. The indignities bred by hospitalization and a calloused staff were seen.

When Sally's husband returned home—the recipient of an accidental minor wound from his own weapon—he discovered his wife had been having an affair with Luke. Bob Hyde's fragile mental stability slipped and he went on a wild rampage, intending to harm both himself and Sally. It was Luke who took matters into his own hands and cooly diffused the situation as a disabled catalyst. The scene also neatly illustrated that Bob had suffered a limitation as injurious as Luke's and, of the two men, was more disabled.

Criticism has been heard from some portions of the disabled community regarding this piece. Luke's character as an affable guy everyone would want to know has been criticized as too perfect. Others have discussed that his political motives were too correct. But character flaws notwithstanding, this piece cannot be ignored. The realistic approach to disability and the existence of humanity and worth found not only in Luke but in other physically limited characters he encountered made this piece different. In a timeline of dramas using characters in wheelchairs, it was the first decent and honest piece to come along since *The Men,* released twenty-eight years before.

Actual disabled performers were used in supporting and background roles of the film.

It shouldn't have taken so long to produce an honest story about a man with a disability (one in equal status has yet to appear about a woman with a disability). And, unfortunately, despite critical and commercial success and numerous Oscars awarded the film, *Coming Home* did little to stem the rushing tide of tragic, embittered characters with severe personal problems.

Leave Yesterday Behind / May 14, 1978 / ABC-TV

Producer: Paul Harrison
Director: Richard Michaels
Writer: Paul Harrison

* Wheelchair-User
* Single White Male
* New Disability

Leave Yesterday Behind

Category: Made-for-TV Movie—
Drama

Plot: A college student is paralyzed in an accident and fights the affections of a girl who falls in love with him.

Veterinary student and polo player Paul Stallings falls off his pony in a match and collapses. A new disability is incurred. Doc, Paul's crusty grandfather, lowers the blow.

> DOC: You suffered a compression fracture of the second lumbar vertebrae with subsequent delayed hemorrhaging.... You've broken your back.... You are—paralyzed from the waist down.
>
> PAUL: ...Oh my God! Oh God! I'm only twenty-one and I'm a helpless cripple!
>
> DOC: Disabled, but not helpless.... You'll be able to use a wheelchair....

Paul asks about his sexual capacity. Doc hedges the issue.

> DOC: I don't know yet. You know Paul, different tracks for different acts.

Paul stays at Doc's farm. Consuelo, the housekeeper, makes Paul's breakfast.

> PAUL: Get ready, I'm coming out, skipping and jumping ... how 'bout if I come out normally, crawling like a lizard?

Paul emerges, dragging himself across the floor on his hands.

> CONSUELO: Use the wheelchair.
>
> PAUL: It's a prison....

In frustrated anger, Paul tosses a dumbbell out the window and spooks a horse pulling a sulky. Marni, a pretty equestrienne, screams at his stupidity. Later, finding he's disabled, she goes to apologize for her anger. Paul tells her to leave.

> MARNI: He thinks a wheelchair gives him a license to be rude....
> [He's] tied to that wheelchair ... lonely....

The two manage to become friends. Marni falls for Paul and her father disapproves. He uses pejorative language.

FATHER: Don't let that cripple come between us.... I'm not gonna let you throw your life away on half a man ... you're in love with a wheelchair.

Paul talks to Doc about the growing relationship and uses typical devaluation. He indicates a lack of sexual capacity.

PAUL: How can I sentence her to pushing a wheelchair for the rest of her life? Remember that time in the hospital when I asked you about sex? You [said] "different tracks for different acts?" ... For me, there is no track. The road's closed. I know that.

DOC: It's possible, but in young men, it's usually temporary, brought on by fear....

Paul admits to Marni he loves her but can't deal with "never being able to dance again." Marni convinces him that his legs are not important.

* * *

Leave Yesterday Behind was played for every tear it could find. Paul was angry, bitter, self-pitying, self-devaluing, and rude. It was amazing Marni found anything good in him. Her acceptance of him elevated her into a saintly position.
Paul was intelligent and possessed of special abilities. He had an interest in creating wire sculptures which he enjoyed. He successfully helped a horse through a bad delivery. He appeared strong and healthy.
Paul asked his grandfather about his sexual capacities and never received a straight answer. The uninformed audience was left with a large question mark. The sexual dynamics of males with spinal cord injuries was ignored. As usual, Paul received no rehabilitation after becoming injured; no psychological counseling was provided. He was left on his own.
Special equipment was misused. Doc obtained a hydraulic lift van to transport his grandson; there were no hand controls or mention of the same. Paul was merely a passenger in the vehicle. Of course, having hand controls would have eradicated an "inspiring" scene when Doc, injured during a storm, did not return to the van. Paul hitched across a muddy field, saved Doc and drove him to safety, using a tree branch to depress the brake and accelerator pedals.
Leave Yesterday Behind was a prime example of why disability programming is termed "three-hankie drama."

Thou Shalt Not Commit Adultery / Nov. 1, 1978 / NBC-TV

Executive Producers: Edgar J. Sherick and Daniel H. Blatt

* Wheelchair-User
* White Married Male

Thou Shalt Not Commit Adultery

Producers: S. Brian Hickox and Brian Glazier
Director: Delbert Mann
Writer: Calder Willingham
Category: Made-for-TV Movie—Drama

* New Disability

Plot: A paraplegic man gives his wife permission to seek sexual gratification from other men.

Jack and Sally Kimball's car is struck by another and overturns. A new disability is incurred. Jack becomes a paraplegic. A lack of sexual capacity is assumed as Sally and Jack retire to separate beds. Jack tells Sally she doesn't have to remain faithful to him and should get out more. In fact, she should go to California on a business trip. Sally reluctantly flies west.

She is attracted to Vic Tannahill and cultivates a friendship, admitting she's married—to a man with a disability. Sally sleeps with Tannahill, who advises her not to feel guilty about being unfaithful.

> TANNAHILL: I know you love your husband a lot and I know he loves you but he can *not* expect you to be faithful to him. I mean, he just can't. That's crazy!

Perception of disabled life from a non-disabled point of view is evident. Pejorative terminology is used.

> TANNAHILL: If I were him—crippled—I'd probably wanna kill myself.... It's just not right for one person to ask another person to give up sex for the rest of their life. It isn't right.

Sally remains with Tannahill a week. On the plane home, she is encouraged to share her troubles with a sympathetic stewardess. Properly informed, the stewardess catches her curious co-workers up on the story.

> STEWARDESS: Her husband's a paraplegic. She just cheated on him.

> STEWARDESS #3: Oh, now the guilt, huh?... You know, if it was me, I'd get a divorce.... You have to live your life.

> STEWARDESS #2: Sex—isn't everything.

> STEWARDESS (unconvinced): Right.

Sally is picked up at the airport by Bill, a friend who advocates open marriage. He deduces she had an affair and condones it because:

BILL: You have a friend, you have a companion, you have a father to your children. But in the real sense, you don't have a husband. You're a widow.

Bill proposes they make a sexual agreement dedicated to their mutual satisfaction. Sally is shocked.

BILL: But don't you think you're gonna have to make some kind of arrangement? If not with me then someone else?... So, you're gonna channel your sexual energies into pottery classes or woodwork or intensive community activities.... What are you gonna do, Sally? Remain faithful to him for the rest of your life?

SALLY: I hope so.

BILL: That's ridiculous! It's impossible. You can't do it.... Your piety is really something.

At home, Sally goes inside where Jack has been waiting.

SALLY: I'm not going on any more trips alone. It's settled, no arguments. From now on, we're going together.

Jack understands and thankfully holds her close. He fights back the tears.

* * *

Within the parameters of this work, *Thou Shalt Not Commit Adultery* is absolutely the most damaging piece ever produced about disability. It is the 180-degree counterpoint to *Coming Home*. The most unrelenting aspect of this film was the perceptions of *all* characters with whom Sally came in contact. When she expressed her husband was disabled, *everyone* "knew" the sexual capacities of a man who was a paraplegic and *all* fully expected her to seek physical satisfaction elsewhere. Jack, Tannahill, the stewardesses, and Bill all felt it was a natural progression. All believed the wife of a man with a degree of bodily paralysis would go out shopping for sex. The general sexual dynamics of spinal cord injured men were not explored or even mentioned; even if Jack was in the inactive percentile, his loss of ability was equated with loss of desire or human sexuality as illustrated by the separate beds the couple took to after the accident. Jack had become an impotent wimp. His "generosity" in letting Sally seek outside satisfaction was a selfless gesture assumed to be noble.

The film enraged the disabled community. The California Association for the Physically Handicapped filed comments with the FCC supporting that such films should be monitored prior to broadcast to determine if the needs of the community represented were being met. *Daily Variety* reported on November 11, 1978:

As a recent illustration of the "insensitivity" of the broadcaster to the feelings and needs of people with disabilities, the comments point to a Nov. 1 NBC-TV telefilm, *Thou Shalt Not Commit Adultery*. The comments claim that the vidpic, by implication at least, suggests that all disabled men are impotent and unable to sexually satisfy their wives.

According to [attorney Stanley Fleishman] ... had NBC been required to ascertain the views and needs of disabled persons, it's unlikely that the web would have exhibited, without some modification, the telepic which portrayed the disabled male as a "stereotype," giving the American public a "grossly distorted" view of handicapped men and their relationship with their mates.

Sally McGraw of NBC's Public Affairs Department made this statement in reply to this author's personal letter of complaint:

December 5, 1978:

We regret your disapproval but feel you have misconstrued the program. This was a drama about particular individuals in a particular situation. It bore no general message about the sexual or other abilities of paraplegics as a group, or the handicapped as a category.... The program standards we follow require a due regard for the special sensitivities of handicapped persons in all our programming, and we believe our record on this is a good one.

Thou Shalt Not Commit Adultery was a gross insult, not only to disabled persons but to the mentality of America at large. It was crass, heavy-handed, and presumptuous. Its existence is even more surprising when it is seen in a timeline of disability drama. It was aired five months after the release of *Coming Home*, a film which honestly depicted the sexuality of a man with a spinal cord injury. It is possible that ...*Adultery* was already in production prior to the May release of *Coming Home;* nevertheless, it should never have been aired.

Thou Shalt Not Commit Adultery purported to have taken cues from a book, *Anger and Despair: Sexual Trauma of the Paraplegic Wife* by Linton. The film must be seen to be believed.

Some Kind of Miracle / Jan. 3, 1979 / CBS-TV

Executive Producers: Lee Rich, Phillip Capice
Producer: George LeMaire
Director: Jerrold Freeman
Writers: Mary and Jack Willis
Category: Made-for-TV Movie— Drama

* Wheelchair-User
* Single White Male
* New Disability
* Equipment: Adaptive writing/ feeding cuff; Braces and crutches

Plot: A young professional couple's future is thrown in jeopardy when one is paralyzed in a surfing accident.

Joe Nykoff and his fiancée, Maggie, are playing on the beach. Joe body surfs and doesn't come up. He eventually surfaces, yelling for help. Maggie runs out. Others help drag Joe from the water. A new disability has been incurred.

> JOE: I can't feel anything ... I don't feel anything from my chest down.

Mom and Dad Nykoff join Maggie in the hospital. Surgeon Mark Spencer shows them Joe's x-rays.

> MOM: Will he be able to walk?
>
> MARK: Well, it's a little too early to say ... I wouldn't be too optimistic.
>
> MAGGIE: ...We were supposed to be married...! Can we have children?
>
> MARK: We don't know yet.

After surgery, Mark says it's a case of wait and see to find if Joe will experience physical return.
Joe is in a rotating frame and concerned about his future.

> JOE: Will I be able to make love?
>
> MARK: It's a little early to tell yet.

Joe is angry and spouts erroneous notions to Maggie.

> JOE: I don't think I can spend the rest of my life in a wheelchair.... I can't stand the idea of being taken care of. And you—how would you like to be a full-time nurse...? Bathe me, feed me, take me to the bathroom, clean me up, no sex—

Joe is transferred to a rehabilitation center. He meets some other men in the ward. He is now able to feed himself with a fork fixed into an adaptive cuff. Hal, his roommate, watches.

> HAL: Hey, you're doin' pretty good with that ... really, you're not bad with a fork. Really, that's pretty good for a quad.
>
> JOE (stops): For a what?

HAL: Quad, man, y'know, you, you're a quad-ri-puh-lee-gic. You eat like that, though, and you're gonna be a super-quad. Really. Most of 'em gotta be fed ... gimps stick together.

Joe improves enough so that he can return to work in a wheelchair. On his first day, he has a bowel accident. He later is able to walk with braces and crutches. He and Maggie will be married.

* * *

Some Kind of Miracle was a trudge through the fear a newly-disabled man experienced. Joe was naturally frightened at his new situation. He talked about killing himself, wondering if Maggie would help him do it. He dwelled constantly on his sexual capabilities. Maggie was carefully warned by Dr. Mark about what she was "in for" should she stay with Joe.

In contrast, no indication of a life with quality was illustrated. Maggie never spoke to a couple in the same situation to find out what it was like for them. Joe never spoke to anyone about it, either. The heavy shroud of negative emotion was never lifted. Hope was something confined to the possibility of walking and enjoying the same sexual relationship again—certainly not a commodity to be applied to something as mundane as achieving independence in daily living skills or understanding life was not over. Even when Joe began to re-enter life, he met with disaster, having an unexpected bowel movement and soiling himself.

Some Kind of Miracle was supposed to chronicle the advent of tragedy and recovery in the lives of two sexually active young people who were exceptionally "modern." As it was, it was a handbook expressing every negative available in the life of someone with a disability.

The Love Boat / "After the War" / Feb. 3, 1979 / ABC-TV

Executive Producer: Aaron Spelling; Douglas Cramer
Producers: Gordon and Lynne Farr and Henry Colman
Director: Roger Duchowny
Writer: Carmen Finestra
Category: Series Television—Romantic Comedy

* Wheelchair-User
* Single White Male

Plot: Julie's class reunion is held on the *Pacific Princess*.

Jack Forbes hopes to see his old pal Mike Kelly at the class reunion. When he sees Mike is in a wheelchair as a result of an injury in Vietnam, he purposely avoids him. His wife convinces him to approach Mike. They have a nice reunion—although Jack experiences guilt. Erroneous notions abound as he talks to his wife.

> JACK: I didn't have the guts to tell him I went to Canada ... Mike's in a wheelchair. We used to play football together; now he can't even pick one up! ... there's Mike, and here I am with a healthy body....

Jack can't take his guilt. He finally talks to Mike who notes Jack's uneasiness.

> MIKE: Don't be embarrassed. I've had to learn to live with this thing. You're my friend. You'll have to learn too.

To Jack's surprise, Mike has known for years about Jack's decision to go to Canada. He supports Jack for doing what he believed in.

> JACK: You're in a wheelchair. And you're forgiving me.

> MIKE: I'm not a saint. There were times when I was so bitter I could taste it, Jack. I hate it. I HATE IT!... The hate was my real disability, not this thing.

> JACK: ...I'm so sorry this had to happen to you.

> MIKE: I am too. I'm just damn glad it didn't happen to both of us.

* * *

"After the War" illustrated a problem more than a disability. Jack had difficulty reconciling his past actions and natural dismay at seeing his old buddy who was now disabled. The story concentrated on the resolution of the problem, not Mike's limitation.

Mike was seen as having a sense of humor, making easy jokes about his hospital stay or his chair. Despite his winning personality, he remained alone on the cruise. He appeared alienated as he sat off to the side watching others do aerobics on deck or in the lounge watching the dancing. This, combined with Jack's line about Mike not being able to pick up a football, could have left the erroneous impression that Mike was relegated to an inactive and nonathletic life simply because he used a chair. A similar mistake was made when Jack indicated he had a "healthy body" and Mike did not, whereas Mike was doubtlessly just as healthy as Jack within his own physicality.

"After the War" was a nice story, different than the regular run-of-the-mill disability drama.

The Paper Chase / "The Man in the Chair" / Feb. 6, 1979 / CBS-TV

Producer: Robert Alley
Story: Jerome Ross; Martin Zwieback

* Wheelchair-User
* Single White Male
* Equipment: Braces and crutches

Teleplay: Jerome Ross
Category: Series Television —
  Drama

Plot: A disabled law student alienates everyone else in his class.

Late entry law student Paul Chandler enters Professor Kingsfield's class. He is supremely confident to the point of being intolerable. Paul is invited to join a study group with Elizabeth Bell, Harry Hart, and others. He is manipulative and begins to ask favors — wants Bell to pick him up books at the library, wants Ford to copy notes for him — and all are willing to comply with his requests.

Paul invites Bell to dinner. She accepts but confides to Hart she only said yes so as not to hurt Chandler's feelings. Pejorative terminology is used by Hart in helping Bell confront her feelings.

> HART: What if he wasn't crippled?
>
> BELL: I just don't want to hurt his feelings.
>
> HART: If you can't be honest with him, be honest with yourself.

Bell has a showdown with Chandler.

> BELL: You are a very attractive man. You're very appealing to a woman. I don't know why I don't feel more. Is it because you're handicapped?
>
> PAUL: I'm not totally handicapped.

The other students realize that Chandler has been controlling them for his own needs. They begin to act jointly as the non-disabled catalysts, overdoing everything for him until he calls a halt to it. Chandler reacts with a large outburst, full of poor images.

> PAUL: ...avoid looking in mirrors because you'll scream "basket case," ... dragging half your body....

Chandler comes to class on crutches, and sports a new attitude.

> KINGSFIELD: In this class, we stand when we speak, Mr. Chandler.

Chandler rises to make his point.

* * *

"The Man in the Chair" was interesting. Despite some well-worn imagery, it possessed some fresh traits. Particularly unique were the reactions of the students — feeling they should help Chandler because he was less fortunate than they in physical attributes; yet, disliking him because he was not a decent person and feeling guilty about it.

Chandler's manipulative behavior fit his character, that of the spoiled rich boy who had only to speak to Mother and all good things were forthcoming. He and his mother were on a first name basis with Professor Kingsfield — a fact he must have thought would help insure him to snag a scholarship Hart desperately needed.

Paul was seen driving a spiffy Targa although he drove with both hands on the wheel without evidence of hand controls. He was also athletic, shooting baskets in the gym, weight lifting, and rope climbing.

The ending was troublesome, what with the request from Kingsfield to stand up. It seemed to indicate Paul's earlier mental aberrations had precluded him from trying to "conform" — which he did for Kingsfield. This subliminal message reiterated that standing/walking was a matter of will and trying and not of physical capacity. It also quietly inferred that since Chandler had seen the malice of his ways, he was now a better person. A "better person" was one who stood, not one who used a chair.

"The Man in the Chair" used updated imagery in a predictable and tired story.

Happy Days / "The Mechanic" / Dec. 4, 1979 / ABC-TV

Producers: Thomas Miller; Edward Milkis
Writer: Fred Fox, Jr.
Category: Series Television — Situation Comedy

* Wheelchair-User
* Single White Male
* Performer with a Disability

Plot: The Fonz hires a worker to help him out at the garage and the man who applies is in a wheelchair.

Overworked Arthur "The Fonz" Fonzarelli puts an ad in the newspaper looking for a mechanic to help him out at the garage. He is surprised when Don, a candidate in a wheelchair, applies for the job. Despite Don's skill, Fonzie holds back at hiring him. Don actively bullies Fonzie into hiring him. The new arrangement seems doomed. Fonzie tells friend Richie Cunningham that Don has a chip on his shoulder.

The cause of Don's disability is discussed as a motor vehicle mishap. Don reveals bitterness as he relays the story.

> DON: The insurance took care of everything — except me walking again.

The Fonz and the Cunningham family are instrumental in non-disabled catalyst roles, helping Don understand his attitude is his real handicap. Don's outlook on life is noticeably brighter when he talks about going to a movie.

DON: I can always get a good seat.

* * *

"The Mechanic" was a ritualistic story where the angry disablee's life was made better by the actions of the series' stars. Don was seen to be athletic, moving purposefully in his chair and later, going to play basketball with Richie and Fonzie. The basketball aspect could be evidence of the industry attempting to update imagery of people with disabilities. Don's light joke about finding a seat at the movies also seemed to be a step in the right direction.

The hiring of a disabled person to play the same was still a fairly untested concept in 1979. The people in charge must be applauded, even in retrospect, for their practice—particularly on a show with the high ratings and popularity of *Happy Days*.

"The Mechanic" demonstrated a person in a chair *could* be employed in a garage position; however, the story used staple elements which painted yet another picture of the angry disabled person who couldn't assimilate a limitation.

Fantasy Island / "The Swimmer" / Apr. 12, 1980 / ABC-TV

Executive Producers: Aaron Spelling; Leonard Goldberg
Producer: Arthur Rowe
Supervising Producer: Michael Fisher
Director: Earl Bellamy
Writer: Tim Maschler
Category: Series Television—Romantic Fantasy Drama

* Wheelchair-User
* Single White Female

Plot: An ex-champion swimmer who now uses a wheelchair journeys to Fantasy Island with hopes to regain her ability to walk.

Terri Sommers arrives on Fantasy Island with her father. The cause of her disability is discussed.

ROARKE: Not long ago, Miss Sommers was one of the top swimmers in the United States, destined to become an Olympic gold medal winner.

TATTOO: Isn't she the girl that had that terrible car accident and the doctors said she was lucky to survive?

Terri and her father have a fantasy—for her to be cured. In between tests, Terri agrees to coach water ballet for some children in the pool. She erroneously indicates that the life of a person using a chair is inactive.

> SOMMERS: [You can work with the kids] as long as you promise not to overdo it.

> TERRI: ...Until I get out of this contraption, no way.

Sommers takes Terri to the pool where she gets a rude shock upon seeing the kids. She uses poor terminology.

> TERRI: Dad! They're crippled!

Terri talks to Mr. Roarke.

> TERRI: Mr. Roarke, you didn't say anything about them being—like this. Learning to do water ballet isn't easy—well, even if you're—normal.

Nevertheless, Terri accepts the job and notices one little boy, Bobby, not joining in. He was once a Little Leaguer but now uses a wheelchair. He won't go in the water.

Terri is told there is no cure for her. Dejected, she plans to leave the island. Bobby sees through her and is somewhat of a disabled catalyst.

> BOBBY: You can't stand bein' like one of us. That's why you wouldn't get into the swimming pool. Isn't it? Isn't it?

Terri makes a decision—to go with life as it is. She tells her skeptical father:

> TERRI: I can't keep living for what might be; I have to start dealing with my life as it IS.

> SOMMERS: Giving up, is that it?

Terri makes an announcement to her water ballet students.

> TERRI: ...What I'm trying to say is, what I mean is—I'm one of you now.

The kids cheer. Mr. Sommers comes around and embraces his daughter.

* * *

"The Swimmer" was another piece illustrating a disability as a personal problem. Terri couldn't deal with herself. She wouldn't even get in the pool, as if trying to deny the fact she had a limitation. It was the rather skewed logic of the disabled child (written from the non-disabled point of view) which straightened her out.

Mr. Sommers' feeling that Terri's acceptance was "giving up" was a typical screen response to the reality that some physical problems cannot be medically repaired. Terri's speech to the kids about being "one of you" was indicative that she felt she was slipping into some kind of subculture. Bobby's indication that she couldn't "stand bein' one of us" was of the same vein.

Special equipment was misused. Both Terri and Bobby used chairs that were much too large for them and hindered their mobility.

Actual kids with disabilities were seen in the pool sequences.

"The Swimmer" sank with its predictable story line, conflict, and resolution. Terri was not explored as a person. She was simply a disability.

CHiPs / "Wheeling" / May 4, 1980 / NBC-TV

Writers: L. Ford Neale & John Huff
Category: Series Television—Police Drama

* Wheelchair-Users
* Single White Males (3)
* Equipment: Car hand controls

Plot: Highway Patrolmen Ponch and Jon can't shake off three men in wheelchairs.

Officers ticket two vehicles for unsafe driving. The perpetrators are drivers with disabilities using their "totally hand-operated" van and car. Artie and his two pals in chairs act as disabled catalysts to a recently-disabled man in the hospital who can't face his new life.

Artie, out on the sidewalk, crashes his car into a female skateboarder. She falls on his lap and they careen downhill. Artie gets a ticket for running a red light in his chair. Ponch makes a curious observation.

> PONCH: Being disabled doesn't give you special privileges when it comes to safety.

Curious about Artie, Ponch and Jon make a visit to the hospital. They talk to a doctor about what happens to persons who become disabled.

> DOCTOR: A "handicap" doesn't mean incapable.

Artie and his pals help catch a hit and run driver by careful driving maneuvers. They are able to entice Brent, the newly-disabled man, to join them when they present him with a souped-up power chair.

Artie drag races with another car. His van is bashed and overturns. He breaks both arms and, hopefully, is out of Ponch and Jon's hair for awhile.

* * *

"Wheeling" offered some good factual information about disability in a lightweight manner. Ponch's statement about "disability doesn't give you special privileges" was out of line. Artie and his friends were just those kind of annoying people who like to toe the line and would do so if they were disabled or not. It also suggests a baseline mode of popular thought — that people with disabilities (probably due to charity and telethon images) get special privileges throughout life rather than face discrimination or other social difficulties due to attitudes about those with limitations.

"Wheeling" illustrated people in chairs who were as stupid, careless, and irresponsible as any other Neanderthal drivers on the street.

Coach of the Year / Oct. 1980

Executive Producer: Joan Conrad
Producer: John Ashley
Director: Don Medford
Director (football segments): Andy Sidaris
Writer: Frank Abatemarco
Category: Made-for-TV Movie — Drama

* Wheelchair-User
* Single White Male
* Equipment: Car hand controls

Plot: Ex-football star, injured in Vietnam, accepts a job at a boys' detention center as an athletic coach.

Ex-NFL football star Jimmy Brandon approaches his old team, the Chicago Bears, for a coaching position years after incurring a disability in Vietnam. He meets attitudinal barriers as the organization tries to shunt him into an unwanted PR position. Brandon surmises his wheelchair-ed presence would make the team aware of their own vulnerability.

> BRANDON: Blinders for everyone, is that it? What does that have to do with coaching?
>
> O'BRADEVICH (bluntly, carefully): It's bad for business, Jimmy, and you and I both know *that's* the bottom line.... You oughta be thankful they're offering you any kind of job at all.

Brandon refuses the job. Bad news comes in droves; his nephew Andy has been arrested for theft and sent to St. Charles Correctional Institute for Boys. Brandon goes to St. Charles to check on Andy. He sees a coach having trouble giving guidance on football plays. Brandon butts in and gives the man some pointers. Marisa, a social worker, sees him and offers him a job as temporary athletic director. He declines.

Brandon heads to a bar to meet Eddie, a man in a chair who runs some sort of bookmaking operation. Brandon tells him about the Bears. He really thought this would be his shot.

> BRANDON: I may be in a chair but I'm still a man. And I want to be treated like a man.

Eddie takes on the role of the disabled catalyst.

> EDDIE: Listen Pal, to hell with them. Stay home. They did this to you. Let the government take care of you. Let 'em pay.

It's enough to send Brandon back to St. Charles.
He meets another attitudinal barrier when a secretary tells the superintendent the new coach has arrived in a wheelchair.

> TURNER: What are they trying to do to me?

Turner tries to dissuade Brandon from accepting the position, telling him he's asking for trouble.

> BRANDON: You're wrong. I already have trouble and the only thing that makes it worse is people making more of me being in this wheelchair than is really necessary.

Brandon is reluctantly hired. He fights for acceptance from the street kids he's coaching. He wins them over. He also trusts them—to the point that he plans a football match off the grounds of the institution, a decision the superintendent advises against.
The game is lost and Brandon wants a rematch. The game is headed for disaster when members of a street gang show up ready to spring one of their own. But on the threshold of winning, the boys go for a hard-won victory and not the easy way out.

* * *

Coach of the Year presented a man in a wheelchair as a talented, fully-faceted person who was dissuaded from pursuing his goal. Brandon was an athletic man, seen weight-lifting, taking passes from the kids, and always in motion. He was tough and took no guff—yet he had a soft side he showed to Marisa, the social worker, and to the kids, buying them Cokes and pizza after a good workout. He was a completely able and healthy man who fought attitudes constantly.
The role of Eddie (played by an actor with a disability) was also nicely played. The other man using a chair was slightly larcenous and ready to do anything for a buck.
Coach of the Year was refreshing as it did not dwell on Brandon's disability, but his *ability* to give the kids something they'd never had.

Skyward / Nov. 20, 1980 / NBC-TV

Executive Producers: Anson Williams and Ron Howard
Producer: John A. Kurt
Director: Ron Howard
Story: Anson Williams
Writer: Nancy Sackett
Category: Made-for-TV Movie—Drama

* Wheelchair-User
* White Female Teenager
* Performer with a Disability

Plot: Julie, a teen in a chair, becomes interested in flying and takes lessons on the sly to rebel from her overprotective parents.

A family moves to new house. All work to get settled except Julie, a teenager using an electric chair. She is told to watch TV. The new house is near an airport. Julie curiously watches planes.

Inaccessibility is discussed when Julie finds the school bathrooms are impossible to enter. Other kids laugh at her trying to fit her chair into a stall. She is humiliated to find all the school can offer her is a bedpan.

Julie sees two gliders in the sky on the way home from school and follows them to a tiny airport. She meets Coop, a grizzled old mechanic working on a plane, who tells her to get him the pliers. She complies and then becomes a regular at the airport.

> COOP: Anybody can learn to fly.
>
> JULIE: Except me.
>
> COOP (sarcastically): ...You don't have to pedal to stay up there.

A moviegoing date with Scott, a cute boy from school, turns into a disaster when Julie's rights are violated. An usher tells them it's against fire laws to have a wheelchair in the aisle. He suggests they leave the wheelchair in the lobby so Scott can carry her in. They decline. In frustrated anger, Julie takes off. She fears Scott's attentions have been a cruel tease. She confides in Billie, an ex-barnstormer turned greasy-spoon cook at the airport.

> JULIE: I try to be like everybody else but I'm not.

Julie is determined to learn to fly. She wants to use her old manual wheelchair because Billie says she needs more physical strength. Her parents try to discourage her from giving up the electric chair.

> MOTHER: You're a *big* girl now.

Julie wins the argument. At the airport, a fellow in a chair shows up and explains aviation hand controls to Julie. In the air, Billie turns the plane over to Julie.

Julie has been lying to Billie and Coop, saying her parents support her learning to fly. She's falsified papers she needs. Her parents believe she is taking a class at the "Y" for disabled teens. Julie's parents discover that Julie is about to solo. They rush to the airport and realize they must let their daughter grow into who she must be.

* * *

Skyward presented a different side of the disabled experience. It was about a teenager who just wanted to grow and find her own way. Julie was a teen who was coddled at home. While her sister was getting chewed out, Julie was told to go watch television. At home, Julie's mother washed her daughter's hair for her and tucked her into bed. In contrast, Coop delegated heavy work to Julie at the airport and she did it.

Julie was a girl who wanted to fall in love and have a boyfriend just like the other girls. Her insecurities were stated, such as fearing Scott's attentions were a tease or not being able to plan a date like the one at the theatre. She crossed the line too far to prove herself, but it was a part of the growing process.

Skyward was honest and interesting. It also led to a TV-movie sequel, *Skyward Christmas* the following year.

ABC Afterschool Special / "Run, Don't Walk" / Mar. 4, 1981 / ABC-TV

Executive Producer: Henry Winkler
Producer: Ervin Zavada
Director: John Herzfeld
Writer: Durrell Royce Crays
Category: Made-for-TV Movie— Children's Programming

* Wheelchair-Users
* White Teenaged Couple
* Equipment: Car hand controls, Sport chair

Plot: A recently disabled high school girl returns to classes and finds her rights in jeopardy.

Samantha Anderson returns to high school in a wheelchair a year after an equestrian accident. She tries to remain unobtrusive while Johnny Jay, a classmate in a chair, draws attention to the fact that the school bathrooms are inaccessible to students using chairs. He tries to recruit an uninterested Sam to help the cause.

JOHNNY: Your rights are being violated here!

Sam wants nothing to do with his crusade. Accessibility is discussed as Sam is excused from class to use the restroom and can't get in.

Miss Jenkins, a young teacher, is out training for an upcoming 10K race. She goads Sam into joining her workout and seeing how fast she can go in her chair. Sam begins to run regularly with the teacher, despite her mother's objections. She wants to enter the 10K.

Johnny is advocating a school walk-out as he recruits non-disabled students to support his bathroom cause.

Johnny gives Sam a ride home on a rainy day in his hand-controlled van. He tells her he was "born like this." Accessibility is again mentioned as Johnny says he is mad about narrow restaurant doors, people who park in handicapped zones, block curbs, and so on. Sam has difficulty understanding this and Johnny's being "handicapped twenty-four hours a day." She devalues herself.

> SAM: Maybe you like being stared at like a freak but I don't!

Johnny acts as somewhat of a disabled catalyst when he gives her the business card of a man who makes lightweight racing wheelchairs.

Sam's hopes of entering the 10K are dashed when a letter from the racing committee denies her entry. She indicates attitudinal barriers she's been learning about.

> SAM: They're afraid I'll get hurt ... when you're in a wheelchair, that's all people see. Only thing that doesn't work are my legs. The rest of me is *me*.

Johnny is told that construction to update the lavatories will begin "next year."

> JOHNNY: That's a long time to wait to go to the bathroom ... it's not just personal. *Nobody* in a wheelchair can use these bathrooms.

Johnny is suspended for advocating a walk-out.

Sam watches the clock. At noon, she goes outside and gets Johnny's protest sign from the garbage. Kids start walking out in support. The principal acquiesces. Johnny returns to classes as construction is beginning.

Sam shows up for the 10K with school friends in support, carrying placards that read, "Let Sam Run!" Johnny cheers her on. She is allowed in the race as a test case, but she must start last. She pushes herself up into the pack, trying to be the best she can be.

* * *

"Run, Don't Walk" was a nicely done, entertaining story with a resounding message. It took a rare approach, juxtaposing the physical barriers represented by the school bathrooms, with attitudinal ones: Sam's fight to join a race with everyone else.

Sam was illustrated as a normal teen who was trying hard to understand why the loss of her walking ability should infringe upon her personhood. Her first response was to ignore her disability and the fight Johnny was waging. But when it hit home, she took it to heart and went to support her rights.

Johnny was a rather brash teen, a very real kid who was popular in school by warrant of his flamboyant personality. The movie focused on the issues the two teenagers wrestled with rather than the limitations of their physicality. The two likeable characters posed the question of what was more disabling: their conditions or the physical barriers around them.

"Run, Don't Walk" deserved an audience much larger than the small, youthful one it may have garnered.

The Ordeal of Bill Carney / 1981

Executive Producer: Deanne Barkley
Producer: Jerry London
Co-Producer: Renee Wayne Golden
Director: Jerry London
Writer: Tom Lazarus
Category: Made-for-TV Movie — Drama

* Wheelchair-Users
* Single White Male (#1); Married White Male (#2)
* New Disability (#1)
* Based on a True Story
* Equipment: Hydraulic lift van; Adaptive writing/feeding cuff; Car hand controls

Plot: A quadriplegic man goes to court to maintain custody of his sons.

Bill Carney, a single father of two sons, goes out for weekend military reserve duty. His jeep flips over and tumbles down a steep hill. A new disability is incurred. Carney is told by doctors at the V.A. he will not walk but will be able to regain use of his arms.

> DOCTOR: Rehabilitation is up to you.

Carney is approached by Jack Hollister, a representative of a disabled veterans association and who uses a chair. Hollister acts as a disabled catalyst.

Carney wishes to marry his live-in girlfriend, Lisa, but needs a divorce from his first wife. Hollister suggests attorney Mason Rose, a man in a wheelchair. Rose is quite political, working on access cases that deny him and other persons with disabilities their civil rights.

Ellen Carney, Bill's ex, responds to his divorce suit by suing Carney for custody of their two sons, believing he is unable to be an appropriate parent in light of his new physical situation. She has not contacted the children in five years.

> MASON: Ten to one the only reason she's asking for custody is that poor bastard's in a wheelchair.

Access is discussed as Rose, Carney, and the attorney's assistant go to a highly recommended restaurant and find it is inaccessible. Rose talks with the manager and tells him the establishment will be served with papers charging discrimination in the morning. The group dines on take-out pizza in the parking lot to make their point.

Carney and Lisa are having problems as the realities of his limitation are setting in—coupled with a judge awarding custody of the kids to Carney's ex-wife. Carney is depressed about the changes in lovemaking abilities.

BILL: I thought of how it won't be like that anymore.

Lisa leaves Carney, describing him as a man who is letting himself be defeated.

Rose and Hollister encourage Carney to fight for his boys. They take the case all the way to the Supreme Court, where Bill is given custody of his children. The case has established a law stating that persons with disabilities cannot be denied their parental rights simply on warrant of their limitation. Their abilities in a parenting situation will establish critieria for custody allowance.

* * *

The Ordeal of Bill Carney came out just months after the real-life Carney won custody of his two sons. In depicting an issue and not the physical limitation itself, many of the common pitfalls of disability drama were avoided. After the disabling injury, Carney was shown receiving rehabilitation. The audience saw him learning to retrain muscles. Special equipment was casually introduced: a cuff to hold a pen so he could write, a hydraulic lift van, etc. Both Jack Hollister and Mason Rose drove. Hand controls were illustrated.

The use of two men with disabilities as mentors was a treat. Hollister was a supportive yet rather brash character. He was there when Bill needed him. The character of Mason Rose was the high point of the movie. He was a multifaceted man who would roll up his sleeves and dive into his next project. He was married, and although he indicated rough times had occurred in the past between him and his wife, they now shared a warm relationship. He was a father who swam with the kids in the pool and barbecued burgers on the grill. He drove a luxury car and had a big house, evidence of a successful career. His was a character far and beyond his disability.

Actors with disabilities were seen in the background of the movie.

The Ordeal of Bill Carney was a rare disability movie and should be seen.

Whose Life Is It, Anyway? / 1981 / MGM

Executive Producers: Martin C. Schute and Ray Cooney

* Wheelchair-User
* Single White Male

Whose Life Is It, Anyway?

Producer: Lawrence P. Bachman
Director: John Badham
Screenplay: Brian Clark and Reginald Rose
Based on the Stage Play: *Whose Life Is It Anyway?* by Brian Clark
Category: Feature Film—Drama

* New Disability

Plot: A man who is paralyzed in an accident fights for the right to die.

A sculptor is injured when his car hits a truck that has run a red light. A new disability is incurred; Harrison is a quadriplegic. Harrison is able to move only his head. Six months after the trauma, his hospital room is a lively center of activity. Nurses, a Jamaican orderly, girlfriend Patty, and Dr. Claire Scott are all part of the scene.

> DR. SCOTT: I think we can start stepping up your physical therapy now.
>
> HARRISON: To what purpose?
>
> DR. SCOTT: To what purpose? So you can start feeling more comfortable and start leading a more normal life.
>
> HARRISON: More normal, huh?

Dr. Michael Emerson, the man responsible for saving Harrison, checks him over after a student nurse's mishap knocks Harrison out of bed.

> DR. EMERSON: Well, Mr. Harrison, we seem to be out of the woods.... We'll send you to a rehab where you'll be comfortable.

Poor language and devaluation are utilized by Harrison.

> HARRISON: I get it. You mean you just grow the vegetable here. The vegetable is stored somewhere else....

Harrison's black humor emerges when Dr. Scott enters his room.

> HARRISON: I was just practicing lying here.

Harrison engages in a verbal battle with Dr. Emerson, refusing the physician permission to sedate him.

> HARRISON: The only thing that I have left is my consciousness. And I don't want that paralyzed as well.... I've decided I don't want to stay alive.

Negative aspects are seen when Harrison is sedated against his wishes. He dreams of watching Patty dancing and seeing himself sketch and sculpt her form. The camera dwells on Harrison's now-still hands.

Patty comes in to see Ken. He won't kiss her.

> HARRISON: Without self-pity, I am no longer someone to love. I'm an object ... I know you love me. And when I was Ken Harrison, I loved you. But that was a long time ago.... I want you to walk out of here and not come back.... Everytime I look at you, I see what I cannot do and what I will never do again and I can't stand it. I know you love me, Patty. But if you don't want to torture me, you'll go. Please.

Harrison meets chipper Mrs. Boyle, who seems to be some kind of social worker. Devaluation is seen again when she introduces herself.

> MRS. BOYLE: Mr. Harrison.
>
> HARRISON: I used to be.
>
> MRS. BOYLE: ...I've come to see if I can help you.... You're going to be able to operate a reading machine and I think an adapted typewriter and even a calculator.
>
> HARRISON: Gee and *wow,* the three R's! Doesn't exactly make an abundant life.

Harrison's barbed tongue leads Mrs. Boyle to decide he is "not ready" for this conversation. She leaves.

Lawyer Carter Hill meets with Harrison at the artist's request. Harrison wants Hill to represent him in a case to permit him to be discharged from the hospital even though he realizes it means his death due to lack of kidney function. Psychiatrists are sent in to determine if Harrison is clinically depressed.

Patty agrees that Ken should be allowed to die. She reveals her feeling to Dr. Scott.

> PATTY: I loved the late Ken Harrison. And I grieve for his death ... Ken Harrison is gone ... just let him do what he wants to do. Let him go.

A hearing is held in the hospital with Judge Wyler to determine if Harrison can leave the hospital. Harrison argues his case. Poor language and negative aspects are illustrated.

> HARRISON: I do not want to die because as far as I am concerned, I am dead already.... I cannot believe that this—condition constitutes life in any real sense of the word.... I'll spend the rest of my

life in this hospital with everything geared just to keeping my brain alive....

After painful deliberation and study of previous similar cases, Judge Wyler renders his decision. He uses interesting language.

WYLER: I therefore order that he be set free.

* * *

Whose Life Is It Anyway? was a fascinating movie. Excellently scripted and adroitly performed and filmed, it is something worth watching. Its value lies in the writing and performances and overall cinematic look.

As an image of disability, it was murderous and damaging. Ken Harrison was never offered any type of psychological counseling or therapy after he was severely disabled. One scene illustrated him lying on a mat having his head rotated by a therapist. No special aids to permit him independence were seen. He read in one scene with the help of a nurse holding a book. The so-called "introduction" of special aids by Mrs. Boyle was scary. An employee better suited for work at Disneyland was sent to tell a severely-disabled artist that a reading machine could help him.

Harrison was never given any type of mentor. He was never introduced to an alternate perspective. Even the judge, who carefully studied previous cases to help him make a decision, never consulted a quadriplegic in similar circumstance to Harrison. The non-disabled viewpoint of Harrison was an opposition to Dr. Emerson's life-at-any-price concept. But an argument expressing a quality life in spite of the severe physical limitation was not presented.

In the months Harrison spent in the hospital, his sole contacts with the outside world were the staff and Patty. He was whisked away to a basement area once where Jamaican orderly John had smuggled in his reggae band to play for the artist. He was shown listening to music. With so little stimulus, an intelligent man might wish for death.

An interesting sidelight to the film was its marketing campaign. As a "depressing" Christmas release, it needed help at the box office. TV promos with composer Arthur Rubenstein's upbeat orchestral overture indicated it was a celebration of life and choice. Initial newspaper ads were a picture of a smiling Harrison in bed with Patty bending over him to kiss him. As the campaign progressed, the bed was airbrushed out and the picture was canted so that the two lovers appeared to be upright.

Despite technical expertise and critical acclaim, no perspective of life with a disability was illustrated in *Whose Life Is It, Anyway?* It runs a close second to *Thou Shalt Not Commit Adultery* in overall poor imagery and information.

The Love Boat / "Love Will Find a Way" / Nov. 20, 1982 / ABC-TV

Executive Producers: Aaron Spelling; Douglas Cramer
Producers: Ben Joelson, Art Baer and Henry Colman
Director: Richard Kinon
Writers: Ann Gibbs and Joel Kimmel
Category: Series Television — Romantic Comedy

* Wheelchair-User
* Single White Male
* Performer with a Disability

Plot: The Hamiltons are looking forward to meeting their daughter's fiancé, Arthur, not knowing he uses a wheelchair.

Buck and Hanna Hamilton join their daughter, Elaine, on the *Pacific Princess* to meet Arthur, Elaine's fiancé. They are amazed to see he uses a wheelchair. The cause of his disability is described as a skateboard accident while a teen. Buck and Hanna are in shock. Arthur is upset with Elaine for not telling her parents about him.

> ELAINE: Arthur ... the closest they've ever been to anyone in a wheelchair is an *Ironside* rerun.

A worried Buck speaks with Arthur in private about the impending marriage.

> BUCK: Arthur, you're handicapped.

> ARTHUR: No, *you're* handicapped by the way you think.

Erroneous notions are brought to fore.

> BUCK: Think of ten years from now ... do you really think it's fair to expect Elaine to play nursemaid for the rest of her life?

Buck has affected Arthur. The young man talks to Elaine. Devaluation appears.

> ARTHUR: I've come to depend on you a great deal ... maybe we're getting dependence mixed up with love ... we're happy right now but — what about ten years from now? ... I'm doing this because I love you.

He calls the wedding off. Elaine's subsequent misery has gotten Hanna thinking. Buck says yes, he would have married Hanna if she had been in a wheelchair.

HANNA: I wonder if *our* parents would have approved.

Buck changes his mind and goes to talk with Arthur. The young man evidences more devaluation.

ARTHUR: You finally showed me that I was telling myself too many lies.

Buck becomes the non-disabled catalyst.

BUCK: ...I think you're telling yourself a lot of lies now.

For an early Christmas gift, Buck "gives" Arthur to Elaine.

* * *

"Love Will Find a Way" was a story so predictable, it wasn't worth watching. It would be natural for parents to have concerns about their daughter marrying a young man in a wheelchair. Buck's patronizing and condescending reaction to Arthur — while appropriate for the paternal character — was made completely unpalatable by Arthur's quiet acquiescence. Arthur, who had lived for many years with his chair, knew his capabilities and strengths whereas Buck was reacting to his own mistaken beliefs.

Buck indicated his was an athletic, outdoorsy family. Arthur never indicated a person in a chair could be the same. Thus, the act of Elaine marrying "down" to him was a saintly one.

The resolution of the story was weak. Instead of Buck and Hanna gaining some type of insight into Arthur's potential as a husband, Buck accepted the liaison to assuage both Elaine's and his own misery. Although he recognized he would have married Hanna if she had been in a chair and would have had to fight parental opposition, he "gave in" rather than accepting Arthur for the person he was. Arthur was very passive and did little to prove he was the right person for Elaine. Instead, in classic devaluation, he accepted someone else's judgment.

On the positive side, the piece used an actor with a disability. He was seen as a person with a sense of humor. He did not remain in his chair for all of his scenes. In one, he was out of it, lounging on the bed in his cabin, feet propped on his wheelchair while he read a book. Arthur was employed as a high school English teacher. He was knowledgeable about wines and had, to Buck and Hanna's amazement, traveled in Europe. The active and healthy young man seemed to be the last person who would need a "nursemaid."

"Love Will Find a Way" had honorable intentions but went along with pure formula.

Cagney and Lacey / "Hot Line" / Nov. 22, 1982 / CBS-TV

Executive Producer: Barney
   Rosenzweig

* Wheelchair-User
* White Male

Producers: April Smith; Jason Stern
Supervising Producer: Richard M. Rosenbloom
Writer: Frank Abatemarco
Category: Series Television — Police Drama

* Performer with a Disability

A man in a chair working at a messenger service is tapped for information by detectives Cagney and Lacey. He helps them out.

* * *

"Hot Line" positively used a person with a disability in a casual manner. He was simply someone with information, without regard to his limitation.

Cagney and Lacey / "Hopes and Dreams" / Jan. 10, 1983 / CBS-TV

Executive Producer: Barney Rosenzweig
Producer: April Smith
Supervising Producer: Richard N. Rosenbloom
Director: Peter Levin
Writer: Frank Abatemarco
Category: Series Television — Police Drama

* Wheelchair-User
* White Female Teenager
* Performer with a Disability

Plot: A teenaged paraplegic loses hope of walking again when her bicycle is stolen in a robbery.

Detectives Chris Cagney and Mary Beth Lacey are working on a series of robberies. Poor language is used by another policeman when describing the latest victim.

    COP: There's Mrs. Grady ... her daughter's crippled.

Teenaged Jeri is angry about the robbery. Her bike was stolen. After Mrs. Grady and her daughter leave, Lacey comments on the girl.

    LACEY: That's an angry young lady.

The cause of Jeri's disability is discussed.

    CAGNEY: Her mother said she was hit by a car two years ago. She's been in a wheelchair ever since.

Cagney spearheads a campaign to raise money in the station to get the girl a substitute bike. But Jeri doesn't want any part of it and bitterly tells Cagney so.

    CAGNEY: You got a mouth on you, kid.

    JERI: Makes up for my legs.

The doctors had told Jeri she might ride again. She improved after the news. Loss of the bike is equated with loss of hope.

* * *

"Hopes and Dreams" gave no indication that there was any quality life available to Jeri without the hope-filled symbol of the bicycle. The non-disabled viewpoint was seen: acceptance and integration of the disability was equivalent to giving up hope.

Jeri was angry, bitter, and not worth being around, let alone worth drawing a sympathy vote from the policemen to replace her bicycle. Her chair drew their attention, not her "winning" personality.

"Hopes and Dreams" was played for some tears, using standard disability formula.

Fantasy Island / "Candy Kisses" / Jan. 15, 1983 / ABC-TV

Executive Producers: Aaron Spelling; Leonard Goldberg
Supervising Producer: Arthur Rowe
Director: Don Ingalls
Writer: Charlotte Keel
Category: Series Television — Romantic Fantasy

* Wheelchair-User
* Single White Female

Plot: A disabled woman wishes to reverse the effects of an accident in order to have a shot at the blue ribbon.

    Miss Haversham of the Kentucky Havershams arrives on Fantasy Island with a dual fantasy. She wishes to be young again and to be able to walk. The cause of her disability is discussed as a fall from a horse. She wishes to fulfill what she felt was rightly hers—the chance to win the blue ribbon.

    Her fantasy is fulfilled and she is able to rise and walk—and compete. Her disability returns as her fantasy draws to a close.

* * *

"Candy Kisses" was based on the negative premise that nothing in a mature woman's life could ever possibly surpass a lost dream of childhood. The older, disabled Miss Haversham spoke in a whispery voice and required assistance to be wheeled about. In contrast, when her fantasy was fulfilled, she was a frisky daredevil, full of life and laughter. It was easy for the audience to assume her accident had prematurely aged her and robbed her of youthful vitality. The only connection between the two versions of Miss Haversham was the love of horses both had.

"Candy Kisses" was a dull and unimaginative story which silently stated disability was the last stop before death.

Simon and Simon / "What's in a Gnome?" / Feb. 24, 1983 / CBS-TV

Executive Producer: Philip De Guere
Producer: Richard Chapman
Supervising Producer: John G. Stephens
Director: Sigmund Neufeld, Jr.
Writer: Paul Magistretti
Category: Series Television — Detective Drama

* Wheelchair-User
* White Male
* Performer with a Disability

Plot: Detectives Rick and AJ Simon investigate sabotage going on at a soon-to-be-open amusement park.

* * *

"What's in a Gnome?" had Rick and AJ involved in a case where the prime suspect was a Marine veteran of the Vietnam War. Rick, a vet himself, knew of someone who could help dig up computer information. He and AJ went to the home of Doyle, a man who used a wheelchair.

Doyle's role was purely incidental. He played a mean game of ping pong and slaughtered Rick; went to the fridge and pulled out beers for his visitors, then got to work. He dug up information on his computer. He had a sense of humor and appeared busy, bright and had a social consciousness toward his fellow vets. His chair was not mentioned.

"What's in a Gnome?" positively presented a man with a disability as a friendly, outgoing contributor to society.

The Jeffersons / "Father's Day" / Mar. 6, 1983 / CBS-TV

Category: Series Television — Situation Comedy

* Wheelchair-User
* Black Male
* Performer with a Disability

The Jeffersons

Plot: George befriends a "fatherless" boy in the building, only to discover the boy has a father who uses a wheelchair.

George Jefferson befriends young Deron, who says he has no father. George takes the kid bowling and agrees to act as surrogate father in the Father and Son Bowling Tournament.

Louise Jefferson is a coordinator for the apartment building's activities committee. Those who *can* offer their services to those who *can't*. A knock on her door reveals Ray Taylor, a man in a wheelchair. He has come to inquire about the activities program.

LOUISE: What kind of assistance do you need?

TAYLOR: I came to *offer* my help.

Ray is quite a handy fix-it person. He quickly finds a point in common with George: they both like the local pro basketball team. George talks about a recent game where people were standing up in excitement and jumping up and down.

TAYLOR: Tell me about it. I missed the whole fourth quarter!

Taylor notes it has been three years since his accident. His conversation also reveals that he is the father of Deron. George calls Deron on his ruse. The boy admits that Ray is his parent.

DERON: My father has a handicap.

George becomes a non-disabled catalyst in the lives of the Taylors.

GEORGE: Your father has a disability. *You* have a handicap.

George reminds Deron that people using wheelchairs are involved in all sorts of athletics, such as marathoning, tennis, and basketball. With his help, the Taylors strike up a peace.

* * *

"Father's Day" was a nice story which focused on the difficulties a status-conscious boy had with admitting his father had a disability rather than on the physicality of Ray Taylor. Taylor was bright, busy, and possessed of a sense of humor. He was able to poke fun at his limitations without sacrificing his personal integrity. He was depicted as a man who could offer his talents to others in the building and who could parent his son if the boy would let him.

Use of a disabled character like this within a cheerful sitcom illustrated some problems without the seemingly perfunctory heavy-handedness of many dramas. "Father's Day" made many good points without having to hammer them in.

Voyagers! / "Destiny's Choice" / Mar. 12, 1983 / NBC-TV

Executive Producer: James D. Parriott
Producers: Jill Sherman; Harry & Renee Longstreet
Co-Producer: Robert Steinhauer
Director: Paul Stanley
Writer: Jill Sherman
Category: Series Television — Fantasy Drama

* Wheelchair-User
* Married White Male
* Equipment: Braces and crutches
* Suggested by a True Story

Plot: Time-traveling "fix-it" colleagues Phineas Bogg and young Jeffrey Jones make sure Franklin Roosevelt gets involved in politics and not the film industry.

Phineas Bogg, the time-hopping rogue whose job it is to straighten out foul-ups in history, finds himself and adolescent point man Jeffrey Jones on a movie set in 1928. "Wild Frank" Roosevelt is directing the first talking picture. The two Voyagers zip back to 1924 to make sure Roosevelt gets into politics instead of movie-making.

Masquerading as a handyman, Bogg enters the Roosevelt home where polio survivor Franklin lies abed. He has just received a letter from Louie Howell asking him to nominate Al Smith for the presidency.

FRANKLIN: I guess this means I'm still a member of the human race.

Mother Roosevelt vetoes the idea to Franklin and Eleanor with devaluation.

MAMA: But how great an advantage will it be for Mr. Smith to be nominated by a man in a wheelchair?

Franklin agrees with her, with more devaluation.

FRANKLIN: Mama's right.... I can't do Al Smith any good making a nominating speech from a wheelchair.

Bogg takes on the role of the non-disabled catalyst by inferring Roosevelt is a "helpless invalid." Roosevelt is piqued; he requests Bogg's help to get into his wheelchair.

BOGG: The polio paralyzed your arms too, huh?

Roosevelt gets into his chair independently. Bogg gets a pair of crutches from the corner. He encourages Roosevelt to try them. With Bogg's help and guidance, FDR ignores his mother's pleas and pulls himself across the lawn — on his way to the presidency.

* * *

"Destiny's Choice" was a benign little piece which illustrated a mother's overprotection was disabling her son more than his limitation. Although Bogg was clearly a non-disabled catalyst in Roosevelt's life, he wasn't doing anything he didn't do any other week — setting history back on the right course. However, the premise of *Voyagers!* was for Bogg and Jeffrey to act as catalysts to misguided history and get it back on the right track. From that vantage point, it is a bit unfair to criticize the use of Bogg in that formulaic manner.

"Destiny's Choice" was imaginative, but well within stereotypical formula.

Hill Street Blues / "Midway to What?" / Dec. 1, 1983 / NBC-TV

Executive Producer: Steven Bochco
Co-Executive Producer: Gregory Hoblit
Producers: Jeffrey Lewis & Sascha Schneider
Supervising Producer: Scott Brazil
Director: Thomas Carter
Television Story: Jeffrey Lewis; David Milch
Teleplay: Jeffrey Lewis; Michael Wagner; Karen Hall; Mark Frost
Based in Part on an Unpublished Story by: Darrell Ray and Alan Toy
Category: Series Television — Police Drama

* Wheelchair-User
* White Male

Plot: Detective Belker arrests a man using a wheelchair who defaces Belker's car when it is parked in a "handicapped zone."

Detective Mick Belker busts a bookmaking operation at a candy store. Outdoors, he finds a young man in a wheelchair spray-painting his car, which is parked in a "handicapped" zone. Belker lights out after the man, catching him. He books the man at the Hill Street station.

BELKER: Name.

GERRY: Gaffney. Gerry ... "G," as in "gimp."

Gerry claims if a car hadn't been coming around the corner, Belker never would have gotten him.

> BELKER: How fast could you go in that thing?

> GERRY: I been clocked at twenty-three on a straight. See, I got a slightly narrower wheelbase on a twenty-seven inch diameter, double butted tubing in the frame and I sit two inches lower in the seat....

Gerry needs to use the restroom. Physical accessibility is discussed.

> GERRY: Is the stall wheelchair accessible? . . . cause if it ain't, I'm gonna need some help.

The restroom is inaccessible. Belker drops a humiliated and embarrassed Gerry while trying to seat him on the toilet.

Belker later states he may go undercover in a wheelchair. Gerry vetoes the idea.

> GERRY: Takes soul.

Gerry's sentence is to do community service. Belker invites him to a boxing match. Gerry accepts, again mentioning accessibility.

> BELKER: I don't know if this place has a ramp, though.

> GERRY: We'll work it out.

* * *

"Midway to What?" presented a man using a wheelchair as a passionate, politically-active man who was so right, he was wrong. Gerry was *not* invisible. He was a strong-minded, strong-willed individual who earned Belker's grudging respect.

The bathroom scene was graphic and gritty. The logistics involved in Belker's trying to help Gerry get seated in a stall would make any viewer squirm and think, "If they only had a wheelchair stall...."

The use of an athletic man in a chair as part of the slightly-seedy Hill Street precinct population was welcome. Other than his limitation, Gerry wasn't much different from the other inhabitants of the metro area.

"Midway to What?" took a different tack — due to the use of a story written by two men with disabilities. It was done with *Hill Street Blues'* usual finesse and left a lasting impression.

Hill Street Blues / "Honk If You're a Goose" / Dec. 8, 1983 / NBC-TV

Executive Producer: Steven Bochco   * Wheelchair-User
Co-Producer: Gregory Hoblit   * White male

Hill Street Blues

Producers: Jeffrey Lewis & Sascha Schneider
Supervising Producer: Scott Brazil
Director: Arthur Allan Seidelman
Television Story: Jeffrey Lewis; David Milch
Teleplay: Michael Wagner; David Milch; Karen Hall; Mark Frost
Based in Part on an Unpublished Story by: Darrell Ray & Alan Toy
Category: Series Television — Police Drama

Plot: Detective Mick Belker goes undercover using a wheelchair.

At morning roll call, Sgt. Esterhaus makes an announcement.

> ESTERHAUS: Item seven. Detective Belker commences undercover today as one of our city's disabled citizens.... Mick's wheelchair will be circulating proximate to banks in the area....

Gerry Gaffney shows up, asking if Belker is ready for his stint in a wheelchair.

> GERRY: Okay then, let's go, hot shot ... we got it rotten enough out there without some amateur giving us a bad name.

Belker tells Gerry he cannot help the police department. Later on the streets, he is upset to see Gerry trailing him. He takes off after Gerry in his chair, then leaps out and runs him down.

> GERRY: I saw what's been goin' on. Every curb you come to, you get out and lift the chair over. That's good. That's authentic.... You know what your mistake is, man? You think it's just a kind of wheelchair. It's an attitude, man. It's a way of life ... it's like I said, man, no soul.

When Belker is mugged at an automatic teller machine, he gives chase to the bandit. Gerry darts out into the street to help and is hit by a car.

Belker arrests Gerry for interfering. At the Hill Street station, Gerry collapses from internal bleeding and dies. Belker pays Gerry one of his highest tributes.

> BELKER: I respected him.... I shouldn't have yelled at him.

* * *

"Honk If You're a Goose," the next installment of the serial-like *Hill Street Blues'* "Midway to What?" episode, again featured so-right-he's-wrong Gerry Gaffney. Gerry's death was a disappointment — particularly when it was evident he and Belker were entering into an almost-reluctant friendship.

The Fall Guy / "Wheels" / Dec. 21, 1983 / ABC-TV

Executive Producer: Glen A. Larson
Producer: Harry Tomason
Co-Producer: Lee Majors
Supervising Producer: Lou Shaw
Director: Michael O'Herlihy
Story by: Ron Friedman
Teleplay: Richard Raskin
Category: Series Television — Action-Adventure

* Wheelchair-User
* Single White Male
* Performer with a Disability

Plot: Stuntman/bounty hunter Colt Seavers is looking for Travis Tyler — and so is the Mob.

Colt locates ex-stuntman Travis Tyler behind a draped table at a gymnasium in Seattle.

COLT: How'd you jump bail?

TRAVIS: I didn't jump. I rolled.

Travis pulls back from the table in a wheelchair. The cause of his disability is discussed as "a high fall on a picture."

Leslie, Travis' one-time fiancée, is delighted Colt has located her love. When she and Travis re-meet, he displays devaluation and bitterness.

TRAVIS: I told you to forget about me ... you always dreamed about walking down the aisle with a guy in a wheelchair.

LESLIE: Travis, I need *you* — and it doesn't have anything to do with any damn chair.

TRAVIS: That's just sympathy talking because I'm different now.

Travis escapes Colt. The bounty hunter locates him at the same time the Mob does. Colt's car is trashed as they escape the gangsters; Travis' wheelchair is miles away. Colt says he must carry Travis across open country.

TRAVIS: I don't like to be carried.

COLT: You want me to *roll* you down the highway?

Colt transports Travis via piggyback.
A showdown with the Mob reveals they framed Travis. Travis admits he still loves Leslie and the two are married.

* * *

"Wheels" was an unorthodox disability piece with some very enjoyable moments. Travis was a headstrong and arrogant young man who never ceased taking chances. He resented Colt's help but didn't have much choice with the Mob on his tail. He was an agile and athletic young man.

Travis stole and drove Colt's truck using an orthopedic cane to depress the foot pedals. However, no indication was made that he may have had his own vehicle with hand controls. He also recklessly "drove" a souped-up motorized wheelchair with an attached sidecar.

Performers with disabilities were utilized in the production.

Despite lapses into formula, "Wheels" was a different image of a person with a disability.

Terrible Joe Moran / Mar. 27, 1984 / CBS-TV

Producer: Robert Halmi
Supervising Producer: David Kappes
Director: Joseph Sargent
Writer: Frank Cucci
Category: Made-for-TV Movie — Drama

* Wheelchair-User
* White Male
* Performer with a Disability

Plot: An ex-boxer gets to know his wild, estranged granddaughter.

* * *

Terrible Joe Moran was a movie written specifically as the TV-movie debut of a "Golden Age" film star. The star, due to age and physical problems, was using a wheelchair for his own mobility. Thus, he played the "non-disabled" role from a chair. The audience was treated to a performance by a talented actor without regard to his physicality.

Fantasy Island / "The Final Adieu" / Apr. 13, 1984 / ABC-TV

Executive Producers: Aaron Spelling; Leonard Goldberg
Producer: Don Ingalls

* Wheelchair-User
* White Married Female

Supervising Producer: Arthur Rowe
Director: Phillip Leacock
Writer: Brian Bird
Category: Series Television — Romantic Fantasy

Plot: A mistress discovers her male friend's wife uses a wheelchair.

* * *

"The Final Adieu" revolved around a pretty young woman who followed her lover to Fantasy Island with the intention of breaking off the affair. Instead, she backed off when she discovered the man's wife used a wheelchair. Erroneous assumptions about the sexual capabilities of a woman experiencing paraplegia were made when the wife stated she was unable to give her husband "that kind of love anymore." The "other woman" then couldn't go ahead with plans to break up the marriage — feeling she was doing a charitable thing.

Special equipment was misused as the woman with a disability used a chair much too large for her. The quarters occupied by her and her husband were not ramped.

"The Final Adieu" was pure, unadulterated schlock that depended on stereotypical myths to work.

Remington Steele / "High Flying Steele" / June 12, 1984 (rerun) / NBC-TV

Executive Producer: Michael Gleason
Co-Producer: Kevin Inch
Director: Karen Arthur
Writer: George Lee Marshall
Category: Series Television — Detective Drama

* Wheelchair-User
* Single Hispanic Female

Plot: Remington Steele and Laura Holt investigate murders at a circus.

Mr. Steele and Miss Holt are investigating a series of murders at Cordero's Fabulous Funtime Circus. Laura Holt meets Christie Cordero, a one-time trapeze star. Laura expresses her admiration for the latter's high-wire work.

    LAURA: I wanted to be you.

    CHRISTIE: Lucky you weren't lucky.

Christie pulls out in an electric wheelchair, a blanket covering her legs. The cause of her accident is described as a trapeze accident, four years previous.

Laura decides her best bet for nailing the killer would be to set herself up as bait. She "joins" the circus as a new member of the high-wire act. Christie lends Laura an aerialist's costume that used to be hers.

CHRISTIE: It's the one I wore—*that* night.

Laura and Mr. Steele successfully nail the killer.

* * *

"High-Flying Steele" presented a young woman in a wheelchair as pretty and bright. She now worked in the business end of the family circus. However, judging from her comments, one could assume she had not been able to put the accident behind her.

Most surprising, due to the 1980s vintage of this program, was the fact that Christie appeared with a blanket covering her legs—something that was a 1930s or 1940s era "tradition"; legs thought not to be "normal" enough for the sensitivities of the general public were hidden away in such manner.

A small-statured person was seen in the background as a circus performer.

"High-Flying Steele's" image of a woman with a disability was that of a once-active athlete now quiet and businesslike and unable to satisfactorily re-enter life.

Miami Vice / Sept. 15, 1984 / NBC-TV

Executive Producers: Michael Mann; Anthony Yerkovich
Producer: John Nicolella
Director: Thomas Carter
Category: Made-for-TV Movie— Crime Drama

* Wheelchair-User
* White Male Child

Plot: Cops Crockett and Tubbs track down a cop who is on the take.

Scott Wheeler Junior joins in a birthday party. He uses a wheelchair. His dad is a cop on the take from some Miami drug dealers. Crockett and Tubbs nail him. Wheeler needed the money.

WHEELER: ...Scott Junior's medical expenses last year alone....

* * *

The pilot film of the hit TV series *Miami Vice* peripherally featured a cop on the take who had a young disabled son. Scott Junior was a part of the household. A ramp in front of the house permitted him easy access. He played with other children and seemed to be an incidental character, until his disability turned into the pivot point. Scott was negatively transformed into a financial burden.

Miami Vice positively illustrated a child with a disability as part of an average family — as well as unfairly suggesting he was a hardship that forced a good man to go wrong.

Simon & Simon / "What Goes Around Comes Around" / Nov. 2, 1984 / CBS-TV

Executive Producer: John G. Stephens
Producers: Bill Dial and George Geiger
Director: Dennis Donney
Story: Bruce Ferber; David Lerner
Teleplay: David Brown
Category: Series Television — Detective Drama

* Wheelchair-User
* Single White Male
* Equipment: Braces and crutches

Plot: Detective brothers Rick and AJ Simon go undercover at a racetrack to try and determine who is sabotaging a driver's engines.

Rick and AJ trail a saboteur trying to kill driver Dwayne Bellwood. They talk to Orville Kincaid, a man using an electric wheelchair. The cause of the ex-driver's disability is discussed as a "near-fatal accident" four years previous which also involved Bellwood.

Kincaid is an active, busy man, still deeply interested in the world of racing — in fact, too interested. Rick and AJ discern he is behind the sabotage attempts on Bellwood. Revenge is seen as his motive.

ORVILLE: I've been waiting four years to get him to trust me.

* * *

"What Goes Around Comes Around" was a routine story. Bellwood felt guilt for involvement in Orville's accident; Orville manipulated Bellwood into a form of trust in order to strike back at him for the disability incurred.

Diff'rent Strokes / "The Gymnast" / Dec. 1, 1984 / NBC-TV

Executive Producers: Martin Cohan and Blake Hunter
Producer: Bruce Taylor
Supervising Producer: Bob

* Wheelchair-User
* Single Black Male
* Performer with a Disability

Brunner, Ken Hecht
Director: Geren Keith
Writers: Bob Brunner & Ken Hecht
Category: Series Television — Situation Comedy

Plot: An ex-gymnast returns to the Drummond household after an accident which has necessitated his using a wheelchair.

Stuart Thompson, ex-star school gymnast, will attend a dedication reception for the new school gymnasium. Stuart uses a wheelchair. The cause of his disability is discussed as an auto accident. He would have been in the next Olympics if he hadn't been injured.

Housekeeper Pearl is nervous about Stuart's return and little Sam is just plain curious. Pearl uses negative imagery as she talks to Sam.

> PEARL: Don't forget, Stuart is in a wheelchair and will never walk again.

Special visitors for the gym dedicaton are members of the 1984 Olympic Men's Gymnastic Team. They perform and approach Stuart, saying they've heard he used to be pretty good. They compliment him on how well he's doing. Stuart bursts out in anger. He devalues himself and uses poor language.

> STUART: "Way to go." "Stay in shape." ... I fell for that garbage in the hospital.... [He angrily pounds his legs.] These are dead! Get away! I don't need anybody!

Stuart later apologizes to Mr. Drummond for his outburst. He goes to the new gym to apologize to the Olympic team. The team jointly accepts the roles of non-disabled catalysts, expressing there are still athletic options available to Stuart.

> JIM HARTUNG: In the Olympics, there was a wheelchair archer from New Zealand....
>
> MITCH GAYLOR: ...other wheelchair sports ... basketball....

*   *   *

"The Gymnast" began with Stuart as an energetic, busy sort who was realistic about his disability and quite eager to get along with life. He joined in with the rapid one-liner fire typical in sitcoms. He appeared to be a person who was happy to return to life after a personal trauma. But as usual, he resorted to by-the-book responses about the quality of his life.

Curiously, while the Olympic team told Stuart about other athletic avenues he could enjoy, they never mentioned the exciting men's and women's wheelchair exhibition sprints of the 1984 Games.

Actual disabled people were seen in the background of "The Gymnast." The story, however, was pure stereotypical formula.

Alice / "Mel Spins His Wheels" / 1984 / CBS-TV

Executive Producers: Madeline Davis; Bob Carrol, Jr.
Producers: Mark Egan; Mark Solomon; Jerry Madden
Director: Marc Daniels
Writers: Richard Marcus & Porges
Category: Series Television — Situation Comedy

* Wheelchair-User
* Single White Male; Series lead
* Temporary Disability

Plot: A temporary stint in a wheelchair teaches Mel the meaning of "accessibility."

A man in a wheelchair comes in to Mel's Diner to use the telephone for assistance after his car has broken down. He struggles to reach the inaccessible phone. He is also unable to use the too-narrow-to-enter restroom. He tells Mel the place should be made accessible for all patrons.

Mel, preparing wiring in the ceiling for his new widescreen TV, falls and sprains both ankles. He comes in with an electric wheelchair. Mel has to use the telephone. Waitress Alice gives the other workers a knowing look.

> ALICE: I wanna see if Mel can handle a phone call from a wheelchair by himself.

Mel grabs a pair of kitchen tongs to insert his money into the telephone and smugly grins.

His tux for that evening's restaurant award dinner is delivered and hung in the men's room. Mel closes the restaurant and excuses the women to go home and get ready for the party. He heads for the restroom to get his tux.

> MEL: I can't get in there. [The door's] not wide enough.

His wheelchair goes on the fritz. He loses his phone quarter, drops his tongs, and can't make a call for help.

Alice pops back into the restaurant, worried about Mel. She finds him frustrated.

> ALICE: So, what lessons have we learned from this?

At the dinner, Mel can't get onstage to receive his restaurateur's award. He complains to the people running the show.

MEL: You should have a ramp here or something.

The stint in a chair has helped Mel decide to lower the restaurant phone and install wider restroom doors. The widescreen TV will have to wait.

* * *

"Mel Spins His Wheels" was a funny, nicely done story with a good message. The vain, penny-pinching Mel had a hard time understanding any good point until it was pounded into his head. His brief stint in a chair taught him things no one could ever have convinced him were true. Lessons were shared with the audience in a nonthreatening way. The issue of physical accessibility was explored with the typical good humor present in the sitcom.

A performer with a disability played the stranded traveler.

Starman / 1984 / Columbia Pictures

Executive Producer: Michael Douglas
Producer: Larry J. Franco
Co-Producer: Barry Bernardi
Director: John Carpenter
Writers: Bruce A. Evans & Raynold Gideon
Category: Feature Film—Science Fiction

* Wheelchair-User
* White Male

Plot: Responding to the invitation of the 1977 *Voyager* probe, an alien visits Earth.

* * *

Starman briefly featured a person with a disability in an incidental role. Mr. Mark Shermin, heading the Search for Extra-Terrestrial Intelligence, explained to a higher-up that he suspected the hollow object found in the Wisconsin wilderness was an alien ship responding to the recorded invitation sent out years before on the *Voyager* probe. Another specialist adding credence to his theory was a scientist using a wheelchair.

Starman positively depicted a man in a wheelchair as one in a special area of expertise and a part of the community at large.

Finder of Lost Loves / "Deadly Silence" / Jan. 12, 1985 / ABC-TV

Executive Producer: Aaron Spelling & Douglas Cramer

* Wheelchair-User
* Single White Male

Director: Georg Stanford Brown
Category: Series Television—
Romantic Drama

Plot: The Maxwell, Ltd., agency has been hired to locate a musician who wanted to marry Joanna then dropped out of sight.

Joanna, a woman who denied herself of romance while spending years taking care of her invalid mother, hires Daisy of the Maxwell, Ltd. "lost-love locator" agency to find Richard Foster. The pianist claimed everlasting love before disappearing.

Daisy locates Foster. He says he has no desire to see Joanna again. Joanna refuses to accept Richard's proclamation and presents herself to force a showdown. Richard enters—in a wheelchair.

> JOANNA: Oh my God! When—
>
> RICHARD: On the way to the airport.... I was in such a hurry to see you.
>
> JOANNA: Why didn't you tell me?
>
> RICHARD: You spent your whole life playing nursemaid to your mother.... I could never ask you to give up your freedom again....

As Daisy watches through misty eyes, Joanna and Richard vow never to part.

* * *

"Deadly Silence" used a curious mixture of standard old disability elements as well as new imagery. Richard lived with his faithful manservant, a concept from decades past. Although the "not good enough for you anymore" and the "can't ask you to give up your freedom" aspects were as old as the hills, Richard was seen as an active man, playing the piano for recreation, bench-pressing weights, and moving around.

His disability was a teaser in the story. When Daisy confronted him, he was at a piano bench; he was lifting weights; he was at a patio table in a casual chair. Not until Joanna showed up was Richard's chair revealed to the audience.

Special equipment was misused. Richard used an ill-fitting chair that was much too large for him and hindered his mobility.

"Deadly Silence" was worn and tired.

Airwolf / "Inn at the End of the Road" / Jan. 26, 1985 / CBS-TV

Executive Producer: Donald Bellisario

* Wheelchair-User
* Single White Male

Producer: Lester William Berks
Co-Producer: Carol Gillson
Supervising Producer: T.S. Cook
Writer: Westbrook Claridge & Alfonso M. Ruggiero, Jr.
Category: Series Television — Action Adventure

* Equipment: Braces and crutches
* Performer with a Disability

Plot: A group of international terrorists hold an innocent group of citizens hostage in a remote mountain inn.

A remote mountain town becomes the unlikely target of fleeing terrorists in search of a doctor for a wounded member of their group. The killers take hostages to insure "Doc" will help them. One of the hostages is Badger, a man using a wheelchair who also walks with braces and crutches.

* * *

"The Inn at the End of the Road" incidentally used a person with a disability as a full-fledged member of the community. His disability was visible, obvious, and completely ignored in the story. Badger was a person one could lean on even in difficult moments; he was also frightened with the rest of the hostages and able to cry over the death of a friend.

Hill Street Blues / "Davenport in a Storm" / Jan. 31, 1985 / NBC-TV

Executive Producer: Steven Bochco
Co-executive Producer: Greg Hoblit
Producer: Jeffrey Lewis
Supervising Producer: Scott Brazil
Director: Gabrielle Beaumont
Story: Steven Bochco, Jeffrey Lewis, David Milch
Teleplay: Jeffrey Lewis, David Milch, Mark Frost, Roger Director
Category: Series Television — Police Drama

* [Paralysis]
* Black Male Teenager
* New Disability

Plot: A black high school athlete is the victim of senseless bigoted violence from a group of white teenagers.

Lester Eagleton, star high school baseball player, is severely injured when a group of prejudiced white teens beats him up. Possible permanent paralysis ensues. Lester echoes fear and worry.

LESTER: Am I gonna lie here of the rest of my life? I don't even wanna live like this.

Detective Henry Goldblum talks to the father of one of the suspect boys.

HENRY: Are you aware of Lester Eagleton's condition?

Pejorative language is used.

FATHER: He's crippled.

* * *

Within the framework of "Davenport in a Storm," there was no time or necessity for Lester to be anything *but* scared and frightened of what his future held. Also, this segment was not the focal point of the episode. Such a small piece is, however, an extension of some full-blown made-for-TV movies. Lester had no concept of a life after disability and no voices were heard to indicate his life would be anything but tragedy (again, difficult to insert within the framework of this story). Since the etiology of Lester's disability was deliberately inflicted by some cruel and bigoted youths, the events were hard for him and the police to fathom.

"Davenport in a Storm" is brought to mention here as a comparison of how a brief, barely-dwelt upon portion of a story differs little from some two-hour television or feature films.

Highway to Heaven / "A Match Made in Heaven" / Feb. 20, 1985 / NBC-TV

Executive Producer: Michael Landon
Producer: Kent McCray
Director: Michael Landon
Story: James Troesh and Theresa Troesh
Teleplay: Michael Landon
Category: Series Televison—Fantasy Drama

* Wheelchair-User
* Single White Male
* Performer with a Disability
* Equipment: Hydraulic lift van; Personal care attendant; Mouth-stick; Speakerphone

Plot: Mark's cousin falls in love with a man who is a quadriplegic.

Quadriplegic attorney Scotty is working at his computer. He has difficulty concentrating on his work as his attendant and his girlfriend are nuzzling as they watch TV. Scotty feels left out and alone.

Mortal Mark Gordon and angel Jonathan Smith are in town to visit Scotty as well as Mark's cousin Diane. She has just quit her job as an architect after her "big break" design was stolen by a scheming executive. She joins Mark, Jonathan, and Scotty for dinner. She and Scotty hit it off.

Scotty is currently working with the man building the edifice Diane designed. Between Scotty's intervention and some heavenly persuasion via Jonathan, Diane gets her building back. She takes Scotty out to dinner to celebrate. He reluctantly admits to Diane that he needs someone to feed him.

> DIANE: Well, I'm your date. Why shouldn't I be the one?

Mark is concerned about the growing relationship. Scotty and Diane begin seeing each other regularly. She proposes marriage to him. Some devaluation appears.

> SCOTTY: You'd have to spend the rest of your life taking care of me.... I can't even put my arms around you.
>
> DIANE: But I can put mine around you.

Scotty accepts her proposal. As they drive home, a drunk driver causes an accident. The van is on fire. Neither Scotty nor Diane is seriously hurt, but Scotty changes his mind. More devaluation is evident.

> SCOTTY: Do you know what would have happened tonight if somebody hadn't pulled us out of the van? She'd be dead because I couldn't do anything to help her.... I've been kidding myself. I can't be a husband or a father.... I was thinking I was in a park with my kid. He was sailing a boat and fell in. What the hell am I supposed to do, sit there and watch my own child die? Don't you see? She'd have to give up everything to take care of me ... she'd end up as handicapped as I am.

Jonathan and Mark pick Scotty up at the hospital. They make a pit stop at a house belonging to Jack Keller. Jack is a man in a wheelchair who has a wife and an army of boisterous kids. Scotty and Jack talk out by the swimming pool. Jack acts as the disabled catalyst.

> JACK: Look, I agonized about putting this pool in. In my mind's eye, I kept seeing the baby fall in and — well, here I am [in a wheelchair].

The talk helps Scotty change his mind. He and Diane are wed.

* * *

"A Match Made in Heaven" featured possibly the most severely disabled character ever seen onscreen who falls in love and gets married. For that, it was a milestone. The growing relationship was interesting although heavily dependent on devaluation from Scotty. Obviously, there would be a great deal of trepidation from both parties at making this big step. Unfortunately, reluctance did not play into this story. It was just Diane convincing Scotty that she loved him no matter what. In such a new situation for the audience, it would have been interesting and informative to have worked more with a reality-based fear rather than typical and predictable devaluation.

The car accident was a heavy-handed conflict device. No one bothered to remind Scotty that just as he felt he couldn't save Diane, she couldn't save him. It had to do with being unconscious, not disabled.

Erroneous notions were presented in the scene with Jack Keller (an actor with a disability was cast in the role). He was a paraplegic and indicated if his child fell in the swimming pool, he might not be able to effect a rescue. This wrongly stated that persons with such disabilities are unable to swim. However, use of a disabled catalyst to aid Scotty's decision was welcome.

"A Match Made in Heaven" deserves a plus for indicating a person as severely disabled as Scotty could love and enjoy a great many activities within his limitation, as well as love and marriage. But like many other pieces, it fell far short of its potential by its dependence on formula.

The Love Boat / "Charmed, I'm Sure" / Mar. 30, 1985 / ABC-TV

Executive Producers: Aaron Spelling and Douglas Cramer
Producers: Ben Joelson, Art Baer and Dennis Hammer
Director: Richard Kinon
Writer: Fredi Towbin
Category: Series Television— Romantic Comedy

* Wheelchair-User; Paraplegic
* Single White Female

Plot: Ship's photographer Ace sees his old girlfriend on board the cruise ship—in a wheelchair.

Ship's photographer Ace recognizes Staci McNamara, his daredevil college girlfriend, on board the *Pacific Princess*. She's in a wheelchair. The cause of her latest "mishap" is discussed as a skiing accident. Ace discovers the condition is permanent. Natural uneasiness surfaces as Ace talks to his friends about Staci.

ACE: I can't get used to seeing her in that wheelchair.

Ace finds Staci was engaged but broke off the relationship "a couple of months ago." Even Staci's alluring appearance can't help Ace over the hurdle of the wheelchair when they go to her cabin.

STACI: Aren't you gonna help me get undressed?

ACE (uneasy): Oh, I'm sorry, I didn't know you need help.

STACI: Who said anything about *need?*

Ace bows out quickly. He berates himself the next day for walking out on her and turns to Captain Stubing for advice.

ACE: Part of me is deeply attracted to her — and part of me can't get used to seeing her in that chair.... Now she's disabled. I want her to be like she was.

CAPTAIN: I'm sure in a lot of ways, she still is. Staci is a vibrant, delightful young woman. I sure she deserves a man who will love her the way she is — and not remind her of what she was. This might be the time to ask yourself if you're that man.

Ace makes peace with his feelings but Staci rebuffs him with typical devaluation.

STACI: I don't need your charity.... [You want me] like this?

ACE: I don't care about the chair. I care about you. You're beautiful, you're sexy —

Staci has news for him. She's still engaged.

STACI: I love him very much ... I couldn't marry Jeff if I thought he was doing it out of pity. I had to prove to myself that I was — still a woman, still attractive to men.

* * *

"Charmed, I'm Sure" took some contemporary imagery and used them in a tired devaluation story. Staci was bright, chatty, a smart dresser and indicated she was quite capable in her chair. It was unfortunate that special equipment was misused; she was socked into a hospital chair which hindered her mobility.

Staci worked hard to attract Ace — yet when she succeeded, she put him off with the clincher — she was already spoken for. (See *Best Years of Our Lives; Happy Days,* "Allison"; *Rawhide,* "The Empty Sleeve"; *Finder of Lost Loves,* "Deadly Silence" for variations on this theme.)

The most interesting part of the show was Ace's reaction to his friend. He was nervous, uneasy, and too careful. He needed time to assimilate the changes which he did with the help of shipboard friends. He learned Staci was important; her chair shouldn't be allowed to dilute her value as a friend or partner.

His transformation seemed natural and gave a plus to this piece it might not have had otherwise.

"Charmed, I'm Sure" had some glimmers of new imagery in it, but tired old devaluation overshadowed it.

First Steps / Apr. 1985 / CBS-TV

Producer: Ellis A. Cohen
Director: Sheldon Larry
Writer: Rod Browning
Category: Made-for-TV Movie—Drama

* Wheelchair-User
* Single White Female
* New Disability
* Based on a True Story

Plot: Computer science enables a young paraplegic woman to take steps.

To celebrate her high school graduation, Nan Davis goes to a party. She and her boyfriend leave. His car speeds around a curve and jumps the road. Nan's head cracks the passenger window. A new disability is incurred.

> NAN: I can't feel my legs!

Nan's parents arrive at the hospital. A doctor suggests they tell Nan the news right away—that she will not walk again.

> MR. DAVIS: Nan, Nan there's something you need to know ... so you'll know what's wrong with your legs. Honey, you were hurt pretty bad and you probably won't be able to walk anymore.
>
> NAN: Yes, I will.

Attitudinal barriers become evident as Mr. Davis takes Nan downtown in a wheelchair for junk food. Everyone stares at her. Nan is angry and frustrated at her predicament.

> NAN: All of my friends are about to start college. I'm about to start physical rehabilitation—which is a joke as we all know because there is no rehabilitation. I am going to spend the rest of my life in this chair watching my legs shrivel up....

Dr. Jerald Petrofsky has been researching muscle fatigue using temporarily paralyzed cats. He is approached about using the same method on permanently paralyzed humans to stimulate their muscles. It is not a cure for spinal cord injury, he stresses but:

> PETROFSKY: ...only a way of improving the quality of life.

Petrofsky continues his work at Wright State University where the accessible campus has attracted a number of physically disabled students.

Nan reads of Petrofsky's work. He's been working mostly with quadriplegics; he needs a strong paraplegic with upper body strength. Nan seeks him out and gains entry into the program.

Nan successfully learns to ride a stationary bike, then takes five historic steps. At her college graduation, she walks to the podium to collect her diploma.

* * *

First Steps illustrated a young woman in a wheelchair who was totally unwilling to accept the prognosis that she would never walk again. Her shining faith spurred her on, in the non-disabled point of view, to life itself.

There was very little evidence of quality life within a disability. Prior to her injury, Nan was athletic, jogging with her mother. After, she was angry, defensive, and devaluating.

As usual on television, Nan went straight home after incurring her injury. She stated she had physical rehabilitation ahead of her—something she called "a joke," indicating she had nothing to gain in learning to better utilize the uninjured parts of her body or learn techniques to make daily living easier.

Disturbing scenes occurred during the movie. Nan verbally discussed the hurt she felt in seeing the shrinkage of her leg muscles. She indicated maximum shrinkage would be in eighteen months—a time when she would no longer be "sexy." After a time on Petrofsky's equipment, she sat in front of a mirror, stroking her legs proudly, illustrating there is no sexuality or pride in a body that is different.

When Petrofsky arrived at Wright State, he began interviewing potential candidates for the program. In a curiously voyeuristic scene, five different minor characters detailed how they became disabled. Due to the unimportance of their roles, the large admissions seemed out of place and seemed to exist to satisfy audience curiosity.

When Nan received her diploma, the class rose and gave her a standing ovation. The camera panned the crowd and settled on a sullen young woman in a chair (played by the actual Nan Davis), perfunctorily applauding the achievement. It was as if Nan had succeeded while this student had failed.

First Steps was a long and fragmented film that quietly stated life without walking was only a half-life.

Trapper John, M.D. / "A Wheel in a Wheel" / Dec. 1, 1985 / CBS-TV

Executive Producer: Don Brinkley
Producers: Deborah Zoe Dawson
   & Victoria Johns
Director: Michael Caffey

* Wheelchair-User
* Single White Female
* Equipment: Car hand controls

Wheelchair-Users

Writers: Gene O'Neill & Noreen Tobin
Category: Series Television — Medical Drama

Plot: A recently-disabled nurse attempts to return to work at San Francisco General in a wheelchair.

Nurse Maggie Morrow returns to work at San Francisco General six months after an accident without telling anyone she now uses a wheelchair. Nursing staff supervisor Ernestine Shoop is blunt.

> ERNIE: You don't really expect to go back on the floor like this, do you?

Patients and staff complain about the nurse on wheels. Administrator Hackett is vocal in her complaints to Ernie.

> ERNIE: The woman has a right to practice her profession.

> HACKETT: ...we're talking about an employee who may be a hazard to staff and patients.

Maggie tells Doctor JT McIntyre that she believes she will walk again. After all, she can now move her foot a little.

She is placed on a desk duty after missing an important deadline to change a seriously ill patient's IV bottle. Maggie had fallen in the physical therapy room, trying to walk. JT tells Maggie her hope for a cure is wishful thinking. The nurse doesn't show up for work. Ernie goes to Maggie's apartment.

> ERNIE: So you don't like to hear you have a limitation, Maggie. Who does?

> MAGGIE: Ernie, you don't understand ... I had something to hope for. That's all that kept me going. And now it's gone. And *yes,* I am angry ... I've heard about the process a thousand times. First is denial, then depression, then anger—

> ERNIE: Then resolution.

> MAGGIE: If resolution means nursing from a desk for the rest of my life—

Ernie becomes the non-disabled catalyst.

> ERNIE: Resolution means getting up off the dime and back into living.... When you decide to get on with your career, let me know.

Maggie returns to work. Ernie assigns her to the "Rehabilitation Therapy Unit."

* * *

"A Wheel in a Wheel" was a somewhat progressive piece. In it, a professional faced rejection when returning to work after her accident. However, the staple elements held it back: Maggie's not telling anyone she was disabled; her fervent belief that she would walk again; and her anger.

Maggie was depicted as a cheery, attractive young woman who caught young Doctor JT's eye. The two became friends. JT acknowledged Maggie's limitation in a nice scene where he plunked himself into a hospital wheelchair to join her in a game of basketball. She was stubborn and brash and strong-willed. Maggie made good points that her disability hadn't hindered her nursing skills. A left-handed mention of physical and attitudinal barriers could be perceived when Ernie told Maggie the hospital wasn't "equipped for you."

It seemed rather unrealistic that Maggie would return to work and fully expect her duties be restored, particularly when the administration and staff had no idea about her limitation. Had it been mentioned that she was fearful of losing her job by the disclosure or had she actually lost it, then the story could have proceeded with a different flavor. As it seemed, Maggie kept mum about her difference because she hadn't accepted her limitation, as Ernie pointed out to her. The disability was her personal problem. Her wrestling with the staff became her protection from them probing too deeply.

"A Wheel in a Wheel" used fairly upbeat imagery and should be recognized for the attempt to approach disability from a different side—that of the recently-disabled professional attempting to get back to work. It also never escaped formula.

The Hitchhiker / "Killer" / 1985

Producer: Riff Markowitz; Lewis Chester
Co-Producer: Jon Anderson
Director: Carl Schenkel
Story: Richard Rothstein & Christopher Leitch
Teleplay: April Campbell & Bruce Jones
Category: Cable Series Television
  —Mystery

* Wheelchair-User
* Single White Female

Plot: A young woman who uses a wheelchair is all alone in a house with a killer on her trail.

Twenty-three-year-old Meg Kinderley is out in the swimming pool of her family's large and elegant estate. While she is swimming in the pool, her family is murdered. Meg uses a power chair and goes up the ramp into the house. She makes a grisly discovery.

Meg gets a rifle. She finds the phones are dead. While using a lift to go upstairs, the electricity is cut and Meg is stranded halfway. She gets out of her chair and crawls up the stairs.

Her brother Jonathan is in the house. Meg corners him and kills him. *She is the killer.*

* * *

"Killer" was a confusing story. It was unclear how, if Meg was the killer, she committed murder while in the pool. Evidentally, she was psychotic and forgot she did these things. But how she did it was not important.

This piece started out to be another disabled-woman-as-victim story but turned out to be another embittered-disabled-character-on-the-rampage piece. Meg was recently disabled and although she appeared to be assimilating the changes in her life by resuming physical activities; while the family seemed adjusted to her by having a ramp installed as well as the stairway lift, things were not right. Meg took out her frustration on her family.

"Killer" was muddled and dark, presenting a picture of a disabled person as forever depressed and vengeful.

Remington Steele / "Steele, Inc." / Jan. 14, 1986 / NBC-TV

Executive Producer: Michael Gleason
Co-Executive Producer: Gareth Davies
Producer: Kevin Inch
Supervising Producer: Jeff Melvoin
Director: Don Weis
Writer: Brad Kern
Category: Series Television — Detective Drama

* Wheelchair-User
* White Female

Plot: Private investigators Remington Steele and Laura Holt are trying to find who killed a man who is listed on the morgue's rolls as "Remington Steele."

A rich, older woman in a wheelchair is one of the suspects in a hit-and-run murder. Negative aspects are expressed when an impersonator of the dashing Remington Steele locks her in a room with a gaseous substance, convinced she can walk. By literally smoking her out, he expects to find she does not require a wheelchair. He is wrong and the woman is unable to escape this "test."

The discovery that she cannot walk provides Remington Steele and Laura Holt with a telltale clue and reinforces a myth about persons using wheelchairs:

STEELE: How can a woman who can't walk—drive?

Laura concurs this is true.

* * *

"Steele, Inc." featured the character using the wheelchair in an almost-incidental role. Her disability was not discussed until the gassing scene, whereupon the two lead characters deduced and supported the fact that persons who do not walk are unable to drive. While this little segment was a neat tie-up of some loose ends within the story, it compounded a common myth that persons with disabilities are unable to drive.

"Steele, Inc." depended on stereotypical mythology to succeed.

Airwolf / "Tracks" / Mar. 22, 1986 / CBS-TV

Executive Producer: Bernard L. Kowalski
Producers: Alan Godfrey; Rick Kelbaugh
Co-Producers: Carol Gillson and Stephen A. Miller
Supervising Producer: Robert Janes
Director: Ron Stein
Writer: Rick Kelbaugh
Category: Television—Action Adventure

* Wheelchair-Users
* Group Portrayal; Multiracial
* Performers with Disabilities

Plot: A group of paraplegics on a mountain climb are stalked by an insane killer.

Stringfellow Hawke has agreed to act as "safety man" for a group of six men in chairs out to climb up San Jacinto Peak. Kirk, the leader of the group and Stringfellow Hawke's friend, trivializes the difficulties of physical access when he notes:

KIRK: What's a street curb—after you've climbed a mountain?

John, one of the hikers, talks with his wife.

WIFE: I'm still trying to figure out what you're trying to prove.

JOHN: Maybe nothing. Maybe everything.

The versatile group push their chairs uphill over rocky and uneven terrain. They set up camp. The Cat Man, a deranged mountaineer, sights the group and kills a member with his bow and arrow.

Hawke's radio has been damaged. He cannot call for help. The group starts down the mountain when Hawke is nicked by an arrow and tumbles down a hillside. John mobilizes the others into disabled catalyst roles. They rig a wheelchair on a rope and lower John down to Hawke. Hawke is rescued with a broken leg. The Airwolf supercopter flushes the deranged man out. The group jumps the killer.

* * *

"Tracks" utilized disabled characters who had personalities and different strengths. They were busy and active men. Hawke responded to them as equals. Even the rather bitter John was reminded that things were up to him. Success in getting off the mountain clearly depended on all involved, not just one character.

Formula popped up in the idea that in order to achieve a personal triumph over disability, the mountain had to be scaled. That was seen in Kirk's remark about the street curbs and in John's nebulous attempt to prove himself.

At least three of the characters were married. A black character was also the father of two adolescent children. Kirk and John were loved by their spouses; another was quite attracted to Hawke's co-worker Caitland and vice-versa.

The personalities illustrated in "Tracks" and the resourcefulness of the group made it easy to ignore shreds of old formula treatment of disability. By and large, "Tracks" was an adventure tale and not a disability story.

Fantasy Island / "The Golden Hour" / date unknown / ABC-TV

Executive Producer: Aaron Spelling; Leonard Goldberg
Producer: Arthur Rowe
Supervising Producer: Michael Fisher
Director: Earl Bellamy
Writer: Robert Earll
Category: Series Television — Fantasy Drama

* Wheelchair-User
* Single White Female

Plot: A woman's fantasy is for her wheelchair-using sister to meet the pen-pal whose sudden literary silence has plunged her deep into depression.

Sandi Larson and her sister arrive on Fantasy Island. The cause of Sandi's disability is described as an automobile accident which destroyed her modeling career. Fantasy Island host Mr. Roarke negatively describes Sandi's situation to Tattoo, his assistant.

> ROARKE: Her desire to live seemed paralyzed along with her legs until a year ago when she began a pen pal relationship with a man in

Fantasy Island

prison. His letters seemed to fill her with happiness and the desire to live and get well.... She never told her pen pal she was crippled. Then three months ago, his letters stopped coming.... She's been depressed ever since.

Linda Larson's fantasy is to cheer sister Sandi up. Sandi herself denotes more negatives of life in a chair by her glum statement:

> SANDI: I wish I *could* cheer up. But I keep thinking of all the things I can't do anymore.

Michael Banning is flown from military prison in Japan to Fort Leavenworth, Kansas. The plane develops trouble over Fantasy Island and is forced to land. Mike is under Fantasy Island jurisdiction and free to roam. He finds Sandi seated at a table with no wheelchair visible. He joins her.

> MIKE: We could take a walk, if you want, talk, some place in private.
>
> SANDI (quickly): No. No, this is fine.

Mr. Roarke shows up with her wheelchair.

> MR. ROARKE: I thought the two of you might want to move around.
>
> SANDI (upset): Mr. Roarke, how could you?... I want to go back to my bungalow.

Mr. Roarke acts as the non-disabled catalyst.

> MR. ROARKE: I suggest that our lagoon is much prettier. Why don't you take Miss Larson there?

Despite Sandi's protests, Mike takes her to the lagoon. She devalues herself to Mike, wondering why he stopped writing to her.

> SANDI: Since you didn't know about — [she indicates her chair] this thing — why did you stop writing?

Sandi confronts Mike with the news that his letters catalyzed her, got her out of a bed where she lay hoping to die. She demonstrates she can swim now. Not only that, she stands and shuffles three steps to tell Mike he has made a change in her life.

Sandi again employs devaluation in her description of their relationship.

> SANDI: A year ago, you didn't care about anybody. And I was a cripple. Now you tell me you love me and I've taken a couple of steps. I'd say together, we've done a great job.

Banning is being returned to Japan for a new parole hearing, doubtlessly orchestrated by Mr. Roarke.

* * *

"The Golden Hour" featured a woman with a disability as one who was bitter and helpless. Her life held little for her except the small shred of dignity and hope she had gained from the convict's letters.

This story was a typical "overcoming" piece. Being able to walk again had to do with non-wavering hope and strength of will. In Sandi's case, she had given up and had to overcome the personal problem.

"The Golden Hour" was a heartstring tugger, nothing more. There was no life for Sandi within her limitation.

Flipper / title, date unknown

Director: Frank McDonald
Teleplay: Orville Hampton
Category: Series Television—
   Family Adventure

* Wheelchair-User
* Single White Female

Plot: Bud and Sandy are excited to find in their midst famous waterskier Linda Granville, who is now in a wheelchair.

Bud and Sandy are thrilled to discover water skiing champ Linda Granville at the dock. She refuses to autograph her picture. Bud and Sandy then see Linda's wheelchair. The cause of Linda's disability is described as a water skiing mishap when a small motorboat "crashed into her." Her mother harbors guilt about the accident.

> MRS. GRANVILLE: You see, I was partly to blame. I pushed too hard for her success.

Mrs. Granville expresses too many medical opinions have caused Linda to lose hope. A doctor says he can help—

> MRS. GRANVILLE: —but he can't help her unless she's got the will to get well.

> MR. RICKS: She's that bitter.

> MRS. GRANVILLE: She's that disappointed.

Linda endangers the lives of herself and her mother when a hurricane blows in and she refuses to leave the shore area. After the storm, Linda returns to the dock in her chair, playing ball with Flipper. The dolphin gets caught in a net and struggles. Young Sandy tries to free him but needs help. He calls out to Linda.

SANDY: You'd sit there and let him drown!

Linda wheels to dock's edge. She sit-dives from her chair and slowly swims to help Sandy. Flipper is freed. Mr. Ricks dives in to bring her and Sandy in. The swim has an effect on Linda. She thinks she's getting better.

LINDA: I felt a sort of tingling when I tried to swim out to Flipper.

Linda and her mom leave to seek more medical attention.

BUD: And when you come back, you can teach us to waterski!

* * *

In this *Flipper* episode, disability was, again, a matter of not trying hard enough and giving up hope.

The disabled character in this piece was nasty, rude, mean, and miserable. Frankly, the audience could have considered it a treat had Linda kicked off during the storm. Instead, they were forced to suffer through her histrionics. There was no value in this piece whatsoever, nor was any factual information about life with a disability imparted.

Taxi / "The Reluctant Fighter" / date unknown / NBC-TV

Executive Producers: James L. Brooks; Stan Daniels; Ed. Weinberger
Producers: Glen & Les Charles
Director: James Burrows
Writer: Ken Estin
Category: Series Television — Situation Comedy

* Wheelchair-User
* White Male Child

Plot: Tony is going to box old champion Benny Foster and is afraid to beat him when he finds a boy with a disability is the inspiration for Benny's fight.

Sunshine Cab Company driver Tony has a boxing match scheduled. He is excited to meet old champion Benny Foster in the ring. He gets himself psyched up for the bout. Benny discusses his reasons for returning to fighting. It is due to the

BENNY: ...inspiration of a brave little guy.

A young boy named Brian comes in, using a wheelchair. Benny is Brian's hero; Foster wants to make a comeback for the boy.

Tony experiences incredible guilt. He wants to win; he is afraid to beat Foster and hurt Brian. He finally decides to go for it and beats Benny in the ring.

Tony talks to Brian after the fight. Brian tells Tony he has something he wants to give him. He lands a solid punch in Tony's gut, hand wrapped around "a ball bearing from my wheelchair." The active child chases Tony around the arena dressing room—before aligning himself with his new hero.

* * *

"The Reluctant Fighter" used an interesting approach to disability. Tony felt guilty even to *want* to beat Foster after he realized why the ex-champ was returning to the ring. Tony had been conditioned to want to win; he had also been conditioned to help those perceived as needing help. Brian caught him right in the middle. Despite Foster's heavy mental advantage, Tony went and fought—and won.

"The Reluctant Fighter" featured a rather obnoxious child who was a youngster first. The adults around him were the ones concerned about his physical condition.

Deafness

The inclusion of pieces with deaf characters appears in this book as a concession to the hearing world's perception of the deaf as "disabled." Deaf people do not consider themselves disabled. They describe themselves as having a communications difficulty or an "invisible handicap" which is not identified as some physical disabilities are. Some deaf people with whom I have discussed this project did not like the idea of an examination of screen deafness included in a book about disability. Inclusion here is a concession to the mainstream audience who imagine being deaf is the same as using a wheelchair or being blind. They are wrong.

Deafness is the most misunderstood of the popular categories of screen disability. This is due greatly to a continuous debate from educators of deaf children about the best way to teach them. Two widely diversified methods of communication have confused the hearing public and have found their way into popular depictions of deaf characters. A basic understanding of the communication modes is necessary.

A war has long been waged between educators of the deaf as to the best way to teach deaf children how to communicate. "Oralists" advocate teaching a child to speak with his/her voice and to receive communication by speechreading—deciphering lip and tongue movements, facial expressions and body language to obtain understanding. "Manualists" contend that sign language, a visual vocabulary made of handshapes, facial expressions, and spelled words is better. Characters using either mode of communication are seen onscreen but without appropriate interpretation of the anomalies inherit in each mode.

On the surface, oralism seems to be the best mode of communication to the hearing world. There are many deaf persons who communicate easily with hearing people through speech and speechreading.

Digging deeper, successful oralism depends on a variety of factors. Speech training is tedious and some people do not have the patience to perfect it. In some cases, successful training depends on financial capability. Training on a prescribed three-day-a-week basis is not cheap. If the support is not offered in school, if the instructor is not particularly good, children may not benefit. A child whose hearing was lost after learning to speak ("post-lingually deaf") will understand how to create speech, whereas a child born deaf or deafened before speech acquisition ("pre-lingually deaf") has to learn from scratch. The amount of residual hearing a child has also becomes a factor in the success of speech production and in the ability to decipher speech from physical cues.

These varying factors are added to an oft-quoted statistic about the physical visibility of English: 40 percent of the spoken language is visible on the lips. The best speechreaders get 80 percent of that forty. Regional accents, rapidity of speech, amount of obscuring facial hair, laughter and smiles are all variables to contend with. Understanding often depends on guesswork supplied by conversational context. Receptive speechreading is an art that is difficult to master. For some, the extraordinary concentration required is stressful.

Speech production also requires patience and training. Some deaf persons never achieve clear, understandable speech. They prefer not to use their voices which may bring looks of trepidation from hearing people. Or, they may speak but in an unmonitored fashion—unable to hear themselves—and require careful listening to be understandable. Ability to speak varies widely from person to person and is not a reflection of intelligence. However, "deaf-mute" or "deaf and dumb" is still used as a convenient term to describe a deaf person. In this work, such terminology is considered offensive as well as a misnomer.

Another form of communication is sign language. The visual language represents whole words or individual alphabet letters through signs and fingerspelling. The larger movements are produced and processed as quickly through the eyes as speech is through an average hearing ear. In its purest form, ASL (American Sign Language) is a language separate from English with its own grammar, syntax and slang. It differs from Signed English, a modified sign language used in some educational settings to relay information in proper English order to help deaf children with the difficult task of reading and writing a language they've never heard.

Sign language is considered by oralists as a barrier to the hearing world. Advocates for the manual method—particularly deaf people themselves—insist that early acquisition of sign allows a child to develop a language base. Speech will then be easier to learn as a "second language." Signing also permits early vocabulary acquisition. While oralists may spend a year with young deaf children to create a sound that will later be put in a word, children using manual signs can express thoughts. Oralists contend that manual deaf people will always be apart from the mainstream; manualists have a colorful historical and cultural heritage that is inaccessible to oralists. There is a schism between the two worlds. In a nutshell, it's a matter of language versus speech. ("Total Communication" has become the happy medium in some educational situations, using speech [for the oralists] and sign [for the manualists] simultaneously. The signs also help less-skilled speechreaders along by offering a physical cue.)

Schools for the deaf did not develop in the United States until the 1820s, bringing together heretofore isolated individuals into a cohesive unit and giving them a common language of signs. A kind of ethnic subculture has developed with its own language, history, and stories.

In general, the (manual) deaf prefer, like immigrants from other countries, to socialize in enclaves to celebrate and commune with their common language and heritage. Evidence of a deaf community is one of the elements sadly lacking in screen imagery of the deaf.

The potential for dramatic conflict and situations regarding deafness in realistic fashion is almost limitless to those writers wishing to explore. Yet, the common devaluation stories seen in blindness portrayals or wheelchair-user stories abound onscreen. Also seen are many stories of a hearing person becoming the non-disabled catalyst and taking a deaf character under wing to give him/her language. As can be surmised by the brief explanation above, one can assume it is not an easy task. But onscreen, armed with a sign language book and fifteen minutes of patience, any character can effortlessly educate a deaf person. This is tired and poorly conceived. It trivializes the difficulty presented by "the glass wall" as some call the unseen barrier between the deaf and the hearing.

Another trivialization is the concept of the deaf person who does not use his/her voice and, within the story, must learn to speak. This suggests that speech is the only important system of communication, thus denying the existence of a vital community unto itself as well as the validity and heritage of sign language.

This heritage and background is invalidated in the screen stories where music is a focal point: a deaf dancer who can't hear music; a deaf person who falls in love with a musician, etc. At this writing, one major studio in Southern California has a script ready about a deaf girl who wants to hear music!

Another popular stereotypical scene is one I lightly term as the "almost-getting-killed" scene. In it, a deaf person unknowingly walks in the path of a speeding car, out-of-control horse or bicycle. The character narrowly avoids disaster. This suggests deaf people are completely unaware of dangers in their surroundings (insurance companies back up statistics that deaf drivers have better driving records than the hearing—simply because they are so visually-oriented).

As noted, deaf people *are* permitted to drive. This is rarely illustrated onscreen—perhaps because the writer is not sure if it is permitted. And, in one piece, it is blatantly stated that the deaf character is "not supposed to drive!"

In this category of "Deafness," some characters will be described as "Hearing Impaired." This is an unscientific description I am using to note characters who have hearing that is not functioning in an average manner.

Communication methods of deaf characters will be noted in each review. "Expressive" denotes method of self-expression; "Receptive" details how information is received. The methods used are the following:

Speech—Communicating by voice.

Speechreading—Deciphering lip and tongue movements as well as facial expressions and body language to understand.

Sign—Utilizing manual means to express or receive language.

Writing/Reading—Method used by a character who puts thought across to hearing people by writing, typing, etc. and reading their responses the same way.

Gesture — Natural gestures used to put a point across to another person.

"None" refers to characters who use no communication.

[NOTE: The term "native speaker" will pop up within this section. It refers to a deaf performer *or* a hearing performer who learned sign language as his/her first language. In the case of a hearing person, it usually means his/her own family was deaf and sign was the preferred method of communication.]

Special Equipment utilized by characters who are deaf is described here.

Flashing Light Alerts — Devices hooked up to a doorbell or telephone causing a light to flash with the electrical pulse of a buzz or a ring. A "Baby Alert" is a sound sensor placed near a baby. When the baby cries, lights will flash.

Interpreter — A person, usually hearing, who acts as a communications facilitator between deaf and hearing persons and does not inject his/her own opinions, feelings or emotions into the subject. Interpreters act as a neutral relay (in the purest most professional sense).

TTY/TDD — A TTY is a Teletypewriter, an old bulky piece of equipment discarded from companies such as Western Union. In the late 1960s, use of a telephone modem hooked up to a TTY permitted deaf people to use the telephone to call others who had a TTY and type their messages back and forth. The new generation of microchip technology has brought the TDD (Telecommunications Device for the Deaf) into most deaf households. The TDD is a small, attractive electronic machine with a built-in modem used in tandem with a standard desk-set telephone. It is extremely portable.

Hearing Ear Dog — A specially trained dog that acts as an alert to crying babies, knocks at doors, or ringing telephones to those people who require a non-audio alert and prefer canine companionship and security.

In addition to the programs listed, other characters who are deaf can be found in the reviews of *Buck Rogers in the 25th Century,* "Return of the Fighting 69th"; *Code Red,* "Dark Fire"; and *The Twilight Zone,* "Healer."

Johnny Belinda / 1948 / Warner Bros.

Producer: Jerry Wald
Director: Jean Negulesco
Screenplay: Irmgard Von Cube

* Deafness
* Single White Female
* Communication: Expressive —

and Allen Vincent
From the Stage Play by: Elmer Harris
Category: Feature Film — Drama

Sign; Receptive — Sign/Speechreading

Plot: A deaf woman is accused of murdering the rapist who has tried to kidnap "his" son from her.

Helping out at the MacDonald farm, young idealistic Doctor Richardson makes a request of a young woman.

    MacDONALD: She can't hear you. She's deaf — and dumb.

The cause of daughter Belinda's deafness is described as a high fever in infancy.

Richardson once interned with deaf children. He becomes the nondisabled catalyst and uses signs to break through to Belinda. She learns language with rapidity. MacDonald is amazed to learn his daughter can communicate. He asks Richardson how to sign "daughter."

Roguish Laughlin McCormick goes on a drunken bender after an argument with his fiancée, Stella. He rapes Belinda. She is pregnant with his child. An erroneous concept is presented when she silently endures a painful labor.

    AGGIE: Her not makin' a sound — it's uncanny.

The MacDonalds are shunned after Belinda delivers a boy. Richardson offers to marry Belinda. MacDonald devalues his daughter.

    MacDONALD: You only feel a kind of pity for her.

Led by Stella and Laughlin, the townsfolk vote to remove baby Johnny from his mother. Laughlin goes to get the baby. Belinda kills him and is tried for murder. A conviction is imminent until Stella spills all in a burst of conscience.

    *   *   *

Johnny Belinda was an intriguing movie, utilizing prejudices within a remote community to create a dramatic situation. Despite Belinda's rapid proficiency in learning sign from the kind doctor, it was a little far-fetched that she could master speechreading and writing to the extent displayed in the film.

Special equipment was misused when, in court, a sign language interpreter interpreted only questions to Belinda and none of the proceedings.

Although this film was a fair portrait of one deaf person in one situation, it became sort of a Rosetta Stone for later deaf portrayals, as will be seen. At least two remakes have appeared, and in 1986, one studio in Hollywood was discussing remaking it again.

Johnny Belinda treated a deaf young woman as a person with emotions and feelings. It was also written entirely from the hearing person's point of view.

Sincerely Yours / 1955 / Warner Bros.

Director: Gordon Douglas
Screenplay: Irving Wallace
From a Play by: Jules Eckert Goodman
Category: Feature Film—Drama

* Deafness
* Single White Male
* Communication: Expressive—Speech; Receptive—Speechreading
* New Disability

Plot: A pianist loses his hearing.

Concert performer Anthony Warren is gradually losing his hearing due to otosclerosis. Just minutes before his big Carnegie Hall debut, he becomes completely deaf. He uses poor language as he tells his entourage to call off the show.

> TONY: It's no use. Tell [the audience] to go home. I'm deaf, stone deaf.

* * *

Sincerely Yours was a long and soapy drama remake of the 1932 film *The Man Who Played God*. Its main difference was the fact that Tony Warren actively received a few minutes of speechreading training onscreen before demonstrating his remarkable prowess and using it to help the unfortunate. The musical aspects were played for every tear in the book.

Sincerely Yours was an emotional exercise and not a realistic portrayal of the newly-deafened. It wasn't much of a movie, either.

Bonanza / "Silent Thunder" / Dec. 10, 1960 / NBC-TV

Producer: David Dortort
Director: Robert Altman
Writer: John Furia, Jr.
Category: Series Television—Western

* Deafness
* Single White Female
* Communication: Expressive and Receptive—Sign

Plot: Little Joe teaches a deaf girl sign language.

Little Joe Cartright champions Annie Croft, a young deaf woman who dresses in rags and herds lambs. He protects her from Alvy, a cruel, oafish man. Joe brings her a doll for a present. Sam, her father, snorts to Joe:

SAM: Waste of time bringing her anything . . . can't hear, can't talk, don't understand no more than them dumb beasts she tends.

Sam feels Annie is a punishment for his past.
Alvy approaches Annie and takes the doll. He rips the eye off. Annie refuses to be kissed.

ALVY: You can't hear, you can't talk, haven't you got any feelings?

Annie gets a coin from her father's money pouch to replace the doll's eye button. Sam believes she is stealing.

SAM: At least if you can't hear, I know you can feel. . . . Thou shalt not steal!

An erroneous concept is presented as Annie endures a switching in silence.
Joe acts as a non-disabled catalyst by getting a sign language book. He takes on the responsibility of teaching Annie to communicate and expressing to Sam that his daughter is capable of learning. Sam gains respect for her.
Negative aspects are seen as Annie crosses the street, unaware a runaway team is heading for her. She narrowly misses death in an "almost-getting-killed" scene. Annie is grateful to Joe for his help.

ANNIE (signing): You help me talk. I love you.

When Joe tells her he doesn't love her, she runs off. When Sam searches for her, Alvy knocks him off a cliff, intending to kill him. In a showdown between Joe and Alvy, Joe emerges the victor when Alvy stumbles off a ledge.
Sam will be fine. When Annie signs that she loves her father, Sam asks to learn the sign for "daughter."

* * *

"Silent Thunder" felt all the world like a low-budget remake of *Johnny Belinda*. Annie never evidenced frustration when persons like Joe or Alvy or even her father would discourse on at length. She just cocked her head, watched with wide, innocent eyes and appeared to be little more than a child, a characteristic reinforced by Joe's inappropriate gift of a rag doll.
"Silent Thunder" was routine, played for all the drama it could drum up.

The Heart Is a Lonely Hunter / 1968 / Warner Bros.–Seven Arts

Executive Producer: Joel Freeman
Producers: Thomas C. Ryan and

* Deafness
* Single White Male

Marc Merson
Director: Robert Ellis Miller
Screenplay: Thomas C. Ryan
From the Novel by: Carson McCullers
Category: Feature Film — Drama

* Communication: Expressive — Notewriting/Sign; Receptive — Speechreading/Sign

Plot: A lonely deaf man becomes a listening post for people with problems.

John Singer, a man who is deaf, moves to a new town to be closer to the state hospital where his only friend, deaf Spiros Antonopoulis, has been committed. Singer rents a room from the Kelly family who needs money. Mr. Singer's card announces "I am a deaf mute." Fifteen-year-old Mick has had to give up her room for rent. She uses questionable vocabulary in describing the situation.

> MICK: ...a deaf mute person ... a dummy ... creepy having a dummy in my room.

Singer takes his meals at a cafe where a drunk man goes on a rampage and ends up hurting himself by ramming his body into a wall. A black doctor who is an onlooker refuses to treat anyone other than "my own." Mr. Singer gives the physician his card and gets his assistance. Mr. Singer takes the injured man home and pays attention as the man rambles on about his life. Upon awakening in the morning, the fellow is surprised to be given a card by Mr. Singer.

> MAN: A mute? Kee-rist. And I thought all this time you was a good listener!

Mr. Singer approaches the doctor to try and pay for the emergency attention. The doctor refuses.

> DOCTOR: ...if anyone knew about it, I'd be called uppity. Lucky thing for me you can't talk.

Mr. Singer is insulted and storms off. The doctor approaches him to apologize and asks Singer if he will talk to a "deaf mute" patient of the doctor's to find out more about his medical problem.

Understanding how much young Mick likes music, Mr. Singer buys a phonograph and records for her. She spends time in his room, listening to symphonies.

The man who had injured himself leaves town. He bids Singer farewell. He uses pejorative language.

> MAN: Man, I could talk to you. And you listened. You old dummy, you really listened.

The black doctor shares a secret with Singer: he has cancer. He is amazed that he, the man who has always hated whites, shares his secret with a white man.

Singer takes Antonopoulis off the hospital grounds for an outing and is embarrassed by the gross and erratic behavior his friend exhibits in a restaurant. Singer arrives home lonely and depressed, where a lonely and depressed Mick turns to him for comfort. Unable to tolerate his own pain, Singer kills himself.

* * *

The Heart Is a Lonely Hunter was a curious study of a deaf man. Mr. Singer was a metaphor, a characterization of silent wisdom. The quiet and tidy man polished his chess board and tended to his friends.

Mr. Singer was eternally isolated. No acknowledgment was made of a deaf community. The only other deaf person he knew, it seemed, was Antonopoulis, a fat, greedy and emotionally disturbed man. Singer's separateness attracted the confidences of a growing girl, a troubled drunk, and a proud but prejudiced doctor. All confided in him, it seemed, under the assumption he would never tell anyone else what he knew.

In a sense, Mr. Singer was a disabled catalyst. He helped the drunken man straighten himself out. It was Singer's own pride that caused the stiff-necked doctor to lower his own defenses. And, in a summer of difficulty for Mick, he became the one person she could trust. However, Singer did not really help generate positive action. The others talked to him and purged their thoughts. Thusly cleansed, they moved on.

Prior to relocation in the southern town, Singer was illustrated as employed, doing careful monogramming on porcelain gift plates. After moving, he paid rent, purchased a record player and records, offered to pay the doctor — but was never seen working. His source of income was not described.

The Heart Is a Lonely Hunter was a sad and ultimately tragic depiction of a man who was seen more as an oddity than as a contributing member of society.

Here Come the Brides / "Absalom, Absalom" / 1969 / ABC-TV

Executive Producer: Bob Claver
Producers: Paul Junger Witt and
   Stan Schwimmer
Director: Paul Junger Witt
Writer: Michael Fisher
Category: Series Television —
   Romantic Period Drama

* Deafness
* White Male Child
* Communication: None

Plot: Jeremy Bolt befriends a deaf youngster and accepts the responsibility of teaching him to speak.

In the 1870s, Mr. Phineas Beef brings the three Bolt brothers a "gift" from a wild mountain man who has just died—a deaf boy in a cage. The wild man's last wish was for Jason Bolt to assume responsibility for his deaf son. Absalom is completely untamed. Jeremy Bolt feels empathy with Absalom due to his own problem of chronic stuttering.

A school for the deaf will not accept Absalom because he cannot speak. Jeremy decides to teach the child to speak so the school will accept him. Light dawns and Absalom learns to make sounds by placing his hand on Jeremy's lips and throat and imitating them. He makes great progress. Jeremy and his girlfriend take Absalom on a picnic with other children. Absalom shoves little Christopher out of danger when he sees a snake. Christopher falls, unconscious. Jeremy angrily shakes Absalom and the boy runs away. Jeremy gives up his crusade. Absalom returns. Jeremy has discovered the reason for Absalom's "violence" and feels regret.

Absalom's uncle Oliver arrives in Seattle, intending to take Absalom and commit him to an institution. When he finds that Absalom is learning to speak, he is deeply moved. Absalom is accepted at the crowded school for the deaf. Jeremy bids an emotional farewell to his young friend.

* * *

"Absalom, Absalom" was an unrealistic story. Its basic premise was that with only patience and care, a deaf child could be taught to speak.

Sister Agnes, the teacher of the deaf, indicated prejudice and denial of education for deaf children, expressing that some parents tried to pretend their children did not exist and hid them away. Her school was packed due to the lack of education elsewhere.

"Absalom, Absalom" was a pleasant piece with little understanding or information about the deaf included during the story.

The Waltons / "The Foundling" / Sept. 14, 1972 / CBS-TV

Writer: John McGreevey
Category: Series Television—
  Period Family Drama

* Deafness
* White Female Child
* Communication: None

Plot: The Waltons find an abandoned deaf child.

The Waltons find a child on their doorstep. Her name is Holly, says a note pinned to her. There is something different about her.

LIVVY: She hasn't said a word ... like there's a wall around her.

The Waltons

Olivia Walton discerns that Holly is deaf. A doctor concurs.

> DOCTOR: [She's a] perfectly normal child—except she's deaf ... that's why she never learned to talk ... she can be taught to communicate.
>
> LIVVY: Talkin' with their hands—I've seen it. It's beautiful, like the wings of birds.
>
> DOCTOR: Maybe someone will spare a few minutes a day to help her.

Oldest sister Mary Ellen Walton is unsuccessful in trying to teach Holly to fingerspell.

Holly's poor backwoods parents keep a surreptitious eye on their daughter.

> HOLLY'S FATHER: She's got to be put away.
>
> MOTHER: Never!
>
> FATHER: ...[She's] a throwback.
>
> MOTHER: She's smart as anyone.

Holly is left out and alone when the family sits around the radio and enjoys a program. She runs upstairs and cries without audible sobs. John-Boy follows her upstairs. He becomes the non-disabled catalyst as he begins to sign with her.

> JOHN-BOY: ...what it must be like not to hear the radio, birds singing ... too bad missing all that but you can't go through life sad.

When Elizabeth is accidentally locked in a trunk, it is Holly and her newfound ability to communicate which gets help to her. Convinced she can learn, Holly's parents take her back.

* * *

"The Foundling" was another variation on the *Johnny Belinda* theme that anyone with patience can teach a deaf child/person the concepts of language—if one's heart is big enough.

Holly's progress in learning sign language was much too rapid. Her father's pejorative description of her could be considered acceptable due to the character's background and economic status but it was quite tired.

"The Foundling" possessed nothing new or different.

Joyous Sound / 1974

Executive Producer: Robert Golden
Producers: Bonita Granville Wrather, William Beaudine, Jr.
Directors: Jack Wrather, Jack B. Hively, Dick Moder
Writers: Robert Schaefer, Eric Freiwald
Category: Made-for-TV Movie—Drama

* Deafness
* White Female Teenager
* Cure
* Communication: Expressive—Speech; Receptive—Speechreading

(Note: This "movie" was made by editing and joining three episodes of the *Lassie* TV series.)

Plot: An operation might restore a deaf girl's hearing, but in her vulnerable state, no one wants to tell her Lassie is missing.

Elaine Baker watches her adolescent deaf daughter Lucy play with Lassie. She tells Keith that a doctor in Los Angeles thinks Lucy may be able to hear with surgery.

> ELAINE: What if there's no miracle?
>
> KEITH: ...she's suffered a difficulty with courage and dignity. I'm sure that whatever life has to offer her, good or bad, she'll suffer with the same courage and dignity. If there's a chance for a cure, she's entitled to that chance.

Lucy tells Lassie she wants to be able to hear the dog barking.
In Los Angeles, the doctor has determined Lucy is a candidate for surgery. He will operate the next day. Lassie, waiting outside the hospital, takes a walk and gets disoriented and lost.
Lucy undergoes surgery. Doctor Robbins stops at Keith's ranch where Lucy and her mother are staying to remove surgical packing from Lucy's ears. She can't hear. The doctor says swelling is the culprit. Lucy tells her mother and the doctor to be optimistic. Lucy has guessed that Lassie is missing.
While out in a meadow, Lucy's hearing returns and Lassie, back from an odyssey, returns and runs to her.

* * *

Joyous Sound was a syrupy picture of a deaf teen. Lucy was sweet, optimistic, patient, able to speechread anything. She could have won the Daughter of the Year Award—in short, she was not a real person. She was forever courageous and an eternal inspiration to all around her, as judging from Keith's gushy speech. Frankly, Lassie's role in the film was much more interesting and deserving of audience compassion than Lucy's!

Joyous Sound was a saccharine piece written from a hearing person's point of view.

Baretta / "Shoes" / Oct. 27, 1976 / ABC-TV

Writers: Lewis Davidsen & Tony Kayden
Category: Series Television—Police Drama

* Deafness
* Single White Male
* Communication: None

Plot: A deaf shoeshine boy is the only witness to the rape of a nun.

A girl is killed in Tony Baretta's rough side of town. Tony goes to a pool hall trying to dig up information. He talks to Shoes, a young man who doesn't respond. An onlooker uses poor language when he snorts:

ONLOOKER: Talkin' to the dummy.

A man attacks and rapes a nun. Shoes is unaware of the crime. Alerted by some vibrations, the deaf young man chases the culprit and is hurt by the same. The assaulted nun sees him and takes him to the hospital. She runs off, fearful of admitting what has happened. Tony discovers "Shoes" is a deaf shoeshine boy. He uses pejorative terminology to affirm what he's just learned.

TONY: This guy's a deaf mute.

Tony uses Shoes to help track the victimized nun as well as the criminal. He is about to become a victim himself but Shoes tackles the man.

Olive the nun has become interested in deafness. She and Shoes are going to go to school together.

OLIVE: We're going to learn to talk to each other at the same time.

* * *

"Shoes" portrayed a deaf person as lackluster, with limited intelligence, dull and devoid of human emotions or desires. The stereotype seen in "Shoes" was quite disheartening; even more so when noting its vintage.

Starsky and Hutch / "Silence" / 1976

Executive Producers: Aaron Spelling and Leonard Goldberg

* Deafness
* Single White Male (#1)

208   Deafness

Producer: Joseph T. Naar
Director: George McCowan
Story: Donald R. Boyle
Teleplay: Parke Perine

* Single Black Male (#2)
* Communication: Expressive — Fingerspelling/Sign; Receptive — Speechreading

Plot: A deaf man is used as a patsy in a series of crimes.

Detective Hutchinson books two petty thieves. Larry and RC are both ex-cons who are deaf. They live at a halfway house run by Father Ignatius. The cause of RC's hearing loss is discussed.

> IGNATIUS: RC lost his speech and hearing in a prison riot when a guard worked over his head with a billy club.

Larry is illustrated as a simple, gentle man who loves kittens. Ignatius uses that to disclaim Starsky and Hutch's hunch that Larry is behind a series of crimes.

> IGNATIUS: Sweet, smiling kitten lover Larry? ... you know Larry's a deaf-mute. It'd make him a lousy burglar ... they can't hear you so you shouldn't have any trouble sneaking up on them.

Starsky and Hutch learn Larry is an unwitting front man for Father Ignatius, who is actually a con named Bessenger. RC, who works in a print shop, agrees to help the cops find Larry.

Captain Doby calls in an APB on Larry without ever mentioning he is deaf. All criminals are caught and another crime is solved.

* * *

"Silence" used a sweet, innocent and unworldly deaf character as a pawn to a quick-thinking con. Both Larry and RC had amazing speechreading capacities. They never missed a phrase or a word.

Captain Doby was setting himself up for lawsuit possibilities by not informing his troops they were searching for a deaf person who could easily be shot for "failure" to respond.

"Silence" painted a picture of deaf persons as a lower subculture of society with little personality or initiative — except to make kittens and other people happy.

The Hardy Boys / "The Mystery of the Silent Scream" / Nov. 27, 1977 / ABC-TV

Story: Alan Godfrey; Michael Sloan

* Deafness
* Single White Female

The Hardy Boys

Writers: Joe Doston & Michael Sloan
Category: Series Television — Mystery

* **Communication:** Expressive — Sign; Receptive — Speechreading

Plot: A deaf girl speechreads of a scheme to blow up a Las Vegas casino and enlists the help of the Hardy Boys.

Deaf Allycia and her hearing cousin Sally are driving to Las Vegas for a vacation. At a gas station, Sally gets out of the car. Allycia glances around. She speechreads a man speaking into a telephone, some distance away in a phone booth. Without contextual clues, Allycia learns he is threatening to blow up a Las Vegas casino. Frightened, Allycia honks the horn to get Sally's attention. As Sally gets close, Allycia slides behind the wheel and tears off as her cousin gets in. A myth about deafness is perpetuated.

SALLY: You KNOW you're not supposed to drive!

In Las Vegas, the girls become involved with Joe and Frank, the mystery-solving Hardy brothers. Joe is angry when Allycia doesn't respond to him. He grabs her and turns her around.

JOE: Answer me!

SALLY: She can't hear you. She's deaf.... Allycia was driving ... she's not supposed to.

Sally is overprotective of Allycia.

SALLY: Allycia's a vulnerable girl ... pity she can do without.

Allycia is in danger. The man from the phone booth has seen her and recognized her. He sees her signing.

STORCH: The girl's deaf.... She read my lips.

Allycia is taken by the criminals and it is up to the Hardy Boys to find and save her — which they do.

*   *   *

"The Mystery of the Silent Scream" was a "high-concept" story, one that can be summed up in one sentence: "A deaf girl speechreads of a crime and sets out to halt it." Allycia's speechreading was amazing, not hindered at all by distance, lack of context, a person speaking over their shoulder, not facing her or standing sideways.

Use of an actress with minimal signing ability (doubtlessly learned just prior to shooting and rendered poorly) helped establish sign language as an awkward form of communication.

The myth that deaf persons have no usable voice was reinforced as Allycia screamed soundlessly when being abducted by the bad guys.

"The Mystery of the Silent Scream" depended on stereotypical mythology to succeed. There was no understanding about deaf persons past long-established screen images.

James at 15 / "Actions Speak Louder" / Jan. 11, 1978 / NBC-TV

Producer: Martin Manulis, Joseph Hardy
Writer: Ron Rubin
Category: Series Television—Drama

* Deafness
* White Male Teenager
* Equipment: Interpreter
* Deaf Performer
* Communication: Expressive—Sign; Receptive—Sign

Plot: A deaf teen wishes to attend James' public school instead of the special school to which he has always gone.

James Hunter's friend Scott wants to attend James' school, much to the objections of his mother. James' father is told of the situation. Accessibility is an issue he is familiar with.

>MR. HUNTER: New law ... guarantees the handicapped can go to any school....

Mr. Hunter supports Scott's desire but notes to his son that Scott's written "English is not good."

>JAMES: English is a foreign language for him ... never heard a word in his life.

Scott gets into the school. He wants to try out for the soccer team. Scott meets an attitudinal barrier in the person of the coach who uses pejorative terminology.

>COACH: What's the matter? Can't he talk?... Deaf and dumb....

>JAMES: No, he's deaf.

When the coach indicates he has "enough trouble with normal kids," James and his friends get an article printed in the school paper labeling the coach as a bigot. The coach has to let Scott try out. He makes the team.

Life in a hearing environment is not always easy as Scott discovers at a party. He is left out when the other kids turn on the TV and listen to music. He asks Cheri to dance.

> CHERI: Dance? But he can't hear the music!... I don't want some deaf and dumb guy touching me. It makes me sick!

The disappointments cause Scott to want to pull out of the new school. His mother is overprotective. She perpetuates the image of the silent deaf and drags out negative aspects of deafness when she talks to James.

> MOTHER: ... [Scott] cries—doesn't make a sound ... the hearing world has nothing to offer him but pain—the sooner he learns, the better.... Do you know what it's like to be deaf?... Do you know what it's like to be Scott?

James attempts to understand what it is like to be deaf. He stuffs up his ears with ear plugs and ear muffs and can't hear. He goes to the park, sees a street band playing and can't hear the music. He is unable to hear people yelling at him.

Scott helps push the soccer team to victory and himself closer to being accepted by his hearing peers.

* * *

"Actions Speak Louder" was an innovative story. Research on deafness was evident all through the story although it did delve into formula concepts at times, particularly the speeches by Scott's mother. It briefly indicated there was legislation providing public school access to children with disabilities. It expressed that Scott's integration into a public school was rocky but, for him, had its benefits.

Poor language was used by Cheri, but she functioned as a mouthpiece for irrational prejudice.

James' attempt to understand deafness by clogging up his ears was a nice touch, although very unrealistic and melodramatic. The scene would have played better had a deaf catalyst been able to explain to James a deaf person's perspective on the hearing world. As it was, James' "impaired" hearing resulted in evoking pity for Scott.

Actual deaf students were seen in the background at Scott's segregated school. The use of a native speaker in the role of a deaf person was a plus, expertly utilizing sign language and facial expressions to enhance his performance.

"Actions Speak Louder" deserves credit for displaying an issue of relevance to both the deaf and hearing communities.

ABC Afterschool Special / "Mom and Dad Can't Hear Me" / Apr. 5, 1978 / ABC-TV

Executive Producer: Daniel Wilson
Producer: Fran Sears
Director: Larry Elikann
Teleplay: Irma Reichert and Daryl Warner
Category: Made-for-TV Movie—Children's

* Deafness
* Married White Couple
* Communication: Expressive—Sign/Speech; Receptive—Sign/Speechreading
* Equipment: Light alerts for doorbell, alarm clock, TTY

Plot: A hearing girl is ashamed of her deaf parents.

New kid Charlotte "Charlie" Meredith is afraid to tell friends her parents are deaf. At pal David's house, Charlie stops him from telling his brother to quiet down. Strange connotations about life in a deaf household are suggested.

> DAVID: You like noise?
>
> CHARLIE: Yes.

Cousin Martha comes over and puts make-up on Charlie. Charlie recalls staying with Martha's family when she was a little girl and not wanting to leave. More curious ideas about a deaf household surface.

> CHARLIE: Television, music, people laughing all that—I remember, I cried and cried when I had to go back home. It's awful, isn't it? I mean, not wanting to go back to your home and all that quiet again.

Charlie's parents demand she remove the make-up. Charlie runs crying to her room. She sobs to Martha:

> CHARLIE: It's just that they don't have any idea of what's going on in the world. And they're never gonna learn.

Charlie tells lie after lie at school to avoid admitting her parents are deaf. She attacks her angry parents when she stays out late without permission.

> CHARLIE: Why shouldn't I have a life like other kids?... I can't help it if you don't understand how normal people live.

Charlie tells a popular girl that the woman with whom she was signing at a store was her housekeeper. After that, she breaks down and tells her friends that both her parents are deaf. She devalues her family.

CHARLIE: We're all freaks!

Charlie runs home and admits to her parents she's been ashamed of them and lied to her friends.

* * *

"Mom and Dad Can't Hear Me" was meant to be a sensitive drama about misunderstanding between deaf parents and a hearing child. It missed the mark by miles. Charlie believed that her parents were "weird" because they were deaf. It never occurred to her that they were just parents. It probably never occurred to the audience, either, since so many erroneous ideas were presented.

Charlie, it seemed, lived in a drab and silent world. She indicated she had never learned to dance, couldn't speak as a child, didn't have a TV or radio, didn't hear the everyday noise of people living because her parents were deaf. All of the above misled the audience.

The film emphasized differences, not sameness. Martha tried to tell Charlie that she fought with her own parents, too—but Charlie continued to believe her problems were rooted in deafness. The audience was never completely clued in.

The story was careful to define that Charlie's parents could speak, but were unable to monitor their voices. A nice selection of light alerts—for notification when doorbell, phone, or alarm clock rang—were clearly illustrated. The TTY was shown and nicely explained.

The hearing actors playing the parents used sign language badly. Misuse of special equipment was evident since signs were wielded jerkily and awkwardly. The signs Charlie used were similarly rendered. The use of hearing actors in this piece was a sore spot with the deaf community. Two deaf actors were originally cast, only to be told at the last minute that hearing actors had been selected to replace them.

"Mom and Dad Can't Hear Me" intended to be a story about the difficulties of growing up with the added facet of the parents being deaf. However, it came off as something quite different and negative. Charlie understood she was wrong. However, her realization may have come too late to help the audience understand the problem was *hers*—and not her parents' deafness.

"And Your Name Is Jonah" / Feb. 1979 / CBS-TV

Executive Producer: Charles Fries
Producers: Stanley Rubin & Norman Felton
Director: Richard Michaels
Writer: Michael Bortman
Category: Made-for-TV Movie—Drama

* Deafness
* White Male Child
* Deaf Performer
* Communication: None

Plot: A family discovers their institutionalized "retarded" son is, in fact, "only deaf."

The young Corelli family learns ten-year-old Jonah, who is in an institution with developmentally disabled children, was misdiagnosed. He is, in fact, "only deaf." Familial and emotional distress ensue as they try to cope with a child with whom they cannot communicate. Jenny Corelli enrolls Jonah in oral school and works hard with him at home.

Jonah's behavior is hard to fathom. Without a way to express himself, he reacts in bizarre ways that scare the family, such as placing his little brother's Spiderman doll into the oven since the scary face haunted him. Such actions break the family up.

Frustrated with Jonah's utter lack of progress in learning to speak and speechread, as well as her own inability to impart the simplest concepts to him, Jenny Corelli approaches a deaf couple she sees signing on the street. She asks for help. The couple act as the disabled catalysts, bringing Jenny to a social club where she sees deaf people laughing, talking and having a good time — and using sign language. With their help, Jonah begins to learn to sign — and at last, Jenny can tell her son that she loves him.

* * *

"And Your Name Is Jonah" was a powerful drama. It utilized a rarely seen focal point — illustrating the long war waged by educators of the deaf to decide which method is best to teach young deaf children. Jonah became a pawn in the war of methodology.

Jonah was depicted as an energetic, curious boy. He was bright, although there was no way to tap into his intelligence. Alternative forms of communication were explained in the drama; although Jonah himself failed at his speech lessons, other deaf persons were shown as able to speak with explanations why their speech was clear.

The drama wisely utilized a deaf perspective in some scenes. A disturbing segment dealt with Jonah attempting to tell his mother he wanted a hot dog from a nearby vendor. He tried in every way he could to communicate and failed. Jonah began screaming in sheer frustration. Many older deaf viewers related to this scene, recalling difficult moments in their own pasts. One man said he could remember kicking the wall until his feet bled in similar frustration.

Special equipment was used, in this case, an interpreter who acted as the go-between for Jenny and her new deaf friends. Sign language, taught to Jonah by Woody, a young deaf man (also played by a deaf actor) was illustrated as a full and colorful language of its own.

Actual children with Down's syndrome were utilized in the early institution scenes; deaf performers appeared as deaf characters throughout the film; actual deaf children appeared in both Jonah's oral school and manual school.

"And Your Name Is Jonah" was a moving film, using a different and fresh

perspective. Although Jonah's immediate grasp of sign language was rather melodramatic and schmaltzy, it was balanced out by the overall quality of story. The writer extended himself to create something different and it paid off.

The Love Boat / "Sound of Silence" / Mar. 17, 1979 / ABC-TV

Executive Producers: Aaron Spelling; Douglas Cramer
Producers: Gordon and Lynne Farr and Henry Colman
Director: Richard Kinon
Writers: Joyce Armor and Judy Neer
Category: Series Television — Romantic Comedy

* Deafness
* Single White Female
* Deaf Performer
* Communication: Expressive — Sign; Receptive — Sign/Speechreading

Plot: A rock star falls in love with a deaf woman on the cruise ship.

Sarah, a deaf passenger, boards the *Pacific Princess* and greets her old friend, cruise director Julie McCoy. Julie signs, indicating she learned the language when she used to volunteer at Sarah's school.
Gopher has arranged for rock star Deacon Dark to perform on the cruise. Underneath grisly face make-up and a wild wig is Phil Baxter, a man who just wants to be a singer, not an attraction. Phil sees Sarah and Julie at the bar. He says hello.

SARAH (signing): Happy meet you.

Phil is surprised and puzzled. He looks at Julie.

JULIE: Oh, she says that she's happy to meet you, too.

Phil is intrigued and copies the signs. He and Sarah hit it off.
Sarah watches and tentatively applauds Deacon Dark's outrageous performance. Phil meets her later. He is sure he has disappointed her by a tasteless act and leaves. He later apologizes to Sarah and tells her he just wants to write songs, but the make-up, the snakes, and grotesque parts of his act are the vision of his agent. Phil just wants to write songs and sing — in fact, he wrote a song for Sarah. He gives her a piece of paper.

PHIL: Just pretend it's poetry and pretend it's good, okay?

Julie acts as the catalyst in advising a confused and lovesick Sarah what to do.

JULIE: If you feel that strongly, go to him and tell him!

Sarah confronts Phil in the lounge and asks him to play the song he wrote. She places her hands on the piano as he plays.

PHIL: You little devil! You can feel the music with your hands!

Phil insists to his agent that he could make it as a songwriter.

PHIL: I sang my song for Sarah this afternoon and she loved it.

MARTY: ...How many records do deaf people buy?

Phil's new act is a success in the ship's lounge. Marty is sold. Sarah and Phil are very happy together.

* * *

"Sound of Silence" was sappy. Deafness in combination with a musical theme popped up here by the device of the musician falling in love with someone with no firsthand knowledge of the art. Comments from Phil and Marty both assumed a deaf person had no residual hearing. Marty's comment about deaf people buying records was understandable yet precluded the notion that the hearing-impaired *do* buy records and are familiar with current pop figures.

Technical assistance was utilized. Julie signed to Sarah and used appropriate ASL order when talking to Sarah using "total communication," that is, voice with sign.

"Sound of Silence" was a bare-bones love story which substituted deafness and a hearing person's perspective for a plot.

The White Shadow / "A Silent Cheer" / Apr. 28, 1979 / CBS-TV

Executive Producer: Bruce Paltrow
Producer: Mark Tinker
Director: Victor Lobl
Writer: Steve Kline
Category: Series Television — Drama

* Deafness
* Black Male Teenager
* Communication: Expressive — Speech; Receptive — Speechreading

Plot: A deaf student enters Coach Reeves' high school and attempts to hide his deafness.

Jeff Simpson, a deaf high school student, is new in town. His father, Carl, wants him to attend Carver High, the school where ex-NBA star Ken Reeves is the basketball coach.

CARL: You have too much talent to be compromised by a minor handicap.

Jeff speechreads easily and speaks in a clear, monitored voice. His mother would prefer he attend a special school. Jeff enrolls at Carver without revealing his limitation. He manages to slide by in class, although some of the other kids have noticed things about him.

STUDENT: [When you're] talkin' to him, you gotta repeat things twice.

Coach Reeves discerns what Jeff's problem is.

REEVES: You can't hear me, can you?

JEFF: No, not really. But I can read your lips.

The cause of Jeff's hearing loss is described as rheumatic fever. Jeff wants to remain at Carver. He has a fantasy.

JEFF: Can you name one deaf basketball player who ever made it to the pros? Well, I want to be the first.

Reeves informs the other players that Jeff has a limitation. The kids help him maintain Jeff's cover until the big game. It reaches a point where the ruse can no longer be maintained. Jeff transfers from Carver to a school where he can work on his speechreading and basketball.

* * *

This episode of the highly acclaimed *The White Shadow* used a common version of deafness seen on television, that of the speechreading-speaking person no one would ever have guessed was deaf. This story could have been quite good had it brought in the fact that education *was* available to Jeff in Reeves' school by law.

Jeff's deafness was a personal embarrassment he and his father had to overcome. It also seemed incredible that a student could goad a professional educator like Reeves not to blow the whistle on him until the big game was over.

Coach Reeves had an annoying habit of speaking to Jeff using overly exaggerated mouth movements. Such action hinders the intelligibility of spoken words to speechreaders.

Jeff's notation that no deaf players had made it to the pros was an interesting one. A neat avenue for exploration would have been why deaf players had not made the pros: Were they not good enough? or had they been discriminated against? Jeff could have been the one to prove the people with the prejudices were wrong.

"A Silent Cheer" was injured by a lack of deaf perspective, knowledge of then-current legislation, and no real understanding of being a deaf student in a hearing environment.

Voices / 1979 / MGM

Producer: Joe Wizan
Director: Robert Markowitz
Writer: John Herzfeld
Category: Feature Film — Drama

* Deafness
* Single White Female
* Equipment: Flashing light alerts; TDD
* Communication: Expressive — Sign/Speech; Receptive — Sign/ Speechreading

Plot: A deaf young woman who dreams of becoming a dancer meets an aspiring rock-n-roll singer.

Drew, a singer, cuts a record in a do-it-yourself booth at an arcade and sees a girl watching him in amusement. He falls in love and tries to follow her but loses her. He sees her again as she gets on a bus. He follows her to a school for the deaf. He realizes she, too, is deaf.

DREW: You don't hear me at all.

ROSEMARY: [shakes her head "no."]

Drew blathers on and realizes Rosemary cannot follow him.

DREW: I'm talkin' too fast for you to read my lips?

ROSEMARY: [nods]

Although Rosemary is seeing a deaf man, she begins to go out with Drew. She has little trouble speechreading him. Drew gets a sign language book to try and learn signs to better communicate with Rosemary.

Rosemary lives with her hearing mother, who is concerned about this new liaison. She is very overprotective of Rosemary. Drew's little brother Raymond has a question.

RAYMOND: She's deaf — so why don't she talk?

With Drew's goading, Rosemary uses her voice to speak to him in unmonitored tones. She explains she lost her hearing when she was six years old. Her dream is to become a dancer.

Her mother tries to dissuade Rosemary from seeing her new friend. Negatives are planted when Rosemary's mother warns her off.

MOTHER: When he realizes how hard it is to live with a deaf woman, he won't be here any more.

A dance company is having auditions. Drew supports Rosemary to try out. The music is not loud enough for her to feel vibrations in the floor. She fails miserably. Drew acts as the non-disabled catalyst and forces his way into the audition, demanding they give Rosemary another chance after they turn the speakers into the floor so that she can feel the vibrations. She performs admirably.

At a club, Drew and his band perform a song. Drew sings it for Rosemary's benefit.

* * *

Voices was a schmaltz-laden image of deafness. Rosemary was a quiet and timid person, dominated by her mother. Although she was successfully employed as a teacher, she remained at home, putting up with her mother's own special kind of abuse.

It would seem that the premise of the story meant to show the deaf woman and the hearing man had something in common: a dream connected with music. However, it got muddled in a drippy story. Typically, Drew hounded Rosemary to speak — as if a person without usable speech is inferior. Rosemary had a special talent, but it required Drew to help it blossom. It was almost as if the deaf world could not understand Rosemary's artistic aspirations and desires, suggesting such talent and dedication belonged to Rosemary alone and did not include any other deaf people.

Without evidence of a deaf community or any type of deaf cultural background, Rosemary appeared to exist in a ghetto of which she was the shining star who managed to break free, thanks to her hearing boyfriend.

The use of a hearing actress in the lead role led to protests and a boycott of the film by deaf people in some parts of the country.

Voices possessed a curious singular image of deafness. Rosemary's limitation was suggested to be an oddity and only the "love beyond words" (as a TV showing of the film described it) could overcome the differences.

Dummy / May 27, 1979 / CBS-TV

Executive Producer: Frank Konigsberg
Producers: Sam Manners and Ernest Tidyman
Director: Frank Perry
Writer: Ernest Tidyman
Category: Made-for-TV Movie — Drama

* Deafness
* Single Black Male (#1)
* Communication #1: none
* Single White Male (#2)
* Communication #2: Expressive — Speech; Receptive — Speechreading
* Based on a True Story

Plot: A deaf man without language is accused of murdering a prostitute.

Offensive language comes into play with the first lines of the script.

> MYERS: This is a true story. The story of Donald Lang, an illiterate deaf-mute caught in the nightmare of a unique criminal trial....

Donald Lang, a twenty-year-old produce loader, is arrested on suspicion of murder. When he does not respond to police questions, they realize he's deaf. The court refers the case to Lowell Myers, an attorney who is deaf. Myers is drawn to the case and uses terrible terminology.

> MYERS: To me, Donald was what I might have been—a mute victim of a crippling handicap if I hadn't learned to speak, to read, to write before I lost my hearing.

Myers meets Lang and constantly speaks to him, never using gestures or signs. Lang notes Myers' hearing aid. Poor vocabulary—a hallmark of this production—is used again.

> MYERS: No, I can't hear a thing. Stone deaf. I haven't heard anything since I was nine years old.

Joel Smith, D.A., talks to Myers.

> SMITH: The D.A.'s office has never had to try a deaf-mute on a felony before.

At the murder site, Lang acts out a scene—that he was knocked aside and saw another man stab the woman. The cops claim it's a confession and Lang is charged with first degree murder. Without his counsel's consent, Lang is taken to a center for communicative disorders and tested. Dr. Morris testifies at a competency hearing.

> MORRIS: He's a higher level imbecile.... He does not have the mental capacity to understand the indictment against him or to cooperate with his counsel.

The jury declares Lang incompetent. He is sentenced to the Illinois Security Hospital until he "recovers" from his incompetence.

Myers works to get Lang out of the facility.

> MYERS: What he needs is special training. If Donald is mentally okay but unable to stand trial because of his deaf-mute handicap, then he cannot be put into a mental institution for the criminally insane. Instead the court should place him in a special school for deaf-mutes where he will be taught sign language....

After a year of lock-up, Lang is placed in a school. Myers expresses later that Lang learned nothing but "boredom, resentment and frustration."

It takes five years to get the Supreme Court of Illinois to listen to the case. The physical evidence has disappeared from the police files and Myers' witnesses have died or disappeared. Charges are dropped.

Six months later, Lang picks up a prostitute who is later found dead. He is thrown into jail—again, on circumstantial evidence.

* * *

Dummy was about a man who was a victim of bureaucracy his whole life. As a child, Mrs. Lang was unable to get Donald into special schools because of lack of money or the overcrowding of free facilities. He was not accepted into public school's special programs because of a misunderstanding. As an adult, he was a victim of red tape.

The denial of rights to one individual was frightening. Lang was railroaded and it took five wasteful years to make a move on the case. A powerful statement was made in front of a stark backdrop about the injustices doled out to Lang.

However, the film destroyed its own credibility by the poor language used continuously throughout. "Deaf-mute" is a term considered offensive within the deaf community; for outsiders to use it without understanding its connotations would be somewhat palatable; for a lawyer who was, himself, deaf, it was unthinkable. For him to deem Lang had a "deaf-mute handicap" was laughable.

Myers' long, spoken diatribes to Lang were ridiculous. He never tried to discern if Lang had formulated his own type of gestural "home signs" with which he could communicate. Myers never encouraged Lang to mime his feelings—until the fateful scene where Lang's actions were taken as a "confession" by police. Instead, Myers talked and talked and talked while Lang cocked his head intelligently.

An erroneous notion was planted within the drama. Myers spoke well in an unmonitored voice. He expressed he had lost his hearing as a child. His attitude implied that Lang, deaf from early infancy, had not learned to communicate because he never learned to speak. Therefore, speech was equated with intelligence.

Lang was illustrated as a good, dependable worker who liked to clown around. He was a quick learner. His cheerful disposition was eroded by the years in prison where he was molested by male prisoners. Perhaps he never understood why he was there.

Myers' dedication to the young man was admirable and although he talked about "Constitutional rights," he never seemed to mean Donald was being discriminated against on account of a sensory limitation. It was never expressed if the long wait to trial was the result of racial prejudice. A deaf black who murdered a black prostitute could have been deemed "unimportant" by a racist judiciary.

Dummy explored a neglected side of deafness—the rights of those without language. It was also undermined by its horrendous language, lack of deaf perspective, and its subtle skirting of racial and political issues.

Silent Victory: The Kitty O'Neil Story / 1979

Producer: R.J. Lewis
Director: Lou Antonio
Writer: Stephen Gethers
Category: Made-for-TV Movie — Drama

* Deafness
* Single White Female
* Based on a True Story
* Communication: Expressive — Speech; Receptive — Speechreading

Plot: The life of actual deaf stuntwoman Kitty O'Neil is outlined.

Months after a high fever, Mrs. O'Neil takes daughter Kitty to see a doctor. The child has not spoken since the illness. Kitty is diagnosed as deaf. Mrs. O'Neil talks to her little girl.

> MOTHER: Listen to me. You will never use sign language. Look at me. Watch. You will never use sign language, Kitty O'Neil. Do you understand? You will learn to hear with your eyes....

Mrs. O'Neil takes teenaged Kitty to California to try out for Dr. Lee, an Olympic diving coach. Kitty wants to learn to dive from the high tower. At the interview, Mrs. O'Neil camouflages Kitty's deafness by answering all of Dr. Lee's questions. When Kitty finally speaks, Dr. Lee has a question.

> DR. LEE: Kitty, how long have you been hard-of-hearing?

Embarrassment about a limitation is illustrated.

> MOTHER (defensively; upset): How did you know that, Dr. Lee?

> DR. LEE: By the way she talks. That's my specialty.

Kitty is not Olympic material. She goes to Texas to live on her own. At an employment agency, she expresses to Tom, a young man also seeking a job, that she's been denied jobs because she has told prospective employers she is deaf.

> KITTY: I can't get a job that way.

With Tom's help, she fudges through the interview. He wants to strike up a relationship. Kitty devalues herself.

> KITTY: Who'd want a deaf girl?

Kitty is in love with Tom and supports him, until she discovers he is ripping her off. She again devalues herself.

Silent Victory: The Kitty O'Neil Story

KITTY: A little deaf joke, that's all I was to you....

Tom responds, using pejorative language.

TOM: ...I figure you got an even trade, because honey, you had me, a whole guy for two years, normal from top to toe....

Kitty meets and marries Duffy Hambleton, a hearing man at the bank who is deeply interested in motorcycles. Hambleton gets involved in stuntwork for films. Kitty joins him. She gets her first job; they tell the producer of the film that she is a foreigner to disguise the fact she is deaf.

Kitty goes to Mrs. O'Neil's The School of Listening Eyes, where she observes deaf children. Kitty is struck by what her mother did at the school.

KITTY: None of those kids will ever have to go through life passing out little cards that say, "Help me, I'm deaf."

Kitty feels her crusade is to prove to those deaf children what they are capable of. She sets out to break the landspeed record and succeeds.

A little girl approaches Kitty.

LITTLE GIRL (in sign language): We love you.

KITTY: I want you to *talk* to me.

LITTLE GIRL (with voice only): Kitt-ee.

* * *

Silent Victory indicated a woman who was deaf could be involved in anything she wanted—even something as inherently dangerous as breaking the landspeed record in a rocket car. Despite the upbeat imagery of a deaf woman and illustration that deafness was just a hindrance to Kitty, the movie fell into the formula groove.

Although events in the real Kitty's life may have been paralleled by segments of the film, it was annoying to see Mrs. O'Neil's personal triumph of the will become a TV model of a deaf child. The scene where young Kitty mechanically plays Beethoven on the piano and then is applauded by teary-eyed classmates was ridiculous. Why Mrs. O'Neil thought this display of "normal" behavior would benefit her deaf daughter was never expressed. It was interesting to note that while Kitty had learned to play piano, as a young adult, she had no work skills to speak of.

Her mention of job discrimination was never expressed as the same. Using lying and dishonesty to affirm employment were simply not ways of dealing with the social problem. If the actual Kitty *did* achieve work in the same way, the responsibility lay with the writer in indicating the same.

This film came out the same year as *"And Your Name Is Jonah."* The muddled image of deafness became murkier. Jonah "failed" in his speech training and succeeded when he learned to sign. Mrs. O'Neil admonished her young child that she would never sign. Kitty's telling the little girl to "talk to me" was an expression that sign language was bad. The lack of background information could easily confuse an audience.

The unspoken message of this film was that to sign or be deaf was a stigma. Kitty's success was due to the fact that she was "normal."

While *Silent Victory: The Kitty O'Neil Story* presented a deaf woman as one with a sense of humor and who could do whatever she desired, the film sidestepped too many issues to be effective in anything but an "inspirational" way.

Little House on the Prairie / "Silent Promises" / Jan. 28, 1980 / NBC-TV

Executive Producer: Michael Landon
Producer: Kent McCray
Writers: Carole & Michael Paschella
Category: Series Television — Period Drama

* Deafness
* White Male Teenager
* Deaf Performer
* Communication: Expressive and Receptive — Sign

Plot: Laura Ingalls teaches a deaf boy how to communicate.

Farmer Nathan Page comes to town with a teenaged boy on the wagon. His son Daniel is deaf and cannot communicate. Negative aspects are illustrated when firecrackers spook a horse into stampeding. Daniel is nearly killed. Laura Ingalls saves his life.

Doc Baker says Daniel can learn. Doc tells Laura about sign language and lends her some books. She becomes the non-disabled catalyst. She learns sign language and takes on the task of teaching Daniel to communicate.

Nathan is skeptical until Laura proves Daniel has learned by telling him to get coffee for his father and to pick up his spectacles. Nathan is converted. He wants to learn to sign.

NATHAN: I want to tell him I love him.

A little societal prejudice is seen when the indefatigable Mrs. Oleson comments on Daniel's language acquisition.

MRS. OLESON: Made me nervous, seeing his fingers wiggle around like that.

Daniel falls in love with Laura.

DANIEL: I love you.

LAURA: Same, but—

They kiss.

LAURA: No!

Daniel runs away. He returns home and refuses to study. Laura goes to him, deciding on honesty.

LAURA (signing and speaking): ...I don't love you. I want you learn but not for me, for self. I teacher.

DANIEL: More than teacher.

LAURA: No, friend.

Nathan talks to Daniel and gives him a fatherly lecture. Daniel sees the light and comes back, asking Laura to continue her instruction.

* * *

"Silent Promises" was another version of "Johnny Belinda." A concerned citizen who believed in the merits of educating a deaf member of the community took on the responsibility of doing so without special training. Laura progressed rapidly from teaching Daniel concrete nouns to abstracts.

Technical assistance was utilized; the character actor portraying farmer Page was a native speaker of American Sign Language as well as being an author and teacher on the same subject. Therefore, Laura's signs were well-executed with appropriate grammar. Although it is doubtful she could have picked up the conceptual nature of the language from a textbook, it was a pleasure to note the language utilized appropriately.

Of course, the "almost-getting-killed" scene was included.

Executive Producer Landon played a very similar role in a 1960 *Bonanza* episode, "Silent Thunder." There, his character taught a deaf girl and had to tell her they were just friends and not really in love. (See *Johnny Belinda,* 1982, for another version of this "friend" scene.)

"Silent Promises" featured a deaf character as one capable of learning and possessing average emotions. It also was a sappy and routine depiction of a deaf character.

Happy Days / "Allison" / Feb. 12, 1980 / ABC-TV

Executive Producers: Thomas Miller, Edwin Milkis & Garry Marshall

* Deafness
* Single White Female
* Deaf Performer

Deafness

Producers: Jerry Davis, Walter Kemply
Supervising Producer: Lowell Ganz
Writers: Patt Shea, Harriet Weiss
Category: Series Television—Situation Comedy

* Communication: Expressive and Receptive—Sign

Plot: Fonzie falls in love with a deaf girl.

Richie and Fonzie go to the electric company to handle a mistaken $4,000 bill. They are to speak to Allison Curtis, who runs the computer department. Fonzie takes one look and is smitten. Characteristically, he walks up behind her and gives his surefire snap, the one that has girls slavishly following him. There is no response. Shaken, Fonzie confides to Richie:

>FONZIE: She didn't respond ... life as I know it is over!

Richie points out another employee signing with the girl. Allison is deaf.

>FONZIE: My vision of loveliness is deaf!

With expressive mime, the Fonz charm works and he leaves arm in arm with Allison.

Allison's birthday is coming up. Fonz wants to learn the song "Happy Birthday" in sign for her. He and Richie sit down with a sign book. Fonzie masters the song. Allison is pleased.

Richie is concerned. He takes Fonz aside.

>RICHIE: Don't play love her and leave her with this girl.

>FONZ: Who said I'm gonna *leave* her?

Fonzie is shocked when he learns Allison is engaged to Doug—who is hearing.

>DOUG: ...Allison seemed to think I was only asking her out because I felt sorry for her ... dating you made her realize how attractive she really is ... you've made two people very happy. This morning I asked Allison to marry me—she said yes.

* * *

"Allison" was a pleasant story although typical media aspects of deafness showed up. The attractive Allison was bright and employed as a computer clerk. Her buoyant personality was certainly not in tandem with a "you only pity me" attitude the writers assumed she must have. They assumed vulnerability on account of deafness — as illustrated by Richie's warning to the Fonz not to love and leave Allison.

The resolution of the story was worn. See *Best Years of Our Lives; The Love Boat,* "Charmed, I'm Sure"; *Finder of Lost Loves,* "Deadly Silence" for other variations on the same theme.

Inclusion of a native speaking deaf actress in this role enhanced "Allison" greatly.

Barney Miller / "Stormy Weather" / Feb. 12, 1981 / ABC-TV

Executive Producer: Danny Arnold
Producers: Tony Sheehan; Noam Pitlik
Director: Noam Pitlik
Writer: Nat Mauldin
Category: Series Television — Situation Comedy

* Deafness
* Single White Female
* Deaf Performer
* Communication: Expressive — Sign; Receptive — Sign and Speechreading

Plot: A deaf woman is brought into the 12th precinct for soliciting.

A deaf woman is brought into the station after being arrested for solicitation. Wojo has discovered something about her.

WOJO: She didn't hear ... she's deaf.

BARNEY: Oh, I'm sorry.

WOJO: She didn't hear that, either.

The others are confused as to what to do. Dietrich wonders if he should "mime her rights."

Madeline has cards that read, "I am a deaf mute — want to party?" and "My name is Madeline — you here for the convention?"

Levitt can communicate with Madeline since he has a deaf sister. Barney indicates he's sorry.

LEVITT: I'm sure if [Sis] were here she'd appreciate your pity.

Madeline calls a deaf attorney.

Madeline accepts a cup of station coffee and wrinkles her nose in distaste.

MADELINE (signing): Tastes awful!

COP: I don't wanna hear it.

* * *

This episode of *Barney Miller* was quite enjoyable. A deaf person was certainly indicated as another part of the human spectrum in the depiction of a prostitute! Although Madeline's cards read she was a "deaf mute," it was hard to look at this as truly offensive in that it was a play on the cards handed out by the deaf "sellers" who still peddle goods.

Particularly pleasurable was Madeline's uninterpreted conversation with her deaf lawyer (played by a deaf actor). When Barney asked Levitt to interpret, he indicated it was "privileged communication," which it was. Madeline's angry pimp/boyfriend was also deaf and the audience was left to imagine what *their* heated discussion was about (a deaf actor was cast in the role).

This episode was written with a great deal of humor which played more on the discomfort of the cops than on Madeline's limitation. It was worth watching.

Fantasy Island / "Chorus Girl" / Feb. 21, 1981 / ABC-TV

Executive Producers: Aaron Spelling; Leonard Goldberg
Writer: Ron Friedman
Category: Series Television— Fantasy Drama

* Deafness
* Single White Female
* Cure
* Communication: Expressive— Speech; Receptive—Speechreading

Plot: The teacher of a deaf dancer has a fantasy: for his protégé to be able to hear and truly understand music.

Sheila Richards, a deaf dancer, arrives on Fantasy Island with her teacher, Mr. Adams. The instructor believes Sheila's dancing will have no soul until she can hear and understand music.

Sheila is cured of her deafness by the mysterious proprietor of Fantasy Island, Mr. Roarke.

* * *

"Chorus Girl" was based on public mythology—the premise that only those who hear can appreciate rhythm and dance. It was a tedious and predictable formula drama with no different or thought-provoking ideas in it. The story was laughable. Sheila's delight with sudden hearing was derived from a hearing person's concept of regaining sound—not the utter disruptive and unintelligible intrusion it would be to someone born deaf as Sheila was.

"Chorus Girl" was a poor image of a deaf person, created entirely in the hearing person's perspective.

Nurse / "Listen to Me" / Apr. 16, 1981 / CBS-TV

Producer: Robert Halmi
Director: James Sheldon

* Deafness
* Single White Male (#1)

Nurse

Story: Michael McGreevey
Teleplay: Michael McGreevey and Max McClellan
Category: Series Television — Medical Drama

* Single White Female (#2)
* Equipment: Flashing light alert on doorbell
* Deaf Performer (#2)
* Cure (#1)
* Communication (#1): Expressive — Speech/Sign; Receptive — Speechreading/Sign
* Communication (#2): Expressive — Sign; Receptive — Speechreading/Sign

Plot: After the deaf employee in the hospital's gift shop is hit by a car, he seems to have some hearing.

Ben Freeman is a deaf employee at the Grant Memorial Hospital Gift Shop. He is hit by a car. The cause of Ben's hearing loss is discussed as a fall at age 14. Records don't indicate auditory nerve damage. When Nurse Mary Benjamin notes Ben seems to hear the phone ringing in his room, she talks to the doctors. The doctors think a degree of Ben's loss is "hysterical."

Ben's deaf girlfriend is a dress designer. Alma is a savvy woman — and upset at the news when Mary tells her Ben may hear again. Alma's feelings make Ben refuse hearing tests. His reasoning?

> BEN: If the tests are positive and show that an operation would restore my hearing again — don't you see? I move into the hearing world without Alma.

Ben decides to have the tests. Alma is greatly upset. She leaves Ben, saying he would change too much if he could hear.

Alma comes to see Mary. She writes to Mary on the lounge blackboard:

> ALMA: If I lose him, I lose everything.

Mary acts as the non-disabled catalyst, telling Alma to take the risk. Alma returns home.

Ben has an operation. When the packing is removed from his ears, he is able to hear. He joyfully describes sounds to Alma — street sounds, air conditioner, etc.

* * *

"Listen to Me" could have been a great piece, but wasn't. Ben, as a postlingually deaf person, spoke well in a slightly unmonitored voice. He had little problem communicating with hearing people. Ben was, in essence, a hearing person who couldn't hear. Alma was a deaf person with a different cultural background. Had the writer expressed the cultural chasm that Ben barely touched upon when he said he did not want to move into the hearing world without Alma, the story could have been truly different. As it was, it came out as a type of devaluation story—as well as a "cure" piece. Alma feared Ben as a hearing person would leave her behind.

Not surprisingly, the story featured an "almost-getting-killed" scene.

The doctors' feeling that Ben's ability to hear a telephone ring indicated a type of hysterical deafness completely removed the possibility that a deaf person has a degree of residual hearing in certain pitch ranges. "Listen to Me" was a routine story.

(The basic story line of "Listen to Me" was similar to "Walls of Silence," a 1973 episode of *Marcus Welby, MD* where a hysterically deaf teenaged boy didn't want to regain his hearing for fear of losing his deaf girlfriend [see Appendix].)

Trapper John, M.D. / "The Albatross" / Aug. 16, 1981 (rerun) / CBS-TV

Executive Producer: Frank Glicksman
Producer: Don Brinkley
Writer: Charles Larson
Category: Series Television— Medical Drama

* Deafness
* White Female Teenager
* Deaf Performer
* Communication: Expressive/ Receptive—Sign

Plot: Dr. Gates' new patient is a wild young deaf girl.

Dr. Gonzo Gates accidentally injures a girl. She is taken to ICU at San Francisco General. Gonzo has noticed something about her. He voices his observation, using poor language.

GONZO: She's deaf and mute—I think.

Eve Forsythe is like a wild animal. She continuously pits her strong will against Gonzo's. He discovers she is a runaway from the county home for the deaf. Her language skills are minimal. Her recovery is difficult. Gonzo goes to the home for the deaf to try and learn more about her. Mrs. Forsythe, Eve's mother, uses poor language in describing her daughter.

INGRID FORSYTHE: ...a deaf and mute daughter...

* * *

"The Albatross" represented a poor image of deafness. The piece used outdated and poor language, as well as ancient concepts. The "county home for the deaf"? Shades of the nineteenth century!

All the professional medical people used a horrendous choice of words when discussing Eve. Nurse Ernestine Shoop won the prize for most offensive when she referred to Eve as a "weeping deaf-mute orphan."

Despite presence of a deaf performer as well as a noted author/teacher of American Sign Language on the set (who played the superintendent of the home for the deaf), production personnel clearly did not take advantage of the talent at hand to embellish this story with any hint of reality. "The Albatross" was a poor and damaging image of deafness.

Amy (a.k.a. Amy on the Lips) / 1981 / Walt Disney Productions

Executive Producer: William Robert Yates
Producer: Jerome Courtland
Director: Vincent McEveety
Writer: Noreen Stone
Category: Feature Film—Drama

* Deafness
* Group Portrayal; White children
* Deaf Performers
* Communication: Expressive— Sign/Speech; Receptive—Sign/ Speechreading

Plot: Amy Medford goes to work at the Parker School, intending to teach deaf children how to speak.

Amy Medford leaves her husband shortly after the turn of the century. She is haunted by the memories of their dead deaf child. She plans to teach speech to deaf students. The job will not be easy, warns the superintendent.

> FERGUSON: There are those who believe passionately that the deaf can never be taught to speak. I'm afraid you're going to meet some opposition to your work.

Ferguson explains that the school also houses twenty blind students.

> FERGUSON: ...and as you will discover, they don't mix.

One of the deaf boys, teenaged Henry Watkins, defends the blind children when they are picked on by others. Henry also becomes Amy's most devoted student and prize pupil. He learns how to say "mother." He eagerly approaches his visiting mother, a woman who is blind. He kneels in front of her and calls her "Mother."

> MRS. WATKINS: Henry? Is that my Henry? Talkin'?

Mr. Ferguson rushes to get Amy. He briefs her on the way, using poor terminology.

> FERGUSON: Henry's mother is ... stone blind. That's why he feels so close to the blind children. That's why he wants so badly to speak.

Henry becomes useful when the board plans to cut the speech program.

ADMINISTRATOR: Everyone knows the deaf cannot speak!

HENRY: Yes, I can.

Henry has also appointed himself protector of a hulking nineteen-year-old named Mervin. Eugene, another deaf boy, picks on Mervin at every opportunity. Henry scraps with Eugene to defend Mervin, who finally runs away in frustration. Mr. Ferguson guesses he is running towards home on the other side of the railroad tracks. Henry is also gone, looking for Mervin. A negative is implied in Amy's response to the news.

AMY: My god! They could be running down the track but neither of them can hear the train.

A train approaches the boys. Henry dives off the track; Mervin is killed. His grieving parents are so moved when they hear Henry use his voice, they turn their other child, a small deaf girl, over to the school.

MA: She ain't never heerd nothin' in her whole life. You take her and make her talk, like him.

Amy's estranged husband finds her and tries to persuade her to return home. She refuses, having found her niche at the school.

*   *   *

Amy was a sweet movie with unrealistic portrayals of deaf children (as well as blind children). The film suffered from a lack of identity. Amy passionately wanted to teach deaf children to speak in lieu of her own deceased deaf child. She was pitted against an old, established teacher who believed only in sign. But instead of this being a scaled-down version of the educational methodology war between the "oralists" and "manualists," it simply became a personal battle of opinion—Amy versus Malvina.

Scenes with the blind children were very saccharine, such as the concentration on the four-year-old who believed that on his fifth birthday his eyes would open and he would be able to see. The blind children were quiet and well-behaved; they all had stiff necks and wooden stares.

The deaf children were also quiet and well-behaved with the exception of Eugene, who had it out for Mervin. Curiously, after all fights between Henry the Good and Eugene the Bad, no one ever pulled either aside for discipline or to find out what the problem was. Adults coddled one or the other in the fray.

An examination of schooling in a period of time where expectations for such children were low and most schools were "asylums" was an intriguing concept. Unfortunately, the only real indication of this was the battle with the board, who were angry that money and time were being spent to teach the deaf boys to play football like any other school. The subplot—a woman of that time leaving her husband and finding love with a doctor—was also interesting. However, the drippy approach and unrealistic children diluted the story. Henry's learning to speak for a blind mother was almost too much to bear.

A turn-of-the-century deaf education methodology war personified by two individuals and backed up with research would have provided a solid foundation for a meaningful drama. Instead, this piece went for the heartstrings with a vengeance. *Amy* fell far short of its potential.

Family Tree / Jan. 22, 1982–Mar. 5, 1982 / NBC-TV

Executive Producer: Nigel McKeand
Producer: Carroll Newman
Director: Joan Darling (Episode 1)
Writer: Carol Evan McKeand (Episode 1)
Category: Series Television—Family Drama

* Deafness
* White Male Child
* Deaf Performer
* Communication: Expressive—Sign/Speech; Receptive—Sign

Plot: The merge-by-marriage of two families with growing children is not easy for mother Annie's youngest, Toby, who is deaf.

* * *

Family Tree had a short run of six weeks as a test series. It dealt with family drama and the difficulties of trying to pull two different families together.

Toby was Annie Benjamin's youngest child. The cause of his limitation was discussed, described as a bout with meningitis when he was seven. Now approaching adolescence, he used speech to communicate but depended more on sign language for understanding others. His mother and sister used signs and speech while conversing with him in a mode known as "total communication."

Toby took the remarriage of his mother with great difficulty, running away from home in hopes of halting the union. An uncreative guilt aspect was seen when Toby admitted to his mother he felt his deafness caused the breakup of his parents' marriage.

Some of Toby's unique problems were explored during the series. One story dealt with new father Kevin's resisting learning sign to communicate with his stepson—and Toby's complete impatience and disregard for his stepfather's awkward attempts to learn. In one episode, Kevin was explaining about his tools to an uninterested Toby using special equipment, in this instance, his sister as an interpreter. The teenager got so engrossed in Kevin's colorful story that she forgot to interpret for Toby. In angry frustration, the boy lashed out by leaving a prized book of Kevin's outdoors where it was ruined by a lawn sprinkler. Kevin was angry until he discovered the root of Toby's bad behavior.

Another episode had to do with the house being robbed. Negative aspects of deafness could be assumed as Toby was in the house at the time and unaware of the burglary. Annie became overprotective and refused to let Toby attend a school trip to a science fair, feeling he was too vulnerable. She learned though, that her son was growing up and had to make his way in the world. The highlight of this episode was Toby's science project: a miniature working volcano which he blew up late one night while all were asleep. He was amazed when the family, shaken and frightened, converged on the kitchen. Toby was surprised they had been bothered. The noise, he indicated, was negligible. "I'm deaf," he snorted in a superior fashion.

Family Tree utilized very real situations in its stories. The integration of a deaf child as a full-fledged family member was a nice, realistic touch.

CHiPs / "Silent Partner" / Feb. 28, 1982 / NBC-TV

Executive Producer: Cy Chermak
Producer: Paul Rabwin
Writer: Bruce Shelly
Category: Series Television—Police Drama

* Deafness
* White Married Couple
* Single White Female
* Deaf Performers
* Equipment: Flashing light alerts; TDD
* Communication: Expressive—Sign/Speech; Receptive—Sign/Speechreading

Plot: A deaf man, failing to heed the siren of the patrolmen, threatens to sue when arrested for drunk driving.

A burglar steals a car. Earl Sorensen, enjoying a backyard picnic, takes off after the culprit. He does not respond to the sirens of California Highway Patrol officers Poncharello and Baker. He is in an accident.

Officer Jon Baker approaches the man. He smells liquor on the man's breath and hears a voice he perceives is slurred. He begins to arrest Sorensen for drunk driving. Officer Bonnie Clark sees something else. She signs to the man, "Deaf?"

JON: Boy, we got a doozie here!

BONNIE: Jon, he's not drunk, he's deaf.

Sorensen wants to file a complaint against Jon for attempted arrest. Baker agonizes over the incident. Ponch deems it a judgment call.

PONCH: You smelled booze, his speech was slurred, he ignored your warning....

Ponch meets Kim, an attractive young friend of Earl Sorensen and his wife. She is also deaf. Ponch asks Kim to dinner. During the meal, the etiology of Earl's anger is discussed. His deaf son was killed six years earlier when he did not yield to the shouted warning of a policeman.

Ponch gains an introduction to a lively deaf community when he takes Kim to a captioned film. He takes her dancing at a club for the deaf.

With Sorensen's help, the patrolmen are able to track down the car thief.

* * *

"Silent Partner" used a technical consultant and it showed. A different and intriguing story line emerged, bolstered by appropriate use of special equipment. Kim was attractive to Ponch, so much so that the new world to which he was introduced didn't intimidate him.

The causes of the three principal deaf characters' limitations were discussed with Ponch over dinner. Sorensen had lost his hearing at age seven, his wife was born deaf, and Kim had lost hers when she was twelve.

Sorensen was an angry man—and he had reason to be. He blamed the authorities for not being aware that deaf people lived in the community.

Poor camera angles that cut off signs detracted from the program. Hands that signed popped in and out of frame. Bonnie used good signs; the mechanical quality was excusable in that she was a hearing person.

Actual members of the Los Angeles deaf community were seen in the busy background of this piece.

"Silent Partner" offered a different picture of deafness, one not seen often enough.

Johnny Belinda / Oct. 20, 1982 / CBS-TV

Executive Producers: Dick Berg; Malcolm Stuart
Producer: Stanley Bass
Director: Anthony Page
Teleplay: Sue Milburn
Based on the Play by: Elmer Harris
Also Based on a Screenplay by: Irmgard Von Cube & Allen Vincent
Category: Made-for-TV Movie—Drama

* Deafness
* Single White Female
* Communication: Expressive/Receptive—Sign

Plot: An idealistic VISTA volunteer teaches a deaf young woman to communicate.

VISTA volunteer Bill Richman's year-long goal in poverty-stricken Hatcher County is to set up nutritional guidelines, a food co-op, and a community garden. His only friend is local-girl-made-good Julie Sayles, who is a medical practitioner in the community.
Bill finds only one garden in town, tended by a young, disheveled woman. She runs away from him. He tracks her down to the McAdam household to apologize.
Bill orders a sign language book when he discovers Belinda is deaf and has no language or education. Bill teaches Belinda sign. She catches on quickly.
Kyle Hager, Julie's longtime beau, gets drunk at a dance. He trails Belinda home and rapes her. Belinda is pregnant.
After the baby is born, Belinda is furious when she sees Kyle Hager bending over the child at the store. Kyle shoves McAdam off a bridge when the older man accuses Kyle of being the father.
Kyle admits to his new wife, Julie, that the baby is his. He goes to the McAdam place to get it. Belinda shoots him dead. Bill tells Belinda he loves her and will take care of her and the baby.

* * *

This remake of the 1948 *Johnny Belinda* fell far short of the original. Despite a more contemporary setting, it lacked the punch of the earlier version.
Poor disheveled Belinda became tidy and groomed after she learned sign language. A girl too-afraid to approach a VISTA volunteer went to a town dance and enjoyed herself after she learned sign. The wild child who could barely groom herself became a young mother. Such changes, wrought by one non-disabled catalyst, turned this into a *Pygmalion* story. And when pupil expressed love for teacher, the instructor pulled back.
Offensive language was used, such as "deaf and dumb" and "dummy." Such language was used by clearly ignorant characters as in the original.
Bill's introduction to Belinda was in an "almost-getting-killed" scene. She was picking up aluminum cans along the side of the road. Bill nearly hit her with his VW van when she did not heed the horn.
A deaf actress appeared briefly in a small role.
Johnny Belinda was a pale and limp imitation of an older and better film.

Hear No Evil / Oct. 23, 1982 / CBS-TV

Producer: Paul Pompian
Director: Harry Falk
Writer: Tom Lazarus

* Deafness
* Single White Male
* New Disability

Hear No Evil

Category: Made-for-TV Movie —
Police Drama

* **Equipment:** Hearing ear dog; Flashing light alerts for doorbell and phone; TDD
* **Communication:** Expressive — Speech; Receptive — Notewriting/ Speechreading

Plot: A tough cop is deafened in a bomb blast.

San Francisco Police Department Inspector Bill Dragon's private crusade is to get the goods on a motorcycle gang that is suspected of drug dealing and murder. When Dragon gets too close, the gang gets a contract out on him. Despite Dragon's precautions, his jeep blows up from a planted bomb. A new disability is incurred.

Dragon awakens in a hospital. He realizes he can't hear the doctor speaking to him. An audiological exam affirms that Dragon is profoundly deaf. Monday, Dragon's partner, asks speech pathologist Meg about this prognosis.

> MEG: Dragon's hearing loss is total. He doesn't even hear himself speak ... barring an extremely unusual turn, his deafness will be permanent.

Monday brings in a stenographer to type everything he says on a screen. He gives Dragon the latest on the gang's case.

Dragon goes to see Meg in her office. She types out her responses to his questions on a screen. He discusses learning speechreading.

> MEG: It takes years. Speechreading is very imprecise ... experts guess at 75% of the words ... you can learn sign language.
>
> DRAGON: That's for deaf people.

Dragon begins his own surveillance on the hoods, watching from a car. He has a gun. He jumpily pulls the weapon on two teens who are playfully scuffling and bump the car.

Monday hooks a flashing light to Dragon's doorbell. Meg begins speech training in earnest. She also takes Dragon to the SPCA. Bill picks out a dog who will alert him when someone is at the door.

Dragon resumes his surveillance. He goads Lieutenant Healy into letting him lean on one of the hoods just arrested. Dragon convinces the hood to be a grand jury witness against his gang, the break he's waited for. However, the leaders of the gang have vanished. Using a super-telephoto lens and guesswork, Dragon speechreads their whereabouts from another gang member. He is responsible for breaking the case and is awarded his badge back.

* * *

Hear No Evil was an interesting film, due to use of technological innovations and a dose of reality. Dragon did not "courageously" face his new limitation; he hurt. However, he went on. He showed his frustration.

The most refreshing aspect of *Hear No Evil* was Dragon's receptive communication. He could not speechread; nor did he learn in three easy lessons. His pal Monday used expressive body language to communicate with him as did Meg. Both Monday and Meg often typed to him on a typewriter whose print-out appeared on a screen.

Dragon used a modem to receive telephone calls over the same system. Although he was not using a traditional TDD and did not use proper coding signals on the device, it is not considered misuse of special equipment since it is assumed that would have been asking too much of the audience. The point was made that Dragon could communicate by telephone.

His deafness led to an amusing incident where he sold his elaborate stereo system via a newspaper ad. The prospective buyers, upon hearing he was deaf, were quite upset. "How are we going to bargain?" worried one.

Even though Dragon's speechreading improved, it seems unlikely he would be able to follow a conversation through his telephoto lens well enough to find the leaders of the motorcycle gang. However, he also half-guessed at the pertinent information, in all fairness. Also unlikely was Dragon's reinstatement on the police force in his former position. While real-life persons with disabilities are pushed out of their jobs, those onscreen fight back and regain their position.

A deaf actress appeared briefly in one scene. *Hear No Evil* benefitted from research and imagination.

Facts of Life / "The Sound of Silence" / Oct. 27, 1982 / NBC-TV

Producers: Linda Marsh; Margie Peters
Director: Asaad Kelada
Writer: Kimberley Hill
Category: Series Television — Situation Comedy

* Hearing Impairment
* Black Female Teenager; Series regular
* Temporary Disability

Plot: Tootie is afraid to tell anyone she is having difficulty with her hearing.

Tootie, one of the students at the Eastland School for Girls, is acting strangely. Jo is waxing the floor and tells Tootie not to track through the wax. Oblivious to the warning, Tootie walks right on through. Her personality is changing — she's being nasty.

Geri, Blair's cousin who has cerebral palsy, is visiting. She notes Tootie's behavior.

> GERI: Have you been having trouble with your hearing? ... [you're] getting mad 'cause you can't hear them....

Geri says that she herself has a hearing problem along with CP. Natalie is concerned when she learns what's up.

> NATALIE: No wonder you've been acting like such a jerk! You couldn't help it!

Natalie agrees to keep mum about the problem. Tootie also refuses to see a doctor. She is touchy and angry.

A crisis occurs when a delivery boy hits Tootie while riding on his bike. Tootie didn't hear him ringing his bell to move out of the way. It is enough to convince Natalie to tell Mrs. Garrett about the problem. Tootie feels her best friend has betrayed her.

Geri assumes the role of the disabled catalyst. She goes to talk with Tootie. The teenager's fears pour out.

> TOOTIE: I don't wanna be handicapped! Oh Geri, I'm sorry! Please don't hate me—but I don't.

Geri responds with her characteristic humor.

> GERI: ...You think they showed me what they had and I picked cerebral palsy?

Geri convinces Tootie to see a doctor. An infection of fluids in her ear caused the problem and can be easily taken care of without residual effect.

* * *

"The Sound of Silence" was a formulaic story, with Tootie becoming angry and surly at the advent of a difficulty.

The story utilized an "almost-getting-killed" scene where Tootie did not hear an approaching bicycle.

The only interesting aspect of the story was using Geri as a disabled catalyst—and humor to break through to Tootie. Other than that, it was typical.

The Love Boat / "Still Life" / Dec. 4, 1982 / ABC-TV

Executive Producers: Aaron Spelling; Douglas Cramer
Producers: Ben Joelson; Art Baer; Henry Colman
Writer: Harvey Bullock

* Hearing Impairment
* Single Black Male; Series regular
* Temporary Disability

Category: Series Television—
Romantic Comedy

Plot: Isaac experiences a brief hearing loss.

Ship's purser Gopher asks bartender Isaac for help. Isaac doesn't respond. Gorgeous Joyce Murdock literally steals Isaac's breath away. He is smitten with the lovely black woman. Isaac recognizes he is not hearing things and goes to see Doc Bricker. The ship's physician diagnoses that Isaac's head is stuffed up, result of a middle ear infection. It will take a few days to clear up.

Isaac's quiet interlude with Joyce is interrupted by a large group invading the pool area. With all the noise, he is unable to hear Joyce. Angry and frustrated, he lies to her and tells her he has to go on duty. Joyce is left hurt, thinking he is only doing his job, cheering up a lonely female passenger.

Vicki, the captain's daughter, comes to ask a favor. Isaac is surly and angry due to his difficulties.

> ISAAC: Stop bugging me!

Captain Stubing pragmatically reminds Isaac of something.

> CAPTAIN: You've had the opportunity to appreciate something we all take for granted—the gift of hearing.

Gopher has told Joyce why Isaac has been "ignoring" her. Not only does she fully understand, she reaches under her hair and pulls out a behind-the-ear hearing aid. She has a minor hearing loss. She casually jokes about it when Isaac suggests they get to know each other better.

> JOYCE: It sounds interesting—I'd better get a new battery.

* * *

"Still Life" had one redeeming quality: the presence of Joyce, a woman with a minor hearing loss who used an aid. However, a person like Joyce, familiar with hearing problems, might have been more sensitive to what was happening with Isaac and recognizing he was not hearing her.

Other than that, "Still Life" was a typical case of putting a regular character through some trial from which he will recover. (See *Facts of Life*, "Sound of Silence" and *Trapper John, M.D.*, "Hear Today, Gone Tomorrow" for similar hearing loss stories.)

T.J. Hooker / "A Child Is Missing" / Apr. 23, 1983 / ABC-TV

Producer: Jeffrey Hayes
Supervising Producer: Rick Husky

* Hearing Impairment
* Hispanic Male Teenager

T.J. Hooker

Director: Cliff Bole
Writer: Jack V. Fogarty

* Cure
* Communication: Expressive—Speech; Receptive—Speechreading

Plot: Sergeant Hooker realizes a youth arrested on suspicion of murder has a hearing loss.

Sergeant T.J. Hooker discovers that young Danny Perez, booked on suspicion of murder, has a severe hearing loss.

> HOOKER: Kid has a hearing impairment. He can't understand what you're saying unless he can read your lips.

Danny was caught running away from a crime he discovered but did not commit. Hooker is intrigued by Danny. He approaches Mr. Perez, an addict.

> HOOKER: Has Danny ever had a problem with his hearing?
>
> FATHER: He hears what he wants to hear.

Hooker is concerned that without the ability to hear, Danny is unwittingly going to get involved in gang activity.

> HOOKER: He can't hear, he can't learn this is leading him into gang violence.

Hooker acts as the non-disabled catalyst and accepts responsibility for Danny. He has an audiologist see the boy. The audiologist discovers that Danny's hearing can be improved with surgery. However, there is a problem. Danny's father cannot afford the operation and the waiting list at County Hospital is very long—so long, that Danny could get swallowed up in gang warfare before surgery occurs. Hooker manages to get volunteer assistance and the operation is performed on Danny, free of charge. Danny is now able to hear.

* * *

"A Child Is Missing" was a trite story. Presumably, if Danny could hear, he would be more prone to walk the straight and narrow, which fails to explain why so many youths with perfect hearing become involved in violent activities. Therefore, Hooker, a cop known for his own violence, became a father-figure and took on responsibility for the kid. He managed to dredge up free surgery for the boy. Danny was cured and, presumably, inspired to become a philanthropic cop like Hooker.

ABC Afterschool Special / "Tough Girl" / Apr. 27, 1983 / ABC-TV

Producer: Martin Tahse
Director: Robert Thompson
Story: Paul Hunter
Writer: Paul W. Cooper
From the Book: *Will the Real Reni Moore Please Stand Up?* by Barbara Morgan
Category: Made-for-TV Movie — Children's

* Deafness
* Single White Male
* Deaf Performer
* Communication: Expressive — Sign/Notewriting; Receptive — Sign/Speechreading

Plot: The only person a "tough girl" will listen to is a young deaf man.

Reni Lake is arrested when the boy she is with is found to have pot in his car. Her mother and boyfriend are not good influences, so surmises her remarried father. Reni is remanded to his custody.

Reni now has to put up with her nasty and popular half-sister Gretchen. Reni is distressed to learn her father plans to send her to a psychiatrist to discern why she is always in trouble. In anger, Reni runs out of the house. She is almost hit by a car. The car misses her but injures a dog. Reni goes to a nearby house for help. She is referred to another residence where a boy who is good with animals lives.

The young man checks out the dog. He doesn't respond to Reni's questions. He writes on a blackboard:

>JAN: I'm deaf.... I lipread.

Jan indicates discrimination. He is good with animals and wants to become a veterinarian, but he says no vet schools will accept him.

Reni is intrigued by Jan's signs. She gets a book from school to try and learn some rudimentary signs. She goes back to Jan's house.

>RENI (signs): How are you?

Jan claps his hands to his head in surprise.

>JAN (signs): I'm fine!!!

Half-sister Gretchen looks down her aristocratic nose when she learns of the new friendship.

>GRETCHEN: I think you make the perfect couple — he's deaf and Reni's dumb.

When Jan gets accepted at Penn State, Reni turns off. She feels she can't trust anyone, not even him. She decides to run away with her old boyfriend,

Gary. When Gary sees Jan and makes fun of him, Reni gets angry. Gary has called Jan "deaf and dumb." Reni uses a lesser version of poor language.

> RENI: The word is mute, not dumb ... do you realize what he's done with his life?

Reni gets out of Gary's car. She realizes that Jan sees her as she is and honestly cares.

* * *

"Tough Girl" was a nice little piece with a fairly incidental portrait of a young deaf man. Reni and Jan met and hit it off. Reni seemed less inhibited with Jan, possibly because he was not looking at her as an odd "tough girl." She was on the other side, seeing something new and different. He was the first person she let get to know her. Her trying to communicate with him was one of the most positive things she'd done for quite some time.

Reni recognized Jan was "different" and was still able to succeed. She was no longer an outsider. She could go ahead in a world where no one believed in her—except herself. Jan was very much a catalyst in her life.

Jan was a personable young man who had to go out and fight to practice what he was good at. The use of a native-speaking actor was a great plus for this piece. The natural use of signs and facial expressions charged one brief scene. When Reni nervously signed, "How are you?" the look on the performer's face—along with his body language and his signing—was marvelous.

"Tough Girl" positively used a deaf young man to help straighten out a girl who found something in her friendship with him that she had never experienced.

Trapper John, M.D. / "Hear Today, Gone Tomorrow" / Jan. 22, 1983 / CBS-TV

Executive Producer: Frank Glicksman
Producer: Don Brinkley
Director: Vince Sherman
Writer: Jeff Stuart
Category: Series Television— Medical Drama

* Hearing Impairment
* Single Black Female; Series regular
* Temporary Disability

Plot: Nurse Ernestine Shoop experiences a hearing loss.

Nurse Ernie doesn't hear Dr. Trapper John McIntyre's instructions and unwittingly puts a patient in danger. Ernie is surly, having difficulty understanding other people. Audiological testing determines she has otosclerosis.

She claims she is fine — until she is almost struck by a screaming ambulance she doesn't hear coming.

Ernie has an operation and is duly mended.

* * *

"Hear Today, Gone Tomorrow" was old. Ernie was nasty and hot-tempered. She refused to admit she had a problem until the time-honored "almost-getting-killed" scene.

After Ernie's character had been strengthened with this bout of humility, she was restored to her average, sunny self and life could go on as it was.

"Hear Today, Gone Tomorrow" was trite, tired, unoriginal and old.

Voyagers! / "Barriers of Sound" / June 12, 1983 / NBC-TV

Executive Producer: James D. Parriot
Producers: Jill Sherman; Harry & Renee Longstreet; Nick Thiel
Co-Producer: Robert Bennett Steinhauer
Director: Bernard McEveety
Writer: Nick Thiel
Category: Series Television — Fantasy Adventure

* Deafness
* Single White Female
* Communication: Expressive — Speech; Receptive — Speechreading

Plot: Time "fix-it" comrades Phineas Bogg and Jeffrey Jones make sure Alexander Graham Bell invents the telephone.

In Boston, 1875, kids set off a firecracker underneath a wagon. The team of horses bolts and tears off down the street. A young woman ignores the warnings of pedestrians and is almost run over. Phineas Bogg leaps in and saves her.

BOGG: Hey, what's the matter? Can't you hear?

MABEL: No. I'm deaf.

Mr. Hubbard, a patent attorney, is waiting for daughter Mabel at Boston University. He is upset to hear about the close call. An erroneous notion is expressed.

FATHER: Why can't I get it through that pretty head of yours how dangerous it is for a deaf girl to walk the streets alone?

Jeffrey Jones, Bogg's teenaged assistant, strikes up a quick friendship with young Alexander Graham Bell, a teacher of the deaf at the university. Bell has shelved his proposed invention of the telephone, preferring to work instead on the harmonic telegraph. Jeffrey recalls that historically, Bell is supposed to marry a deaf woman named Mabel whose father is a patent attorney and will support Bell's experiments. Jeffrey and Bogg must get the two together to get history back right.

Bogg begins seeing Mabel. She notes societal difficulties.

> MABEL: I'm deaf. Men aren't interested in a deaf wife.... A lot of men approach me because they find me attractive. But you ought to see how the looks on their faces change when I tell them I'm deaf. Suddenly, they don't come around anymore.

Jeffrey convinces Bell to have Mabel over for tea. The inventor complies and tells Mabel about the failed telephone, an instrument to send the human voice through the air. But he can't show it to Mabel. She devalues herself.

> MABEL: Yes, I guess it would be a waste to show me since I can't hear the human voice or anything else.

Bell explains he cannot show her because the device doesn't work. Mabel is relieved, particularly when she discovers Bell's mother is, herself, deaf.

The two begin to get along. Bogg's time calibration device shows a green light, meaning history is back on course.

* * *

"Barriers of Sound" presented a deaf character as bright and friendly without any exploration of deafness. Mabel was a marvelous speechreader and never missed a phrase. She spoke in a natural, monitored voice. Of course, no story about deafness would be complete without the "almost-getting-killed" scene.

A young deaf performer was used as one of Bell's students.

"Barriers of Sound" was an amusing and pleasant program, but it did not present a realistic image of deafness.

Trackdown: Finding the Goodbar Killer / Oct. 14, 1983

Producer: Sonny Grosso; Larry Jacobson
Director: Bill Persky
Writer: Albert Ruben
Category: Made-for-TV Movie— Crime Drama

* Deafness
* Group Portrayal
* Deaf Performers
* Communication: Expressive/ Receptive—Sign

Plot: A detective is trying to unravel the mystery of the "Goodbar Killer."

A detective is on the trail to discover who killed the young female teacher who patronized singles bars before she was murdered. He approaches a cousin of the dead woman and gets his first lead.

> COUSIN: She taught, like—you know, deaf kids.

The detective goes to the school where the victim had taught. In the auditorium, he finds a group of deaf children onstage, rehearsing a song they are signing. He is duly impressed and approaches their teacher after the kids are dismissed.

> DETECTIVE: That's a neat trick! You had 'em eating out of your hand!

> TEACHER: I'm a teacher, not an animal trainer.

* * *

Trackdown: Finding the Goodbar Killer picked up where the 1977 feature *Looking for Mr. Goodbar* left off. Deaf children were illustrated in one scene of the film as busy and involved in their school project. They were not "special," as their teacher pointed out. They were just kids who were deaf and she was just doing her job.

Trackdown: Finding the Goodbar Killer positively illustrated deaf children as average kids.

Trauma Center / "Silent Sounds" / Nov. 24, 1983 / ABC-TV

Executive Producer: Glen A. Larson; Jerry McNeely
Producer: Scoyk, Harry & Renee Longstreet
Director: Vincent Lobl
Writer: Jerry McNeely
Category: Series Television—Medical Drama

* Deafness
* White Male Child
* New Disability
* Communication: Expressive—Speech; Receptive—Speechreading

Plot: A young boy loses his hearing in an accident.

Young Toby is in a car collision. Hearing-impaired paramedic Mr. Six notices something about the boy's responses to medical personnel.

> SIX: Mainly, he was reading lips.

Toby's mother is naturally frightened about what has happened. She notes of Mr. Six:

MOTHER: Your speech isn't quite normal.

Mr. Six acts as a deaf catalyst and a role model for both Toby and his mother.
Toby's mother refuses to accept the possibility that her son may be deaf. Dr. Cutter uses poor language when prescribing some advice.

CUTTER: You don't want him to think of himself ... as a cripple.

* * *

"Silent Sounds" was a pedestrian drama with one large difference—Mr. Six. Using his own experience and background, Six was able to express to both Toby and his mother that although the results of the accident were not the best, they were also not the worst. And he was the right person to assure them of the fact, seeing that he was a busy professional who had integrated a hearing loss into his life.

Other than that, it was a pretty dry piece. Toby's familiarity with the shapes and sounds of everyday speech gave him a tremendous advantage in learning to speechread; however, he caught on much too quickly.

"Silent Sounds" had the welcome addition of a deaf catalyst. Other than that, it was another forgettable piece.

Tin Man / 1983 / Montage Films

Executive Producer: Aaron Biston
Producer: John G. Thomas
Director: John G. Thomas
Screenplay: Bishop Holiday
Category: Feature Film—Drama

* Deafness
* Single White Male
* Temporary Cure
* Equipment: Flashing light alert for doorbell
* Communication: Expressive—Notewriting/Voice synthesizer; Receptive—Speechreading

Plot: A deaf computer genius regains his hearing.

Marcia Bell's car is in the repair shop. She waits in the employees' room. She speaks to mechanic Casey Kane. Poor language is used.

MAN: Ma'am, he can't hear. He's stone deaf.

Marcia is a speech therapist. She discovers Casey does not sign but he can speechread. She goes to his boss to talk about Casey's hearing. A supervisor is present and wants to know what's wrong with Casey's ears. Mr. Maddox lies to the supervisor, saying that Casey has an earache to hide his employee's limitation.

The supervisor uses bad language and states false notions when confronting Casey.

> TYSON: You're deaf! You're stone deaf! You can't hear a thing I'm saying.... If you had an accident, insurance wouldn't cover it!

Boss Maddox steps in.

> MADDOX: Yes they would—because I'd fill out the papers.

> TYSON: Fire him. Today. Do you understand?

When Maddox doesn't comply, both he and Casey are fired.
At home, Casey is surrounded by various electronic devices and gadgets he has created. He has a computer that transforms speech to letters. When he types a response, the device "talks" with a synthesized voice. Using it with a telephone modem, he calls a pizza parlor and threatens the person on the other end, who jeers at the electronic "voice."
Marcia comes by to apologize for causing Casey to lose his job. She sees the invention and is excited by the fact her words are translated to letters on Casey's screen.

> MARCIA: Any deaf person who can read and write can speak to anyone—instantly!

Casey has been deaf since birth. He wants the synth voice to sound more human but says he can't program naturalness without knowing how voices sound.
Marcia takes on the non-disabled catalyst role and talks to a doctor at the hospital. She finds that with a cochlear implant, Casey has a chance to hear. She tells the young man about it, using qualifying terminology.

> MARCIA: You can live a normal life!

Casey isn't wild about hearing people. Nevertheless, he devalues himself.

> CASEY: Everytime I ran into one of you, it was a reminder I was a freak.... I hate being deaf. I'd love to hear more than anything.

After surgery, Casey can hear loud and clear. He learns to play the banjo. He also becomes rich as a corporation subsidizes his inventing. But he begins to suffer ear infections. After evil corporate pirates wreck his talking computer, he loses his hearing—and has learned lessons about the world.

* * *

Tin Man presented a comic-book image of a person who was deaf. A myth about deafness was perpetuated by Supervisor Tyson's claim that insurance rates would rise with a deaf employee on the payroll. The writer clearly had no idea that people who are deaf are protected by the law.

The film also presented new technology—a cochlear implant—as a "cure" for deafness, which it is not. It provides aural stimuli which must be translated by the brain and is not hearing as the average ear perceives it. The scene where Casey woke up with his hearing was simply fantasy.

The use of such technology and the computer's synthesized voice suggested the writer had seen some pop "magazine" television show that illustrated the new horizons opening through technology to people who are deaf.

Tin Man presented a portrait of an isolated deaf genius who needed a hearing person to propel him to the heights.

Hart to Hart / title unknown / Jan. 31, 1984 / ABC-TV

Executive Producers: Aaron Spelling; Leonard Goldberg
Producer: Leigh Vance
Supervising Producer: Hugh Benson
Director: George McGowan
Writer: Larry Forrester
Category: Series Television—Crime Drama

* Deafness
* White Female Teenager
* New Disability
* Cure

Plot: A figure skater's dreams are shattered when she is deafened.

Teenaged Olympic skating hopeful Susan Wilmot and her father are hurt in a car accident arranged by saboteurs whom Susan can identify. A new disability is incurred.

A doctor uses exceptionally unprofessional language to describe Susan's condition.

DOCTOR: Right now, Susan is stone deaf.

Susan continues skating although it is difficult for her.

JENNIFER: ...she can't hear the music she's skating to.

Susan is unable to follow a beat. Her skating career may be over.

The villains identified by Susan are captured. Thanks to Jonathan Hart, a cure is available. Jonathan Hart Industries has developed a little super-duper hearing aid. With it, Susan is able to hear to compete. Another skating competitor indicates that Susan's "got guts."

* * *

Susan Wilmot got a "quick fix" when she lost her hearing in this episode of *Hart to Hart*. Despite the new limitation, she never received any counseling or any special training to help her cope with the loss of her hearing. The general level of understanding of all characters was that if Susan could still compete, she would be fine.

The indication that Susan could not compete without usable hearing was an erroneous concept. The possibility of remaining competitive within the limitation was not explored; instead, the quick fix of a new powerful hearing aid was her way out. This piece was simplistic and trite.

St. Elsewhere / "Hearing" / Feb. 1984 / NBC-TV

Executive Producer: Bruce Paltrow
Producers: John Masius; Tom Fontana
Supervising Producer: Mark Tinker
Director: Charles Braverman
Story: Steve Bello and Robert Daniels
Teleplay: Steve Bello
Category: Series Television — Medical Drama

* Deafness
* Single White Male
* Deaf Performer
* Communication: Expressive — Speech/Sign; Receptive — Speechreading/Sign

Plot: A deaf X-ray technician has problems with a supervisor.

Deaf X-ray technician Lee Tovan is called to help communicate with a hysterical deaf woman in the emergency room. Lee finds out what type of pain the woman is in by using sign language. Dr. Fiscus is able to treat her.

Lee later tells anesthesiologist V.J. Kochar that there are difficulties about working in a hospital.

> LEE: It's hard for me to communicate with anyone in a surgical mask.

Radiology supervisor Al Kleckner doesn't like the idea of a deaf person working for him. He exerts pressure on Lee. Lee speaks to V.J. about his problems. He devalues himself.

> LEE: It'll always be this way. I'm always going to lose.

V.J. acts as the non-disabled catalyst by telling Chief of Staff Dr. Westphall about the problem. Westphall calls Al into the office.

> AL: [Lee's] just not normal.

WESTPHALL: That's baloney and you know it. You can't treat the handicapped like they're contagious. Those people have rights and feelings and dreams like everyone else. And a helluva lot more courage in their day-to-day existence than you and I will ever know anything about or have to deal with.

Westphall tells Kleckner that his job is to give the younger man some humanistic leeway. Lee later approaches Dr. Westphall.

LEE: I could've handled it alone, believe me.... I'm so used to people looking down on me, either by being mean or patronizing....

WESTPHALL: ...I'm not saying all the problems are going to go away.

LEE: In that respect, I'm like everyone else.

* * *

"Hearing" dealt with the attitudes of a man who didn't care for equal opportunity hiring. This fresh approach was due to the story being co-written by a deaf person, who also performed the role.

The fact that Lee had rights was touched upon by Dr. Westphall but quickly squelched in the gushy speech about courage. Such formula sentiment cheapened the whole story.

A deaf actress was used for the role of the hysterical patient.

"Hearing" dealt with an issue of deafness and not the limitation itself.

T.J. Hooker / "Death Strip" / Mar. 10, 1984 / ABC-TV

Executive Producers: Aaron Spelling; Leonard Goldberg
Producer: Jeffrey Hayes
Co-Producer: Jack V. Fogarty; Simon Muntner
Supervising Producer: Rick Husky
Director: Sigmund Neufeld, Jr.
Writer: Patrick Mathews
Category: Series Television — Police Drama

* Deafness
* Single White Female
* Deaf Performer
* Equipment: Flashing light alert for doorbell
* Communication: Expressive — Sign/Notewriting; Receptive — Sign/Speechreading

Plot: A deaf woman is being chased by unknown persons for unknown reasons after her sister is killed.

Betty Parsons has been supplying cop Vince Romano with information to blow open a scam. Someone is on to her and she is killed. Romano approaches Betty's sister. Kate is deaf and Romano signs the bad news to her.

Kate receives some mail shortly thereafter and finds a letter and a photo from Betty, instructing Kate to give it to the police if something bad happens to Betty. Kate rapidly writes her neighbor a note and asks that Romano be contacted to meet her at the restaurant where she is a hostess.

Kate is ambushed in the parking lot by a henchman who steals her purse, searching for the picture. She is beaten.

Romano rhapsodizes to Hooker about the benefits of a friendship with Kate.

ROMANO: It makes your day to talk to her.

Romano and Hooker arrive at the restaurant too late to help. At the hospital, Kate is able to give them a description of her attacker. Romano acts as interpreter.

Kate is caught and kidnapped by the villains but saved by Hooker before they can do her in.

* * *

"Death Strip" used a deaf character in a fairly incidental role. The story did not depend on Kate's communication difficulty to work. It was a basic cop-helps-the-helpless-victim story — but in this case, the victim happened to be a person who was deaf. She was not preyed upon as an easy mark because she was deaf.

Kate was employed, working as a hostess at a restaurant. Such a job suggests the role was written for a hearing person but cast with a deaf performer and inserted with throwaway lines to explain her limitation. Kate lived alone in a nice apartment and was intelligent and vivacious. Romano indicated at story's end that he had a "hot" date with her.

The use of a native speaker enhanced the role. The character of Romano also used nice signs, clearly rendered.

"Death Strip" utilized a deaf person as part of the human spectrum whose life was made better by Sergeant Hooker.

Lottery! / "Win or Lose" / Mar. 22, 1984 / ABC-TV

Executive Producer: Rick Rosner
Producer: Liam O'Brien
Co-Producer: Bob Birnbaum
Supervising Producer: Robert Janes
Director: Barry Crane
Writer: Hindi Brooks
Category: Series Television — Drama

* Deafness
* Single White Female
* Communication: Expressive — Speech; Receptive — Speechreading

Plot: Patrick and Colt seek out lottery winner Sarah Keene.

Lottery!

Miss Sarah Keene is flabbergasted to be told she's won millions in a lottery. She asks Patrick Flaherty and Colt if this is a joke. They respond it is not, but she seems to have not heard.

> PATRICK (surprised): You have to read our lips!
>
> SARAH: I'm deaf. I'm sorry, I forgot to tell you.

Mrs. Keene is thrilled about Sarah's new fortune.

> MRS. KEENE: It means that Sarah can hear again!

However, a visit to a top specialist says there is no cure for Sarah. Sarah indicates she has more on her mind than being able to hear. She confronts her mother, who wants to try another doctor.

> SARAH: I'm just deaf. I'm not dead.

Sarah bursts into the street. She is almost hit by a car she does not hear approaching.

Sarah confides in Patrick. The cause of her hearing loss is discussed. A bad bout of influenza thirteen years earlier damaged her hearing. Sarah's mother feels if she herself had been more responsive to the illness, Sarah would be able to hear.

> SARAH: My mother, wallowing in guilt for what she did.... I can live with [being deaf]. My mother can't ... all I want is to live my life like everyone else; solve my problems like everyone else.

Sarah decides to run away to New York to prove she can make it on her own. Mrs. Keene wants to stop her. Patrick intercedes with timely advice and wisdom.

Sarah is at the airport. She speaks to the airline clerk.

> SARAH: When you talk to me, could you look at me? I'm deaf.
>
> LADY: I'm sorry.
>
> SARAH (brightly): Oh, it's okay. You didn't know.

Mrs. Keene approaches her daughter—to wish her a bon voyage.

* * *

"Win or Lose" began as a formula-type of story then twisted off in another direction. The writer took a larger look at the character created and noted a problem that, to Sarah, was greater than her inability to hear: her overprotective and guilt-ridden mother.

Sarah's speech and speechreading skills were very accurate — to the point that no one would have known she was deaf had she not spoken up. The few signs she used were awkwardly rendered.

Formula treatment did creep in, however, particularly in the "almost-getting-killed" sequence.

"Win or Lose" had some typical elements of a formula drama but wisely based the bulk of the story on a problem outside of the limitation.

AfterM*A*S*H / title unknown / May 6, 1984 (rerun) / CBS-TV

Producer: Dennis Koenig
Supervising Producers: Ken Levine; David Isaacs
Director: Nick Havinga
Writer: Larry Gelbart
Category: Series Television — Situation Comedy

* Hearing Impairment
* Single White Male; Series regular
* Cure
* Equipment: Hearing aid

Plot: Father Mulcahy has his impaired hearing restored.

Father Francis Mulcahy is the chaplain at a Missouri veterans' hospital after returning home from the Korean War. He has surgery to repair a perforated eardrum.

A black veteran falls down in the cafeteria. He is told to stand up on his leg.

EDWARDS (bitterly): If I had my leg, I'd stand on it.

The amputee Edwards has problems accepting an artificial limb. Mulcahy counsels him. Edwards points to the priest's hearing aid.

EDWARDS: At least you can wear something that can help you.

MULCAHY: So can you.

Mulcahy determines the veteran is having problems accepting a "white" flesh-toned leg. Under his direction, the limb is painted brown. Edwards adopts the device.

Surgical packing is removed from Mulcahy's ear and he is able to hear.

* * *

In the last episode of the long-running TV favorite *M*A*S*H,* "Goodbye, Farewell and Amen," the mobile hospital's chaplain lost a good deal of his hearing in a blast. His limitation carried over to the spinoff series. Mulcahy remained hearing-impaired for a few episodes before undergoing surgery.

Mulcahy was realistic about the loss, feeling it gave him a place to better counsel the vets in his charge. He also indicated it was a bother. His hearing aid's hyper-amplification, while helpful, was a nuisance. In this episode, he mentioned that while other people heard the movie they attended, he could hear the people in the back "making babies." The difficulties he faced were dealt with honestly and with the humor typical for the series.

Mulcahy's limitation gave him a better understanding of the men he worked with; it would have been interesting to have seen the character remain hearing-impaired and to have seen his experiences. It seemed, however, that the writers thought they had exhausted the story possibilities in regard to Mulcahy's limitation. His cure got them out of their supposed dilemma—when, in fact, they had barely scratched the surface of what the problem could mean in terms of development of conflict and growth. Still, they must be commended for not giving Mulcahy a "quick fix." They tried to explore how such a limitation would affect the priest for a few shows.

Actors with disabilities were seen in the background of the episode.

Fame / "Signs" / May 10, 1984 / Syndicated

Consulting Producer: David De Silva
Director: William Claxton
Writers: Michael Hoey; Valerie Landsburg
Category: Series Television—Drama

* Deafness
* Single White Teenager; Series regular
* Temporary Disability
* Communication: Expressive—Speech/Sign; Receptive—Speechreading/Sign

Plot: Chris faces deafness after a head blow.

While dancing at the School for the Performing Arts, student Chris Donlon hits his head and is out cold for a few moments. When he rouses, he has a buzzing in his ears. The buzzing overcomes the sound of voices. He misses the ringing of the class bell.

    MR. MORLOCH: Final bell, Donlon. You deaf or something?

Chris goes to see an audiologist. A technician types to him on a screen.

    CHRIS: If you're gonna tell me I'm deaf, I already know that.

    TECHNICIAN: ...That's what you have to prepare yourself for, Chris, the possibility [your hearing may never return].

Chris rejects the suggestion that he transfer to a school for the deaf. In class, his friends—who believe his hearing will return in a week—cover for him. He manages to speechread a bit.

Danny informs Mr. Morloch that Chris can't hear. Morloch indicates the School of the Arts is not able to teach Chris. Chris is morbid about his future.

> CHRIS: Not much call for a deaf singer.

Chris enrolls at the school for the deaf. He meets the principal, who is deaf himself.

> PRINCIPAL: [We're going to] start you on a program of lipreading and signing . . . everything depends on you.

The fright of being transplanted into a world he does not understand is helped when Chris meets Christina, a deaf girl. She speechreads, speaks, and signs.

Chris' hearing spontaneously pops back in and he thankfully returns to his old school.

A dance routine is stuck in a creative rut so Chris calls on Christina and some of her schoolmates to help out. Together, the hearing and deaf students do a routine of vocal song, sign-song and dance.

* * *

In "Signs," as is par for the TV course, Chris was not offered any counseling or special rehabilitation after losing his hearing. He was plunked in the middle of what would be a whole new world for him while hoping for a maybe — that his hearing would return.

It was distressing to find that in the world of the series, a School of the Performing Arts, education was not available for a hearing-impaired student (not only Chris, but any). Such a notion precluded the possibility that talented dancers without hearing could exist and was reinforced when the deaf students did not dance in the big production. And, despite laws that permit students with limitations a free public education with resource teachers to aid in special areas, no indication was made that Chris might be able to return to his preferred school with such support. Once he was deaf, he was shoved off into the school for the deaf where he would naturally be an outcast, always branded a hearing person despite his loss. He belonged to the mainstream culture.

Deaf actors were used in various roles. The principal at the school for the deaf, a classroom teacher, and Christina were all deaf performers. Actual deaf students were used in the background of the school scenes.

"Signs" had two big pluses: the use of deaf performers and the joint production between talented students of the two cultures and schools. Other than that, the piece was pretty routine.

Gimme a Break / "The Earthquake" / Feb. 9, 1985 / NBC-TV

Executive Producers: Rod Parker, Hal Cooper and Mort Lachman

* Deafness
* Hispanic Female

Gimme a Break

Director: Hal Cooper
Writer: Rod Parker
Category: Series Television — Situation Comedy

* Deaf Performer
* Communication: Expressive/Receptive — Sign

Plot: An earthquake traps Nell in a library basement with a woman who is deaf.

Nell goes to the library to straighten out a mistaken bill for $1,600 received for a book that's one week overdue. While in the basement accounting office, an earthquake hits. A beam falls down and blocks off the exit. Nell and another woman are trapped. Nell's requests for help to move the beam are ignored.

NELL: Lady, are you deaf?

The other woman begins to rapidly sign.

MONICA (signs): Can't hear, can't speak.

Nell's bright idea to communicate via pad and paper is thwarted when she discovers the other woman speechreads and writes only Spanish.

NELL: I'm gonna die and have nobody to complain to!

Nell's fearful stream of jabber annoys Monica; Monica's heated signed conversation with herself annoys Nell. They strike up an uneasy liaison when an aftershock sends them under a desk. Nell begins to sing "Ave Maria" for comfort. Monica, recognizing the words, joins in with sign.

* * *

"The Earthquake" had a big plus—the casting of an actress who was very talented and was herself, deaf. The situation created was interesting—Nell, who was never at a loss for words, stuck with someone who couldn't hear her.

A marvelous scene occurred when Nell paced up and down, moaning that she was trapped with this woman who just waved her arms around. When Nell's tirade was over, Monica treaded the same path, griping in sign that she was stuck with a woman who talked, talked and talked. Although her comments were not accessible to the hearing audience at large, the intent was clear.

The inclusion of "Ave Maria" as a binding element was a little schmaltzy, but interesting to note the song was as important to the deaf character as the hearing one.

"The Earthquake" was pleasurable and light. It provided a nice sense of sameness between the two women. Monica didn't know English; Nell didn't know Spanish or sign—both were equal in the situation and both were very funny.

MacGruder and Loud / title unknown / Feb. 26, 1985 / ABC-TV

Executive Producers: Aaron Spelling and Douglas Cramer
Producer: Robert Justman
Executive Supervising Producer: E. Duke Vincent
Supervising Producer: Robert Collins
Director: Richard Compton
Writer: Jill Gordon
Category: Series Television — Police Drama

* Deafness
* Male Teenager
* Communication: n/a

Plot: Policeman Malcolm MacGruder shoots a fleeing perpetrator who didn't heed his warning and finds out he's deaf.

Two suspects flee after shooting a cop. Cop MacGruder threatens to shoot a young suspect if he does not halt. When the call is ignored, MacGruder shoots and injures a teenager. The kid has a card on him that reads, "I am deaf." The boy is a fifteen-year-old who did not hearing the warning.
MacGruder tortures himself over the incident.

> MacGRUDER: If he'd just done something with his hands — made a sign —

MacGruder is suspended from the force for the duration of the investigation. "Officer Shoots Deaf Boy" makes the news headlines.
With the help of a friend, MacGruder learns to sign, "I'm sorry." He goes to the hospital to tell the boy how he feels.

* * *

This episode of *MacGruder and Loud* brought to light a different problem. A young deaf boy, frightened, did not respond to a cop's warning — a warning he could not hear. It was a problem with a basis in reality.
The deaf character was minor. The story dealt with MacGruder's guilt over the incident and his trying to come to terms with what he had done.
This piece illustrated the necessity that persons in the service of the public need to be aware of possibilities in terms of the public they deal with — in this case, a citizen who did not hear threats of police.

Murder, She Wrote / "Sudden Death" / Mar. 3, 1985 / CBS-TV

Executive Producer: Peter S. Fischer

* Deafness
* White Female Child

Producer: Robert F. O'Neill
Director: Edward M. Abroms
Writer: Robert E. Swanson
Category: Series Television—
   Mystery

* **Communication:** Expressive—
Sign; Receptive—Speechreading

Plot: Jessica finds herself mixed up with murders in a professional football organization.

Mystery writer Jessica Fletcher has inherited stock in the Leopards, a pro football team. She checks out the organization to determine if she will keep the stock or not. While at the field watching practice, she is nearly run down by a "Helmetmobile" driven by Jill Farrell, the daughter of football star Zak Farrell. Jessica is unperturbed, telling the girl she didn't expect to get run over by a "hat." Jessica realizes the girl is deaf when the child corrects her using signs.

ZAK: "Helmet"—she reads lips very well.

The Farrells receive anonymous phone calls, threatening them. Jill was adopted illegally through an attorney. The caller threatens to blow the whistle on them. Zak believes the caller was Kreuger. When Kreuger is killed, Zak becomes a prime suspect.

Thanks to Jessica's sleuth-work, Zak is off the hook. Jessica decides to get out of the football business and gives her stock in the team to Jill.

*   *   *

"Sudden Death" used a deaf child in an almost-incidental role. Her limitation had little to do with the story. Although Jessica treated Jill as she would any child, while speaking to her, she overenunciated her words in an attempt to help Jill speechread her better, an action that distorted her mouth movements. No one pointed out that such exaggeration would have made it hard for Jill to speechread her. Consequently, all of Jessica's statements to the girl were belabored and hard to listen to.

But, then again, Jill's speechreading skills were too amazing. She managed to pick up abstracts in conversations, such as Jessica's statement that she and Jill "hit it off" or the fact that Jill would be "partners" with her father now that she owned stock.

The signs Jill used were technically correct but rendered mechanically. The nicest impression left by this piece was that the child was cherished, wanted, and loved by her parents. Her father jokingly projected his daughter would be the "first female quarterback."

"Sudden Death" presented a deaf child as one who simply could not hear.

St. Elsewhere / "Bang the Ear Drum Slowly" / Mar. 20, 1985 / NBC-TV

Executive Producer: Bruce Paltrow
Supervising Producer: Mark Tinker
Producer: John Masius; Tom Fontana
Coordinating Producer: Abby Singer
Director: David Anspaugh
Story: John Masius & Tom Fontana
Teleplay: Stephen Willey
Category: Series Television — Medical Drama

* Hearing Impairment
* Single Black Male; Series regular
* Temporary Disability

Plot: A temporary hearing loss helps Luther evaluate his future.

Orderly Luther Hawkins and maintenance man Raleigh go to the basement to look at the ancient boiler. The pilot light is out. When Raleigh lights it, it explodes. Luther's hearing is muffled. Raleigh is out cold. Luther staggers from the basement and gets help. Raleigh dies as Luther wanders outside of the emergency room in a daze.

LUTHER: I can't hear.

Luther needs immediate surgery to have his eardrum reconstructed. Surgery is successful.

* * *

"Bang the Eardrum Slowly" took a little different tack than the basic regular character-faces-a-temporary-disability story. First, it was brief, used to bring the character to a point of transition in his life. Luther felt God didn't want him to be an orderly anymore.

The most interesting thing about the segment was the use of point-of-view. A handheld camera shot everything Luther was seeing. The sound was muffled. He really did not know what was happening. He was examined and told via note that an operation was necessary. He just went along with the flow. Happily for Luther, a reconstruction was successful and his hearing was restored.

"Bang the Eardrum Slowly" pointed out that understanding without language is a difficult process. Luther's temporary limitation was a time of shock, not one of typical devaluation and bitterness.

A Summer to Remember... / Mar. 27, 1985 / CBS-TV

Executive Producer: Max Keller and Robert Lloyd Lewis
Producer: Michelline Keller
Director: Robert Lloyd Lewis
Story: Scott Swanton and Robert Lloyd Lewis
Teleplay: Scott Swanton
Category: Made-for-TV Movie—Drama

* Deafness
* White Male Child
* Deaf Performer
* Communication: Expressive/Receptive—Sign

Plot: A deaf boy befriends an escaped signing orangutan.

A van transporting an orangutan from the Radford Research Institute, San Francisco, is in a crash caused by a drunk. The animal disappears. Toby Wyler, a deaf child, spots the animal. He believes he's seen Bigfoot. His family thinks he is imagining things.

Toby and his sister make a startling discovery—not only is the animal in their tree house tame, he also signs.

Mother Jeannie is concerned. Toby seems to be withdrawing even more. He doesn't get along with his new stepfather, who can't communicate with him.

She is also worried that Toby will not use his voice. The cause of his limitation is described as an illness years before. Toby has not spoken since becoming deaf.

    JEANNIE: Toby *will* talk again.

The orangutan is adopted by a nearby circus. The kids release Casey.

Dolly, the researcher from San Francisco who has been searching for Casey, launches a search. It is Toby who finds Casey and uses his voice to trumpet the discovery.

* * *

A Summer to Remember took a story from the newspapers—about primates learning sign language—and plugged it into a story about kids and their new stepfather. The addition of a deaf child in a family situation was welcome.

Toby was a busy and very intelligent boy. He was also very headstrong and temperamental. He was a handful for his mother and an enigma to his new stepfather. Surprisingly, he was not the one to note the orangutan signed, his hearing sister made the discovery. The two, like any brother and sister, remained confederates in keeping this secret from the adults.

Despite its good points, the story was difficult to believe. The inclusion of the staple "Toby *will* talk again" was tedious. Being a post-lingually deafened child meant that Toby had good language; for him not to use his voice as if in embarrassment after losing his hearing was a formulaic devaluation device.

A Summer to Remember was pleasant and forgettable. (See Appendix: *The Red Hand Gang* for a similar story.)

Airwolf / "Jennie" / Nov. 23, 1985 / CBS-TV

Executive Producer: Bernard L. Kowalski
Producer: Robert Janes
Co-Producers: Carol Gillson and Stephen A. Miller
Supervising Producer: Everett Chambers
Director: Bernard L. Kowalski
Writer: Katharyn Powers
Category: Series Television— Action Adventure

* Deafness
* Group Portrayal; Hispanic children
* Deaf Performers
* Communication: Expressive/ Receptive—Sign

Plot: On a mission in a South American jungle, Hawke meets up with American schoolteacher Jennie and a group of deaf students.

Jennie, an American schoolteacher, was out on a day hike with her deaf students. While gone, government troops destroyed the village. She and the children are on their way to Santa Teresa for shelter and safety.

Hawke has been dispatched to South America to rescue scientist Jason Keith, who has been imprisoned. As the two men trek across the jungle, they are trapped in a swamp and "captured" by Jennie and her gun-toting charges. Noble/inspiring connotations are derived.

> KEITH: ...captured by a bunch of deaf kids?

> JENNIE: They're hearing impaired and they're young but everyone of them has a lot more courage than most adults have ever known.

Hawke is intrigued by Jennie and her profession.

> HAWKE: Must take an awful lot of patience.

> JENNIE: Only because they're kids. The other is just a language barrier.

The children are cooperative. The eldest saves Keith's life when he spots a snake. Solita, the teenaged girl who is second in seniority, carefully protects the little ones—yet is ready to jump in and club a bad guy tracking down Keith and Hawke.

The group makes it to Santa Teresa in safety, thanks to a concerted group effort.

* * *

"Jennie" used deaf youngsters in a semi-incidental fashion. Their deafness had nothing to do with the story but added a little extra interest. The kids were resourceful and mature and not particularly different from any other kids their age.

Especially nice was Jennie's inference that neither she nor the children were particularly special.

"Jennie" used deaf children as part of the general spectrum of society, those whose lives were endangered by politics and policies and not their limitations.

Love Is Never Silent / Dec. 9, 1985 / NBC-TV

Executive Producer: Marian Rees
Co-Executive Producer: Julianna Fjeld
Producer: Dorthea G. Petrie
Director: Joseph Sargent
Teleplay: Darlene Craviotto
Based on the Novel: *In This Sign,* by Joanna Greenberg
Category: Made-for-TV Movie—Drama

* Deafness
* White Married Couple
* Deaf Performers
* Equipment: Interpreter
* Communication: Expressive/Receptive—Sign

Plot: A hearing teenager is the communication link between her world and that of her deaf parents in the 1930s.

The Ryders appear to be an average Depression-era family—husband, wife, and two small children. The parents are deaf and the children are hearing. After her brother Bradley's accidental death, young Margaret becomes the communicator for the family, interpreting the words of salesmen, funeral directors, and just plain folk into sign for her grizzly, gentle father and her rigid, unemotional mother. Adolescence is difficult for her as she attempts to grow and her parents try to keep her with them. Her marriage is a sore spot for them as they are losing the link they have with the hearing world.

* * *

Love Is Never Silent was a rare drama. It took itself into the realm of deafness as seen by the deaf or people close to the community. It was not a projection of deafness as imagined by a hearing writer. It featured a unique aspect of deaf culture: the need for a hearing person to bridge the gap between the two worlds. In the film, the daughter was the link, straddling the fence between her own impetuousness and her sense of responsibility to her parents.

Love Is Never Silent featured a limitation but was not focused on it. It was about children and parents and the unrealistic expectations that can arise in a close-knit family. It was about a clash of cultures—Margaret's hearing world and the deaf background of her parents.

The Ryders were illustrated as concerned parents, both employed. Abel Ryder worked in a print shop and Janice was a garment worker.

The movie also featured stunning performances by deaf actors, both of whom were singled out in reviews. A deaf actress was also seen in the background, portraying one of Janice Ryder's co-workers at the garment factory.

In addition to almost-universal rave reviews, the production garnered two Emmys at the 1986 Emmy Awards for Best Director and the Emmy equivalent of best picture of the year.

Love Is Never Silent was a story exploring the aspects of life within a limitation—and not a melodramatic vehicle simply designed for tears or moral uplifting.

CBS Schoolbreak Special / "Have You Tried Talking to Patty?" / Jan. 14, 1986 / CBS-TV

Producer: Diane Asselin
Director: Donald Petrie
Writers: Alan L. Gansberg and Judith M. Gansberg
Category: Made-for-TV Movie—Children's

* Deafness
* White Female Teenager
* Deaf Performer
* Communication: Expressive—Speech; Receptive—Speechreading

Plot: A deaf teenager, feeling left out when her hearing friends pay more attention to boys than to her, falls in with some punk kids.

Patty Miller attends a hearing high school and is able to speechread well. She attends regular classes but also has a tutor. She, like her two best friends, is worried about getting a date for the dance coming up.

Her friends look out for her, trying to solve special problems that may come up during a necking session.

> GIRL: How's she gonna manage if she has to keep on the lights the whole time to read his lips?

When her friends "defect," going after the boys they want to date, Patty also defects, hanging out with some "punk" girls who think dances are stupid. Patty's new friends line her up with a date, a punk boy from another school.

Patty's grades begin to slip. And boys are starting to notice her, but for the wrong reasons. They've heard she went out with the biggest make-out artist at Central High. One of the boys trying to pick her up is Kevin, the guy her old best friend is crazy about. The friend believes Patty is stabbing her in the back.

Patty goes to the store with her punk friends and begins shoplifting like they tell her. She is rescued from getting arrested by the nephew of the manager, a boy who likes Patty. Her "friends" vanish.

It's enough to shake Patty up and she returns to her normal self. She makes up with her friends and goes to the dance with them since they discovered the truth about the boys they liked. Patty dances with the boy from the market, having learned a valuable lesson.

* * *

"Have You Tried Talking to Patty?" was an interesting little drama about conformity. Patty's deafness was almost incidental—she was just another teenager who felt out of place and at a point in her life where no one liked or understood her—a universal problem not exclusive to deaf teens. The story could have existed without Patty's limitation. As it was, it just presented a deaf high school student going through growing pains.

Spenser for Hire / "When Silence Speaks" / Feb. 11, 1986 / ABC-TV

Executive Producer: John Wilder
Producers: Dick Gallegly; Robert Hamilton
Supervising Producer: William Robert Yates
Director: Ray Austin
Writer: Robert Hamilton
Category: Television—Detective Drama

* Deafness
* Single White Female
* Deaf Performer
* Communication: Expressive— Sign/Notewriting; Receptive— Speechreading/Sign

Plot: Private investigator Spenser is retained to locate a missing person by a deaf woman.

Joan Cugell, an advice-to-the-lovelorn columnist, approaches private investigator Spenser to track down a reader with whom she had begun a relationship. The fact that Joan is deaf intrigues Spenser. He is able to communicate with Joan through writing and by the fact his girlfriend Susan recalls sign taught to her long ago by a deaf cousin.

Spenser locates the missing person.

* * *

"When Silence Speaks" used a deaf character as a character *first*. Deafness had nothing to do with the role. Joan Cugell had overstepped her professional bounds and become involved with a reader and pursued a correspondence with him. The man knew the writer was deaf. He vanished, due to a laser breakthrough he had made. The villains wanted his information for money. Thanks to Joan, Spenser located the man and foiled the dastardly plot of the bad guys.

Joan's deafness was dealt with in a few throwaway lines. A rendition of the "almost-getting-killed" scene was included. The deaf cousin from whom Susan had learned sign had died at a young age when she was hit by a speeding car. "Of course," sighed Susan, "she couldn't hear it."

The role, announced the producers to *TV Guide* magazine prior to air, was not written for a deaf person. When the actress was hired, reworking was done to accommodate her. The portrayal was, therefore, that of a faceted human being with interests and feelings. Deafness had nothing to do with the story.

"When Silence Speaks" positively featured a deaf character as a part of everyday life. Focus remained on the missing person and Spenser's search, not on Joan's communication differences.

Alfred Hitchcock Presents / "A Very Happy Ending" / Feb. 16, 1986 / NBC-TV

Executive Producer: Christopher Crowe
Producer: Alan Barnette
Supervising Producer: Andrew Mirisch
Director: Tom Rickman
Writer: Tom Rickman
Category: Series Television — Occult/Suspense

* Deafness
* White Male Child
* Cure
* Communication: Expressive — Speech; Receptive — Speechreading/Sign

Plot: A deaf child blackmails a hit man to do away with his father.

Little rich boy Pagie Fisher is being chauffeured to the airport by an antagonistic driver and his helpmate/nanny, Martha.

> DRIVER: He can't hear me, he can't hear nothin'!
>
> MARTHA: ...He can read your lips.
>
> DRIVER: Not if he can't see 'em.

But Pagie has "heard." Illustrating amazing speechreading skills, Pagie has followed the conversation from the dark car's backseat via a rearview mirror.

At the airline terminal, the boy wanders. His eyes light upon two men near a phone booth. He comprehends they are hit men. While he watches, Irish Charlie does in the other man. Pagie finds Charlie on the same plane. He lifts Charlie's driver's license and switchblade and uses them to blackmail Charlie into doing a job for him—to "hit" his wealthy and never-home father. If Charlie complies, Pagie will keep mum about the murder.

At Pagie's home the next day, Charlie awaits the arrival of Mr. Fisher. He talks to Pagie. The cause of the boy's deafness is discussed as a fever when he was seven.

> PAGIE: When I lost my hearing, it was like [my father] couldn't stand to see me any more.

The hit is thwarted when Mr. Fisher turns out to be Charlie's boss. Charlie is taken away but survives.

Mr. Fisher gives Pagie a gift. He puts a hearing aid into his boy's ear. Charlie approaches, intending to get Mr. Fisher. Pagie tells Charlie he is able to hear now. Charlie decides not to kill the other man.

* * *

"A Very Happy Ending" was a story which required public mythology to have credibility. In this case, the watcher was to believe a child, without context, could speechread across a crowded airport terminal well enough to discern details of a "hit." Pagie was one of TV's talented speaking/speechreading persons one would never guess was deaf.

Pagie was a precocious, spoiled rich kid who wanted his father's love more than his birthday party complete with a mini-Mercedes. He was a bright child, understanding too well what a "hit man" was and how he could be utilized.

"A Very Happy Ending" was a tale that did not require deafness to propel it along; one could only wonder why the writer even bothered to insert it.

Magnum, P.I. / "One Picture Is Worth" / Oct. 8, 1986 / CBS-TV

Executive Producer: Donald Bellisario
Co-executive Producer: Charles Floyd Johnson
Producers: Jay Huguely; Rick Weaver
Supervising Producer: Chris Abbott-Fish
Director: Ray Austin
Writer: James L. Novack

* Deafness
* Single White Female
* Communication: Expressive— Speech/Sign; Receptive—Speechreading

Deafness

Category: Series Television — Detective Drama

Plot: Private investigator Thomas Magnum must protect a deaf witness to a hold-up.

Linda Andrews goes to a police line-up to identify the man she saw commit murder in an Oahu bank. Assistant D.A. Carol taps her on the shoulder to remind her the suspects cannot see her. Private investigator Thomas Magnum looks on.

> CAROL: I keep forgetting.
>
> MAGNUM (whispering): Is she deaf?

The cause of Linda's deafness is discussed as a boating accident five years ago. Thomas is goaded into providing protection for her. She will stay at the estate where Thomas acts as live-in security. At the estate, major domo Higgins knows who Linda is — an internationally acclaimed artist. Higgins uses a few signs with Linda. She speechreads every detail of one of his memoir-type yarns.

Linda turns on the TV and speechreads a TV newscaster stating she has been identified as the "mystery witness" at the bank hold-up. The killer is out on bail. Linda flees in fear.

Magnum tracks down Linda at her secret hideaway. Linda is angry at the intrusion. Erroneous notions about people who are deaf are suggested by her outburst.

> LINDA: You don't know what it's like to have to depend on people to take care of you all of the time. You're never safe anywhere. I learned that five years ago. I don't need to learn it again from you. Just go away.

Magnum becomes somewhat of a non-disabled catalyst.

> MAGNUM: You think just because you're deaf you have to take on the whole world by yourself?
>
> LINDA: After the accident and I lost my hearing, I felt so helpless. I promised myself I was never ever going to feel that way again.

The killer has trailed Linda. He stalks her little cottage with two henchmen. Linda speechreads them through binoculars. Magnum engages in a gun battle. When he indicates he's running low on bullets, Linda thinks quickly and makes Molotov cocktails. They get the three criminals.

* * *

"One Picture Is Worth" illustrated a deaf woman as one who was talented and creative. It also reinforced myths about deafness. Linda was a tremendous speechreader. She was able to understand everything Magnum said without being hindered by the thick mustache on his upper lip. Not only that, she fully understood him as he spoke while driving—his face in profile or three-quarter angles while watching the road. She easily understood Higgins, the TV, people across the room, and the conversation of three killers as seen through binoculars.

Linda's mode of communication was appropriate, seeing as how she was described as being a deafened adult. However, she spoke in a clear, monitored voice—and even hummed without pitch problems. She used a little bit of sign with Higgins. In one sense, special equipment could be considered misused as the signs were rendered awkwardly and in one case, unintelligibly. English signs were used (as opposed to Ameslan), which could be considered appropriate as Linda was only recently deafened. Ameslan would not be natural to her.

Linda was shown driving a car without any problems. "One Picture Is Worth" illustrated a deaf woman as one who was capable and interesting; however, she also did not portray a person who was deaf—only one who had to face the speaker some of the time.

Children of a Lesser God / Oct. 1986 / Paramount Pictures

Producer: Burt Sugarman and Patrick Palmer
Director: Randa Haines
Writers: Hesper Anderson and Mark Medoff
Based on the Play by: Mark Medoff

* Deafness
* Single White Female
* Deaf Performer
* Communication: Expressive/Receptive—Sign

Plot: A speech teacher of deaf children falls in love with a deaf woman.

James Leeds begins teaching speech to deaf high school students. He is a bit of a maverick and the kids respond to his wild tactics. At the school, he spies an angry deaf woman who is hotly signing to a cafeteria worker. Leeds is completely captivated. He discovers she is Sarah, an ex-student who is now a custodian at the school.

Leeds manages to meet Sarah. Despite her almost-constant rebuffs, he is attracted to her beautiful, defiant anger. She is very intelligent, too intelligent, he feels, to be stuck in a nowhere job. He tries to convince her to let him work with her, to teach her to speak.

LEEDS: Don't you want to be able to get along in the world?

Sarah explains she gets along just fine.

The two fall into a tempestuous relationship. Leeds tries to determine the source of Sarah's anger; at the same time he constantly tries to pull her into his world.

After a party the couple attends given by Sarah's deaf friends, the crisis comes to a head. Sarah notes the achievements of one of the deaf women at the party, a vivacious and intelligent person who did not use her voice. Sarah demands the same freedom: to be herself and not have to speak. She devalues herself in a shrieking speech, the first time Leeds has heard her voice.

> SARAH: Hear me now! Hear my voice! Am I beautiful now?... I'm a fucking freak!

The couple is torn apart while Sarah leaves to find herself. The two meet again, reluctant but ready to enter into a new relationship.

* * *

Children of a Lesser God was a screen version of a Tony Award–winning play. The film was visually stunning. The performances were strong and directed. The film received almost-universal good reviews. Yet, its central theme was one seen many times: a hearing person trying to get a deaf person to speak.

The kids in Leeds' class were all successful, except one. He sat sullen and quiet while the others danced around, signing, and using their voices to accompany a rock song. His non-participation suggested he was a failure.

Sarah was a failure as well. The unspoken feeling was that if she could speak, she wouldn't be stuck in a dead-end job. However, Leeds was not allowed to be an easy savior. He had to fight Sarah and was forced to listen to her. She wanted to marry and have children. *"Deaf* children," she stated pointedly. She admired the smart and savvy woman who did not use her voice. Her own strength of character prevented Leeds from being a catalyst in her life.

Sarah had reservations about men due to difficulties in her past. It was three-quarters into the movie before the audience recognized the same. Her anger toward men—personified by Leeds—could have been perceived by a noninitiated audience well-conditioned to devaluation scenes to be anger at her limitation.

People who saw both the stage and the screen version complained the film was "too easy" and "too Hollywood." The stage-Sarah involved Leeds in the political aspects of being deaf; the movie relied heavily on the speech theme.

The movie was the first feature which offered a deaf performer star billing. It also presented an entirely different image of deaf people. They were vital, busy and attractive people. The kids in Leeds' school were like teenagers anywhere—affecting extremes in fashion, enjoying sports, and having fun. Had the film relied less on the speech theme and delved more explicitly into Sarah's personal tug-of-war, it could have avoided the dips into formula.

Actual deaf performers were used in the background of the film.

Children of a Lesser God positively illustrated deaf people as busy and vibrant members of society. It also did little to shatter myths.

Mannix / "Silent Cry" / date unknown / CBS-TV

Writer: Arthur Weiss
Category: Series Television — Crime Drama

* Deafness
* Single White Female
* Deaf Performer
* Equipment: Fan alert for doorbell
* Communication: Expressive — Sign; Receptive — Speechreading

Plot: A deaf woman lipreads a murder plot and seeks help.

Deaf actress Jody Wellman exits the Pacific Repertory Theatre of the Deaf. It is a rainy evening. As she takes a few breaths of air, her eyes light on a man in a telephone booth across the street. She speechreads him, understanding he will kill a woman. Terrified, she hurries to the police.

The police try to get her to remember the names spoken by the man. She can't. Joe Mannix is intrigued. He helps her out.

Jody is stalked by the killer and saved in the nick of time by Mannix in a deserted warehouse.

* * *

"Silent Cry" was based on the premise that speechreading is an easy art. Perhaps Jody was one of the lucky few who could speechread accurately. But to believe she could understand a man at a three-quarter angle — talking into a telephone — in a telephone booth — across the street — at twilight — in the rain — was stretching it a bit too far!

Jody was seen as a vivacious, intelligent woman in an interesting artistic profession.

The myth that deaf persons have no usable voice was reinforced when, in the deserted warehouse, Jody saw Mannix was in danger from the killer and made no sound to warn him. Also, the possibility that someone like Jody could have residual hearing was canceled out when a gunshot was fired in the warehouse and she did not respond.

"Silent Cry" was built on erroneous myths of deafness. Its one saving grace was the casting of a deaf actress in the role of the deaf actress.

Amputation

Characters who have lost one or more limbs either surgically or traumatically are referred to in the Amputation category. Characters in this category are overwhelmingly male, possibly due to the association of limb loss with war injuries or motorcycle accidents. They are described by the particular limb loss they are experiencing; e.g., "Amputation; single leg" or "Amputation; single arm."

Characters who function without one arm or one hand are the most visible onscreen. Those living with one lower limb are second in visibility. Third-most-seen type of amputee is loss of one leg and one arm on the same side of the body. Characters who have lost two hands or two legs are the least visible (a few triple amputees have been seen onscreen but usually in small, background roles).

Many amputee characters use a prosthesis, an artificial limb that restores a degree of function. Seen onscreen are leg prostheses of various sorts and arm prostheses. Despite the complexities in creating a device for heavy use in the action of weight-bearing and walking, little examination has been made onscreen of what is involved in using an artificial leg. Despite progress in developing a foot with a natural "spring" in it, screen characters appear ignorant of the nuances due to the level of writer understanding. A character is fitted with an artificial leg and appears to be "cured."

Arm prostheses are more visible to the audience. Cosmetic hands or functional hooks are both used by screen characters. In general terms, a cosmetic hand is a natural-appearing device. Although flesh-toned compounds are now used to cover the mechanism, some characters still appear with the outdated concept of a black-gloved hand; the glove disguises a mechanism and appears frightening. Despite its pleasing appearance, a cosmetic hand is limited in function. It provides an open or closed grip. A hook is, in the most simple terms, a curved, two-sided clip which is pulled open into two halves by actively tensing a cable, usually by means of a harness worn about the shoulders. A pull forward of the *opposite* shoulder provides the tension to open the hook. (Hooks and cosmetic hands are driven in a variety of ways; this is the most base description.) A hook is very functional but cosmetically inacceptable to many.

Onscreen single-leg amputees appear to be average people — or "supercrip" overachievers. In contrast, stories about arm/hand amputees frequently use an "embittered" characterization. This bitterness leads to one of the single most frightening (and erroneous) traits in disability drama: the use of an arm prosthesis as weaponry. This refers to instances where a prosthesis is used as a skewer, "heavy, metal clublike" object, or slashing tool to wreak havoc on society. These frightening weapons show up in "average" TV drama *(Hawaii Five-O* "Hookman" or comic book–like action-adventure films.

(Pieces like *Barbarians from the Year 3000* are not included in this resource due to the blatant comic book nature of the finished product. In *Barbarians,* a woman with an iron hand unsheathed deadly finger-claws to slash a person's cheek. Also not included is the short-lived CBS-TV series *Otherworld,* in which an average family found itself in a frightening parallel universe. A headmaster at the teenaged boy's military academy had an artificial hand which doubled as a flame thrower when intimidation was required. The TV series *V* featured a single-arm amputee alien who attached a barbed whip to his prosthetic mount when he needed to "take care" of someone. Again, these comic book examples are an illustration of the far-reaching effects of the "trait" seen in more traditional drama.)

Special equipment used in stories featuring amputees includes:

Prosthesis—A mechanical replacement for a leg or an arm.

Skiing Outrigger—This device was created to permit leg amputees to ski. It is a short ski mounted on a lightweight arm-cuff type crutch ("Canadian Cane"). A cable control on the hand grip controls the angle of the ski. It is used on the side of the body without the leg and acts as both a ski pole and second ski for balance.

In addition to the programs listed, other amputee characters can be found in the reviews of *AfterM*A*S*H* (Mulcahy's hearing restored); *Beg, Borrow ...or Steal; Buck Rogers in the 25th Century,* "Return of the Fighting 69th"; *The A-Team,* "Water, Water Everywhere"; *Highway to Heaven,* "One Fresh Batch of Lemonade"; and *Just the Way You Are.*

Kings Row / 1941 / Warner Bros.–First National Pictures

Executive Producer: Hal B. Wallis
Associate Producer: David Lewis
Director: Sam Wood
Screenplay: Casey Robinson
From the Novel by: Henry Bellamann
Category: Feature Film—Drama

* Amputation; double leg
* Single White Male
* New Disability

Plot: A young man leaves his home town to study psychiatry.

Turn-of-the-century town Kings Row is home to privileged Parris Mitchell and his good friend Drake McHugh. Parris goes away to Vienna to study to become a doctor. Drake remains the playboy squire of Kings Row. He is in love with Louise Gordon, daughter of the town's doctor. Her father disapproves of the liaison and breaks them up. Drake begins to date Randy Monoghan, a childhood friend from the wrong side of the tracks. Drake plans to go into real estate.

Drake's future is destroyed when a crooked bank president absconds with his trust fund. Drake is penniless and forced to find a job. He approaches Mr. Monoghan for work. Monoghan gets him a job on the railroad.

A load of tiles falls on Drake at the train yard and he is "run over" by a train. Doctor Gordon is called and determines Drake's legs must be amputated. Drake awakens to find his legs gone.

> DRAKE: Where's the rest of me?

Drake remains in bed at the Monoghan house. Randy marries him for reasons she later describes to Parris, a budding psychiatrist.

> RANDY: I didn't marry Drake out of pity, Parris. I've never loved anyone else ... [after the accident] I didn't love him any less, only differently.

Drake and Randy sell real estate lots to workers. Drake looks over the diagram of parcels and uses pejorative language in discussing his achievement.

> DRAKE: Not bad for a girl and an old cripple piled up in bed.

Parris suggests Drake and Randy build a place themselves. Randy is enthusiastic but Drake vetoes the possibility.

> DRAKE: Randy ... promise me I'll never have to go outside of this house until I'm dead.

Parris is concerned about Drake's outbursts. He confides to Randy that Drake needs to be able to move independently.

> RANDY: [My brother] gave him a wheelchair once for a present. [Drake] would have killed him if he could....

Louise Gordon has had a breakdown and is Parris' patient. She reveals she believes her father took Drake's legs to stop the two from seeing each other. Tod Monoghan backs this up.

> TOD: [Sam Winters said] the bones in neither [leg] was broke up one bit.

Parris goes to confront Drake with the truth. He uses offensive language.

> PARRIS: He wanted to see you turn into a lifelong cripple, mentally as well as physically.

DRAKE: Where did Gordon think I lived, in my legs? Did he think those things were Drake McHugh?

Drake indicates he is ready to move on and begin his life again.

* * *

Kings Row took an interesting approach to disability. Randy was firm and matter-of-fact when dealing with her beloved Drake. Parris, studying medicine then branching off into the new science of psychiatry, treated Drake's disability from a mental standpoint. Drake was tentatively moving ahead with his life by marrying Randy and getting involved in a money-making scheme. The revelation of the twisted work done by Doctor Gordon gave him a lift, finding some relief in the truth. Drake appeared ready to go on with life and told Randy they *would* get a house and have a party—a distinct change from the man who was afraid to go outside. Parris was the non-disabled catalyst, but it was Drake who made the decision to go on.

Kings Row was interesting, due to the lack of tears. Although it contained its share of clichés, it was different. The recognition of psychiatry/psychology as a treatment factor in the rehabilitation process further distinguished it, although a more in-depth study from that angle would have been welcome.

The Stratton Story / 1944 / MGM

Producer: Jack Cummings
Director: Sam Wood
Story: Douglas Morrow
Screenplay: Douglas Morrow and Guy Trosper
Category: Feature Film—Drama

* Amputation; single leg
* Married White Male
* New Disability
* Based on a True Story

Plot: Major leaguer Monty Stratton loses his leg in a freak accident.

Major league pitcher Monty Stratton goes rabbit hunting in the off-season. His shotgun accidentally discharges and injures his leg. An infection sets in. His wife, Ethel, signs a release permitting the surgeons to amputate Monty's right leg. Monty is heavily depressed. His personal pain is exacerbated when his young son takes his first steps.

MONTY: What's so wonderful about it? He's got two legs, hasn't he?

Monty begins to wear his artificial leg as his son improves upon his own tottering performance.

In an effort to help Monty, Ethel goads him into throwing a baseball around for recreation. Monty can't keep his balance and he falls. He works hard to improve. With the help of Barney, his old scout/mentor, it is arranged for Monty to pitch in the All Star Game. Monty plays. He falls when running to first base but makes light of his mishap.

>   MONTY: Guess I started my slide too soon.

Monty recognizes his dream to play again. He knocks in a run and strikes out the last batter. A gushy indication of "courage" follows.

>   NARRATOR: Monty Stratton has not won just a ball game, he's won a greater victory as he goes on pitching, leading a rich, full life. He stands as an inspiration to all of us, as living proof of what a man can do if he has the courage and determination to refuse to admit defeat.

* * *

The Stratton Story was a film which ended on an upbeat tone, no doubt as a piece to encourage those who had lost limbs in the war. Monty was left out in the cold after losing his leg. As usual, he was given no support or rehabilitation by any type of professional personnel. He returned to his mother's farm with his wife and son and had to make his own way through his anger and despair. He was elevated to a heroic status simply because he succeeded on his own — with help from a loving wife and a baseball.

Monty was an active, athletic man, but his activeness was not meant to indicate persons with his disability were likewise. It was simply to prove that for Monty to be content again, he must play baseball. The "quick fix" gave value to Monty's life.

The Stratton Story was an entry in the inspiring "supercrip" sweepstakes.

The Best Years of Our Lives / 1946 / Samuel Goldwyn Pictures

Producer: Samuel Goldwyn
Director: William Wyler
Story: MacKinlay Kantor
Screenplay: Robert Sherwood
Category: Feature Film — Drama

* Amputation; double hand
* Single White Male
* Equipment: Prosthetic hooks
* Performer with a Disability

Plot: Three war veterans return home to Boone City, including Homer Parrish, who lost both hands in the war.

During a flight home from the war, Fred Derry, Al Stevenson, and amputee Homer Parrish meet. Despite initial awkwardness from Stevenson and Derry, Parrish wins them over by a demonstration of the dexterity his hooks afford him by lighting smokes for the trio. The cause of his disability is described as a result of severe burns on a ship. His hooks are pretty handy, he tells them.

> HOMER: I can dial telephones, I can drive a car, I can even put nickels in a juke box.

Despite his upbeat outlook, Homer is concerned about his girlfriend, Wilma.

> HOMER: She's never seen anything like these hooks.

At home, Homer is uneasy at his family's scrutiny. At Butch's bar, he explains how everyone was awkward that they had hands and he didn't. Girlfriend Wilma confronts Homer about the status of their relationship. He puts her off. He devalues himself when he sees his sister and her friends spying on him and Wilma.

> HOMER: Wanna see how the hooks work? You wanna see the freak?

Homer frightens the children by smashing his hooks through the window and brandishing them at the kids who back away in fear. Homer immediately regrets his actions and apologizes to Louella and Wilma.

> HOMER: All I want is for people to treat me like anybody else instead of pitying me ... I've just got to learn to get used to it and pay no attention.

Wilma confronts Homer again late one evening. Her parents want her to go away so she will forget about him. Homer supports the idea with typical devaluation.

> HOMER: I want you to be free, Wilma, to live your own life. I don't want you to be tied down forever just because you've got a kind heart.... You don't know what it would be like to have to live with me. Have to face this every day, every night—

Homer takes Wilma up to his bedroom to show her "what happens." As she watches, he removes his prostheses.

> HOMER: This is where I know I'm helpless. My hands are down there on the bed. I can't put them on again without calling to somebody for help. Can't smoke a cigarette or read a book. If that door should blow shut, I can't open it and get out of this room. I'm as dependent as a baby that doesn't know how to get anything except cry for it.

Wilma assures Homer she loves him and "always will." They marry.

Although Samuel Goldwyn was warned that an amputee was not good box office, he stuck to his casting in *Best Years of Our Lives*. The complex and powerful film skillfully meshed three stories—one of which was Homer Parrish's. Despite Homer's difficulties in adjusting to civilian life and himself, the overall impression left by this movie was that Homer was *able*. Homer used his hooks for such fine tasks as lighting cigarettes, ripping a pin off another man's lapel, tapping out a tune on the piano, stuffing cash in his wallet, and even putting a wedding ring on Wilma's finger. His limitations were how others reacted to him and how he himself was learning to assimilate the difficulties into his life.

The lapses into devaluation were somewhat countered by the clear-cut demonstration of abilities Homer possessed.

One erroneous negative was illustrated in the film. Homer said he was unable to get into his prostheses independently—when, in fact, the actor had the ability to do so. This "dramatic license" was disturbing, leaving a lingering impression that Homer was helpless. Wilma was therefore elevated to a higher plane of human understanding in wanting to be involved with him.

One poignant scene stood out. Homer, after scaring Louella, tiptoed into her bedroom late that night. He silently and gently drew the covers up over her in a rarely seen illustration of tenderness associated with a person utilizing prostheses. Hooks-as-weapons are much more prevalent.

The Best Years of Our Lives illustrated a man with a disability as one who was tender and capable. He was a bit afraid of the future but willing to go on. He was a person with opinions and feelings who was capable of being a friend.

Chamber of Horrors / 1966 / Warner Bros. Pictures

Producer: Hy Averback
Director: Hy Averback
Story: Ray Russell & Stephen Kandel
Screenplay: Stephen Kandel
Category: Feature Film—Horror

* Amputation; single arm
* Single White Male
* Prosthesis Used as Weaponry

Plot: An insane man chops off his hand to escape prison—then proceeds to murder all those who convicted him.

Jason Crevette, a disturbed man in Victorian times, is captured for crimes. On his way to jail, he uses a fire-ax to free his handcuffed hand from an iron wheel. He chops off his right hand, jumps into a river, and is presumed dead.

Jason "Carroll" goes to New Orleans for an arsenal of weapons to attach to the mount of his prosthesis. He uses the hook attachment to trap a man's wrist to a table. He strokes the cheek of a woman with his metal hook.

JASON: Does this shock you, my dear?

He kills Judge Randall, the man who originally sentenced him to prison. He uses a meat cleaver in place of his hook for the job. He uses his hook like an icepick to spear the meat and wraps the body pieces in brown butcher paper for the police to find. Next, he uses a skewer to go after Dr. Romulus, the physician who declared him insane. Sergeant Tim Albertson, the original arresting policeman, is shot by a gun concealed in Crevette's cosmetic hand.

A museum of wax horror figures has revered Crevette by re-creating him in wax. Pepe, a small-statured man, has worked on the statue.

PEPE: I say it is a masterpiece! And I helped.

HAROLD KNAUBEN-BLOUNT: ...Three-foot-nine in stature, nine-foot-three in ego.

Crevette breaks into the museum to go after his last victim, Tony Draco. His meat cleaver is at the ready. Ironically, he is killed when skewered by the prosthetic-mounted weapon on the wax figure of himself.

* * *

Chamber of Horrors was a Grade F horror movie and a Grade F depiction of a person without a hand. Crevette was certified as being off-the-beam from the beginning; to expect different behavior after he was disabled would be too much. However, his disability was a factor in his crimes. He used the prosthesis to help kill—since, obviously, those who had convicted him were at fault for him chopping off his own hand. Ol' Jason wasn't quite working with a full deck, you see!

Jason delighted in terrorizing people with his prosthesis. Marie, a woman he had snared to help him lure the victims to him, had to put up with him stroking her face with his hook and running it through her hair. Crevette's breathy voice and menacing attitude made the hook seem to be a frightening thing—which it was intended to be in the film. Poor imagery and erroneous notions abounded. The weapons Crevette attached to the mount for his prosthesis were hideous and frightening. The cleaver was amazing.

The peripheral character of the small-statured Pepe was a busy and creative man with a sense of humor. He was treated as a full-fledged member of the museum staff. His friends gently teased him about his size, like Knauben-Blount's chide.

Chamber of Horrors was a poor and completely ludicrous portrait of disability—which, no doubt, it was intended to be.

The Wild, Wild West / "The Night of the Lord of Limbo" / 1966 / CBS-TV

Producer: Bruce Lansbury
Director: Jesse Hibbs

* Amputation; double leg
* Single Male

Amputation

Writer: Henry Sharp
Category: Series Television—
Western Action Adventure

Plot: An amputee veteran of the Civil War enlists the aid of James West in a plot to go back in time to recover his lost legs.

Special Agent James West goes to Vicksburg in search of his missing partner, Artemus Gordon. West embarks to Live Oak Manor to see Colonel Noel Bartley Vautrain, his only lead to Artemus' disappearance.

Vautrain appears in a wheelchair with a blanket over his legs. It was not Artemus he wanted, but West himself. Bitterness surfaces. Revenge as a motive is expressed.

> VAUTRAIN: Because, for seven long years, I have wallowed in my hate for you.... It was ... [an] unimportant little skirmish ... during the late war between the states. The gallant James West stumbles upon a wounded soldier in the field, a soldier whose legs are shattered....
>
> WEST: So, that was you. I remember applying tourniquets but I never thought you'd—
>
> VAUTRAIN: That I'd live? Oh yes, oh yes, I lived. You saved my life. *[enraged]* But for what? A life sentence in this prison on wheels?

Vautrain backs from the dinner table and rips the blanket from himself, revealing two legs amputated above the knees.

> VAUTRAIN: As you can see, my legs are gone. You are going to help me recover them.

Vautrain has discovered a method of traveling into the fourth dimension. He intends to relive the battle, assassinate General Grant, and escape with his legs intact. Although the transportation to the wartime past is successful, Vautrain is pinned by a falling pillar when his house is shelled by mortars and cannon. His "new" legs are crushed. He dies. West and Artemus return to the present.

* * *

"The Night of the Lord of Limbo" used the vehicle of the vengeful person with a disability manipulating others to get what he believes he rightfully deserves. Vautrain was a mean-spirited, angry, embittered man whose hatred fueled his energy. He wanted retribution for the sin West had committed— letting Vautrain live with a disability. This episode presented an amputee as a cold and cruel wreck of a human being.

Lancer / "Death Bait" / 1969 / CBS-TV

Producer: Alan A. Armer
Director: Robert Butler
Writer: Jack Turley
Category: Series Television—
  Western

* Amputation; single arm
* White Male
* Prosthesis Used as Weaponry

Plot: A sinister man with one arm appears in town looking for the Lancers' hired hand, Jelly Hoskins.

A cold and frightening man enters the saloon with an equally-frightening dog. The man has one hand; the other is a metal-capped "prosthesis" with a chain dangling from it. A jerk of his arm and clank of the chain signals his dog to attack. He is Sheriff Gannett and he is looking for Jelly Hoskins.

　　　GANNETT: I owe him something.

Murdoch Lancer is alone on the ranch with young ward Teresa and Jelly. An unseen gunman sends hot coals into Murdoch's face, temporarily blinding him. Jelly knows who is out there. He tells Murdoch he worked for four "drovers" a few years back in Texas—only to find they were killers. They hurt the sheriff pretty bad. Jelly ran, fearing he couldn't prove his innocence.

The cause of Sheriff Gannett's disability is discussed. When the four criminals handcuffed him to an ironwood tree, his only recourse was to use a knife to cut off his hand. Revenge is his motive to locate Jelly.

Gannett terrorizes Murdoch and the girl when Jelly goes to get help. Jelly's quick-thinking makes Gannett a target for Teresa's shotgun.

　　　　　*　　*　　*

"Death Bait" used a frightening portrayal of a person with a disability. Gannett, angry at his humiliation at the hands of criminals years before, held them responsible for the loss of his hand. He was out to settle the score.

The odd "prosthesis" on Gannett's arm was created to inspire dread. The clanking sound of the chain was meant to add to frightening spectre.

"Death Bait" suggested a person with a missing limb was mentally unstable and vengeful, forever seeking retribution.

Hawaii Five-O / "Hookman" / 1973 / CBS-TV

Executive Producer: Leonard
  Freeman
Producer: William Finnegan
Supervising Producer: Bob
  Sweeney

* Amputation; double hand
* Single White Male
* Prosthesis Used as Weaponry
* Performer with a Disability

Amputation

Director: Allen Reisner
Writers: Glen Olson and Rod Baker
Category: Series Television — Police Drama

Plot: McGarrett is looking for a cop killer who leaves behind the murdering weapon with gold personalized name plates of the victims.

Five-O Detective Steve McGarrett is stymied by the murders of police friends. His only clue is that the killer leaves behind the weapon. There are no fingerprints, but each gun has affixed to it a nameplate with the deceased's name. The cop killer is a man with two prosthetic hooks. McGarrett is next on his list.

The killer is staking out McGarrett when interrupted by a painter. He hides behind a door and uses his prosthesis for weaponry as he slams a hook into the man's back. McGarrett goes to the morgue for an autopsy report on the painter.

> CORONER: There was a complete transection of the column and the spinal cord. Death instantaneous.
>
> McGARRETT: ...What about the weapon?
>
> CORONER: Metal, heavy, clublike.

A game of cat and mouse ensues. The murderer is shown able to drive a car with a stick shift and leads McGarrett on a wild chase. He avoids capture.

A telltale clue appears when the killer's car is found in the harbor. A prosthetic arm is found hanging from the wheel. McGarrett puts two and two together. Kurt Stoner is his man, a recent parolee from prison. The cause of Stoner's disability is discussed. While holding dynamite charges in his hands during a bank robbery twelve years past, the explosives went off. Revenge is illustrated as a motive for Stoner's criminal acts, picking off the police who were first on the scene at the robbery.

> LT. DAN WILLIAMS: Stoner got ten to life. The government paid for his artificial hands and trained him. He became expert, worked in the metal shop.
>
> McGARRETT: But he forgot he was caught in the act of robbing a bank and threatening people. He hated those hooks so he blamed us....

McGarrett tracks Stoner and breaks into his seedy apartment to find Stoner gone. Stoner calls on the telephone, telling McGarrett to look in the bureau drawer for a surprise. McGarrett does and finds a pair of hooks with his own name engraved on them.

Stoner is killed before he is able to get Steve—with the automatic rifle ready with a nameplate reading "McGarrett."

* * *

"Hookman" was an interesting piece. Since the character of Stoner was indicated as being a criminal prior to his disability, it was no surprise to find him still wreaking havoc on society. Typically, he was aggressive in matters of violence. His motive was identical to that of Crevette in *Chamber of Horrors*.

The most interesting aspect of this episode, despite the poor and frightening image of a man utilizing prosthetic tools, was the concentration on Stoner's hooks. The performer, a hand amputee, used the aids dexterously; he was shown able to do fine tasks, such as inserting a key in a lock, tapping letters into a metal plate, removing his sunglasses, and so on. Also, he completed numerous nefarious tasks, such as fitting together weapons from his arsenal and firing them to kill his prey. He was athletic: running, climbing fire escapes, etc. The director used many close shots of the hooks at work. This educational aspect helped balance the poor images a bit.

"Hookman" benefitted from good direction, but suffered from negative and damaging imagery.

The Desperate Miles / 1975

Executive Producer: Joel Rogosin
Producers: Robert Greenwald & Frank Von Zerneck
Director: Daniel Haller
Story: Arthur Ross
Teleplay: Arthur Ross and Joel Rogosin
Category: Made-for-TV Movie—Drama

* Amputation; single leg
* Single White Male
* Based on a True Story

Plot: A Vietnam vet wheels his way from Los Angeles to San Diego.

Vietnam vet Joe Larkin is an athletic man, running on his one natural and one artificial leg. The cause of his disability is described as a land mine explosion in Southeast Asia. His leg pains him after a tumble. Doctor Bryson suggests Joe cancel his proposed walk from Los Angeles to San Diego, a distance of 110 miles. Joe is unconvinced.

After breaking his residual leg in a fall, he learns he will have to use a wheelchair from now on. Joe's mother hears the news sorrowfully.

> MRS. LARKIN: Well, I think if he has to give up trying to live his life the way he's used to, he'll die. That's all he knows. That's all he has.

Joe decides to go ahead with his trip, using his chair. It's for him and for the guys in the ward: Rhodes, the double leg amputee; Ruiz, the cynical single legger; and Jason, a fellow who remains in bed without speaking. Al is behind Joe. All want him to complete the trip but seem to doubt his ability to succeed.

Joe shoves off with a cart attached to his chair. A sign reads, "Boost the morale of the handicapped." Ruiz cynically views the situation after seeing Joe in a TV news report.

> RUIZ: After all, if he makes it, something really fantasic happens, right? I mean, we all get up and walk out of here or something!

Joe's girlfriend intimates to Mrs. Larkin that she fears success for Joe will spell the end of their relationship. Erroneous aspects are suggested by Mrs. Larkin's comment.

> MRS. LARKIN: We don't have to lose him, just because he's no longer dependent on us.

Back in the hospital, Al has begun to study business law. Ruiz is skeptical about this endeavor. Accessibility is discussed.

> RUIZ: Can you see him practicing law on wheels? He won't even be able to make it up the steps of the courthouse.

Joe makes it to San Diego. Waiting for him at the top of the last hill are some of the guys from the ward, cheering him on. Jason, watching Joe's televised progress up the last hill, pulls himself from his bed and into a standing position.

Joe makes it, snatching his winning bet from Ruiz's hand.

* * *

The Desperate Miles featured conflicting attitudes about disability. Joe insisted he was not different from anyone else, in essence, assimilating his disability. However, his lack of good sense about proper care of his residual leg indicated rejection of the same.

Larkin was an independent leader to the men in the hospital, all of whom thought they were less-than-average people. Even Dr. Bryson felt that way. Bryson worried about the "morale" of the other men who unrealistically looked to Joe as the open door to their own futures.

Mrs. Larkin thought Joe must do what he had to do or die. His girlfriend feared she would lose him if he became "independent." Thus, it was very hard to locate a single prevailing attitude throughout the film.

The athletic Joe had great compassion for others who had been injured in the war. However, he was also quite taciturn and revealed little about himself. He never fully articulated why he was making the trip.

Some attitudinal barriers and natural awkwardness were shown when a double leg amputee vet started work as a used-car salesman and had to face the surprise of would-be customers.

The Desperate Miles avoided the traps of a triumph-over-disability movie, but still indicated that once a mountain was climbed, nothing could stop this man.

Police Story / "Captain Hook" / 1975 / NBC-TV

Executive Producer: Stanley Kallis
Producer: Christopher Morgan
Director: Richard Benedict
Writer: Frank Telford
Category: Series Television — Police Drama

* Amputation; single hand
* Single White Male
* Equipment: Prosthetic hook
* Prosthesis Used as Weaponry
* New Disability

Plot: An amputee cop must fight to try and regain his position on the police force.

Officer Joe Waldron throws himself on an exploding bomb during a police call. The action costs him his right hand. Partner Ted Stuart loses his left. Joe is approached by a veteran of the department. Barton, who'd long ago lost an eye, acts as a disabled catalyst within the story.

> BARTON: I'm no missionary ... I wouldn't be here if I didn't know it was true. If you wanna try—really try, your whole character can be wrapped up in that mitt. [indicates Joe's gauze-wrapped wrist] Character. It can become the proudest part of your body.... Hey man, I'm not here to show you. I'm only telling you you'll surprise yourself ... be more man than you were before.

Joe sees Dr. Murphy about a prosthesis. He is shown a cosmetic hand and then a hook.

> DOCTOR MURPHY: It may not look like much—but it works. It's called a prosthesis.

> JOE: Prosthesis. Why don't you call it what it is? It's a hook, a damn ugly hook!

Attitudinal barriers are illustrated as Joe returns to work, regaining employ with the police department. He is unable to convince his superiors, even after hard practice with his prosthesis, that he is capable of resuming street duty. He refuses to be relegated to paper-pushing.

> JOE: I want to do police work ... *real* police work.

CAPTAIN: You can't.

JOE: Why? Why can't I?

CAPTAIN: Because you can't write reports.

An interesting and thought-provoking scene occurs at the bank. Joe's straggling left hand signature does not match that of his on-file right hand signature card. The embarrassing encounter leads to his meeting Jennie Hill, a teller with whom he falls in love and marries.

Joe runs into ex-partner Ted Stuart. Stuart has chosen a cosmetic hand to replace his missing left one. Stuart notes Joe's stare at the black-gloved device.

STUART: Useless, but not offensive [like a hook].

Out on an undercover assignment, Joe uses his prosthesis as weaponry when he slams the hook down to trap a suspect's hand.

Joe is athletic, able to complete all tests administered by the department. Departmental policy is the culprit though, in Joe's inability to retain his job despite outstanding performance. His anger and frustration at the attitudinal barriers keep him going. Joe continues to get the runaround.

His initial fear and distress at incurring a disability are gradually erased. The emotionally induced stutter goes away and he grows confident and sure of himself as he uses—and respects—his prosthesis. His job is cinched after a difficult chase nets two suspects. He sees Barton and indicates his prosthesis.

JOE: Everything you said in the hospital came true. I *am* proud of this damn thing.

* * *

"Captain Hook" was a neatly crafted story which recognized departmental policy and prejudice as the factors handicapping a police officer and not his loss of a hand. Notable were careful camera angles which disguised the fact the actor portraying Joe Waldron wore a prosthesis over his hand. Conspicuous use of the hook and the illusion of it being a part of the actor's arm allowed a viewer's eye to concentrate on and be impressed by the abilities the prosthetic tool afforded. Seeing the hook used as weaponry in the context of this story was disappointing.

Joe was energetic, bright, and highly motivated. He wanted nothing more than to regain his former status as a street cop—which was a realistic aspiration—after he learned to deal with his disability.

"Captain Hook" illustrated that unwarranted prejudice and cosmetic drawbacks were more disabling than the loss of his hand.

Posse / 1975 / Bryna Films

Executive Producer: Phil Feldman
Producer: Kirk Douglas
Director: Kirk Douglas
Story: Christopher Knopf
Screenplay: William Roberts and Christopher Knopf
Category: Feature Film — Western

* Amputation; single arm, single leg
* Single White Male
* Equipment: Crutch
* Performer with a Disability

Plot: Is famous lawman Howard Nightingale supporting justice or his bid for election?

Hellman, a newspaper owner and reporter of the *Tesota* (Arizona) *Sentinel*, begins to dig to find if the criminal brought in by Marshall Nightingale was set up. Hellman has a disability but moves easily with a crutch. Nightingale forbids Hellman to interview the convict being held in a local jail.

HELLMAN: [Afraid I'll hit him with my crutch?]

The cause of Hellman's disability is not discussed, although one surmises it is a war injury. His commanding officer, he tells Nightingale, became a general.

HELLMAN: I became a civilian.

Hellman follows the Nightingale story as it unfolds.

* * *

Posse presented an active, intelligent, and probing man as one who also had a disability. Hellman's limitation was incidental. The few throwaway lines were possibly to satisfy audience curiosity about the man. The story was about the somewhat shady Nightingale. Hellman was just another fellow with a nose for news. He was the "boss" at the paper and his word was law. And he wanted to know what was going on with Nightingale.

Posse depicted a man with a disability as a contributing member of the community.

Just a Little Inconvenience / Oct. 2, 1977 / NBC-TV

Executive Producer: Lee Majors
Producer: Allan J. Balter
Writer: Theodore J. Flicker & Allan Balter
Director: Theodore J. Flicker

* Amputation; single arm, single leg
* Single White Male
* Performer with a Disability
* Equipment: Crutch; artificial

Amputation

Category: Made-for-TV Movie — Drama

limbs; skiing outrigger

Plot: Two old skiing friends take to the slopes again after one becomes an amputee.

Frank Logan and Ken Briggs, longtime skiing hotshots, serve together in Vietnam. Logan makes a tactical decision that saves the outfit, while Briggs makes an impulsive decision that costs him his left arm and left leg.

Logan meets Briggs again in 1971 at a San Francisco bar. Logan states it's good to see him.

> BRIGGS: You haven't seen me.... I don't think you're gonna like it, either.

Briggs knocks over a cocktail table and stands, revealing his missing limbs.

Logan approaches people at the hospital to find out how he can help Briggs. After rebuffs from Briggs and advice from an old skiing instructor, Logan designs a skiing program for amputees. Briggs is the unwilling test participant. Briggs is angry and bitter, blaming Logan for his disability.

> BRIGGS: I know whose fault it is I'm a crip.

Logan gives up. The desertion gives Briggs food for thought and he returns to the mountain to apologize. The two men renew their friendship.

Briggs is spurred on to ski when he meets Nikki Clausing. He is wearing his artificial limbs; she does not suspect he has a disability until they meet to ski the next day. She stares in shock at his pinned-up sleeve and pant leg. Briggs devalues himself.

> BRIGGS: Disgusting, isn't it?

He tears off down the hill, successfully skiing for the first time. When Logan tries to congratulate him for the feat, Briggs again devalues himself.

> BRIGGS: I put on a freak show for the whole mountain.... I can go anywhere on the hill turning people's stomachs.

Nikki goes to see Ken and chews him out.

> NIKKI: You have to test everybody, don't you? So you can be smug and superior when we're unable to keep from reacting when you shoved your stumps in our faces!

Briggs later apologizes. Nikki promises him a skiing date. When she stands him up, Logan confronts her. She isn't sure, she admits, she wants all the complications that go along with an amputee. She later returns to satisfy her curiosity.

Just a Little Inconvenience

She is, as Briggs aptly describes, taking another look. She is ashamed and still doesn't know if she will see him again. She admits she cares for him after he lands back in the veteran's hospital with a broken leg from skiing.

Briggs proposes. Nikki wants to think about it. She also tells Briggs that Logan still suffers from guilt, feeling that he was responsible for Briggs' injury. Briggs approaches Logan.

> BRIGGS: I was the only one that made a dumb decision that day—and even that's turned out okay. Frank, look at me. I may be missin' some parts but I'm a happy man.

Nikki agrees to marry Briggs. He exuberantly races Logan down the toughest run on the mountain.

> LOGAN: Not bad, considering a handicap.

> BRIGGS: Handicap? Oh, you mean this? It's no handicap, it's just a little inconvenience.

* * *

Just a Little Inconvenience was a different portrayal of disability. Although Briggs illustrated classic devaluation, anger, and bitterness, he worked his way out of it.

The relationship with Nikki was interesting. Instead of becoming the saint who loves the disabled character despite all odds, she was very concerned. Terminology—such as "amputee"—concerned her. She admitted she wasn't sure she could get past the curiosity stage.

The scene where Nikki angrily accuses Briggs of "shoving your stumps in our faces" was odd. Their preliminary meeting gave Briggs no easy opportunity to express he had a disability—nor was it warranted. Her surprise at finding he was an amputee was natural. Although he took her reaction personally, he certainly wasn't "testing" her as she accused. His subsequent apology was confusing. She should have apologized for her own bad behavior. The scene played was formulaic: he was the bitter disabled person trying to shock the non-disabled public.

The "testing" notion was also stated by a veterans hospital doctor, who told Logan that Briggs did not use his artificial limbs because "he wants us to suffer every time we see him." (See *Night Court*, "Walk Don't Wheel," for another rendition of the "testing" scene.)

Briggs was an athletic and energetic man with a sense of humor. He was working hard to assimilate all of his difficulties, managing to work them out during the course of the movie. People with actual disabilities were seen in the hospital segments.

Just a Little Inconvenience presented a fair image of a man attempting to assimilate a disability into his life.

What Really Happened to the Class of '65? / "Class Hustler" / Dec. 15, 1977 / NBC-TV

Writer: Peter Fischer
Category: Series Television—
Drama

* Amputation; single leg
* Single White Male

Plot: One of the graduates of the Class of '65 loses a leg in Vietnam.

Class huckster Eddie Casselio returns from Vietnam minus a leg. Cause of his disability is discussed as a war injury. He constantly tries to prove himself, racing around on crutches. A medico worries about Eddie's rapidity in assimilating his disability. Possible negative connotations appear in Eddie's blunt replies.

> DOCTOR: ...rapid adjustment to your situation.
>
> EDDIE: Situation?
>
> DOCTOR: Your disability.
>
> EDDIE: Oh! You mean the stump!

Eddie decides he needs to prove himself and wants to swim 26 miles from the Southern California coast to the island of Catalina. In an inspirational climax, Eddie makes the swim to Catalina.

* * *

"Class Hustler" provided little that was new or different. A determined little guy refused to let the loss of a leg get him down and took on a great task to assure himself he was still a member of the human race.

Characters portrayed as disabled were seen in the background of hospital scenes such as a man with one arm playing the piano. Carlos, a peripheral character, used a prosthetic hook and used it very openly. The camera deliberately recorded his movements in a manner that was interesting and educational.

"Class Hustler" was routine, a "quick fix" story. If Eddie could swim to Catalina, he could go ahead in life.

Police Story / "End of the Line" / 1977 / NBC-TV

Executive Producer: David Gerber
Producer: Liam O'Brien
Co-Producer: Mel Swope
Director: Michael O'Herlihy

* Amputation; single arm
* Single White Male

Police Story

Writer: Sean Blaine
Category: Series Television — Police Drama

Plot: An embittered ex-cop goes after those responsible for the loss of his limb.

Red Avery is an insurance investigator. The ex-cop returns to his old police precinct years after losing his arm. He is assigned to help officers Pete and Gino nail supermarket robbers. Avery's insurance company covers the supermarket chain. Pete is not happy about the idea he and his partner are to be:

> PETE: ...saddle[d] ... with this one-armed rent-a-cop.

An officer in charge explains the case to Pete and Gino.

> ZIGGY: Any questions?

> PETE: Just one. What happened to his arm?

The cause of Avery's disability is discussed.

> ZIGGY: About six years ago — bandit took it with a shotgun.

Avery more than proves himself in the field by running, climbing, and showing he is still a good cop. However, Pete begins to suspect Avery's motive for being on this case.

> ZIGGY: You're saying he wormed his way in here for revenge?

Pete guessed right. Avery has realized the supermarket robbers had the same M.O. as the crooks he was chasing when he lost his arm. His surveillance of them with his police stint reaffirms these are the same guys. Revenge as a motive for antisocial behavior is seen. Avery turns into a bloodthirsty man as he seeks retribution. He is stopped.

* * *

"End of the Line" was a poor image of man who had lost an arm. Although he was employed, athletic, and seemed to be a decent fellow, the story implied his six years of progress were due to the lure of revenge. His disability had warped him.

Starsky and Hutch / "Quadromania" / May 10, 1978 / ABC-TV

Executive Producer: Aaron Spelling, Leonard Goldberg
Producer: Joseph T. Naar
Director: Rick Edelstein
Writer: Anthony Yerkovich
Category: Series Television — Police Drama

* Amputation; single arm, single leg
* Single White Male
* Prosthesis Used as Weaponry
* Equipment: Prosthetic hand and leg

Plot: Detectives Dave Starsky and Ken Hutchinson are on the trail of a taxicab killer who has a strange modus operandi: one-handed strangulation with "a grip like a set of bolt cutters."

Captain Doby is briefing detectives Starsky and Hutch on the taxicab killings, using inappropriate language.

> CAPTAIN DOBY: Suspect in the first murder was described as a sixty-year-old skid row cripple.

Hutch notes the similarities of the cases.

> HUTCH: They all belong to the same one-arm strangulation club.

The murderer is stage actor Lionel Fitzgerald II who lives with his blind grandfather. Lionel walks with an ominous shuffle. Gramps helps Lionel with the disguises worn for his evil deeds, believing the actor is applying make-up for his comeback appearance at a theatre. Lionel uses interesting language to explain to Gramps the reason for making-up at home.

> LIONEL: That make-up man down at the Savoy has got about as much finesse as a bloody stump.

The cause of Lionel's disability is discussed as a hit-and-run accident where he lost his arm and leg. Revenge is the motive for his criminal actions; he is attempting to kill the taxi driver who injured him.

Lionel gets in a cab. He removes his glove and places his artificial hand around the driver's neck. He kills him with a squeeze. Starsky and Hutch discover an old newspaper article in the dead cabbie's locker, "Actor Crippled by Hit-and-Run Driver." They zero in on Lionel.

Lionel no longer considers himself a member of the human race. Bitterness and pejorative imagery are present in his description of an all-night movie house.

> LIONEL: It's a refuge for the misfits, the deserted — the crippled.

* * *

"Quadromania" painted a frightening portrait of disability. The demented Lionel was bitter, vengeful, used offensive language himself, and illustrated life within his disability as a horrendous and repulsive thing. He suffered from devaluation, as evidenced in his "movie house" speech. Frightening shadows about the distorted and far-fetched capabilities of an artificial hand were seen.

No doubt was left in the minds of the audience that an artificial hand could wreak the described havoc. A close shot of the prosthetic limb and its "iron fingers" silently expressed the dangerous potential.

Curiously enough, two intelligent and decidedly liberal police detectives had no qualm about accepting the fact that a disability had turned an actor into a murderer. Starsky mused that Lionel lost "his arm and his leg — and most likely, his mind."

"Quadromania" perpetuated the cruel, embittered image of disability designed for horror films.

Father Murphy / "Establish Thou the Work of Our Hands" / 1978 / NBC-TV

Executive Producer: Michael Landon
Producer: Kent McCray
Director: Leo Penn
Writer: Paul W. Cooper
Category: Series Television — Family Drama

* Amputation; single hand
* Black Male Teenager
* New Disability

Plot: Father Murphy takes in a troublesome youth who finds his niche in driving a team — and loses it when he loses a hand.

Father Murphy is concerned about accepting 'Lijah, a trouble-prone ex-slave, into his orphanage. Mose, his black assistant, assumes responsibility for the boy. 'Lijah makes trouble at every turn. Murphy decides to take him on a long freight haul. 'Lijah steals gold from Mose and joins Murphy on the trail — planning to hightail at the right moment.

A transformation occurs. 'Lijah demonstrates an interest in driving the team of huge work mules and shows great natural ability to do so. He proves his mettle when he stays up all night to poultice the aching leg of one of the animals. He gives the stolen gold to Murphy to return to Mose.

A wheel on the wagon requires adjusting. Murphy lets the willing 'Lijah handle it. The jack slips and the wagon falls, crushing 'Lijah's right hand and wrist. Murphy rushes the fever-wracked boy to the nearest town for a doctor. Gangrene has set in. Murphy accepts responsibility and gives the doctor his consent to amputate 'Lijah's hand.

Back at the school/orphanage, 'Lijah remains sullen and angry, alone in his room.

> 'LIJAH: Look at this, mister. You did this to me. You owe me a hand.

Murphy acts as the non-disabled catalyst.

> MURPHY: You owe yourself a life. Is this how you want to live it? Feelin' sorry for yourself? Go right ahead. Don't expect any help from me.

Two of the other children whittle a wooden hand for 'Lijah. He is angry at the gift. But it plants an idea in Murphy's head. He goes down to the forge and creates a metal hand with separated fingers so 'Lijah can handle reins and still be a driver. The boy turns his back on the offer; but when he goes to leave the school on an animal given him, he finds the hand hanging in the tack room. He tries it and finds he can still drive. He skillfully handles a team through town as a proud Murphy and Mose look on.

* * *

"Establish Thou..." was a typical characterization of disability. 'Lijah was angry, blamed Murphy, hated the world, and so on. The one difference in this story was the illustration that with a simple aid, 'Lijah's self-respect — of which he'd had precious little prior to his accident — was restored. He had a special talent and the prosthesis permitted him to utilize that talent. Other than that, 'Lijah was a cardboard cutout of disability in a "quick fix" role.

The Love Boat / "Aftermath" / Feb. 10, 1979 / ABC-TV

Executive Producers: Aaron Spelling; Douglas Cramer
Producers: Gordon and Lynne Farr and Henry Colman
Director: George Tyne
Story: Sue Masters and John Walsh
Teleplay: Lee Aronsohn
Category: Series Television — Romantic Comedy

* Amputation; single hand
* Married White Male

Plot: Doc Bricker's old mentor Dr. Aikers boards the cruise ship — minus a hand.

Dr. Arthur Aikers takes a cruise on the *Pacific Princess* along with his wife. He lost a hand in a car accident and indicates his black-gloved hand is "plastic." Aikers is angry and bitter about the circumstances of his life. When asked by his wife what his plans are for the day, he replies:

> AIKERS: I think I'll spend the day lying on deck with the other invalids.

Mrs. Aikers confides in Doc that her husband has changed.

> MRS. AIKERS: Since the accident, he feels useless ... he won't listen to anyone.

Aikers' attempts at self-effacing humor reveal his self-devaluation and bitterness.

> AIKERS: I wish this ship had television. I'd like to watch a rerun of "The Fugitive" and root for the one-armed man ... maybe I'll go find a bridge game that's short a hand.

Mrs. Aikers is under a great deal of stress. She blames herself for her husband's accident. She pops pills when she cannot cope with his anger and accidentally overdoses. The action catalyzes Aikers to get on with his life.

> AIKERS: I was so busy feeling sorry for myself I didn't see what was happening to you.

* * *

"Aftermath" was a predictable little melodrama. Man has accident, hates himself; woman has guilt complex and hurts herself. Now man has the will to get well. According to both Aikers and his wife, life held little after he became disabled.

Crossbar / 1979 / Crossbar Productions

Executive Producer: Stanley Colbert
Producer: Brian Walker
Director: John Trent
Story: Bill Boyle
Screenplay: Keith Leckie
Category: Feature Film—Drama

* Amputee; single leg
* Single White Male
* Equipment: Crutches; Prosthetic leg

Plot: After losing a leg, on Olympic hopeful continues his quest for a medal.

Olympic bronze medalist Aaron Kornylo loses his right leg in a farming accident. He believes his high-jumping career is over. His old girlfriend Katie returns to offer support. Aaron indicates evidence of some prejudice toward him now that he is an amputee. He didn't get a coaching job for kids at a local school.

> AARON: Now I'm not good enough to nursemaid a bunch of kids, college coaches don't want to know I'm alive, and my old man wants to plant me here like one of his vegetables.

Katie sets up an appointment for Aaron about another coaching job. He purposely botches his chance. He uses devaluation to fight Katie's righteous anger.

> AARON: They arrest people for beating up on cripples.

Aaron begins jumping again with Katie coaching. She suggests Aaron try out for the "disabled games." Aaron vetoes that. He wants to go for the Olympic trials.

Miles Kornylo uses bad language and devalues his son when Aaron asks for a loan to go to the trials.

> MILES: I won't let you make a freak show of yourself....

> AARON: The only one that thinks I'm a freak is my own father.

Although Aaron's jumps qualify him for entry, the Olympic committee has a problem with him. Attitudinal barriers are evident as Mr. Carver indicates letting Aaron compete would be bad.

> CARVER: How do you respond to an amputee? Guilt? Embarrassment? Thankful that it isn't you? That you're still whole? We can't subject the other team members to those emotions on the field. How can they do their best under such circumstances? That's why we have the disabled games.

The Kornylos fly to Toronto. Miles is ready to go to bat for his son.

> WALLACE: ...there are other considerations ... your son does have a right to jump—except when it interferes with the other athletes. Now we believe your son would represent a diversion to them.

> MILES: Like a—freak show.

Miles visits a committee member at home to get an answer to why Aaron is disqualified.

> CARVER: It's just the effect his handicap might have on the other athletes.

Miles has gotten signatures from the other members of the committee agreeing to let Aaron compete. Carver refuses to sign. The other athletes vote to allow Aaron entry and threaten a boycott if he is barred. Carver signs. Aaron jumps seven feet on his leg. He tells Katie he doesn't need the Olympics anymore—he knows he can do anything he wants.

* * *

Crossbar was a fairly typical "triumph over disability" drama with a difference. Aaron met clearly articulated prejudice and attitudinal barriers as he assimilated the loss of his leg. However, his family coming to support him was the case of one group supporting one person. It was never expressed that a group's rights were being denied. The proposed boycott of the team members was to let their old teammate back into the fold, not to give a qualified athlete a shot.

Katie acted as a non-disabled catalyst. Since she was his girlfriend as well as a track and field athlete, her support seemed natural.

Within this film, the "disabled games" were considered by Aaron to not be competitive enough for him; the committee people suggested the "disabled games" existed for the comfort of those without disabilities.

It is unclear if the actor portraying Aaron was a performer with a disability or if masterful editing of a disabled athlete made it appear he did have a limitation.

Crossbar was a "quick fix" drama. If Aaron could high jump again, he could go on living. It was entertaining with some different slants to it.

My Kidnapper, My Love / Dec. 8, 1980 / NBC-TV

Executive Producers: Roger Gimbel and Tony Converse
Producer: James Stacy
Director: Sam Wanamaker
Teleplay: Louie Elias
Based on the Novel: *Dark Side of Love* by Oscar Saul
Category: Made-for-TV Movie— Drama

* Amputation; single arm, single leg
* Single White Male
* Performer with a Disability
* Equipment: Prosthetic arm and leg; crutch

Plot: A disabled newspaper vendor "kidnaps" a sick runaway for the ransom, unbeknownst to the "victim."

Denny, a New Orleans newspaper vendor who is an amputee, picks up a sick teenager and brings her home to warm her up. He comes on to her and she fights him off. He uses poor descriptive terminology.

GIGI: I thought it would be safe, being with a—

DENNY: A cripple? You think I ain't human? You think I ain't got feelings? I'm not all gone, dummy.

Gigi is looking for a friend who no longer lives in town. Denny reluctantly permits her to stay with him. 'Maker, Denny's bookmaker and anything-for-a-buck brother, identifies Gigi by the expensive wristwatch Denny has lifted from her to sell. Gigi is an heiress who is worth big bucks. 'Maker owes money to everyone in town, including the crime kingpin, King of Spades. Denny, by association, is in danger.

KING OF SPADES [warningly]: Takes two legs to dodge cars crossing the street.

'Maker makes plans for the ransom drop. Denny calls Gigi's parents, after dressing up in a trenchcoat and putting on his prosthetic limbs for disguise. Denny feels the ruse is foolproof. Matters are complicated as Denny falls in love with his "victim."

The ransom drop goes without a hitch. A cop corners Denny, noting 'Maker has paid all his debts and left town. Denny has managed to get his old boat going again after years in dry dock. But the police can't prove complicity. Gigi tells her parents she is going away with Denny.

* * *

In *My Kidnapper, My Love* a limitation was almost purely incidental, disposed of in a few natural throwaway lines. 'Maker, as a person experiencing some type of lung disorder, frequently needed oxygen to get his wheezy breathing under control. He was more disabled than the healthy amputee Denny.

Denny was a busy and athletic man. He worked out with a punching bag and moved easily with a crutch. He used his artificial limbs only when he wished to disguise himself.

Gigi was a teenager with dyslexia who had run away from home after finding out she was pregnant. Police approached her old teacher to get information about her. Actual kids with disabilities were seen in the background at the school.

My Kidnapper, My Love was about a person and a situation—not a disability.

Trapper John, M.D. / "Days of Wine and Leo" / Mar. 15, 1981 / CBS-TV

* Amputation; double hand
* Single White Male
* Equipment: Prosthetic hooks
* Performer with a Disability

Trapper John, M.D.

Plot: A disabled Korean War veteran falls in love for the first time.

Dr. Trapper John McIntyre's old army buddy, Dr. Leo Hearkins, arrives at San Francisco General. The diagnostician lost his hands in the Korean War and uses prosthetic hooks. Gonzo reaches out for a handshake with Leo then hesitates. Leo gives him a smile.

>LEO: You won't hurt them. They're war surplus.

Trapper offers Leo a hospital position as a diagnostician. Leo accepts on a trial basis. Leo is brought in on the case of an ex-stripper who has injured her neck in a fall. Liz is intrigued in the man with the hooks.

>LIZ: You play gin with those?

>LEO: If the stakes are right.

Liz is clearly interested in Leo. She gently chides him for his shyness when she knows he's interested in her. She wants him to put his arms around her. Erroneous notions in the form of a joke appear.

>LEO: Can you imagine the scar tissue my wife would develop from being hugged?

Trapper reveals he was responsible for Leo's presence on the chopper that crashed in Korea and cost Leo his hands. Leo learns this and fears Trapper's longtime friendship was motivated by guilt. He plans to leave San Francisco.
Liz takes a turn for the worse and requires surgery. Leo stays to help her. He forgives Trapper.

* * *

"Days of Wine and Leo" was a nice story when formula didn't creep in. There was a fun chemistry between Leo and Liz, expressed in easy jokes and flirtatious lines. It was delightful seeing an older man with a disability illustrated as sexual and attractive to a pretty and vivacious woman.

Leo's line about "the scar tissue my wife would develop" was delivered jokingly; however, due to the many times hooks/prostheses have been illustrated as weaponry, it is easy to assume this was not perceived as humor in many viewers' minds.

Trapper's guilt trip was pure formula. He could certainly have suffered angst for many years since he was the one on the chopper that crashed (he had persuaded Leo to sub for him). But for Leo to believe that Trapper's continued friendship in the days after the accident and in the thirty-plus years after the war was motivated by guilt was silly. It just didn't wash with the image of the busy and secure professional who had come to terms with some difficulties in his past and clearly enjoyed life.

"The Days of Wine and Leo" deserves a nod for its presentation of a double hand amputee as a hearty and healthy man who was a professional in his field. The love story was satisfying, due to the chemistry of the two persons involved.

Something Wicked This Way Comes / 1983 / A Bryna Company Production / Buena Vista

Producer: Peter Vincent Douglas
Director: Jack Clayton
Screenplay: Ray Bradbury
Based on the Novel by: Ray Bradbury
Category: Feature Film — Horror/Occult

* Amputation; single arm, single leg
* Single White Male
* Equipment: Crutch
* Performer with a Disability

Plot: The mysterious carnival that has come to town does strange things to many residents.

In Will Halloway's adult reminiscence of a dead autumn, several faces come to mind. He remembers people in the town, including tavernkeeper Edgar Barnum, a man with one arm and one leg who used a crutch for mobility. Will recalls Edgar was once a football star.

>ADULT WILL (v.o.): Edgar Barnum, yesterday's football hero, still haunted by forty-yard runs down the dark fields of his dreams.

Will recalls the odd carnival that arrived late one night. Edgar, like everyone else in town, goes to check out the fun. He is transfixed as he enters the house of mirrors. Young Will and his friend see what has Edgar's attention. The mirror's reflection casts an image of a non-disabled man. Edgar goes inside. The boys never see him come out.

* * *

Something Wicked This Way Comes featured a busy and talkative proprietor of a town tavern as a man with a disability. Edgar Barnum discussed football constantly, recalling his glorious past with only a shade of remorse. However, his attention to a past in which he could no longer be competitively included suggested he had never fully assimilated his limitation.

His role was semi-incidental in that others in the town saw things in the carnival they wished: a barber saw himself the object of exotic women's attention; an old maid schoolmarm saw herself as young and beautiful. Barnum saw himself as non-disabled. In that sense, he was not focused upon as a disabled character, but one with some shreds of fantasy he dealt with — like everyone else.

His fate was a little sketchy. Confusing events triggered the climax of the unsettling and eerie movie and made it hard to understand.

Small-statured persons were seen in the background of the carnival sequences.

Something Wicked This Way Comes used a person with a limitation as part of the overall story without unduly focusing on a disability.

AfterM*A*S*H / title unknown / Dec. 12, 1983 / CBS-TV

Executive Producer: Burt Metcalfe
Producer: Dennis Koenig
Supervising Producers: Ken Levine and David Isaacs
Director: Nick Havinga
Writers: Everett Greenbaum and Eliott Reid
Category: Series Television — Situation Comedy

* Amputation; single leg
* White Male
* Equipment: Prosthetic leg

Plot: Klinger is distressed to find an old friend has returned from the Korean War minus a leg.

Max Klinger, now working at a Missouri veteran's hospital, is happy to see Pete Sax, an old buddy of his. Pete looks and sounds great although he says he has checked into the hospital about his leg.

Klinger is uneasy when he discovers Pete lost a leg in the war. He avoids his friend and frets over the changes the war has wrought. He discusses his feelings with priest Father Mulcahy.

> KLINGER: [We used to play football together.] He was a hell of a man.
>
> MULCAHY: And my guess is he still is.

Klinger forces himself to face Pete again, noting that his friend walks with a swinging leg gait, using no cane or crutches. When Pete tells Klinger he drove to the hospital, the latter is astonished.

> KLINGER: You drove?
>
> PETE: I did. I do. Don't you?

* * *

This spinoff series from the popular *M*A*S*H* program, took the war home — as it was in the veterans hospital. In this episode, a real drama was enacted — the uneasiness of a friend learning that someone he knew had incurred a disability. Klinger's avoidance of Pete and his failure to follow through on a date to get together were resultant of his concern. However, in the course of the story, he recognized Pete was still a person Klinger wanted in his life.

Pete was illustrated as a smiling, humorous man who was busy and had things to do.

Actors with disabilities were seen in the background of this episode.

AfterM*A*S*H presented a man with a disability as a person who was going on despite a major change in his life.

The Terry Fox Story / 1983

Executive Producer: Guistan I. Rosenfeld
Producer: Robert Cooper
Director: R.L. Thomas
Story: John Kasten; Rose Kasten
Writer: Ed Hume
Category: Made-for-Cable Movie — Drama

* Amputation; single leg
* Single White Male
* Based on a True Story
* Equipment: Prosthetic leg
* Performer with a Disability

Plot: A young college student amputee decides to run across Canada to raise money for cancer research.

* * *

The Terry Fox Story was a dull and long movie about a young man who would never say die. Fox lost his leg after a bout with cancer. In true screen tradition, he received no counseling or rehabilitative therapy to learn what his limitation meant. He was fitted with a prosthetic leg, then decided to run for cancer research. The film chronicled the run which was stopped by a recurrence of the cancer. Fox died before completing the run.

An important issue was sidestepped in the film. While the world works hard and spends tremendous sums of money to create weapons that destroy human life or severely alter it, the public is expected to support research for catastrophic disease or trauma as an act of charity. With sufficient funds, such acts as "heroism" would be unnecessary.

The film was a "triumph-over-disability" drama with nothing new, interesting, or enjoyable. This one was a good bet for a work-out of the tear glands.

Powerhouse / "One of the Gang" / June 15, 1984 / PBS-TV

Executive Producer: Ira Klugerman
Producer: J. Allman
Director: Jack Zafran

* Amputation; single arm
* White Male Teenager
* Equipment: Prosthetic hook

Writer: J. Allman
Category: Series Television—
  Childrens'

* Performer with a Disability

Plot: The Powerhouse gang tries to help an ex-boxer find his cache of diamonds.

O'Toole, a long-ago member of the Powerhouse gang, made a name for himself in his youth as a boxer. Now, after a stroke, he is in a nursing home and unable to clearly speak. A villain is tormenting O'Toole, trying to find out where O'Toole hid some diamonds long ago.

Mike is a new member of the gang. He is a kid with a prosthetic arm. He helps the gang discover old O'Toole's cache of diamonds in the clubhouse.

* * *

"One of the Gang" was a wonderful little drama. In the space of a half hour, Mike was introduced; experienced prejudice from another member of the gang who thought he was incapable of doing anything; illustrated a picture-taking talent; developed pictures in the darkroom; and was ultimately the hero of the story. His prosthesis was conspicuously used throughout the episode.

Mike was angry to be pushed aside by the other kids, left out of their important "mission" because the others deemed he could get hurt. He knew the reason. He proved his mettle by illustrating his hook didn't make him different; it put him on an equal basis with the other boys.

"One of the Gang" gave a fair portrayal of a character with a disability and was worth seeing.

St. Elsewhere / "Give the Boy a Hand" / Jan. 23, 1985 / NBC-TV

Executive Producer: Bruce Paltrow
Producers: John Masius & Tom
  Fontana
Supervising Producer: Mark
  Tinker
Director: Janet Greek
Story: John Masius & Tom
  Fontana
Writer: Mitchell Fink and Mark
  Ross

* Amputation; single hand
* White Male
* Equipment: Prosthetic hook
* Performer with a Disability

Plot: Dr. Victor Ehrlich needs a "hard-hitting" subject for his TV spot and decides to do something on disability.

Amputation

In the hospital cafeteria, Elliott crashes into a hospital worker carrying a tray. The worker insists on picking up the broken glass using a prosthetic hook he calls "Old Floyd."

Ehrlich, wracking his brain for a subject on which to base his next TV news "Health Spot," seizes the opportunity to approach Powers.

> EHRLICH: I'd like to ask you about the problems you experience as a handicapped person.
>
> POWERS: It's DISABLED, not handicapped ... you got a week?

Elliott watches Ehrlich and Powers move off. He is writhing in guilt.

> ELLIOTT: I just yelled at a guy who's crippled!
>
> FISCUS: It's DISABLED.

Ehrlich does his "Health Spot." He mentions physical and attitudinal barriers confronting persons with disabilities. But his "hoof-in-mouth" disease gets the better of him and he tells a tasteless joke about an amputee "who didn't have a leg to stand on."

He approaches Powers in the cafeteria to find out how the other man liked the report. Powers employs a unique response. He takes Ehrlich's glasses and orders him to read the menu on the wall. Ehrlich cannot.

> POWERS: You're disabled, like me.... I'm an ordinary guy without a hand ... all we're asking is the same chance you give anyone else.

* * *

The always well-done *St. Elsewhere* did it again with "Give the Boy a Hand." Powers was illustrated as a capable cafeteria worker, just an ordinary guy, as he stated. Conspicuous use of his prosthesis helped educate the audience and allowed them to see it as a satisfactory substitute for a hand.

The scene where Powers illustrated that Ehrlich was also disabled without his own special aid was a nice one. And yes, Dr. Ehrlich was fired from his "Health Spot" after his tasteless discussion of disability!

"Give the Boy a Hand" was a brief and enjoyable portrayal of a person with a disability.

Night Court / "Walk, Don't Wheel" / Sept. 19, 1985 (rerun) / NBC-TV

Executive Producer: Reinhold Weege

* Amputation; double leg
* Single White Female

Night Court

Producer: Jeff Melman
Director: Reinhold Weege
Writer: Reinhold Weege
Category: Series Television — Situation Comedy

* Performer with a Disability
* Equipment: Wheelchair; Prosthetic legs

Plot: When Harry turns down a disabled law student's invitation to a party, she takes it personally.

Kristen is a law student and a leg amputee. She asks Harry Stone for a date and becomes angry when he turns her down, even though his reason is a mayor's function on Saturday at which he's to speak. Devaluation and bitterness are evident.

HARRY: Kristen, I really DO have a date at the Mayor's on Saturday.

KRISTEN [heavily]: Oh, I'm sure. What about Friday? Dining with the Governor?

HARRY: I can understand why you're bitter.

KRISTEN: No, you can't.

Harry gives the mayor's invitation away to D.A. Dan Fielding as Kristen watches.

HARRY: Well, now I'm free. So, is that invitation ... still open?

KRISTEN: I'm sorry, but I don't need ... your sympathy.... The little gimp gets her feelings hurt so you make a grand gesture. I suppose that makes you feel like a great big hero.... There's nothing to talk about.

HARRY: You're right.... There's nothing to talk about. I wouldn't go to that dance with you if you were the last person on earth.

KRISTEN: Hey, you can't say that. I'm disabled!

HARRY: You sure are. [taps his forehead] Up here.

Kristen comes to realize Harry was not trying to dodge her and she is guilty of trying to test people. On Saturday, Kristen comes in to pick up Harry. She is standing, wearing her artificial legs.

BULL: Why haven't you been using them?

KRISTEN: Ask Harry.

* * *

"Walk, Don't Wheel" illustrated an energetic, bright law student. Initially, she was seen as having a sense of humor, but all was lost in this formula treatment of Kristen's disability being a personal problem she was unable to deal with. Consequently, no one could say the right thing to her without her taking it wrong. It was up to Harry to set her straight. The insinuation that she did not use her artificial legs in a bid to elicit shock or sympathy indicated mental instability.

The title "Walk, Don't Wheel" (not screened for the audience) was further indication of the misunderstanding possessed by the writer. Prostheses are sometimes painful to the user; Kristen's not using them could have been a matter of personal comfort, not "testing." However, the audience was left with no doubts as to why they weren't worn. "Walk, Don't Wheel" was a poor and damaging image of disability.

Hill Street Blues / "Seoul on Ice" / Oct. 18, 1985 / NBC-TV

Executive Producer: Jeffrey Lewis
Co-Executive Producer: David Milch
Producer: Michael Vittes
Supervising Producer: Scott Brazil
Director: John Patterson
Writers: Jeffrey Lewis; David Milch
Category: Series Television—Police Drama

* Amputation; single leg
* Single White Male

Plot: A young amputee running to raise money for research has his van robbed.

Young Matt, an amputee, is running across the country to earn money for cancer research. As "Matt's Run for Research" passes through the locale of the Hill Street Station, his van is ripped off. All the money collected along the way is stolen.

Always seeking to polish his own tarnished halo, Chief Daniels approaches Coach McGonegeal, Matt's trainer, who is making a great deal of noise about the theft.

CHIEF DANIELS: Are you associated with the courageous runner?

In private, Daniels is more blunt and uses bad language.

DANIELS: The robbery of this cripple has just frosted me.

The crime is solved when it turns out that Coach McGonegeal stole the goods.

* * *

"Seoul on Ice" picked up on a story that had hit the newswires earlier that year when a young runner (inspired by Canada's Terry Fox) who had lost a leg to cancer ran across country to increase awareness and raise money for research. *Hill Street* picked up on the story and added a little twist — an inside job of theft.

Matt was an athletic, busy young man who was upset because his routine was disrupted by this unwanted intrusion of theft, police, news media, etc. He simply wanted to get back to his work. The concentration on the technical aspects of the run kept the story from being an "inspiring" one. Also, the concept of the coach as the culprit helped destroy the sanctimonious imagery often associated with people who are involved with the community of those with disabilities.

A brief scene featured a man in a wheelchair talking to police. He described seeing Matt's van, the one with "that crippled boy's picture on it." It seemed odd that he would use such poor language.

"Seoul on Ice" featured a character with a disability as part of the *Hill Street* cosmos.

Cagney and Lacey / "The Gimp" / Jan. 27, 1986 / CBS-TV

Executive Producer: Barney Rosenzweig
Producers: Ralph Singleton; Patricia Green
Co-Producer: P.K. Knelman
Supervising Producer: Liz Coe
Director: Sharron Miller
Story: Norman Chandler Fox
Teleplay: Cynthia Darnell
Category: Series Television — Police Drama

* Amputation; single arm, single leg
* Single White Male
* Equipment: Wheelchair
* Performer with a Disability

Plot: Detective Cagney is utterly frustrated in her attempts to nail a mugger who is attacking people using wheelchairs.

Ted Peters has been hassling Detective Christine Cagney by phone for information on the progress of her wheelchair-muggings investigation. Cagney is called out into the winter cold to meet Peters in the parking bay. Accessibility is discussed.

> CAGNEY: What, he can't find the front door? ... Mr. Peters? Where the hell are you? And why —

Peters appears in a wheelchair.

> PETERS: —the hell didn't I come into the building? Well, ask the truck driver why he's blocking this ramp.

Ted Peters is a busy professional man, employed as the head of the Eisley Foundation, which runs "centers for people with disabilities." He is realistic, bright, and politically active in matters that concern the disabled community. The cause of his disability is described as an auto accident in which he was at fault.

Cagney opts to go undercover using a wheelchair in hopes of getting mugged herself. She camps out in Peters' apartment since it is "wheelchair accessible."

Using a chair, Cagney is confronted with physical barriers. She can barely reach the coin slot of an inaccessible pay phone. She must accept the help of a pedestrian to get down a curb which is not ramped. Attitudinal barriers are also seen. Cagney waves at a curious child who looks at her chair. He waves back and is reprimanded by his mother "for staring at the lady." Men don't respond to her except as "a crip." As she tells Peters:

> CAGNEY: I knew it was going to be rough getting around, I expected that. But I tell you, the people in this city, they don't even *look* at you. They all look up here.

Cagney indicates an average eye level with her hand.

> CAGNEY: And the ones that *do* look at you, they're so damn patronizing, you just want to kill them.

Peters is a sexual, tender man. He touches Cagney and massages her sore neck. They consummate their interest and Cagney runs out. She tells partner Mary Beth Lacey she doesn't want to hurt him. She is concerned he won't fit into her busy, active life.

The mugger is caught and Cagney decides she can handle a relationship with the disabled man. Ironically, Peters tells her *he* has no place in his busy, active life for a relationship.

* * *

"The Gimp" was a different kind of story—and one of the best disability pieces ever produced. Peters was illustrated as a busy man, a workaholic who had fully integrated a severe limitation into his life. He was attractive to other women, a fact which initially surprised Cagney. He was athletic, working out with weights at home and moving well in a chair. Peters was simply a man who knew what he wanted out of life. He was a unique character with a personality far and beyond his disability.

An interesting sidelight to "The Gimp" was audience reaction to the story and character. An interview I did with various personnel at *Cagney and Lacey* revealed that "The Gimp" generated an "overwhelming" amount of mail from viewers, *all* of it positive. The character of Ted Peters was described as "very sexy," by one viewer. Another felt Peters was an appropriately strong-willed partner for the independent Cagney. Still another felt this character was *the* one who could take care of Cagney—not an easy position for any man, as avid fans would note.

Performers with disabilities were utilized for the program. "The Gimp" was wonderful.

A Winner Never Quits / Apr. 14, 1986 / ABC-TV

Executive Producers: Daniel Blatt and Robert Singer
Producers: James Keach and Lynn Radnor
Director: Mel Damski
Writer: Burt Prelutsky
Category: Made-for-TV Movie—Drama

* Amputation; single arm
* Single White Male
* Based on a True Story

Plot: Pete Gray, who lost his right arm in a childhood accident, is determined to make it to the big league of baseball.

In 1925, ten-year-old Pete has a dream: to play major league baseball. A childhood accident left him with only one arm. As the last one picked for sandlot ball, his future as a player is bleak. Some devaluation shows up.

> PETE: Can't be a major league baseball player. Can't play in Yankee Stadium with one arm. I know one thing—without two arms, even Babe Ruth would be selling pencils.

Older brother Whitey takes Pete under his wing and trains him.

As an adult, Pete is turned away from a semi-pro team having open tryouts. He even tries to get into the army to fight World War II but is classed 4-F. In 1943, Pete gets signed to the Memphis Chicks, whose owner sees him as an attraction.

> MR. TATUM: You're gonna be the biggest thing to hit Memphis since Barnum and Bailey came to town ... you are gonna sell a lot of tickets.
>
> PETE: Why don't you just buy yourself a freak show?

Pete begins dating a waitress named Annie. She wants him to visit war veterans at the hospital.

> PETE: I'm sorry but I'm not joining the freak of the month club.

In California, a ten-year-old boy loses his arm in a freak accident. His hopes of playing ball are dashed until his father reads about Pete Gray. Mr. Tatum arranges for the family to come to Memphis to meet Pete. The athlete resists the plan. He notes everyone will make a big deal over the kid today but then—

> PETE: He's gotta go through the rest of his life being ridiculed, pitied, stared at ... it's a charade and I don't want no part of it.

When Pete meets the kid, he exhibits a soft side and acts as the disabled catalyst for the boy.

Gray is picked as Most Valuable Player of the Southern League. He visits vets at the V.A. and he is signed by the major leagues for the St. Louis Browns. At Yankee Stadium, he replaces another player and saves the game.

* * *

A Winner Never Quits had its share of devaluation, but generally was a nice portrayal of a person with a disability. Gray was an interesting character—aggressive, arrogant, athletic, a brawler and a fighter. He was also an artist, enjoying sketching. He wasn't very likeable and didn't care—he just wanted to play baseball. He got peeved at the world—if he could slam a baseball 380 feet with a bat, why couldn't he fire a gun for the army?

His reaction to the boy with a similar disability was interesting. He wanted nothing to do with the kid until the boy showed up in his locker room. Then he let down his walls, finally letting a soft side show. It was an interesting type of character development; it was a relief to not have someone jumping up to save another with his own inspiring courage. Pete seemed to say he was Pete and that was it. He wasn't what all those other folks made him out to be.

Pete was seen cutting up the dance floor with pleasure, beating his brother Whitey in a game of pool and, as to be expected, exceptionally capable with a baseball mitt and bat.

Performers with disabilities were utilized in the veterans hospital scene.

A Winner Never Quits was an intriguing story about a man who simply wanted what he felt he deserved.

The Ted Kennedy Jr. Story / Nov. 4, 1986 / NBC-TV

Executive Producer: Robert E. Fuisz
Producers: William F. Storke; Alfred R. Kelman
Director: Delbert Mann
Writer: Roger O. Hirson

* Amputation; single leg
* White Male Child
* Based on a True Story
* New Disability
* Equipment: Prosthetic leg; Crutches; Cane; Skiing outrigger

The Ted Kennedy Jr. Story

Category: Made-for-TV Movie—
Drama

Plot: The famed Kennedy family is tested again when twelve-year-old Teddy's leg is amputated.

Teddy Kennedy, Jr., son of the Senator, is an active boy in 1973. He makes the football team at school although plagued by a sore knee. He is finally taken to see a doctor about a bruise that won't go away.

When the bruise and soreness remain after treatment, a biopsy is taken from the bone tissue of the leg. It is discerned that the boy has osteochondrosarcoma—cancer of bone and cartilage. The doctors recommend to Senator Kennedy that Teddy's leg be amputated above the knee.

KENNEDY: Are you telling me there is no way to save my son's leg?

The Senator approaches his son and tells him about the impending surgery.

TEDDY: I don't wanna lose my leg. Please Dad, I don't wanna lose my leg.

After surgery, Teddy pushes himself and is soon walking, using a temporary leg and crutches. He chooses an artificial leg to replace his own. Teddy learns to ski. He joins a school excursion to Ireland despite illness from chemotherapy. When his father flies to Ireland to get him, Teddy convinces the senator to let him continue the trip—just like the other boys.

* * *

The Ted Kennedy Jr. Story was a dull and unmoving attempt to chronicle a difficult period in the lives of the Kennedy clan. To the film's credit, it did not wallow in scenes of devaluation from Teddy. It focused on the Senator virtually facing the crisis alone as his wife, Joan, was undergoing alcohol rehabilitation. He had to bolster Joan to support Teddy.

After losing his leg, Teddy did not receive any type of counseling. He did not undergo any rehabilitation. He woke up with a temporary leg and took it home.

The effort of the film to indicate it was the story of a remarkable boy showed up conspicuously. In one scene, Teddy wished to take a shower—something requiring caution. He wanted that shower and told himself to "do something about it." He picked up a wooden chair from his bedroom and dragged it into the tub, seating himself to do the chore. His mother was duly impressed and told him it was a good idea. Therefore, Teddy was seen as resourceful and special; in fact, "shower chairs" of various kinds are items on the market to permit older or disabled persons the luxury of a shower in safety.

The high point of the piece was the tag. The actual Ted Kennedy, Jr., appeared as his adult self and made a speech to the audience. He had been, he stated, involved in "a human rights struggle, called the Independent Living Movement, for persons with disabilities.... The opportunities in life which able-bodied people take for granted just aren't available to millions of people.... There are many barriers which are in our way ... we ... have to open our minds to end the worst kind of isolation, fear and pity and allow people who may be differently-abled to participate in life as well."

Other than the stirring reminder that the community of people with disabilities was not fairly represented in society, *The Ted Kennedy Jr. Story* was melodrama.

Developmental Disability

Within the context of this work, television and film characters whose level of intellectual and social development are below-average are described as Developmentally Disabled. Most of these characters have some degree of mental retardation.

Developmentally disabled characters are often seen as forever-childlike people who are complacent and smiling. Such characterizations ignore basic human emotions and needs. Happily, the screen image of those with developmental disabilities has been changing. The presence onscreen of performers who are, themselves, disabled in this capacity has been a positive trend. These characters are often seen with a range of feelings and abilities to offer.

Only one characteristic pops up with frequency in pieces about developmental disability. The Special Olympics—athletic competitions for those with developmental disabilities—have become well-publicized events around which local dignitaries and media celebrities gather. Recognition of the events is high from the general public—which includes writers. Though the Special Olympics has been a welcome addition to the screen portrayals of persons with developmental disabilities, the events are also in danger now of becoming a stereotype. A number of stories in this category revolve about the Special Olympics.

Also, see *Highway to Heaven,* "A Special Love" for an additional Olympics offering. *Medical Center*'s "The Albatross" also features a developmentally disabled character.

A Child Is Waiting / 1963 / United Artists

Producer: Stanley Kramer
Director: John Cassavetes
Writer: Abby Mann
Category: Feature Film—Drama

* Developmental Disability
* White Male Child

Plot: A woman goes to work as a paid assistant at a state home for developmentally disabled children.

Miss Jean Hansen begins work at the state institution for children with developmental disabilities. Matty, a teacher/nurse, talks to Jean about the children and why it is important they be there.

> MATTY: Treatment and education for these children is a fairly new thing.

On Visitor's Day, excitement prevails as families come to visit. Ruben Widdicome, a boy whose father dumped him at the school one day, waits and waits for visitors who never come. Jean hurts for the boy who is fast becoming her favorite.

> WOMAN: Ruben's mother won't come. She hasn't come for two years.

Dr. Clark comments on the same.

> DR. CLARK: You know, sometimes I think we should be treating the parents instead of the kids.

Jean thinks Ruben's parents may have changed. After all, they are college-educated people.

> DR. CLARK: What makes you think that having a college degree and a good income helps one to understand any better?

Concerned at Jean's personal involvement with one child, Dr. Clark assigns her to another cottage. Jean takes matters into her own hands and goes to visit the Widdicomes.

> MR. WIDDICOME: I wish he were dead.

Dr. Clark chews Jean out for her action.
The children put on a play. Surprisingly, Mr. Widdicome shows up. He can't bear to look at the stage. He does, reluctantly, and is amazed at what he sees — a school play.

* * *

A Child Is Waiting was an absorbing and interesting look at developmental disability through the eyes of adults. Dr. Clark was the professional who had to fight for every penny doled out to his institution; Jean Hansen was a person who thought her heart was in the right place; and Mr. Widdicome anguished over his "defective" son.

This film stressed the fact that these children had abilities and were able to function. Dr. Clark stressed that discipline was a part of their lives as it was for any average child. He also drily noted — after a meeting with state bureaucrats — that longevity of a "controversial" program such as his depended on finance; there was little support elsewhere. He had to fight for educational classes in the curriculum.

Actual children with disabilities were used in the film, a fact moviegoers were "warned" about to "prepare" them.

A Child Is Waiting was a detailed piece which illustrated a different aspect of developmental disability, indicating that the children were human and needed love, attention and education like any others—not sympathy.

Starsky and Hutch / "Nightmare" / 1976 / ABC-TV

Executive Producers: Aaron Spelling; Leonard Goldberg
Producer: Joseph T. Naar
Director: Randall Kleiser
Writer: Steve Fisher
Category: Series Television—Police Drama

* Developmental Disability
* Single White Female

Plot: A developmentally disabled young woman is raped and beaten.

Lisa, a nineteen-year-old developmentally disabled young woman, is raped and beaten on her way to the library. Detectives and friends Starsky and Hutch meet with Lisa's mother at the hospital.

> MOTHER: Maybe the fact that she's retarded might help her forget a little easier.

Lisa is a target for the criminals who hurt her. One goes to her house when she is alone, intent on killing her. Lisa thinks fast, throwing hot coffee at him. She locks the door and attempts to phone for help, but she is thwarted by a recording. She hides from the man pursuing her and pushes a large shelf unit over on him. Starsky and Hutch arrive to save her in the nick of time.

Lisa is put on the witness stand for a pre-trial hearing. The Public Defender describes Lisa as a "mentally deficient" woman of nineteen with the mind of a ten-year-old. Starsky reinforces Lisa's childlikeness when he tells her she is lucky she can still play games, like Pretend. Her mother details the difficult past.

> MOTHER: Lisa was three when we found out she was—
>
> HUTCH: Special?
>
> MOTHER: Yes.

She squeezes Hutch's arm as if in thanks.

> MOTHER: What mommy wouldn't love a child that never grows up?

* * *

"Nightmare" featured opposing images of developmental disability. Lisa was shown as bright, capable of taking care of herself, thinking independently, and having achieved such skills as reading. Her mother trusted her to go to the library by herself or to stay home alone. At the same time, she was portrayed as childlike, playing with dolls and wearing kiddie pajamas to bed. Her mother reinforced this by the inscription on Lisa's birthday cake: "Happy Birthday to My Big, Beautiful Girl." The babyish pajamas and the dolls utilized the "adult-child" approach to developmental disability, that is, the case of arrested growth, resulting in a never-never land of forever childhood.

"Nightmare" had one or two good points but was not a fair image of this particular disability. It also featured the disabled-woman-as-victim approach.

One Day at a Time / title unknown / Oct. 23, 1978

Writer: Bud Wisen
Category: Series Television — Situation Comedy

* Developmental Disability
* Single White Male

Plot: A developmentally disabled young man proves he can be a good worker.

When apartment super Schneider hurts his back, he needs to hire someone to help him get by. Barb suggests Jackie, a friend of hers.

BARB: Jackie is exceptional.

JACKIE: That means I'm slow but people say exceptional.

Mother Anne Romano is condescending to Jackie. Barb explains the concept of mainstreaming to her mother. Attitudinal barriers are touched on.

BARB: Jackie ... has a hard time getting a job because he's discriminated against....

SCHNEIDER: What's his problem?

BARB: Let me put this delicately — he's mentally retarded.

SCHNEIDER: [Jackie] ... is a looney?

BARB: He's just slow! He'd be perfect for the job.

Schneider hires Jackie. When there is a gas leak, Jackie is able to follow Schneider's orders on the walkie talkie and shut off the main. Working with Schneider has been a benefit, decides Jackie.

JACKIE: He yells at me. He thinks that I can do things then I think I can do them ... he doesn't make me feel different ... people never let me try to do things because I'm slow.

This episode of *One Day at a Time* was a nice story. It dealt with Jackie's suitability for the job at hand and not his disability. Schneider learned he could trust the boy.

Jackie exhibited some "super-crip" tendencies, that is, he did everything so exceptionally well with little faltering that his disability appeared to be nonexistent — except in other people's eyes. Despite some lapses, this was a very fair piece and a good portrayal.

A Special Kind of Love (a.k.a. "Special Olympics") / 1978

Executive Producer: Roger Gimbel
Co-Executive Producer: Tony Converse
Producers: Merrit Malloy & Marc Trabulus
Director: Lee Phillips
Writer: John Sacret Young
Category: Made-for-TV Movie — Drama

* Developmental Disability
* White Male Teenager

Plot: After Grandma Elmira's death, the Gallatzin family must shift their lives to adjust, including developmentally disabled Matt.

Widower Carl Gallatzin is a trucker on the move. His mother, Elmira, keeps high school sports star Mike on an even keel and acts as mother for adolescent Janice. She is also the catalyst in wanting to keep fourteen-year-old developmentally disabled Matt home instead of in the state institution. Elmira's death sends the family in a topspin and seemingly seals Matt's fate to remain in the institution. Both Janice and Mike persuade their father to let Matt come home and attend a nearby school. Carl agrees.

At the new school, Matt is enamored by the sports program which leads to participation in the Special Olympics. He qualifies for the games and enters, becoming a winner.

* * *

A Special Kind of Love dealt with family difficulties, not disability. Matt was just another part of the family struggling to cope after Grandma Elmira's death. Older brother Mike's own image was shattered when he lost an important track meet and saw his girl kiss another boy. Young Janice bridled under the new and sudden burden of responsibility she had in the home. In the explosive household, Matt's hyperactivity was too much too bear.

The athletics at the new school gave Matt a place to channel his energy. Older brother Mike learned patience as he tried to train the younger boy to high jump while attempting to mend his own image. His growth from calling Matt a "retard" to learning how to best teach him to high jump was refreshing. The Special Olympics benefitted the floundering family as much as it did Matt, giving them a thread to tie them together.

Children with disabilities were utilized freely in the background and in the Special Olympics sequence. *A Special Kind of Love* was nicely and fairly done.

Like Normal People / 1979

Producer: Joanna Lee
Director: Harvey Hart
Writer: Joanna Lee
Based on the Book: *Like Normal People* by Robert Meyers
Category: Made-for-TV Movie — Drama

* Developmental Disability
* Single White Couple
* Based on a True Story

Plot: Two developmentally disabled adults meet opposition when they announce they wish to marry.

Roger Meyers is a bright and imaginative poet and artist. At age eighteen, he is interested in girls. He has a developmental disability. He joins the local YMCA to use the pool. He has a Red Cross lifesaving card which he proudly displays.

    ROGER: See, you don't have to be smart to swim good.

Roger likes a little eleven-year-old girl to whom he sends a valentine. He is subsequently investigated by police when the girl receives a pornographic letter. Prejudice is illustrated as the police infer that someone with a mental limitation is in a medieval "sex fiend" category. Roger is innocent of the deed.

Roger is very attracted to Virginia, a young woman at his independent living center/school. They begin a courtship. School officials warn them to stop seeing each other. Roger stands up for their rights.

    ROGER: ...When normal people love each other, they hold hands and they kiss.... We're gonna be like normal people.

Roger and Virginia move into the community as part of a transitional living program. They want to marry. Mr. Davis, a school official, prohibits the marriage.

    DAVIS: I believe in helping the retarded. But I also believe [that] kind of normalcy ... is a cruel delusion. And I believe any talk of marriage between retarded people is a social obscenity.... They must not reproduce.

Program co-ordinator Stein tells him Roger and Virginia will be thoroughly counseled on reproduction and their options then left to their own decisions. If Davis doesn't like it:

STEIN: I will consider it a violation of their civil rights and I will haul your rear end into court.

Virginia and Roger make plans. Virginia goes to the doctor. She comes home and talks to Roger.

VIRGINIA: No babies, Roger. It's better for us ... we did the right thing....

The couple is married.

* * *

Like Normal People was a film which presented two developmentally disabled persons as people. They were not children; they had a great capacity to feel. Roger was directed. When his father told him a man who wanted to be married needed a job, Roger found himself a job, traveled to the site on a bus and inquired within.

A confusing element of this story was the segment regarding children. Stein counseled the two on reproduction, birth and then augmented it with practical questions, such as, "What do you do if the baby cries at three in the morning?" Roger was stymied for a solution. The following scene had Virginia coming in from a doctor's appointment saying "No babies." It wasn't expressed if she was unable to bear children — or if her "we did the right thing" statement was meant to imply she was voluntarily sterilized. It was quickly pushed aside and ignored.

The film attended to Roger's older brother's lifelong struggle not to be jealous of the special attention Roger got. Even as an adult when trying to expand his writing career, his mother wanted him to share Roger's poetry with agents. Robert had to tersely remind her he had his own life.

The piece focused on the rights of those with developmental disabilities. A small segment dealt with "normalization," indicating that Roger and Virginia should be considered successful students due to their degree of independence. But the sponsoring institution tried to squelch the ultimate "normalization." More examination of such administrative contradictions would have given the movie more of an edge.

Like Normal People had some good merits.

The Kid from Nowhere / Jan. 4, 1981 / NBC-TV

Producer: Gilbert Cates
Director: Beau Bridges
Writer: Judy Farrell
Category: Made-for-TV Movie — Drama

* Developmental Disability
* White Male Child
* Performer with a Disability

Plot: A mother overprotects her developmentally disabled son, finding it increasingly hard to cope with him as he approaches adolescence.

* * *

The Kid from Nowhere was a nicely-done piece. It was the story of a single parent who was completely devoted to her child with Down's syndrome. She had worked hard with him, had a very special rapport with him, but was finding his mood swings as he approached adolescence hard to deal with. The attempts of people at the boy's school to put him into an athletic program which would lead to entry in the Special Olympics were vetoed by the concerned mother.

After a difficult period, the mother recognized her son could achieve and also, more importantly, that he was growing up and had to find his own special niche in the world. She understood that she could not make all of his decisions.

The concentration on the problems of the mother who denied herself a personal life out of guilty devotion to the boy singled this story out from other similar "Special Olympics" stories. It was the tale of her growth and how she learned that her son was a person who had the right to fail and learn from his mistakes. Most refreshing was the indication the boy was stubborn and had his own turbulent emotions.

A love story made up the subplot. The mother fell in love with the boy's coach. His experience with similarly disabled children had given him a different outlook. He was comfortably casual and at ease with her son, a fact which made her think the boy wasn't getting enough attention. Again, she realized the boy was at an age where she must pull back.

The Kid from Nowhere was a carefully done piece and worth seeing.

Bill / 1981 / CBS-TV

Producer: Mel Stuart
Director: Anthony Page
Story: Barry Morrow
Writer: Corey Blechman
Category: Made-for-TV Movie — Drama

* Developmental Disability
* Single White Male
* Based on a True Story

The Kid from Nowhere; Bill

Plot: A developmentally disabled man is released from the institution in which he has lived for forty-six years.

Bill Sackter leaves Faribault, the "State School for the Feeble-Minded and Epileptic" in the 1960s, after nearly half a century of residence. Social worker Orville Farley finds him a residence.

> MRS. VOSS: He can't read or write, can't tell time and he's got a bad leg too? Why'd they let him out?
>
> FARLEY: Community placement, it's a new concept.
>
> MRS. VOSS: ...he's probably no crazier than anyone else walking the streets.

Bill is regularly arrested for various reasons. He is an easy mark for con men. He cannot resist people and always believes in the best of each person he meets.

Barry Morrow, a young filmmaker, reluctantly attends a staff Christmas party at the country club where his wife works. His eye is caught by Bill, who works in the kitchen. Barry is intrigued by the man. Barry and his wife, Bev, unofficially adopt Bill. When Barry gets a job in another state, he manages to get custody of Bill and transfers him with the family. Bill gets a job at the university making coffee. He boards in a house run by Mae, an elderly lady.

When Barry gets the job of a lifetime across the country, he must tell Bill. Bill does not want to go. Someone, he reasons, needs to take care of the coffee pots, has to help Mae with the housework, and must play the harmonica for the children at the school. Bill has found his niche and wishes Barry the best.

* * *

Bill was a wonderful and lovingly written drama. Bill Sackter came out of the institution with the wariness and weariness of an adult, but with the innocent curiosity of a young man. He was eager to see the world. And when the world took advantage of him, he felt betrayed. The advent of Barry in his life was a turning point. Although Barry was a non-disabled catalyst, he did what the social services at the time were not doing. He helped Bill learn to take a bus and get by on his own. He believed in Bill. In exchange, Bill gave him everything he had—love.

The story was not sappy. The character was faceted and had a distinct personality. He had been abused—he constantly referred to himself as a "crack-minded old man"—and was never encouraged to strike out on his own in the institution. Outside, he learned and grew.

Bill was compelling, moving and emotional. It deserves to be seen.

Two of a Kind / Oct. 9, 1982

Producers: Stanley Kallis; Lee Rich; Malcolm Stuart
Co-Producer: Bonnie Raskin
Director: Roger Young
Writer: James Sadwith
Category: Made-for-TV Movie — Drama

* Developmental Disability
* Single White Male

Plot: A developmentally disabled young man and his grandfather are "two of a kind."

Noel Minor is twenty-one and developmentally disabled. He is progressing well in a workshop that is teaching him independent living skills. Grandpa Ross Minor, Noel's "Papa Ross," is in a nursing home after the death of his wife. He is withdrawn, never responding to those around him.

Noel loves his grandfather and rides his bike to see him every day. His attention helps Papa Ross break out of his severe depression. But while the old man responds to Noel, the Minors and the staff in the nursing home believe Ross is catatonic.

When Mrs. Minor discovers the goal of the workshop is to enable Noel to have an apartment of his own, she pulls him out of the program—despite the objections of her husband. Frank Minor wants Noel to be independent since he claims his wife uses Noel as a shield between the two of them. Mrs. Minor decides to leave her husband and take "Noel-y" with her. Noel rebels, lashing out angrily for his mother calling him the diminutive "Noel-y." He bursts out of the house and takes her car.

He "kidnaps" Papa Ross from the nursing home. They spend a wonderful day together. Papa Ross does not wish to return to the nursing home; Noel does not wish to go with his mother. Papa Ross has a solution. The two will get an apartment together.

* * *

Two of a Kind illustrated a young developmentally disabled man as one who had the right to grow up despite what his mother wanted. The juxtapositioning of the young man bursting to learn and to be out on his own with the old man who was, he felt, being warehoused, was nicely done. Papa Ross seemed to be of a more pragmatic old school, whereas Mrs. Minor felt Noel was hers to take care of.

Within the drama, it was easy to see that the independent living skills center was the appropriate place for Noel to be. He told Papa Ross he had learned to handle money and how to ride the bus. He learned to tell time and how to cook. When his mother removed him from the program, he was deeply depressed. Mrs. Minor thought he'd get over it in a few days—as always, badly underestimating her son.

Noel was headstrong and often in the wrong, but he was learning. With the no-nonsense guidance of Papa Ross, he found an ally and a teacher. In Noel, the old man found energy and a fresh outlook on what had become a very tired life.

A performer with a disability had a small role as Irene, Noel's girlfriend at the workshop, who encouraged him to strike out on his own.

Two of a Kind illustrated that a person with a disability had a great deal to give. As Papa Ross noted, Noel was the only person smart enough to break through to him when his own children and hospital counseling staff could not.

Facts of Life / "Different Drummer" / Nov. 10, 1982 / NBC-TV

Writers: Dianne Messina and Lou Messina
Category: Series Television—Situation Comedy

* Developmental Disability
* White Male Teenager

Plot: Blair falls for a mildly retarded young man and begins to remake him into her own image.

The new part-time delivery boy is Leo, a very attractive young man who is also developmentally disabled. Blair is attracted to him.

ROY: I guess with his looks, it doesn't matter he's retarded.

Blair and Leo go out to a movie on Saturday night. Blair later expresses to her friends they had a good time.

BLAIR: He laughed in all the right places.

JO: That's more than we can say for most of your dates.

Blair has ambitious plans to help Leo.

BLAIR: Now that I know Leo's potential, I can open up new horizons for him.

Blair's single-handed attempt to be a major catalyst in Leo's life is commented on by Jo.

JO: ...Blair decided to become the Miracle Worker....

Blair is schooling Leo in painting but he doesn't perform in the way she thinks he should. In frustration, Leo leaves.

BLAIR: I'm just trying to help him!

MRS. G: [You're trying to change him.]

Leo becomes a disabled catalyst in Blair's life. She learns a lesson in that every person is different. She and Leo make up, but he will paint what *he* sees—not what Blair thinks he should see.

* * *

"Different Drummer" took a fairly standard disability theme and turned it around. Blair was not a saint for attempting to show Leo the way. She was an obstruction to his natural progression.

Leo was attractive, talented and employed. He was a character who had potential—provided someone like the overbearing Blair did not hinder him. "Different Drummer" was a pleasant episode.

CHiPs / "Something Special" / Nov. 21, 1982

Executive Producer: Cy Chermak
Supervising Producer: Paul Mason
Writers: Pamela Ryan and Beverly Bloomberg
Category: Series Television—Police Drama

* Developmental Disability
* White Male Teenager
* Performer with a Disability

Plot: A developmentally disabled adolescent runs away from a father who can't accept his son.

California Highway Patrol officer Frank "Ponch" Poncherello works as a coach with young Nicky Grievey, a developmentally disabled youngster. He is helping the boy prepare for the Special Olympics competition. Nicky's dad doesn't want to watch his boy. Nicky says his dad doesn't care. The thought harms his performance.

Ponch approaches the Grieveys to discuss the problem.

MELISSA: It's difficult for [my husband] to deal with Nicky's handicap.

Gordon is piqued at the intrusion and the descriptions of Nicky.

GORDON: You make it sound so *nice* ... he's retarded.

Nicky overhears as Ponch takes on a non-disabled catalyst role.

PONCH: Your son's tryin' to be a champion too—in his own class.... You got something special.

Ponch and partner Bobby get a radio report that Nicky has run away. The boy has left home in confusion and followed a frog. He ends up beneath a dry spillway of a dam. Water begins seeping down, indicating a flood is about to occur. Ponch and Bobby rescue the kid as the floodgates open.

Gordon attends the Special Olympics. Nicky falls in his race, then comes from behind to take second place.

NICKY: I lost, Dad.

GORDON: You're a champion, Son. Don't you forget it.

* * *

"Something Special" was a sweet little story, illustrating a developmentally disabled child as one with thoughts and feelings of his own. He wanted to win, wanted the respect of his father, much like any other kid.

Actual children with disabilities were seen in the Olympics montage.

The use of a developmentally disabled actor in this episode gave an extra sheen of authenticity to the production.

Fame / "Love Is the Question" / Jan. 27, 1983 / NBC-TV

Producer: David De Silva
Director: Robert Scheerer
Writer: Leah Markus
Category: Series Television—
  Drama

* Developmental Disability
* White Male Teenager

Plot: A developmentally disabled teenager attends the School of the Performing Arts part-time and falls in love with Julie.

* * *

"Love Is the Question" was a student-loves-teacher story. Troy, a developmentally disabled teen, went to the School of the Performing Arts in the afternoons. Always feeling like an outsider, he gravitated toward fellow student Julie, who tutored him in music theory. He fell in love and she had to hurt him by telling him it was not mutual. However, Troy made a place for himself and proved he *could* be a part of the high-energy educational institution.

The love aspect of the story was a formula trend which greatly weakened it. "Love Is the Question" was quite forgettable.

Bill—On His Own / Nov. 9, 1983 / CBS-TV

Executive Producer: Alan
  Landsburg

* Developmental Disability
* Single White Male

Producer: Linda Otto *Based on a True Story
Director: Anthony Page
Writer: Barry Morrow
Category: Made-for-TV Movie—
  Drama

Plot: Bill Sackter, a developmentally disabled man, attempts to make it on his own.

Bill—On His Own takes up where its predecessor, *Bill,* left off. Mentor Barry Morrow and his family have moved to California. Bill is living in a home run by an elderly woman with other adults who have various developmental limitations. Bill is busy, interested in people, and has a little job—running a coffee corner at a college campus student lounge.

A young female student decides he needs more education and finds out how limited her patience is when she grows frustrated with Bill, unable to teach him. Rather than her becoming a catalyst in his life for change, Bill assumes that role for her, helping her understand some very basic things about people through his unclouded eyes.

Bill also has an outside interest. He wants to have a Bar Mitzvah despite the fact he is well into his fifties or sixties. He is able to complete the ceremony with the help of a concerned rabbi.

Bill is illustrated as a multifaceted, busy human being whose limitations are not tragedies but learning experiences for himself and others.

* * *

Bill—On His Own followed the Emmy award-winning *Bill,* the true story of a man who spent fifty years or so in a mental institution before a concerned young filmmaker "adopted" him and introduced him to the world. The sequel revolved about the idealistic young student who wanted to "improve" Bill. The lesson illustrated "right" and "appropriate" for some may be unnecessary baggage for a different person.

Bill—On His Own quietly asserted that Bill was a person in his own right. His disability was not depicted to garner pity or tears, but to illustrate the different capacities all people have—including those like Bill. The matter-of-fact study kept the story from being a "triumph-over-disability" one. The drama was an honest portrayal of a developmentally disabled older adult and well-worth watching.

Testament / 1983 / Paramount

Producer: Lynne Littman * Developmental Disability
Director: Lynne Littman * Asian-Pacific Male Teenager
Story: Carol Amen * Performer with a Disability
Writer: John Sacret Young

Category: Made-for-TV Movie—
Drama

Plot: Life creeps on in a small California town after a nuclear holocaust.

* * *

Testament, a chilling and heart-breaking drama of life after nuclear warfare, featured a developmentally disabled character in a small role. Hiroshi was the adolescent developmentally disabled son of Mike, the local gas station owner in the small town. The boy survived the initial blast along with his father. Hiroshi was later discovered alone in his father's garage, saying his dad had "gone away." He was taken in by the central family.

Hiroshi was a beloved child and one worth saving. He was a member of the community—although he did not really understand what had happened to the world beyond the town. [It should be noted that Hiroshi is the *only* Asian-Pacific character logged in this entire collection of disability portrayals.]

Testament used a developmentally disabled character in a natural way within a strong and powerful drama.

Money on the Side / July 11, 1984 / ABC-TV

Producer: Hal Landers
Supervising Producer: Audrey Blasdell-Godard
Director: Robert Collins
Story: Mort Fine
Teleplay: Eugene Price; Robert Collins
Category: Made-for-TV Movie—
Drama

* Developmental Disability
* White Male Child

Plot: The lives of ordinary housewives who turn to prostitution for "money on the side" are explored.

Janice Vernon is a housewife searching for an alternate means to get cash. She has a son, Scottie.

> JANICE: [When Scottie] was born with his "special problems," we had to redefine [our lives]....

Janice turns to prostitution. She wants money because of Scottie.

> JANICE: He needs a special class in a special school in San Francisco.

Her husband Nels refuses to believe that.

NELS: He's just slow, that's all.

Janice erroneously indicates that Scottie's developmental problem is also a health difficulty. She compares him with her other children.

JANICE: Three beautiful kids—all perfect ... but with Scottie, he's not healthy ... he's different.

She keeps her husband up-to-date on Scottie's progress.

JANICE: By the end of the year, he'll be able to button his own shirt.

Nels explodes.

NELS: Some school for idiots! [How will it look on his record? How will he be able to get into college?]

* * *

Money on the Side concentrated on the financial difficulties associated with having a child who is disabled. Never was Scottie looked at as a child. He was something that cost money and upset the balance between his parents.

Janice loved Scottie and compromised her own values to get him the type of education she knew he needed. This story skipped over the fact that children with disabilities are afforded free public education.

Nels was a close-minded man who could not admit he had helped create a child that was less than perfect. His calling the child an "idiot" fit his character, although use of such language in reference to developmental disability was wrong. His feelings and his embarrassment all contributed to Janice's secret life and subsequent arrest.

Money on the Side used a character with a disability as one who had caused emotional distress in a family.

The Fall Guy / "The Winner" / Dec. 19, 1984 / ABC-TV

Executive Producer: Glen Larson
Co-Executive Producer: Lee Majors
Producer: Andrew Schneider and Sam Egan
Supervising Producer: Lou Shaw
Director: Ray Austin
Writers: Lou Shaw and Sam Egan
Category: Series Television— Drama

* Developmental Disability
* White Male Child
* Performer with a Disability

Plot: A young developmentally disabled boy attaches himself to stuntman/bounty hunter Colt Seavers.

Developmentally disabled Jason Corey and his older brother, Sean, are on a bus heading to Los Angeles for the Special Olympics. Left alone in the bus station while Sean makes a phone call, Jason follows a cat. He ditches under Colt Seaver's truck and sees two men knock a third out. Jason retrieves an envelope from the man's pocket and climbs into the back of Colt's truck while the thugs search for him and the envelope.

Colt is surprised to find a boy in the back of his truck. He's frustrated when the kid won't tell him his name—his older brother told him "don't talk to strangers."

Howie, Colt's friend, surmises that the youngster is different. Some good educational information is presented.

> HOWIE: Colt ... he has Down's syndrome ... it's an abnormality that occurs when a child is born with one extra chromosome ... it's pretty common, about one birth in seven hundred. Usually causes some degree of mental retardation.
>
> COLT: You mean that poor little kid will never be like other kids?
>
> HOWIE: Well, it's not the end of the world. Of course, he'll have his limitations but that doesn't mean he's not capable of a lot.

Despite the criminals in pursuit, Jason manages—on his own initiative—to get to the Special Olympics, where he doesn't win. Colt assures him he *is* a winner anyway.

* * *

"The Winner" was a wonderful story about a motivated and directed child who wanted to get to the Special Olympics. Jason was presented as a busy boy, intelligent in his own right and capable of being a child even Colt Seavers couldn't resist. Educational points were sprinkled throughout the program, such as Jason's ability to read or get into trouble. Jason was a growing boy much like ones everywhere.

The portrayal by a youngster with Down's himself heightened this Christmas show and made it worth remembering and seeing again. Adult actors with disabilities were seen in the background of this episode as well as developmentally disabled children during the Special Olympics sequence.

"The Winner" was an entertaining piece with a great deal of subtle educational points.

Welcome Home, Jellybean / 1984

Executive Producer: Harry Ackerman

* Developmental Disability
* White Female Child

Producer: Cynthia A. Cherbak
Director: Robert Mandel
Writer: Cynthia A. Cherbak
Category: Made-for-TV Movie—
 Children's

Plot: A family brings their developmentally disabled child home from the institution where she's lived her whole life.

The life of the Osney family changes greatly when they bring Geraldine, their developmentally disabled daughter, home from the institution where she has always lived. Teenager Neil is glad to have her home, remembering how much Geri always hated to see them leave on visiting days.
 Geri is almost too-excited to see the world. On an elevator, she presses buttons, enjoying the blinking lights.

 MAN: Children like that shouldn't be allowed on elevators!

Geri's nightly head-banging, unintelligible speech, tearing bright labels off of cans, her destruction of Neil's homework and Mr. Osney's piano composing time strain the family to the limit.
 Mr. Osney moves out of the apartment to get some quiet where he can work. He urges Neil to join him. Neil is playing in a school talent show where he will perform a piano piece written by his dad. It's hard to practice with Geri around.
 Mrs. Osney enrolls Geri in school. She is empathetic to Geri's frustrations.

 MOTHER: Less smarts doesn't mean less feelings.

 Neil meets with his dad, who again asks his son to move in with him. He discusses Geri.

 DAD: She's never gonna have any kind of real sense.

 NEIL: She has her own kind of sense.

 At the school talent show, Mrs. Osney enters with Geri in tow. Geri begins to excitedly scream, "Jellybean! Jellybean!" her rendition of her name. Beef, a tough hot-shot who doesn't like Neil, takes up the "Jelly-*Bean!* Jelly-*Bean!*" chant with his crowd. Neil flees the stage.
 He calls his father, ready to live with him. But when his dad comes to pick him up, he changes his mind because his mother needs him and he loves Jellybean.

* * *

Welcome Home, Jellybean was a nice drama about the changes a family had to make when their developmentally disabled child came home to live. Geri was a sweet girl—but difficult to live with. Her exuberant behavior knew no bounds. Mr. Osney was forced to deal with something he had tried to avoid for years. His wife had suffered guilt with Geri away and wanted to try having her at home.

Neil was patient with his little sister, helping her and trying very hard to understand what went on inside her head. He was somewhat of a liaison between his parents simply because his father couldn't face the child he had helped create.

Geri was loved and wanted. She also presented difficulties that the family needed to work through. *Welcome Home, Jellybean* was an interesting and sensitive look at relationships between family members when a disabled child comes home to live. Life with Geri was not easy—but it was not bad, either. It was different.

The Love Boat / "Letting Go" / May 4, 1985 / ABC-TV

Executive Producers: Aaron Spelling and Douglas Cramer
Producers: Ben Joelson, Art Baer and Dennis Hammer
Director: Robert Scheerer
Writer: Michael Grace
Category: Series Television— Romantic Comedy

* Developmental Disability
* White Male Teenager

Plot: A mother learns she must let go of her developmentally disabled son.

Insurance agent Helen Williams takes a European cruise with her son, Curtis. Vicki Stubing, daughter of the captain, hits it off with Curtis. The two go onshore together. Due to Curtis' impetuousness, they miss the boat.

Helen talks to Vicki when they get back on. Curtis was "brain-damaged" at birth and, as a result, is slightly retarded. Vicki is not put off. She likes the way Curtis looks at life. Helen tells Vicki that with special schools Curtis has made great strides. Curtis is aware of his mother's protective shield.

CURTIS: ...I'm slow—simple. What does she say? Retarded?

When Curtis and Vicki are stranded and temporarily lost, the young man takes control of the situation and sees them through. Helen finally realizes her boy has grown up and is capable of making decisions and mistakes on his own.

* * *

"Letting Go" was a nice little story which permitted the character with the disability to grow. Curtis knew what his mother thought about him — relying on the label "retarded" to permit her to protect him. Curtis termed himself slow, as well as capable. He outgrew his mother's structured walls and Vicki's concerns about her own well-being when they were lost. "Letting Go" proved, in the long run, to be a fairly positive story about a person with a mild developmental disability. Curtis was a character beyond his limitation.

Hotel / "Imperfect Union" / Oct. 9, 1985 / ABC-TV

Executive Producers: Aaron Spelling; Douglas Cramer
Producer: Henry Colman and Geoffrey Fischer
Supervising Producer: E. Duke Vincent
Director: Charles Dubin
Writer: Geoffrey Fischer
Category: Series Television — Drama

* Developmental Disability
* Single White Couple

Plot: A runaway developmentally disabled couple check into the hotel, intent on getting married.

* * *

"Imperfect Union" featured developmental disability as a state of terminal childhood and arrested development. Robert Bianco and his love, Annie, demonstrated youthful exuberance as they attempted to prove they deserved a life together. They demonstrated their mettle by remembering such real-world things as "call the concierge" if there was a problem. When the two got separated in a busy shopping district, Annie called the concierge back at the hotel and the lovebirds were reunited!

Although persons with developmental disabilities *are* capable of sharing a life and responsibilities and though this episode's basic premise was worthwhile, the illusion presented by these characters was that they had escaped from Miss Nancy's schoolroom and were more qualified to share crayons than intimacy. One had the feeling a game of "Doctor" would follow.

These were nothing more than children in adult bodies, pure personifications of innocence and wonder. While "Imperfect Union" deserved a nod for its attempt to humanize this limitation, its lack of honest investigation cut off its circulation.

St. Elsewhere / "Lost and Found in Space" / Nov. 13, 1985 / NBC-TV

Executive Producer: Bruce Paltrow
Producers: John Masius; Tom Fontana
Co-Producer: Abby Singer
Supervising Producer: Mark Tinker
Director: Robert Becker
Story by: John Masius and Tom Fontana
Teleplay: Bob Rosenfarb
Category: Series Television— Medical Drama

* Developmental Disability
* Single White Couple

Plot: After suffering minor injuries in a bus crash, two developmentally disabled young adults indicate an interest in one another.

* * *

"Lost and Found in Space" used developmental disability in an interesting story.

Buddy and Pru, recuperating from a minor bus accident in which they were slightly injured, talk. Buddy indicated he would like to kiss Pru. Pru held back then joined in. The two adults explored each other quite fully and intimately. The facts were revealed to medical personnel, who were concerned about lawsuits from the parents.

Buddy and Pru were individuals with personalities and interests. Pru was an interesting mixture of a young woman with limited intellectual capacity but much curiosity; she was grown-up and innocent at the same time. Buddy was more aggressive. He told Pru it was all right to have fun and that's all they were doing.

The ever-critical Dr. Craig went to tell Pru she had done wrong and found himself at a loss to defeat her logic expressing why it was all right to have "fun." Pru was featured in a subsequent episode where she was discovered to be pregnant.

"Lost and Found in Space" illustrated a hot topic in the area of developmental disability—that is, the right to enjoy sexual intercourse and the right to learn about the possible consequences.

Punky Brewster / "The Gift" / Nov. 24, 1985 / NBC-TV

Producer: Rick Hawkins
Supervising Producer: Gary Menteer

* Developmental Disability
* Single White Female

Director: Art Dielhenn
Writer: Rick Hawkins
Category: Series Television —
  Situation Comedy

Plot: Linda, the "slow" janitor at Punky's school, is teased by the children.

Teacher Mike Fulton notices Linda the janitor listening to his classical recordings as he works after school. He talks to her, realizing she has a developmental disability.

> LINDA: This is the first job anybody would ever gave me. My mom says I will get fired but my dad says "Go for it, Cupcake...." I always wanted to go to regular school like everybody else but they wouldn't let me because I was too dumb.

Little Punky Brewster makes friends with Linda, sharing stickers with her. Linda reveals that many kids make fun of her. At home, Punky's foster father, Henry, expresses to the little girl the beauty of individuality. When Punky indicates she feels sorry for Linda, Henry tells her:

> HENRY: You're looking at what she *doesn't* have.

During music appreciation time, Mike teaches the class about music and instruments. Linda gravitates toward the class and pretends to play the violin with spray bottle and duster. The children laugh and Linda runs away, mortified. Mike tells the class they hurt Linda's feelings.

> ALLEN: Can't hurt *her* feelings. She's a retard.

> MIKE: Where do you get off laughing at someone's disability?

Mike orders Allen to write a three-page report on the Special Olympics, due in the morning.
Linda is off, crying. Punky approaches her and reassures her she is Linda's friend. She acts as the non-disabled catalyst.

> LINDA: I'm too dumb to be anybody's friend. I hate being dumb ... why do I act so stupid?... I'm grown up and I'm still dumb and I always will be.

> PUNKY: You know what, Linda? I think it's time we stop thinking about the things you don't have — and start thinking about the things you *do* have.

Back in the classroom, Mike gives Linda a violin. She is able to pick it up and play it almost immediately, garnering the respect of the children.

* * *

"The Gift" is notable for its use of a different aspect of developmental disability. The "Savant Syndrome" is an amazing and astounding talent that comes from someone who, in other areas of cognitive development, lacks average abilities. Linda possessed remarkable musical prowess.

As a show geared for children, educational lessons were delivered. Particularly nice was Henry's discussion of individuality. He also told Punky he was glad she was Linda's friend.

The nasty Allen acted as a mouthpiece for all prejudice; the teacher's assigning him a three-page report on the Special Olympics was simplistic and harsh and would probably make the kid resistant to any lesson. A classroom project on the Special Olympics would have been more appropriate.

Punky's assumption of the non-disabled catalyst role was, as usual, heavy-handed and predictable. However, it was nice to see a developmentally disabled person employed and earning a wage. Linda was very careful about doing a good job.

"The Gift" has its share of formula. Nevertheless, it provided its young audience with some good lessons and food for thought about the capabilities a person like Linda may possess.

Airwolf / "And a Child Shall Lead" / 1985 / ABC-TV

Executive Producer: Bernard L. Kowalski
Producer: Robert Janes
Co-Producers: Carol Gillson and Stephen A. Miller
Supervising Producer: Everett Chambers
Director: Allen Reisner
Writer: Stephen A. Miller
Category: Series Television — Action Adventure

* Developmental Disability
* White Male Teenager
* Performer with a Disability

Plot: When a kidnapped aerodynamic designer has a heart attack, the villains go after his developmentally disabled son, who has a special talent.

Stringfellow Hawke and Dominic Santini go to a picnic for St. Julia's School. Hawke has a rendezvous planned with Bobby Phelps, a boy who is developmentally disabled. He gives his young buddy a helicopter ride and an astronaut's medal made of a special alloy.

Bobby is the son of an aerodynamics engineer and has a very special gift. He is able to draw anything he sees.

> PHELPS: Bobby was born with extraordinary ability. Although he's below average in general mental development, he sees things in great detail and can reproduce them.... Bobby can draw anything.

Phelps' new wing design is of great interest to some villains. He is kidnapped. Hawke is unable to trail the getaway vehicle by air. Maxwell has nabbed Phelps for his new wing designs. Phelps collapses with a heart attack. A doctor recommends a hospital or Phelps will die. The doctor is forced to remain with Phelps. Maxwell requires the design in two days. He has another idea. Since Bobby has doubtlessly seen the wing designs, he can reproduce them.

> MAXWELL: I mean, the kid's retarded but he can draw anything he sees.

Bobby is taken from school. Maxwell tells Bobby he can help his dad by reproducing the drawings of the airplane wing. Bobby complies — until, with the help of a doctor, he escapes with a note to tell any passer-by to call the police.

The ultra-high tech *Airwolf* helicopter is scanning an area thought to hold Phelps from various leads. Scanners pick up a reading from the medal Hawke gave to Bobby. The boy is rescued but can't recall the way back. He devalues himself.

> BOBBY: I'm too dumb [to remember].

With the graphic pad and light pen on Airwolf at his disposal, Bobby draws the house he escaped from. Using scanners, the building is located from the air. *Airwolf*'s firepower disables Maxwell's escape.

* * *

"And a Child Shall Lead" portrayed a youngster who was developmentally disabled as one who was capable and assertive. Bobby was illustrated as having a special talent: his ability to reproduce on paper anything from memory. He was seen as trying hard to learn to read and complaining about his homework. He had a healthy interest in girls and enjoyed drawing them. He enjoyed his friends and seemed to be curious about everything around him.

Bobby was not just a pawn in the story. He was a key player, one who held some cards of his own. He is instrumental in saving his father and stopping the new designs from falling into the wrong hands.

Actual children with disabilities were seen in the background of the episode.

"And a Child Shall Lead" presented a rounded portrait of a teenager who was developmentally disabled.

Night Heat / "Snow White" / 1985 / CBS-TV

Executive Producers: Sonny Grosso; Larry Jacobson
Producer: Andras Hamori

* Developmental Disability
* White Female Teenager

Director: Mario Azzopardi
Writer: Peter Mohan and Tim Dunphy
Category: Series Television—Police Drama

Plot: A developmentally disabled girl is the only person who can lead the police to a pair of young bloodthirsty hooligans wanted for a murder.

After a stop at the market, Debbie Loris walks home. She sees a pair of teenagers dressed in full combat regalia attack and shoot a man. Randy and Lou, the would-be soldiers, recognize the witness.

> RANDY: She's retarded. She probably forgot it by now.

Debbie's mother is worried when her daughter does not come home.

> MOTHER: I never should have let her go out alone.... She really can't take care of herself.... It's not like with other children. She's retarded.

Lou has ordered Randy to kill Debbie.

> RANDY: You wouldn't understand [why I'm supposed to kill you].

> DEBBIE: Because I'm different?

Debbie goes home. Her mother surmises Debbie was with a boy and is quite upset. In fear, Debbie runs off and goes to the abandoned station house used by Randy and Lou as their headquarters. Randy jumps Lou in a kamikaze move to prevent him from throwing a grenade at the approaching cops.

* * *

The Canadian production of "Snow White" was a terribly violent piece. In it, a developmentally disabled adolescent was treated as an innocent young child. Debbie was a living metaphor of eternal childhood pitted against horrendous evil.

"Snow White" possessed absolutely no facts about disability.

Highway to Heaven / "Alone" / Jan. 8, 1986 / NBC-TV

Executive Producer: Michael Landon
Producer: Kent McCray
Director: Michael Landon

* Developmental Disability
* White Male Teenager

Writer: Michael Landon
Category: Series Television —
   Fantasy Drama

Plot: Angel Jonathan Smith and his mortal sidekick Mark Gordon help a developmentally disabled runaway youth to find a home.

Arnie, a homeless teen, lives in a cardboard box on the streets. He steals cat food from a store to take care of his kitty. His one wish in life is to have a family who loves him. Angel Jonathan and his pal Mark find Arnie is their next "mission." Jonathan tells Arnie he is an angel.

>ARNIE: I thought you only saw angels if you're dead. Am I dead?

>JONATHAN: No, you're not dead. You're special.

Jonathan takes Arnie along as he and Mark go to work at the home of a rich man who has a sick son. The father blames the boy for his wife's desertion; Larry tries to remain sick to bring his folks together. Arnie exhibits simple, childlike wisdom to the man.

Jonathan manipulates a situation so Larry can see his mother. The father is angry and tells the workers to leave. Feeling at fault, Arnie runs away and returns to his box in the alley.

Jonathan and Arnie are the catalysts in bringing the family together. The family adopts Arnie.

* * *

"Alone" was played for tears. Arnie was the forever-childlike version of developmental disability enjoyed by writers. He liked his kitty, believed in angels, and wanted a mommy and daddy. It wouldn't have been surprising if Big Bird had come down to the alley to play.

This story addressed an important issue: homeless persons who may require special assistance and who are not getting it on the streets. However, the approach and pat solution was hard to stomach, as was the entire episode.

Arnie was seen to be a character surviving on his wits who had learned to steal to support himself and his cat. A character with such tenacity would have to be aggressive, regardless of intellectual capacity. Had Arnie shown difficulties in adjusting to the idea of having friends and family, perhaps the story would have been truer.

"Alone" was soapy melodrama, meant to be moving. It failed to hit the mark by relying on cuteness.

Kate and Allie / "Chip's Friend" / 1986 / CBS-TV

Executive Producers: Mort Lachman; Merril Grant

* Developmental Disability
* Single White Male

Kate and Allie

Producers: Bill Persky; Bob Randall
Co-ordinating Producer: George Barimo
Director: Bill Persky
Writers: Anne Flett & Chuck Ranberg
Category: Series Television — Situation Comedy

Plot: Chip befriends a homeless man who is developmentally disabled.

Chip sneaks his pal Louis in the house when it is empty. Louis is an adult. He is developmentally disabled and quite a student of television. Chip offers him a glass of milk.

> LOUIS: Milk has something for everybody. I learned that on TV.... I like the shows where people win valuable prizes the best.

Louis lives in basements. He's been on his own since his mother died. Chip offers the use of the basement in the apartment. It will be their "secret." Kate and Allie soon discover the man in the basement and allow him temporary sanctuary. Upstairs, Kate and Allie discuss him.

> ALLIE: How does he live on his own? What if he gets on the wrong bus? Or he tries to pay for something and they overcharge him?
>
> KATE: Heck, that happens to me. That's not being handicapped; that's being in New York!

Kate tries to explain Louis' limitation to Chip.

> KATE: Chip, you know that all people are born different, right? ... people like Louis are different in a special sort of way....

Kate explains that a part of Louis "never grew up."
Louis awakens early and cooks breakfast. Allie terms his haphazard table settings "perfect," fearful of hurting his feelings. Kate is more pragmatic and tells him a few things need to be adjusted. She teaches him about different bowls and glasses. Kate privately explains to Allie:

> KATE: He's never gonna learn anything if we condescend to him.

Allie catches on quickly. When she notes Louis' shirt is torn, she shows him how to mend it himself.
Kate discovers Louis is eligible for federal aid. She also finds a good living center for him where he can continue to grow and learn.

* * *

"Chip's Friend" was a nice story. Louis was a person in his own right, with interests and talents of his own. He was very responsible, enjoyed routine household chores, and liked to draw. He had a good ear for catch phrases from television and often quoted them in his everyday conversation. He knew, he said, "the secret" to making good coffee.

"Chip's Friend" positively gave a developmentally disabled character a personality. He was an intriguing and interesting person who had potential to expand in his own way. He was explored in greater depth in subsequent episodes of the sitcom.

Small-Stature

Persons who, at an adult age, have achieved a height of 4'10" or less are classified as Small-Statured. While not recognized as "disabled" in many governmental definitions, this group of the populace is attempting to change that.

Physical difficulties often occur in small-statured people, requiring multiple surgeries to allow them to go ahead with their daily lives. Being unable to classify themselves in a "disabled" category means they are excluded from legislation to protect the rights of or aid to people with disabilities. They are included here because they are people with a physical difference and have been exploited and portrayed just as characters with more "traditional" disabilities have been.

Group portrayals are more prevalent in pieces with small-statured persons than any other disability group. This is the singlemost prevailing "trait" of productions featuring small-statured performers. Because of their size, actors who are small continue to be stereotyped as circus performers or as holiday elves.

A small-statured member of the Screen Actors Guild revealed to me he felt most roles using performers of his size were "demeaning." He hopes that small-statured persons will be portrayed more often "as everyday human beings, not as clowns. You always see them playing clown roles.... I have a daughter ... I want her to be proud of her mother and father who are short-statured—and not clowns."

Special equipment noted in this section include the following:

> **Extension Pedals for Vehicle Control**—Items which attach to the pedals in a car so that a person with shorter-than-average legs can use the vehicle.
>
> **Built-up Seat**—A seat placed upon the average car seat to enable the user to operate the vehicle at an average and safe eye level.

In addition to the programs listed, small-statured characters are also mentioned in the reviews of *Love Leads the Way; Remington Steele*, "High Flying Steele"; *Chamber of Horrors; Something Wicked This Way Comes; The Elephant Man;* and *Magnum, P.I.*, "I Never Wanted to Go to France, Anyway...."

NOTE: Small-statured performers will not be noted as "Performers with

Disabilities" simply because average-statured actors are not cast as small ones, whereas non-disabled performers often appear as blind people, those in wheelchairs, etc.

The Terror of Tiny Town / 1938 / Columbia

Producer: Jed Buell
Associate Producer: Abe Meyer
Director: Sam Newfield
Writer: Fred Myton
Category: Feature Film — Western

* Small-stature
* Group Portrayal

Plot: Buck loves Nancy but the feud between their families puts their love in jeopardy.

* * *

The Terror of Tiny Town has to be seen to be believed. Producer Jed Buell took a Grade B Western (maybe a C!), added music, singing cowboys, a family feud, a love story — and a cast made up entirely of small-statured performers.

The film assumed all of these people were everyday, average cowfolk, and in that respect, it was different. The performers were able to create characters without regard to size: the crusty old rancher Tex, lovely Nancy, and Otto, the funny German cook. Unfortunately, the abundance of sight gags reduced the group to buffoons and helped the film gain its cult status as one of the worst movies ever made. Otto the cook crawled *into* cupboards for his pots and pans. When Nancy, the pretty young heroine, needed a short cut to the door, she ducked *under* a desk. At the dance, the bull fiddle was played by two men — one standing on a chair to work the fingerboard and the other on the floor to ply the bow. The cowboys all rode Shetland ponies and the characters ducked under the swinging doors of the saloon. They jumped up to reach the hitching posts. These things placed the actors in the position of being funny scrambling little people, never to be taken seriously.

Bonanza / "Hoss and the Leprechauns" / 1963 / NBC-TV

Producer: David Dortort
Director: John Florea
Writer: Robert V. Barron
Category: Series Television — Western

* Small-stature
* Group Portrayal — White Males

Plot: Hoss Cartwright has a hard time convincing his family he saw little men dressed in green.

The Cartwrights think Hoss has flipped his lid when he claims to have seen a group of little men in green suits burying a chest of gold. However, the elusive quintet turns out to be acrobats.

> PROFESSOR McCARTHY: Gentlemen, allow me to introduce you—McCarthy's Leprechauns. They sing, they dance, and as you've seen, they're daring and accomplished acrobats.

McCarthy apologizes for "the lads," five small-statured men.

> SMALL MAN: Yeah—and you cheated us out of all our savings—the money we were going to buy the farm with.

> TIMOTHY: And our families are still back east, waiting for us to send for them. That's why we began panning for gold. We were broke.

The sheriff throws McCarthy out of town.

A crowd gathers outside the sheriff's office, curious to see the group. The men fear ridicule from the people of Virginia City. Their concern is substantiated when the door opens and onlookers peep inside.

> CHARLIE: There they are! What are they? They're the funniest little critters I ever did see!

The small men are angry at the intrusion and reaction. Hoss steps in as a non-disabled catalyst.

> HOSS: Now, wait a minute.... Don't you go sellin' those folks short out there. You're makin' the same mistake they're makin'. You're judging them before you even know them.

The men follow Hoss outside.

> CHARLIE: Hey Hoss, be careful you don't step on one of those little fellers. You might squarsh him.

The crowd roars.

Hoss begins to explain about the group, breaking down some attitudinal barriers from both sides.

> HOSS: Timothy and the others ... think you're makin' fun of 'em 'cause you don't want 'em around. Of course, you noticed that they're different from you. They're a whole lot littler.... These fellers are here for the same reason most of us are.... We got five brand new families here in Virginia City that's gonna raise their younguns, buy clothes, and buy food and get haircuts.... I figure every one of us is gonna benefit from their being here.

The townsfolk welcome the newcomers to Virginia City.

* * *

"Hoss and the Leprechauns" began as one of the comic romps that sometimes popped up on the series, with poor Hoss trying to explain he really *did* see five small men with a hoard of gold. It turned into a different story of five people who had been exploited and were taking matters into their own hands. The attitudes of the people in Virginia City seemed quite real and prejudiced both sides in the situation. Hoss felt he could be an appropriate mediator since he was so very big and often felt the odd man out himself.

"Hoss and the Leprechauns" was entertaining although quite patronizing in its treatment of the small-statured men.

The Wild, Wild West / "The Night the Wizard Shook the Earth" / Oct. 1, 1965 / CBS-TV

Producer: Fred Freiberger
Director: Bernard Kowalski
Writer: John Kneubuhl
Category: Series Television—Western

* Small-stature
* Single White Male

Plot: Dr. Miguelito Loveless plans to blow up 5,000 people unless the Governor of California reverts to him ownership of lands belonging to his ancestors.

Secret Service agent James West is protecting Professor Neilson, a man who has invented a powerful explosive. Neilson is killed by a small-statured man and West finds himself in the clutches of a new enemy—the small Dr. Miguelito Loveless.

Loveless claims his ancestors owned vast amounts of land in California before it was seized by the Spanish. He is demanding return of the land from the Governor. If his demands are not met, he will blow up 5,000 people that night—and once a week from then on.

West wriggles his way out of another sticky situation and saves the city and state. Dr. Loveless is sent to prison.

* * *

"The Night the Wizard Shook the Earth" was the debut of recurring character Dr. Miguelito Loveless. He appeared in at least ten episodes during the series' run to bedevil James West.

Loveless was presented as a worthy adversary to West. He was athletic and shown in hand-to-hand combat with three burly average-statured fellows whom he kept at bay. He was articulate and refined, keeping a private aviary in his home. He entertained many lovely women, all of whom seemed eager to do his bidding. He sang sweet ballads and hesitated to harm a fly. He was also straight out of a comic book.

His great genius had conceived, in his Victorian era, planes, television, automobiles, and radio. These inventions were to enrich the world, he said. But when crossed, the genius reverted to a child—a sick, manic child.

Loveless' evil-doing seemed to be in revenge at the world for his size. (He mentioned other people as "healthy" and intimated that he himself had suffered pain for so long that he no longer felt it.) In comparison to other small-statured characters, Loveless was not an impotent, bumbling fool, but a character to be dealt with. West treated him as he did all his other enemies.

"The Night the Wizard Shook the Earth" illustrated a small-statured man as a potential contributor to society, provided he could do away with his criminal bent. He was also as cruel and nasty as any traditional comic book villain.

Ship of Fools / 1965 / Columbia Pictures

Producer: Stanley Kramer
Director: Stanley Kramer
Screenplay: Abby Mann
From: Katherine Anne Porter's
Ship of Fools
Category: Feature Film—Drama

* Small-stature
* Single White Male

Plot: Personal conflicts abound on a cruise ship crossing the Atlantic.

A ship leaves Veracruz, Mexico, in 1933. Its first-class passenger contingent is largely German, including Carl Glochen, a small-statured man who describes himself as one of the "fools" on the ship and a "dwarf."

Glochen and Jewish Mr. Leventhal are the only two Germans on board not seated at the Captain's table. Leventhal asks if Glochen is sure he's not Jewish to have warranted being ostracized. Glochen indicates societal barriers.

> GLOCHEN: No. I have my own minority group.

Glochen indicates he's been an outsider looking in when he asks a young artist about the status of the younger man's relationship with a young woman. Glochen apologizes for being nosy.

> GLOCHEN: You know, the distasteful curiosity of the non-participant.

Glochen notes he travels often, his parents bankrolling the trips.

> GLOCHEN: They are more comfortable when I'm not around.

* * *

Ship of Fools utilized a small-statured man as one of the personalities sentenced to talk, talk, talk his way across the Atlantic Ocean. Carl Glochen was a sensitive man who prided himself on being somewhat of a philosopher and analyzer of life. He was highly intelligent and articulate, discussing politics and other subjects. He was well aware of the difficulties his size had caused, particularly among his own family. He was pragmatic about the same but seemed to harbor more hurt deep inside.

Glochen was stared at by others on board the ship but made friends and was soon taken in stride, mixing and matching with other passengers.

Ship of Fools illustrated a small-statured man as one who was urbane and learned with interests and intellect.

Star Trek / "Plato's Stepchildren" / Nov. 22, 1968 / NBC-TV

Executive Producer: Gene Roddenberry
Producer: Fred Freiberger
Co-Producer: Robert H. Justman
Director: David Alexander
Writer: Meyer Dolinsky
Category: Series Television — Science Fiction

* Small-stature
* Single White Male

Plot: Captain Kirk and his landing party become the unwilling puppets to a cruel master on the planet Platonius.

The *Enterprise* responds to a distress call from a planet thought uninhabited. The place is rich in kyronite deposits. They are greeted by Alexander, a small-statured man.

> ALEXANDER: I sing, I dance, I play all variety of games and I'm a good loser, a very good loser.

The average-statured population of Platonius came from a distant star eons ago. Parmen, the leader, is abed with an injured leg and dangerous fever. It is rapidly evident the Platonians have amazing psychokinetic powers. Parmen's delirium causes statuary and items to fly about. Only Alexander does not possess the Power.

> KIRK: Alexander, are there other Platonians like you?... Who don't have the psychokinetic ability?

Simplistic societal prejudice is noted.

ALEXANDER: ... They make fun of me for my size. But to answer your question, I'm the only one who *doesn't* have it. I was brought here as the court buffoon, that's why I'm everybody's slave and I have to be ten places at once and I never do anything right ... they say I'm a throwback.

Parmen requests Dr. McCoy to remain on Platonius as the physician. When McCoy refuses, Parmen cruelly manipulates Kirk and Mr. Spock into bizarre actions to force the doctor to change his mind.

Alexander reveals that the Platonians developed the Power when they arrived on this planet. Dr. McCoy discerns that a chemical in the native food, "broken down by pituitary hormones," is responsible for the Power.

ALEXANDER: Oh, you mean the same thing that kept me from having the Power made me a dwarf.

McCoy prepares injections of kyronite for Mr. Spock and Captain Kirk in order to be able to combat Parmen. Alexander refuses to be injected.

ALEXANDER: You think that's what I want? Become one of them? Become my own enemy?

Kirk's Power is stronger than Parmen's and forces a showdown. The *Enterprise* and its crew are free to go. Alexander will beam aboard the starship with the group. Kirk radioes Scotty.

KIRK: I've got a little surprise. I'm bringing a visitor aboard.

* * *

"Plato's Stepchildren" was a different kind of story. Alexander was simply part of the spectrum in a multiracial, multi-"ethnic" galaxy of humanoid beings. He was devalued and degraded by the Platonians because of his size and the fact that he did not develop the "divine" Power.

Alexander found the visit of the *Enterprise* crew very enlightening. He saw the cruelty of the Platonians for what it was. Previously, he had accepted it as their reaction to his small size. He demonstrated violent emotions, wishing to kill Parmen for his flagrant violations of personal privacy. Alexander also showed presence of mind in not wanting to develop the power which had made his life miserable for centuries.

Captain Kirk was slightly patronizing to Alexander, not affording him full status as an adult. Mr. Spock and Dr. McCoy did not seem to have the same problem. Fortunately, when Alexander took a long pottery shard, intending to slash Parmen, Kirk stopped him with talk — although it appeared he could have easily physically subdued the smaller man. Such a reaction gave Alexander's anger due respect and did not subordinate it like the tantrum of a child.

"Plato's Stepchildren" was an interesting story in which small stature was secondary to the fact the chracter did not have a corrupting Power.

Goodnight, My Love / Oct. 17, 1972

Producer: Ward Sylvester
Director: Peter Hyams
Writer: Peter Hyams
Category: Made-for-TV Movie—
 Crime Drama/Comedy

* Small-stature
* Single White Male

Plot: Two detectives search for a missing man in 1940's Los Angeles and wind up being targets for a killer.

Detectives Francis Hogan and his small-statured assistant, Arthur Boyle, take on the case of Susan Lakely who wishes to find her missing boyfriend. The investigation turns a corner when Hogan is beaten by an assailant. He glares at bystander Boyle.

> HOGAN [sarcastically]: Thanks for the help.
>
> BOYLE: Well, what do you want me to do? Punch him in the knee?

Horse racing fits in as an angle. Hogan and Boyle question some jockeys at the track. The men are very helpful. Hogan admiringly tells Boyle as they leave:

> HOGAN: Those jocks sure seem to like you.
>
> BOYLE [smugly]: We have a certain—rapport.
>
> HOGAN: 'Course, you're the only one that ever looked up to them.
>
> BOYLE [drily]: Yo-ho, Francis.

* * *

Goodnight, My Love was a period drama highlighted by classy direction. Detectives Hogan and Boyle were a team. Hogan was a real curmudgeon. Boyle was an articulate man who talked about food constantly and ate his way through the movie. He was an expert pickpocket and lockpicker, and could sling a line of bull with dapper perfection. Hogan was excitable; Boyle was dry.

Boyle did all the behind-the-wheel chores for the two. An amusing scene occurred at a classy restaurant where the parking valet nearly killed himself trying to scrunch in over Boyle's built-up seat. Scenes like this one and the lazy jokes about the jockeys made for comfortable viewing without sacrificing Boyle's integrity. Boyle was multifaceted, bright, and fun.

Curiously, when Hogan and Boyle were met by other people, Hogan was greeted and responded to but Boyle was overlooked. It is unclear whether this represented an attitudinal barrier or an oversight on the part of the writer.

Goodnight, My Love was a plus, due to the chemistry of the two principals. Little attention was paid to Boyle's size; the focus wisely remained on the story.

The Love Boat / "The Little People" / Mar. 31, 1979 / ABC-TV

Executive Producers: Aaron Spelling; Douglas Cramer
Writer: Barry Blitzer
Category: Series Television — Romantic Comedy

* Small-stature
* Married White Couple

Plot: An average-sized son takes his small-statured parents on a cruise for their wedding anniversary and falls in love with a young woman who is nervous about "Them."

Doug's small-statured parents are delighted to have been treated to a cruise on board the *Pacific Princess*. Doug is equally delighted to meet Beth, a girl with whom he quickly falls in love. Doug and Beth are enjoying a drink when she spots the two small people at the bar.

> BETH: Oh! I didn't know they allowed children at the bar — oh! They're —
>
> DOUG [smiling]: They call themselves "little people."

Beth indicates fear that children of hers could turn out that way. Doug is reluctant to tell her that the two are his parents. Fearing she is prejudiced, Doug breaks off with her. Beth forlornly mopes about the ship and accidentally meets Doug's parents — still not knowing they are his kin. She finds out their son took them on the cruise and that they have two children, a boy who is average-statured and:

> MOTHER: One married daughter, compact-sized, like us.

Beth hits it off with the two.
She and Doug talk at night in the lounge. Doug decides to be frank.

> DOUG: Those two small people dancing over there? They're my folks.

Doug and Beth want to get married. Doug discusses the possibility of their own children being like his folks.

DOUG: A chance in a million they will be small.

Beth indicates meeting the couple has changed her views.

BETH: A couple of days ago, that would have scared the daylights out of me but [after knowing your parents, I don't care].

* * *

"The Little People" presented a portrait of a family, rare in depictions of small-stature. An educational aspect was involved, informing the audience that small persons may have average-sized children.

The character of the mother was quite real, concerned about her son. She was vivacious and appropriately maternal. The father, however, was saddled with many bad "short" jokes which he used constantly, to the point of being tiresome. The couple were displayed as older and wiser, particularly when meeting Beth and talking about their son — not knowing this was the girl he was moping over.

"The Little People" was a different type of story and portrayed small-statured persons in a fair light, as part of a vacationing family unit. All the "short" jokes aside, it possessed good elements.

CHiPs / "Counterfeit" / 1979 / NBC-TV

Producer: Cy Chermak
Director: John Florea
Writer: Brian Coffey
Category: Series Television — Police Drama

* Small-stature
* White Male
* Equipment: Extension pedals for vehicle control; Built-up seat

Plot: A small-statured man, angry at taunts from those of average size, retaliates.

A man driving on the freeway is so busy watching a woman in the next car that he causes an accident. A small-statured man gets out of the injured car.

O'HARA: Oh, now, let's hear some crack about I'm so small, you didn't see me.

ATTORNEY: You've got to admit, it's a pretty big car for a man your size.

Mr. James O'Hara is sure attending CHP officers Baker and Poncherello will stick him with responsibility because he's short. He complains to his average-statured bartender brother that he is tired of turning the other cheek at the jeers he receives. A woman at the bar begins to taunt him about being short.

Later, O'Hara is bothered by some rowdy kids out on the highway. Attitudinal barriers are illustrated.

> ROWDY #1: He's a leprechaun!... Hey Shorty, your mother know you got the car?

The kids try to harass O'Hara on the road. He bashes them and causes a multicar pile-up. Witnesses support he had been victimized by the youths and he is not at fault.

After discerning that part of O'Hara's anger is due to an inability to accept his size, Officer Baker becomes the non-disabled catalyst.

> BAKER: Give yourself some credit would ya? And stop blaming yourself for your size. Oh, and give us tall guys a break, would you?

* * *

"Counterfeit" used a typical slant to a disability story. O'Hara was a disgruntled man who hated the world because he was small. His brother noted O'Hara used to be able to ignore the taunts; supposedly, O'Hara was now at wit's end at how to deal with everyday slobs.

In the course of the story O'Hara was unfairly abused, but his size was never far from mind. After being bashed by the attorney's car, the second thing out of his mouth was the line, "let's hear some crack about I'm so small, you didn't see me."

O'Hara was an angry man, presumably because society was constantly wronging him. Such an obvious surface exploration of social prejudice shortchanged "Counterfeit."

Buck Rogers in the 25th Century / "Shgoratchx!" / 1980 / NBC-TV

Executive Producer: John Mantley
Producer: John G. Stephens
Supervising Producer: Calvin Clements
Director: Vincent McEveety
Writer: William Keys
Category: Series Television— Science Fiction

* Small-stature
* Group Portrayal—Six White Males; One Black Male

Plot: The *Searcher* intercepts a ship with a crew of seven small-statured aliens.

The *Searcher* locates a derelict ship which is drifting into the freight lanes. Buck Rogers and Hawk shuttle over to investigate. A group of small-statured, bizarrely uniformed aliens converge upon Buck and Hawk, firing harmless little pellets from some weapons. The six white characters introduce themselves as generals and indicate the lone black is a private. The characters are quickly seen to be irresponsible and childlike. They discuss the role of Private Zedht.

> GENERAL XCES: We give orders, he takes orders.
>
> HAWK: Is that—not confusing?
>
> GENERAL ZOMAN: Is not confusing. He never obeys.

Private Zedht nods.

> HAWK: If he does not obey, what good does it do giving him orders?
>
> GENERAL XCES: What good is it to be a general if you do not have someone to give orders to?
>
> BUCK [to Hawk]: You ready to give up?

The Zirdonians are carrying sola bombs that can blow up. For safety, their ship is taken in tow by the *Searcher*. Hawk is bewildered by the aliens.

> HAWK: I have never quite seen anything like them.
>
> BUCK: I have. They used to hang out with a very pretty lady named Snow White.

The aliens are welcomed aboard the Searcher.

> PRIVATE ZEDHT: I'm hungry.
>
> GENERAL #3: Yes, hungry.
>
> GENERAL #4: Famished!
>
> GENERAL ZOMAN: Very famished!
>
> GENERAL #5: Ravenous!
>
> GENERAL #6: Starving!
>
> GENERAL XCES: Food!
>
> GROUP [in unison]: Yes! Yes! Yes!
>
> BUCK: Come on, gentlemen, I'll see what I can do.

GROUP: Yes! Yes! Yes!

The appearance of a female, Colonel Wilma Deering, is new and strange to the Zirdonians.

GENERAL: Look, she's got bumps!

The aliens begin spinning around in swivel chairs and playing with bridge controls and endanger the ship. Their antics damage a robot used for information gathering and navigation. The *Searcher* narrowly escapes collision with a sun.

* * *

"Shgoratchx!" used a group of small-statured males in a variation of funny, mischievous elves. They acted irresponsibly, ate constantly, littered, disobeyed directions, tried to "examine" the female Colonel Deering by "offthinking" her clothes, and so on. The generals blustered around giving orders that Private Zedht never carried out. Buck became the father figure; in one scene; he had to hold the hand of a disobedient Private Zedht. Terms like "keep them out of trouble" subordinated the aliens.

They had some unique qualities, such as their "offthink" and "onthink" abilities, which permitted them to fix the damaged memory of the robot and repair the *Searcher*. It must be noted, though, that they were the cause of the damage in the first place.

"Shgoratchx!" indicated small-statured persons as irresponsible, silly, and devoid of any adult qualities. In defense, it can be argued that the Zirdonians were not meant to represent small-statured humans, but aliens from another star system.

Under the Rainbow / 1981 / Orion Pictures

Director: Steve Rash * Small-stature
Category: Feature Film—Comedy * Group Portrayal

Plot: A duke, a duchess, a dog, a secret service man, spies and small-statured actors cross paths in a raucous hotel.

* * *

Under the Rainbow was billed as a comedy; by a stretch of the imagination, it could be termed one. The action took place in 1939 when Rollo, a small-statured man, fell off a roof and hit his head. He came to with a large group of small-statured people on their way to Hollywood to play Munchkins in the *Wizard of Oz*. Rollo joined the group, who proceeded to turn a sedate hotel into a shambles.

The antics of the group made up the backdrop for a fifth-rate spy spoof. They cavorted in a manner reminiscent of *The Terror of Tiny Town*. Small persons used the dumbwaiter to travel between floors and fought duels using kitchen knives for swords. They hung and swung on the chandeliers. Curiously enough, the characters often appeared in their "Munchkin" costumes despite the fact the cavorting took place off the movie set for *Wizard of Oz*.

Rollo was a warm and heroic character, a leader in a pinch. His counterpart was a German spy named Hitler, who stomped about searching for a map of America's mainland defenses prior to World War II.

The disjointed story was further muddled when, à la *Wizard of Oz,* it seemed Rollo never went to Hollywood but dreamed the whole thing after falling from the roof.

Under the Rainbow seriously devalued and demeaned the integrity of small-statured men and women.

Little House: A New Beginning / "Little Lou" / Oct. 25, 1982 / NBC-TV

Executive Producer: Michael Landon
Producer: Kent McCray
Director: Victor French
Writer: Michael Landon
Category: Series Television — Family Drama

* Small-stature
* Married White Couple

Plot: A small-statured man, attempting to find work to support his family, meets prejudice in Walnut Grove.

Lou Bates, a small-statured clown with a circus, rushes to Walnut Grove for Doc Baker. He is looking for a physician as his small-statured wife has gone into labor. Lou is nervous about impending fatherhood. He describes his trepidation to John Carter but uses a little devaluation when he intimates the child will be all right.

LOU: As long as it's healthy — y'know, Big People.

Alice gives birth to a girl. She asks Lou not to rejoin the circus. She dies.

Lou begins job-hunting to support his daughter and mother. He meets attitudinal barriers in the person of Mrs. Oleson when applying for a job at Oleson's Mercantile. Mrs. Oleson will not hire him because he's small.

John Carter arranges for Lou to go for an interview at the bank. Although suitably impressed by Lou's accounting skills, Mr. Anderson is afraid to hire him — as Mrs. Oleson threatens to remove her account from the bank if he does, an account which is the lifeblood of the institution. John Carter goes to bat for Lou, telling Mrs. Oleson:

JOHN: He's a fine man trying to earn a living.

More attitudinal barriers are seen.

MRS. OLESON: He's deformed. He's not like us. He's a troll. He spent his whole life in a sideshow ... he's not *like* us.

In retaliation, John cancels his account at the store and Oleson's restaurant.

A robbery at the store has Nels Oleson confused. A doll was taken, suggesting a child committed the crime; food was stolen — but no money is missing. The window used to facilitate the entry is too small for a grown person to get through.

MRS. OLESON: But a dwarf could [get through].

Confronted with the crime and caught with the goods, Lou is incarcerated.

Nancie Oleson, the spoiled adopted daughter of the storeowners, tumbles down a well being drilled. The opening is too small for a man to get down to rescue her — Lou is the logical choice. He is lowered into the well and saves Nancie's life. Mrs. Oleson agrees to drop all charges and Lou is hired at the bank as a teller.

* * *

"Little Lou" was a nice story although Mrs. Oleson's heavy-handed prejudice made the piece quite predictable, and, in a sense, trivialized discrimination as being one loud-mouthed woman's opinion. However, it nicely showed that her feelings handicapped a capable man and led him to commit a crime to feed his infant daughter and aging mother.

An educational aspect was illustrated in indicating Lou's mother was an average-statured woman. His daughter was also average.

Although Mrs. Oleson used terminology that could be considered offensive, she was the out-and-out villain of the piece and such expressions were completely in character. Others did *not* use such language.

"Little Lou" was a story almost identical to "It's a Small World" that aired on *Bonanza* in the late 1960's (see Appendix).

Trapper John, M.D. / "A Little Knife Music" / July 8, 1984 (rerun) / CBS-TV

Executive Producer: Frank Glicksman
Producer: Don Brinkley
Director: Earl Bellamy
Writer: John Whelpley

* Small-stature
* White Female; White Male; White Infant

Small-Stature

Category: Series Television —
Medical Drama

Plot: A couple is distressed to find their young daughter will be small statured.

A babysitter has rushed her infant charge to the hospital after a fall. The baby's respiratory distress is alleviated but X-rays reveal something else.

> DOCTOR [looking at X-rays]: Where'd you get these? The humane society?

Dwarfism is the diagnosis. David and Marsha Huber, Kelly's parents, are in shock when shown the X-rays and use poor language.

> MARSHA: She looks deformed — crippled.

> DAVID: She's broken! She's twisted, inside out . . . you can't let her suffer like that.

David denies permission for medical treatment, feeling it would only prolong the agony for both Kelly and the family. Meanwhile, Dr. Trapper John McIntyre suggests Dr. Heller may be able to help. He's a surgeon with considerable background in the medical problems experienced by the small statured. Trapper talks to Dr. Gonzo Gates about it.

> GONZO: [Heller works] with dwarves?

> TRAPPER: They call themselves "Little People."

Megan Malone, a small-statured woman who is a hospital employee, recognizes the call going out to Dr. Heller as meaning one of "her own" is in need. She manages a peek at the X-rays and tells Morty Cavanaugh, a fellow member of a Little People's theatre group, that they must help this little girl.

> MEGAN: It's one of the bad ones.

The theatre people raise money for plane tickets for Gonzo to go to Seattle and learn from Dr. Heller what can be done for Kelly.
Morty acts as the disabled catalyst for Marsha and David, assuring them their daughter is going to grow up and live a full life. The support helps the couple agree to surgery to help their daughter.
Dr. Neilson, a physician who has lost his confidence, learns a great deal while working with Kelly and decides to work with Dr. Heller to learn more. Mort and Megan and the little people's group help his decision along by paying his plane fare in hopes of insuring help for some of their own problems in the future.

"A Little Knife Music" was different from most disability drama in that it brought in a group interested in supporting their own rights as catalysts. Both Morty and Megan were illustrated as busy, capable people with outside interests who were, nonetheless, politically involved in the community. Both acted as realistic and bright counsel for Kelly's grieving parents. Megan was employed at the hospital; Morty was the brash and loud-mouthed stage director at the Little People's theatre. They catalyzed both their community and the family in need.

Attitudinal barriers were touched upon when someone stated, "It's not their size that's the problem. It's the attitude of people around them." Dr. Neilson's reaction toward baby Kelly, calling her "Li'l Darlin'" was welcome, treating her as a real infant and not a "dwarf."

Many small statured people were seen in the background of this episode, either as members of the theatre group or persons being seen by Dr. Heller in his clinic. Special note was made of the fact Dr. Heller's secretary was a small-statured woman.

Use of the words "crippled" and "deformed" were not classed as pejorative. Through Morty and Megan's assistance, Marsha and David learned these were misnomers. Morty's use of the word "freak," however, was questionable. He was making a point to David, telling him many people "don't want a freak in the family."

"A Little Knife Music" approached a disability from a different standpoint and should be applauded for such.

The Ice Pirates / 1984 / MGM/UA

Producer: John Foreman
Director: Stewart Raffill
Writers: Stewart Raffill and Stanford Sherman
Category: Feature Film—Science Fiction

* Small-stature
* White Female; White Male

Plot: A group of galactic pirates steals water for a dry galaxy until commandeered by a princess to locate her father.

* * *

The bizarre rough-and-tumble worlds of the tongue-in-cheek adventure *The Ice Pirates* featured all sorts of interesting characters. On one planet where the renegades stopped in search of a particular man, a small-statured alien shoeshine man said there would be no more spit in the polish until a water ship came in.

Head pirate Jason visited a bar after narrowly escaping castration and enslavement. One of the people who gleefully greeted him was a small-statured waitress.

The Ice Pirates used small-statured persons in an incidental way, as part of a multiracial, multihued galaxy of life forms.

Swing Shift / 1984 / Warner Bros.

Executive Producers: Alex Winitsky and Arlene Sellers
Producer: Jerry Bick
Director: Jonathan Demme
Writer: Rob Morton
Category: Feature Film — Drama

* Small-stature
* White Female

Plot: Life changes during World War II when women go to work in the factories.

* * *

Swing Shift used a small-statured woman in a supporting role as one of the thousands who went to work in an aircraft factory during the Second World War. "Stretch" was just one of the girls, working and helping to end the war.

Crazy Like a Fox / "Requiem for a Fox" / Oct. 20, 1985 / CBS-TV

Executive Producers: Frank Cardea, George Schenk, John Baskin, Roger Shulman
Co-Producer: Carl Kugel
Director: Vincent McEveety
Writer: Thomas A. Chehak
Category: Series Television — Crime Comedy/Drama

* Small-stature
* Married White Male

Plot: A small-statured professional wrestler hires investigator Harry Fox when death threats start worrying him.

Harry gets tickets to the wrestling match, featuring Mighty Moe Young. His grandson Josh is quite excited.

> JOSH: I watch him all the time on TV. He took out the Lubner with a full body slam. He's mean, he's awesome — and he's a midget.

Cindy freezes, having been warned by a psychic that Harry should "Beware of midgets."

> CINDY: Did you say midget?
>
> HARRY: Well, they like to be called "Little People."

Harry and attorney son Harrison go to talk to Moe, who claims he's worried about death threats he's receiving. He indicates he is married and a parent by noting the scare has forced him to send his children to private school for their safety. Harry suspects more than a grudge against Moe as he reveals to Harrison:

> HARRY: I think there's a lot more goin' on here than someone tryin' to scare a Little Person.

Moe is murdered in the empty arena. Harry guesses Moe was killed because the wrestler figured out Bert, part-owner of the Grand Arena, was trying to buy out the place from his partner, using force.

* * *

"Requiem for a Fox" used a small-statured man in an imaginative way. Moe was intelligent, articulate, and concerned about his future and that of his family. His height had little to do with the part, other than making him quickly identifiable as the one of whom Harry had to "beware."

Night Court / "Dan's Boss" / Nov. 14, 1985 / NBC-TV

Executive Producer: Reinhold Weege
Producer: Nat Mauldin
Supervising Producer: Jeff Melman
Director: Jeff Melman
Writer: Bob Stevens
Category: Series Television— Situation Comedy

* Small-stature
* White Male

Plot: Dan Fielding is horrified to discover his new boss is a small-statured man.

A small-statured man approaches prosecutor Dan Fielding and Judge Harry Stone in the courthouse cafeteria. He asks for directions.

> DAN: First left, take the corridor then follow the Yellow Brick Road.

The toadying prosecutor is horrified to find the man is Vincent Daniels, his new boss. Daniels wants to see Dan pronto. Later, despite Daniels' impressive credentials, Dan thinks the situation ridiculous.

> DAN: Did you ever discuss jurisprudence with a muppet?... They turn around and give [the job] to Santa's favorite elf.

Dan oversteps the bounds of decency when he angrily picks up Daniels and sets him on a table.

> DAN: You want to see eye to eye?

Harry is upset at his recently fired colleague.

> HARRY: Dan, everyone has the right to work.

> DAN: Of course they do! In circuses, amusement parks—

Dan apologizes and Daniels agrees to rehire him.

> VINCENT: But most of all, I'm taking you back because it will give me the opportunity to make your life a living hell.... I am the nastiest little man God ever put on the earth.

* * *

"Dan's Boss" brought out the absolute worst from the character of Dan Fielding. Unwilling to listen to anyone, Fielding was horrified to know he would be answering to a small-statured boss.

Vincent Daniels was illustrated as an articulate and professional man who knew his job. However, he became mean and angry, forcing Dan to handle his laundry, wax his car, and front him for loose change. Daniels indicated his father had left the family years ago, feeling guilt about his son's size, thinking he was a "punishment from God." However, that did not excuse him from practically emulating Dan's poor behavior once Dan knew to whom he must answer.

"Dan's Boss" started out with an interesting premise but became irrational and unbelievable. It was so heavy-handed, it lost credibility. It presented an unbalanced image of a small-statured man.

The Golden Girls / "A Little Romance" / Dec. 14, 1985 / NBC-TV

Executive Producers: Paul Junger Witt and Tony Thomas

* Small-stature
* Single White Male

The Golden Girls

Producers: Kathy Speer and Terry Grossman
Co-Producer: Marsha Posner Williams
Director: Terry Hughes
Writers: Barry Fanaro & Mort Nathan
Category: Series Television — Situation Comedy

Plot: Rose falls for an urbane, intelligent man who is small-statured.

Although deeply attracted to Dr. Jonathan Newman, Rose is a bit nervous to introduce the small man to roommates Dorothy and Blanche. Jonathan recognizes the fact that his size is discomfiting to the assembled women.

> JONATHAN: All in all, I'm pretty happy with who I am.

> ROSE: Oh god, it gives me goosebumps when he talks like that!

Dorothy is sold on the man.

> DOROTHY: What a delightful man. He has the most positive attitude of anyone I have ever met.

Dorothy's acid-tongued mother, Sophia, enters. All the women freeze, fearful of what she will say when she sees Jonathan.

> SOPHIA: That guy over there — is he a midget?

> DOROTHY: Yes, Ma.

> SOPHIA: Thank god! I thought I was having another stroke!

Rose discusses Jonathan with the other women after accepting a dinner date with the man for the next evening. She confides to her friends that Jonathan may pop the big question. She is troubled by her own reaction to the thought. Her own attitudinal barriers are revealed.

> ROSE: When we're around other people, I'm uncomfortable. I know they're staring at him and talking about us and it bothers me ... how big a man is shouldn't make or break a relationship.

A dream helps Rose decide to say yes if Jonathan should ask her to marry him.

The two go to a fancy French restaurant. Jonathan wants to talk seriously about their relationship. There are things, he notes, that can never be worked out between them.

ROSE: It doesn't bother me that you're small.

JONATHAN: Small? No, I meant I can't see you anymore because you're not Jewish.

*   *   *

"A Little Romance" was an amusing story which explored some interesting possibilities in a relationship between a small man and an average-statured woman. Although the "short" jokes got a little tiring (Blanche concerned about serving "shrimp" and Dorothy announcing the main dinner course was "short ribs" or declarations of "it's a small world," etc.), the piece is important as it illustrated a favorite character in a popular comedy having a relationship with a small man. The jokes were carefully delivered and did not damage the integrity of the character. They were not out of line for the characters or the type of humor present in the series.

Jonathan was an intelligent man who was a Harvard graduate. He was well-traveled, witty, and urbane. In fact, one might even wonder what he saw in Rose, a woman whose bulb burned a little dimmer than others.

Rose's reluctance was quite realistic. She had to work her way through the problem and was thwarted when Jonathan sadly pulled the plug on their relationship.

Another small-statured actor appeared in Rose's dream sequence.

"A Little Romance" was a story which amusingly discussed a realistic problem within the prescribed sitcom format. This episode was an Emmy award–winner for Best Writing.

Simon and Simon / "Burden of the Beast" / 1985 / CBS-TV

Executive Producers: John G. Stephens; Richard Chapman
Producers: Mark A. Burley, Mary Eagle and Michael Piller
Supervising Producer: Bill Dial
Director: Sigmund Neufeld, Jr.
Story By: Paul Magistretti and Paul Robert Coyle
Teleplay: Paul Robert Coyle
Category: Series Television — Crime Drama

* Small-stature
* White Male

Plot: Stretch Mooney helps out detectives Rick and A.J. Simon as an undercover man.

Stretch masquerades in an ape costume during an undercover operation. The small-statured man pulls a gun on a surprised suspect.

STRETCH: Freeze, Turkey. Drop it. Don't you understand English? I said *drop* it!

Rick praises Stretch.

RICK: Nice going, Stretch.

STRETCH: It's eighty degrees in the shade, I'm in an ape costume and your a.c.'s on the blink. This *is* above and beyond the call of duty, guys.

* * *

"Burden of the Beast" featured the semi-recurring character of Stretch Mooney, a sort of freelance helper to the detective team. Stretch appeared in an incidental role without regard to his size and was seen as a busy, capable, complaining human being with a personality.

The serio-comic series used Stretch in situations the average-statured actors could not adequately handle due to their size; it was assumed the character was meant to be half-comic.

In "The Skull of Nostradamus" episode (10/31/85; writer: W. Reed Moran), Stretch appeared to help Rick and A.J. track down the member of a group of Druids who was making death threats. On Halloween, the small-statured man was goaded by the brothers to dress in a costume and pretend he was a kid. They needed him to knock on doors and peer into houses to locate the appropriate one where the Druids were meeting.

A.J.: You think Stretch can pass as a ten-year-old?

RICK: Yeah, as long as they don't smell his cigar breath.

Stretch was always quick to let the Simons know his integrity was wounded by such actions.

Both "Burden of the Beast" and "The Skull of Nostradamus" used a small-statured character in an interesting manner.

The Bride / 1985 / Columbia

Producer: Victor Drai
Director: Franco Roddam
Writer: Lloyd Fonvielle
Category: Feature Film — Drama

* Small-stature
* Single White Male

Plot: The monster created by Baron von Frankenstein meets up with a small-statured traveler.

The monster created by Frankenstein is banished from the castle of the nobleman after Eva, a female, has been created. Although initially meant to be a companion for the monster, the Baron sees an opportunity to shape Eva into the perfect woman for himself.

The monster wanders and meets Rinaldo, a small-statured man full of ideas and stories. Rinaldo easily accepts the monster's offbeat appearance. He intimates it gives him something in common. As far as the monster loving a woman:

> RINALDO: You and I are bound to have trouble in that direction.

The two new friends support themselves in a strange way. The creature approaches the local vicar for work, carrying a bag over his shoulder. As the vicar turns him down, Rinaldo, in the bag, handily cuts a small hole in the sack from which he lifts cash from the collection box.

In a town, Rinaldo and his friend meet prejudice.

> TAVERNKEEP: We don't want your sort 'round here.

Rinaldo gives his friend the name of Victor. The two head for Budapest. Once in the city, they try to get work at a circus. The owner says he doesn't "need a midget." But he needs Victor's strength to drive tent pegs. Rinaldo gets them both signed in a package deal. He has a trapeze act where he unexpectedly dives from the high swing as the crowd screams. A harness protects him in the fall. Despite the popularity of the act, the owner confides to another he doesn't like "that dwarf."

Rinaldo performs his act. His harness has been sabotaged and he crashes to the ground. He dies in Victor's arms. With his circus money, Victor returns to Frankenstein's castle, where he saves Eva from the cruel advances of the Baron.

* * *

The Bride was a curious film. More concentration was given to Victor and Rinaldo than to "The Bride" herself. The travels of the two were infinitely more interesting.

Rinaldo was an intelligent and articulate man who had received an education somewhere. It was very easy to assume that the lack of opportunities available to him in the early 1800s had prevented him from success. His head for business had the effect of rising the ire of the circus owner. His intelligence often led to cockiness. In a tavern, with Victor to protect him, he strode purposefully up and down the length of the bar, making demands of the tavernkeep. Once ale caused Victor to pass out, the two were carted out of the tavern and dumped in a river.

The two men traveled in a curious fashion. Victor often picked Rinaldo up and set him on his shoulder. Such a move was condescending to the smaller man, although the character himself seemed happy enough with the arrangement.

Rinaldo never suspected Victor's origins. He once said that Victor was the best friend he had met in all of his travels. Victor was innocent and did not patronize or abuse Rinaldo. Victor afforded the personal audience Rinaldo deserved by warrant of his personality and wit but had been denied because of his size.

"The Bride" nicely illustrated a small-statured man as a human being with all the plusses and minuses anyone can have. Rinaldo's quick brain and opportunistic nature added interest to an otherwise dull movie.

St. Elsewhere / "Family Affair" / Feb. 12, 1986 / NBC-TV

Executive Producer: Bruce Paltrow
Producers: John Masius; Tom Fontana
Co-Producer: Abby Singer
Director: Bruce Paltrow
Story: John Masius; Tom Fontana
Teleplay: Eric Overmeyer
Category: Series Television — Medical Drama

* Small-stature
* Married White Couple; White Male Teenager

Plot: Dr. Victor Ehrlich encounters a small-statured boy and approaches the teen's parents to seek medical treatment.

Dr. Victor Ehrlich's family counseling group at the Southside Youth Center includes fifteen-year-old Lewis. The teenager is measured by Ehrlich and found to be 4'1". Ehrlich notes during the examination that the boy is on the small side.

LEWIS: Nothing wrong with being short!

EHRLICH: Unless Disney's hiring.

Angrily, Lewis bolts out of the room.
Ehrlich believes tests at St. Eligius Hospital might find that a growth hormone could help Lewis attain a more average height. He goes to Lewis' address and finds the door opened by a small-statured man, Vern Appleton.

VERN: I'm Lewis' father.

Ehrlich wants the parents to take Lewis in for tests. The two veto the idea. Vern gets angry at Ehrlich for butting in.
Ehrlich later describes his day to a colleague at the hospital and includes this accomplishment:

EHRLICH: ...angered an elfin family....

The Appletons bring Lewis in. Tests determine he is a candidate for growth hormone and will grow. Devaluation shows up when Vern, hearing the news, suddenly leaves. He reveals to Ehrlich he thinks his son won't be able to respect a small father if the boy grows to average height.

* * *

The attention of "Family Affair" on the small-statured family was minor but interesting. Of particular note was the indication of an average home with a mother, father, and son, all of whom were small-statured. Lewis was a rather rowdy boy, ready to swagger and act tough with his street friends or proposition a nurse at St. Eligius.

At a glance, Dr. Ehrlich's terminology and odd humor might seem pejorative, but it must be noted that the character was a boor afflicted with terminal foot-in-mouth disease. His remarks were in character and easily recognized as such.

The devaluation Vern experienced was disappointing. Feeling his son would not respect him was just too predictable and unsatisfying.

"Family Affair" presented a routine storyline; even so, existence of a small-statured family unit was appreciated despite the predictability.

Miami Vice / "Tale of the Goat" / Apr. 25, 1986 / NBC-TV

Executive Producer: Michael Mann
Producer: John Nicolella
Co-Producers: Richard Brams; Donald L. Gold
Consulting Producer: Liam O'Brien
Supervising Producer: Ed Waters
Director: Michael O'Herlihy
Writer: Jim Trombetta
Category: Series Television — Crime Drama

* Small-stature
* Black Male

Plot: Haitian voodoo crime kingpin Legba returns to Miami.

When Haitian hood Legba returns to Miami alive, small-statured Baron Sandy is one of the killing hoods attached to the voodoo king. He is the "Baron of the graveyard," states Legba, using his pickax to dig graves. He helps "take care" of people who get in the way of Legba.

* * *

"Tale of the Goat" used a small man in an incidental role, as part of the creepy and evil entourage with which Legba surrounded himself. Baron Sandy was a muscular man and a snappy dresser. His height was of no consequence.

While certainly not a role model, Baron Sandy *was* an illustration that people come in all shapes, sizes, colors and personify both good and evil. Baron's evilness was not seen as being related to anger about his size; therefore, it was not perceived as a negative.

The Wizard / "El Dorado" / Sept. 9, 1986 / CBS-TV

Executive Producers: Douglas Schwartz and Michael Berk
Producer: Paul B. Radin
Director: Peter H. Hunt
Story: Michael Berk, Douglas Schwartz, Paul B. Radin
Teleplay: Michael Berk & Douglas Schwartz
Category: Series Television — Adventure/Fantasy

* Small-stature
* Single White Male
* Equipment: Extension pedals for vehicle control

Plot: Government agent Alex Jagger's new assignment is to protect toymaker/inventor Simon McKay from anybody who may want to use his genius for the wrong reasons.

Alex Jagger is assigned to keep an eye on Simon McKay, "The Wizard," a toymaker genius who occasionally does work for the Department of Defense. McKay is small-statured.

McKay is meeting a boy from the Starlight Foundation, a child with leukemia whose fondest wish is to meet the Wizard. McKay is realistic about his size.

> BRIAN: Simon, what's it like being small? I mean, grown up but not —
>
> McKAY: ...I don't think about being small.... You don't measure a person by his height. It's the size of their heart that really matters. And you know, we've all got something in common.... We're all different.

Brian is dying. His only chance for survival is to undergo a bone marrow transplant. The only possible candidate is a missing brother. McKay impulsively hunts down the brother who is in trouble. He is brought back to help Brian — who now has a chance for life.

* * *

Within the first five minutes of "El Dorado," the debut episode of *The Wizard,* it was evident that it was something different. Simon McKay was illustrated as a genius, a toymaker who could design for the government; therefore, he was afforded special protection in the persons of Darcy and the abrasive Jagger. McKay was dry-humored, intelligent, and very talented. He played the drums when he wanted to think. He had the wisdom and know-how of an adult but the adventurous nature of a child. He indicated he never had much of a childhood once his family discovered he would never grow tall.

In almost total departure from standard story lines featuring small-statured characters, McKay was the catalyst for every and anything. He was the brains and the motivater. McKay was able to exhibit a personality and even his weaknesses, such as eating candy, which he had vowed to give up. His soft heart led them into quite a scrape in South America, but it paid off for Brian.

McKay drove a car. His controls on the pedals of the automobile caused fits of consternation to the average-statured agents when they were forced to take the wheel while being chased by villains.

"El Dorado" portrayed a real and sensitive character who just happened to be small *and* the world's greatest inventor. McKay continued to aid people and society in the series' brief one-season run.

Other Disabilities

The Hunchback of Notre Dame / 1939 / C & L Films, Inc.

Producer: Pandro S. Berman
Director: William Dieterle
Screenplay: Sonya Levien
Adaptation: Bruno Frank
Category: Feature Film — Drama

* Unique body and facial configuration; Deafness
* Single White Male
* Communication: Expressive — Speech; Receptive — Gestures

Plot: A disabled bellringer saves the life of a gypsy girl.

In medieval Paris, tales are told of Quasimodo, the "hunchbacked," deaf bellringer of the cathedral of Notre Dame. A young girl screams that Quasimodo has crossed her path. Her grandmother orders her to go home and light a candle.

Quasimodo gets caught up in ribald revelry in the streets. He is elected "King of Fools" and paraded about. He exults in the "acceptance" of the heckling crowd.

Esmeralda, a gypsy girl, dances in the street to earn a few pennies. When she faces arrest, she seeks sanctuary in the church. John, a clergyman, is smitten with her. He tells her she will be taken care of by the bellringer. When she sees Quasimodo, she flees the church in fear. Quasimodo chases her down, grabs her, and runs. Quasimodo is captured. He is flogged and placed on public display. He is abused by a jeering crowd. He wants water and only Esmeralda will give it to him.

John cannot stop thinking of Esmeralda. He murders Esmeralda's lover and lets her take the fall. If she dies, he rationalizes, it will break the spell he claims she has cast on him. Esmeralda is sentenced to die. As the gallows rope is about to be put around her neck, Quasimodo swings down from the tower to save her. He takes her up to the tower as the people rejoice that she has sanctuary in the church.

Quasimodo has been shunned all his life. He gives Esmeralda food and tells her:

> QUASIMODO: I'm going away so you don't have to see my ugly face when I eat.

Esmeralda draws him back to sit with her while she eats.

QUASIMODO: I'm deaf too. It's horrible . . . I'm not a man, I'm not a beast, I'm about as shapeless as the man in the moon.

A political battle rages. Should the church offer sanctuary to foreigners like the gypsies? An angry lynch mob prepares to storm the cathedral. Quasimodo watches the crowd from the tower. He pushes beams and stones out to disperse the crowd. He dumps molten metal on the floor that drains from the mouths of stone gargoyles to shower on the crowd. The mob flees and Notre Dame is safe. He kills John when John tries to get Esmeralda.

The King pardons Esmeralda. Quasimodo watches her leave with another man.

* * *

The Hunchback of Notre Dame featured a man with multiple disabilities who was forever shunned by society. Quasimodo had been raised by the church when he had been left a foundling on their steps years before. He became the bellringer of the cathedral and lost his hearing from the ringing of the bells.

His disabilities were compounded by the superstitions of the people. He was believed to be possessed. He was also never taken seriously. In a curiously disjointed scene, he burst in on Esmeralda's trial and claimed he murdered her lover. He was laughed at by the crowd. Even Esmeralda, tender-hearted though she was, easily forgot he saved her. She left Paris with the man she loved and never looked back to the tower where the miserable Quasimodo wondered why he was not made of stone like the gargoyles around him.

Quasimodo was a directed character once he had a cause. Esmeralda became that cause because she was beautiful and she had given him water. He was also a little off-the-beam, presumably because of his cloistered existence and the maddening clang of the bells. He was never considered to be a man with thoughts and feelings of his own. He chased down Esmeralda out of a gross animal instinct, it seemed, casting negative connotations over his mental stability. Even Esmeralda's attention seemed to be that given by a person to a starving animal. She never gave him credit for being a lonely man who had been psychologically damaged by many factors of the contemporary society.

The Hunchback of Notre Dame portrayed an isolated man with a disability as one who was forever excluded and eternally separate.

The Spiral Staircase / 1946 / A Selznick Release

Producer: Dore Schary
Director: Robert Siodmak
Screenplay: Mel Dinelli
Based on the Novel: *Some Must Watch* by Ethel Lina White
Category: Feature Film — Drama

* Elective mutism
* Single White Female
* Cure

Plot: A murderer is killing off "defective" women. Helen, a mute servant, seems to be next on his list.

A small town in the early years of the century is terrorized by the murders of three women. All had some type of physical disability. Helen, a servant in the wealthy Warren household, is mute. The cause of her disability is described as a traumatic reaction to seeing her house burn down as a child with her family inside. Helen was unable to scream for help and has remained silent ever since.

Helen is attractive and has the interest of Dr. Parre, a newcomer to the town. He gives her a lift in his buggy and indicates her silence is a case of her not trying to speak.

> DR. PARRE: I got to wondering just how long you were going on like this—I mean doing the work you're doing at the Warrens. You wanted to be a nurse or a teacher. You mean, you're going to give up that without making an effort to get your voice back again?

Helen is distraught by this discussion. Back at the Warren house, she sees Mrs. Oakes, the head housekeeper who has a concern about the murders. She uses pejorative language in describing the victims.

> MRS. OAKES: First, there was that girl with the scar on her face, then there was that poor, simple-minded creature and now this cripple. It seems like—

It seems like Helen may be next.

Helen finds herself the potential victim of the killer. She is saved at the last minute by old Mrs. Warren, who drags herself from her deathbed to shoot the killer. Cure occurs when Helen's silence is shattered by her own scream. The psychological block is gone and she is able to use the telephone to whisper to Dr. Parre to come to help.

* * *

The Spiral Staircase was a classy thriller with every step carefully mapped toward its climax. Helen's disability made her a predictable victim in the story, as one of the "imperfect" people. The murderer told her she was "imperfect" and that there was no room for such in the world. The disability worked in the story as it was the killer's motivator; it was also stereotypical in that, supposedly, the disabled target could not escape a dangerous situation without help.

Helen was bright, energetic, and full of life. She possessed a light and cheerful personality. Despite what could be considered period stereotyping, *The Spiral Staircase* indicated a woman with a disability as one who was capable and her own person—even though it was in the tired disabled-woman-as-victim mold.

See also the remake of this movie (1975).

The Miracle Worker / 1962 / United Artists
(A Playfilm Production)

Producer: Fred Coe
Director: Arthur Penn
Screenplay: William Gibson
Based Upon the Stage Play by: William Gibson
Category: Feature Film — Drama

* Deafness and Blindness
* White Female Child
* Based on a True Story
* Communication: None

Plot: A young, inexperienced teacher takes on the job of attempting to teach an unruly child who is blind and deaf.

Captain Arthur Keller and Mrs. Kate Keller in Tuscumbia, Alabama, are at wit's end as how to handle their daughter Helen, who is deaf and blind. The cause of Helen's disability is discussed as a high fever in infancy.

Captain Keller is persuaded to write to the Perkins School for the Blind in Boston. Miss Anne Sullivan, a visually-impaired graduate of the same institution, is dispatched to Alabama. Anne's introduction to Helen assures her the child is intelligent — particularly when Helen locks Anne in her room and successfully hides the key from her family.

> ANNE: There's nothing impaired in that head. It's like a mousetrap.

Helen is the "tyrant" of the family, as Anne notes. At dinner, Helen goes from plate to plate and grabs food. Anne begins to assert her authority, accusing the parents of negligence.

> ANNE: It's less trouble to feel sorry for her than to teach her anything!

Anne convinces the Kellers she needs time alone with Helen, time without parental interference. She goads the Captain into letting her and Helen remain — unhindered — in a small house on the Keller estate. There, she gets Helen to tolerate her. Helen begins to learn to dress herself. She allows Anne to groom her. Anne fingerspells words in Helen's hand. Helen quickly parrots without comprehension.

Mrs. Keller peeks in every day, unbeknownst to Helen. Anne brings up an attitudinal barrier.

> ANNE: Mrs. Keller, I don't think Helen's worst handicap is deafness or blindness — it's your love. You're so sorry for her, you've kept her like a pet. Why, even a dog you housebreak.

After two weeks in the cottage, the Kellers want Helen back. They are pleased with her new calm behavior. Anne is not.

CAPTAIN: We are more than satisfied. You've taught her to behave....

ANNE: ...I wanted to teach her what language is. Obedience without understanding is a—blindness, too.

At home, Helen tests her family by misbehaving and spilling a water pitcher at the table. She is turned over to Anne. Anne forces Helen to help her refill the pitcher. As water gushes over Helen's hands at the pump, Anne's incessant fingerspelling in the child's palm continues. And this time, Helen understands.

* * *

The Miracle Worker augments the legend that has become Helen Keller. Powerful imagery makes up the film. The scenes of Helen groping across a field, arms and face to the sky; her busy hands touching every and anything—faces, clothes, objects, food; the surprisingly physical and heated battles between the two combatants make this movie impossible to forget. The performances were electrifying. Likewise, the climactic scene at the well was emotional and powerful. It was virtually impossible to *not* be moved as Helen finally understood despite the subsequent melodrama.

In the overwhelming tide of imagery from the film and the undying respect the mainstream culture had for the achievements of Helen Keller, the film seems to be part of the Helen Keller mystique, inseparable from the actual woman—and her actual limitations. Anne Sullivan became the hallmark of the dedicated teacher and the ultimate catalyst, disabled or non-disabled. In that sense, it was impossible to look at this film as anything but the Helen-Keller-and-Teacher story, plain and simple.

Little information about the education of persons who are deaf and blind was presented.

A TV movie based on the same script aired in 1979 with less impact than the original (see Appendix, TV Movies, *The Miracle Worker*). A 1984 TV movie "followed up" the story (see *Helen Keller: The Miracle Continues*).

The Miracle Worker should be seen for its cinematic value and integrity. It is, however, a story of two driving personalities with little exploration into the meaning of deafness coupled with blindness.

The Affair / 1973

Producers: Aaron Spelling; Leonard Goldberg
Director: Gilbert Cates
Writer: Barbara Turner
Category: Made-for-TV Movie—Drama

* Orthopedic
* Single White Female
* Equipment: Crutches

Plot: A songwriter who uses crutches falls in love for the first time.

Mr. Marcus Smith visits the Patterson home for business. His eye is caught by a pretty young woman on horseback. He later finds she is Courtney Patterson, daughter of the man with whom he is doing business. He approaches her in the house. He is surprised to see a pair of crutches on the floor.

MARCUS: Are these yours?

COURTNEY: Why? Are they yours?

MARCUS: No.

COURTNEY: Then they must be mine.

The cause of Courtney's disability is described as a bout with polio when she was a child.

Marcus is intrigued with Courtney, who is a successful songwriter. The two begin a romance. Courtney is uncertain; she's never had a relationship before even though she's in her thirties. They go away for a weekend and Courtney grows cold and distant in fear. Marcus brings her home.

She meets his kids from his first marriage. The group goes down to the pier. Courtney sits and watches as Marcus and the kids scramble everywhere. The romance sours. Courtney is despondent and attempts suicide.

* * *

The Affair was a long and tedious movie with the consistency of molasses. Courtney was, as she admitted to Marcus, her father's "personal triumph of the will." He had felt guilty after she had survived polio and took her everywhere to give her advantages. She had gotten everything she wanted. She had been a poster child for a charity.

Despite her career as a songwriter and having worked in recording studios, she had never met anyone before Marcus. Of course, the failure of a first love is the most painful. The movie indicated that a woman who had never been through the process as a teenager was so emotionally devastated by the hurt that she tried to take her life. From the movie's viewpoint, polio had denied Courtney an emotional maturation. She was a scared child in a woman's body.

The scenes at the pier were interesting. The children and Marcus appeared to be the perfect family, laughing and playing together. Courtney, due to access problems (which were not discussed) and physicality, could not join in with them. She sat and watched them from afar, appearing forever isolated.

The most interesting scene occurred as the Patterson family ate. Courtney's brother gave her a gift. He had found and framed a poster of her as a child reading "Fight Polio." Courtney thought the gift a lark; her father was upset to see her making fun of it. There was a wealth of possibilities in exploring the exciting media-feed life of a poster child and the reality of an adult existence by the same. The movie chose to dwell on more "traditional" disability themes.

The Affair was a long and tedious film which illustrated a woman with a disability as scared, brittle, and emotionally backward.

Little House on the Prairie / "The Voice of Tinker Jones" / 1974 / NBC-TV

Category: Series Television— Family Drama

* Speech-impaired
* Single White Male
* Communication: Expressive— mime, drawings, gestures

Plot: A speech-impaired coppersmith takes matters into his own hands when the town of Walnut Grove squabbles over a church bell.

Traveling Tinker Jones arrives in Walnut Grove to sell his wares. He is a favorite with children as he is always giving them metal toys he has made himself. He has no usable voice and communicates with mime and pictures. Little Laura Ingalls is curious about the man.

> LAURA: I wish Tinker could talk so we'd know for sure if he was happy.

The church needs a bell. Storeowner Harriet Oleson wants a large one. As the town's richest woman, she will contribute a bell and a plaque in the name of herself and her henpecked husband, Nels. However, there is a stipulation: the bell is to be used exclusively for church services and not for the school classes held in the same building.

Mrs. Oleson's decision sets the entire town at each other's throats, arguing and bickering over how to resolve this situation. Tinker gets fed up with the fighting. He recruits the kids to bring in the metal toys he's made them. Together, he and the children build a cast, melt the toys, and mold a bell to end the squabbling.

* * *

"The Voice of Tinker Jones" was a sweet little story. The man with the disability possessed a personality and ideas. He was the only one able to resolve a burning issue that enflamed the whole town.

Jones was the catalyst in enlisting ranks of his devoted youthful friends. He used pictographs to delegate jobs and had their complete trust. He had a heart and was dedicated to ending the struggle. As the bell rang out, Laura noted that Tinker Jones *did* have a voice, one heard by the entire town.

"The Voice of Tinker Jones" presented a man with a disability as a concerned community member.

The Spiral Staircase / 1975 / Raven Films

Executive Producer: Josef Shaftel
Producer: Peter Shaw
Director: Peter Collinson
Screenplay: Andrew Meredith
Based on the Screenplay: *The Spiral Staircase* by Mel Dinelli
Based on the Novel: *Some Must Watch* by Ethel Lina White
Category: Feature Film — Drama

* Elective mutism
* Single White Female
* Cure

Plot: Helen, a young woman who can't speak, seems to be next on a murderer's list.

A blind woman is stalked and killed by an assailant.

> DOCTOR RAWLEY: Five people — each with a physical disability — have been murdered.

Rawley's patient and love interest is Helen Mallory. He cannot find any organic reason why Helen Mallory is unable to speak. The cause of her disability is described as a traumatic reaction to seeing her family perish in a fire.

On a dark and stormy evening, people in the wealthy Sherman house are battening down the hatches. Old Mrs. Sherman tells her granddaughter Helen to leave the house that night, but Helen stays.

Helen is targeted by the murderer but rescued in the nick of time by her grandmother, who has pulled herself out of her bed.

Helen races to the telephone to call Dr. Rawley to come to the house. Without thinking, she speaks into the phone and hears her own voice.

* * *

The Spiral Staircase was a remake of the 1946 original, using a contemporary setting. Helen was a busy and directed young woman. She was also frustrated by her inability to speak and was seeking to remedy the situation. She was lively and functioned well, communicating by writing notes, mouthing words, and mime.

In the original, Helen seemed to be the next logical target for the killer. The remake attempted to make a stronger point for the "imperfect" women to be targeted. A great focus was placed on a blind woman who was gunned down while walking with her dog guide. This greater concentration changed the focus. The blind woman became a *specific* target — watched and followed; her murder was the result of a premeditated plan. Therefore, the random aspect of killing "imperfect" women was lost; Helen seemed a less likely target than the blind woman.

Even if she was the logical victim, special equipment was available in 1975 to help someone like Helen use a telephone. A wealthy household like that of the Shermans would have been able to afford a TTY for the deaf or speech-impaired. Therefore, the deliberately helpless situation was manipulated. The woman with the disability was a helpless pawn without means to help herself. Helen was just prey to a killer.

The Spiral Staircase presented a woman with a disability as warm, attractive and bright, but ultimately helpless in the old disabled-woman-as-victim framework.

Deadman's Curve / Feb. 3, 1978 / CBS-TV

Executive Producers: Roger Gimbel; Tony Converse
Producer: Pat Rooney
Director: Richard Compton
Teleplay: Darlene Young
Based on a *Rolling Stone* magazine article by: Paul Morantz
Category: Made-for-TV Movie — Drama

* Brain-injury — aphasia; Partial paralysis
* Single White Male
* New Disability
* Based on a True Story

Plot: The meteoric career of singers Jan and Dean is halted when Jan is seriously injured in an auto accident.

Two Southern California high school kids make it big in the music business in the late 1950s. Jan Berry is the heart and soul behind a long series of surf and hot rod records that become hits. Dean Torrence is the loyal friend who adds the signature falsetto voice.

Jan receives a draft notice in the mail. He angrily goes to the draft board where he is assured, star or not, Uncle Sam wants him. The egocentric star stalks off and jumps into his car. He roars off and crashes into a parked truck. A new disability is incurred.

Jan remains comatose in the hospital for months. When he comes out of it, the doctors diagnose he is aphasic.

    MRS. BERRY: He's like a baby!

The doctor expresses that Jan can learn.

Jan has one wish: to reunite with Dean and appear onstage one more time — which they do.

* * *

Deadman's Curve illustrated a man continuing to live after a severe brain injury. After the accident, Jan was illustrated as the same, egocentric character he had been prior to the crash. However, the film expressed that recovery depended on his strong will, illustrated in a scene where Jan refused to use a wheelchair despite difficulties in walking due to residual paralysis of his right side.

After the accident, Jan was illustrated going to speech therapy, working hard to learn to reform sound and words. The movie indicated that his aphasia was not a short-term thing but a problem he would continue to work through. His speech improved slightly throughout the film but the difficulty was not easily disposed of (see *Long Journey Back* for a comparison).

An interesting sidelight to the film was an illustration of the power of network TV. After the movie aired (and garnered respectable ratings), interest in the 1960s stars was rekindled to the extent that the actual Jan Berry and Dean Torrence began a successful touring career which they presently do on a part-time basis.

Deadman's Curve fairly illustrated the difficulties facing a man experiencing a severe brain-injury.

Long Journey Back / Feb. 15, 1978

Executive Producers: Lee Rich; Philip Capice
Producer: Robert Lowenheim
Director: Mel Damski
Story: Judith Ramsey
Teleplay: Audrey Davis Levin
Category: Made-for-TV Movie — Drama

* Brain-injury — aphasia; Amputation — single leg
* New Disability
* White Female Teenager
* Equipment: Cane; Prosthetic leg

Plot: A teenager, disabled in a school bus crash, fights her way back to an average life.

The Cassala family's plans for a Mexican vacation are shattered when a school bus carrying their elder daughter, Celia, is struck by a train on the way home from school. A new disability is incurred.

> DOCTOR ROBERTS: We can't save the leg ... there appears to be extensive brain damage....

Family stress is highlighted. Younger daughter Amy is virtually pushed aside as the focus of the family's life shifts to the hospital where Celia is in a coma. Upon awakening, the diagnosis is aphasia.

> DOCTOR ROBERTS: Amnesia and aphasia are caused by brain damage. Amnesia means loss of memory; aphasia is the loss of speech and the ability to convey and understand ideas.... Think of her as a baby who has to relearn everything.

Five months after the accident, Celia enters a rehabilitation program. Her speech is rapidly improving. She is fitted with a cosmetic leg and learns to function with it. Celia's improvement continues. She returns to school and, in an attempt to help her classmates better understand, does an oral report on her experience, displaying artificial limbs for the other kids to see.

> CELIA: I wrote this report for you but it's really for me, to help you understand that I'm different, not better or worse, just different. I can never fully adjust to that until you do. I used to want to go back to what I was, but now I'm just happy to be here. Any questions?

* * *

Long Journey Back took a fairly routine triumph-over-disability story and treated it with honesty, utilizing technical assistance. Celia's problems were not just hers, they affected her little sister and the relationship between her parents. Her father had a great deal of difficulty coping with the situation.

Celia's recovery from aphasia was very rapid and too easy. The amputation was expressed as being more serious. Celia *did* indicate in her school report, "Now and then, I'll have trouble remembering, putting thoughts in order...." The audience was barely aware that the difficulty remained.

A nice scene dealt with Celia returning home late from a date. For the first time since her accident, her father stopped pussyfooting around and chewed her out. Celia was delighted, gleefully telling her father, "You're giving me hell!" It was an indication that life was settling back down to a norm.

Appropriate terminology was used throughout the film. Celia's rehabilitation at the hospital was nicely documented. Actual people with disabilities were seen in the background of the rehab sequences.

Long Journey Back had plenty of soapy elements and teary scenes, but the information doled out during the telecast and the concentration on family problems and not just Celia gave it an edge over the average inspiring triumph drama.

The Waltons / "The Ordeal" / Feb. 16, 1978 / CBS-TV

Writer: Paul West
Category: Series Television — Family Drama

* Orthopedia; nerve damage
* White Female Child; series regular
* Equipment: Braces and crutches
* Temporary Disability

Plot: Elizabeth Walton loses the use of her legs after an accident.

Elizabeth Walton climbs a stack of cut logs to try and put a fallen baby bird back into a nest. She slips and the logs fall on her. Mother Olivia Walton notices something.

OLIVIA: Her legs aren't movin'.

The Walton family waits for word at the hospital. Oldest sister and nursing student Mary Ellen gives them some information.

MARY ELLEN: [She has] multiple fractures of both legs.

The doctor steps in.

DOCTOR: Considerable damage to the nerves.

Elizabeth is fitted with braces and uses crutches. She struggles to move about. She casts negatives over the life of a person with a degree of paralysis.

ELIZABETH: It's like I'm half a person—this half is alive and that half is just draggin' along.

More negatives are assumed as Elizabeth stares sadly at horses trotting, knowing she is missing out. Her problem is seen to be one of her not trying to get better. Her friend Amy uses poor language trying to make this point.

AMY: Do you wanna be a cripple all your life?

Elizabeth stands off alone, watching other children play a game into which she cannot join.
Cure is seen as Elizabeth spontaneously regains use of her legs and is able to run and jump about happily.

* * *

"The Ordeal" was a tired story. It required a gushing of pity from the audience to propel it. Elizabeth's difference and natural misery were focused on; she was never given a chance to discover her own resources. A cure was her only avenue to a happy, healthy, and productive life. This episode was an unbalanced image of disability.

One Day at a Time / June 5, 1978 (rerun) / CBS-TV

Producer: Norman Paul
Writers: James B. [?] Johnson; Pat Harrington, Jr.
Category: Series Television— Situation Comedy

* Epilepsy
* White Female Teenager

Plot: Ann Romano fires her new secretary when she sees her taking pills.

One Day at a Time

Ann Romano interviews teenaged Leslie for a clerical job. Ann is amazed that someone who types ninety words a minute hasn't been snapped up by another employer. She hires Leslie.

At home, Ann's daughters hear the news and begin to talk.

> JULIE: She needs that job.
>
> BARB: [Mom] can lose *her* job.
>
> JULIE: If you tell Mom, I'll never forgive you.

Ann wants to know what is going on.

> BARB: It's about Leslie—she's a doper ... sits in class, all spaced out.

Ann is leery. She sees Leslie taking a pill at work. Minutes later, she calls Leslie. The young woman does not respond. She sits and stares.

Barb's warning comes back. Ann confronts her employee.

> ANN: Leslie, what went on just now ... you were sitting, staring ... you were on some kind of a trip.
>
> LESLIE: No, I wasn't on a trip!

Ann fires Leslie. Julie informs her mother that Leslie is epileptic.

> ANN: She doesn't fall down and have convulsions—
>
> JULIE: That's the kind of seizure Leslie has ... she'd rather be known as a doper than an epileptic.

Leslie is given a chance to state her case. An attitudinal barrier is seen as Leslie describes how people draw away from one who is "an epileptic" and Ann sees herself.

> LESLIE: They used to think epileptics were witches and burned them at the stake ... there are two million in the country, taught to lie—it's not a disease, it's a condition.

* * *

This particular episode of the popular sitcom successfully treaded a thin line between comedy and pathos. Without devaluing Leslie, the piece was funny and sharp, yet delivered a resounding message in a brief half hour. Excellent information was expressed through the script. Best of all, Leslie's problem was explored through the attitudes and reactions of others: Barb's sneering contempt of "the doper" and Ann's wary eye when she, too, believed Leslie to be on drugs. Leslie proved she was capable of performing excellently on the job, yet it was Ann's fear that kept her from succeeding.

Another nice touch was the fact that Ann's realization was not simple and pat. Although she was relieved to discover Leslie was not a substance-user, she maintained a prejudice toward the girl which would still need to be worked out.

Some pejorative language popped into the script, such as when Leslie described a seizure as "rolling around on the floor like a mad dog." It seems doubtful that one sensitive to the difficulty would further devalue herself by such a description. It would seem to be more of a picture placed deliberately by the writers to make a point. However, this episode was excellent and well worth viewing.

Magnum, P.I. / "Don't Say Goodbye" / Mar. 26, 1980 / CBS-TV

Executive Producer: Donald Bellisario
Producer: J. Rickley Dumm
Director: Winrich Kolbe
Story: T.J. Miles
Teleplay: T.J. Miles and Babs Greyhosky
Category: Series Television — Crime Drama

* Blindness; Wheelchair-User
* White Female

Plot: Agatha Kimball hires Thomas Magnum to pay off a blackmailer who claims to have some dirt on her granddaughter.

Private investigator Thomas Magnum is hired by old Agatha Kimball, a wealthy blind woman who uses an electric wheelchair. She's being blackmailed by someone who claims to have "enlightening information" about her beloved granddaughter, Amy.

Agatha misses the sloping ramp that leads outdoors and falls out of her chair. The misplacing of the ramp is the most recent accident in a series of mishaps. Agatha insists she is all right and greets Thomas. She touches his face, noting his thick mustache.

AGATHA: You've still got it. I'm glad.

Agatha wants Thomas to pay off the extortionist and to keep the information to himself. Magnum's investigation reveals that granddaughter Amy is an imposter, replacing the real Amy who had died. However, "Amy" loves Agatha and does not care for her money. Agatha had guessed the ruse long ago and kept quiet, just happy to be reunited with a long-lost granddaughter who showed her affection.

* * *

"Don't Say Goodbye" used the disabled-woman-as-victim theme. She was also being deceived by a fake granddaughter who assumed an old blind woman would never know the difference. Agatha *did* know the difference but kept mum.

The disability made Agatha an easy target for someone who wanted to inherit her money. The ramp was deliberately moved to cause her to spill out from her chair; she was also pushed into the swimming pool by her assailant. It would seem that Agatha, due to age and infirmities, was incapable of defending herself in any way.

Her touching Magnum's face and commenting on his mustache could be considered a type of face-feeling—but she reached to pat his cheek in a grandmotherly sort of way then her hand traveled over to see the mustache. It appeared to be an affectionate gesture, not the standard face-feel.

"Don't Say Goodbye" illustrated an older lady with multiple limitations who was comfortable with herself and who enjoyed other people. She was also cherished and valued by others around her. Her disabilities made her a vulnerable target. Without them, there would have been no story.

The Elephant Man / 1980 / Paramount Pictures

Executive Producer: Stuart Cornfeld
Producer: Jonathan Sanger
Director: David Lynch
Screenplay: Christopher De Vore; Eric Berren; David Lynch
Based On: *The Elephant Man and Other Reminiscences* by Sir Frederick Treves; *The Elephant Man — A Study in Human Dignity* by Ashley Montagu
Category: Feature Film—Drama

* Unique body and facial configuration
* Single White Male

Plot: A London doctor wonders if he has rescued a "freak" from a carnival or simply put him on display for more genteel audiences.

Dr. Frederick Treves, noted surgeon and lecturer, approaches Bytes, a sleazy carnival barker who exhibits "a freak" called "The Elephant Man." Treves pays for a private showing.

Treves strikes up a deal with Bytes. He wishes to lecture on The Elephant Man—John Merrick—at his anatomy class. Bytes agrees. Merrick is later beaten by Bytes. Treves is summoned to minister to Merrick and orders the man to be hospitalized. He soon discovers that the silent Merrick not only understands him but can read. Merrick possesses a superior intelligence.

TREVES: Why didn't you tell me you could read?

MERRICK: I was frightened.

Treves takes Merrick home for tea with him and his wife. Merrick cries, not accustomed to being treated in a genteel manner.

A stage actress, Mrs. Kendal, reads about Merrick in the newspaper. She goes to meet him. And where goes Mrs. Kendal, follows the cream of London society. Merrick becomes a popular figure in the Victorian city. A nurse in the hospital is angry about the visitors. She talks to Treves.

NURSE: They only want to impress their friends ... if you ask me, he's only being stared at all over again.

Treves suddenly feels he has something in common with Bytes.

An unscrupulous nightwatchman at the hospital sells tickets for the masses to see Merrick. They scream at his countenance and torment him. One of the crowd is Bytes — who steals "his" man back. Merrick is tortured by Bytes and re-exhibited with the circus. Small-statured carnies help spirit Merrick away in the dead of night and send him back to London.

Merrick is tormented and bedeviled by the curious who wish to know what is under the hood he wears. He is cornered in a washroom.

MERRICK: I am not an animal! I am a human being!

Merrick is taken to the theatre for the first time in his life. Mrs. Kendal draws all attention to him in his private box. London gives him a standing ovation.

Back in his room, Merrick readies himself for bed. He prepares to sleep lying flat — an action he knows will mean his death.

* * *

The Elephant Man was a unique study of open and veiled prejudice. Merrick was explored compassionately by Treves. The surgeon knew he could not cure Merrick, but he did what he could to make Merrick comfortable and give him the dignity he deserved. Merrick was much better off in Treves' world.

Yet, in his desire to share society with Merrick, he discovered he was no better than Bytes. Bytes brought in money by subjecting Merrick to the cold stares of a carnival mob. Treves earned popular status when society came to visit Merrick. The trappings of a lavish tea party did not differ much from the carnival. Until confronted by the nurse, he never thought the visits were of a voyeuristic nature.

The scene where Merrick was applauded by London society in the theatre was a subtle rendition of the "King of Fools" segment seen in *The Hunchback of Notre Dame*. The world loved Quasimodo and Merrick — for a few minutes.

The stunning and stark film must be applauded for the careful introduction of Merrick. The advance publicity campaign illustrated a hooded figure, leading to much speculation about what was under the hood. Merrick was introduced slowly. His first full-face introduction was in partial shadow and removed any shock value the face would have to the audience. The viewers had a sense of something quite unusual, but through Treves, had already sensed Merrick's pain and humanity.

The Elephant Man quietly discussed the nature of prejudice. It also illustrated inhumanity was not dependent on the nature of the physical body but of the mind.

Touched by Love (a.k.a. "To Elvis, with Love") / 1980 / Columbia Pictures

Producer: Peter Strauss
Director: Michael Viner
Screenplay: Hesper Anderson
Based on Book: *To Elvis, with Love* by Lena Canada
Category: Feature Film — Drama

* Cerebral Palsy
* White Female Child

Plot: A withdrawn girl with cerebral palsy responds only when her letter to Elvis Presley is answered.

* * *

Touched by Love was a sentimental story. A nursing trainee spending an early 1960s summer at a camp for children with disabilities was drawn to one withdrawn youngster. The child was an Elvis Presley fan and wrote him a letter, hoping and hoping to get an answer from the star. Everyone, including trainee Lena Canada, was sure her hopes would be dashed. Only the child was not surprised when a letter full of encouragement and hope came from the superstar, spurring on the child to improve to the best of her abilities. She corresponded with the star and lived for his letters.

The premise of this true story was sweet. However, in execution, it was played for every tear in the book.

Rowdy and rambunctious kids with disabilities were used in the camp sequences.

Touched by Love illustrated a child with a disability as one who was forever innocent and full of shining, untarnished hope.

The Miracle of Kathy Miller / Oct. 5, 1981 / CBS-TV

Producers: Bernard Rothman; Jack Wohl
Director: Robert Lewis

* Brain-injury — aphasia; partial paralysis
* White Teenaged Female

Writers: Mel & Ethel Brez
Category: Made-for-TV Movie—Drama

* New Disability
* Based on a True Story

Plot: A teenaged girl is brain-injured in a hit-and-run accident and fights her way back into the world.

Teenaged jogging enthusiast Kathy Miller is hit by a car as she crosses a busy thoroughfare. A new disability is incurred.

> DR. CHRISTIANSON: There appears to be some damage to the brain stem.

Kathy slips into a coma. Family strain and stress ensues while waiting for her to awaken. She gradually rouses from the coma and is diagnosed as brain-injured. A poor description of her condition is rendered by a doctor talking to the Millers.

> DOCTOR: Kathy is an infant.

He suggests placing Kathy in an institution.
The Millers bring Kathy home and devote themselves to helping her come back. Kathy gradually is able to walk although experiencing paralysis of her right side. She works to overcome the aphasia that makes her speech difficult. Kathy is painfully aware of the changes that have occurred in her life. Her friends find it hard to visit her. They are not patient enough for her halting speech.

> KATHY: I loooooook stu—pid.

Kathy decides she wants to be able to run again. She works hard until she builds up her endurance. She enters a ten-kilometer race with her mother and slowly makes it across the finish line hours later.

* * *

The Miracle of Kathy Miller was a routine triumph-over-disability story but it contained some good elements. The focus on Kathy's difficulties with her old friends were done well and brought to light that the social barriers she had to face were sometimes as difficult as the physical ones.
Although the story followed Kathy's recovery, it focused on return of her physical abilities through hard work. Some indication was made of a social recovery but not in ratio to the physical.
The Miracle of Kathy Miller was an average piece with insertion of some very good and thought-provoking scenes. It was a "quick fix" story—if Kathy could run again, she would be all right.

Cutter's Way / 1981 / MGM/UA

Producer: Paul R. Gurian
Director: Ivan Passer
Screenplay: Jeffrey Alan Fiskin
Based on the Novel: *Cutter and Bone* by Newton Thornburg
Category: Feature Film—Drama

* Amputee—single hand; Orthopedic disability; Single eye
* Married White Male
* Equipment: leg brace

Plot: A Vietnam vet has delusions of wealth when his best friend recognizes a rich man as one who may have committed a murder.

Alex Cutter is a disabled Vietnam veteran with a penchant for booze and wild fantasies. When friend Richard Bone tries to smooth over feathers Cutter has ruffled at a bar by explaining Cutter was a war hero, Alex replies:

CUTTER: I wasn't in any war.

Cutter's erratic behavior has sent his wife, Mo, to the edge. She tries to seduce Bone, who feels an obligation to Cutter. Mo feels she is:

MO: Playing second fiddle to a one-eyed cripple—

Bone's car breaks down in an alley. He glimpses a man and a big car. A dead body is found nearby the next day and Bone is hauled in for questioning as a suspect. When he glimpses millionaire J.J. Cord in a parade, he feels *that's* the man. Cutter dreams up a wild blackmail scheme. Mo scoffs at Cutter's latest fantasy. She indicates he has been emotionally disturbed for some time.

MO: [I've been] waiting for you to get the nerve to start living again....

Cutter intends to see his plot through, with or without the support of Bone.

* * *

Cutter's Way illustrated a disabled Vietnam veteran as a disturbed alcoholic with dreams of grandeur. Cutter, when drunk, was abusive, angry, and wildly reckless. One night when arriving home late, he repeatedly smashed into a neighbor's car. He had a natural talent for pulling the wool over the eyes of others—and managed to suavely convince the police it was an accident, due to not being able to see out of one eye. He reminded his irate neighbor, "I'm a cripple," as if that should absolve him from responsibility.

Cutter had a lonely wife who loved him and didn't know why; a good friend in drifter Bone, who had some deep obligation to the veteran; and a rich polo-playing friend who also supported him. Cutter leaned on all for emotional support but never articulated his love for them.

Despite the reckless and irresponsible actions Cutter often displayed, he was also a creative and engaging character whose fantasies seemed to keep him away from full reality. It was assumed his experiences in combat and subsequent disabilities were the rationale for his flakiness.

Cutter moved quickly when needed and even went on a wild rampage on horseback to complete his destructive fantasy. His death resulting from the ride was a case of the disabled character seeing justice through, then dying before reaping pleasure from the same.

Cutter's Way used a character with multiple disabilities as a sorry and disturbed man who was an interesting and engaging personality—and ultimately tragic.

The Love Boat / "I Don't Play Anymore" / Jan. 23, 1982 / ABC-TV

Executive Producers: Aaron Spelling; Douglas Cramer
Producers: Ben Joelson, Art Baer and Henry Colman
Director: Bob Sweeney
Writer: Lan O'Kun
Category: Series Television— Romantic Comedy

* Arthritis
* Single White Male

Plot: A famed concert pianist refuses to play for a rich man with ample bucks.

Millionaire Gillian Stockwell and his wife, Millie, greet famed concert pianist Paul Krakower on the *Pacific Princess*. Krakower will not shake hands with Stockwell, nor will he play on the ship.

> KRAKOWER: I'm sorry, I don't shake hands ... I don't shake anybody's hand.... I don't play anymore.

A maid is in Krakower's cabin to turn down the bed and notices his painful movements. He drops and breaks a water glass, unable to hold on to it. He uses poor terminology when Irene dutifully asks if she can help.

> KRAKOWER: I'm not a cripple.

Stockwell wants Krakower to play for Millie's birthday.

> KRAKOWER: I told you, I don't play anymore.

Krakower realizes Irene has an orthopedic problem. he takes her out to apologize for his earlier surliness.

Stockwell offers Krakower $10,000 to play. Krakower says even for $25,000, he couldn't. Krakower tells Irene about the man's offer, but it's too painful to play and no, there is no cure.

> KRAKOWER: What's the problem with your foot, if you don't mind my asking?

Irene relates a long-ago car accident caused the injury. It could be rectified with money and courage—

> IRENE: —and I've never had very much of either.

When Stockwell ups his offer to $25,000—the cost of the operation Irene requires—Krakower goes to the lounge and practices. Doc watches and sees Krakower shake his hands and grimace in pain. Bricker gives him medication for temporary relief of inflammation.

Krakower plays one song that evening and takes Stockwell's check for $25,000. He gives it to Irene. She says she doesn't have the courage to go through the operation alone.

> KRAKOWER: Irene, I may not be able to hold on to a glass of water—but you just wait to see how tightly I hold on to you.

* * *

"I Don't Play Anymore" was a characteristically saccharine and simplistic story common to this series. Krakower never articulated what his disability was. He simply appeared surly until the audience recognized there was a problem. He mentioned he had "inflammation" and swelling of his knuckles, but again, never expressed he had arthritis.

Krakower's life seemed dark and limited in contrast to the glittering existence he'd known as a star. He described the ability to help Irene as a "brief reprieve" to once again "make the world beautiful." He evidently felt there was nothing left for him.

"I Don't Play Anymore" indicated there was nothing left after disability—except maybe love and the ability to do something noble for others.

Little House: A New Beginning / "The Wild Boy" Parts I and II / Nov. 1 and 8, 1982 / NBC-TV

Executive Producer: Michael Landon
Producer: Kent McCray
Director: Victor French
Writer: Vince Gutierrez

* Speech-impaired
* White Male Child
* Deaf Performer

Category: Series Television—
Family Drama

Plot: Mr. Edwards takes in a "wild boy" from a sideshow—a boy who is mute.

Dr. McQueen, a traveling salesman, sells "magic elixir." He augments his income by selling tickets to see "something" in the tent—The Wild Boy of the North. In Walnut Grove, curious kids sneak into the tent to see the "wild boy." When the boy escapes, it is Jenny who befriends him and hides him from Dr. McQueen's search. The boy can understand Jenny and writes his name—Matthew. He is unable to speak.

Mr. Edwards takes Matthew in, washes and clips him. He is concerned about the nightmares the boy has. The doctor discovers McQueen had kept the child sedated with his "magic elixer." Matthew's irrational and "wild" behavior was withdrawal from morphine.

Laura Ingalls takes Matthew, Mr. Edwards, and Jenny under her wing to teach them all sign language. Matthew picks up language very quickly, delighted to be able to express himself.

McQueen sues for custody of "his" child. The circuit judge denies him the right and claims Matthew belongs in an asylum. An impassioned signed farewell speech from Matthew that is reverse-interpreted by Mr. Edwards and Laura changes the judge's mind. Matthew will stay with Mr. Edwards.

* * *

"The Wild Boy" used creative casting. The part of a hearing child without speech was played by a young deaf actor with intelligible speech. The youth easily portrayed a hearing person.

Special notation must be made of the camera angles used by the director. Most signs were fully in frame, without the annoying use of standard head-and-shoulders shots of deaf characters where hands pop in and out of frame (akin to hearing only every other word).

The character was used in at least one other episode of *Little House: A New Beginning* when Matthew's father returned to retrieve him. The boy made a difficult decision to leave Mr. Edwards and live with his parent.

"The Wild Boy" dealt with prejudice similarly to a 1968 *Here Come the Brides* episode entitled, "Absalom, Absalom."

Quincy / "Unreasonable Doubt" / Nov. 10, 1982 / NBC-TV

Producers: Michael Braverman;
Jerry Taylor
Supervising Producer: Sam Egan
Writer: Lee Sheldon
Category: Series Television—
Drama

* Orthopedic Disability
* Single White Male
* Equipment: Braces and crutches

Plot: A disabled pathologist in the coroner's lab believes the death of a disabled baby was no accident.

Wally Ross is a hardworking pathologist on crutches at the coroner's lab. He gets involved with medical examiner Quincy's case regarding a dead baby whose premature demise is described as accidental. Ross suspects otherwise.

The baby had a deteriorating condition leading to facial distortion and mental retardation. Ross speculates the thought of having an "imperfect" child led a parent to murder the infant. Bitterness is illustrated when Ross responds to another employee about coming in the next day.

> ROSS: I think I may be able to *drag* myself into here again tomorrow.

Quincy acts as the non-disabled catalyst, discerning that Ross' father was ashamed of his disabled child. Ross' anger and resentment toward his parent have led him to synthesize his own experience with that of the dead child — whose death *was* an accident.

* * *

"Unreasonable Doubt" was an "embittered crip" story. Despite being mobile on both crutches and in a wheelchair, and despite being intelligent and employed, Ross' whole life was governed by the fact that he was not accepted by his family. In one scene, he even tore up photos of himself as a child where he posed with his father. He used demeaning and pejorative imagery, referring to himself and including his remarks about the baby as "some diseased little creature." He was so sure he was right about a motive behind the little boy's death, he fought Quincy all the way and nearly destroyed himself in the process.

A more interesting examination may have been a reversal of roles — where Quincy suspected murder and the man with a disability proved him wrong. "Unreasonable Doubt" was disturbing, highlighting a portrait of disability with dark hues.

T.J. Hooker / "Hooker's Run" / Feb. 4, 1984 / ABC-TV

Executive Producer: Aaron Spelling; Leonard Goldberg
Producer: Jeffrey Hayes
Co-Producers: Jack V. Fogarty; Simon Muntner
Supervising Producer: Rick Husky
Director: Cliff Bole
Writer: Simon Muntner
Category: Series Television — Police Drama

* Orthopedic Disability
* White Male
* Equipment: Braces and crutches
* Performer with a Disability

Plot: A desk clerk at the seedy hotel where grand jury witness Angie has hidden is a man with a disability.

* * *

"Hooker's Run" used a disabled character as part of the populace. The desk clerk, as shabby as the hotel in which he worked, was seen getting his crutches, crossing the floor, and answering the telephone. His disability was easily visible and identifiable; he was just a man at work who needed a shave. The brief scene easily expressed that all sorts of people populate this world.

Why Me? / Mar. 12, 1984 / ABC-TV

Executive Producers: Malcolm Stuart, Dalene Young
Producer: Robert Papazian
Co-Producers: Irwin Steinberg, M. Lowell, Michelle Mayosse
Director: Fielder Cook
Writer: Dalene Young
Category: Made-for-TV Movie—Drama

* Facial Scarring
* Married White Female
* New Disability
* Based on a True Story

Plot: A nurse is facially disfigured in an auto accident and fights to rebuild her life while a doctor reconstructs her face.

Leola Mae Harmon has a bad car accident. A new disability is incurred when her face is severely injured. She is horrified to see her reflection in a mirror. She blames the doctor for saving her life.

> LEOLA: Who gave you the right?

She pejoratively describes herself as "Frankenstein's wife." Her medical training has given her some background in plastic surgery and so she knows nothing can be done. Doctor Jim Stallings is realistic with Leola.

> DOCTOR STALLINGS: Things could be worse.

Leola insists on going home to try and salvage her personal life. Her husband, Brian, is unable to make love to her. He cannot handle what has happened. He tells Doctor Stallings:

> BRIAN: She was really beautiful. People would turn and take a second look ... she's deformed.

> DOCTOR STALLINGS: She's more than a face.

The advent of disability destroys Leola's marriage.
It takes the dedication of Doctor Stallings and the inspiring courage of Leola Harmon to forge ahead with more surgery to come.

* * *

Why Me? was a tedious and predictable melodrama. A pretty nurse became "ugly" in an accident, had problems with her husband, and underwent surgery to remake her face. She rebuilt her life with the love and dedication of a saintly doctor. Most of all, she illustrated pluck and dignity as she courageously triumphed.

A little background on plastic surgery propped up this weak Pygmalion story. The script was constructed to build up to the first operation, which came one hour and twenty minutes into a two-hour story. There was no evidence of someone like Leola undergoing psychological counseling after such a trauma.

Why Me? was long, boring, and emminently forgettable despite good acting performances.

Fantasy Island / "Roarke's Sacrifice" / Apr. 21, 1984 / ABC-TV

Executive Producers: Aaron Spelling; Leonard Goldberg
Producer: Don Ingalls
Supervising Producer: Arthur Rowe
Writer: Don Ingalls
Category: Series Television — Fantasy Drama

* Orthopedic Disability
* Single White Female
* Equipment: cane

Plot: An ex-dancer, disabled by an accident, goes to Fantasy Island to be able to dance just one more time.

Julie Mars, an old flame of the mysterious Mr. Roarke, arrives on Fantasy Island. Mr. Roarke sadly watches her make her way off the seaplane and tells his assistant, Lawrence:

MR. ROARKE: I was responsible for her accident.

The cause of Julie's disability is described as an auto accident which occurred after a falling out with Mr. Roarke. Roarke suffers from guilt.

MR. ROARKE: I've always blamed myself for not stopping you.... I'm so sorry it happened.

Julie appears to be quite integrated in her new life.

> JULIE: And the only thing that's changed is that I walk with this cane.

Mr. Roarke grants Julie's fantasy and takes away her disability. She is able to dance. He watches her.

> MR. ROARKE: What a joy to see you happy again.

A Broadway promoter sees Julie dance and wants her to make a comeback in a one-woman show. Julie approaches Roarke and begs to be permanently cured. She uses pejorative language when she describes a man who watched her dance.

> JULIE: I was dancing. An old man with a cane was watching me. I remembered I was a cripple, too.

More offensive language appears when Roarke tells Julie he can make her cure permanent.

> JULIE: Then it's really true! I won't be crippled again!... I'm whole again!... I can't go back to that—the self-pity, the absolute despair in knowing I can never dance again.

Roarke cures her but to do so, must erase all her memories of their previous love. He renounces his own feelings for her in return for this miracle.

* * *

In "Roarke's Sacrifice," disability was a fate worse than death. The guilt aspect, the poor language chosen by the writer, the assumption life without dance was not worth living, all added up to typical fare. Julie constantly devalued her disabled self, indicating a person with an orthopedic difficulty was not "whole."

"Roarke's Sacrifice" was a "quick fix" piece crafted from sappy and tired formula.

Helen Keller: The Miracle Continues / May 30, 1984 / syndicated

Executive Producer: David Lawrence
Director: Alan Gibson
Writer: John McGreevey
Category: Made-for-TV Movie—Drama

* Blindness; Deafness
* Single White Female
* Face-feeling
* Based on a True Story
* Equipment: Interpreter
* Communication: Expressive—

speech/fingerspelling; Receptive —fingerspelling/tactile speech-reading

Plot: Helen Keller enters college and adult life.

* * *

Helen Keller: The Miracle Continues took up years after *The Miracle Worker* left off. The college life of the young woman was explored. She faced loneliness due to the communication barrier between her and her classmates. She was a social creature, craving conversation, attending dances, but really only knew the voices of the few who took the time to converse with her.

Special equipment was considered misused. Although as a conscientious teacher Anne Sullivan involved her pupil in everything, Helen was constantly talked over. Things were not interpreted for her—although a woman as bright as she would surely be aware of the "missing" conversational pieces.

A disturbing sequence involved Peter, a young man with whom Helen fell in love. He cared deeply for her and wanted to marry her. Helen was as elated as any young woman. Face-feeling was illustrated as Helen touched Peter's face for information on how he looked. However, Anne Sullivan and those who seemed to effectively control Helen's life, dissuaded Peter from his pursuit, expressing they had put too much work into her to let her throw away everything for love. Peter left and Helen was confused and heartbroken.

Helen Keller: The Miracle Continues presented a fair portrait of a woman who was both hearing and visually impaired, permitting the audience to see the personality, intelligence, and humor beyond that communication barrier. However, on the whole, it left only a minor impression.

Hotel / "Confrontations" / Sept. 12, 1984 / ABC-TV

Executive Producer: Aaron Spelling; Douglas Cramer
Producers: Joseph B. Wallenstein; Bill & Jo La Mond
Supervising Producer: E. Duke Vincent
Director: Henry Harris
Writer: James Fritzhand
Category: Series Television—Drama

* Elective mutism
* Single White Female

Plot: A young woman without speech runs away from her mother during a vacation at the St. Gregory Hotel.

A mother arrives at the St. Gregory Hotel with her strangely silent daughter, Andrea. The woman uses inappropriate terminology to describe her daughter's difficulty.

>   MOTHER: My daughter suffers from hysterical aphasia ... she's as helpless as a child.

Andrea gets out of the hotel and sees a street mime. She enjoys his silent communication. He passes the hat. She follows him to his place.

>   MICHAEL: You can't—

Andrea shakes her head no.

>   ANDREA [signing]: [Think you nice.]

>   MICHAEL: Sorry, never learned to sign.

The cause of Andrea's disability is described as a traumatic reaction to seeing her father burn to death in a car accident ten years previously. Michael's love and attention restore Andrea's voice, saving her from the institution in which her mother was planning to place her.

* * *

"Confrontations" bore a resemblance to both versions of *The Spiral Staircase,* in which a traumatic reaction to tragedy resulted in a loss of voice. The instant rapport Andrea felt with the mime was similar to *Clown White.* The mother's decision to place her intelligent daughter in an institution—when she obviously had bucks to spend on treatment, judging from a vacation at the ultra-posh St. Gregory—was reminiscent to the stepmother in *Cinderella.* In fact, this piece *was* a fairy tale. It just lacked the happy birds and smiling rabbits for support.

Jessie / title unknown / Oct. 23, 1984 / ABC-TV

Executive Producer: David Gerber
Producer: R.W. Goodwin
Supervising Producer: Stanley Kallis
Director: James Sheldon
Writer: Sy Salkowitz
Category: Series Television—Police Drama

* Severe burns
* White Male
* New Disability

Plot: Police psychiatrist Jessie Hayden has a new patient: a cop who has been badly burned.

Police officer Pat McLaughlin is ambushed by an arsonist. He is torched and catches on fire.

DOCTOR: Keep the blisters intact. Be especially gentle with his face.... There's not much he'll be able to do.

Police psychiatrist Jessie Hayden is handling McLaughlin's case. She looks him over, noting his burned face.

JESSIE: You are one ugly son-of-a-gun.

PAT: At least you don't blow smoke rings like the others.

Jessie is instrumental in helping Pat get back on the track again.

* * *

This episode of *Jessie* featured the familiar get-the-guy-back-on-the-track theme with a difference. Jessie was not merely a good friend with unerring common sense, but a trained professional whose job it was to help McLaughlin reason out what had happened to him. It was up to McLaughlin to do what he wanted with his life. Therefore, Jessie's work was not considered in the "non-disabled catalyst" mode. She was simply doing her job, which was counseling traumatized cops.

This episode also used technical assistance and contained some useful, factual information about serious burns.

This story bore a great resemblance to the 1976 *Police Story* episode entitled, "Firebird," also produced by David Gerber.

T.J. Hooker / "Lag Time" / Mar. 23, 1985 / ABC-TV

Producers: Mark Rodgers and Chuck Bowman
Co-Producer: Kenneth Koch
Supervising Producer: Rick Husky
Director: Sigmund Neufeld
Story By: William Keys
Teleplay By: William Keys and Rick Kelbaugh
Category: Series Television—Police Drama

* Orthopedic disability
* White Male
* Equipment: Braces and crutches
* Performer with a Disability

Plot: Sergeant Hooker and sidekick Romano are on the trail of a cop killer.

A cop-killing perpetrator is using a special kind of bullet. Hooker is hitting all of his information rats for help on finding the supplier. One of the people he approaches for aid is a man using crutches. The reluctant snitch identifies the bullets.

* * *

"Lag Time" casually featured a man with a disability as part of the scene in Hooker's precinct. His disability was purely incidental. His information for the cops was much more important.

Diff'rent Strokes / "The Special Friend" / May 4, 1985 / NBC-TV

Executive Producers: Martin Cohan and Blake Hunter
Producer: Bruce Taylor
Supervising Producers: Bob Brunner and Ken Hecht
Director: Gerren Keith
Writers: Bob Brunner and Ken Hecht
Category: Series Television—Situation Comedy

* Epilepsy
* Single White Female

Plot: Arnold and Sam are scared when a friend has an epileptic seizure in front of them.

Teenaged Arnold and little Sam hang out in the park where they are friends with Karen, a street artist. Mr. Drummond prefers the boys play with kids their own age. They go to tell Karen they can't see her anymore. To their astonishment, she falls to the ground and begins to twitch.

SAM: It's Karen! She's dying!

A cop calls for an ambulance. Sam and Arnold are distraught. At home, they try to describe to Mr. Drummond what occurred.

ARNOLD: Karen—she freaked out on us.

SAM: Yeah. Her body just went crazy. She fell down and flopped all over the ground.

Drummond realizes Karen had a seizure. He tells the boys they should be more understanding. He goes to the park himself to see Karen. She knows the boys are scared. She also indicates societal barriers have helped force her to become a street performer.

KAREN: Nobody wants to hire someone like me.... I used to be a kindergarten teacher ... I had a seizure in front of my class once. It was suggested I not come back because it scared the children. And you know what, it made sense to me so I quit.... I looked for a job for over a year ... everytime my employers got my references ... well, here I am.

Drummond wants Karen to explain to the boys that she is all right. Karen says the kids will only remember the seizure, not their friendship.

At home, Arnold and Sam make fun of Karen. Housekeeper Pearl is upset, ordering them to stop their cruel jokes. She admits she has epilepsy herself. She says she studied to be a legal secretary, but no one wanted to take her for a job. She convinces the boys to go and talk to Karen. Arnold becomes the non-disabled catalyst when Karen rebuffs their advance.

> ARNOLD: But what you're doing is wrong too ... it means you've given up ... you've told us you went to college. Is this what you went to college for?
>
> KAREN: It's the only thing I can do.
>
> ARNOLD: You don't know that.... Karen, there are organizations for people who have epilepsy. Our housekeeper ... told us these organizations are for counseling and job placement.... If you're not gonna try, you've lost me and Sam for friends.

Karen promises to try the placement center.

* * *

"The Special Friend" gets a few points for its sensitive exploration of a rarely seen problem on television. Karen's difficulties were dealt with on a simple level that was not threatening to viewers. However, when a teenager stepped in and blamed Karen for "giving up" and said he and his brother wouldn't be friends with her again until she tried, the piece plunged into formula and destroyed its integrity.

Pearl mentioned that although she loved being a housekeeper, she had studied to be a legal secretary—but was unable to get a job. Instead of looking at this as a discrimination issue, Pearl indicated not everyone was as "understanding" as Mr. Drummond when it came to hiring a person with a disability. Thus, an examination of an attitudinal barrier was ignored. And Mr. Drummond was elevated to a higher plane of humanity for his magnanimous heart.

"The Special Friend" illustrated a person with epilepsy as bright, talented, and attractive—but Karen's failure to have a regular job was due to her "giving up." Since she couldn't overcome society's hurdles, she was at fault for her failures. It took Arnold to help her see the light in true sitcom fashion—while ignoring a complex and pervasive social problem.

North and South—Pts. II, III, IV, V & VI / Nov. 3-10, 1985 / ABC-TV

Executive Producers: David L. Wolper & Chuck McClain

* Orthopedic disability
* Single White Male

Other Disabilities

Director: Richard Heffron
Story By: John Jakes
Writers: Paul F. Edwards, Patricia Green, Douglas Heyes, Kathleen A. Shelly
Category: Television Mini-Series — Period Drama

* Equipment: Cane
* New Disability

Plot: Northerner George Hazard and Southerner Orry Main become best friends at West Point Academy and manage to hold their friendship together during the years leading up to the Civil War.

George and Orry are sent to Mexico after graduation from West Point Academy to fight in the war. At Churubusco, Orry is wounded in the leg. A new disability is incurred. Orry is abed for months before getting to his feet on crutches. He is angry and sullen.

> ORRY: It won't get any better.

> GEORGE: It won't get any worse, either.

Orry is shipped home to Mont Royal, the family plantation in South Carolina. He walks with difficulty, using a cane. he becomes reclusive and begins drinking heavily. George stops to visit on his way home to Pennsylvania. He gets angry at Orry.

> GEORGE: All you can do is sit there and feel sorry for yourself.

Orry's leg shows improvement but remains stiff. He must use his cane. He is concerned about re-meeting Madeline, the married neighbor with whom he has a secret liaison.

> ORRY: I don't want you to feel sorry for me.

> MADELINE: I *don't* feel sorry for you. I still love you.

Orry continues to live his life, active in the saddle and running the plantation.

Years later, as the whirlwind of political rhetoric and events propel the country toward war, Orry undertakes a dangerous trip north to close out a business deal with old friend George. He tells George he's been offered a commission in the Confederate Army.

> ORRY: A brigadier with their new war department. I guess a bad leg is no handicap at that rank.

* * *

North and South illustrated a character who went on with his life without regard to his limitation. Orry initially experienced despair and devaluation over his "bad leg," but soon the problem was integrated within his life. He went on, paying little attention to his cane.

North and South presented a person with a disability as a concerned citizen in a difficult period of history.

Trapper John, M.D. / "Game of Hearts" Parts I & II / 1985 / CBS-TV

Executive Producer: Don Brinkley
Producers: Deborah Zoe Dawson & Victoria Johns
Director: Michael Caffey
Writer: John Whelpley
Category: Series Television — Medical Drama

* Multiple sclerosis
* Single White Female
* New Disability

Plot: Gonzo's new girlfriend is diagnosed as having multiple sclerosis.

After a spill from a bike caused by blurring vision, veterinarian Dr. Fran Brenner is examined by Dr. Gonzo Gates, her new boyfriend. All signs point to multiple sclerosis.

Frannie walks in on an occupational therapist discussing kitchen wheelchair access with a group of people with disabilities. After they clear out, Frannie sits in a wheelchair as if trying it on for size. She is frustrated in her attempt to fill up an ice cube tray, needing a long-handled ladle to reach the water faucet handles and being unable to carry the tray on her lap. The freezer door is too high from the chair and Frannie dumps the water all over herself.

Gonzo tries to be there for Frannie but she responds with angry devaluation.

> GONZO: Look Frannie, I know you're frustrated and you're angry.... I don't care what's wrong with you. It doesn't matter.
>
> FRANNIE: ...Maybe not today. What about tomorrow? What about when my eyes go? What about when my legs go? Are you going to be there to clean up the mess when my bladder goes? ... will you love me when you spend your entire life being nursemaid to me? Will you love me then?
>
> GONZO: Yes.
>
> FRANNIE: No you won't.

She tells Gonzo to leave her alone. Undaunted, he drags her along to a park where a busy picnic is going on. Frannie sees the banner announcing it is a gathering of the M.S. Society.

> FRANNIE: Oh. I see. Thank you. Rub my nose in it.

> GONZO: Why are you so quick to put yourself in permanent disability? ... you see anyone there feeling sorry for themselves?

They approach an artist welding another piece on a large metal sculpture. He says he used to paint landscapes and carve miniatures but has graduated to bigger pieces since his M.S. eye difficulties accelerated. He peers at Frannie. He acts as a disabled catalyst.

> ARTIST: You just found out, didn't you? Don't let it kill your will. M.S. is a cagey thief—but you can outfox it.

Frannie later approaches Gonzo.

> FRANNIE: That was a really dirty trick you pulled on me, leaving me at the picnic like that. It was manipulative, it was calculating—and it worked.

Frannie tells him that she loves him.

> FRANNIE: You were right. I *was* crawling into some hole of self-pity. But all those people with M.S., it was just the slap in the face I needed.

* * *

"Game of Hearts" was a routine wallow in anger, devaluation, and self-pity. With the love of Gonzo, Frannie would pull through. The only different aspect was the inclusion of a group of cheerful, happy picnickers who had M.S. to help Frannie come to terms with her new situation.

Actual people with disabilities were used in the background of "Game of Hearts." The supporting role of the occupational therapist was filled by an actress with a disability. However, "Game of Hearts" was old and dull.

A Time to Live / Oct. 28, 1985 / NBC-TV

Executive Producer: Judith A. Polone
Producer: Blue André
Director: Rick Wallace
Teleplay: John McGreevey

* Muscular dystrophy
* White Male Child
* Equipment: Wheelchair

A Time to Live

Based on the Book: *Intensive Care*
by Mary Lou Weisman
Category: Made-for-TV Movie—
Drama

Plot: A mother devotes her life to her ten-year-old son who has muscular dystrophy.

Peter Weisman's muscular dystrophy is diagnosed while still a toddler. A frightened Larry and Mary Lou Weisman are informed what this means by a physician.

> DOCTOR: Quite simply, it's the progressive atrophying of all the muscles. The disease is born with the baby, it grows with the baby. Even as the baby's muscles are developing, the disease is destroying them, turning them to fat.

Peter is overprotected and a source of constant worry. Mary Lou's obsessive attention and subsequent martyrdom when it comes to her son rule her life. She blames her husband for not doing enough; he, in turn, blames her for not sharing the difficulties. Mary Lou devotes herself to "Pocket" so fully that her other son, Adam, is virtually ignored. Attention is constantly shifted to Peter.

Father Larry advocates surgery for Peter. A special kind of operation will keep him out of a wheelchair for another year. He expresses an erroneous notion.

> LARRY: It's better than being a prisoner in a wheelchair.

* * *

A Time to Live was an "inspiring" drama about relentless "courage" in the face of adversity. In other words, it was played for every tear in the book. Very little emphasis was placed on the relationship or obligations between Peter and Adam. An interesting scene occurred when Adam, bragging about his excellent grades, was thoughtlessly put down by his mother. When Peter said he wasn't a genius like his brother, Mary Lou stepped in to tell Adam that grades weren't as important as being a good, kind person. Adam lashed out at Peter, knocking him down. He was chastised: "You can't do that to Peter, no matter how much you want to." It seemed there might be an interesting love/hate rivalry to be examined between the boys but the audience was not privy to it. Such omissions focused attention on Peter's physicality and ignored his feelings.

Peter's condition took him from an ambulatory state to an electric wheelchair. Naturally, the change was difficult for the family. However, the freedom afforded the boy and the greater range of exploration possible for him in a chair was never seen. The wheelchair was not a ticket to independent movement. It was a "prison."

Peter was a bright, animated boy with interests. He was very in tune with the world — although little attention was actually paid to his own development and accomplishments. The audience never learned much about his social life.

Accessibility was briefly discussed. At a theatre to see a live show, Larry was told Peter must sit in special wheelchair seating. Larry made an issue out of it and Peter was allowed to remain in the aisle. However, accessibility was not indicated as a social issue or a right. It was just another problem this indefatigable family battled.

Peter experienced some prejudice at school. He was not permitted to sit where he wished in the school cafeteria. He ran around with a protest sign on the back of his wheelchair but the issue was never resolved. Another school scene was troublesome. Some older tough kids locked the brakes to Peter's wheelchair, leaving him stranded in the hall. The boy was in a dour mood when he arrived home. Mary Lou never investigated the etiology of Peter's gloom. She cajoled him into a good mood by "spiking" his hair and setting him in front of his drums to bang along with a tape of a rock group. This subordinated Peter's personality and concerns. As long as he was smiling at home, Mary Lou felt all was well.

Weepy music dominated the soundtrack, manipulating the audience to tears at the ultimately tragic ending. *A Time to Live* was a cathartic work-out for the tear glands.

Hotel / "Saving Grace" / Dec. 4, 1985 / ABC-TV

Executive Producer: Aaron Spelling; Douglas Cramer
Producers: Henry Colman and Geoffrey Fischer
Supervising Producer: E. Duke Vincent
Director: Jerome Courtland
Story: Donna Pekkonen and Andrew Laskos
Teleplay: Andrew Laskos
Category: Series Television — Drama

* Wheelchair-User; Amputation — single arm
* Married White Male
* Equipment: Prosthetic hook
* Performer with a Disability

Plot: Two visitors at the St. Gregory include a dancer and her recently-disabled choreographer husband.

Jeremy Hall and Natalie Rogers, a famous choreographer and dancer husband-and-wife team, are visiting San Francisco. Jeremy is frustrated at himself while trying to choreograph. Poor language is used to describe his chair.

> JEREMY: How am I supposed to show [the dancers] what it should look like when I'm stuck in this iron maiden?

Jeremy is exceptionally bitter about his disability. He devalues himself to his wife.

> JEREMY: You had a wonderful career — till you started nursemaiding me.... What do you, pity me? Does that turn you on?
>
> NATALIE: I care about you. I want to help.
>
> JEREMY: Well then, you care more than I do. I'm not worth it.... Sorry. Why do you stay? Don't I embarrass you?
>
> NATALIE: How could I ever be embarrassed about loving a man?

The cause of Jeremy's limitation is described as a hit-and-run accident a year before. Natalie was the driver, unbeknownst to her husband. She stays with him out of guilt.

> NATALIE: I put him in that chair for the rest of his life. I can't ever leave him.

Jeremy indicates he is sexually inactive when his wife makes advances to him. Negative aspects are illustrated.

> JEREMY: You know, I can't give you what you want.... You're free to sleep with whomever you wish.

Drunk and angry, Jeremy starts to rape Natalie. The acts becomes a love scene. Natalie wakes up contented. Now sober, Jeremy devalues himself, displays bitterness and anger and every other ugly emotion.

> JEREMY: [You're] happy? Like a social worker and her charity case?... I'm sorry, Natalie, but from now on, I'm gonna get my physical therapy in the gym.

St. Gregory's Peter McDermott counsels Jeremy on how much Natalie loves him.

Natalie leaves Jeremy. The action catalyzes him. He slowly *walks* onstage at the theatre and admits he loves her and needs her.

* * *

"Saving Grace" had only one thing worth watching: the very brittle performance of the actor playing Jeremy.

Special equipment was misused. The wheelchair Jeremy used was a standard prop chair and not a chair with double pushrims that a hand amputee would use.

"Saving Grace" presented an exceptionally poor and damaging portrait of a person with a disability.

Magnum, P.I. / "I Never Wanted to Go to France, Anyway..." / Jan. 2, 1986 / CBS-TV

Executive Producer: Donald Bellisario
Producer: Chris Abbot-Fish
Co-Producers: Jay Huguely; Jill Sherman Donner
Supervising Producer: Charles Floyd Johnson
Director: Arthur Allan Seidelman
Writer: Reuben Leder
Category: Series Television — Detective Drama

* Facial scarring
* Single White Male

Plot: Thomas Magnum goes undercover at a traveling circus to find out who is killing off performers.

Private eye Magnum hires on as a maintenance man at a circus to find out who has been killing off performers. While working in the Tower of Terror, Magnum is startled by a man whose face cannot be seen in the dimness. The man dons a plastic hockey mask before emerging in the light. He introduces himself as Gus "The Geek" Zimmer. Gus's self-devaluation is evident in his introduction.

> GUS: I really wasn't trying to make you sick. It's the only place I can catch a few winks without people bothering me and I don't have to wear the mask.

The cause of Gus' disability is described as a bad fire. He devalues himself more when he tells Magnum why he remains with the circus.

> GUS: Not much of a retirement program [available] for geeks.

Magnum nails Gus as the criminal who killed performers and circus owner Inky Gilbert. He wants to know the reason.

> GUS: Why? You're askin' me why?

Gus removes the always-present hockey mask to reveal a face with scar tissue left from bad burns. His bitterness pours out.

Magnum, P.I.

> GUS: ...Take a good look. I had a fiancée and a job to come back to [after World War II]. When I took the bandages off and looked in the mirror, I knew it was never gonna happen. I didn't want to put anyone through the grief of having to look at me and smile and be brave and try to keep from throwin' up at the same time.

Gus was Inky's "silent partner" *and* his presumed-dead-in-the-war brother. He had "died" in Africa to spare his loved ones the pain of his diability. He claims he didn't kill Inky for monetary gain.

> GUS: What would a geek want with money?

Magnum reacts with a speech reminiscent of the non-disabled catalyst category.

> MAGNUM: Maybe some kind of real life ... where you don't have to drool and moan and chase live rats around three times a day ... where you can rent an apartment, watch TV, pretend you're just like everyone else.

Gus expresses Magnum is ignorant in these matters.

> GUS: But you don't know what it's *really* like. And unless you swallow a bucketful of fire ... someday, you never will.

A small-statured man was seen leaving the circus after another murder had occurred. Magnum's voice-over reverie revealed interesting stereotypical thoughts about the man, who was departing with another performer.

> MAGNUM [v.o.]: There's something disturbing and sad when you see something out of its normal element, like ... those carnies who have no idea that there's another world out there — much less have the ability to cope in it.

* * *

"I Never Wanted to Go to France, Anyway..." used an accident and outdated view of life within disability. Gus was bitter and angry. He felt his life could only be lived out as a "geek," hiding behind a mask which gave a frightening undertone to whatever was living behind it.

Magnum's comment about the small-statured carnie insinuated a circus was the only suitable place for a person like that to live.

"I Never Wanted to Go to France, Anyway..." featured *Phantom of the Opera* elements as well as suggestions from *Tomorrow Is Forever*.

A Fighting Choice / Apr. 13, 1986 / ABC-TV

Producer: Nelle Nugent
Director: Ferdinand Fairfax
Writer: Craig Buck
Category: Made-for-TV Movie — Drama

* Epilepsy
* White Male Teenager

Plot: A sixteen-year-old who wants a cerebral commissurotomy to stop his epileptic seizures takes his parents to court to permit surgery.

Sixteen-year-old Kellin Taylor is on an experimental drug program to curtail his daily Grand Mal epileptic seizures. Five months into the program, he has not had a seizure and is enrolled in public school for the first time. His history grades are bad and he is assigned a tutor, Suzy Fatelli. Kellin is attracted to the girl and makes a date to go jogging with her.

>   FATHER: Does Suzy know you're an epileptic?
>
>   KELLIN: I haven't had a Grand Mal seizure in five months, Dad.

He lies and tells his parents Dr. Tobin said jogging was fine. He also doesn't mention the small seizure he had at school.
That night, Kellin has a Grand Mal. He keeps it to himself — and misses his jogging date with Suzy. He admits to her why he stood her up. She is moved.

>   SUZY: I can't believe how hard it was for you to tell me that . . . Kellin, it's nothing to be ashamed of. . . .

Kellin tells her what exactly happens to him and what she should do if he has a seizure, such as making sure there are no breakables nearby. She shouldn't stuff anything in his mouth.
Dr. Tobin recognizes by Kellin's test that he had a Grand Mal. He tells the Taylors that Kellin has developed a resistance to the drug and will probably return to daily seizures after a time.
In a letter, Dr. Tobin tells Kellin's parents to reconsider the radical option of cerebral commissurotomy: separating the two halves of the brain to stop seizures. Kellin finds the letter and goes to see Dr. Tobin himself with Suzy in tow.
The Taylors will not permit the surgery. Kellin wants to sue his parents. He talks to a civil rights lawyer that visited his school. The suit nearly destroys the family, but Kellin wins the right to have surgery.

* * *

A Fighting Choice was a powerful drama that was compelling and emotional. Kellin's only option to stopping his daily Grand Mal seizures was surgery, which he would undergo as soon as he was eighteen. His parents expressed there was too much risk. But Kellin couldn't imagine living again with daily seizures. He recognized he was not permitted his due process and decided to go to court.

The story was very tight. It indicated Kellin's type of epilepsy was rare; therefore, commissurotomy was a last-ditch medical option. It discussed how to deal with a person having a seizure. Kellin's graphic seizures onscreen were quite educational. A great deal of information about the disability was imparted.

Still, there was room for more. Even though Kellin's first girlfriend was scared—she cared for him; his parents who had changed cities and jobs to allow Kellin to be closer to treatment loved him deeply, but vetoed surgery, afraid of losing him. Little brother Harvey was constantly pushed aside, not let in on what was happening until he confronted his parents. He wondered why a newspaper knew Kellin was suing his parents before he himself did.

Tying all of this together was an exploration of Kellin's right to pursue surgery. The courtroom portion of the drama was completely in Kellin's favor and in that way, a bit predictable, although fascinating. The father's acceptance of his son's victory was evident when he decided not to appeal the case.

Superfluous to the movie was the surgery scene, which was anti-climactic. *A Fighting Choice* dealt with rights—and not just a disability.

Trapper John, M.D. / "Going, Going Gonzo" / 1986 / CBS-TV

Executive Producer: Don Brinkley
Producers: Deborah Zoe Dawson; Victoria Johns
Director: Victor Lobl
Writer: John Whelpley
Category: Series Television—Medical Drama

* Hemiplegia; aphasia
* Single White Male; series regular
* New Disability

Plot: Dr. Gonzo Gates has a stroke.

Gonzo and his fiancée, Frannie, are planning on beginning a long-delayed vacation. After surgery on a basketball star, Gonzo collapses at the elevator.

> TRAPPER: He had a stroke ... bad heart valve started the whole thing ... he's going to pull through.
>
> FRANNIE: ...What about brain damage?
>
> TRAPPER: ...We'll know more when he regains consciousness.

Gonzo awakens and speaks garbled jargon.

> FRANNIE: He can't walk, he can't talk, he's here but he's gone. Can't you see it in his eyes? He's gone.

Gonzo initially works at therapy then gives up. Everyone at San Francisco General acts as a non-disabled catalyst.

> ERNIE: It's been two months now and some of us around here would like to see a change in attitude—particularly your fiancée. That's Frances—remember her?

Trapper comes in to see his protégé who is sleeping.

> TRAPPER: This all you gonna do? Sleep your life away? Come on, Gonz, how're you gonna make this any better for yourself? Talk to me!

Frannie comes in.

> FRANNIE: To hell with you, you stupid sick son-of-a—you lied to me. You told me you were gonna take care of me. You can't even take care of yourself.

Gonzo tells her he loves her. He gets back into his therapy with renewed vigor.

Gonzo checks out his basketball star patient. He looks at the X-rays and makes suggestions on treatment. Frannie is pleased at his recovery. It was important to her because:

> FRANNIE: I needed you to need me. ... the M.S.—I'm just not frightened of it any more.... I grew more and more dependent on you ... helping you fight back helped me fight back. We're not a crippled couple here. We're much stronger.

Gonzo is reinstated on the hospital payroll as the chairman of the in-house review board. However, as pleased as he is, he has an announcement to make.

> GONZO: What I really want is to be a surgeon again. That's just not gonna happen. I know that and I think you know that, too.

He and Frannie are going to get married and start anew in a different place.

* * *

"Going, Going Gonzo" was written to enable the actor who had been portraying the doctor for seven years an exit to pursue other projects. Thus, he sustained a disability that wasn't quite "cured" after an hour; but he wouldn't be around for the audience to see him live with it, either.

Gonzo had a marvelous recovery from his stroke. At the end of the hour, his speech was a little halting but clear; he had discarded a cane and was using his right hand quite well. The story stated more than four months had elapsed since his stroke; one wonders why his basketball playing patient was still in the hospital rather than recovering at home!

Although rehabilitation was mentioned and even showed via a few shots, the doctors and nurses who were friends of Gonzo did the most visible administering of treatment.

Frannie's inclusion in the segment where everyone figuratively slapped Gonzo in the face was technically that of a disabled catalyst. But, since M.S. was not specifically mentioned until well after that scene (and presupposing the audience had missed "Game of Hearts" where Frannie and her disability were introduced), she must be considered a non-disabled catalyst. She also was not speaking from her own experience.

"Going, Going Gonzo" was a teary wallow in melodrama. Gonzo's easy recovery, his reinstatement on the staff, and his fighting to overcome the odds placed this piece in the unimaginative and predictable category.

The Love Boat / "What's a Brother For?" / date unknown / ABC-TV

Executive Producers: Aaron Spelling; Douglas Cramer
Producers: Gordon and Lynne Farr and Henry Colman
Director: James Sheldon (?)
Writer: Tom Dunsmuir
Category: Series Television — Romantic Comedy

* Orthopedic disability
* Single White Male
* Equipment: Braces and crutches

Plot: Two brothers, one disabled and one not, take a cruise on the *Pacific Princess*.

* * *

"What's a Brother For?" was a routine approach to disability. The non-disabled brother suffered extreme guilt that he himself was not disabled. He tried to assuage that by spending as much time as he could with his disabled brother. Together, they played Scrabble, chess, and other games. When a woman entered the life of the non-disabled brother, his sibling manipulated him into feeling bad for not spending time with him. Eventually, the disabled brother saw the error of his ways.

"What's a Brother For?" indicated a person with a disability as overly cerebral, inactive, and manipulative.

Happy Days / "The Tall Story" / date unknown / ABC-TV

Executive Producers: Thomas Miller; Edward Milkis; Garry Marshall
Producer: Jerry Paris; Ronny Hallin
Director: Jerry Paris
Writer: Barry Rubinowitz
Category: Series Television— Situation Comedy

* Epilepsy
* Black Male Teenager

Plot: Roger tries to recruit a tall and talented player for the basketball team.

High school basketball coach Roger convinces Johnny, a talented player, to come to practice to try out for the team. Roger thinks the team has a good shot at winning with his unexpected new talent. Johnny tells him he can't play. Roger discovers the reason.

> ROGER: It seems that Johnny has epilepsy ... it's not a contagious disease.

Johnny's father is concerned that the boy may have a seizure while playing and embarrass himself and the family. Roger acts as the non-disabled catalyst and convinces the father that Johnny has a right to play a game in which he excels.

* * *

"The Tall Story" took a simplistic look at epilepsy by condensing it to a father's overprotectiveness versus a "forward-thinking" high school coach's better judgment. Little information was provided in the piece.

Multiple Disabled Characters

Pieces featuring more than one major disabled character in a single production.

Tell Me That You Love Me, Junie Moon / 1970

Producer: Otto Preminger
Director: Otto Preminger
Screenplay: Marjorie Kellogg
Based on the Novel by: Marjorie Kellog
Category: Feature Film—Drama

* (#1) Facial scarring
* (#2) Wheelchair-User
* (#3) Epilepsy
* (#1) Single White Female
* (#2) Single White Male
* (#3) Single White Male

Plot: Three disabled friends who meet in the hospital decide to move in together.

Warren, a young gay man who is a paraplegic, requests help from the hospital social worker. Junie Moon, a woman with a scarred face, Arthur who is an epileptic, and Warren wish to move in together. The social worker is skeptical.

> WOMAN: ...How would you manage? Cooking, cleaning, and laundry, just finding a place to live? Many people might refuse to rent to you.
>
> WARREN: They couldn't! We represent at least three different minority groups.

Junie Moon has her bandages removed. Warren and Arthur react when they see her. They swallow. Junie devalues herself.

> JUNIE MOON: Listen, I saw myself today and it's pretty gruesome. Let's call off this dumb plan ... you and Warren can live together. You don't need a freak like me.
>
> ARTHUR: We're all freaks. Don't try to steal the show.

Out of the hospital, Junie is unsuccessful in finding a place for them to rent. She is laughed at by children and stared at by would-be mashers. She recognizes the "housing shortage" as discrimination.

> JUNIE MOON: No one else will rent to us because of the way I look.

Junie's persistence finds them a small, old-fashioned bungalow. The fellows move in. Accessibility is briefly mentioned when Warren heads toward the bathroom.

> WARREN: Damn! Every bathroom door in America is a half an inch too narrow.

Arthur can't get his old job back. Poor language is used when it is described that he "had a fit" in the street and went to the hospital. He finds work at Mario's Fish Market, but Mario reneges when an anonymous phone caller terms Arthur "a lulu" and a sex pervert. Mario later hires Arthur back.

Mario likes Junie Moon. He bankrolls a vacation for the three, lending his truck and bankbook for them to go away to a hotel by the ocean. The three travel under the guise of being a reclusive society woman, her brother and her secretary. The hotel is inaccessible; Beachboy, a strong, well-built black man, carries Warren and his chair up the stairs. Beachboy later carries Warren by tossing him over his shoulder.

Arthur and Junie Moon fall in love.

* * *

Tell Me That You Love Me, Junie Moon was one of the most bizarre representations of disability ever filmed. The three characters had nothing in common except they all possessed a limitation and an inferiority complex. Junie was psychologically damaged by the abusiveness of a date who had hurt her by pouring battery acid on her. Arthur had been put into a state institution when young by his parents. Warren was a well-read and exceptionally bright fellow. Yet, their diverse personalities and backgrounds were ignored. They were lumped together as "disabilities" and nothing else mattered. All three expected little of themselves and of life—after all, they were "freaks."

Most outrageous and offensive was the mode of transport Beachboy used for Warren. He picked him up and slung him over his shoulder, Warren's head hanging down his back. Beachboy took him to restaurants and bars in this manner and Warren never said a disparaging word.

The three never gave any indication of wanting to go ahead in life. They accepted living in a beat-up old bungalow, putting up with the peeping eyes of a neighbor—which indicated again they saw themselves in a category of inferiority.

Tell Me That You Love Me, Junie Moon may have had some theatrical value as a story of three people with nothing else and nowhere to go who were drawn to each other. But as imagery of disability, it was maligned and damaging to the perceptions of the public at large.

Medical Center / "Albatross" / Nov. 3, 1971 / CBS-TV

Director: Ric Benedict
Writer: Rich Shapiro
Category: Series Television—
   Medical Drama

* (#1) Developmental Disability
* (#2) Wheelchair-User; paraplegic
* (#3) New Disability
* (#1) Single White Male
* (#2) Single White Male

Plot: A newly-disabled man is reluctant to have his mildly retarded brother tested.

Jonathan, a developmentally disabled young man, goes on an outing with his brother, Steve. His unbridled exuberance causes a car accident. Both are sent to the University Medical Center for treatment.

Steve is to be married in two weeks to Carol. She says she will take care of Jonathan after he is released from the hospital. Steve refuses permission for the doctors to test Jonathan, equating old tests with the new.

Steve develops complications that require surgery. Dr. Joe Gannon warns him that paralysis could result. Gannon explains the circumstances to Jonathan and patronizingly tells him to "be a good boy."

Chief of Surgery Paul Lochner reminds Gannon that Jonathan is not a child.

> PAUL: That "boy" is there is a fully grown, twenty-six year old man.

Steve's status has deteriorated. He has lost sensation and mobility in his legs. Gannon goes in to operate to relieve pressure on the spinal cord. A new disability is seen as Gannon's warning has become reality.

> JOE: Steve's awakened. He's—paralyzed from the waist down.

Erroneous information and pejorative language is conveyed through a disappointed Steve. He believes he can no longer care for his family.

> STEVE: I'll be in beds or a wheelchair for the rest of my life . . . they need me whole, not busted up like a puppet with the strings cut . . . no, I won't marry [Carol] now, not under these conditions.

Jonathan stays alone, makes his breakfast, washes the dishes, and puts them away. When Carol drops in, she is surprised to find he is capable of taking care of everything. However, she is not as sure about Steve. She hints he will not be an "appropriate" husband now.

CAROL: I always thought the man I married would take care of me, not the other way around.

Steve's bout with pneumonia leaves him more depressed. Gannon is the non-disabled catalyst, telling Steve how the blind and deaf learn to become self-sufficient. He accuses Steve of keeping Jonathan a kid.

Carol tells Joe she's not sure she can handle Steve's injury. But she's willing to try. She comes to take Steve home.

* * *

"Albatross" painted an interesting portrait of how love actively handicapped a developmentally disabled adult from achieving his potential. Jonathan was capable of many things his brother was not aware of. He indicated he had learned these things in school. It took the drastic accident and subsequent injury to help Steve see the light.

Steve was sent home from the hospital without being told of any kind of rehabilitation. Gannon's lecture on persons who are blind or deaf to a man who would be using a wheelchair was like comparing apples and oranges. The non-disabled writer's view portrayed all three disabilities as similar when each has its own separate set of difficulties and possibilities. Gannon's lecture also suggested Steve's future well-being was up to him, never indicating psychological counseling or rehabilitation procedures were available to him.

As a newly-disabled character, Steve certainly had little idea of his own potential; still, to relay such misleading information through him without a counterbalance left erroneous impressions. Steve felt he would be in a bed, felt he was a "puppet with the strings cut," and so on.

"Albatross" presented a different side of developmental disability and a staple image of a person experiencing paraplegia.

Beg, Borrow ... Or Steal / Mar. 20, 1973 / NBC-TV

Producer: Stanley Kallis
Director: David Lowell Rich
Story: Grant Sims and Paul Playdon
Teleplay: Paul Playdon
Category: Made-for-TV Movie — Drama

* (#1) Wheelchair-User; paraplegia
* (#2) Amputation; double hand
* (#3) Blindness
* (#1) Single White Male
* (#2) Single White Male
* (#3) Single White Male
* Equipment: (#2) Prosthetic hooks; (#3) Mobility cane, Braille

Plot: Three disabled roommates pull off a museum heist.

Attitudinal barriers are seen when Cliff Norris, a man who ably performs tasks with prosthetic hooks, is dismissed from a trial job position as an electronics assembler.

CLIFF: I know what he's saying. He's saying, "He's too slow. Insurance rates will go through the roof." Ramsey had rocks in his head for giving me a chance in the first place.

Les is blind, operating a small key-duplicating business in a kiosk near the beach.

Vic Cummins, a man using a wheelchair, is also out of work. Laid off from his job as security consultant for the soon-to-be-open Franklin Museum, he plots a museum robbery, intending to sell plans for a heist to pros. The money will keep open the laundromat the three men own. But the pros turn down the plans as too risky.

Desperate for money, Vic contemplates the roommates doing the job themselves. He appears somewhat vengeful at the turn of events and uses offensive language when told the plan doesn't make sense.

VIC: Our lives barely make sense. All three of us put together barely make one man.

Cliff is also guilty of using poor terminology when reacting to Vic's suggestion the roommates pull off the heist.

CLIFF: Vic, three top [professional crooks] turned it down because it was too tough—three *whole* human beings.

Les indicates a shred of vengeance when he reluctantly joins the escapade.

LES: ...Every time we reached out, we got kicked in the teeth. I think [society] owes us that chance. And I think we have the right to collect.

After successfully pulling off the crime, the three are approached by Hal, a guard at the museum. He has figured out who broke in and confronts the men.

HAL: ...if you're counting on a twelve-handkerchief jury, forget it. You don't give those stones back, they'll throw the book at you.

His friend the D.A. says if three handicapped fellows pulled off a crime just to prove a point and give back the booty, the court will go easy on them. Vic indicates that their disabilities lessen the crime and devalues the group again.

VIC: Oh, there's a lot of glory in putting *us* away.

The men decide to give the stones back. Hal, the guard, co-signs a bank loan so they can reopen the laundromat.

* * *

Beg, Borrow ... Or Steal was a rather creative movie despite its stereotypical imagery. Vic was athletic—although his rope-climb up the side of a three story building to break into a museum window seemed to be stretching it a bit. He was shown driving a car although his hand controls were never seen.

Cliff's character was the most interesting, due to the dextrous use of prosthetic hooks a non-disabled actor wore over his own arms. He performed fine motor tasks in sequences that were interesting and educational, such as doing assembly work, depressing a shutter on a camera, threading a needle, and finally, excavating the jewels from the "Great Captain" statue.

Les was the only one illustrated as having outside interests. In his case, ice skating was a sport he took great pleasure in and did well.

Beg, Borrow ... Or Steal attempted to make the point that three unique persons were fighting a system that would not let them succeed. However, their angry methods of achieving their just due in society cut this story down to more routine—although entertaining—disability fare.

Buck Rogers in the 25th Century / "Return of the Fighting 69th" / Oct. 25, 1979 / NBC-TV

Producers: John Gaynor & David J. O'Connell
Director: Philip Leacock
Writer: David Bennet Carren
Category: Series Television—Science Fiction

* (#1) Deafness
* (#1) Communication—Receptive: Speechreading; Expressive: Sign Language
* (#1) Deaf Performer
* (#2) Amputation; single hand
* (#2) Prosthesis Used as Weaponry
* (#3) Facial scarring
* (#1) Single White Female
* (#2) Single White Female
* (#3) Single White Male

Plot: A deaf slave girl helps Buck Rogers foil an evil plan to destroy the Earth.

Roxanne Trent, a woman with an artificial metal hand, orders her deaf servant Alicia to groom her. When Alicia is slow to reply, Roxanne uses her prosthesis as weaponry and grips Alicia's arm. Roxanne exhibits anger and bitterness.

> ROXANNE: You think I'm hideous. You think you're better than me because you have two normal hands.

Commander Corliss, Roxanne's lover, is a man with a scarred face. A metal plate fitted with a bulbous magnifying eye is attached to his head. The cause of his and Roxanne's disabilities are described as results of Colonel Wilma Deering's attack on them three years previously. Revenge is seen as a motivating factor.

    CORLISS: We're going to pay them back.

The old freighter is loaded with twentieth-century nerve gas that will destroy the Earth in three days. Captain Buck Rogers and Colonel Deering join the retired 69th Marine Space Squadron who can pilot them through the asteroid belt hiding Corliss' ship.
    Roxanne uses her prosthesis to intimidate Alicia. She puts a hole through a wall while swinging at Alicia. She takes Alicia's cherished memory globe with pictures of her family inside and shatters it with a squeeze.
    Buck and Wilma are captured by Corliss' fighters. Corliss and Roxanne face Wilma and Buck. Corliss is bitter.

    CORLISS: That's right—you haven't seen your handiwork, have you?

Roxanne nearly crushes Wilma's hand in her own while Alicia looks on. Buck has noticed something and signs to Alicia, discovering she is deaf. She was taken prisoner five years ago. Buck tells her he learned sign language "a long time ago."
    Alicia helps Buck and Wilma escape captivity. They get in their ship just before the 69th squadron destroys Corliss' base in a bombing raid.
    Buck throws a party for the squadron where he reunites Alicia with her parents. While searching for the family, he did something else. Cure looms in Alicia's future.

    BUCK: I also dropped by the medical directory. Alicia's scheduled for electronic surgery next month. A little retraining, she'll be able to hear in no time at all.

    *   *   *

"The Return of the Fighting 69th" used a deaf character as a menial who "doesn't have the mind" for communication as the short-sighted Roxanne put it. Roxanne and Corliss were living cartoon characters but were noted for the traits they had that also exist in more traditional drama.
    Alicia was a sensitive young woman, always dreaming of home. Her quick-thinking saved Buck and Wilma from certain death. She was a "happens-to-be" character. The role did not depend on deafness.
    Roxanne and Corliss were exaggerated villains. Roxanne enjoyed being cruel and using her prosthesis to keep up a good front. Both she and Corliss hated the way they were and wanted to destroy the entire Earth as revenge for their situation.
    "Return of the Fighting 69th" utilized a deaf character in a small role with

little regard toward deafness. It also illustrated others who'd survived a traumatic injury as ones who were mentally unstable. Despite cartoon overtones, this piece differed little from other dramas.

Code Red / "Dark Fire" / Nov. 15, 1981 / ABC-TV

Story: Ray Brenner
Teleplay: Jackson Gillis
Category: Series Television — Rescue Drama

* (#1) Blindness
* (#2) Wheelchair-User
* (#3) Deafness
* (#2) Performer with a Disability
* (#3) Deaf Performer
* (#3) Communication: Expressive — Sign; Receptive — Speechreading
* (#1) Single White Female
* (#2) Single White Male
* (#3) Single White Female
* Equipment: Braille, wheelchair ramp, mobility cane, hydraulic lift van, TDD

Plot: An unscrupulous real estate entrepreneur is trying to force people with disabilities out of their living center.

Fire Chief Rorchek is called to the scene when a bus blows up in front of a community home for people with disabilities.

> RORCHEK: Every single person in there is handicapped in some way.

A fireman rushes in to evacuate the residents. In the kitchen, he finds a woman calmly taking muffins out of the oven.

> FIREMAN: You can't hear me — you can't speak.

None of the residents are seriously injured, although Kathy, a blind young woman, must spend time in the hospital. Young Ted Rorchek, son of the fire chief and a firefighter himself, is attracted to Kathy. His natural uneasiness is banished by Kathy's vivacity.

> KATHY: Have you ever been with a blind person?... Just relax.

Ted is rapidly falling in love with Kathy. He takes her out but she holds back at romancing him. He's concerned.

> KATHY: [You think I'm] holding off because I'm not attracted to you? ... I am ... but until this blind girl learns to handle this seeing world ... I can't let anyone [be my eyes].

Mr. Melton, the heavy who is trying to run the disabled people off the property, returns. Kathy has remained home alone to work while the rest of the residents are out, enjoying a sports event with a group of firemen.

Melton has a can of gasoline. He slips down the stairs, unconscious. Kathy hurries out. The gasoline spills and drips into the heater and explodes. Kathy is quick and resourceful, getting a blanket with which to cover Melton. She reads the Braille number of the fire department on the telephone and calls for help. She drags Melton outside.

TED: You saved his life.

KATHY: Some days I get lucky, I guess.

* * *

"Dark Fire" was an interesting but disjointed piece. It had some good points; at times, it was terribly silly.

A group of people with various disabilities were illustrated in a group situation. They seemed to be one big, happy family.

Kathy was a warm and intelligent character. She had a buoyant personality that attracted Ted Rorchek and rightly so. She indicated she had been blind since she was a little girl; it was a little curious that she indicated she needed basic independent living instruction. She misused special equipment, using her mobility cane in the house.

A supporting character was Victor, a young man using a wheelchair. Danny Rorchek adopted him, winning a bet when Victor shinnied up the firemen's pole at the station. It was a heavy-handed "let's-show-them-what-the-disabled-can-do" type of situation.

Inclusion of a deaf person in such a living center was questionable. The community home was not illustrated as a center for independent living, but a *home* for people with disabilities. A deaf person with a communication difficulty did *not* belong there (the others did not seem to belong, either).

After the bus explosion, firemen began evacuating the place. A fireman rushed into the kitchen where the deaf woman was calmly reaching into the oven. The explosion would have sent shock waves through the house the woman should have felt. Her lack of awareness also precluded the possibility that she had residual hearing and heard the bomb. She was also unperturbed to find a full-rigged fireman standing behind her, continuing to take the muffins out before turning to the firefighter as if saying, "Now, what was it you wanted?" It became a variation of the almost-getting-killed scene, expressing a deaf person was in imminent danger.

"Dark Fire" had some good educational information within its disabled-persons-as-victims story.

Little House: A New Beginning / "Marvin's Garden" / Jan. 23, 1983 / NBC-TV

Executive Producer: Michael Landon
Producer: Kent McCray
Director: Michael Rhodes
Writer: Michael Landon
Category: Series Television — Period Family Drama

* (#1) Brain-injury; aphasia
* (#1) White Female Child; series regular
* New Disability
* (#2) Blindness
* (#2) White Male

Plot: A doctor with failing vision helps a little girl with a brain-injury.

Old Doctor Marvin's eyesight is failing to the point he knows he will no longer be able to practice medicine.

A group of kids plays at the nearby swimming hole. Jenny loses a locket in water and goes to look for it. She gets stuck under some tree roots and fails to surface. One of the boys saves her.

Jenny can walk, but is left with speech problems and motor problems "due to lack of oxygen." Laura and Almanzo take Jenny to the city to see another doctor. The prognosis is uncertain. Laura cries to Almanzo.

Doctor Marvin's sight is so poor he can't pass the physical Doc Baker wants to give to him. He is forced into retirement. Marvin putters in his garden. He becomes a disabled catalyst, telling Laura that Jenny could come and help him. She could walk over. He understands her difficulties and she can help him locate things he cannot see.

* * *

"Marvin's Garden" was just another of this series' "heartwarming" contributions to television history. Jenny was an unfortunate little girl who, instead of playing with her friends, retreated to the protective security old Doc Marvin could give her. In the long run, it was better for her since Laura tended to be oversolicitous to the girl after her injury.

The two became friends. Jenny's discovery of a bird with a broken wing that Marvin mended seemed to be a metaphor for the two of them. "Marvin's Garden" expressed that while there was life ahead for both of these characters, it would tend to be quiet and gentle.

The A-Team / "Water, Water Everywhere" / Apr. 24, 1984 (rerun) / NBC-TV

Executive Producer: Stephen J. Cannell
Producer: John Ashley

* (#1) Wheelchair-User
* (#2) Amputation; single leg
* (#3) Amputation; single arm

Supervising Producer: Jo Swerling, Jr.
Director: Arnold Laven
Story: Sidney Ellis
Teleplay: Sidney Ellis and Jo Swerling, Jr.
Category: Series Television — Action Adventure

* Equipment: Prosthetic hook, prosthetic leg
* (#1, #2, #3) Performers with Disabilities
* (#1) Single White Male
* (#2) Single Black Male
* (#3) Single White Male

Plot: The A-Team aids a group of Vietnam vets battling a greedy land developer who is trying to force them off of their land.

Jamie, Les, and Dave, three disabled men, are renovating the Stagecoach Inn in Deadwood, an old ghost town. Their dream is to turn it into a resort. However, Mr. Gaines, a developer who owns most of the county and its politicians, is trying to force the men to sell. After they are beat up by Gaines and his toughs, they call on the A-Team.

The A-Team assists them in tapping into the artesian well underneath the land so that Gaines' plans to dry and burn them out are for naught.

* * *

The only interesting thing about "Water, Water Everywhere" was the fact that three actors with disabilities were able to add to their résumés and pick up a paycheck.

Although it could easily be stated that the A-Team was the non-disabled catalyst in the lives of three entrepreneurs, it must also be noted that the *raison d'être* for *The A-Team* was to help anyone being trampled by corrupted villains. These victims, for reasons unknown, never went to the proper authorities for help. They relied on the strongarms and firepower of the underground A-Team.

"Water, Water Everywhere" was a picture of three men with disabilities who wanted to keep a dream alive — and did so with the aid of the A-Team.

Highway to Heaven / "One Fresh Batch of Lemonade" Pts. I & II / Oct. 24–31, 1984 / NBC-TV

Executive Producer: Michael Landon
Producer: Kent McCray
Director: Michael Landon
Writer: Dan Gordon
Category: Series Television — Fantasy Drama

* (#1) Amputation; double leg
* (#2) Wheelchair-User
* (#1) New Disability
* Equipment: Mouthstick
* (#2) Performer with a Disability
* (#1) White Male Teenager
* (#2) Single White Male

Plot: Angel Jonathan Smith and his mortal sidekick's latest mission is to help a teenaged amputee get back into life.

Multiple Disabled Characters

PART I

Star high school baseball player Deke Larson, Jr., hotdogs on his motorcycle after a game. He is struck by a pick-up truck and loses both legs below the knee.

Angel missionary Jonathan Smith and his mortal helpmate Mark get jobs at the rehab hospital where Deke is recuperating. Deke Larson, Sr., sees his own dreams go up in smoke with his boy's disability. He cannot face the teenager.

Deke's cheerleader girlfriend visits and reports that everybody sends hello. Bitterness is evident in Deke's reply.

DEKE: Everybody? Every *able*-body?

Jonathan acts as a non-disabled catalyst by reminding Deke he is not a "cripple" as he terms himself. He can use a wheelchair. Jonathan brings a book for Deke to read.

JONATHAN: It's about a guy like you — handicapped.

The book is *Eleanor and Franklin*.

In the therapy room, Deke sits morosely. Scotty, a quadriplegic, sits nearby. He reads, using a mouthstick to turn the pages of the book. He knocks the book over. He asks Deke to pick it up for him. Deke replies he can't.

SCOTTY: Hey man, ain't you got arms?

Scotty is taking law classes in preparation of his bar exam.

Mark goes to see Deke Larson, Sr., and details the younger Deke's progress.

MARK: He'll be up on crutches any day now.

DEKE SR.: Some kind of progress.

Eleanor, a high school girl, brings Deke his homework. Deke uses devaluation and pejorative language when questioning her duties.

DEKE: Are you doing a report on cripples or something?

PART II

Deke gets his prosthetic legs. Despite improved mobility, he feels sorry for himself. He is bitter as he talks to Eleanor who has become a friend.

DEKE: You finally got a boyfriend who couldn't run away from you.

Jonathan has convinced Deke he still has a future in athletics. Deke begins training in men's gymnastics to perform on the horse. He discovers his coach is the person whose truck hit him. More bitterness pours out.

> DEKE: This is the "Let's Feel Sorry for Deke" club, isn't it?

Scotty acts as a disabled catalyst for Deke.

> SCOTTY: Throwin' away what I'll never have—it drives me crazy! ... (if I had use of one arm) I wouldn't have to have some nurse wipe me when I go to the bathroom.... I am more than the parts of my body that don't work.

Scotty is nervous about his bar exam. Jonathan reminds him non-disabled guys are scared, too. Despite his realistic front to Deke, Scotty indicates shaky thoughts about himself.

> SCOTTY: Sure they are, but they're different.... I'm not like everybody else.

Scotty passes the bar. And Deke will compete in a gymnastics meet. He hopes his father will come.

> DEKE: I'm gonna show him I'm still a winner.

Mark informs Deke Sr. his son will compete. Mr. Larson uses bad language in response.

> DEKE SR.: ...a freak show ... a crippled gymnast.

Mark and Scotty attend the meet. Jonathan railroads Mr. Larson into attendance. Deke begins his routine and falls. The audience sits in stunned silence. A proud Mr. Larson rises and starts to applaud. He is finally able to accept his son's difference.

* * *

"One Fresh Batch of Lemonade" was intended to be inspirational. However, pure repetition of plot from similar pieces rendered it long and stale. The story did offer a fresh aspect in the character of Scotty, a forward-thinking and ambitious young man who was moving ahead with a severe physical limitation. Educational information was delivered within the story as Scotty was seen propelling his own chair. He was shown turning the pages of a book, using the simple instrument of a mouthstick. He was intelligent and had a nice sense of humor. When embarrassed by a patronizing man in a restaurant who wanted to buy him a drink, his anger was held in check although he indicated jokingly he was glad he had restrained himself. "I damn near asked him to step outside." He was an appropriate catalyst for the angry teenager.

Other than the introduction of the to-be-semi-recurring character of Scotty in this popular series, the story was dry.

Actual performers with disabilities were seen in the background.

"One Fresh Batch of Lemonade" was an uninspired "triumph over disability" and a "quick fix" piece. If Deke could be an athlete again, he would be fine (see *Highway to Heaven* — "A Match Made in Heaven," "The Monster," and "A Special Love" for the chronological appearances of Scotty).

Mask / 1985 / Universal

Producer: Martin Starger
Co-Producer: Howard Alston
Director: Peter Bogdanovich
Writer: Anna Hamilton Phelan
Category: Feature Film — Drama

* (#1) Unique facial configuration
* (#2) Blindness
* Face-feeling
* (#1) White Male Teenager
* (#2) White Female Teenager
* Based on a True Story

Plot: The uncommon love between a drug-using biker mother and her uniquely disabled son binds them together.

Rocky Dennis is a teenaged rock 'n' roll lover who has a large face so startling that others think he wears a mask. His head has grown large and disproportionate. His drug-using mother, Rusty, takes him to his new school to enroll him in the ninth grade. Social barriers are in evidence.

> MR. SIMS: This is a public junior high school, Ms. Dennis. There are special schools — with wonderful facilities that might be more appropriate for his needs.
>
> RUSTY: ...Do you teach Algebra and Biology and English here?
>
> MR. SIMS: Of course.
>
> RUSTY: Those are his needs.
>
> ROCKY: ...Don't worry, Mr. Sims. I look weird but otherwise, I'm real normal. Everything'll be cool.

Rocky fits into his new school and begins to make friends. His extracurricular hours are often spent with his pal Ben. The two are saving money to take a motorcycle tour across Europe.

Rusty's drug use bothers Rocky and he does all he can to get her off of the substances. She is too much for Rocky to bear. He leaves for the summer, working as a counselor's aide at a camp for blind children.

At camp, Rocky meets and immediately falls for Diana, a blind teenager who is a horse wrangler. Since she was born blind, Rocky's attempt to describe things frustrate her. The sighted writer's point of view is evident when Diana asks Rocky to describe himself. After fudging, he tells her:

> ROCKY: ...I've got this real strange disease and it makes my face look unreal.

Diana reaches out to touch his face. He stops her.

> DIANA: Come on, Rocky, don't be a chicken.

Face-feeling is seen as she touches his cheek, forehead, chin—

> DIANA: You look pretty good to me.

The sighted writer's viewpoint is again prevalent in a scene set in the camp kitchen. Rocky gets a rock from the freezer and another from the fridge. He puts the "freezer" stone into her hand.

> ROCKY: This is blue.

> DIANA: It's freezing! It's blue?

> ROCKY: This is green.

> DIANA: Rocky, I think I understand.

Rocky gets another from a pan on the stove.

> ROCKY: Now, this is red.... And when it cools down, it'll be pink.

> DIANA: Rocky, I understand!

Rocky's teenaged dreams come true when Diana kisses him. He is brought back to reality when her parents come to pick her up from camp and see him. They try to rush Diana away.

Rocky's disease creeps up on him. After seeing Diana and finding she still loves him, Rocky dies.

* * *

Mask presented a character who was a well-rounded human being despite a rare and misunderstood disability. Rocky collected old baseball cards, was bright and personable, and planned his motorcycle trip. He was a person far and beyond his mostly cosmetic limitation.

Rocky was an attractive character who garnered the support of the audience by warrant of his warm personality and gentle sense of humor. He confronted attitudinal barriers every day and recognized the unfairness of them.

Diana was fiercely independent. She loved horses, cared for them and indicated she had one outside of camp. She had no difficulties about her limitation. Her parents, she noted, were a problem.

Disappointing in this film was the color scene (see *Simon and Simon,* "I Heard It Was Murder," for another version of this segment). It was a predictable sighted writer's fantasy scene.

Actual children with disabilities were used in the background of the camp segment, all metaphors of innocence since they did not judge Rocky by his appearance.

Mask presented a fair portrait of a youngster with a severe disability as well as one of a young blind woman.

The Twilight Zone / "Healer" / Oct. 11, 1985 / CBS-TV

Executive Producer: Philip de Guere
Producer: Harvey Frand
Supervising Producer: James Crocker
Director: Sigmund Neufeld
Writer: Michael Bryant
Category: Series Television — Fantasy/Occult

* (#1) Wheelchair-User
* (#2) Deafness
* (#2) Communication: Expressive —n/a; Receptive—Sign
* (#1, #2) Cure
* (#1) White Female Child
* (#2) White Male Child

Plot: A burglar steals a "healing" stone from a museum and becomes a faith healer.

John "Jackie" Thompson finds that the stone he burgled from a museum has strange healing qualities. He heals a wound he receives from thugs and revives his dead huckster/promoter friend, Harry, after a heart attack. Under Harry's guidance, Jackie hits the faith-healing circuit and becomes a smash, due to his record of successful cures.

A young girl in a chair is brought to "Brother" John. The cause of her disability is discussed as the result of being hit by a car three years earlier.

JACKIE: All that concerns us is seeing Amanda walk again.

Jackie warms up his audience and uses negative imagery to gain their sympathy and support for Amanda. He looks skyward for supplication.

JACKIE: [Don't let this child spend a lifetime unable to experience the simple joy] of a walk through the new-mown grass....

Jackie's stone, hidden in his palm, glows and heals Amanda.

Even Jackie is impressed by this feat. He uses poor language when he and Harry discuss the show later on.

JACKIE: That little lame kid was something, huh?

A deaf child is brought to John backstage before another show by his mother.

MOTHER [in voice and sign]: He can't hear. He was born deaf.

HARRY: Oh, you poor child.

An odd mystical man appears and tells Jackie he has misused the power of the stone by turning its goodness to personal gain. It now refuses to glow. Jackie's old wound comes back and he is dying. He gives the stone to the deaf boy and the child heals Jackie. Jackie then uses the artifact on the boy's ears. Another cure is evident as the kid smiles and gazes in wonder. The process is complete as he understands everything that is said to him. Jackie relinquishes the stone to the mystical man.

* * *

"Healer" used tired pictures that seemed as if they were lifted from a charity telethon: the poor, helpless children, doomed to a tragic life. The story required healing to be dramatically effective and in that sense, use of a disabled child and a deaf child could not be a point of criticism. The small usage of the children gave no indication that they were capable of being happy, healthy kids without running through the new-mown grass or having hearing.

There was a lack of careful thought from the writer about what sudden hearing would bring into the life of a child born without it. If the boy were miraculously cured, the world would present a noisy, frightening, and unintelligible cacophony, which he would be unable to decode or understand. Of course, such reality would have destroyed the concept of this story. Still, such approaches are never seen. The boy was born deaf and, unto himself, he was perfectly normal. The child's entire life could have been ruined by a cure his mother had hoped and prayed for. The avenues for such exploration are endless.

"Healer" was a story that required miraculous cures to work. It required a baseline audience acceptance that disability or being deaf was inferior to their own concept of physical or sensorial "normality." It also perpetuated disability and being deaf as eternal tragedies.

Highway to Heaven / "The Monster" Parts 1 & 2 / 1985 / NBC-TV

Executive Producer: Michael Landon
Producer: Kent McCray
Director: Victor French

* (#1) Facial birthmark
* (#2) Blindness
* (#3) Wheelchair-User
* (#2) Cure

Writer: Dan Gordon
Category: Series Television — Fantasy Drama

* (#1) Single White Male
* (#2) Single White Female
* (#3) Married White Male
* Face-feeling
* Equipment: Mobility cane; Hydraulic lift van; Personal care attendant

Plot: Apprentice angel Jonathan Smith and his mortal sidekick have a double mission: to help prove a man with a "monstrous" birthmark on his face did not attempt murder and to get quadriplegic Scotty's marriage back on the track.

PART I

Rachel McCulloch's introduction to her aunt's new handyman, Jonathan, is bristling. The young blind woman's statements allude to hypersensitive perception.

> RACHEL: I hope you can do your work quietly. Blind people have sensitive hearing, you know that.

Jonathan is fixing up her little cottage. Rachel imparts erroneous aspects about being blind.

> RACHEL: I have absolutely no interest if this room gets a fresh coat of paint of not.

Blindness as a lightless condition is reinforced when Rachel discovers a lamp on the table.

> RACHEL: Jonathan, I'm blind.... Ergo, I don't care about the color of the walls or how many lights you put in this place.... I don't plan on entertaining this season. I'll tell you where I want the furniture and then I want you to bolt it down, or nail it, whatever.

Scotty, a lawyer who is a quadriplegic, blames lack of clientele on his disability. Marital stress ensues.

Rachel meets Julian Bradley, a young man with a large birthmark covering half his face. He is the town "monster," remaining in his dark and shuttered cottage except at night. The two are attracted to each other. To discourage Rachel's fear about the community's legend about Julian-the-Monster, the young man says his name is "Clark." Face-feeling is illustrated.

> RACHEL: Could I touch your face? Please—it makes it easier to talk to someone if you know what they're like.

Julian is captivated when Rachel declares he is "handsome." The two agree to meet for dinner at Rachel's; Rachel suddenly orders her handyman to paint and light up the cottage.

Highway to Heaven

Scotty and Diane argue after Scotty accuses Diane of fooling around. They separate.

At dinner, Rachel tells "Clark" she will have an operation that may restore her sight. He is angry and admits he is Julian. He devalues himself, assuming if she can see, she will shun him like all the rest. He runs off. Rachel follows him into the woods and stumbles, falling down a hill. Police find Julian bending over her unconscious form and arrest him for attempted murder.

PART II

Despondent, Scotty rolls his wheelchair into a swimming pool, determined to end his misery. He is rescued by angel Jonathan, who acts as the non-disabled catalyst by lecturing him. Jonathan tells Scotty he *has* a case—the defense of Julian Bradley.

In cheap manipulation, District Attorney Thrasher uses every pejorative in the book to catapult audience support to Rachel's corner with his opening statement at the trial.

> THRASHER: The victim was blind, helpless—she was not able to see, as you are, the monster who loomed before her ... the one victim who lived in a world of darkness and when he found her, like a fiend from a horror movie ... he attacked her.... The defense will attempt to show you that this poor blind girl, did, in fact, care for Julian Bradley.... And I submit to you that this is a perversion of the very notion of love....

Scotty begins with a statement to the jury. His notes fall and are replaced upside down. Composure shot, he is undone by a severe bout of muscle spasms. At a recess, he is depressed. Diane approaches him and tells him she loves him. Confidence restored, Scotty continues the trial. Attitudinal barriers are touched upon.

> SCOTTY: If Julian didn't look the way he looks, and if the medieval legends about him hadn't sprung up in this town, he wouldn't be here.... There *is* a monster in this room.... It's prejudice.

Scotty wins the case and Rachel regains consciousness. Doctors have operated and restored her sight.

Diane and Scotty mend their differences. They are reunited and plan to celebrate the new caseload the trial has generated by trying to conceive a child.

Julian refuses to see Rachel. She pushes her way into his house and assures him she loves him even though she can see him. Julian joins her for a walk in the sunlight.

* * *

"The Monster" had it all. It was a contrived piece, utilizing outmoded concepts about disability to propel the story. It was a close relative to *The Light That Came,* a theme seventy-six years old!

All three characters with disabilities were portrayed as bright, articulate, intelligent people; Scotty indicated a severely disabled person is capable of practicing law and having children; Julian was an artist; however, the negatives heavily outweighed these attributes.

Rachel's blindness was a clumsy metaphor for innocence untainted by visual prejudice; therefore, the love between Julian and her seemed false. Scotty's lack of faith in himself, and his marriage falling victim to his anger, were intended to illustrate that his problem was the attitudinal barriers that prevented clients from seeking his legal advice. But his attempted suicide clearly indicated emotional difficulties that, by law of TV averages, *had* to be associated with his physical limitation. His muscle spasms in court seemed associated with his fear and devaluation, not physiological happenstance.

The case against Julian was so loaded it was embarrassing to watch. It was hard to sit through this piece without cringing — or laughing.

"The Monster" was supposed to be a heart-tugger. Instead, it featured little that was new, innovative, fresh, or even remotely interesting.

Just the Way You Are / 1985

Executive Producer: Jerry Zeitman
Producer: Leo L. Fuchs
Director: Edouard Molinaro
Writer: Allan Barns
Category: Feature Film — Drama

* (#1) Orthopedic disability
* (#2) Amputation; single leg
* (#1) Single White Female
* (#2) Single White Male
* Equipment: Leg brace; Prosthetic leg; Skiing outrigger

Plot: A flutist who walks with a brace on one leg replaces her brace with a cast at a ski lodge in Europe to see what it's like to be "normal."

Susan Berlanger, a professional flute player, had viral encephalitis as a child and wears a leg brace. Devaluation is evident when she is incredulous that a guy has fallen for her. She has a running phone romance with Jack, the fellow at her answering service. More devaluation is evident as she constantly turns down the opportunity to date him. An attitudinal barrier is seen when Jack poses as the "Gorilla Gram" man to finally meet Susan. When he sees she is disabled, he leaves without revealing his identity.

Susan is exceptionally self-conscious about her brace. She gets an idea. She cancels a couple of her European recital dates. She wants a doctor to put a cast on her leg. She will go to Switzerland for a vacation at a prestigious ski lodge and pretend to have a broken leg. The doctor worries she is taking an "emotional risk" but thinks it is an "ingenious idea."

In Switzerland, she becomes friends with François Rossignol, who has a limp from a long-ago auto accident. At a party, she is afraid to dance with an attractive racer and has to be forced out onto the dance floor. She finds she can dance and begins to enjoy herself. Her facial expressions draw the eye of Peter, a photographer who is neglecting his ski-bunny girlfriend while paying attention to Susan.

Peter approaches her with prints of his photos, saying her face is hiding some secret. He is intrigued and wants to know more. Susan and Peter are taking the tram to the top of the moutain when François hops on, revealing he is a leg amputee. Peter stares sadly.

PETER: How did you lose it?

François looks down at his leg.

FRANÇOIS: Lose what? Oh my *god!* Where is it?

Nicole, Susan's roommate at the ski lodge, is attracted to François but rejects him. Susan asks why, since Francois has "everything."

NICOLE: Everything—except two legs.

Nicole admits it is her problem. Susan can't believe it would matter. It brings to mind the ruse she is perpetrating on everyone—especially Peter.

The vacation ends and Susan's cast is removed and replaced with her leg brace. Peter discovers what secret Susan has been harboring and still wants to be with her.

* * *

Just the Way You Are was a very superficial look at a difficult problem. Susan was a healthy, intelligent, and talented young woman. With a burgeoning musical career and European recital dates, she should have been on top of the world. However, the old standby, devaluation, stepped in.

Had Susan recognized that it was other people who made such a big thing about her disability—and perhaps had some type of wager or challenge going, the trip to Switzerland to compare a "non-disabled" experience with her average, everyday life would have been interesting. But, as usual, the problem was her own and her ploy was, in fact, running away from the notion that attitudes around her caused her difficulties. The only way Susan could be herself was to hide her own reality and try to be something and someone she was not.

The peripheral character of François was a busy and active young man. He was wealthy and quite a jet-setter. Susan seemed amazed that Nicole should be concerned about his missing limb, which she shouldn't have been. Susan wanted to deny her own limitation; why should another person's rejection of a disability surprise her? The story might have hung together better had the realization about François been a catalyst in her own life. She might have emotionally supported him and realized the two of them were just citizens of the world like the rest. Unfortunately for Susan, this never happened.

Another interesting misconception in this film was stated by the doctor. He claimed Susan was taking a "risk" by pretending to have a temporary limitation rather than her lifelong one. What was the risk? That Susan might discover she was an average person upon whom society had erected a few barriers?

Done correctly, *Just the Way You Are* could have been a type of *Gentleman's Agreement* film. As it was, it was a below-average romance.

Highway to Heaven / "A Special Love" Parts I & II / Sept. 24–Oct. 1, 1986 / NBC-TV

Executive Producer: Michael Landon
Producer: Kent McCray
Director: Michael Landon
Writer: Dan Gordon
Category: Series Television — Fantasy Drama

* (#1) Wheelchair-User
* (#2) Developmental Disability
* (#1) Married White Male
* (#2) White Male Child

Plot: A developmentally disabled youngster joins the Special Olympics in order to be adopted by Scotty and Diane Wilson.

PART I

Mark and Jonathan are going to stop off to see Scotty and Diane. Their new assignment is a coaching job at the Special Olympics.

Scotty and Diane have been frustrated in their attempts to have a child. Scotty visits the hospital.

> SCOTTY: When you're in a chair, you wonder what other parts don't work the way they should.

Diane learns *she* is the one unable to have children.

Jonathan works to get young Todd Bryant into the Special Olympics. The boy lives in a home with other developmentally disabled children. Todd is not interested and devalues himself.

> TODD: I'm not good at nothin'. I'm dumb.

Scotty and Diane decide to adopt. The couple comes to the training area for the Special Olympics. Todd has been convinced to try out for the games. He comes and meets Scotty. Scotty gives Todd the baseball cap he would have given to his own little boy. He wants Todd to run fast for the both of them. Diane is taken by Todd. She wants to adopt him even though he is approaching adolescence. Scotty doesn't like the idea.

Todd says he will win his Olympics heat to prove he is worthy of Scotty's love. Scotty pulls back, afraid the boy is getting too attached. Besides, his natural parents won't give him up, even though they haven't seen him since he was a baby.

PART II

On the day of the meet, Scotty agrees to be at the finish line for Todd. The boy loses the race.

TODD: I didn't win. I wanted to show you that I could do stuff because I wanted [you to be my dad].

Scotty invites Todd to come home for the weekend with him and Diane. Todd hugs Scotty when Scotty indicates he can't use his arms to hug Todd. Both Scotty and Diane want Todd.

Jonathan goes to see Todd's biological parents, who feel a quadriplegic wouldn't be a good guardian. They take court action to bar Scotty and Diane from contacting their son. The older Bryant son discovers for the first time that he has a brother and confronts his mother.

MOTHER: Your brother is retarded. He is one of the tragedies of my life. He will never get better ... he is in one of the finest facilities in the state ... better than some cripple could give him.

With Scotty's aid, Todd sues his parents. He must undergo a competency hearing.

Unbeknownst to Todd, his natural parents are at the hearing. He performs well and they relinquish him to Scotty and Diane.

* * *

"A Special Love" was another "heartwarming" disability story. The recurring character of Scotty was a large plus in this episode. In this, his fourth outing on *Highway to Heaven,* he grew considerably. His disability was virtually incidental to the story. He was a disappointed man who wanted a child. Todd wasn't the one he anticipated but he fell in love. He worked hard to teach the boy everything he could.

The Special Olympics sequence was nicely done, but by the time it aired, the Special Olympics seemed in danger of becoming a stereotype in stories about developmental disability.

Actual developmentally disabled children were utilized in the episodes.

"A Special Love" was predictable and forgettable.

Endnote

It took nine months to pull together eleven years of a collection. Upon finishing, I have one reaction: I can't believe the repetition.

A friend was recently in a meeting with a man who is the executive producer of a popular network show. A script revolving about disability was being discussed. My friend saw it and found the piece was "the same old stuff." He casually suggested to the producer that if this maladjusted character were presented, it might be nice to balance the role with another disabled person who had successfully assimilated his/her own limitation. The producer looked bored. "I don't believe in that kind of censorship," he replied.

In the fall of 1986, one major studio in Southern California was trying to find a deaf actress to play the part of a deaf woman who wants to hear music. Another studio was discussing a remake of *Johnny Belinda*.

Since completing the manuscript, I have seen perhaps fifty new disability pieces on television—most discovered through random channel-switching. A blind woman begged for a cure from a man she thought was a healer. In another story, a recently-disabled dancer wanted to leave her wheelchair and dance again. A hearing-impaired teacher helped out a series star; he, in turn, brought a new electronic device to her deaf students to enable them to "hear."

Does it ever end?

All of these pieces would be welcome if they resembled reality in some way. The hit comedy *Kate and Allie* introduced "Louis," a developmentally disabled man in the spring of 1986. He was featured in three new episodes in 1987. He was explored as a very real person. *L.A. Law* introduced "Benny," a developmentally disabled office worker. But why are these the exceptions to the rule?

I met with a friend who is also a producer. I asked him if he thought a disability had been featured very often on television. He responded, "No, I don't think so." I'll never forget the look on his face when I showed him my basic reference list. He flipped through the pages one by one, his eyes getting bigger by the minute. He looked up at me. "Now I see there's been a hell of a lot."

Believe me, there has been. I feel like I've seen *every* piece ever made about disability. Fortunately, I haven't and that's probably why I enjoy a degree of sanity. But I've been collecting for eleven years. Yes, there have been changes. The most welcome is the increased usage of performers with disabilities or deaf actors onscreen. And on television, commercials have featured people with disabilities as a part of life, part of a consumer public who enjoy hamburgers, jeans, beer, and new cars. This positive trend is heartening.

For once, episodic television and movies should take a cue from the commercials.

LAURI KLOBAS
Pacific Palisades, California

Appendix: Additional Disability-Related Productions

Series Television Episodes

BLINDNESS

(1960) *Wanted: Dead or Alive* (title unknown).* A dying blind man who wants to see his son before he dies does not realize his "son" is an imposter.

(3/22/62) *Rawhide* "Incident of the Child Woman."* Trail boss Gil Favor is temporarily blinded in an ambush by villains.

(10/5/62) *Rawhide* "Incident of the Portrait."* A thief who joins the drovers' train is worried when he sees the person he is to drive is the young woman whose house he just robbed — but finds out she is blind.

(1962) *The Rifleman* (title unknown).* Mark meets a blind man looking for the man he feels was responsible for his blindness.

(1968) *The Mod Squad* (title unknown). Linc Hayes falls in love with a blind poetess.

(1968) *Ironside* "The Light at the End of...." Chief Robert Ironside must protect a blind witness to a crime.

(1968) *The Wild, Wild West* "The Night of the Sabatini Death." Blind Sylvia Nolan is the key to the murder of Mr. Sabatini.

(1968) *Bonanza* (title unknown). Little Joe is temporarily blinded in a nitro blast.

(10/5/69) *The Bold Ones* "What Price a Pair of Eyes?" A woman whose sight is sacrificed in an operation to save her life becomes the perfect test subject for new electronic sensory aids being developed. Actual blind children appear in the background.

---

*An asterisk indicates a program shared with me from the collection of Michael Bryan Kelly, M.A., Ph.D.

Appendix: Additional Disability-Related Productions

(11/30/69) *Lassie* "More Than Meets the Eye." Lassie helps a frightened blind girl learn confidence. Actual blind children appear in the episode.

(3/3/70) *Marcus Welby, M.D.* "The Merely Syndrome." A young blind man and woman both undergo surgery to restore their sight. When the fellow regains his sight, the still-blind girlfriend fears losing him.

(4/14/71) *Medical Center* (title unknown). Dr. Joe Gannon is temporarily blinded.

(1973) *Longstreet* "Leave the Wreck for Others to Enjoy." Blind insurance investigator Mike Longstreet combats depression about his limitation by being the disabled catalyst for a self-pitying, embittered, blind young man. Actual blind children appear in the background.

(1974) *MacMillan and Wife* (title unknown). Police commissioner Stewart MacMillan calls on the blind musician son of a famous tobacco expert to help identify a blend of tobacco found at the scene of a crime. A performer with a disability appears in the role.

(1974) *Kung Fu* (title unknown). Caine utilizes the services of a blind man to locate a hidden cave he recalls from childhood. A performer with a disability is cast in the role.

(6/1/77) *Charlie's Angels* "The Killing Kind." Female undercover detectives help a blind man.

(1977) *Big Hawaii* "Blind Rage." An embittered blind man holds Barrett's niece Karen hostage as he prepares retribution for Barrett "causing" his disability.

(1/26/78) *Police Woman* "Blind Terror." Policewoman Pepper goes undercover as a blind woman to protect the blind witness to a crime.

(6/17/78) *The Young and the Restless.* David, an old flame of Jill's, shows up with a new fiancée who is blind.

(1978) *Starsky and Hutch* "Blindfold." Dave Starsky feels responsible for a woman blinded as a result of a stray bullet fired during an undercover operation — not realizing she was in on the crime.

(1980) *Buck Rogers in the 25th Century* "The Guardians." A strange box with which Buck has been entrusted causes strange dreams. Colonel Wilma Deering's nightmare of becoming blind is temporarily true.

(1980) *Fantasy Island* "Nona." A blind man has a fantasy: to be able to see in order to track down the missing movie star he has loved for years.

(11/12/84) *Scarecrow and Mrs. King* "Brunettes Are In."* Mr. Sinclair, the blind head of a charity for which Amanda King is working, isn't what he seems.

(2/22/86) *Fortune Dane* (pilot, pt. II).* A blind airport fruit vendor supplies keys to lockers used by criminals for transferring drugs or dollars.

(date unknown) *The Rifleman* (title unknown).* Lucas is temporarily blinded when a load of blasting powder goes off in his face. A vengeful enemy sees his chances of getting even have never been better.

(date unknown) *Rawhide* (title unknown).* Gil Favor is framed for horse stealing. Blind sheriff Tom Wilson is one of the suspects who stole Favor's $50,000 from the jail's safe. Has an early version of a *Wait Until Dark* type scene where Tom's wife, Clara, douses the lamp so Tom and a villain are on equal terms in a dark barn.

(date unknown) *Rawhide* (title unknown).* Wishbone faces temporary (hysterical) blindness.

(date unknown) *Mission: Impossible* (title unknown). Special agent Jim Phelps masquerades as a blinded FBI agent.

(date unknown) *Marcus Welby, M.D.* (title unknown). A diabetic teenager neglects necessary treatments and loses her sight.

(date unknown) *Night Gallery* "Witness Within." A story involving a blind woman.

WHEELCHAIR-USERS

(3/31/61) *Rawhide* "Incident of His Brother's Keeper."* Rancher Paul Evans who uses a wheelchair is losing his wife to his brother.

(ca.1959–1963) *Laramie* (title unknown).* Jess Harper offers help to rancher Bryan James, a man in a wheelchair.

(1963) *Rifleman* (title unknown).* After a fall from a horse, Mark McCain cannot use or feel his legs.

(ca.1963–1964) *Route 66* (title unknown).* When three girls find out a rich man is looking for a young woman who needs financial help, they jump into wheelchairs to garner his sympathy.

(1963–1964) *East Side, West Side*. Social worker Neil Brock organizes a group of paraplegics. They are concerned — their friend Sam claims he knows a doctor who can make him walk.

442   Appendix: Additional Disability-Related Productions

(1964) *Bonanza* "The Miracle Maker." A charlatan claims he can help a young woman who uses a wheelchair to walk again.

(1973) *Search for Tomorrow*. Doug Phillips is left a paraplegic after an auto accident. He becomes a quadriplegic after he and his wheelchair are hit by a car.

(1978) *The Young and the Restless*. After surviving temporary paralysis from a gunshot wound, conniving Mrs. Chancellor fakes a disability after her recovery to garner love and sympathy.

(1980) *Little House on the Prairie* "Dearest Albert, I'll Miss You." Albert Ingalls doesn't tell his new pen pal Leslie that he is short and unathletic—and Leslie doesn't tell him she uses a wheelchair. An actress with a disability appears in the role.

(1981) *The Incredible Hulk* (title unknown). David Banner becomes a paraplegic and finds that the strength of his alter-ego, the Hulk, helps him recover.

(2/23/84) *Simon and Simon* "Under the Knife." Detectives Rick and A.J. Simon set out to prove a man suing for malpractice is not actually paralyzed.

(11/25/84) *Trapper John, M.D.* "A Fall to Grace." Chief of Surgery Trapper John McIntyre is temporarily paralyzed by Guillain-Barré Syndrome.

(date unknown) *Rawhide* "Incident of the Dark Side of the Street."* A character witness for the family whose son was lynched is a man in a wheelchair.

(date unknown) *Marcus Welby, M.D.* (title unknown). A vibrant and talented young woman is left paraplegic after surviving a bout of meningitis.

(date unknown) *Hawaii Five-O* (title unknown). Steve McGarrett is on the trail of an embittered Vietnam vet in a wheelchair who's planting bombs and shooting people.

DEAFNESS

(1970) *The Man and the City* (title unknown). Mayor Alcala helps a deaf couple fighting discrimination—they are being denied the right to adopt a hearing child. A deaf actress and a native speaker signer play the parents.

(1970) *Night Gallery* (title unknown). A deaf woman speechreads of a murder plot across a smoky room.

(1/14/71) *Matt Lincoln* (title unknown). Young, "with it" psychiatrist Lincoln treats a famed concert pianist who goes deaf.

(1972) *Medical Center* "Wall of Silence." Dr. Gannon believes that deaf teenager Kyle is hysterically deaf.

(1973) *Search for Tomorrow.* Matt has fallen in love with Melissa, a deaf woman. A deaf actress appears in the serial role.

(1974) *Medical Center* (title unknown). Dr. Joe Gannon treats a rock star who loses his hearing.

(1974) *Harry O* "Silent Kill." Offbeat cop Harry Orwell helps a deaf man framed for arson. A deaf actor appeared in the role; actual deaf children seen in the background.

(1974) *Marcus Welby, M.D.* "A Child of Silence." A little deaf girl runs away, fearing an operation that could restore her hearing.

(1974) *Emergency!* (title unknown). Paramedics Gage and DeSoto are called to a supermarket where a deaf woman has gone into labor.

(1975) *Streets of San Francisco* (title unknown). Inspector Stone faces possible deafness for an hour.

(1976) *Mary Hartman, Mary Hartman.* Cathy Shumway's new boyfriend Steve is deaf. "Well," sighs her mother, "at least they won't fight."

(11/12/77) *The Red Hand Gang* (title unknown). The Red Hand Gang, youthful neighborhood crimebusters, welcome deaf Holly to their ranks. Features an "almost-getting-killed" scene.

(1977) *Westside Medical* (title unknown). A deaf woman has her hearing restored and wonders if she can share both the deaf and hearing worlds. A deaf performer appears in the episode.

(1977) *The Bionic Woman* "The Vega Syndrome." An alien probe has affected everyone at a military base—except Jamie and a deaf teenager.

(5/31/78) *America 2-Nite* (title unknown). "Ronnie Matlin," a deaf puppeteer, takes the stage with his signing puppet while Barth and Jerry act as voice interpreters for those who are, "unfortunately, not deaf." Features a deaf performer.

(1983) *General Hospital.* Luke, recuperating from an injury, is intrigued by a young deaf boy he sees in the hospital's physical therapy room. Features a deaf performer.

444   Appendix: Additional Disability-Related Productions

(date unknown) *The Rifleman* (title unknown).* Mark begins to teach Jake's deaf daughter Abby how to read and write.

AMPUTATION

(1953) *China Smith* "The Night the Dragon Walked."* Opportunist China Smith comes across an amputee beggar on a wheeled platform with a tin cup as he tries to discover who is threatening his friend.

(4/2/65) *Rawhide* "The Empty Sleeve."* Years after losing an arm in the Civil War, Tom Cowan faces the young wife who believed he was dead, telling her it was for her benefit he never came back.

(1976) *Hallmark Hall of Fame* "Peter Pan." Captain Hook uses his prosthesis to threaten and maim.

(10/1/83) *Cutter to Houston* (debut). The doctors treat a man who loses his arm in an oil rig accident.

(1983) *Matt Houston* "Here's Another Fine Mess." Houston is on the trail of two killers who do a Laurel and Hardy lookalike act — whose "Laurel" is a man with a prosthetic arm.

(date unknown) *Medical Center* (title unknown). Dr. Gannon treats J.K. Rutledge, a baseball star who has just lost his leg.

DEVELOPMENTAL DISABILITY

(1959) *The Rifleman* (title unknown).* Davy Pardee is the developmentally disabled brother of an escaped outlaw who joins his brother in a life of crime.

(1960) *The Rifleman* (title unknown).* Reuben Miles, a "slow in the head" fast draw and crack shot, is taken advantage of by his mentor.

(1960) *Bonanza* "The Ape." Hoss befriends a developmentally disabled man who is as big and strong "as an ape."

(9/21/65) *Rawhide* "Walk into Terror."* Developmentally disabled Jerry Boggs is constantly manipulated by ex-miner Ed Rankin.

(2/3/71) *Medical Center* "Secret Heritage." Dr. Gannon believes he can help a developmentally disabled young woman in an institution.

(1973) *Medical Center* (title unknown). A developmentally disabled delivery boy falls in love with a cardiac patient at the hospital.

(2/2/74) *All in the Family* "Gloria's Boyfriend." A developmentally disabled grocery store boxboy teaches Archie Bunker a lesson.

(5/6/76) *Harry O* "Portrait of a Murder." Harry sets out to prove a 19-year-old developmentally disabled youth did not commit a murder.

(1977) *Baretta* "Buddy." Tony Baretta befriends a young man with a developmental disability who is blamed for his mother's murder.

(10/7/78) *The Incredible Hulk* "Rickey." David Banner encourages the brother of a developmentally disabled young man to put his sibling in school.

(1/19/84) *Simon and Simon* "Bloodlines." The responsible stableman at the Diamond C thoroughbred ranch where Rick and A.J. are investigating the disappearance of a horse is developmentally disabled—or is he?

(1985) *Hill Street Blues* "An Oy for an Oy." Officers Hill and Renko assist a developmentally disabled man who is out on the streets.

(date unknown) *The Rookies* (title unknown). A young man with a developmental disability witnesses a murder, but is unable to tell the police about it.

SMALL-STATURE

(1956) *Superman* "Mr. Zero."* Small-statured Martian Mr. Zero uses his "freeze finger" to help Superman capture crooks.

(1961) *Rawhide* "Incident of the Prairie Elephant."* "Shorty," a circus performer, runs the circus after the owner gives him the organization.

(2/13/67) *The Monkees* "Monkees at the Circus." A small-statured man is a member of the circus the Monkees try to help out of a slump.

(9/29/67) *The Wild, Wild West* (title unknown). Dr. Loveless is—dead? His uncle, Dr. Leibknict bears a startling resemblance to the nemesis of James West.

(10/2/67) *The Monkees* "Monkee Mayor." The baby in a baby carriage poised for candidate Mike's kiss turns out to be a small-statured man in a bonnet.

(1977) *Charlie's Angels* (title unknown). Bosley has caught the eye of an aggressive small-statured woman when he and the "angels" go undercover at the circus.

(date unknown) *Bonanza* "It's a Small World." A small-statured man turns to theft when social prejudice bars him from a job (see *Little House: A New Beginning,* "Little Lou" for an updated version of the same story).

446   Appendix: Additional Disability-Related Productions

OTHER DISABILITIES

(1949) *The Lone Ranger* (title unknown).* Ex-con Clem Jones, a man with a disabled arm, is framed for robbery.

(1956) *The Lone Ranger* (title unknown).* The Ranger is tracking down the outlaw brother of a Civil War veteran without a voice.

(2/7/57) *Playhouse 90* "The Miracle Worker." A dramatization of teacher Anne Sullivan's preliminary work with pupil Helen Keller.

(2/20/59) *Rawhide* "The Incident at Barker Springs."* New drover Lance Ford mysteriously wears a neckerchief over his face all the time.

(7/10/59) *Rawhide* "Incident of the Roman Candles."* An outlaw with a disabled leg seeks revenge on a bounty hunter whom he blames for his disability.

(1960) *Rifleman* (title unknown).* Mark C's throat was slashed by kidnapping Indians and he lost his voice. He now "speaks" with a knife since a knife took his voice.

(1961) *The Rifleman* "The Wyoming Story"—Parts I & II.* Lucas goes undercover as a U.S. Marshal and stalks out crooked Indian Agent Ross, a man with a large X-shaped scar where one eye used to be.

(1/20/61) *Rawhide* "Incident of the Broken Word."* A bitter, angry woman who walks with a cane is a suspect in a murder.

(1/5/62) *Route 66* "To Walk with the Serpent."* Buz and Tod help stop a crazed man with a disabled right hand and arm from blowing up an audience at a political rally.

(5/16/63) *Rawhide* "A Woman's Place."* A peripheral character, the Mayor's wife, plans to leave her husband before he learns of her disability, a creeping paralysis.

(5/1/66) *Perry Mason* "The Case of the Positive Negative."* A man with a limp is a suspect in Perry's current murder case.

(10/5/67) *Cimarron Strip* "The Blue Moon Train."* "Dum Dum" is a non-speaking villain helping an ex-con free a group of convicts on a prison train.

(1976) *Police Story* "Firebird." A cop whose hands and face are severely burned in a helicopter crash fights to return to his job (see *Jessie* for updating of this story).

(6/1/78) *Barnaby Jones* "Shadow of Fear." A boy without speech helps Jones nab a villain who has kidnapped Betty.

(1978) *The Waltons* "Grandma Comes Home." Grandma Walton returns home from the hospital after a stroke has left her partially paralyzed and aphasic. An actress with a disability is used for the role.

(date unknown) *Marcus Welby, M.D.* (title unknown). A painter sees her artistic career and marriage going up in smoke as she faces multiple sclerosis.

(date unknown) *Marcus Welby, M.D.* (title unknown). Throat cancer and a laryngectomy mean the end of an air traffic controller's career.

(date unknown) *CHiPs* "Blabbermouth." CHP officer Bonnie's stuttering CB radio pal is the only person who can determine if her car accident was caused by hallucination.

(date unknown) *Little House on the Prairie* "Town Party, Country Party." A sprained ankle gives Laura an idea of what life is like for a schoolmate with a club foot.

MULTIPLE DISABLED CHARACTERS

(1958) *Zorro* (title unknown).* Zorro's non-speaking helpmate Bernardo pretends to be deaf to uncover the plot being hatched by a fake blind beggar.

(1976) *The New Avengers* "Target."* An arm amputee jungle expert is given a fatal dose of curare by a small-statured villain.

Feature Films

BLINDNESS

(1935) *Magnificent Obsession.* A rich playboy becomes a surgeon after his reckless ways cause a woman's blindness. Remade in 1954.

(1942) *Saboteur.** A man who has escaped from custody for a crime he did not commit finds refuge in the home of a blind man.

(1942) *Eyes in the Night.* A blind detective aids two women.

(1944) *Dead Man's Eyes.* A man who said he would bequeath his eyes to a blind man for a transplant operation is murdered.

(1951) *On Dangerous Ground.* A young blind woman affects a tough cop.

(1951) *Night Without Stars* (British). A partially-sighted lawyer becomes involved with a murder on the Riviera.

(1956) *The Betrayal* (British). A blinded ex-pilot vows to locate the voice he heard, the traitor who cost four men their lives.

(1969) *80 Steps to Jonah*. A camp for blind children changes the life of a drifter wanted by the police.

(1980) *If You Could See What I Hear*. Based-on-a-true-story account of blind singer Tom Sullivan's life.

(1984) *Blind Date*. A man who is blind regains the ability to see with the help of a technological implant.

(1984) *Splash!* Alan, the man who's fallen in love with a lovely woman-cum-mermaid, must chastise her when she snatches pencils from the tin cup of a blind beggar on the streets of New York.

WHEELCHAIR-USERS

(1931) *City Streets.** A kindly man helps an orphan who uses a wheelchair.

(1937) *Moonlight on the Range.** A no-good has his eye out for Wendy, a young woman whose father uses a wheelchair.

(1937) *Roll Along, Cowboy.** A woman may lose her ranch—and her only chance to pay for an operation for her son in a wheelchair.

(1941) *The Officer and the Lady.** A woman won't marry the policeman she loves for fear he will end up in a wheelchair just like her ex-cop father—who is kidnapped by the man who disabled him.

(1943) *Song of Texas.** Roy Rogers and Trigger pay a visit to children with disabilities in a hospital ward.

(1946) *It's a Wonderful Life*. Crochety old miser Potter who makes George Bailey's life miserable is a man using a wheelchair. Played by an actor with a disability.

(1948) *Last of the Wild Horses.** A rancher who uses a wheelchair is victimized by his hired hands.

(1948) *The Dead Don't Dream.** This entry in the Hopalong Cassidy series features Hoppy and sidekicks staying in a town where mysterious deaths have occurred. Hoppy suspects innkeeper Potter, a man in a wheelchair, as the evil culprit.

(1951) *When Worlds Collide*. Angry and bitter Sidney Stanton is a millionaire in a wheelchair. He will pay any price to buy a berth on the spaceship trying to escape the doomed Earth.

(1960) *Sunrise at Campobello*. Up-and-coming politician Franklin D. Roosevelt works to succeed in his chosen profession after surviving polio.

(1978) *The Other Side of the Mountain — Pt. II*. The continuation of *The Other Side of the Mountain* takes Jill Kinmont into a marriage.

(1981) *For Your Eyes Only.* * An evil man in a wheelchair has it out for Agent 007 and learns a deadly lesson in the opening of this James Bond film.

(1983) *Twilight Zone — The Movie.* * A nasty boy with frightening powers gets angry at his sister and "wishes" her into a wheelchair.

(1986) *Peggy Sue Got Married*. One of Peggy Sue's confidantes is a woman in a wheelchair.

DEAFNESS

(1932) *The Man Who Played God*. A concert pianist who loses his hearing spends his lonely days in his apartment, speechreading people in the park through binoculars and sending them money. Based on a play and an old silent film; remade as *Sincerely Yours* in 1955.

(1951) *Thundering Trail.* * A "deaf-mute" ranch handyman is actually a spy for some villains.

(1959) *For the First Time*. An opera star falls in love with a beautiful deaf girl.

(1962) *Gigot*. A sad and sweet deaf man befriends a little girl in Paris.

(1968) *Psych-Out*. A deaf teenager tries to hunt down her brother in the Flower Power empire of Haight-Ashbury, San Francisco.

(1977) *Looking for Mr. Goodbar*. A teacher of deaf children prowls singles' bars at night.

(1981) *Choices*. A hearing-impaired teenager who wants to play football finds his limitation a problem.

AMPUTATION

(1935) *The New Frontier.* * Wagonmaster Tom Lewis is a single arm amputee.

(1944) *Crime by Night.* * A man with one arm is the prime suspect for the murder of his father-in-law.

(1953) *Man from the Alamo.* * Fred Gage is a single arm amputee member of the wagon train.

(1980) *Bronco Billy.* Lefty, a cowboy who is a single arm amputee, is part of Billy's rag-tag cowboy road show.

(1983) *Trading Places.* A con man poses as a seedy, double leg amputee war vet in order to panhandle with more success.

(1984) *Lassiter.* A slick jewel thief is blackmailed by the U.S. government to steal some diamonds. His "fence" is a single arm amputee.

DEVELOPMENTAL DISABILITY

(1965) *Rapture.* A developmentally disabled girl falls for a fugitive.

(1972) *You'll Like My Mother.* A pregnant young woman who is recently widowed goes to meet her in-laws for the first time and finds her only ally in a creepy house is a developmentally disabled young woman.

SMALL-STATURE

(1932) *Tarzan, the Ape Man.* * Tarzan's woman is captured by a band of black small-statured natives.

(1939) *Three Texas Steers.* * This entry of The Three Mesquiteers series features a small-statured circus "tarzan."

(1939) *The Wizard of Oz.* A group of happy, dancing and cheerful small-statured people inhabit Dorothy Gale's dream.

(1968) *Madigan.* * The brother of the man Madigan is searching for is a dapper, small-statured man.

(1969) *The Comic.* * A small-statured man briefly appears as a silent movie actor in "Billy Bright"'s movies.

(1976) *The Amazing Dobermans.* A small-statured man works with the owner of marvelously trained dogs.

(1981) *Time Bandits.* A group of boisterous and roguish small-statured men pop in and out of time periods.

(1983) *Hot Stuff.* * Rocky, a small-statured criminal, is one of the toughs being set-up by the cops in a fencing operation.

OTHER DISABILITIES

(1925) *Phantom of the Opera.* A composer with a scarred face hides behind a mask and kidnaps a woman.

(1934) *Randy Rides Alone.* * Harmless "Mat the Mute" may not be quite what he seems.

(1941) *Face Behind the Mask.* A man whose face is injured hides behind a mask and sets out to live a life of crime.

(1943) *Phantom of the Opera.* A composer with a scarred face hides behind a mask and kidnaps a woman.

(1944) *Tomorrow Is Forever.* The disabled German refugee Elizabeth meets bears an uncanny resemblance to her dead husband. A classic "I-couldn't-ask-you-to-give-up-your-own-life-for-me" type of devaluation story.

(1957) *The Story of Esther Costello.* A wealthy society woman champions a young woman who is blind and deaf.

(1981) *Eyes of a Stranger.* A multiply-disabled woman may be the next victim of a murderer.

(1982) *Basket Case.* A man comes to New York City with his severely disabled telepathic twin brother in a basket.

MULTIPLE DISABLED CHARACTERS

(1909) *The Light That Came.* A woman with facial scarring finances an operation for a blind musician she loves — even though she fears if he can see, he will shun her.

(1932) *Freaks.* A now-cult classic about the "freaks" in a carnival sideshow. Performers with disabilities are cast in the unsettling piece.

(1966) *An Eye for an Eye.* Two men with disabilities track down murderers.

(1980) *Inside Moves.* A recently-disabled young man finds comfort in a bar where other people with disabilities hang out.

Made-for-TV Movies

BLINDNESS

(9/23/69) *Seven in Darkness* — ABC. Seven blind people, on their way to a convention for the blind, are the only survivors when their small plane crashes.

452   **Appendix: Additional Disability-Related Productions**

(2/23/71) *Longstreet* — ABC. Insurance investigator Mike Longstreet loses his wife and his sight when an enemy plants a bomb. He begins the process of getting himself back on the track. Pilot to *Longstreet* TV series, 1971-1972.

(10/16/71) *In Broad Daylight* — ABC. A blind movie star plans to kill his wife.

(1973) *The Cay* — NBC. Two shipwrecked survivors after a German U-boat attack in World War II are Old Timothy, a black man, and young Phillip, a white child who has lost his vision in the explosion.

(1974) *Journey from Darkness* — NBC. A blind student fights the system and prejudice to get into med school — a prerequisite before he can reach his career goal of a psychiatrist. Based on a true story.

(1978) *Love's Dark Ride* — NBC. A theme park architect blinded in a gunshot accident goes on to build his fantasy park. Based on a true story.

(1980) *To Race the Wind* — CBS. A blind student enters law school and falls in love for the first time. Based on a true story.

WHEELCHAIR-USERS

(3/28/67) *Ironside* — NBC. Robert Ironside, chief of detectives of the San Francisco police force, survives an assassination attempt and requires a wheelchair for mobility. Pilot film for the TV series.

(10/10/72) *Night of Terror* — ABC. A woman in a wheelchair is a potential victim for a killer who traps her on the second floor of a house with no elevator.

(1974) *It's Good to Be Alive.* A pro baseball player becomes a quadriplegic in an auto accident. Based on a true story.

(1978) *The Great Wallendas.* One of the members of the Wallenda high-wire performing act falls and injures his spinal cord. Based on a true story.

(1980) *Act of Love.* A man goes on trial for the murder of his paralyzed brother, an act he claimed was a "mercy-killing."

(1985) *In Like Flynn* — CBS. A shadowy man in a wheelchair plans to destroy lives and property for his own selfish reasons.

DEAFNESS

(10/22/67) *Johnny Belinda* — ABC. Remake of the 1948 feature film about a deaf woman who is raped and bears a child.

(1980) *Wonderworks* "Clown White." A deaf child at an oral school exhibits sudden bad behavior. He stows away on a class bus and loses himself in the city where he is entranced and befriended by a mime who breaks through the boy's shell.

AMPUTATION

(1979) *Aunt Mary*. An older woman who is a leg amputee does what she loves best — counsels youngsters and coaches their baseball team. Based on a true story.

(1982) *The Blue and the Gray — Pt. III*. Jonas Steele comes home from the American Civil War minus an arm.

(5/10/83) *American Playhouse* "Fifth of July" — PBS. A gay Vietnam veteran who is a double leg amputee has a bizarre family reunion at his house.

DEVELOPMENTAL DISABILITY

(3/24/79) *No Other Love*. Two developmentally disabled adults meet in an independent living skills center and fall in love. Very similar to *Like Normal People*.

(9/9/83) *Lottery!* — ABC. The pilot film for the series has Colt and Patrick looking for lottery winner "P. Moreno," whom they discover is developmentally disabled.

SMALL-STATURE

(1982) *Being Normal* (British). A couple recounts the difficult series of events in realizing one of their daughters is not growing as she should and follows their decision to subject her to hormone-growth therapy.

(1983) *A Touch of the Tiny Hacketts* (British). A man who captured a would-be burglar in his home is honored and revered — until people learn the would-be thief is a small-statured man who is now in the hospital with a concussion. Supposedly a comedy.

(12/84) *The Night They Saved Christmas* — ABC. Three children and the wife of an Arctic pipeline worker help save Santa and the North Pole from destruction brought about by pipeline dynamiting. A large group of squabbling, arguing, and noisy small-statured "elves" people North Pole City.

(1984) *It Came Upon the Midnight Clear* — Syndicated. A dead man gets his last wish — to return to earth to try and find the meaning of Christmas to share with his grandson. The spirit of the holiday is lacking in a storefront tableau where three small-statured men portraying "elves" are fighting, squabbling, and getting into dreadful mischief.

OTHER DISABILITIES

(1979) *The Miracle Worker*—NBC. A TV movie remake of the 1963 chronicles the meeting of teacher Anne Sullivan and Helen Keller, a wild child who is deaf and blind.

(1981) *The Patricia Neal Story*—CBS. A Based-on-a-True-Story account of actress Patricia Neal's recovery after a stroke.

(4/27/83) *Muggable Mary, Street Cop*. A woman whose son is hydroencephalitic tries to join the police force to qualify for the city's medical plan.

(1983) *Phantom of the Opera*. A TV-movie remake of the story of a composer who hides in an opera house behind a mask.

MULTIPLE DISABLED CHARACTERS

(1981) *The Acorn People*—NBC. A group of children with disabilities play themselves in a drama about the life of a summer camp counselor whose life is changed when he meets up with them.

(3/30/85) *The Fourth Wise Man*—ABC. A blind man and two youths without legs are part of the "colony of misfits" visited by a man seeking Jesus.

The Regulars

A few characters with disabilities have appeared in regular or recurring roles in various TV episodes.

BLINDNESS

(1972–1973) *Longstreet*. Insurance investigator Mike Longstreet continued his successful career after being blinded. With the help of his guide dog Pax, his boss Duke, and assistant Nikki, Mike battled fraud in New Orleans. The show introduced many high-tech tools that could be utilized by persons with low or no vision; however, it was never expressed that some of these aids were not available to the general public due to cost. Despite the upbeat imagery present in the show, it had its moments of melodrama, such as when Mike stood in front of a mirror. Nikki asked him what he saw when he stood there. After a painful pause, Mike replied, "A memory."

(1978-198?) *Little House on the Prairie.* Mary Ingalls, daughter of Charles Ingalls, lost her sight in a two-part episode of *Little House* (see "I'll Be Waving As You Drive Away"). She remained blind for the rest of her tenure on the program.

(1986) *Mr. Sunshine.* Mr. Paul Stark was a blind professor in this trial-run sitcom (see *Mr. Sunshine*).

WHEELCHAIR-USERS

(1967-1975) *Ironside.* Chief of detectives Robert Ironside lost his position on the San Francisco police force after a would-be assassin's bullet injured his spine. After his introduction to a wheelchair, Ironside fought to retain his position. Despite the fact the character had integrated a disability into his life, the disabled community felt numerous aspects of the show were negative. Ironside was constantly surrounded by his staff, which implied he was unable to live alone. Although a police van was renovated for him with a lift, he never drove. Driving chores were left to his devoted staff, who seemed to have no lives of their own. Contrary to popular belief, he *did,* in at least one episode, encounter a flight of stairs and was unable to follow an attractive woman into her apartment for a nightcap.

(1975-1976) *Bronk.* Special assignment cop Alex Bronkov's daughter was Ellen, a young woman in a wheelchair.

(1982-1983) *Tales of the Gold Monkey.* A performer with a disability was a regular cast member in this 1930's action-adventure series. As Gushie, co-owner of the Monkey Bar, he was in danger of villains and got thrown across the room like anyone else. His disability was not discussed. He was just another sweaty citizen of the island.

(1984-1986) *T.J. Hooker.* A performer with a disability was cast in the recurring role of Lieutenant Pete O'Brien, a cigar-chomping, hard-nosed cop who was Hooker's superior. O'Brien's wheelchair was not discussed. He was seen driving a car and in total command of the situations at hand. He used a little bit of personal empathy to help Hooker's partner Romano when he was temporarily blinded in 1984 (see "Target: Hooker").

(date unknown) *Diff'rent Strokes.* A regular visitor to the Drummond household was a classmate of Arnold's who used a wheelchair. A performer with a disability was cast in the recurrent, wisecracking role.

DEAFNESS

(1983) *Family Tree.* Toby Benjamin was the deaf son of Annie Benjamin Nichols on the short-lived *Family Tree.* A deaf performer was cast in the role.

(1983-1984) *Trauma Center.* One of the efficient paramedics for the trauma team at the hospital was the huge and gentle Mr. Six, a man with a hearing impairment (played by a hearing-impaired performer). Six occasionally mentioned his background—such as being teased back in grammar school about his slightly-unmonitored speech—and was teased about his limitation by friends. One of the hospital regulars sighed and said to him, "Mr. Six, why is it whenever I talk to you, I get the feeling you've turned off your hearing aid?" (see *Trauma Center,* "Silent Sounds").

AMPUTATION

(1/16/84) *AfterM*A*S*H.* Dr. Boyer joined the staff at the veteran's hospital mid-season. The surly, sharp-tongued surgeon revealed he lost a leg in Korea.

DEVELOPMENTAL DISABILITY

(1959-1965) **Rawhide.* Harkness Milligan Mushgrove the Third was better known as Mushy, the cook's "louse." In the 10/11/60 episode, "Incident of the Slavemaster," the cook Wishbone told Mushy, "You have a boy's brain in a man's body." Other episodes featured Mushy's "slowness."

SMALL-STATURE

(date unknown) *The Odd Couple.* Sloppy sportswriter Oscar Madison's bookie was a small-statured man who popped up every now and then with a good tip.

(date unknown) *Baretta.* One of with-it cop Tony Baretta's informants was a small-statured man.

(1978-1983) *Fantasy Island.* Small-statured Tattoo was mystical Mr. Roarke's right-hand man on Fantasy Island. Tattoo was often sympathetic to the guests but often caused trouble, as well, getting into pickles. He was never presented in a very serious light, providing instead, comic relief—although often at the expense of his own integrity. Tattoo had the judgment of a child and required chastising from Mr. Roarke quite often. However, in one episode, he *did* reveal that people often treated him like a little boy instead of a man.

OTHER DISABILITIES

(1957-1959) **Zorro.* The fop Don Diego who became the dashing Zorro to help fight injustice in early California was aided by a non-speaking manservant, Bernardo. Bernardo communicated with Zorro by using mime and gestures. He was permitted to come up with ideas of his own, although he never seemed to have full personhood status—possibly due to the social strata in which he lived.

(1968-1970) *Here Come the Brides*. The youngest of the three Bolt Brothers in 1870's Seattle was Jeremy. After his mother died, the boy couldn't say "Amen" at the gravesite without stuttering. Now, years later, his stammer made him the butt of jokes from loggers on the Bolts own Bridal Veil Mountain. He rarely spoke until he met Candy, one of the 100 "brides" shipped in from New England, who felt what he said was more important than how he said it. Jeremy's emotionally-induced stutter decreased after a visiting charlatan rainmaker worked with him. Toward the end of the series, his stutter only surfaced when he was tremendously excited or upset.

(1978-1979) *The Waltons*. In the sixth season of the family favorite, *The Waltons*, the actress portraying hard-to-please Grandma Walton had a stroke. She continued her role as Grandma after a period of recuperation. She experienced residual language difficulties and partial paralysis after the stroke. The disability was integrated into the series with care. A poignant episode featured everyone fussing over Grandma and gradually pushing her aside. Within the story, she had retained her ability to write. Unable to verbalize her pain and frustration to the family, Grandpa discovered her personal journal which he read aloud, detailing Grandma's private anguish at being pushed aside. The family realized what they had done. Her character "passed away" in 1979.

(1982-?) *Facts of Life*. Wealthy Blair Warner, a student at the Eastland School for Girls, was occasionally visited by her cousin Geri, an aspiring comedienne with cerebral palsy (a performer with a disability was cast in the role). Geri's introduction as a recurring regular came as the school was preparing for a big dance—and Blair was concerned over how she would ever locate a date for Geri. Geri had no trouble attracting a date; in fact, when she was gone all night, Blair became angry and overprotective—at which time Geri reminded her she was old enough to make her own decisions and get hurt like anyone else.

(1983-1983) *Trauma Center*. The anesthesiologist at the hospital was Sniff, a man who walked with braces and crutches (played by an actor with a disability).

(1983-1988) *St. Elsewhere*. Hospital administrator Dr. Donald Westphall was a crack shot when it came to dealing with the problems of St. Eligius. However, at home, it was a different story as the widower was lost and confused when it comes to dealing with his low-verbal, autistic son, Tommy. During the course of the series, Westphall put Tommy into a school program where he was progressing—but felt so horrible about not having the boy at home that he removed Tommy from school, whereupon the child regressed. Tommy remained an enigma for Dr. Westphall.

(5/83-) *The Young and the Restless*. Carole Robbins, an efficient secretary, kept Jack Abbott's office running. Carole's disability, an orthopedic limitation which necessitated the use of a leg brace and a cane, was discussed in the serial. A performer with a disability was cast in the role.

References

Actors' Television Credits 1950-1972, James Robert Parish. Scarecrow Press, 1973.

The Complete Directory to Primetime Network TV Shows, Tim Brooks, Earl Marsh. Ballantine Books, 1981.

Leonard Maltin's TV Movies, 1985-1986, Leonard Maltin. Signet Books, 1984.

Physical Disability—A Psychosocial Approach, second edition, Beatrice A. Wright. Harper & Row, 1983.

The Source Book for the Disabled, edited by Glorya Hale. Imprint Books Limited, London 1979; Bantam Books edition, 1981.

The Story of My Life, Helen Keller, Doubleday, 1954.

The Unseen Minority: A Social History of Blindness in America, Frances A. Koestler. McKay, 1976.

Index

Titles of movies, including made-for-television movies, are in *italics;* titles of television shows, in **boldface**. Titles of episodes of television shows are placed within quotation marks.

A

A-Team: "Waste 'Em!" 92–93; "Water, Water Everywhere" 422–423
Abatemarco, Frank 150, 162
Abbot-Fish, Chris 267, 406
ABC Afterschool Special: "Blind Sunday" 42–43; "Mom and Dad Can't Hear Me" 212–213; "Run, Don't Walk" 153–155; "Tough Girl" 242–243
Abroms, Edward M. 259
Ackerman, Harry 329
The Acorn People 454
Act of Love 452
Aediken, Simon 112
The Affair 373–375
AfterM*A*S*H 456; Klinger's amputee friend 301–302; Mulcahy's hearing restored 254–255
Airwolf: "And a Child Shall Lead" 335–336; "Inn at the End of the Road" 178–179; "Jennie" 262–263; "Tracks" 189–190
Aldrich, Robert 199
Alexander, David 346
Alf: "For Your Eyes Only" 109–111
Alfred Hitchcock Presents: "A Very Happy Ending" 266–267
Alice: "Alice's Blind Date" 77–78; "Mel Spins His Wheels" 176–177
All in the Family: "Gloria's Boyfriend" 445
All of Me 95–96
Allen, Ray 63
Alley, Robert 144
Allman, Jack 302
Alston, Howard 426
Altman, Robert 200

The Amazing Dobermans 450
Amen, Carol 326
America 2-Nite: deaf comic 443; wheelchair access 134–135
American Playhouse: "Fifth of July" 453
Amy 231–233
Amy on the Lips see *Amy*
And Your Name Is Jonah 213–215
Anderson, Hesper 269, 385
Anderson, Jon 187
Andre, Blue 402
Anspaugh, David 260
Antonio, Louis 24, 222
Armer, Alan A. 281
Armor, Joyce 215
Armstrong, Adrienne 110
Arnold, Danny 45, 227
Aronsohn, Lee 294
Arthur, Karen 66, 172
Ashby, Hal 135
Ashley, John 92, 150, 422
Asselin, Diane 264
Aunt Mary 453
Aurora 85–87
Austin, Ray 265, 267, 328
Averback, Hy 278
Azzopardi, Mario 337

B

Bachman, Lawrence P. 157
Badham, John 157
Baer, Art 83, 160, 182, 239, 331, 388
Baim, Gary L. 57
Baker, Rod 282

Balluck, Don 53
Balter, Allan 287
Barbarians from the Year 3000 273
Baretta 456; "All That Shatters" 129–132; "Buddy" 445; "Shoes" 207
Barimo, George 339
Barkley, Deanne 155
Barmak, Ira R. 108
Barnaby Jones: "A Focus on Fear" 62–63; "See Some Evil, Do Some Evil" 30–31; "Shadow of Fear" 447
Barnes, Steven 98
Barnette, Alan 107, 111, 266
Barney Miller: "Community Relations" 45–46; "Stormy Weather" 227–228
Barns, Allan 432
Baron, Allen 47
Barr, Douglas 104
Barron, A. 42
Barron, Robert V. 342
Bartlett, Juanita 62
Barton, Frank 22
Basket Case 451
Baskin, John 96, 358
Bass, Stanley 235
Bateman, Kent 105
Beaudine, William, Jr. 206
Beaumont, Gabrielle 179
Becker, Robert 333
Beg, Borrow . . . Or Steal 416–418
Being Normal 453
Bellamann, Henry 273
Bellamy, Earl 147, 190, 355
Bellisario, Donald 178, 267, 382, 406
Bello, Steve 250
Benedict, Richard 285, 415
Benson, Hugh 249
Benton, Robert 88
Berg, Dick 235
Berk, Michael 104, 367
Berks, Lester William 179
Berman, Pandro S. 18, 369
Bernardi, Barry 177
Bernhardi, Lee 102
Bernstein, Jonathan 105
Berren, Eric 383
The Best Years of Our Lives 276–278
The Betrayal 448
Bick, Jerry 358
Big Hawaii: "Blind Rage" 440
Bill 320–321, 326
Bill—On His Own 325–326
The Bionic Woman: "The Vega Syndrome" 443

Bird, Brian 172
Birnbaum, Bob 252
Biston, Aaron 247
Black, Noel 98
Blaine, Sean 291
Blasdell-Goddard, Audrey 327
Blatt, Daniel H. 138, 309
Blechman, Corey 320
Blees, Robert 14
Blind Date 448
"Blind Sunday" 42–43
Blind Terror see *See No Evil*
Blinn, William 72
Blitzer, Barry 349
Bloomberg, Beverly 324
The Blue and the Gray, Pt. III 453
The Blue Gardenia 12–13
Bochco, Steven 167, 168, 179
Bodeen, DeWitt 8
Boehm, Sidney 9
Bogdanovich, Peter 426
The Bold Ones: "What Price a Pair of Eyes?" 439
Bole, Cliff 68, 241, 391
Bonanza: "The Ape" 444; "Bullet for a Bride" 16–18; "Gabrielle" 15–16; "The Horse Breaker" 120–121; "Hoss and the Leprechauns" 342–344; "It's a Small World" 445; "The Miracle Maker" 442; "The Return" 121–123; "Silent Thunder" 200–201; (Joe is blinded) 439
Bonerz, Peter 110
Borowsky, Mar vin 6
Bortman, Michael 213
Bowman, Chuck 87, 397
Boyle, Bill 295
Boyle, Donald 208
Bradbury, Ray 300
Brams, Richard 366
Braverman, Charles 250
Braverman, Michael 390
Brazil, Scott 167, 169, 179, 306
Brenner, Ray 420
Brez, Ethel 386
Brez, Mel 386
The Bride 363
Bridges, Beau 320
Bright Victory 10–12
Brillstein, Bernie 109
Brinkley, Don 185, 230, 243, 355, 401, 409
Bronco Billy 450
Bronk 455
Brooks, Hindi 252

Brooks, James L. 193
Brown, David 174
Brown, Georg Stanford 178
Browning, Rod 184
Brunner, Bob 54, 175, 398
Bryant, Michael 428
Buck, Craig 408
Buck Rogers in the 25th Century: "The Guardians" 440; "Return of the Fighting 69th" 418–420; "Shgoratchx!" 351–353
Buckner, Robert 10, 11
Buell, Jed 342
Bullock, Harvey 63, 239
Burditt, George 56
Burley, Mark A. 362
Burrows, James 193
Butler, Robert 281
Butterfield, Roger 6
Butterflies Are Free 28–29

C

Caffey, Michael 185, 401
Cagney and Lacey: "The Gimp" 307–309; "Hopes and Dreams" 162–163; "Hot Line" xvi, 161–162
Cahn, Barry 94
Campbell, April 187
Can You Feel Me Dancing? 105–107
Canada, Lena 385
Cannell, Stephen J. 60, 62, 92, 422
Capice, Phillip 141, 378
Cardea, Frank 96, 358
Carpenter, John 177
Carr, Thomas 13, 15
Carren, David Bennett 418
Carrington, Jane-Howard 19
Carrington, Robert 19
Carrol, Bob, Jr. 77, 176
Carsey, Marcia 99
Carson, Robert 5
Carter, Thomas 167, 173
Caspary, Vern 12
Cassavetes, John 313
Cates, Gilbert 320, 373
The Cay 452
CBS Schoolbreak Special: "Have You Tried Talking to Patty?" 264–265
Chaffey, Don 70
Chamber of Horrors 278–279, 283
Chambers, Everett 262, 335
Chapin, Doug 80

Chaplin, Charles 4
Chapman, Richard 75, 164, 362
Charles, Glen 193
Charles, Les 193
Charlie's Angels: Angels undercover at circus 445; "The Killing Kind" 440
Chase, David 60, 62
Chase, Frank 120, 122
Chehak, Thomas 358
Cherbak, Cynthia A. 330
Chermak, Cy 234, 324, 350
Chester, Lewis 187
A Child Is Waiting 313–315
Children of a Lesser God 269–270
China Smith: "The Night the Dragon Walked" 444
ChiPs: "Blabbermouth" 447; "Counterfeit" 350–351; "Silent Partner" 234–235; "Something Special" 324–325; "Wheeling" 149–150
Choices 449
Cimarron Strip: "The Blue Moon Train" 446
City Lights 4–5
City Streets 448
Claridge, Westbrook 179
Clark, Blake 90
Clark, Brian 157
Clarke, Cecil 31
Claver, Bob 24, 203
Claxton, William 51, 53, 255
Clayton, Jack 300
Clemens, Brian 27, 31, 35, 124
Clements, Calvin 351
Clements, Calvin, Jr. 81, 82
Coach of the Year 150–151
Code Red: "Dark Fire" 420–421
Coe, Fred 372
Coe, Liz 307
Coffey, Brian 350
Cohan, Martin 174, 398
Cohen, Barney 133
Cohen, Ellis A. 184
Cohen, Eric 33
Cohen, Randy 94
Colbert, Stanley 295
Collins, Anne 68
Collins, Robert 258, 327
Collinson, Peter 376
Colman, Henry 47, 63, 143, 160, 215, 239, 294, 332, 388, 404, 411
The Comic 450
Coming Home 135–136
Compton, Richard 107, 258, 377

464 Index

Conrad, Joan 150
Converse, Tony 85, 297, 317, 377
Cook, Fielder 392
Cook, T.S. 179
Cooney, Ray 156
Cooper, Hal 256
Cooper, Paul W. 74, 242, 293
Cooper, Peter H. 108
Cooper, Robert 302
Coopersmith, Jerome 22
Corea, Nicholas 65
Cornfeld, Stuart 383
The Cosby Show: "A Touch of Wonder" 99
Cos*t*igan, James 128
Courtland, Jerome 231, 404
Coyle, Paul Robert 362
Cramer, Douglas 47, 63, 68, 78, 81, 83, 143, 160, 177, 182, 215, 239, 258, 294, 331, 332, 349, 388, 395, 404, 411
Crane, Barry 252
Craviotto, Darlene 263
Crays, Durrell Royce 153
Crazy Like a Fox: "Hearing Is Believing" 96-97; "Requiem for a Fox" 358-359
Crime by Night 449
Crocker, James 98, 428
Cromwell, John 8
Crossbar 295-297
Crowe, Christopher 266
Crowley, Matt 66
Cucci, Frank 171
Cummings, Jack 275
Curtis, Brice Cohn 123
Cutter to Houston 444
Cutter's Way 387-388

D

Dallenback, Walter 70
Damski, Mel 309, 378
Daniels, Marc 176
Daniels, Robert 250
Daniels, Stan 112, 193
Darling, Joan 233
Darnell, Cynthia 307
Daves, Delmar 6
Davidsen, Lewis 207
Davies, Gareth 188
Davis, Ed 95
Davis, Jerry 226
Davis, Madelyn 77, 176
Davis, Peter S. 133

Dawson, Deborah Zoe 185, 401, 409
The Dead Don't Dream 448
Dead Man's Eyes 447
Deadman's Curve 377-378
De Guere, Philip 75, 97, 164, 428
Delmar, Vina 116
Demme, Jonathan 358
Denker, Henry 90
De Silva, David 72, 255, 325
The Desperate Miles 283-285
De Vore, Christopher 383
Dial, Bill 75, 174, 362
Dielhenn, Art 334
Dieterle, William 369
Diff'rent Strokes 455; "The Gymnast" 174-176; "The Special Friend" 398-399
Dimsdale, Howard 41
Dinelli, Mel 370, 376
Director, Roger 179
Dismukes, Charles E. 130
Divorce Court 94-95
Dobkin, Lawrence 30
Dolinsky, Meyer 346
Donner, Jill Sherman 406
Donney, Dennis 174
Donovan, Arlene 88
Dortort, David 15, 16, 120, 121, 200, 342
Doston, Joe 209
Douglas, Gordon 200
Douglas, Kirk 287
Douglas, Lloyd 14
Douglas, Michael 177
Douglas, Peter Vincent 300
Dowd, Nancy 135
Downing, Stephen 70, 87
Drai, Victor 363
Dubin, Charles 332
Duchowny, Roger 143
Dugan, John T. 52
Dumm, J. Rickley 382
Dummy 219-221
Duncan, Frank 99
Dunphy, Tim 337
Dunsmuir, Tom 411

E

Eagle, Mary 362
Earll, Robert 190
East Side, West Side 441
Eastlake, Carlton 107
Edelstein, Rick 292
Edwards, George 25

Edwards, Paul F. 400
Egan, Mark 77, 176
Egan, Sam 328, 390
80 Steps to Jonah 448
Eleanor and Franklin 127–128
The Elephant Man 383–385
Elias, Louie 297
Elikann, Larry 42, 212
Ellis, Sidney 423
Ellsworth, Whitney 13
Elstad, Linda 72
Emergency! 443
The Equalizer: "Counterfire" 111–112; "Nocturne" 107–108
Estin, Ken 112, 193
Evans, Bruce A. 177
ExoMan 132–133
Eye for an Eye 451
The Eyes Have It 31–33
Eyes in the Night 447
Eyes of a Stranger 451

F

Face Behind the Mask 451
The Facts of Life 457; "Different Drummer" 323–324; "The Sound of Silence" 238–239
Fairfax, Ferdinand 408
Falk, Harry 236
The Fall Guy: "Wheels" 170–171; "The Winner" 328–329
Fame: "Love Is the Question" 325; "Signs" 255–256; "Solo Song" 72–73
Family: "See Saw" 49–50
Family Tree 233–234, 455
Fanaro, Barry 361
Fantasy Island 456; "Candy Kisses" 163–164; "Chorus Girl" 228; "The Final Adieu" 171–172; "The Golden Hour" 190–192; "Nona" 440; "Roarke's Sacrifice" 393–394 "The Swimmer" 147–149
Farr, Gordon 47, 102, 143, 215, 294, 411
Farr, Lynne 47, 143, 215, 294, 411
Farrell, Henry 25, 119
Farrell, Judy 320
Father Murphy: "Establish Thou the Work of Our Hands" 293–294
Feely, Terence 31, 35
Feldman, Edward 125
Feldman, Phil 287
Felton, Norman 213
Fenton, Frank 8

Ferber, Bruce 174
Ferraro, Delores 77
Ferrer, Mel 19
Ferrini 85
Fields, Herbert 116
Fifth of July 453
A Fighting Choice 408–409
Finder of Lost Loves: "Deadly Silence" 177–178; debut 83
Fine, Mort 327
Finestra, Carmen 99, 143
Fink, Mitchell 303
Finnegan, William 281
First Steps xvi, 184–185
Fischer, Geoffrey 332, 404
Fischer, Peter 258, 290
Fisher, Michael 81, 147, 190, 203
Fisher, Steve 315
Fisken, Jeffrey Alan 387
Fjeld, Julianna 263
Fleischer, Richard 27
Flett, Anne 339
Flicker, Theodore J. 287
Flipper 192–193
Florea, John 342, 350
Fodice, Ian 35, 124
Fogarty, Jack V. 62, 241, 251, 391
Fontana, Tom 250, 260, 303, 333, 365
Fonvielle, Lloyd 363
For the First Time 449
For Your Eyes Only 449
Forbes, Bryan 123
Foreman, Carl 117, 357
Foreman, John 357
Forrester, Larry 249
Fortune Dane 441
Fournier, Rift 130
The Fourth Wise Man 454
Fox, Fred, Jr. 146
Fox, Norman Chandler 307
Franco, Larry J. 177
Frand, Harvey 98, 428
Frank, Bruno 369
Frank, Morris 90
Frankovich, M.J. 28
Freaks 451
Freeman, Jerrold 141
Freeman, Joel 201
Freeman, Leonard 22, 281
Freiberger, Fred 344, 346
Freiwald, Eric 206
French, Victor 354, 389, 429
Friedgen, Julie 96
Friedman, Ron 170, 228

Friedman, Stephen 95
Fries, Charles 213
Fritzhand, James 395
Frost, Mark 167, 169, 179
Fuchs, Leo L. 432
Fuisz, Robert F. 310
Furia, John, Jr. 200
Fusco, Paul 110

G

Gallegly, Dick 265
Gansberg, Alan L. 264
Gansberg, Judith M. 264
Ganz, Lowell 226
Garnett, Tay 16
Gaynor, John 418
Geiger, George 174
Gelbart, Larry 254
Gelman, Laurie 110
General Hospital 443
Gerber, David 290, 396
Gershe, Leonard 28
Gethers, Stephen 222
Gibbs, Ann 160
Gibson, Alan 394
Gibson, William 372
Gideon, Raynold 177
Gigot 449
Gilbert, Kenneth C. 62
Gillis, Jackson 13, 420
Gillson, Carol 179, 189, 262, 335
Gimbel, Roger 85, 297, 317, 377
Gimme a Break: "The Earthquake" 256–257
Glazier, Brian 139
Gleason, Michael 172, 188
Glicksman, Frank 230, 243, 355
Godfrey, Alan 130, 189, 208
Gold, Donald L. 366
Goldberg, Leonard 49, 66, 70, 147, 163, 171, 190, 207, 228, 249, 251, 292, 315, 373, 391, 393
Golden, Renee Wayne 155
Golden, Robert 206
The Golden Girls: "A Little Romance" 360–362
Goldwyn, Samuel 276
Good Times: "The Encyclopedia Hustle" 33–34
Goodman, Jules Eckert 200
Goodnight, My Love 348–349
Goodwin, R.W. 396

Gordon, Dan 423, 430, 434
Gordon, Jill 258
Gordon, Lawrence 81
Gottleib, Alex 12
Grace, Michael 331
Grant, Merril 338
The Great Wallendas 452
Greek, Janet 303
Green, Guy 18
Green, Patricia 307, 400
Greenbaum, Everett 301
Greenberg, Joanna 263
Greenwald, Robert 105, 283
Greyhosky, Babs 382
Gross, Jack J. 8
Grossman, Terry 361
Grosso, Sonny 245, 336
Groves, Herman 34
Gurian, Paul R. 387
Gutierrez, Vince 389

H

Haines, Randa 269
Hall, Karen 167, 169
Haller, Daniel 283
Hallin, Ronnie 412
Halmi, Robert 171, 228
Hamilton, Robert 265
Hammer, Dennis 83, 182, 331
Hamori, Andras 336
Hampton, Orville 192
Hands Across the Table 116–117
Happy Days: "Allison" 225–227; "Fonzie's Blindness" 54–56; "The Mechanic" 146–147; "The Tall Story" 412
Hardy, Joseph 210
The Hardy Boys: "The Mystery of the Silent Scream" 208–210
Harpster, Michael 133
Harrington, Curtis 25
Harrington, Pat, Jr. 380
Harris, Elmer 199, 235
Harris, Henry 395
Harrison, Paul 136
Harry-O: "Eyewitness" 34–35; "Portrait of a Murderer" 445; "Second Sight" 2, 37–38; "Silent Kill" 443
Hart, Harvey 318
Hart to Hart: deaf ice skater xvi, 249–250; "Hart of Darkness" 67–68
Hausman, Michael 88

Index

"Have You Tried Talking to Patty?" 264–265
Havinga, Nick 254, 301
Hawaii Five-O: "Blind Tiger" 22–24; embittered Viet vet/wheelchair 442; "Hookman" 273, 281–283
Hawkins, Jimmy 90
Hawkins, John 44
Hawkins, Rick 333
Hayers, Sidney 92
Hayes, Jeffrey 68, 70, 240, 251, 391
Hear No Evil 236–238
The Heart Is a Lonely Hunter 201–203
Hecht, Ken 175, 398
Heerman, Victor 14
Heffron, Richard 400
Helen Keller: The Miracle Continues 394–395
Heller, Lukas 119
Heller, Rosilyn 57
Hellman, Jerome 135
Hello 89–90
Hensley, J. Miyoko 105
Hensley, Steven 105
Here Come the Brides 457; "Absalom, Absalom" 203–204; "Two Worlds" 24–25, 75, 390
Hertzog, Lawrence 66
Herzfeld, John 153, 218
Heyes, Douglas 400
Hibbs, Jesse 279
Hickox, S. Brian 139
Highway to Heaven: "Alone" 337–338; "A Match Made in Heaven" 180–182; "The Monster" xii, xiii, 429–432; "One Fresh Batch of Lemonade" 423–426; "A Special Love" 434–435
Hill, Kimberley 238
Hill Street Blues: "Davenport in a Storm" 179–180; "Honk If You're a Goose" 168–170; "Midway to What?" 167–168; "An Oy for an Oy" 445; "Seoul on Ice" 306–307
Hirson, Roger O. 310
The Hitchhiker: "Killer" 187–188
Hively, Jack B. 206
Hobin, Bill 56
Hoblit, Greg 167–168, 179
Hocken, Sheila 80
Hoey, Michael 255
Hoffman, Charles 12
Holiday, Bishop 247
Hot Stuff 450
Hotel: "Confrontations" 395–396; "Imperfect Union" 332; "Saving Grace" 404–406
How Awful About Allan 25–27
Howard, Ron 152
Huff, John 149
Hughes, Terry 361
Huguely, Jay 267, 406
Hume, Ed 302
The Hunchback of Notre Dame 369–370, 384
Hunt, Peter H. 104, 367
Hunter, Blake 174, 398
Hunter, Paul 242
Hunter, Ross 14
Husky, Rick 70, 87, 240, 251, 391, 397
Hyams, Peter 348
Hyland, Dick Irving 8
Hyman, Kenneth 119

I

Ice Castles xv, 57–59
The Ice Pirates 357–358
If You Could See What I Hear 448
In Broad Daylight 452
In Like Flynn 452
Inch, Kevin 172, 188
The Incredible Hulk: Banner loses the use of his legs 442; blind pianist 65–66; "Rickey" 445
Ingalls, Don 163, 171, 393
Inside Moves 451
Ironside 452, 455
Ironside: "The Light at the End of...." 439
Irving, Richard 132
Isaacs, David 46, 254, 301
It Came Upon the Midnight Clear 453–454
It's a Wonderful Life 448
It's Good to Be Alive 452

J

Jacobson, Larry 245, 336
Jakes, John 400
James At: "Actions Speak Louder" 210–211
Janes, Robert 189, 252, 262, 335
The Jeffersons: "Father's Day" 164–165
Jenkin, Len 49
Jessie 396–397

468 Index

Joelson, Ben 83, 160, 182, 239, 331, 388
John, Tom 102
Johnny Belinda (1948) 198–200
Johnny Belinda (1971) 452
Johnny Belinda (1982) 235–236
Johns, Victoria 185, 401, 409
Johnson, Bruce 59
Johnson, Charles Floyd 60, 62, 267, 406
Johnson, Dennis 133
Johnson, James B. 380
Johnson, Kenneth 65
Jones, Bruce 187
Jones, Marc 92
Jones, Robert C. 135
Journey from Darkness 452
Joyous Sound 206–207
Just a Little Inconvenience 287–289
Just the Way You Are 432–434
Justman, Robert 258, 346

K

Kallis, Stanley 285, 322, 396, 416
Kandel, Stephen 278
Kane, Arnold 102
Kantor, MacKinlay 276
Kappes, David 171
Kasten, John 302
Kata, Elizabeth 18
Kate and Allie: "Chip's Friend" 338–340
Katselas, Milton 28
Katz, Stephen 92
Katzman, Leonard 22
Kayden, Tony 207
Keach, James 309
Keane, E. Arthur 38
Keel, Charlotte 163
Keith, Gerren 398
Kelada, Asaad 238
Kelbaugh, Rick 189, 397
Keller, Max 261
Keller, Michelline 261
Kellogg, Marjorie 413
Kelman, Alfred R. 310
Kemeny, John 57
Kemply, Walter 226
Kendrick, Baynard 11
Kennedy, Bob 42
Kenwith, Herbert 33
Kern, Brad 188
Kern, Dale 104
Keys, William 351, 397
The Kid from Nowhere 320

Kimmel, Joel 160
Kings Row 273–275
Kinon, Richard 160, 182, 215
Kipling, Rudyard 5
Kleinbart, Philip K. 105
Kleiser, Randall 315
Kline, Steven 216
Klugerman, Ira 302
Knelman, P.K. 307
Kneubuhl, John 344
Knopf, Christopher 287
Knott, Frederick 19
Koch, Kenneth 87, 397
Koenig, Dennis 254, 301
Kolbe, Winrich 382
Konigsberg, Frank 219
Korty, John 80
Kowalski, Bernard L. 129, 189, 262, 335, 344
Kramer, Stanley 117, 313, 345
Krasna, Norman 116
Krasny, Paul 96
Krost, Barry 80
Kugel, Carl 358
Kung Fu 440
Kurt, John A. 152
Kushner, Donald 94

L

Lachman, Mort 256, 338
La Mond, Bill 395
La Mond, Jo 395
Lancer: "Death Bait" 281
Landers, Hal 327
Landon, Michael 43, 44, 52, 53, 74, 180, 224, 293, 337, 354, 389, 422, 423, 429, 434
Landsberg, Cleve 105
Landsburg, Alan 325
Landsburg, Valerie 255
Lang, Fritz 12
Lang, Richard 34
Lansbury, Bruce 279
Laramie 441
Larry, Sheldon 184
Larson, Charles 230
Larson, Glen 170, 246, 328
Lash, Joseph P. 128
Laskos, Andrew 404
Lassie: "More Than Meets the Eye" 440
Lassiter 450
Last of the Wild Horses 448

Index

Laven, Arnold 423
Laven, Harold 60
Lawrence, Anthony 15
Lawrence, David 394
Lawrence, Vincent 116
Lazarus, Tom 155, 236
Leacock, Phillip 49, 172, 418
Lear, Norman 33
Leave Yesterday Behind xvi, 136-138
Leavitt, Ron 55
Leckie, Keith 295
Leder, Reuben 406
Lee, Joanna 318
Leitch, Christopher 187
Le Maire, George 141
Lerner, David 174
Lester, Mark L. 133
Leven, Audrey Davis 378
Levien, Sonya 369
Levin, Lissa 99
Levin, Peter 162
Levine, Ken 46, 254, 301
Levitt, Alan J. 56
Levitt, Gene 30
Lewis, David 273
Lewis, Jeffrey 167, 169, 179, 306
Lewis, R.J. 222
Lewis, Robert 385
Lewis, Robert Lloyd 261
Lieberstein, Daniel 107, 111
The Light That Came xii, xiii, 113, 432, 451
The Light That Failed 5-6, 9
Like Normal People 318-319, 453
Linder, Leslie 27
Linton 141
Little House: A New Beginning: "Little Lou" 354-355; "Love" 74-75; "Marvin's Garden" 422; "The Wild Boy" 389-390
Little House on the Prairie 455; "Blind Journey" 52-53, 98; "Dearest Albert, I'll Miss You" 442; "The Enchanted Cottage" 53-54; "The Hunters" 43-45; "I'll Be Waving As You Drive Away" 51-52; "Silent Promises" 224-225; "Town Party, Country Party" 447; "The Voice of Tinker Jones" 375
Littman, Lynne 326
Lloyd, David 101
Lobl, Victor 74, 216, 246, 409
Locke, Peter 94
Lofaro, Raymond 133
London, Jerry 155
The Lone Ranger: excon, disabled arm 446; Ranger tracks voiceless war vet 446
Long Ago Tomorrow 123-124
Long Journey Back 378-379
Longstreet, Harry 166, 244, 246
Longstreet, Renee 166, 244, 246
Longstreet 452
Longstreet 454; "Leave the Wreck for Others to Enjoy" 440
Look Back in Darkness 35-36, 108
Looking for Mr. Goodbar 449
Lottery! 453
Lottery!: "Win Or Lose" 252-254
The Love Boat: "After the War" 143-144; "Aftermath" 294-295; blind passenger plays helpless 78-79; "Charmed, I'm Sure" 182-184; "Eye of the Beholder" 63-65; "Eyes of Love" 47-48; "I Don't Play Anymore" 388-389; "Letting Go" 331-332; "The Light of Another Day" 83-84; "The Little People" 349-350; "Love Will Find a Way" 160-161; "Message for Maureen" 129; "Sound of Silence" 215-216; "Still Life" 239-240; "What's a Brother For?" 411-412
Love Is Never Silent 263-264
Love Leads the Way 90-92
Love's Dark Ride 452
Lowell, M. 392
Lowenheim, Robert 378
Luck, Coleman 107, 111
Lynch, David 383

M

Maas, Audrey 127
McAdams, James 107, 111
McAll, Mitzi 110
McClain, Chuck 399
McClellan, Max 220
McCowan, George 208
McCray, Kent 74, 180, 224, 293, 337, 354, 389, 422, 423, 429, 434
McCullers, Carson 202
McDonald, Frank 192
McDougall, Don 120
McEveety, Bernard 244
McEveety, Vincent 87, 231, 351, 358
McGowan, George 249
McGreevey, John 85, 204, 394, 402
McGreevey, Michael 229
MacGruder and Loud 258
McKeand, Carol Evan 233

McKeand, Nigel 49, 233
MacMillan and Wife 440
McNeely, Jerry 246
McRaven, Dale 59
Madden, Jerry 176
Madigan 450
Magistretti, Paul 164, 362
Magnificent Obsession (1935) 447
Magnificent Obsession (1954) 14–15
Magnum, P.I.: "Don't Say Goodbye" 382–383; "I Never Wanted to Go to France, Anyway . . ." 406–407; "One Picture Is Worth" 267–269
Majors, Lee 170, 287, 328
Malloy, Merrit 317
Maltz, Albert 6
The Man and the City 442
Man from the Alamo 450
The Man Who Played God 449
Mandel, Robert 330
Manings, Allan 33
Mann, Abby 313, 345
Mann, Delbert 90, 139, 310
Mann, Michael 173, 366
Manners, Sam 219
Mannix: "Silent Cry" 271
Mantley, John 351
Manulis, Martin 210
Marcus, Richard 176
Marcus Welby, M.D.: air controller has laryngectomy 447; artist with M.S. 447; "A Child of Silence" 443; diabetic teen loses sight 441; "The Merely Syndrome" 441; young woman paralyzed— meningitis 442
Markowitz, Riff 187
Markowitz, Robert 218
Markus, John 99
Markus, Leah 325
Marsh, Linda 238
Marshall, Garry 54, 59, 225, 412
Marshall, George Lee 172
Marshall, Peter 123
Marshall, Tony 59
Martin, Quinn 30
Mary Hartman, Mary Hartman 443
Maschler, Tim 147
M*A*S*H: "Out of Sight, Out of Mind" 46–47
Masius, John 250, 260, 303, 333, 365
Mask 98, 426–428
Mason, Paul 324
Mason, Sarah Y. 14
Masters, Sue 294

Mastrogeorge, Harry 63
Mate, Rudolf 9
Mathews, Patrick 251
Matt Houston: "Here's Another Fine Mess" 444; "The Outsider" 81–82
Matt Lincoln 443
Mauldin, Nat 227
Mayosse, Michelle 392
Medford, Don 130, 150
Medical Center: "Albatross" 415–416; baseball star loses leg 444; dev. disabled delivery boy 444; Gannon blinded 443; musician goes deaf 443; "secret Heritage" 444; "A Touch of Sight" 41; "Wall of Silence" 443
Medical Story: "Million Dollar Baby" 38–39
Medoff, Mark 269
Melman, Jeff 305, 359
Melvoin, Jeff 188
The Men 117–119
Menom 85
Menteer, Gary 333
Meredith, Andrew 376
Merson, Marc 202
Messina, Dianne 323
Messina, Lou 323
Metcalfe, Burt 46, 301
Metzger, Alan 111
Meyer, Abe 342
Meyers, Robert 318
Miami Vice 173–174
Miami Vice: "Tale of the Goat" 366–367
Michaels, Richard 136, 213
Milburn, Sue 235
Milch, David 167, 169, 179, 306
Miles, T.J. 382
Milkis, Edward 54, 146, 225, 412
Miller, Jack 24
Miller, Michael 105
Miller, Robert Ellis 202
Miller, Sharron 307
Miller, Stephen A. 189, 262, 335
Miller, Susan 80
Miller, Thomas L. 54, 146, 225, 412
The Miracle of Kathy Miller 385–386
The Miracle Worker (1963) 372–373
The Miracle Worker (1979) 454
"The Miracle Worker" (Playhouse 90) 446
Mirisch, Andrew 266
Mission: Impossible 441
Mr. Belvedere: "Heather's Tutor" 99–100
Mr. Sunshine 455; pilot 101–102
Mitchell, Shelley 24

Mittleman, Rick 104
The Mod Squad 439
Moder, Dick 206
Mohan, Peter 337
Molinaro, Edouard 432
"Mom and Dad Can't Hear Me" 212-213
Money on the Side 327-328
The Monkees: "Monkee Mayor" 445; "Monkees at the Circus" 445
Montagu, Ashley 383
Moonlight on the Range 448
Moran, W. Reed 363
Morantz, Paul 377
Morgan, Barbara 242
Morgan, Christopher 285
Mork and Mindy: "Mork Learns to See" 59-60
Morris, Linda 102
Morrow, Barry 320, 326
Morrow, Douglas 275
Morse, Sid 63
Morton, Rob 358
Muggable Mary, Street Cop 454
Mumford, Thad 110
Muntner, Simon 87, 251, 391
Murder, She Wrote: "Sudden Death" 258-259
My Kidnapper, My Love 297-298
Myton, Fred 342

N

Naar, Joseph T. 208, 292, 315
Nathan, Mort 361
Neale, L. Ford 149
Neer, Judy 215
Negulesco, Jean 198
Neufeld, Sigmund 164, 251, 362, 397, 428
The New Avengers: "Target" 447
The New Frontier 449
New Love American Style: "Love & Reading Music" 102-104
Newfield, Sam 342
Newman, Carroll 233
The Next Victim 124-125
The Next Voice You See see *Look Back in Darkness*
Nicolella, John 173, 366
Night Court: "Dan's Boss" 359-360; "Walk, Don't Wheel" 289, 304-306
Night Gallery: deaf girl speechreads murder plot 442; "A Portrait" 21-22; "Witness Within" 441

Night Heat: "Snow White" 336-337
Night of Terror 452
Night Song 8-9
The Night They Saved Christmas 453
Night Without Stars 448
No Other Love 453
North and South 399-401
Novack, James L. 267
Nugent, Nelle 408
Nurse: "Listen to Me" 228-230
Nyby, Christian, II 75

O

O'Brien, Liam 252, 290, 366
O'Connell, David J. 418
The Odd Couple 456
Officer and the Lady 448
O'Herlihy, Michael 170, 290, 366
O'Kun, Lan 83, 388
Olek, Henry 95
Olenicoff, S. Rodger 57
Olson, Glen 282
Omerod, James 124
On Dangerous Ground 447
One Day at a Time: developmental disability 316-317; epilepsy 380-382
O'Neill, Gene 186
O'Neill, Robert F. 259
The Ordeal of Bill Carney 155-156
Ordinary Heroes 107-109
O'Riordan, Shaun 31
The Other Side of the Mountain 125-127, 449
The Other Side of the Mountain, Pt. II 449
Otto, Linda 326
Overmeyer, Eric 365

P

Page, Anthony 235, 320, 326
Palmer, Patrick 269
Paltrow, Bruce 216, 250, 260, 303, 333, 365
Panzer, William N. 133
Papazian, Robert 392
The Paper Chase: "The Man in the Chair" 144-146
Paris, Jerry 54, 412
Parker, Rod 256
Parriott, James D. 166, 244

Parsons, Harriet 8
Paschella, Carole 51, 52, 224
Paschella, Michael 51, 52, 224
Passer, Ivan 387
A Patch of Blue 18-19
Patchett, Tom 109
The Patricia Neal Story 454
Patterson, John 62, 306
Paul, Norman 380
Peerce, Larry 125
Peggy Sue Got Married 449
Pekkonen, Donna 404
Penn, Arthur 372
Penn, Leo 293
Perine, Parke 208
Permut, David 90
Perry, Frank 219
Perry, Sue 94
Perry Mason: "The Case of the Positive Negative" 446
Persky, Bill 245, 339
Peter Pan 444
Peters, Margie 238
Pettus, Ken 122
Petrie, Daniel 127
Petrie, Donald 264
Petrie, Dorthea G. 263
Petrocelli: "To See No Evil" 40
Phantom of the Opera (1925) 407, 451
Phantom of the Opera (1943) 451
Phantom of the Opera (1983) 454
Phelan, Anna Hamilton 426
Phillips, Lee 317
Piller, Michael 362
Pitlik, Noam 45, 99, 112, 227
Places in the Heart 88-89
Playdon, Paul 416
Playhouse 90: "The Miracle Worker" 446
Police Story: "Captain Hook" 285-286; "End of the Line" 290-291; "Firebird" 397, 446
Police Woman: "Blind Terror" 440
Polone, Judith 402
Pompian, Paul 236
Ponti, Alex 85
Ponzi, Maurizio 85
Porges 176
Porter, Katherine Anne 345
Posse 287
Powerhouse: "One of the Gang" 302-303
Powers, Katharyn 262
Prelutsky, Burt 309
Preminger, Otto 413
Pressburger, Lawrence 42
Price, Eugene 327
Pride of the Marines 6-8, 9, 11, 109
Psych-Out 449
Punky Brewster: "The Gift" 333-335

Q

Quincy: "Unreasonable Doubt" 390-391

R

Rabwin, Paul 234
Radin, Paul B. 104, 367
Radnor, Lynn 309
Raffill, Stewart 357
The Raging Moon see *Long Ago Tomorrow*
Ramsey, Judith 378
Ranberg, Chuck 339
Randall, Bob 339
Randy Rides Alone 451
Ransohoff, Martin 27
Rapture 450
Rash, Steve 353
Raskin, Bonnie 322
Raskin, Richard 170
Rauseo, Vic 102
Rawhide 456; blind sheriff 3, 441; "The Empty Sleeve" 444; "Incident at Barker Springs" 446; "Incident of His Brother's Keeper" 441; "Incident of the Broken Word" 446; "Incident of the Child Woman" 439; "Incident of the Dark Side of the Street" 442; "Incident of the Portrait" 439; "Incident of the Prairie Elephant" 445; "Incident of the Roman Candles" 446; "Walk Into Terror" 444; Wishbone is blinded 441; "A Woman's Place" 446
Ray, Darrell 167, 169
The Red Hand Gang 443
Rees, Marion 263
Reichert, Irma 212
Reid, Eliott 301
Reiner, Carl 95
Reisner, Allan 282, 335
Remington Steele: "High Flying Steele" 172-173; "Steele, Inc." 188-189
Reynolds, Gene 46
Rhodes, Michael 422
Rich, David Lowell 416

Rich, John 101
Rich, Lee 141, 322, 378
Rickey, Patricia 99
Rickman, Tom 266
The Rifleman: blind man seeks revenge 439; Davy Pardee—dev. disabled brother of an outlaw 444; Lucas is blinded 441; Mark begins to teach deaf girl 444; Mark loses use of his legs 441; Reuben Miles—"slow in the head" but a fast draw 444; voiceless man 446; "The Wyoming Story" 446
Roberts, William 287
Robinson, Casey 273
Robinson, Phil Alden 95
Robson, Mark 10
The Rockford Files: "Black Mirror" 60–62; "Love Is the Word" 62
Roddam, Franco 363
Roddenbery, Gene 346
Rodgers, Mark 397
Rogosin, Joel 283
Roll Along Cowboy 448
The Rookies 445
Rooney, Pat 377
Rose, Reginald 157
Rosenberg, Meta 60, 62
Rosenbloom, Richard M. 162
Rosenfarb, Bob 333
Rosenfeld, Guistan I. 302
Rosenstock, Richard 55
Rosenzweig, Barney 161, 162, 307
Rosner, Rick 252
Ross, Arthur 283
Ross, Jerome 144
Ross, Mark 303
Rothman, Bernard 385
Rothstein, Richard 187
Route 66: three girls masquerade as disabled females 441; "To Walk with the Serpent" 446
Rowe, Arthur 147, 163, 172, 190, 393
Ruben, Albert 245
Rubin, Ron 210
Rubin, Stanley 213
Rubinowitz, Barry 412
Ruggiero, Alfonso M., Jr. 179
"Run, Don't Walk" 153–155
Runfolo, Peter A. 107, 111
Russell, Ray 278
Ryan, Pamela 324
Ryan, Thomas C. 201

S

Saboteur 447
Sackett, Nancy 152
Sackheim, William 21
Sadwith, James 322
St. Elsewhere 457; "Bang the Ear Drum Slowly" 260; "Family Affair" 365–366; "Give the Boy a Hand" 303–304; "Hearing" 250–251; "Lost and Found in Space" 333
Salkowitz, Sy 396
Salt, Waldo 135
Saltzman, Phillip 62
Samish, Adrian 30
Sandrich, Jay 99
Sanger, Jonathan 383
Sargent, Joseph 171, 263
Saul, Oscar 297
Scarecrow and Mrs. King: "Brunettes Are In" 441
Schaefer, Robert 206
Scharlach, Ed 59
Schary, Dore 370
Scheerer, Robert 325, 331
Schenck, George 96, 358
Schenkel, Carl 187
Schneider, Andrew 328
Schneider, Sascha 167, 169
Schute, Martin C. 156
Schwartz, Douglas 104, 367
Schwimmer, Stan 24, 203
Scoyk 246
Search for Tomorrow: Doug Phillips injured 442; Matt falls in love with a deaf woman 443
Sears, Fran 212
Second Sight: A Love Story 80–81
See No Evil 27–28
Seidelman, Arthur Allen 169, 406
Seller, Tom 16
Sellers, Arlene 358
Seltzer, David 125
Serling, Rod 21
Seven in Darkness 451
Shaftel, Josef 376
Shapiro, Rich 415
Sharp, Henry 280
Shaw, Lou 170, 328
Shaw, Peter 376
Shaye, Robert 133
Shayne, Bob 33
Shea, Patt 226
Sheehan, Tony 45, 99, 227

Sheldon, E. Lloyd 2
Sheldon, James 228, 396, 411
Sheldon, Lee 390
Shelly, Bruce 234
Shelly, Kathleen A. 400
Shepherd, Scott 107, 111
Sher, David Douglas 75
Sherick, Edgar J. 138
Sherman, Harry R. 127
Sherman, Jill 166, 244
Sherman, Robert 62
Sherman, Stanford 357
Sherman, Vince 243
Sherwood, Robert 276
Ship of Fools 345-346
Shulman, Roger 96, 358
Sichel, John 31
Sidaris, Andy 150
Siegel, Lionel 132
Silent Victory: The Kitty O'Neil Story 222-224
Silverberg, Robert 98
Simon and Simon: "Bloodlines" 445; "Burden of the Beast" 362-363; "I Heard It Was Murder" 2, 75-77, 428; "The Skull of Nostradamus" 363; "Under the Knife" 442; "What Goes Around Comes Around" 174; "What's in a Gnome?" 164
Simoun, Henry 132
Sims, Grant 416
Sincerely Yours 200, 449
Singer, Abby 260, 333, 365
Singer, Robert 309
Singleton, Ralph 307
Siodmak, Robert 370
Sirk, Douglas 14
Skyward 152-153
Slavin, George F. 30
Sloan, Michael 208
Smith, April 162
Smith, Barbara Elaine 49
Soloman, Mark 77, 176
Some Kind of Miracle 141-143
Something Wicked This Way Comes 300-301
Song of Texas 448
A Special Kind of Love 317-318
Special Olympics see *A Special Kind of Love*
Speer, Kathy 361
Spelling, Aaron 25, 47, 49, 63, 66, 68, 70, 78, 81, 83, 143, 147, 160, 163, 171, 177, 182, 190, 207, 215, 228, 239, 249, 251, 258, 292, 294, 315, 331, 332, 349, 373, 388, 391, 393, 395, 404, 411
Spenser for Hire: "When Silence Speaks" 265-266
Spielberg, Steven 21
The Spiral Staircase (1946) 196, 370-371, 396
The Spiral Staircase (1975) 376-377, 396
Splash! 448
Stacy, James 297
Stanley, Paul 166
Star Trek: "Plato's Stepchildren" 346-347
Starger, Martin 426
Starman 177
Starsky and Hutch: "Blindfold" 440; "Nightmare" 315-316; "Quadromania" 292-293; "Silence" 207-208
Stein, Jeff 99
Stein, Ron 189
Steinberg, Irwin 392
Steinhauer, Robert Bennett 166, 244
Stephens, John G. 75, 164, 174, 351, 362
Stern, Jason 162
Stevens, Bob 77, 359
Stewart, Lisa 94
Stone, Noreen 231
Storke, William F. 310
Storm, Howard 59
The Story of Esther Costello 451
The Stratton Story xv, 275-276
Strauss, Peter 385
Streets of San Francisco 443
Stuart, Jeff 243, 320
Stuart, Malcolm 235, 322, 392
Stuart, Mel 320
Stunts 133-134
Sugarman, Burt 269
A Summer to Remember . . . 261-262
Sunrise at Campobello 449
Superman: "Around the World with Superman" 13-14; "Mr. Zero" 445
Susskind, David 127
Swanson, Robert E. 259
Swanton, Harold 44
Swanton, Scott 261
Sweeney, Bob 281, 388
Swerling, Jo, Jr. 92, 423
Swing Shift 358
Swope, Mel 72, 290
Sylvester, Ward 348

T

T.J. Hooker 455; "Blind Justice" 2, 70–72; "A Child Is Missing" 240–241; "Death Strip" 251–252; "Hooker's Run" 391–392; "Lag Time" 397–398; "Target: Hooker" 87–88
Tahse, Martin 242
Tales of the Gold Monkey 455
Tarzan, The Ape Man 450
Taxi: "Louie and the Blind Girl" 112–113; "The Reluctant Fighter" 193–194
Taylor, Bruce 174, 398
Taylor, Jerry 390
The Ted Kennedy, Jr. Story 310–312
Telford, Frank 285
Tell Me That You Love Me, Junie Moon 413–415
Tenowich, Tom 59
Terrible Joe Moran 171
The Terror of Tiny Town 342
The Terry Fox Story 302
Testament 326–327
Thiel, Nick 244
Thomas, John G. 247
Thomas, R.L. 302
Thomas, Tony 360
Thompson, Robert 242
Thompson, Robert E. 34
Thomsen, Gene 37
Thornburg, Newton 387
Thorpe, Jerry 34
Thou Shalt Not Commit Adultery 138–141
Three Texas Steers 450
Three's Company: "Jack's Navy Pal" 56–57
Thundering Trail 449
Tidyman, Ernest 219
Time Bandits 450
A Time to Love 402–404
Tin Man 247–249
Tinker, Mark 216, 250, 260, 303, 333
To Elvis, With Love see *Touched by Love*
To Race the Wind 452
Tobin, Noreen 186
Tomason, Harry 170
Tomorrow Is Forever 407, 451
A Touch of the Tiny Hacketts 453
Touched by Love 385
"Tough Girl" 242–243
Towbin, Fredi 182
Toy, Alan 167, 169

Trabulus, Marc 317
Trackdown: Finding the Goodbar Killer 245–246
Trading Places 450
Trapper John, M.D.: "The Albatross" 230–231; "Days of Wine and Leo" 298–300; "A Fall to Grace" 442; "Game of Hearts" 401–402; "Going, Going Gonzo" 409–411; "Hear Today, Gone Tomorrow" 243–244; "A Little Knife Music" 355–357; "A Wheel in a Wheel" 185–187
Trauma Center 455–456, 457; "Silent Sounds" 246–247
Trent, John 295
Treves, Sir Frederick 383
Trivers, Barry 37
Troesh, James 180
Troesh, Theresa 180
Trombetta, Jim 366
Tronson, Robert 35
Trosper, Guy 275
Turley, Jack 281
Turner, Barbara 373
Turner, Dennis 80
The Twilight Zone: "Healer" 428–429; "To See the Invisible Man" 97–99
Twilight Zone: The Movie 449
Two of a Kind 322–323
Tyne, George 294

U

Under the Rainbow 353–354
Union Station 9–10, 105

V

V 273
Valens, E.G. 125
Van Boom, Gregory 102
Van Normann, Alessandro 85
Vance, Leigh 249
VEGA$: "Out of Sight" 68–69
Vincent, Allen 199, 235
Vincent, E. Duke 68, 81, 258, 332, 395, 404
Viner, Michael 385
Viola, Joe 70
Vittes, Michael 306
Vogel, Virgil W. 121
Voices 218–219

Von Cube, Irmgard 198, 235
Von Zerneck, Frank 283
Voyagers!: "Barriers of Sound" 244–245; "Destiny's Choice" 166–167

W

Wagner, Michael 167, 169
Wait Until Dark 2, 19–21, 23, 67, 68, 71, 97, 104, 108, 441
Wald, Jerry 6, 198
Walker, Brian 295
Wallace, Irving 200
Wallace, Rick 402
Wallenstein, Joseph B. 395
Wallis, Hal B. 273
Walsh, Diane 105
Walsh, John 294
Walsh, Thomas 9
The Waltons 457; "The Foundling" 204–205; "Grandma Comes Home" 447; "The Job" xvi, 36–37; "The Ordeal" 379–380
Wanamaker, Sam 297
Wanted: Dead or Alive 439
Warner, Daryl 212
Waters, Ed 107, 111, 130, 366
Watkins, William 80
Wayne, Paul 56
Weaver, Rick 267
Webster, Tony 47
Weege, Reinhold 304
Weinberger, Ed 193
Weis, Don 83, 188
Weisman, Mary Lou 403
Weiss, Arthur 271
Weiss, Harriet 226
Welcome Home, Jellybean 329–331
Wellman, William A. 5
Werner, Tom 99
West, Paul 379
Westside Medical 443
What Really Happened to the Class of '65?: "Class Hustler" 290
Whatever Happened to Baby Jane? 119–120
Whelpley, John 355, 401, 409
When Worlds Collide 449
White, Ethel Lina 370, 376
The White Shadow: "A Silent Cheer" 216–218
Who's Killing the Stuntmen? see *Stunts*
Whose Life Is It Anyway? 156–159

Why Me? 392–393
The Wild, Wild West: Dr. Leibknict 445; "The Night of the Lord of Limbo" 279–280; "The Night of the Sabatini Death" 439; "The Night the Wizard Shook the Earth" 344–345
Wilder, John 265
Willey, Stephen 260
Williams, Anson 152
Williams, Marsha Posner 361
Williams, Matt 99
Willingham, Calder 139
Willis, Jack 141
Willis, Mary 141
Wilson, Daniel 42, 212
Wilson, Hugh 69
Winitsky, Alex 358
Winkler, Henry 101, 153
A Winner Never Quits 309–310
Wisen, Bud 316
Witt, Paul Junger 24, 203, 360
Wizan, Joe 218
The Wizard: "El Dorado" 367–368; "Seeing Is Believing" 104–105
The Wizard of Oz 450
WKRP in Cincinnati 69–70
Wohl, Jack 385
Wolper, David L. 399
Wonderworks: "Clown White" 396, 453
Wood, Sam 273, 275
Wrather, Bonita Granville 206
Wrather, Jack 206
Wrye, Donald 57
Wyler, William 276

Y

Yarnell, David 102
Yates, Robert 22
Yates, William Robert 231, 265
Yerkovich, Anthony 173, 292
You'll Like My Mother 450
Young, Dalene 377, 392
Young, John Sacret 317, 326
Young, Roger 322
Young, Terence 19
The Young and the Restless 457; David's new fiancee is blind 440; Mrs. Chancellor fakes a disability 442

Z

Zafran, Jack 302
Zavada, Ervin 153
Zeitman, Jerry 432

Zinnemann, Fred 117
Zorro 456; Bernardo pretends to be deaf 447
Zwieback, Martin 145